W. W. Norton & Company has been independ when William Warder Norton and Mary D. Herte. tures delivered at the People's Institute, the adult education division of New York City's Cooper Union. The firm soon expanded its program beyond the Institute, publishing books by celebrated academics from America and abroad. By mid-century, the two major pillars of Norton's publishing program—trade books and college texts—were firmly established. In the 1950s, the Norton family transferred control of the company to its employees, and today—with a staff of four hundred and a comparable number of trade, college, and professional titles published each year—W. W. Norton & Company stands as the largest and oldest publishing house owned wholly by its employees.

A History of
Modern Europe

A HISTORY OF MODERN EUROPE

Third Edition

VOLUME 1
From the Renaissance to the Age of Napoleon

JOHN MERRIMAN
Yale University

W. W. NORTON & COMPANY
New York · London

Copyright © 2010, 2004, 1996 by John Merriman

Editor: Steve Forman
Project editor: Kate Feighery
Production manager, College: Eric Pier-Hocking
Composition: Westchester Book Group
Manufacturing: RR Donnelley—Harrisonburg

The Library of Congress has cataloged the one-volume edition as follows:

Merriman, John M.
  A history of modern Europe : from the Renaissance to the present / John
Merriman.—3rd ed.
    p. cm.
  Includes bibliographical references and index.
  ISBN: 978-0-393-93433-5 (pbk.)
  1. Europe—History—1492–   I. Title.

D228.M485   2009
940.2'1—dc22   2009027982

ISBN: 978-0-393-93384-0 (pbk.)

W. W. Norton & Company, Inc., 500 Fifth Avenue, New York, N.Y. 10110
www.wwnorton.com

W. W. Norton & Company Ltd., Castle House, 75/76 Wells Street, London
W1T 3QT

5 6 7 8 9 0

For Laura Merriman and
Christopher Merriman

CONTENTS

PART TWO   STATEMAKING

PART THREE NEW CULTURAL AND POLITICAL HORIZONS

PART FOUR REVOLUTIONARY EUROPE, 1789–1850

MAPS

MAPS

JOHN MERRIMAN is Charles Seymour Professor of History at Yale University, and regularly teaches the survey of modern European history at Yale. He received his Ph.D from the University of Michigan, and is the author and editor of many books on the history of modern France, including *The Margins of City Life: Explorations on the French Urban Frontier, The Red City: Limoges and the French Nineteenth Century, The Agony of the Republic: The Repression of the Left in Revolutionary France, 1848–1851*, and most recently *The Dynamite Club*.

PREFACE

Caught as we are in a global economic crisis, the interconnections of economies, nations, and societies around the world could not be clearer. The ongoing social and cultural turmoil of immigrant communities excluded from the mainstream by the former imperial powers demonstrates that history does not go away: the effects of Europe's imperial ambitions and vast empires, although they no longer exist, remain with us. The relatively recent disappearance in 1989–1992 of a more recent empire, that of the Soviet Union, has also had an enormous impact on Europe, and indeed much of the world, transforming international relations while presenting imposing challenges. Russia, to be sure, remains a major power, but it is commonplace now to consider the United States as the one remaining superpower, with an informal empire stretching across the globe through its great economic, political, and military influence.

Empires have greatly shaped European history since the Renaissance. Trade with Africa, Asia, and the Americas led to colonization and empire. Within Europe, rivalries between empires—such as those of England and Spain in the sixteenth and seventeenth centuries, the Ottoman Turkish Empire and the Austrian Habsburg and Russian Empires, and Britain and France in the eighteenth century—reflected both the consolidation and expansion of state power and also shaped the evolution of warfare. During the first fifteen years of the nineteenth century, Napoleon's empire extended through much of the European continent and led to conquests as far as Egypt.

The rise and fall of empires—Portuguese, Spanish, Dutch, Ottoman, British, French, and that of the Soviet Union—is a major theme developed in the third edition of *A History of Modern Europe*. More than ever, the history of Europe cannot be understood without attention to Europe's interaction with cultures in the rest of the world. Europeans, to be sure, have for centuries learned from Muslim, Asian, African, and American cultures. The influence of the Ottoman Empire in Eastern Europe and the Balkans commands additional attention in this volume. At the same time, through commercial contact, conquest, and intellectual, religious, and political influence, as well as, finally, decolonization, the European powers and cultures have affected the histories of non-Western peoples. The construction of stronger and more efficient states facilitated the development of national identities—consider, for example, the role of the British Empire in the emergence in the eighteenth and nineteenth centuries of the sense of being British, and of the wrenching bewilderment among many Britons when the empire ended after World War II. At the same time, national identities developed in the newly independent states that were once colonies. Reflecting recent scholarship, this third edition describes in greater detail the end of the British Empire in Africa, specifically the bloody story of decolonialization in Kenya.

The third edition emphasizes the dynamism of European trade, settlement, and conquest and their great impact not only on Asia, Africa, and the Americas, but also on the history of European peoples. Comparisons are made between the Spanish Empire in Latin America and the English colonies in the Americas. Unlike the Spanish Empire, trade was the basis of the burgeoning English Empire. The Spanish Empire reflected the combination of the absolutism of the Spanish monarchy and the determination to convert—by force if necessary—the indigenous populations to Catholicism. In sharp contrast, many settlers came to the North American English colonies in search of religious freedom. And, again in contrast to the building of the Spanish Empire a century earlier, the English colonists sought not to convert the indigenous peoples to Christianity, but rather to push them out of colonial areas of settlement. While the Spanish colonies reflected state centralization, their English counterparts evolved in a pattern of decentralization that would culminate in the federalist structure of the United States. British rule in India, particularly interesting because of the cultural interaction that took place there, receives more well-deserved attention. And so does the expansion of Dutch rule in Southeast Asia and the response of China and Japan to the Western powers.

Many of the chapters have been usefully reduced in size. There are other changes, as well. The section on the middle classes has been moved to Chapter 14, "The Industrial Revolution," so that "Liberal Challenges to Restoration Europe" stands alone as Chapter 15. In the twentieth century, Joseph Stalin and Stalinism have been moved from the chapter on "Revolutionary Russia and the Soviet Union" (Chapter 23) to the discussion of the Europe of dictators (Chapter 25). I have amplified the discussion of the National Socialism of the Nazis and fascism as a European-wide phenomenon during the inter-war period. The post–World War II chapters have been reorganized and streamlined. Decolonialization and the Cold War, certainly two of the major occurrences in the decades that followed the war, have been combined in Chapter 28. The final chapter has been shortened and brought up to date.

We move away from the traditional textbook strategy of continually contrasting Western and Eastern Europe. For example, the third edition of *A History of Modern Europe* places the emergence of the concept of political sovereignty not only in early modern England and the Dutch Republic, but also in the Polish-Lithuanian Commonwealth during the early modern period. We offer expanded coverage of the heroic rising of the Jews of the Warsaw ghetto against the Nazis in 1943, and of the Warsaw Uprising little more than a year later. We explore the roots of the economic and political problems that continue to beset Western and Eastern Europe, for example by demonstrating how the simmering ethnic tensions that burst into bloody civil war in Bosnia after the disintegration of Yugoslavia echoed the quarrels that eroded the stately Habsburg monarchy a century earlier.

The third edition draws on exciting studies in the social history of ideas, approaches that stand at the intersection of intellectual, social, and cultural history. Volume 1 explains how artistic patronage during the Renaissance and the Golden Age of Dutch culture reveals some of the social foundations of art. Recent studies on the family economy, village and neighborhood life, and the changing structure of work have all enriched this book's account of the transformation of European society from an overwhelmingly peasant society into an increasingly urban and industrial world. The account of the emergence of mass politics in the nineteenth century draws on recent studies of popular culture and the symbolism and power of language.

We retain a narrative framework with the goals of both analyzing the central themes of the European experience and telling a story. Each chapter can be read as part of a larger, interconnected story. Moreover, this book stresses the dynamics of economic, social, political, and cultural change, but within the context of the amazing diversity of Europe. The history of modern Europe and its influence in the world presents extraordinary characters, well known and little known. The text brings the past to life, presenting portraits of men and women who have played major roles in European history: religious reformers such as Martin Luther and Jean Calvin; Queen Elizabeth I, who solidified the English throne, and Maria Theresa, who preserved the Habsburg monarchy; King Louis XIV of France and Tsar Peter the Great, two monarchs whose reigns exemplified the absolute state; great thinkers like Kepler and Voltaire; Napoleon, heir to the French Revolution, but also in some ways a despot in the tradition of absolute rulers, and perhaps even an originator of total war. Inevitably, we discuss the monstrous Adolf Hitler, examining the sources of his growing popularity in Germany in the wake of World War I, and Joseph Stalin, discussing his Communist state and murderous purges. But ordinary men and women have also played a significant role in Europe's story, making their own histories. This book thus evokes the lives of both leaders and ordinary people in periods of rapid economic and political change, revolution, and war.

The growth of strong, centralized states helped shape modern Europe. Medieval Europe was a maze of overlapping political and judicial authorities. In 1500, virtually all Europeans defined themselves in terms of family, village, town, neighborhood, and religious solidarities. Over the next three centuries, dynastic states consolidated and extended their territories while increasing the reach of their effective authority over their own people. Portugal, Spain, England (and later as Great Britain), France, the Netherlands, and Russia built vast empires that reached into other continents. The European Great Powers emerged. With the rise of nationalism in the wake of the French Revolution and the Napoleonic era, demands of ethnic groups for national states encouraged the unification of Italy and Germany and stirred unrest among Croats, Hungarians, and Romanians, who were anxious for their own national states. Ordinary people demanded freedom and political sovereignty, with revolution both a reflection of and a motor for political change. The emergence of liberalism in the nineteenth century and the quest for democratic political structures and mass politics have transformed Europe, beginning in Western Europe. Even the autocracies of Russia and Central and Eastern Europe were not immune to change, and there the quest for democracy still continues.

While discussing dynastic rivalries and nationalism, the book also considers how wars themselves have often generated political and social change. French financial and military contributions to the American War of Independence further accentuated the financial crisis of the monarchy of France, helping to spark the French Revolution. French armies of military conscripts that replaced the professional armies of the age of aristocracy contributed to the emergence of nationalism in Britain and France in the eighteenth century. The defeat of the Russian army by the Japanese in 1905 brought political concessions that helped prepare the way for the Russian Revolution of 1917. The German, Austro-Hungarian, Ottoman, and Russian Empires disappeared in the wake of World War I and World War II; the economic and social impact of these wars generated political instability, facilitating the emergence of fascism and communism. World War I and the role played by colonized peoples gave impetus to movements for independence within the British, French, and Dutch Empires that would ultimately be successful, transforming the world in which we live.

Like politics, religion has also been a significant factor in the lives of Europeans and, at times, in the quest for freedom in the modern world. Catholicism was a unifying force in the Middle Ages; for centuries European popular culture was based on religious belief. Imperial missionaries carried their religions into Africa and Asia in the aggressive quest for converts. Spanish conquerors forced indigenous populations in the Americas to convert to Christianity. Religion has also been a frequently divisive force in modern European history; after the Reformation in the sixteenth century, states extended their authority over religion, while religious minorities demanded the right to practice their own religion. Religious (as well as racial and cultural) intolerance has scarred the European experience, ranging from the expulsion of Jews and Muslims from Spain at the end of the fifteenth century, to Louis XIV's abrogation of religious toleration for Protestants during the seventeenth century, to the horror of the Nazi Holocaust during World War II. Religious conflict in Northern Ireland and the bloody civil war and atrocities perpetuated in Bosnia in the 1990s recall the ravaging of Central Europe during the Thirty Years' War.

The causes and effects of economic change are another thread that weaves through the history of modern Europe. The expansion of commerce in the early modern period, which owed much to the development of the means of raising investment capital and obtaining credit, transformed life in both Western and Eastern Europe, and directly led to the European empires that followed. The Industrial Revolution, which began in England in the eighteenth century and spread to continental Europe in the nineteenth, depended on a rise in population and thus of agricultural production, but also manifested significant continuities with the past. As important as were inventions, the Industrial Revolution also drew on technology that had been in place for centuries. It ultimately changed the ways Europeans worked and lived. Here, too, European empires are an important, fascinating part of the story.

European history remains crucial to understanding the contemporary world. The political, religious, economic, and global concerns that affect Europe and the world today can best be addressed by examining their roots and development. Globalization has carried movement between the continents to new levels. For centuries, Europe sent waves of emigrants to other parts of the world, particularly North and South America. Now the pattern has been reversed. The arrival of millions of migrants from other continents, particularly Africa and Asia, has posed challenges to European states and Europeans. Moreover, the poverty of some of the states of Eastern Europe and the Balkans, and the tragic events in Bosnia in the 1990s, have increased immigration into Western European countries. Immigrants have added to the religious and cultural complexity of European states. As globalization continues to transform Europe and the world, it becomes even more important and exciting to study the continent's history. With the initiation of a new single currency within most of the member states of the European Union and the continued expansion of that organization, Europe has entered a new era, even as a daunting global economic crisis and the threat of terror in the post-9/11 world present some unprecedented challenges. This third edition enhances our understanding of Europe and the world today, as we contemplate not only the distressing failures and appalling tragedies of the past, but also the exhilarating triumphs that have been part of the European experience.

ACKNOWLEDGMENTS

Charles Tilly died during the time I was working on the third edition of *A History of Modern Europe*. His friends, colleagues, and former students—I am all three—miss him very much. He taught me that it is better not to see history as a series of bins that one opens and then shuts before getting on to the next topic, but rather to look for the big news, the major themes, that have been the dynamics of change and provide revealing continuities, even amid astonishing change. At the same time, he believed in keeping ordinary people fully in view by analyzing, describing, and evoking their histories.

I remain indebted to many colleagues and friends who shared their knowledge, expertise, and suggestions with me, including David Underdown, Laura King, Richard Brodhead, Daniel Orlovsky, Mark Steinberg, John Lynn, Mark Micale, Linda Colley, Roberto González-Echevarria, Ivo Banac, Vincent Moncrief, Laura Engelstein, Geoffrey Parker, David Marshall, David Bell, and my late friend Robin Winks. I also want to thank Jeffrey Burds, Harold Selesky, Leslie Page Moch, Richard Stites, David Cannadine, Jim Boyden, Paul Hanson, Michael Burns, Ivan Marcus, Thomas Kaiser, Christopher Johnson, Louise Tilly, Paul Monod, Judy Coffin, Mark Lawrence, John Sweets, Harold Nelson, Kathleen Nilan, Henry Hyder, Jim McClain, Alan Forrest, Martin Ultee, George Behlmer, Mary O'Neal, Mary Jo Maynes, Thomas Head, Jonathan Dewald, Johan Åhr, Margaret McLane, Jan Albers, Martha Hoffman-Strock, Tom Maulucci, Michael Levin, Daryl Lee, Max Oberfus, and my dear friend Peter McPhee. I am particularly grateful to Joel Mokyr for his many helpful suggestions. Special thanks also to Jeffrey Brooks, Eric Jennings, Christopher Reid, and Aristotle Kallis. I also greatly appreciate suggestions given by Doron Ben-Atar, Robert Brown, Alexander Ganse, Bradley Woodworth, David Goldfrank, Adel Allouche, Leon Plantagna, Michael Sibalis, James McMillan, Steven Wheatcroft, Rachel Fuchs, Kenneth Loiselle, and Maya Jasanoff.

For the third edition, my thanks to Elinor Accampo (University of Southern California), Paul Freedman (Yale University), Wayne te Brake (Purchase College), Timothy Snyder (Yale University), Anders Winroth (Yale University), Andrew Devenney (Central Michigan University), Nicholas Murray (Adirondack Community College), Paul Deslandes (University of Vermont), Alex Porter, Zech Jonathan, Anne Riegert (Université de Rouen), Sven Wanegffelen (Université de Rouen), Steven Pincus (Yale University), Carol Merriman, Lindsay O'Neill (University of Southern California), Charles Beem (Michigan State University), Brian McClure (Michigan State University), Charles Keith (Michigan State University), Valerie Hansen (Yale University), Paul Bushkovitch (Yale University), Charles-Édouard Levillain (University de Lille), Robert Schwartz (Mount Holyoke College), Jay Winter (Yale University), Sarah Cameron (Yale University), Keith Wrightson (Yale University), Francesca Trivellato (Yale University), Steve Sawyer (American University of Paris), Steven Englund (American University of Paris), Michael Driedger (Brock University), Charles Lansing (University of Connecticut), Brian Peterson (Union College), Michael Mahoney (Yale University), Chuck Walton (Yale University), David Large (Montana State University), Frank Snowden (Yale University), Daniel Brückenhaus (Yale University), Jonathan Sperber (University of Missouri), and especially to Piotr Wandycz (Yale University), Victoria Johnson (University of Michigan), Christine Brouwer (Yale University), Michael Galgano (James Madison University), Bruno Cabanes (Yale University), and Gary Shanafelt (McMurry University). The third edition benefited greatly from conferences organized by the Civic Space Institute at the Larzowski School of Law and Commerce in Warsaw. Thanks to my colleagues and friends Andrzej Kaminski (Georgetown University and the Larzowski School of Law and Commerce), Jim Collins (Georgetown University), Wojciech Falkowski (University of Warsaw), Krzysztof Lazarski (Larzowski School of Law and Commerce), Daria Nałęcz (Larzowski School of Law and Commerce), Randy Roberts (Purdue University), Gabor Agoston (Georgetown University), Ashley Dodge, and Ted Weeks (University of Southern Illinois).

I have the greatest admiration for W. W. Norton, which remains a very special independent publisher. My friend Donald Lamm, former chairman of the board and former president of Norton, has always embodied the best in publishing. He and Steve Forman, a wonderful editor and valued friend, first proposed this project to me. Alan Cameron in London's Norton office has long provided support. Sandy Lifland's deft and patient work as developmental editor contributed greatly to the first edition. Sarah England, then Steve's assistant and now an editor at Norton, was extremely helpful throughout the preparation of the second edition, and Kate Feighery and JoAnn

Simony were for the third edition. A special thanks to Carol Merriman, who has patiently lived with and encouraged this and other projects for many wonderful years.

The third edition of *A History of Modern Europe* is dedicated to Laura Merriman and to Christopher Merriman, with much love.

Balazuc (Ardèche),
March 5, 2009

A HISTORY OF
MODERN EUROPE

PART ONE

FOUNDATIONS

As Europe emerged from the Middle Ages, a dynamic era of trade, statebuilding, and global discovery began that would for centuries affect the lives of rich and poor alike, not only in Europe but across the oceans as well. Spanish and Portuguese conquerors and merchants expanding their trade routes laid the foundations for the first transoceanic European empires. During the Italian Renaissance, which lasted from about 1330 to 1530, humanists rediscovered texts from classical Greece and Rome. Renaissance artists and scholars celebrated the beauty of nature and the dignity of mankind, helping shape the intellectual and cultural history of the modern world. Moreover, after a period when almost all of Western Europe adhered to Roman Catholicism, abuses in the Church would lead to cries for reform that would not be stilled until most of Europe was divided between Protestants and Catholics. By 1540, the Reformation had carved out large zones of Protestant allegiance in central and northern Europe, as well as in England and parts of France. Religious conflict and wars would tear Europe apart, leading to reform in the Church but leaving permanent religious divisions where once there had been near-uniformity of belief and worship.

CHAPTER 1

MEDIEVAL LEGACIES AND TRANSFORMING DISCOVERIES

Jacob Fugger (1455–1525) was one of the sons of a weaver who settled in the southern German town of Augsburg. At age fourteen, he joined his brothers as a trader in spices, silks, and woolen goods. He traded, above all, with the Adriatic port of Venice, where he learned double-entry bookkeeping (keeping track of business credits and debits), which was then unknown in the German states. Jacob Fugger amassed a vast fortune, and he began to loan sizable sums to various rulers in Central Europe. Fugger's name soon became known "in every kingdom and every region, even among the heathens. Emperors, kings, princes, and lords sent emissaries to him; the pope hailed him and embraced him as his own dear son; the cardinals stood up when he appeared." When asked if he wanted to retire, Jacob Fugger replied that he intended to go on making money until he dropped dead.

The family history of the Fuggers intersected with economic growth and statemaking in Central Europe. The Fuggers emerged as the wealthiest and most influential of the international banking families that financed warring states, answering the call of the highest bidder. In 1519, the Fuggers helped Charles V become Holy Roman emperor by providing funds with which the scheming Habsburg could bribe the princes who were electors to vote for him. The Fuggers raised and transported the money that made possible imperial foreign policy. Loaning money to ambitious rulers, as well as to popes and military entrepreneurs, the Fugger family rose to princely status and facilitated the consolidation of territorial states and the emergence of a dynamic economy not only in the Mediterranean region but also in the German states and northwestern Europe by helping merchants and manufacturers find credit for their enterprises.

The growth of trade and manufacturing ultimately changed the face of Europe. The expanding economy contributed to a sense that many Europeans

(*Left*) Jacob Fugger, merchant-banker and creditor of rulers and popes, traded with the port of Seville (*right*), a stepping-off point for colonization of the New World.

had in 1500 of living in a period of rebirth and revitalization. In Italy, the cultural movement we know as the Renaissance was still in bloom, and it was spreading along trade routes across the Alps into northern Europe (see Chapter 2). The by-products of trade and exploration were an increasing exchange of ideas and a growing interconnectedness among European states.

Although famine, disease, and war (the horsemen of the apocalypse) still trampled their victims across Europe, significant improvements in the standard of living occurred. The European population rose in the late fifteenth century and continued to rise throughout the sixteenth century. Europe's population stood at about 70 million in 1500 and around 90 million in 1600 (well less than a third of that today). These gains overcame the horrific loss of one-third of the European population to the Black Death (the bubonic plague) in the mid-fourteenth century. The expansion of the population revived European commerce, particularly in the Mediterranean region and in England and northwestern Europe, where the Fuggers and other merchant-bankers were financing new industry and trade. Towns multiplied and their merchants grew more prosperous, building elegant houses near markets.

The pace of change was quickened by several inventions that would help shape the emergence of the modern world. Gunpowder, first used in China and adopted by Europeans in the fourteenth century, made warfare more deadly, gradually eliminating the heavily armed knight. The invention of the printing press in the mid-fifteenth century engendered a cultural revolution first felt in religious life, with the Bible and other religious texts now more widely available to be read, discussed, and debated. The compass, first used to determine direction by Chinese and Mediterranean navigators in the eleventh or twelfth century, now helped guide European exploration across the oceans.

Spanish and Portuguese conquerors and merchants seeking riches in the New World established the first European transoceanic empires. Population growth; the growth of trade and manufacturing, which facilitated the exchange of ideas and gradually increased the standard of living; the use of gunpowder and the compass; and the development of printing all stimulated and facilitated the establishment of colonies across the oceans by the European powers.

MEDIEVAL CONTINUITIES

England and France emerged as sovereign states, standing as exceptions amid the territorial fragmentation that characterized medieval Europe. Smaller territories also began to coalesce into larger units and rulers consolidated and extended their authority. European society took on the shape it would have for centuries, with three orders—clergy, nobles, and peasants—standing in relationships of mutual obligation to each other. Material well-being remained at a subsistence level for most peasants but nonetheless improved overall as commercial trade across greater distances began to rise in the eleventh century. Moreover, small-scale textile manufacturing developed as towns grew, particularly in Italy and northwestern Europe during the twelfth and thirteenth centuries.

The Fragmentation of Europe

With the end of the Roman Empire in the fifth century, Europe experienced an influx of new peoples. From the east came the Magyars (Hungarians), who settled in Central Europe, where they were converted to Christianity. From Scandinavia came the so-called Northmen (Norse or Vikings), who reached Ukraine, and who for the most part became Christians. Arabs invaded Europe in the eighth century, subsequently expanding their influence into North Africa, as well as Spain. Mongols poured into what is now Russia and Ukraine, sacking Kiev in the 1230s, before their empire began to collapse in the fifteenth century. The princely state of Muscovy, which had been one of their tributaries, gradually expanded in size, reaching the southern Ural Mountains and the Caspian Sea and emerging as a dynastic state. This multitude of influences contributed to both the political and cultural fragmentation of Europe.

In 1500, Europe was a maze of about 1,500 fragmented states. Economic, political, and judicial institutions were overwhelmingly local. Territories and cities were subject to a confused array of overlapping jurisdictions. The city-states of Italy and the trading towns of northern Germany managed to preserve their independence from territorial rulers. The town walls that protected residents against bandits and disease (during times of plague and epidemics) stood also as symbols of urban privileges. Paris, for example, was dotted with enclaves of ecclesiastical authority.

Part of Europe's fragmentation was due to its three systems of law: civil, canon, and customary. The legal concepts, principles, and procedures of civil law evolved from Roman law, which was based on the rational interpretation of written law applied to human affairs. Civil laws were decreed and thereby sanctioned by rulers, whose authority stemmed in part from their right to make or impose laws. The development of civil law, then, was conducive to the development of sovereign states by closely associating the power of rulers of states with the force of law. Canon law, established by the pope for the Western Church, codified in Latin the canons of Church councils and the revealed authorities of the Bible and Church fathers. As with civil law, canon law helped affirm, at least in principle, the authority of spiritual rulers—the popes, cardinals, and bishops—by closely linking the law to the authority of the rulers in general, whose subjects owed them personal allegiance.

Yet, to be sure, in the late Middle Ages, cross-cutting allegiances—the most common being to both secular and ecclesiastical authorities—were often the norm. Subjects of competing authorities used the system to exploit jurisdictional conflicts to their own ends, whenever possible. This sometimes served to reinforce the influence of multiple authorities. Thus, the effective authority of rulers could end up being rather distant.

Customary, or common law, was a codification of established custom, implying a constant reference to decisions taken earlier by judges. It was the usual mode of law in all areas where Roman law was not used. In Western Europe, customary law developed out of the customs of feudalism (see below), a set of reciprocal economic, social, and political relationships that encouraged decentralized power structures.

In England, where common law unified the customary law for the whole land, laws were overseen by local courts, which contributed to the decentralization of English royal authority. Unlike Roman law, which helped shape the sense that the ruler was a sovereign lawgiver who could override custom, customary law helped corporate groups (such as guilds, which were craft associations) or individuals assert their interests and rights by establishing precedents that, at least in principle, could override the ruler's intervention in the legal process.

Europe's political fragmentation was accompanied by cultural fragmentation, reinforced by the many languages spoken. Latin, the language of culture, was still spoken in university towns—thus the "Latin Quarter" in Paris. Distances and difficulties in travel and communication were also imposing. It sometimes took months for mail to arrive. The shortest time to travel from Madrid to Venice was twenty-two days, and the longest, in bad weather, was four times that.

At the Crossroads of Cultures

Europe stood at the crossroads between civilizations and religions (see Map 1.1). After the collapse of the Roman Empire, Christendom had been split between the Roman Catholic Church and the Eastern Orthodox Church following the Great Schism between the two churches in 1054. The claim by the bishop of Rome—the pope—to authority over all Eastern Christians (as well as a festering doctrinal dispute over the nature of the Holy Trinity) led to the break, culminating in the pope's excommunication of the patriarch of Constantinople. By 1500, the Eastern Orthodox Church held the allegiance of most of the people in Russia and the Balkans. The Roman Catholic and Orthodox worlds met in the eastern part of Central Europe, with Poland, Bohemia, and Hungary looking to the West.

Christianity, as an alternate source of allegiance and power claiming to be a universal state (with its own language, Latin), presented a potential impediment to state authority. It also provided a common culture that engulfed much of Europe. As both the Church and the monarchies became more centralized, conflict between them became inevitable. The Church itself had been a centralized religious authority since the end of the Roman Empire, which left the papacy in Rome independent of secular rule. After the middle of the eleventh century, the popes were elected by the Church cardinals, each of whom had been appointed by a previous pope. Bishops and abbots pledged obedience to the pope in return for tenure over abbey lands and ecclesiastical revenues.

In the Ottoman Empire, religious and political sovereignty rested in the same person, the sultan. In contrast, rulers of territorial states in Europe had succeeded in making themselves largely autonomous from Church authority. Although the Church was wealthy and powerful (owning about 25 percent of the land of Catalonia and Castile and perhaps 65 percent in southern Italy), princes were unwilling to let the Church interfere with their authority, even though ecclesiastical leaders in many cases had crowned them. During the fourteenth and fifteenth centuries, rulers refused to allow ecclesiastical courts in their territories. The pope commanded his bishops and other clergy to be loyal to the rulers of secular states.

During the medieval period, Western Christians attempted to win back lands conquered by Muslims, especially seeking to recapture Jerusalem. The first of eight "Crusades" that lasted to 1270 began in 1095. In 1204, believing the Eastern Orthodox religion to be heresy, the Crusaders conquered the Eastern Orthodox Byzantine Empire, which had extended from eastern Italy to the Black Sea's eastern end. In the mid-fourteenth century, the Ottoman Turks conquered two-thirds of Anatolia, much of the Balkan Peninsula, and Greece. By 1400, Islam stretched from southern Spain and North Africa all the way to northern India and beyond to islands in Southeast Asia. During the fourteenth and early fifteenth centuries, the Byzantine Empire (which was Greek in culture and Eastern Orthodox Christian in religion) was

MAP 1.1 THE OTTOMAN EMPIRE, c. 1500

AUSTRIA

HUNGARY

MOLDAVIA

WALLACHIA

SEA OF AZOV

BLACK SEA

PERSIA

DULKADIR

EGYPT

ANADOLU

KARAMAN

CYPRUS

Constantinople

BOSNA

SERBIA

RUMELI

AEGEAN SEA

CRETE

MEDITERRANEAN SEA

ADRIATIC SEA

NAPLES

SICILY

0   250 miles
0   250 kilometers

Ottoman Empire, 1503

reduced to a small area straddling the straits between Asia and Europe, which included its capital, Constantinople (modern Istanbul). Finally, the Ottoman Turks captured Constantinople after a lengthy siege in 1453, the final act of the decline of the Byzantine Empire. During the next four decades, the Ottomans doubled their European territory, conquering Serbia in 1459, Bosnia in 1463, Albania in 1479, and Herzogovina in 1483. The addition of Hungary extended the Ottoman Empire to the Danube River.

The Ottoman Turks possessed a large army—much of it recruited from converts to Islam, notably the infantry (the janissaries)—and a strong navy. Effective diplomacy complemented military strength. During the first half of the sixteenth century, the Ottomans also absorbed Egypt and moved into Iran, reaching Baghdad in what is now Iraq in 1534, and then the Persian Gulf. This was the apogee of the Ottoman Empire, which made use of loyal elites at the local level to bring in the revenues that financed the state. For the next several centuries, Roman Catholic Europe would view Islam as a perpetual threat to its religion and culture. Yet a sizable majority of the myriad populations the Ottoman Turks ruled remained Christian and were allowed to continue to practice their religion. Despite the existence of a common Islamic high culture, the Islamic Ottoman Turks accepted non-Muslims in their empire, and the latter always represented a significant majority of the population. In contrast, Christian states systematically persecuted and expelled Muslims. For centuries, Western writers outdid each other in describing the Ottoman Turks as "the scourge of God," barbaric, despotic, and cruel. However, the Russian Orthodox Church (which was greatly influenced by its Byzantine heritage), Greek Orthodox Church (also an Eastern Orthodox Church), Roman Catholic Church, and the Islamic religion coexisted remarkably well in the Balkans under Ottoman Turkish rule. The Ottomans established the *millet* system, which allowed autonomy for religious minorities, with leaders of religious communities appointed by the sultan.

Much of Europe thus confronted a huge semicircle of states under direct or indirect Turkish control. The Western powers, which had launched Christian crusades against the Muslims, now were forced into a series of defensive wars against Islam, which to the West was embodied by the Ottoman Empire. To aid in their defense, the Venetians constructed a series of fortifications along the Adriatic coast.

The Structure of Society

Medieval society was roughly divided into three social groups: the clergy, who prayed and cared for souls; nobles, who governed and fought; and peasants, who labored in the fields. Burghers, town residents whose entrepreneurial activity made possible the economic dynamism of medieval Europe between 1000 and 1350, were, despite their increasing importance, outside this classical typology.

The clergy had many roles, serving as priests, teachers, judges, nurses, landlords, and chaplains. But they could only be tried in ecclesiastical courts, and, in the evolution of the modern state, their status as a group apart would come into question. The secular clergy (that is, priests who did not belong to a specific religious order) ministered to the population as a whole. Most of the secular clergy were as poor as their parishioners, but bishops generally were from noble families. The regular clergy included hundreds of thousands of monks and nuns living in monasteries and convents according to strict religious rules, cut off from the outside world by their vows (and in some places legally considered dead).

Nobles owned most of the land, with their status and income stemming from this, as well as from their military functions. Noble titles connoted superiority of birth, and noble families usually intermarried. Nobles were not supposed to work but were to stand ready to defend their monarch and the interests and honor of their families.

Peasants, who made up about 85 percent of the population of Europe in 1500, lived in villages or in small settlements on the lands of nobles, dependent on the latter for protection in exchange for labor. Peasants had no legal status, with the exception of those (for the most part in Western Europe) who owned land. In some places, they were considered barely better than animals by the lords who oppressed them and the clergy who told them their lot in life was to suffer in anticipation of heavenly rewards.

Villages or, within towns, parishes formed the universe of most Europeans. Local solidarities took precedence over those to the rulers of states, whose effective reach in many places remained quite limited. Many villages were, for all intents and purposes, virtually self-governing; village councils decided which crops would be planted on common land and set the date

The poor man, the artisan, and the lord in the late fifteenth century. Note the subservient role of women and children in each family.

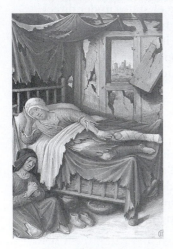  

plowing was to begin. Such councils coexisted with the seigneurial authority of lords.

At least a fifth of the European population lived in dire poverty. For ordinary laborers, three-quarters of their earnings went to purchase food. Towns and cities were crowded with poor people struggling to get by. A pope complained of vagrants in Rome "who fill with their groans and cries not only public places and private houses but the churches themselves; they provoke alarms and incidents; they roam like brute beasts with no other care than the search for food." The poor wandered everywhere their feet could carry them, finding work where they could, sometimes begging, sometimes stealing. Acts of charity, encouraged by the Catholic Church, which viewed such acts as essential for salvation, helped many poor people survive. But while poor beggars from within communities were tolerated and sometimes given assistance, townspeople and villagers alike feared the poor outsider, particularly gypsies. Banditry was pervasive most everywhere, for example, between Venetian and Turkish territory, between the Papal States and the Kingdom of Naples, and in the Pyrenees Mountains. The story of Robin Hood, the thirteenth-century English bandit and popular hero alleged to have stolen from the rich to give to the poor, had its continental counterparts.

Feudalism

Feudalism developed during the ninth and tenth centuries in response to the collapse of the authority of territorial rulers. Between about A.D. 980 and 1030, law and order broke down in much of Europe, and violence became the norm. This unstable period was characterized by warfare between clans and between territorial lords, attended by retinues of armed men, as well as the ravages of predatory bands. The power structure (king, lords, vassals, and peasants) that emerged in feudal times was a reaction against the anarchy and instability of earlier years. Feudalism also should be seen in the context of an overwhelmingly agricultural economy, where rulers and lords retained great estates.

Despite an increase in the power of great lords, there remained a crucial difference between a king and a lord. Kings were anointed by the ecclesiastical authority in a sacred rite, and therefore claimed to rule "by the grace of God" even when they were incapable of coercing the great lords and their families. The mighty lords imposed obligations of loyalty and military service on "vassals." Their vassals received, in exchange, protection and the use of lands (called fiefs) to which, at least in principle, the lords retained rights. The heirs of vassals would inherit the same conditions, although a vassal had to pay the lord a fee upon inheriting an estate. Vassals agreed to fight for their lord for a certain number of days a year and to ransom the lord if he were captured. For their part, lords adjudicated disputes between vassals. Vassals could join together to oppose a king who failed to meet his

In this Italian miniature from 1492, a vassal kneels to formally certify his allegiance to his lord and cement their mutual obligations to each other.

obligations; likewise, a king or lord could punish a vassal who neglected his obligations to his lord. Elaborate ceremonies featuring solemn oaths, sworn before God and blessed by churchmen, specified the mutual obligations of lord and vassal. "You are mine," a powerful lord in Aquitaine in what is now southwestern France reminded a vassal, "to do my will." Thus, feudalism was a system in which the more powerful extracted revenue or services from the less powerful, with the peasantry, at the bottom of social hierarchy, the weakest of them all.

Feudalism finally waned in the monarchical states in the late fourteenth century with the emergence of stronger state structures, as well as the reimposition of the authority of the Roman Catholic Church in much of Europe. Thus, feudal relationships dissolved as the strength of rulers increased and the independence of nobles declined in stronger states. Royal courts gradually usurped the judicial authority of nobles (although in some places not entirely). Furthermore, the development of a money economy (payment in gold or silver, or in coins minted by rulers) increasingly made feudal relationships obsolete. One sign of this was the shift to cash payment by peasants to lords, instead of payment in services, crops, or animals.

The Black Death of the mid-fourteenth century also helped sound the death knell of feudalism in Western Europe by killing off one-third to one-half of the population (see "A Rising Population," p. 19). As wages rose because of a shortage of labor, peasants were able to improve their legal status. The plague had also killed many lords. When lords tried to reimpose feudal relationships, some spectacular rebellions occurred. Resentment against royal troops (along with the imposition of new taxes) contributed to peasant rebellions in Flanders (1323–1328), northern France (the Jacquerie of 1358), and the Peasants' Revolt in England in 1381. There was also unrest among the urban poor, as ordinary people resisted attempts to return to the way things were before. States took advantage of the chaos by assessing new taxes, such as the hearth tax (a tax on households). By increasing their authority, the monarchies of Western Europe gradually brought the feudal era to a close.

A Subsistence Economy

Agriculture lay at the base of the European economy, in which the ownership of land was the principal determinant of status. Peasants were constantly engaged in a protracted and, more often than not, losing battle against nature. Much land was of poor quality, including hilly and rocky terrain or marshland that could not be farmed. In most of Europe, small plots, poor and exhausted soil, and traditional farming techniques limited yields. Steep slopes had to be cleared and terraced by hand. Peasants plowed with hand "swing" plows. Furthermore, villages held some land in common, originally granted by lords. This was economically wasteful, but for centuries common land offered the landless poor a necessary resource for survival. And under the best of circumstances, peasants had to save about one-fifth to one-eighth of their seed for replanting the following year.

Peasants owed their lords most of what they produced. Peasants also had to pay part of what meager benefits they managed to extract from the land to lords, by virtue of the latter's status and ownership of land. Lords increasingly found it more advantageous to rent out plots of land, and gradually many commuted labor services to cash, which they spent on goods, including luxuries, available at expanding markets and fairs. These included silk, cotton, and some spices that traders brought from the Levant (countries bordering on the eastern Mediterranean). Peasants (like other social groups) also had to tithe (give 10 percent of their revenue) to the Church. These tithes had traditionally been in-kind, but they were increasingly monetized during the late Middle Ages. In a fundamentally subsistence economy, this left the rural poor—that is, most families—with little on which to get by.

Yet even with the rise in population, lords in the thirteenth century had faced frequent shortages of labor and were forced to grant favorable terms to peasants. Many peasants in Western Europe succeeded in purchasing their freedom, transforming their obligations into rents paid to the lords. Nonetheless, even free peasants still had to pay feudal dues to lords and fees for the right to mill grain, brew beer, or bake bread, monopolies that the lords retained.

Serfdom began to disappear in France and southern England in the twelfth century. Rulers had reason to encourage the movement toward a free peasantry in Western Europe, because free peasants could be taxed, whereas serfs—who were legally attached to the land they worked—were entirely dependent on the lords who owned the land. In Western Europe, the free peasantry reflected the growth in the authority of rulers and a relative decline in that of nobles. In the West, most peasant holdings were increasingly protected by civic law or by custom.

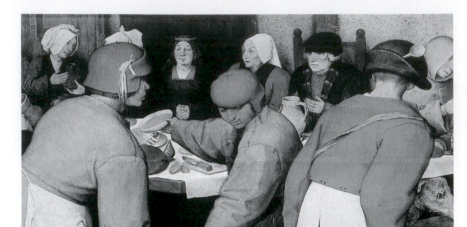

Pieter Bruegel the Elder: *The Peasants' Wedding* (1568). On that special day, they would probably eat as well as they ever would.

In contrast to the emergence of a free peasantry in the West, most peasants in Eastern and Central Europe lost their freedom during the sixteenth century, forced to become serfs as landowners sought to assure themselves of a stable labor supply. This in itself was a sign that nobles there were carving out territorial domination virtually independent from that of kings and other rulers, as in Poland.

Many people were constantly on the move in Europe. Free peasants moved toward the frontiers of Europe in search of land, which they brought under cultivation. Peddlers, artisans, and agricultural laborers traveled great distances in search of work. Shepherds led their sheep from the plains to summer pastures at higher elevations, and then back down in the fall (transhumance). Hundreds of thousands of rural people also migrated seasonally from the Pyrenees, Alps, and other mountainous regions to undertake construction work in towns, or to follow the harvests. Roads were also full of vagabonds and beggars.

Most poor families survived by eating bread and not much else. For peasants, meat was something that lords and burghers ate, fruit was rare, and vegetables were poor; rye bread, soup, and perhaps peas, cabbage, and beans were the staples of the peasant's diet, depending on the region. In southern France, grain made from chestnuts served as the bread of the poor. The Mediterranean lands produced olives and wine, as well as wheat.

Beer was limited to northern Europe, particularly the German states, England, and Scandinavia.

Agricultural growth, which had been steady until the beginning of the fourteenth century, slowed down until the mid-fifteenth century in the wake of the Black Death. But once the population began to grow again, plots that had been abandoned were plowed once more. In regions of relatively fertile land, the "three-field system" became more common. This left about a third of all land fallow (unplanted) in order to replenish its fertility during the growing season. This mode of agricultural production necessitated relatively sizable landholdings, and thus could not be used on small peasant plots. But over the long run it increased agricultural yields. Yet this did not necessarily aid the peasant family, because dependency on a seigneur could force them to give more attention to cultivation in the interest of the lord, leaving less time to supplement the family economy by hunting, fishing, or looking after livestock. Overall, however, farming techniques and tools improved during the fifteenth century. Innovations such as the use of mills and metal harvesting implements were introduced, although not adopted in some places until much later. These methods would remain basically the same until the nineteenth century.

Free peasants contributed to the rise in agricultural production. Not all peasants were desperately poor. Many could survive (and a minority did quite well) when famine, disease, and war left them alone, selling in the nearest market what produce they had left over after replanting and obligations to lords and the Church had been paid up for that year.

The medieval innovation of the three-field system allowed for the renewal of one field by leaving it fallow for a season.

The growth in the European population during the medieval period depended on these modest increases in agricultural yields. Some lords became market-oriented farmers in response to increased population. This in itself increased agricultural production. In England, Flanders, northern France, and Sicily (as well as North Africa), grain was intensively cultivated for the market. Urban growth encouraged cash-crop farming, enriching nearby landlords, merchants, and wealthy peasants. Prosperous agriculture was to be found in the rich valley of the Po River in central Italy, the plains of Valencia in Spain, and the Beauce, between the Loire River and Paris. Landowners brought more land under cultivation, cleared forests, drained marshes and swamps, and where possible, irrigated arid fields.

Religion and Popular Culture

Religion played an enormous part in the lives of Europeans in the Middle Ages. Christianity shaped a general system of belief and values that defined the way most people viewed themselves and the world in which they lived. The Church, its faith and learning preserved during the so-called Dark Ages before the medieval period, viewed itself as a unifying force in Europe. This gave the clergy great prestige and moral authority as distributors of the sacraments (above all, penance, the forgiveness of sins), without which Christians believed that salvation could not be achieved. When preachers passed through villages, the faithful waited long into the night to have their confessions heard. One of Europe's most traveled routes took pilgrims from many countries to the shrine of Santiago de Compostela in northwestern Castile (Spain). The Church blessed oaths of fealty (loyalty) sworn by vassals to lords and rulers, and it took an important role in the rites of passage (birth, marriage, death). The Italian Renaissance (see Chapter 2), to be sure, would rediscover the dignity of humanity, but did so within the context of Christian belief.

Religious themes and subjects permeated virtually all medieval art and music. In the twelfth century, magnificent Gothic cathedrals began to be built. The construction of these colossal churches often lasted as long as a century, absorbing enormous resources, and paid for by gifts, large and small, from people of all walks of life. Church bells tolled the hours (clocks would remain novelties until the end of the sixteenth century) and called people to Mass.

Western Christendom was interlocked with Western civilization, although Muslim and Jewish heritages remained strong in Spain and Turkish-controlled areas. Jews remained outcasts, although in general they did not live apart from the Christian population until the fifteenth century, when they were forced to do so by civil and ecclesiastical authorities. The popes forced Jews in Rome to wear distinctive badges; Venice established the first Jewish "ghetto" in 1516. Many Jews, forbidden to enter certain trades, were forced to wander in search of towns where they could live in relative peace.

Storytellers, both amateur and professional, kept oral traditions of popular culture alive at a time when most people were illiterate. Accomplished storytellers passed on their tales during evening gatherings, when villagers, principally women, gathered together to mend garments, tell stories, and keep warm. Many of these stories and tales reflected the fatalism of societies in which most people died relatively young.

Most people believed in magic and the presence of the supernatural on earth. By such views, sorcerers or saints could intervene between people and the bad luck that might befall them. Primitive healers were believed to stand between disease and survival. People believed that rubbing certain saints' images could bring good fortune. When the wine harvest failed in some parts of France, villagers whipped statues of the saints that had failed them. Superstitions abounded. In some places it was believed that it was a good sign to encounter a wolf, deer, or bear, that a stork landing on a house assured its occupants of wealth and longevity, that meeting a white-robed monk in the morning was a bad omen and a black-robed one a good one, that a crow cawing over the house of someone sick meant death was on its way, and that a magpie announced a cure. In the Balkans, garlic was believed to ward off evil. Such beliefs helped peasants cope with a world in which droughts, harvest failures, accidents, and myriad fatal illnesses could bring personal and family catastrophe. "Cunning folk" and witches were believed by many to determine earthly events. A "cunning man" might discover the identity of a thief by placing papers with names inside little clay balls; the guilty party's name would be the first to unravel inside a bucket of water.

A village festival.

Religious holidays and festivals interspersed the calendar year, still governed by the agricultural calendar. At the beginning of Lent in some places in Western Europe, frolicking young men carried torches of blazing straw through the village to ensure agricultural and sexual fertility. Carnival was the highlight of the year for most people in early modern Europe. People ate and drank as at no other time, tossing flour, eggs, and fruit at each other and playing games. Carnival also stood the world on its head, if only briefly. The poor acted out the misdeeds of the wealthy in elaborate plays. Ordinary people could poke fun at the powerful in elaborately staged farces and parades by spoofing the behavior of judges, nobles, and clergymen.

The Emergence of Early Modern Europe

The late Middle Ages brought significant economic, social, and political changes that shaped the emergence of early modern Europe. Following the devastation of the Black Death in the fourteenth century, Europe's population slowly revived and then grew. More land was brought into cultivation, providing a greater supply of food. Yet the balance between life and death remained precarious; famine, disease, and war still intervened frequently to check population growth.

However, the continent's trade and manufacturing developed rapidly, particularly in the Mediterranean region (especially the Italian city-states) and in northwestern Europe. Prosperous banking families provided capital for traders and manufacturers, as they did for states, and basic mechanisms for the transfer of credit evolved. Trade with Asia and the Middle East developed at a rapid pace, catching up with the amount of trade Europeans carried out with the Muslim world. Towns grew in size, and their merchants became more prosperous, reflecting the importance of trade and textile manufacturing on urban growth. As they grew richer, some merchant families purchased land and noble titles. Merchants became important figures in every state. Many nobles resented the new status of these commoners, believing the old saying, "The king could make a nobleman, but not a gentleman." The growing prosperity of the entrepreneurial elite of many towns in Western Europe reflected their relative independence from territorial rulers. One of the characteristics of this independent status was the proliferation of guilds and other organizations that reflected a more dynamic economy.

Yet some aspects of the modern state system were already in place. During the period from 1350 to 1450, the rulers of France, Spain, England, Scotland, Denmark, Norway, Sweden, and Hungary consolidated and extended their authority over their territories, eroding the domains of feudal lords and ecclesiastical authorities. The Iberian Peninsula was divided between Castile and Aragon—joined through the marriage of Queen Isabella and King Ferdinand in 1469, forming contemporary Spain—and Portugal, the borders of which have not changed since the late Middle Ages. The basic layout of three Scandinavian states already existed. And important states of East Central and Central Europe (Hungary, Bohemia, and Poland-Lithuania, a confederation created in 1386 and which early in the sixteenth century extended from the Baltic to the Black Sea), were already reasonably well defined. Even the Swiss cantonal federation had emerged. Most of the small territorial fragments lay in the German states or Italy.

A Rising Population

Europe's population had almost doubled between 1000 and 1300, rising from about 40 million to about 75 million people. But early in the fourteenth century, the population began to decline, probably because of rampant disease. Then, in the middle of the century, the Black Death ravaged Europe, killing between a third and half of the European population. Spread by fleas carried by rats, the bubonic plague reached Constantinople from Asia in 1347. Within three years, it had torn through Europe. Victims died horrible deaths, some in a few days, others lingering in agony. Some villages were completely abandoned, as people tried to flee the path of the scourge. In vain, states and cities tried frantically to prevent the arrival of travelers, fearful that they carried plague with them.

For the next century, births and deaths remained balanced (with higher mortality rates in cities wiping out increased births in the countryside). Europe only began to recover during the second half of the fifteenth century, thanks to a lull in epidemics and the absence of destructive wars. However, the population did not reach the level it had been at in 1300 until about 1550, when it began to rise rapidly, particularly in northern Europe (see Table 1.1).

Europeans remained perpetually vulnerable to disease and disaster. The bubonic plague was the worst of epidemics, but influenza, typhus, malaria, typhoid, and smallpox also carried off many people, particularly the poor, who invariably suffered from inadequate nutrition. Moreover, Europeans looked to the heavens not only in prayer but also to watch for the bad weather that could ruin harvests, including storms that brought flooding. Famine still devastated regularly, a natural disaster that checked population growth, killing off infants, children, and old people in the greatest numbers. "Nothing new here," a Roman wrote in the mid-sixteenth century, "except that people are dying of hunger."

Life for most people was short. Life expectancy, once one had made it out of infancy and childhood alive, was about forty years. Women lived longer than men, but many of them died during childbirth. About a fifth of all babies born died before they reached their first birthday. Of 100 children born, less than half lived to age twenty and only about a fifth celebrated a fortieth birthday. Christ, who died at age thirty-three, was not considered to have died young.

Table 1.1 The European Population in the Sixteenth and
Seventeenth Centuries (in millions)

	1500	1600
Spain and Portugal	9.3	11.3
Italian states	10.5	13.3
France	16.4	18.5
Low Countries*	1.9	2.9
British Isles	4.4	6.8
Scandinavia	1.5	2.4
German states	12.0	15.0
Switzerland	0.8	1.0
Balkans	7.0	8.0
Poland	3.5	5.0
Russia	9.0	15.5

*Currently Belgium, the Netherlands, and Luxembourg.
Source: Richard Mackenney, *Sixteenth-Century Europe: Expansion and Conflict* (New York: Macmillan, 1993), p. 51.

The balance between life and death was precarious. In most towns, deaths outnumbered births almost every year. Prosperous families had more children than the poor (the opposite pattern of today). The exposure and abandonment of newly born infants was common. Furthermore, couples may have limited births through sexual abstinence. The fact that one partner often died prematurely also served as a check on population. So too did relatively late marriage. Most English men married at between twenty-six and twenty-nine years of age, women between twenty-four and twenty-six years.

The choice of a marriage partner was important for economic reasons (although in parts of Western Europe, up to a fifth of women never married). Marriages were often arranged—parents played a major and often determining role in choosing partners for their children. For families of means, particularly nobles, the promise of a sizable dowry counted for much. Yet some evidence suggests that by the end of the sixteenth century, at least in England, the inclinations of the bride and groom were sometimes difficult to ignore. For the poor, marriage could offer the chance of improving one's situation. Thus, a young woman whose family could provide a dowry, however modest, or who had a skill, was an attractive prospective spouse, as was a young man with a trade.

Wives remained legally subservient to their husbands, although in the "economy of makeshifts" in the poor household their role as managers of income and as workers gave them some minimal degree of equality. Sexual infidelity, while common, ran against the grain of a popular sense of justice, which placed a premium on loyalty and mutual obligation between marriage partners. Such liaisons might also jeopardize the system of inheritance and the protection of family property by leading to the appearance of unanticipated offspring, in an age when contraceptive techniques were rudimentary and not well known. Still, about a fifth of English brides were pregnant at the time of their wedding, as sexual relations between couples expecting to marry were very common.

Kinship and village solidarities defined the lives of ordinary people. In some places, extended families were common; that is, parents and sometimes other relatives lived with couples. In some places, such as England, the nuclear family (a couple and their children) was the most common household. When children of the lower classes began their working lives—usually at the age of fourteen or fifteen, or earlier for some apprentices—their obligations to their parents did not end. Often, however, they left home in search of work, rarely, if ever, to return. The poor turned to family and neighbors for help in bad times, as well as for help with harvests, if they owned land.

An Expanding Economy

One of the hallmarks of medieval society had been the marked expansion of trade and manufacture that began in the eleventh century. During the twelfth and thirteenth centuries, merchants greatly increased the amount of products carried on land routes and in the low galley-ships that hugged the Mediterranean coastline, more confident than ever before that their goods would find purchasers. In the markets of Flanders and northern France, olive oil, fruit, and wine from the Mediterranean region were exchanged for timber, cereals, and salted herring.

With the expansion in commercial activity, a money economy slowly developed. Yet trade and barter remained important, particularly for peasants, most of whom were part of a subsistence economy. Currency still did not penetrate some mountainous regions.

Yet overall, the late Middle Ages brought a significant rise in the availability of credit to states and entrepreneurs. Banking families in Venice and other Italian city-states were already well-established in the thirteenth century. Some merchants were no longer itinerant travelers, but rather sedentary entrepreneurs able to raise capital, such as from borrowing from banking families or other merchants or moneylenders, and extend and obtain credit. They also developed bills of exchange (see Chapter 5), which were orders drawn upon an agent to pay another merchant money at a future date, perhaps in another country and in another currency. Here and there, merchants began to work on a commission basis, and some specialized in transporting goods. They began to keep registers of profits and losses, using double-entry bookkeeping. All these changes facilitated a commercial boom in the sixteenth century, even if the multiplicity of states and the tolls between and within them hindered commerce.

The sixteenth century also brought a marked increase in basic manufacturing, which in some regions may have multiplied by 500 percent. The

Bankers sitting behind their *banco* (counter) doing business.

extraction of iron, copper, and silver quadrupled, for example, in Central Europe. Large-scale production, however, was limited to mining and textiles, as well as to arms manufacturing and shipbuilding.

The production of textiles, whether for distant markets or local consumption, dominated the manufacturing economy. Techniques for the production of silk had been imported from China into Europe by Arabs in the tenth century. First centered in the Italian states, production spread during the second half of the fifteenth century across the Alps to the German states, France, and Spain, which no longer depended on imported silk from Persia and Asia.

The manufacture of cloth developed in Tuscany, northern France, Flanders, and the Netherlands. The woolens industry of Flanders, which had begun during the medieval period, boomed, centered in the towns of Ypres, Ghent, and Bruges. England, which continued to export wool to the continent, became a major producer of woolen goods in the fourteenth century. Antwerp emerged as Europe's first important center of international trade.

Urban merchants and artisans were organized into guilds, which regulated production and distribution, thus protecting, at least in principle, guild members and consumers. The structure of craft production was organized hierarchically. Apprentices who learned their craft became journeymen and, if all went well, could eventually become masters, joining a masters' guild and employing journeymen and training apprentices. Most cloth was finished in towns by craft artisans. Through the guilds, masters could preserve the quality of work within their particular trades and, at the same time, the reputations of their town. During the fourteenth and fifteenth centuries, it became increasingly difficult for journeymen to become independent master craftsmen. Early in the sixteenth century, some German journeymen refused to work for masters who paid them less than they desired or had been used to receiving.

In the cottage (domestic) industry, merchant-capitalists put out spinning, weaving, and other work into the countryside. Here a woman is spinning in her home.

Some craftsmen worked outside the walls of cities or in the countryside to avoid guild monopolies and specifications on wages and piece rates. Likewise, merchant-capitalists who owned raw materials put out spinning, weaving (sometimes renting out looms), and other work into the countryside, where labor was cheaper. Rural production spread rapidly in northern Italy, the Netherlands, northern France, and England between 1450 and 1550. Hundreds of thousands of peasants produced woolen or linen yarn or wove it into cloth; then urban workers dyed, bleached, or shrunk the cloth, which merchants then sold. This "cottage industry" (also sometimes called "domestic industry") would remain an important part of the manufacturing process well into the nineteenth century.

The Growth of Towns

During the twelfth and thirteenth centuries, European towns grew rapidly in both number and size, reflecting economic development and increased security in medieval Europe. Fortified stone ramparts, gates, and towers gave towns unique visible characteristics. Towns were the residence of most courts (including municipal courts), hospitals, and fraternal associations, such as religious confraternities and guilds. Town halls and churches were the cornerstones of the medieval towns. In addition to the "bourgeois" or "burghers" (townspeople), most towns had a relatively large number of clergy living within their walls, ministering to the needs of the population or living a cloistered existence in convents and monasteries.

Most major towns in Europe were founded before 1300. In Poland, about 200 new towns were created between 1450 and 1550, adding to the 450 already in existence. Northern Italy and the Low Countries had the densest networks of towns. However, even there town dwellers remained a relatively small minority of the population, no more than about 15 percent. In 1500 only about 6 percent of Europeans resided in towns of more than 10,000 people. In the German states, about 200 of 3,000 towns had more than 10,000 residents. Only Constantinople, Naples, Milan, Paris, and Venice had more than 100,000 inhabitants.

In Italy, Venice, Florence, Genoa, Milan, and Pisa became independent city-states in about 1100, establishing control over surrounding smaller towns and villages. The decline of the Byzantine Empire and the inability of the Holy Roman Empire to establish its authority throughout Italy prevented the development of large territorial states on the peninsula. The prosperity of the city-states, too, impeded the creation of a single state, or even two or three major ones. Freed of feudal overlords, the dynamism of these city-states underlay the Renaissance (see Chapter 2). Venetian and Genoese merchants sent trading fleets carrying goods to and from the Levant and beyond, as well as along the spice routes to Central Asia, India, and China (visited by the Italian adventurer Marco Polo during his long voyage from 1275 to 1292).

In northern Europe, as well, the growth of cities and towns was linked to the expansion of long-distance trade and commerce. In northern Germany, independent trading towns were enriched by the Baltic grain trade, as Polish landowners, like their Hungarian and Bohemian counterparts, exported grain to the Netherlands and other Western countries. Lübeck and Hamburg with other northern German trading cities formed the Hanseatic League, which at first was a federation established to defend against banditry. These towns began to thrive in the mid-twelfth century, establishing networks of trade that reached from London all the way to Novgorod in northwestern Russia. The Polish Baltic port of Gdańsk had its own currency, fleet, army, and diplomats. Likewise, towns in southern Germany formed leagues to resist territorial lords and to protect trade routes. The fairs held outside the towns of Champagne in northern France, as well as in Lyon and Beaucaire farther south on the Rhône, served as trading points between northern Europe and Mediterranean merchants. The market function of trading towns swelled their populations. Landowners, particularly in regions of commercialized agriculture, sold their produce in the town markets.

Medieval Europe boasted major urban centers of learning. Paris (theology), Montpellier (medicine), and Bologna (Roman law) were major university centers. Oxford and Cambridge Universities were founded in the thirteenth century. Universities existed not in the sense that we know them today. Rather, the term referred to a corporately organized body of students or masters in one town. By 1500, dozens of towns had universities. And, in turn, literacy (limited to a small proportion of the population) rose faster in towns than in the countryside, as the equivalent of secondary education— limited to a privileged few—shifted from rural monasteries to town church or grammar schools.

Town governments were dominated by oligarchies of rich merchants, guild masters, and property owners (in Italian towns, nobles were part of these oligarchies). Despite the fact that many peasants still lived in towns, working fields outside town walls during the day and returning home before the gates slammed shut at nightfall, town and country seemed in some ways worlds apart.

Municipal Liberties

In feudal Europe, towns stood as zones of freedom, because their residents were not, in most cases, bound by service obligations to lords. Contemporaries held that "town air makes [one] free." No town person in Western Europe could be a serf. Urban freedoms had to be obtained from lords, however. Towns purchased charters of exemption from taxes in exchange for payments. Urban oligarchs jealously guarded this municipal independence against nobles and rulers eager to attain revenue and political consolidation. In some cases, rulers actively sought alliances with towns against nobles. Towns could also loan money to kings waging war against recalcitrant vassals or other rulers, including popes. Where territorial rulers were weak, as in Italy and the German states, towns obtained the greatest degree of freedom. Towns developed less rapidly in areas where rulers and nobles exercised strong authority.

Traditions of municipal liberties would leave a significant heritage in Western Europe, ultimately shaping the emergence of constitutional forms of government. Whereas social relationships in the countryside were largely defined by personal obligations, in towns these were replaced by collective rights through guilds and other associations. In England, northern France, the Netherlands, Flanders, and Switzerland, urban medieval confraternities struggled to maintain their independence from rulers and rural nobles. Lacking the associational infrastructure of many towns in Western Europe, however, Eastern European towns were not able to stem the tide of the increasing power of nobles and, in the case of Russia, the tsars. As the Muscovite state expanded its authority, the tsars ran roughshod over urban pretensions. Most towns in the East enjoyed none of the special charters of rights that characterized towns in the West. Russian rulers considered towns their personal property, and Russian lords demanded the service and allegiance of townspeople.

The Emergence of Sovereign States

Although the term "state" was not yet being used to denote a political entity, by 1500 the largest monarchical kingdoms (see Map 1.2) were taking on some of the characteristics of the modern state. During the late fifteenth century, France, Spain, and England evolved into "new monarchies." What was "new" about them was their growing reach, an evolution begun

MAP 1.2 EUROPE IN 1500 Europe in 1500 was a maze of fragmented realms although sovereign monarchical states were beginning to emerge.

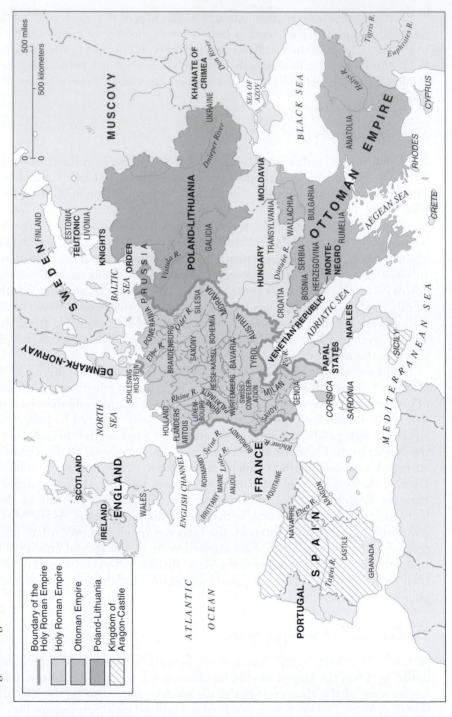

in the late medieval era. While monarchies grew stronger in Western Europe, however, they were actually weakened in Eastern and East Central Europe during the late Middle Ages. Struggles for power, civil war, and the growing domination of lords hindered the emergence of strong states there at least until the late sixteenth century.

Sovereign states emerged in Western Europe during the medieval period as rulers moved toward greater authority and independence. Yet, to be sure, these states were not "nation-states" in the modern sense, in which citizens feel that they belong to a nation by being, for example, Spanish, French, or Italian. Such national states, defined by ethnic bonds and cultural and linguistic traditions, would only develop beginning in the mid-eighteenth century and, above all, the nineteenth century. Medieval rulers governed a complex hodgepodge of territories, semi-independent towns, feudal vassals, and corporate institutions such as guilds that were largely independent of the crown, exchanging personal and/or corporate privileges for loyalty.

Between the tenth and fifteenth centuries, the kingdoms of France, England, and Spain grew into sovereign states as their rulers consolidated their territories by establishing their primacy over rivals. These rulers made laws and imposed administrative unity to a degree that was unprecedented. They asserted their authority, but not domination, over the nobles of the territories they claimed. Royal authority directly touched more subjects than ever before. Monarchs could raise and command armies, mint money, impose taxes, summon advisers, and appoint officials to represent and enforce their will.

The French kings, their territories clustered around Paris, had little real power during the medieval period. Until the mid-fifteenth century, the kings of England held Normandy, Brittany, Maine, Anjou, and Aquitaine, and the counts of Flanders held wealthy lands in what is now northern France and southern Belgium. During the Hundred Years' War (1337–1453), French kings raised the funds and armies necessary to expel the English from France (with the exception of the Channel port of Calais). During the last half of the fifteenth century, the French kings ended the *de facto* independence of large, prosperous provinces that were technically fiefs of the crown. In 1482, France absorbed Burgundy, whose powerful dukes were related to the kings of France, and a decade later the regent for Charles VIII (ruled 1483–1498) invaded Brittany, adding it to France. Through timely royal marriages and warfare, the French monarchs established the foundations for a stronger, more centralized monarchy.

England, too, emerged as a stronger monarchical state during the late medieval period, but with significant differences from its continental counterparts. The vassals of King John (ruled 1199–1216) and the people of London rebelled against more taxes he imposed to finance his attempt to recover continental territories lost to France. In 1215, the king was forced to sign the Magna Carta, the "great Charter of Liberties." John agreed to

The seal of King John (1215) on the Magna Carta, a cornerstone of English common and constitutional law.

impose major taxes only with the permission of a "great council" that represented the barons and to cease hiring mercenaries when his barons refused to fight. Later in the century, King Edward I (ruled 1272–1307) summoned barons, bishops, and representatives from England's major towns in the hope of obtaining their agreement to provide funds for another war against the king of France. From that "parley," or "parliament," came the tradition in England of consultation with leading subjects and the origins of an English constitutional government that constrained royal authority. The division of Parliament into two houses, the House of Lords and the House of Commons, which consisted of landed nobles and representatives of towns, developed during the reign of Edward III (ruled 1327–1377). Parliament's role as a representative institution increased as the king required new taxes to fight the Hundred Years' War against France. Parliament approved these levies.

In Central Europe, the Holy Roman Empire was not really a sovereign state. It dated from A.D. 962, the year when German nobles elected a ruler. By the end of the thirteenth century, the principle that the Holy Roman emperor would be elected, and not designated by heredity, had been established. Considering themselves the successors of the Roman Empire, the Holy Roman emperors saw themselves as the protectors of the papacy and of all Christendom. This involved the emperor in the stormy world of Italian politics.

The Holy Roman Empire encompassed about 300 semi-autonomous states, ranging from several large territories to a whole host of smaller states, principalities, and free cities that carried out their own foreign policy and fought wars. The emperor, selected by seven princes, could not consolidate his authority, levy taxes, raise armies or, increasingly, enforce his will outside of his own hereditary estates.

The Austrian Habsburgs, the ruling house in the German Alpine hereditary lands, had gradually extended their territories in the fourteenth and fifteenth centuries between the Danube River, the Adriatic Sea, and the Little Carpathian Mountains in Eastern Europe. Beginning in 1438, when the first Habsburg was elected Holy Roman emperor, until 1740 (when the male line was extinguished), only Habsburgs held the title of Holy Roman emperor. Smaller states, such as the thirteen cantons of Switzerland, struggled to maintain their autonomy against rising Habsburg power.

Developing State Structures

The growth in the number of royal officials helped rulers consolidate more effective power. Rulers had always had some kind of advisory council, but the importance of their advisers grew in the fourteenth and fifteenth centuries. Chanceries, treasuries, and courts of law represented an early stage of bureaucratization. Serving as royal officials, some humble men of talent began to reach positions of influence within states.

Rulers still earned revenue from their own lands. But in order to meet the expenses of their states, they drew income from taxation, the sale of offices (posts in the service of the monarch that were often both prestigious and lucrative) and government bonds, and the confiscation of land from recalcitrant nobles. Like other rulers, popes also centralized administration and finances, selling posts. Rulers imposed taxes on salt, wine, and other goods, impositions from which nobles and clergy were generally exempt. States in the sixteenth century became the great collectors and distributors of revenue. Moreover, the gradual growth of public debt was another sign of the increased authority of monarchical states. Royal dependency on the loans of merchant-bankers enriched the latter, providing more capital for their ventures. Rulers, surrounded by courtiers and councils, lived in a grander fashion. As they worked to consolidate their authority and territories, thrones became increasingly hereditary. As even wealthy people were apt to die young, such succession arrangements, which varied throughout Europe, mattered considerably.

With the strengthening of sovereign states in the fifteenth century, which entailed the loss of the right to have armies of retainers, nobles depended more on monarchies for the sanction of their power and honor. More of them came to court and served as royal officials. The sale of royal offices, especially in France and Spain, encouraged loyalty to the throne. Royal courts now adjudicated property disputes, gradually eroding noble jurisdiction over the king's subjects, although in France and many of the German states nobles retained rights of justice over peasants.

In the fifteenth century, regular channels for diplomacy emerged among the states of Europe. The Italian city-states were the first to exchange permanent resident ambassadors. By the middle of the century, Florence, Milan, Venice, and the kingdom of Naples all routinely exchanged ambassadors, who provided news and other information, while representing the interests of their states.

Limits to State Authority

Significant constraints, however, still limited the authority of rulers. We have seen that the privileges of towns, established through the purchase of royal charters of financial immunity, tempered royal power. Some regions (for example, Navarre in Spain), nominally incorporated into realms, maintained autonomy through representative institutions. And, to be sure, distance and physical impediments such as mountains and vast plains also prevented the effective extension of royal authority.

Even more important was the tradition that assemblies of notable subjects had rights, including that of being consulted, as in the case of England cited above. In the thirteenth century, rulers had convoked assemblies of notable subjects to explain their policies and to ask for help. Because they depended on those whom they assembled to provide military assistance when they required it, they also heard grievances. From this, parliaments, assemblies, diets, and Estates developed, representing (depending on the place) nobles, clergy, towns, and, in several cases, commoners.

Early in the sixteenth century, an Italian exile told the king of France what the monarch would need to attack the duchy of Milan: "Three things are necessary: money; more money; and still more money." The most powerful states—France, Habsburg Austria, and Spain—could raise sizable armies with relative ease. But, to meet the extraordinary expenses of wartime, they increasingly borrowed money from wealthy banking families. Rulers also utilized subsidies from friendly powers, imposed special taxes and forced loans, and sold offices. Sixteenth-century inflation would make wars even more expensive.

Royal levies to finance warfare through direct taxation could only be imposed with the consent of those taxed, except peasants, who had limited rights. The dialogue between rulers and assemblies, and the strength and weakness of such representative bodies, over the centuries would define the emergence and nature of modern government in European states.

The princes of the German states had to ask assemblies of nobles for the right to collect excise taxes. In Poland-Lithuania and Hungary, noble assemblies were more important than royal authority. In Bohemia, the rights of towns partially balanced noble prerogatives. Rulers could suspend decisions of those "sovereign" bodies, yet such assemblies could not be completely ignored because rulers needed their support, or at least compliance, particularly in time of war.

The prerogatives of nobles and churchmen also impeded royal authority. They invariably resisted royal taxes, which fell on the poor—the vast majority of the population—whom no one represented. Nobles still had to be convinced or coerced to provide armies. Kings became, at least in principle, supreme judges (though not for the clergy, as ecclesiastics were generally tried in Church courts), with royal courts offering litigants and petitioners a final appeal.

The struggle between rulers and the popes dated to the late eleventh century, when the popes and Holy Roman emperors had struggled for primacy. During the "lay investiture crisis," which began in 1060, the popes had contested the right of lay rulers to appoint bishops and invest them with signs of spiritual authority, normally a staff and a ring. (The dispute ended in 1122 when Emperor Henry V relinquished the imperial claim to the power to

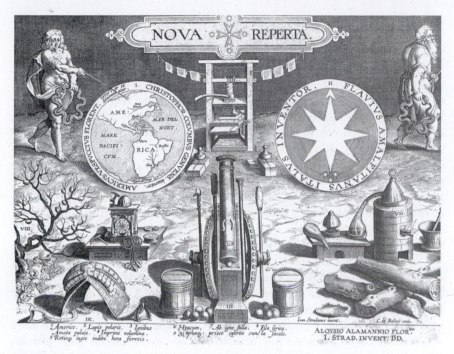

Theodore Galle's *Nova reperta* ("New discoveries") celebrates the discovery of the New World and forms of the new technology (gunpowder, the compass, the clock, the saddle with stirrups).

invest bishops with spiritual authority, and the pope recognized the emperor's right to give fiefs to the bishops once they had been consecrated, which left them with the status of vassals recognizing the lay authority of the emperor.) The clergy generally taught obedience to secular as well as ecclesiastical rulers. Furthermore, in the late medieval period, kings were able to further consolidate their power when popes granted the rulers of France, Spain, and some German towns certain rights over the clergy, including that of naming bishops.

TRANSFORMING DISCOVERIES

In the late Middle Ages, stunning developments in warfare and exploration transformed Europe and its relationship with the rest of the world. Moreover, the invention of printing created a culture of books, facilitating the spread of knowledge, ideas, and debate, at a time when exploration led to developing trade networks across the oceans, conquest, and empires.

Gunpowder, Warfare, and Armies

Warfare became more pervasive in the early modern period because of dynastic quarrels between rulers as they sought to consolidate or increase their territories. Although kings still depended on nobles to raise armies and to command on the battlefield, the face of battle was revolutionized in the late medieval period. Invented in China, gunpowder was brought to Europe in the thirteenth century by the Arabs. Gunpowder moved warfare from "chiefly a matter of violent housekeeping" between lords and vassals to sometimes massive struggles between dynastic rivals. First used in battle in the early fourteenth century, gunpowder could propel arrows and, increasingly, lead bullets. Gunpowder soon became the explosive for early versions of rifles, or muskets, which could be standardized in caliber and ammunition and for which clockmakers could produce spring-driven wheel locks that functioned as firing mechanisms.

Gradually replacing the lance, sword, crossbow, and longbow in battle, the rifle eroded the role of the noble as a privileged warrior since heavily armored knights could now be more easily shot off their horses by guns than unseated by lances or brought down by arrows. This reduced the role of cavalry in battle. Cavalrymen now wore light armor, and, while they might well carry a lance, they also sometimes were armed with pistols. Pikemen, however, remained essential to any army; their thirteen-foot-long weapons, made of a long wooden pole topped by a sharp iron point, protected the infantry while soldiers reloaded. The furious attack of pikemen could tear apart the rows of riflemen as they knelt to reload.

Now exploding artillery shells could wound or kill many combatants at once. At the Battle of Novara (1513) in northern Italy, where Swiss soldiers defeated a French army, artillery fire killed 700 men in three minutes. Deadly bombardments during battles had a devastating effect on the morale of the enemy. Naval battles grew fiercer as cannon replaced rams on warships. The sleek galleys that raced along the coast of the Mediterranean during the warm summer months gave way to ships large enough to transport heavy cannon. The threat from enemy artillery forced the construction of massive fortifications around towns, which left the defense with a solid advantage in warfare. Sieges lasted longer than ever before. Victorious armies, frustrated by lengthy sieges, sometimes slaughtered the surviving civilian population.

Although frontier garrisons, artillery units, and the king's household guards were virtually the only true standing armies, their size increased during the wars of the late fifteenth and the sixteenth centuries. During the Hundred Years' War (1337–1453), major battles were fought with between 7,000 and 15,000 soldiers on each side. During the struggles between the Austrian Habsburg and French Valois dynasties on the Italian peninsula in the fifteenth and sixteenth centuries, armies reached 25,000 men in size. Some nobles still had private armies but served their kings as commanders and cavalrymen.

Mercenaries, the original "free lances," increasingly replaced feudal levies (and urban militias, where they existed) in armies mobilized by rulers to defend or expand their territorial interests. These might include Albanians, Englishmen, Scots, Greeks, Poles, and Swiss pikemen. Mercenaries received modest, though irregular, pay and expected acceptable rations and the opportunity to pillage the towns they conquered. Assuming these conditions were met, they seem to have deserted far less frequently than soldiers recruited by states from their own populations.

Yet most states had some kind of conscription, whether a formalized draft of men between the ages of fifteen and sixty or a hasty roundup when war approached. Loyal nobles, royal officials, and paid recruiters provided soldiers. Peasants made up more than three-quarters of armies, as they did the European population. Criminals also ended up in armies, often as the price of their release from prison or from execution, though they might well carry with them forever a branded letter as part of their sentence (such as the letter "V" for the French word *voleur*—thief).

Conditions of military service were difficult at best. In addition to barely adequate lodging and food, infractions of rules were dealt with harshly, including the infamous and often fatal "running the gauntlet" through troops lined up on both sides, dispensing blows with sticks or swords. Officers dispensed justice without trial or appeal, and sentences were carried out immediately. The severed heads of deserters or other serious offenders were impaled on pikes for several days at the entrance to a camp, sending a clear message.

Except for royal guards, artillery units, and other specialized forces, uniforms were rare in any army, although most soldiers sported some type of identification, such as an armband or a tunic bearing a national or regional symbol like the English red cross, the barred cross of Lorraine, or the lion of Lyon.

Epidemics and disease—dysentery and typhoid, among others—carried off far more than did wounds received in battle. But casualty figures were also alarming, however inaccurately kept. The wounded often died from inadequate—even for the time—medical treatment and from neglect.

The Printing Press and the Power of the Printed Word

The advent of printing in Europe in the fifteenth century in some ways marked the end of the medieval period. The invention of woodblock printing and paper had occurred in China in the eighth century; both reached Europe from the Arab world via Spain in the thirteenth century. Before the arrival of these technologies, monks and scribes had copied books on parchment sheets; a single copy of the Bible required about 170 calfskins or 300 sheepskins. Because it was much cheaper than parchment, paper more readily accommodated scholars, officials, and merchants. But the process of copying itself remained slow. Cosimo de' Medici, the Florentine banker and patron of Renaissance art, hired 200 scribes to copy 200 volumes in two years' time.

All this changed in the fifteenth century when Flemish craftsmen invented a kind of oil-based ink. This and the innovation of a wooden hand press made possible the invention of movable metal type in the German cathedral town of Mainz in about 1450 by, among several others, Johannes Gutenberg (c. 1395–1468). His stunningly beautiful Latin Bibles are treasured today. Printing shops soon started up in the Italian states, Bohemia, France, and the Netherlands, and in Spain and England by the 1470s (see Map 1.3). By 1500, about 35,000 books were published each year in Europe, and a century later the number had jumped to between 150,000 and 200,000 books.

Books provided scholars with identical ancient and medieval texts to discuss and critique. Accounts of discoveries and adventures in the New World filtered across Europe from Spain, England, and France. The number of scholarly libraries—which were really just private collections—grew rapidly. New professions developed: librarians, booksellers, publishers, typesetters,

MAP 1.3 SPREAD OF PRINTING THROUGH EUROPE, 1450–1508   Towns and dates at which printing shops were established throughout Europe.

and editors. Moreover, with the greater dissemination of knowledge came an increase in the number of universities, rising from twenty in 1300 to about seventy in 1500.

More people learned how to read, although literate individuals remained far in the minority. In Florence and other prosperous cities, the rate of literacy may have been relatively high, although in the Italian city-states as a whole it is unlikely that more than 1 percent of workers and peasants could read and write. The literate population of the German states in 1500 was about 3 or 4 percent. But among the upper classes many more people developed the habit of reading.

Not all that was published pleased lay and ecclesiastic leaders, and printing made censorship considerably more difficult. No longer could the destruction of one or two manuscripts hope to root out an idea. Thus, Pope Alexander VI warned in a bull in 1501: "The art of printing is very useful insofar as it furthers the circulation of useful and tested books; but it can be very harmful if it is permitted to widen the influence of pernicious works. It will therefore be necessary to maintain full control over the printers."

Exploration and Conquest in the New World:
The Origins of European Empire

By the last decade of the fifteenth century, the inhabitants of the Iberian Peninsula already had several centuries of navigational and sailing accomplishments behind them. The Portuguese, who had the advantage of the magnificent port of Lisbon, had captured a foothold on the Moroccan coast in 1415, beginning two centuries of expansion. Early in the fifteenth century, they began to explore the west coast of Africa and had taken Madeira and the Azores islands in the Atlantic. Their goal was to break Muslim and Venetian control of European access to Asian spices and silk.

King Ferdinand and Queen Isabella of Spain initially rejected the request of the Genoese cartographer and merchant Christopher Columbus (1451–1506), who sought financial backing for an ocean voyage to reach the Indies. In 1492, however, fearing that Portuguese vessels might be the first to reach the wealth of Asia by sea, the royal couple consented to support the expedition.

Late in 1492, Columbus set sail with three ships. He believed the earth was a perfect sphere, and since Africa stood in the way of a voyage sailing to the east, he thought it possible to reach the Orient by sailing west across the Atlantic Ocean, which he believed to be narrow. After more than nine weeks on the open seas, the small fleet reached not Asia but rather the small Caribbean island of San Salvador in the Americas. He then came ashore in Cuba and finally Hispaniola (now the Dominican Republic and Haiti). "What on earth have you come seeking so far away?" he was asked. "Christians and spices," he replied. But he also probably believed that he would find gold, and asked the Indians he encountered on the shore in sign language if they knew where some could be found. Columbus was impressed with the beauty of Hispaniola (although he remained convinced that he had discovered islands near India) and the "docility" of the indigenous people. Yet, in the absence of gold, he suggested that the Spanish crown could make Hispaniola profitable by selling its people as slaves, a looming tragedy. Columbus, whose greatest contribution was to find a way across the sea using the trade winds, made three subsequent voyages of discovery, the last beginning in 1502, after which he gave up his search for a passage to Asia.

Portugal, a much poorer state than Spain, struggled to defend its trade routes against Spanish encroachments. In 1487 Bartholomew Dias (c. 1450–1500) first rounded the Cape of Good Hope, the southern tip of Africa, reaching the Indian Ocean, and then Calcutta on the southwest coast of India. The cargo of spices the Portuguese explorer Vasco da Gama (c. 1460–1524) brought back to Lisbon from India in 1498 paid for his costly expedition sixty times over. The Portuguese established fortified bases along the Indian Ocean, including at Goa. The maritime route across the Indian Ocean to the South China Sea could now compete with the overland spice and silk routes that had long linked Europe to the markets of the East. However, the Portuguese found that a thriving maritime trade network

Portuguese, wearing Western attire, meeting robed Japanese upon disembarking in 1542.

already existed between China, Japan, Southeast Asia, India, the Persian Gulf, and East Africa. The European trading presence was new. An Indonesian ruler remarked of the Portuguese adventurers, "The fact that these people journey so far from home to conquer territory indicates clearly that there must be very little justice and a great deal of greed among them." This had made them "fly all over the waters in order to acquire possessions that God did not give them."

In 1493, Pope Alexander VI divided the non-Christian world into zones for Spanish and Portuguese exploration and exploitation (see Map 1.4). His proclamation seemed to justify conquests, as well as the conversion of indigenous peoples. He awarded Portugal all of sub-Saharan Africa and Asia; Spain, the pope's ally, received most of the Americas. Portugal claimed Brazil, which became the largest colony in the Americas, established in the second half of the sixteenth century.

Soon more and more Spanish explorers reached the Americas. Vasco Núñez de Balboa (c. 1475–1519) established Spanish sovereignty over what is now Panama. Cuba, in turn, fell, and then served as a staging point for the conquest of Mexico by Hernando Cortés (1485–1547), which opened a new chapter in European expansion. Cortés, who first crossed the Atlantic in 1506 to Hispaniola, landed on the coast of Mexico in 1519. He went to see the Aztec ruler, Montezuma. The Aztec capital of Tenochtitlán (present-day Mexico City) was then larger than any other European city except Constantinople. Montezuma sent him away, although he later sent him gifts of gold and silver. Despite the fact that he had been ordered to limit his expedition to exploration and trade, Cortés was determined to conquer Mexico in the name of Emperor Charles V. The interests of the Spanish crown would remain paramount in the construction of Spain's overseas empire. Cortés formed alliances with Montezuma's non-Aztec peoples, who naively hoped that Cortés might help them achieve independence. The Spanish adventurer then conquered Mexico with no more than sixteen horses and six hundred soldiers, with the help of his Native American allies.

Farther south, Francisco Pizarro (c. 1476–1541) led his men in the conquest of the Inca Empire in Peru. Although the Incas were a people rich in precious metals and culture, they had never seen iron or steel weapons before, nor did they have draft animals. When Pizarro's horses lost their shoes in Peru and there was no iron available to replace them, he had them shod in silver. In the 1540s more silver was discovered in Mexico, and also in the Andes Mountains, completely transforming the economy of Spanish conquest. Imported silver enhanced the integration of the Spanish Empire into the expanding trade of Europe.

The victory of the conquistadors (conquerors) was the victory of steel-bladed swords over stone-bladed swords. Moreover, the surprise element of cannon contributed to the Spanish victory in the Americas and of the Portuguese in Southeast Asia. A witness to a Portuguese attack in 1511

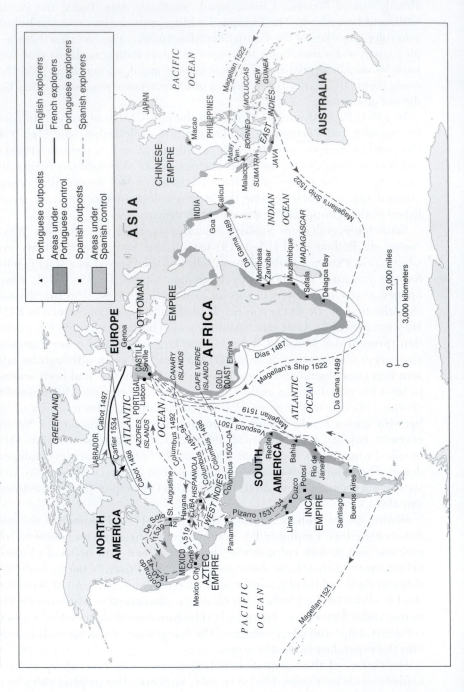

MAP 1.4 EXPLORATION AND CONQUEST, 1492–1542 Pope Alexander VI divided the non-Christian world into zones for Spanish and Portuguese exploration and exploitation. Portuguese, Spanish, French, and English explorers set out to find new routes to Asia, the New World, and around the world.

Aztec emissaries agreeing to a treaty with Cortés, who is seated with his interpreter standing to his left.

remembered, "the noise of the cannon was as the noise of thunder in the heavens and the flashes of fire of their guns were like flashes of lightning in the sky: and the noise of their matchlocks was like that of ground-nuts popping in the frying-pan."

Steeped in tales of crusading chivalry and conquest, the conquerors set out looking for adventure and wealth. Cortés, for example, was of a modest Castilian noble family; his father had fought against the Moors in southern Spain, and thus was himself a veteran of another imperial conquest, the Reconquista, which had expelled the Moors from the Iberian Peninsula. "We came here to serve God and the king," said one Spaniard in the Americas, "but also to get rich." Most died young, far from home, their dreams of wealth shattered by the harsh realities of life in what seemed to them a strange and often inhospitable world. Ferdinand Magellan (c. 1480–1521), the Portuguese-born explorer, was killed by angry islanders on a Pacific beach. His crew nonetheless circumnavigated the globe, having proven that a southwest passage to India did exist, returning to Spain in 1522.

Many of the conquistadors, and many of the later settlers (mostly men) who were attracted by tales of gold and silver, died in the New World; during the first ten years of Spanish settlement of Hispaniola, as much as two-thirds of the European population perished. However, many times more of the native people they encountered perished as a result of contact with the newcomers. The smallpox the Spanish brought with them wiped out people who had no immunity to diseases brought from Europe. The indigenous population of Mexico fell from about 25 million—or more—in 1520 to perhaps as few as 1 million in 1600. The native population of Peru fell from about 7 million in 1500 to half a million in 1600. Other European diseases, including measles, typhus, and bubonic plague, decimated the native population. In Guatemala, a Mayan Indian kept a chronicle of the ravages of European disease among his people: "Great was the stench of the dead. After our fathers and grandfathers succumbed, half of the people fled to the fields. The dogs and vultures devoured the bodies. . . . We were born to die." In turn, the Indians gave the Spanish syphilis, which then spread in Europe.

The exchange of diseases was a tragic consequence of the meeting between the Old and New Worlds, but there were beneficial exchanges as well. Before the arrival of Europeans, there were no domesticated animals larger than the llama and alpaca in the Americas, and little animal protein in the Indian diet. Spaniards brought horses and cattle with them. Sheep had accompanied Columbus on his second journey. The 350 pigs brought to Cuba by Columbus had multiplied to over 30,000 by 1514. They provided manure for farming but ate their way through forest land and eroded the indigenous agricultural terrace system, upsetting the ecological balance of conquered lands.

Every year the Spanish galleons returned with tobacco, potatoes, new varieties of beans, cacao, chili peppers, and tomatoes. These crops contributed to an increase in the European population. Maize fed European farm animals. In turn, the Spaniards planted wheat, barley, rice, and oats in their colonies.

In 1565, a Spanish galleon completed a voyage of global trade by sailing across the Pacific Ocean from Manila to unload cinnamon on the coast of Mexico. Spanish ships returned with silver, which could purchase silks, porcelain, spices, jade, and mother-of-pearl brought by Chinese junks to the Philippines. Shipping routes led from Seville to the Caribbean and to the ports of Veracruz in Mexico and Cartagena in Colombia. They returned with Mexican and Peruvian silver that replenished the coffers of European princes and merchants. All five continents—Europe, Asia, Africa, North America, and South America—thus moved closer together in reciprocal economic relationships that represented the beginnings of a globalization of trade.

The Spanish sought not only trade with the Americas but also empire. Spanish legal documents affecting the new colonies declared that Indians would keep all lands they already held, but that all other territories henceforth belonged either to the crowns of Spain or were to be divided up among the conquerors as booty. The Spanish proclaimed the *requerim-*

iento, which required that Indians accept both Spanish rule and Christianity. The conquistadors built new towns, placing the church, town hall, and prison around a central marketplace (*plaza*), as towns developed on a rectangular grid plan.

In return for the pope's blessing of the colonial enterprise, missionaries began to arrive in the Americas, hoping to convert the Indians to Christianity. The harsh reality of the colonial experience for the natives, however, was largely untempered by the good intentions of some, but not all, of the missionaries. "For this kind of people," snapped a Portuguese priest in Brazil in 1563, "there is no better way of preaching than the sword and the rod of iron." A Spanish judge in Mexico said of his people that they "compelled [the Indians] to give whatever they asked, and inflicted unheard-of cruelties and tortures upon them."

Spaniards, Portuguese, and other Europeans sought to impose their culture on the peoples they conquered, although Christian teaching made only limited headway in India and virtually none in China. Unlike its view of Muslims, the Church did not consider Indians infidels, but rather as innocents who could be taught Christian beliefs. "Are these Indians not men?" asked a Dominican priest in Santo Domingo in a sermon to shocked colonists in 1511, "Do they not have rational souls? Are you not obliged to love them as you love yourselves?" A papal pronouncement depicted the Indians as "true men . . . capable not only of understanding the Catholic faith, but also, according to our information, desirous of receiving it." The Spaniards already had experience in dealing with the diversity of language and culture on the Iberian Peninsula, although nothing like what they found in the Americas. In the 1590s, a Franciscan friar boasted that he had built over 200 churches and baptized more than 70,000 Indians. In Latin America, Christian belief sometimes merged with local religious deities, customs, and shrines to create a distinctive form of Christianity.

Obligatory labor service, brutally enforced, first formed the relationship between rulers and the ruled. The crown of Castile established a system of encomienda, by which Spanish settlers would hold Indians "in trust," but not their lands. They could exact tribute in kind or labor. The system gradually ended and a wage system—not much better—came into place. Moreover, repartimiento allowed royal officials to force Indians to work for specific periods. In Central America, Spanish colonists invoked the medieval Christian concept of a "just war" against "heathens" as a justification for enslavement.

The Church and the crown periodically tried to protect the Indians against the harsh treatment accorded them by many of their Spanish countrymen in the name of profit. Bishop Bartolomé de Las Casas (1474–1566), whose father had accompanied Columbus on his second voyage to the Americas and who had himself been a conquistador before becoming a priest, spoke out against the treatment of Indians. He saluted the "marvelous government, laws, and good customs" of the Mayas of Central America, whom he wanted placed under the authority of the Church. Charles V ordered a pause in Spanish conquests until such moral issues could be considered, but the Spanish destruction of what they considered pagan temples and idols continued and the empire continued to expand.

As the Indian population was depleted through disease, overwork, and brutality, the Spanish looked for new sources of labor. Domestic slavery still existed in Italy, Spain, and Muscovy in the sixteenth century, as well as in the Arab world, and some Indians in the New World also had slaves. By the fifteenth century, Portuguese traders along the coast of West Africa had begun to make profits selling Africans as servants in Lisbon or as sugar plantation workers in the Portuguese Atlantic islands. Portugal soon dominated the African network of slave-trading, which depended on chieftains and traders in African kingdoms, merchants in Seville and Lisbon, settlers in Mexico and Peru, and Brazilian sugar growers. The Spaniards believed that Africans could best survive the brutally difficult work and hot climate of America. Between 1595 and 1640 about 300,000 slaves were transported to the Spanish colonies in the Americas, and five times that many would be shipped during the next century.

Gradually, more Spanish settlers arrived to populate the American colonies, including small traders, shoemakers, blacksmiths, and masons. (In Paraguay, the governor asked that no lawyers be allowed to emigrate, "because in newly settled countries they encourage dissension and litigation.") By the mid-sixteenth century about 150,000 Spaniards had crossed to America, and by the end of the century about 240,000 Spaniards had emigrated there. Most never returned to Spain.

In 1552, a Spanish official wrote King Charles V (ruled 1516–1556, Holy Roman emperor 1519–1558) that the discovery of the East and West Indies was "the greatest event since the creation of the world, apart from the incarnation and death of Him who created it." But Michel de Montaigne (1533–1592), a French writer who had met Indians brought back from Brazil, offered another view in 1588, when he observed that "so many goodly cities [were] ransacked and razed; so many nations destroyed and made desolate; so infinite millions of harmless peoples of all sexes, states, and ages, massacred, ravaged and put to the sword . . . ruined and defaced for the traffic of pearls and pepper."

Conclusion

The economic and political structures of early modern Europe drew on the dynamism of the medieval period. Demographic vitality finally overcame the catastrophic losses brought by the Black Death. Within Europe, commerce and manufacturing expanded. Mediterranean traders roamed as far as the Middle East and even Asia. And although much of Central Europe and the Italian peninsula remained a hodgepodge of small states, rulers in

France, England, and Spain had consolidated their authority, and sovereign monarchical states began to emerge.

Above all, three salient movements of change brought the Middle Ages to an end. The first was the Renaissance, or cultural rebirth, which began in the mid-fourteenth century in the Italian city-states (see Chapter 2). The commercial prosperity of Florence, above all, but also of Venice and other independent city-states made possible this period of extraordinary accomplishment in literature and painting. The invention of printing began to transform one culture after another. Second, the exploration and colonization of the New World would ultimately help end the Mediterranean Sea's role as the center of European prosperity and would lead to Spain's emergence as a world power, along with England and the Netherlands (see Chapters 5 and 6). Colonization brought the establishment of European empires abroad; between 1500 and the late eighteenth century, more than 1.5 million Europeans crossed the ocean to live in the New World. Third, the Reformation (see Chapter 3), which began in the second decade of the sixteenth century, challenged the unity of the Roman Catholic Church and its dominance in much of Europe.

CHAPTER 2

THE RENAISSANCE

In 1508, Pope Julius II summoned Michelangelo from Florence to the papal city of Rome. He commissioned the artist to paint frescoes (paintings on plaster) on the ceiling of the new Sistine Chapel, a ceremonial chapel next to the papal residence in the Vatican. With some reluctance (since he considered himself primarily a sculptor), Michelangelo agreed to undertake the project. He signed a contract that stipulated a payment of 3,000 ducats and began work that very day in May.

During the long, difficult years of intense creativity, Michelangelo often lay on his back, staring at the ceiling (still the best position from which to study his masterpiece), before climbing up the scaffolding to work. His frescoes, depicting Creation, Original Sin, the Flood, and the ancestors of Christ, are a triumph of religious painting. However, Pope Julius II, offended by the nude figures in the *Last Judgment* frescoes, ordered painters to cover the nudes with fig leaves. As a result, Michelangelo left Rome in disgust. He left behind what is arguably the most beautiful pictorial ensemble in Western painting.

Michelangelo's work represents the epitome of art during the Renaissance, a time of cultural rebirth. From about 1330 to 1530, the city-states of the Italian peninsula emerged as the intellectual and artistic centers of Europe. It was a period during which classical texts were rediscovered, thereby reviving the ideas, architecture, arts, and values of ancient Greece and Rome. By celebrating the beauty of nature and the dignity of mankind, Renaissance artists and scholars helped shape the intellectual and cultural history of the modern world. During the fifteenth century, Michelangelo, as well as Leonardo da Vinci and many other Renaissance sculptors and painters, enjoyed the patronage of wealthy families and produced some of the immortal works of the European experience. From about 1490 to 1530, Rome, too, was the center of a final period of artistic innovation, the High Renaissance, during which time the popes, including Julius II, commissioned paintings, sculptures, and churches.

Yet, weakened by internal political turmoil, the Italian city-states were ravaged by foreign invaders beginning in 1494. Unable to resist French invasion and then Spanish domination, after 1530 the city-states were no longer able to support artistic glories, and the Renaissance ended in a mood of discouragement, in striking contrast to the contagious optimism that had characterized its greatest moments.

THE CITY-STATES OF THE ITALIAN PENINSULA

The city-states were the fundamental political unit of the Italian peninsula, the most urbanized part of the Western world, even though the vast majority of the population of the Italian peninsula still lived in the countryside. In 1200, there were several hundred independent city-states on the Italian peninsula; gradually, however, that number was reduced, as many were absorbed as subject territories by more powerful city-states. A century later, at least twenty-three cities in the northern and central parts of the peninsula had populations of more than 20,000. It was within these city-states that the achievements of the Renaissance took place.

The city-states of Renaissance Italy were the most urbanized part of the Western world. Pictured here is the Loggia dei Lanzi, the principal gathering place in Florence. In the foreground, one can see priests and nuns praying while Florentine citizens go on about their day.

Thriving Economies

The economic prosperity and social dynamism of the city-states made the cultural achievements of the Renaissance possible. The city-states had become independent and prosperous because of the expansion of commerce during the eleventh and twelfth centuries. The Italian peninsula formed a natural point of exchange between East and West.

Intensively studied in the twelfth and thirteenth centuries, Roman law provided a framework for order and the development of political life within the Italian city-states. The Roman Empire had depended on a network of largely autonomous cities and towns, particularly in the plains of the northern part of the peninsula. These had been linked by a system of roads, unrivaled in Europe, all of which, as the saying goes, eventually led to Rome.

The people of the Italian peninsula had suffered the ravages of the Black Death and the other epidemics of the fourteenth century, but the ensuing economic recession, which led to declines in manufacturing and population in the central Italian region of Tuscany, did not affect much of the northern part of the peninsula, which still prospered. Drawing wool from England and Spain, Florence's textile industry employed about 30,000 workers. The finished Florentine cloth and woolen goods were then traded throughout the Mediterranean, and to Burgundy, Flanders, England, and as far as Asia. Agriculture thrived in the broad river valleys of Tuscany and Lombardy. The production of grains, vegetables, and wine, aided by the drainage of swamps and marshes and by irrigation, not only fed the urban population but also provided an agricultural surplus that could be invested in commerce and manufacturing. The proximity of Mediterranean trade routes bolstered international trade and small-scale manufacturing and brought prosperity to ambitious Italian merchants.

The development of banking during the early fourteenth century helped finance internal trade and international commerce. By the beginning of the fifteenth century, the Church's condemnation of usury no longer was taken to apply to banking, as long as the rates of interest were not considered excessive. Florence's gold florin became a standard currency in European trading centers. The bankers of that city, with agents in Avignon and many other cities throughout its trading network, were central to European commerce and monarchical and papal finances. Unlike traders elsewhere in Europe, Florentine merchants had broad experience with bills of exchange and deposit, which provided credit to purchasers. There were, however, risks to such loans. In the fifteenth century, the king of England forced Florentine merchants to loan him money, or face expulsion from the realm and lose all their assets there. But he defaulted on the loans after his invasion of France failed during the Hundred Years' War, and several major Florentine merchant companies went into bankruptcy.

Venice and Genoa were also major trading and banking cities, as well as centers of shipbuilding and insurance. Each city had long traded with the

This miniature depicts the Piazzetta of the Republic of Venice, with all the activity of a major Adriatic port.

East Indies and the Far East. Venice, in particular, had been a major center of trade and transcultural exchange between the Christian West and Muslim East since the eighth century. Venice linked sea routes with the long overland routes to Constantinople through the desolate mountains of the Balkans. Merchants hedged their bets on whether their shipments would fall victim to the sudden Mediterranean storms, to roving pirates, or to some other mishap on the overland route through Central Asia. The merchants carried fine woolens and linen from the Italian peninsula and northern Europe, as well as metals, to the East. They returned with cotton, silk, and, above all, spices, including pepper, cinnamon, nutmeg, ginger, and sugar, which arrived via Alexandria or Constantinople from the East Indies, luxury goods to awaken the palates of wealthy Europeans. Merchants from both East and West used towns in Crimea, a peninsula extending into the northern Black Sea, as intermediary points for trade from Muscovy, Persia, India, and China (see Map 2.1).

Merchant capitalism eroded the power of the nobility by expanding the ranks and influence of townsmen. The wealth and status of urban merchants—although nobles also engaged in trade—allowed them to

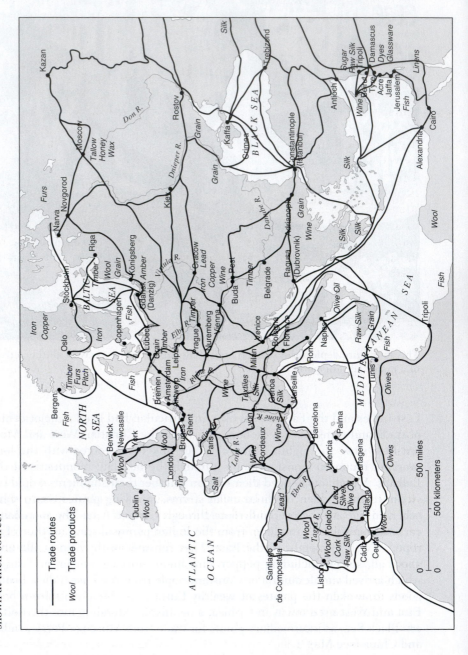

MAP 2.1 REACH OF TRADE DURING THE FIFTEENTH CENTURY Major trade routes, both by land and sea, led from the Italian city-states of Venice, Genoa, and Florence, as well as from northern Europe and the Baltic regions. The Italian city-states formed a natural point of exchange between East and West. Products that were traded are shown at their source.

dominate the oligarchies that ruled the city-states. Prosperity increased the strong sense of municipal identity and pride; the Florentine political theorist Niccolò Machiavelli insisted, "I love my native city more than my own soul."

Social Structure

The social structure of the Italian city-states resembled that of other urban centers of trade and manufacturing in England, France, Flanders, and Holland. In the city-states, the *pòpolo grasso,* or "fat people," were the elite, including nobles, wealthy merchants, and manufacturers. The *mediòcri* were the middling sort, including smaller merchants and master artisans. The *pòpolo minuto,* or "little people," made up the bulk of the urban population. In cities, artisans and laborers were burdened by high taxes on consumption. Urban elites owned much of the richest land of the hinterland, which was worked by tenant farmers, sharecroppers, and agricultural laborers, as well as by peasant landowners. In the northern and central part of the Italian peninsula, most peasants were free to be miserably poor, while in the southern part many still owed obligations to their lords.

The "fat people" of the city-states comprised no more than 5 percent of the population. The great patricians assumed the status of princes of their cities, whether as dukes, cardinals, or, in the case of Rome, as the pope himself. Although social differences remained sharp in Italian city-states, as everywhere, commercial wealth made possible some degree of social mobility, above all in Florence, the wealthiest city. New families, enriched by commerce, rose into the ruling elite, although opportunities to do so declined noticeably by the end of the fifteenth century.

An elaborate and highly ritualized etiquette based upon mutual flattery maintained social distance. The wealthiest families became even richer despite the recession that extended throughout much of the fourteenth and fifteenth centuries; their prosperity made them even more eager not to be taken for anyone of more modest station. Thus, one of the powerful dukes of Milan insisted that his wife be called *Illustrissima* ("Illustrious One"). Flattery and subservience could be found in every greeting, and in every letter penned to a prince: "Nothing in the world pleases me more than your commands," and the ominous "I live only insofar as I am in your excellency's graces," which was sometimes true enough.

Urban patriarchs dominated their cities through power and patronage. They dispensed titles, privileges, and cash as they pleased. The duke of Ferrara affirmed his power by going door to door once a year to "beg" on behalf of the poor, an inversion of reality that served to define his authority and the subordination of everyone else. But princes and patriarchs also ruled through intimidation, occasionally eliminating enemies with astonishing cruelty.

Renaissance Political Life

The originality of the Italian city-states during the Renaissance lay not only in their remarkable artistic accomplishments but also in their precociously innovative forms of political structure. The organization of some of the city-states into constitutional republics was closely linked to the cultural achievements of the Renaissance. Nonetheless, there was nothing democratic about the city-states of Renaissance Italy, for the elites had brutally crushed the popular uprisings of artisans and shopkeepers that occurred in Siena and other towns during the fourteenth century.

Fourteenth- and fifteenth-century republics were constitutional oligarchies dominated by the most powerful families who filled the executive bodies, legislative or advisory councils, and special commissions that governed each city-state. The percentage of male citizens enjoying the right to vote ranged from about 2 percent in fifteenth-century Venice to 12 percent in fourteenth-century Bologna, the former percentage seeming most representative of the restricted nature of political rights in Renaissance Italy. Venice, Siena, Lucca, and Florence (at least until the waning days of domination by the powerful Medici family) were the most stable oligarchic republics of Renaissance Italy; Genoa, Bologna, and Perugia went back and forth between republican and despotic governments (see Map 2.2).

Some of the other city-states became outright hereditary despotisms (*signori*) run by a single family. Milan, a despotism under the control of the Visconti family, had grown prosperous from metallurgy and textile manufacturing. Francesco Sforza, a *condottieri* (mercenary of common origins), who had married the illegitimate daughter of the last Visconti duke in 1447, helped overthrow the republic less than three years later. Sforza imposed his family's rule with the support of Milanese nobles. The Sforza family thereafter skillfully played off rivalries between other powerful families, sometimes implementing their will with sheer force. The duke of Milan tolerated a council of 900 men drawn from the city's leading citizens, but he appointed magistrates and officials—and in general ruled—as he pleased. Likewise, princely families, such as the Este family of Ferrara and the Gonzaga family of Mantua, ran the smaller city-states.

By contrast, Venice, an energetic, prosperous Adriatic port city of lagoons and canals built on a number of small islands, remained in principle a republic. Its constitution offered a balance of political interests: the *doge*, an official elected for life by the Senate, served as an executive authority whose prerogatives were not that far from those of a monarch. The Great Council, consisting of about 2,500 enfranchised patricians, elected the Senate, which represented the nobility, an increasing number of whom were ennobled merchants living in elegantly decorated houses facing the canals. No one represented the poor, more than half the population of Venice.

Like the monarchies beyond the Alps, the Italian city-states developed small, efficient state bureaucracies, as the despots or oligarchs (a few men

MAP 2.2 CITY-STATES IN RENAISSANCE ITALY, 1494   The city-state was the fundamental political unit of the Italian peninsula; the number of city-states was reduced as many of them were absorbed by the more powerful city-states.

or families running the government) of each city improved the effectiveness of state administration. Thus, Florence and Venice had special committees responsible for foreign affairs and commerce. Many offices were sold or filled by members of the leading families linked by marriages. Personal relations between powerful families, for example, between the Medicis and the Sforza, facilitated diplomacy. The Medici engaged financial specialists for the management of the fiscal policies of their city and their family, although the latter, to the detriment of Florence, almost

Portrait of Francesco Sforza, one of the elite *pòpolo grasso*.

always took precedence. ("Better a city ruined," said Cosimo de' Medici, "than lost.")

The *condottieri* were central to the political and military situation in Italy. A military ethos permeated the courts of the Italian princes. A young prince learned military exercises, including jousting (horseback combat with long lances that could occasionally be deadly), and he began to hunt, sometimes using falcons. Some dukes hired themselves and their private armies out to the highest bidders, such as powerful Italian princes, the king of France, or the Holy Roman emperor.

Renaissance princes and oligarchs surrounded themselves with an imposing retinue of attendants. The court of Urbino, not particularly wealthy compared to some of the others, employed a staff of 355 people. This number included 45 counts of the duchy, 17 noblemen of various pedigrees, 22 pages, 5 secretaries, 19 chamber grooms, 5 cooks, 19 waiters, 50 stable hands, and 125 servants and jacks-of-all-trades, including the *galoppini*, who galloped around on a variety of errands.

Florence, Milan, Venice, Naples, and the Papal States were as aggressive as France and the other monarchies beyond the Alps. They dominated their weaker neighbors through force, intimidation, and alliances, picking them off one by one, as in chess. When they were not battling each other, Florence and Venice combined to limit Milanese control to Lombardy, while establishing their own authority over their respective regions. Venice controlled territory from the Alps to the Po River. Genoa, bitterly divided between merchant factions and nobles living in the hills above the Mediterranean port, struggled to maintain its autonomy because it lay physically exposed to more powerful Milan, as well as to the kingdom of France.

The Papal States, which bordered Tuscany east of the Apennines and to their south, functioned like any other city-state. The pope, too, was a temporal, as well as a spiritual, prince. He was elected for life by cardinals, the highest bishops of the Church, who were, in turn, appointed by the pope. Like monarchs and urban oligarchs, popes had to contend with the ambitious nobles of the Papal States. They, too, conspired with and sought alliances against other city-states. The eternal city was only the peninsula's eighth largest city in the late fourteenth century, ruled by a beleaguered papacy amid distant echoes of past glories. The city-states were increasingly freed from the authority and interference of the papacy. This began with the "Babylonian Captivity" (1309–1378), when the popes lived in Avignon under the direct influence of the king of France and, for a time, a rival pontiff claimed authority from Rome (see Chapter 3). The declining role of the papacy in temporal Italian affairs further aided the rise of Florence, Milan, and Venice.

Florence: Anatomy of a Renaissance City

Florence was the cradle of the Italian Renaissance, fulfilling the prediction of the Tuscan poet Dante Alighieri (1265–1321) that a new civilization would arise on the Italian peninsula. Indeed, early in the Renaissance, the language of the region, Tuscan, emerged as the "courtly language" used by an increasing number of educated Italians beyond Tuscany.

The walled city dominated its rich hinterland of gentle hills and prosperous plains. The Arno River, which flows through Florence, was navigable from the Mediterranean port of Pisa except during the summer months. In 1406, Florence conquered Pisa, another center of textile production, once a worthy challenger of Genoa for maritime trade but now divided into quarreling factions. This window on the sea aided Florentine commerce, enabling the city to become a maritime power.

Several other factors contributed to Florence's becoming the center of the revival of classical learning. Roman law and Latin had long been the foundation of training of Florentine ecclesiastics, lawyers, and notaries. Although the influence of the Church remained strong, the Medici rulers encouraged a cultural movement that had strong secular elements. Both Christian and secular traditions, then, infused Florentine civic life.

The combination of a dynamic craft tradition and an economy closely tied to the production of luxury goods made Florence receptive to artistic innovation. The city honored the accomplishments of its citizens—including cultural achievements. Lastly, Florence's reputation as a relatively educated city helped attract talented newcomers from rural Tuscany and other regions. It had many schools, including a university, and boasted a rate of literacy unmatched in Europe. In the fifteenth century, at least 8,000 children in a population of 100,000 attended church and civic schools, as well as private academies. It was said that even laborers could recite Dante's verses by heart.

The bell tower of the Palazzo Vecchio, the government building completed early in the fourteenth century, watched over the dynamic center of international banking, commerce, and the manufacture of cloth, woolens, silk, and jewelry. By the middle of the fourteenth century, Florence had become the fifth largest city in Europe. Before the plagues of the 1340s, about 100,000 people lived there. After falling by half, Florence's population revived during the next half-century, equaling that of London and

A Florentine council in session.

Seville, but not Venice and Naples, each of which then had at least 100,000 inhabitants.

Wealthy merchants, the *grandi,* governed Florence with the support of merchants, lawyers, and craftsmen of more modest means. Organized into seven major guilds, the merchants and manufacturers, particularly the cloth merchants, kept the fourteen lesser guilds (whose members included artisans and shopkeepers) in a subordinate position. The guilds elected the nine members of government, the *Signoria,* which administered the city. The Signoria proposed laws and conducted foreign affairs. Its members led the processions through the narrow streets during the various religious holidays. Two assemblies, the Council of the People and the Council of the Commune, served as a legislature. Citizens wealthy enough to pay taxes elected the 600 to 700 members of these councils, which met as needed to approve the decisions of the Signoria.

During the fifteenth century, the business of government went on in the palaces of the wealthiest citizens of Florence. The elite feared that the poor would revolt as they had in 1378 in the uprising known as the Ciompi, or "the wooden shoes," so named because many of the laborers could only afford such footwear. Suffering from economic hardship and aided by disgruntled members of the lower guilds, the cloth workers had risen up in a bloody insurrection in the hope of expanding the guild system already in power. The possibility of another uprising of the poor thereafter remained in the memory of the "fat people," causing them to keep the workers in a position of resentful subservience.

The renewal, then, of the Florentine elite with new families provided change within continuity, despite no small degree of political turbulence in the fifteenth century. The crowning cultural achievements of the Renaissance were not only rooted in Florence's prosperity but also in the relative social and political stability within that innovative city-state.

In 1434, Cosimo de' Medici (1389–1464) and his family seized control of Florentine political life. The family drew its great wealth from banking and the manufacture and commerce of textiles. Supported by a few patrician families, Cosimo banished prominent members of the most powerful rival clans. The Medici now controlled the offices of government. They manipulated the electoral process masterfully, using their wealth to curry support. Cosimo reflected the marketplace toughness of his family.

Florentine nobles generally accepted Medici rule because stability contributed to prosperity. Wealthy families continued to conspire against each other, even as Florence warred against Venice, but the powerful families remained staunchly patriotic, devoted to their city. Nonetheless, some Florentine nobles continued to oppose the Medici. In the Pazzi conspiracy of 1479, Lorenzo the Magnificent (1449–1492), Cosimo's grandson, survived an assassination attempt during Mass. Several hours later, four of the enemies of the Medici were hanging upside down from a government building, including the archbishop of Pisa. Lorenzo composed verses to be placed under their heads and commissioned Sandro Botticelli (c. 1445–1510) to paint them as they swung. Renaissance culture and the often violent political world of the city-states here converged.

The establishment of a Council of Seventy, which elected committees assigned responsibility for domestic and foreign affairs, helped the Medici tighten their grip on the reins of the Florentine republic. Lorenzo extended the family's banking interests and its influence with the pope in Rome. Among the many honors bestowed on the Medici family, Lorenzo considered the papal nomination of his thirteen-year-old son to the rank of Church cardinal "the greatest achievement of our house."

A DYNAMIC CULTURE

Economically and intellectually dynamic, Florence emerged as the center of the Renaissance. As Florence solidified its leading position on the Italian peninsula, its people rediscovered and celebrated classical learning. While glorifying antiquity, Renaissance poetry, prose, and painting emphasized the dignity of the individual, made in the image of God. It gradually moved concepts like beauty and virtue away from theological constraints.

The Rediscovery of Classical Learning

The Tuscan poet Petrarch (Francesco Petrarca, 1304–1374) was among the earliest and most influential of those who rediscovered and celebrated the classics of Latin antiquity. Petrarch, the son of a Florentine notary, learned Latin from a monk who inspired the boy to pursue his fascination with the classical world, which he came to view as a lost age. As a young man, Petrarch lived in Avignon, among an international community of lawyers and churchmen at the papal court during the "Avignon Papacy" (1309–1378), when the popes were subject to the influence of the kings of France. There he copied ancient works from manuscripts and books. Petrarch and his friends searched far and wide for more classical manuscripts. They uncovered the *Letters to Athens* of the Roman orator and moralist Marcus Tullius Cicero (106–43 B.C.), among other texts, stored in the cathedral of Verona. The study of Cicero led Petrarch to see in classical philosophy a guide to life based on experience.

Petrarch's successors found and copied other classical manuscripts. Among them were classical literary commentaries, which provided humanists with a body of information about the authors in whom they were interested. Scholars brought works of classical Greek authors, including the playwright Sophocles, from Constantinople and from the libraries of Mount Athos, an important center of learning in the Eastern Orthodox Church. Knowledge of Greek texts (as well as certain Arabic and Hebrew texts) spread slowly through Italy after the arrival of Greek teachers from Constantinople.

The development of printing (see Chapter 1) permitted the diffusion of a variety of histories, treatises, biographies, autobiographies, and poems. Printing spread knowledge of classical texts and the development of textual criticism itself. Many Renaissance scholars considered Cicero to represent the model of the purest classical prose (although others considered him too long-winded), and by 1500 more than 200 editions of his works had been printed in Italy, including his influential *On Oratory* and his letters. Libraries were established in many of the Italian city-states, including Florence, Naples, and Venice, and provided scholars with common texts for study.

From Scholasticism to Humanism

The Romans had used the concept of *humanitas* to describe the combination of wisdom and virtue that they revered. The term came to refer to studies that were intellectually liberating, the seven liberal arts of antiquity: grammar, logic, arithmetic, geometry, music, astronomy, and rhetoric (the art of expressive and persuasive speech or discourse). Medieval scholasticism was a system of thought in which clerics applied reason to philosophical and theological questions. Those teachers and students who shifted their

A humanist educator and his charges.

focus from the scholastic curriculum—law, medicine, and theology—to the curriculum of Latin grammar, rhetoric, and metaphysics became known as "humanists." They considered the study of the "humanities" to be essential for educating a good citizen.

Renaissance humanists believed that they were reviving the glory of the classical age. They considered their era greater than any since the Roman Empire. They also believed the Italian peninsula, although divided by political units, dialects, and by the Apennine Mountains, shared a common, distinct culture.

Venerating classical civilization, the humanists turned their backs on medieval scholasticism, which they believed was composed of irrelevant theological debates and encouraged ascetic withdrawal from the world. Scholastics celebrated the authority of Church texts and revered the saint, the monk, and the knight. Petrarch rejected idle philosophic speculation or even knowledge that seemed irrelevant to mankind. He mocked scholastics, remarking that they can tell you "how many hairs there are in the lion's mane . . . with how many arms the squid binds a shipwrecked sailor. . . . What is the use, I pray you, of knowing the nature of beasts, birds, fishes and serpents, and not knowing, or spurning the nature of man, to what end we are born, and from where and whither we pilgrimage."

The humanists proclaimed the writers of antiquity to be heroes worthy of emulation. Although virtually all humanists accepted Christianity, and clerical religious culture persisted intact, humanism stood as an alternative approach to knowledge and culture. Humanists believed that a knowledge of the humanities could civilize mankind, teaching the "art of living." Petrarch insisted that the study of classical poetry and rhetoric could infuse daily life with ethical values.

Unlike the scholastics, humanists believed that it was not enough to withdraw into philosophy. Petrarch rediscovered the classical ideal that the philosopher, or humanist, was a wise man who could govern. Cicero had written that what made an individual great was not the gifts of good fortune, but the use to which he put them. The active life, including participation in public affairs, had formed part of his definition of true wisdom. From the literature of the Greek and Roman past, humanists looked for guides to public life in their own city-states. The first half of the fifteenth century is often referred to as the period of "civic humanism" because of the influence of humanists and artists on the city-states themselves. Like the classic writers of ancient Rome, Renaissance writers were concerned with wisdom, virtue, and morality within the context of the political community. Humanists wrote boastful histories of the city-states, philosophical essays, stirring orations, and flattering biographies, as well as poetry, eagerly imitating classical styles.

The Renaissance and Religion

While rediscovering classic texts and motifs, the Renaissance remained closely linked to religion. Dante's *Divine Comedy* (1321), an allegorical poem, provides the quintessential expression of medieval thought by its demonstration of the extraordinary power that both Latin classical learning and Christian theology exerted on educated thought and literature. In his voyage through Hell, Purgatory, and Heaven, Dante encounters historical figures suffering terrible agonies for their sins, waiting expectantly for admission into Heaven, or already reaping the benefits of having lived a good life. Renaissance humanists could reject medieval scholasticism without turning their backs on the Church. Indeed, they claimed that they were searching for the origins of Christianity in the classical world from which it had emerged.

Although not the first to do so, humanists took classic texts, which were pagan, and ascribed to them meanings prophetic of Christianity. For example, the *Aeneid,* the long epic written by Virgil (70–19 B.C.), had been commissioned by the Roman emperor Augustus in the hope that it would offer the most favorable image of himself and of the empire, that is, of Rome bringing peace and civilization to the world. The hero of the *Aeneid*, Aeneas, personifies the ideal qualities of a Roman citizen, wanting to fulfill his patriotic duties, seeking glory for the empire but never for himself. The humanists transformed Aeneas's journey into an allegory for the itinerary of the Christian soul, appropriating antiquity into theology by viewing it as a foreshadowing of the true religion.

The place of the Church in Italian life remained strong during the Renaissance, the relative decline in the papacy's temporal power notwithstanding. There was thus considerable continuity between the medieval period and the Renaissance in matters of religion. There were at least 264 bishops in Italy, as many as in the rest of the Christian world. In 1427, Florence had more than 1,400 clerics out of a population of 38,000 living in ecclesiastical institutions. Religious festivals dotted the calendar. The colorful Venetian water processions of elaborately decorated gondolas, jousting, boat races, and the annual horse race (*palio*) sponsored by rival neighborhoods in Siena still bear witness to the playful but intense festivity of the Renaissance city-states, a festivity that gave ritualized religious expression to civic and political life.

The Renaissance Man and Woman

Renaissance literature and poetry, preoccupied with nature, beauty, and reason, placed the individual at the forefront of attention. Renaissance writers praised mankind as "heroic" and "divine," rational and prudent, rather than intrinsically unworthy by virtue of being stained by original sin, as Church theologians held. This, too, represented a revival of the classic vision of the moral greatness of the individual and his or her ability to discover truth and wisdom.

By this view, the lay person could interpret morality through the ancient texts themselves, without the assistance of the clergy. Once someone had learned to read Latin and Greek, neither ecclesiastical guidance nor formalized school settings were necessary for the accumulation of wisdom. Universities in general remained under the influence of the theological debates of scholasticism, although the universities of Florence, Bologna, and Padua gradually added humanist subjects to their curricula. Relatively few humanists emerged from the universities, which remained training grounds for jurists, doctors, and clerics.

"These studies are called liberal because they make man free," a humanist wrote; they are humane "because they perfect man . . . those studies by which we attain and practice virtue and wisdom; that education which calls forth, trains and develops those highest gifts of body and of mind, which ennoble man." The young Giovanni Pico della Mirandola (1463–1494) exclaimed, "O highest and most marvelous felicity of man! To him it is granted to have whatever he chooses, to be whatever he wills." Pico described the individual as an independent and autonomous being who could make his own moral choices and become, within the context of Christianity, "the molder and sculptor of himself."

The political theorist Niccolò Machiavelli (1469–1527), too, found personal fulfillment in the study of the classics. He had been employed in the Florentine chancery, serving as a diplomat. Purged when the Medici overthrew the republic in 1512, he took up residence in the countryside. Machiavelli complained that his days consisted of mundane exchanges with rustics. But "when evening comes I return home and go into my study. On the threshold I strip off my muddy, sweaty, workday clothes, and put on the robes of court and palace, and in this graver dress I enter the antique courts of the ancients and am welcomed by them, and there again I taste the food that alone is mine, and for which I was born. And I make bold to speak to them and ask the motives of their actions, and they, in their humanity, reply to me. And for the space of four hours I forget the world, remember no vexation, fear poverty no more, tremble no more at death: I pass indeed into their world." Machiavelli evoked the exhilaration of the individual discovering the joys of antiquity.

The development of the autobiography in literature reflected the celebration of the individual, however much the genre was limited to public people and the image that they sought to present of themselves, revealing virtually nothing of private life. In the first half of the fifteenth century, the portrait and the self-portrait emerged as artistic genres; princes, oligarchs, courtiers, and other people of wealth joined Christ, the Virgin Mary, and popular saints as subjects of painting.

A growing sense of what it meant to be "civilized" arose in the Italian city-states and highlighted the place of the individual in society. The Italian patrician may have been cleaner and more perfumed than people elsewhere in Europe. Books on good conduct and manners emerged. The writer Baldassare Castiglione (1478–1529) urged the person of taste to show that "whatever is said or done has been done without pains and virtually without thought" as if correct behavior had become part of his or her very being. Women, he contended, should obtain a "knowledge of letters, of music, of painting, and . . . how to dance and be festive."

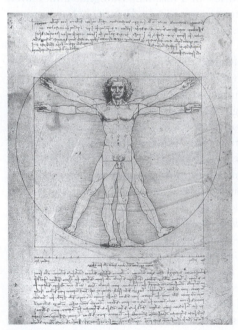

A drawing by Leonardo da Vinci that illustrates his understanding and appreciation of human anatomy.

Castiglione's *The Courtier* (1528) described the ideal courtier, or attendant at a court, as someone who had mastered the classics and several languages, and who could paint, sing, write poetry, advise and console his prince, as well as run, jump, swim, and wrestle. This idea of a "universal person," or "Renaissance man," had existed for some time, although, of course, not everyone had the leisure or resources to study so many subjects.

Although he was not a humanist and could not read Latin, Leonardo da Vinci (1452–1519)—painter, sculptor, scientist, architect, military engineer, inventor, and philosopher—became the epitome of the "Renaissance man." The illegitimate son of a notary from a Tuscan village, he was apprenticed to a Florentine painter at the age of twelve. Following acceptance into the master's guild in Florence, he remained in the workshop of his master until moving in 1482 to Milan, where he enjoyed the patronage of the Sforza family. Taking the title "Painter and Engineer of the Duke of Milan," Leonardo taught students in his workshop and undertook scientific studies of human and animal anatomy. His drawings were the first modern scientific illustrations. Leonardo began compiling his prodigious notebooks, in which he jotted down his ideas, perceptions, and experiences. He also sculpted an equestrian monument, designed costumes for theatrical performances, worked as a military engineer, and decorated palaces. In 1500, Leonardo returned to Florence, then went back to Milan six years later, beckoned by the governor of Francis I, king of France. When the Milanese freed themselves from French hegemony, he went south to Rome, where Pope Leo X (pope 1513–1521) provided him with a salary. In 1516, the French king brought Leonardo to his château on the Loire River at Amboise, where he sketched court festivals, and served as something of a Renaissance jack-of-all-trades before his death in 1519.

If the Renaissance is often said to have "discovered" mankind in general, this meant, for the most part, men. The Church considered women to be sinful daughters of Eve. Legally, women remained subordinate to men; they could own property and make their wills, but they could not sell property without their husbands' permission. Both rich and poor families continued to value boys more than girls; poor families were far more likely to abandon female babies or to place them in the care of a distant wet nurse. Many families viewed girls as a liability because of the necessity of providing a dowry, however large or small, for their marriage. Some families of means sent daughters off into convents. Because of the strict gender division within the Church, women there could aspire not only to holiness and sainthood, but also to leadership in a world of women. Life in a convent left them free to study.

Some patricians, however, educated their girls as well as their boys in the humanities. These girls studied letters, orations, and poems with tutors. A small number of women went on to write because they could not enter learned professions. Isotta Nogarola (1418–1466), a fifteenth-century humanist from Verona, abandoned secular life for quiet religious contemplation and scholarship. In her discussion of the fall of mankind in the Garden of Eden, she apologized for the weakness of women's nature, and she lamented that she fell short of "the whole and perfect virtue that men attain." Several women, however, managed to become publishers, booksellers, and printers, including several nuns who set the type for works by Petrarch. The achievement of such status required literacy and family connections to the trade—for example, being the widow or daughter of a printer and thus having family links to a guild. It was rare for a female printer to sign her name to her work, and her status was viewed as provisional—until, for example, a male heir came of age.

Overall, the Renaissance did not bring about any significant loosening in the restrictions placed on women, and women's social and personal options may even have been reduced. In the Italian city-states, women had less of a role in public life than they had enjoyed in the courts of medieval Europe. They presided over social gatherings, but for the most part in a ritualized, decorative role. Although Renaissance authors idealized love and women, the role of women continued to be to serve their fathers, husbands, or, in some cases, their lovers. When the education of young women clashed with a father's plans for his daughter to marry, marriage won out without discussion. Men's feelings were the focus of considerable attention by Renaissance writers; women's feelings and opinions usually were assumed to be unimportant. To be sure, women in large, powerful families like the Sforza, Este, and Gonzaga exerted influence and were patrons to artists. Yet the subjects they commissioned artists and sculptors to portray were essentially the same as those of their male counterparts, and, in patriarchal households, their husbands made the decisions.

Renaissance Art

When the German painter Albrecht Dürer (1471–1528) visited Venice on one of his two trips to the northern Italian peninsula, he was surprised and delighted by the fact that artists there enjoyed considerably more status than in his native Nuremburg: "Here," he wrote, "I am a gentleman, at home a sponger."

The prestige and support given to the Renaissance artist created a nurturing environment for the remarkable artistic accomplishments that characterize that special period's place in history. Great works of Renaissance architecture, painting, and sculpture are still studied by specialists and appreciated by millions of people each year.

Architecture

Despite the Renaissance concept of the "ideal city" of architectural harmony, reflected in the first treatises on architecture, Florence, Siena, Perugia, and other Italian cities retained their medieval cores, which contained their markets and their public buildings, such as the town hall. But during the fifteenth century, the narrow streets and alleys of many Italian cities became interspersed with splendid buildings and dotted with works of art commissioned by wealthy families.

Florence underwent a building boom during the fifteenth century. Construction of its elegant residences stimulated the economy, providing employment to day laborers, skilled artisans—brick- and tilemakers, masons, roofers, carpenters, cabinetmakers, and joiners—and decorative artists, including goldsmiths, sculptors, and painters. Renaissance architecture emphasized elegant simplicity, an expansion of the simple rustic fronts that had characterized medieval building. Renaissance architects combined plain white walls with colorful, intricate arches, doors, and window frames. In the fifteenth century, expensive palaces of monumental proportions with columns, arches, and magnificent stairways were considered sensible investments, because they could later be sold at a profit.

Like writers and painters, Renaissance architects looked to antiquity for models. Filippo Brunelleschi (1377–1446) first applied theories of classical architecture to the Foundling Hospital in Florence, the earliest building constructed in Renaissance style. Fourteenth-century architects planned churches in the form of a circle, the shape they thought was in the image of God, with no beginning and no end. But they may also have drawn on Rome's Pantheon, a round classical temple. After going to the papal city to study the ruins of classical architecture, Brunelleschi solved daunting technical problems to construct the vast dome, or cupola, of that city's cathedral (Duomo). The magnificent structure, completed in 1413 after work lasting more than a century, reflects the architect's rejection of the northern Gothic architectural style, with its pointed arches, vaulting, and flying buttresses. Inspired by excavations of classical ruins and the rebuilding of Rome in the late fifteenth century, architects began to copy classical styles closely, adding ornate Corinthian columns and great sweeping arches.

Patronage and the Arts

Renaissance art could not have flourished without the patronage of wealthy, powerful families, though commissions by guilds and religious confraternities were not uncommon. Artists, as well as poets and musicians, were eager, like Leonardo, to be invited into a patrician's household, where there were few or no expenses, and time to work. Lesser artists painted coats of arms, tapestries, and even portraits of the prince's pets—dogs and falcons.

Some humanists not fortunate enough to be given the run of a powerful patrician's place found posts as state secretaries, because they could draft impressive official correspondence. They tutored the children of patrician families, and a few worked as papal courtiers. Such humanists penned orations, scrupulously imitating Cicero, for formal state receptions, clamorous festivals, and funerals. Pope Leo X, a Medici who composed and played music himself, brought to his court a number of distinguished artists, in addition to Leonardo da Vinci, and musicians, as well as humanists whom he employed as officials and envoys. At the same time, the genres of wit and satire developed and became part of the ribald and "sharp-tongued" life of the political and social world of the city-state. Her well-heeled friends winked and joined in the laughter when Isabella of Mantua dressed one of her dwarfs as a bishop to greet a visiting dignitary. The biting satires and lampoons of Pietro Aretino (1492–1556), who enjoyed in succession

Pope Leo X, here presented
by Raphael with two cardinals, brought artists and
musicians to his court.

the patronage of a banker, a cardinal, the duke of Mantua, the Medici of
Florence, and a Venetian doge and nobleman, spared neither secular nor
ecclesiastical leaders from mocking jokes and rhymes. Aretino attacked
social climbers and the venality of offices in the city-states with particular
venom. He spared the one person he referred to as divine—himself.

Because the classical texts suggested that the active life included playing a
salutary role in one's community, humanist families of means believed that
they should demonstrate wisdom by making good use of their riches. Commissioning works of art seemed to confirm moral leadership, and therefore
the right to govern. Wealthy families also used art to reflect the image that
they wished to give of themselves, for example, commissioning portraits to
impress the family of a prospective spouse.

The Medici of Florence, the greatest of the secular patrons of the arts,
commissioned buildings, paid for the elaborate decoration of chapels and
altarpieces, and restored monasteries. Although wags suggested that he may
have been more interested in the expensive bindings of the books he purchased than in their contents, Cosimo de' Medici collected manuscripts and
even read some of them. The wealthy banker oversaw the construction of
fine palaces and churches. Michelangelo (1475–1564), who designed the
Medici tomb in the church of Saint Lorenzo in Florence, was but one sculptor who enjoyed the favor of the Medici.

The long economic recession of the fifteenth century may have actually
contributed to the arts. Finding insufficient profits in commerce and manufacturing for their money, patrician families spent considerable sums on
paintings and sculpture. This may, in turn, have accentuated the recession
by turning productive capital away from economic investments. At the
same time, so the argument goes, the recession offered families of means
more time to devote to culture.

Masaccio's *Adoration of the Magi* (1426).

Patrons of the arts often specified not only the subject of the work they were commissioning but certain details as well, requiring, for example, that specific saints be depicted. The size of the work of art and its price were also specified, of course, including the cost of blue pigment or gold for paintings and bronze or marble for sculptures. Cherubs cost more. Although one of the dukes of Ferrara paid for his paintings by their size, increasingly patrons paid the artist for his time—and thus his skill—as well as for the materials he used. The contract for a work of art might specify whether it was to be completed by the artist himself, or if assistants from the master's workshop could be employed for certain parts. Patrons sometimes appeared on the canvas, as in the case of *The Adoration of the Magi* (1426) by Tommaso di Giovanni Masaccio (1401–1428), which includes portraits of the notary who commissioned the painting and his son. Conversely, patricians occasionally commissioned artists to humiliate their enemies, as when a painter in Verona was paid to sneak up to the walls of a rival palace and paint obscene pictures.

Renaissance Artists

Because of its basis in the craft tradition, in the medieval world painting was considered a "mechanical" art. This made the status of the artist ambiguous, because he sold his own works and lacked the humanist's education. Michelangelo's father tried to discourage his son from becoming a sculptor, an art that he identified with stone cutting. Michelangelo himself sometimes signed his paintings "Michelangelo, sculptor," as if to differentiate himself from a mere painter. Yet, in his treatise on painting (1435), the humanist Leon Battista Alberti, irritated by contemporary insistence that painting was a "mechanical art," insisted that the artist was no longer a craftsman but a practitioner of a "high art."

Of the artists whose social origins are known, the majority had fathers who were urban shopkeepers or artisans, most often in the luxury trades.

Next in number—surprisingly—came the sons of nobles, perhaps reflecting the relative decline in noble fortunes during the Renaissance. Then came the children of merchants and educated professionals such as notaries, lawyers, and officials. A few painters, like Raphael (1483–1520), were sons of artists. Only a handful were the sons of peasants.

The contemporary association between craftsmen and painters was appropriate, because, like the former, artists entered a period of apprenticeship. Architects and composers lacked such formal training. The painters' guild of Venice required five years of apprenticeship, followed by two years of journeyman status, requirements similar to those by which silversmiths, shoemakers, cabinetmakers, and other craftsmen were trained. Some masters had sizable workshops, where apprentices trained and often lived together, sometimes working on the same paintings (which is one reason it is difficult to authenticate some canvases). Because women could neither become apprentices nor attend universities, there were no prominent female Renaissance artists until well into the sixteenth century.

Indeed, artists claimed that they deserved more esteem than a craftsman. Leonardo praised the painter, who sits "at his easel in front of his work, dressed as he pleases, and moves his light brush with the beautiful colors . . . often accompanied by musicians or readers of various beautiful works." The artist's quest for the humanist ideals of beauty and God helps explain the rise of some artists of the Renaissance period from practitioners of a "mechanical art," to the description of Michelangelo offered by a Portuguese painter: "In Italy, one does not care for the renown of great princes: it's a painter only that they call divine." Not all painters ascended to such heights, of course, but in general the status of the artist rose during the Renaissance. Michelangelo, Leonardo, Raphael, and Titian (Tiziano Vecellio, c. 1490–1576) lived as gentlemen, the last knighted by Holy Roman Emperor Charles V. Some artists and writers were crowned with laurels—thus the designation of "poet laureate"—by their adoring city-states.

Painting and Sculpture

The rediscovery of antiquity, nature, and mankind transformed European painting. Renaissance artists reflected the influence of the neo-Platonists. In the late fifteenth and early sixteenth centuries, the neo-Platonists appropriated Plato's belief that eternal ideas—such as beauty, truth, and goodness—existed beyond the realm of everyday life. Humanists believed that the mind could transcend human nature and come to understand these eternal ideas. The artist could reproduce the beauty of the soul through imagination and, in doing so, reach out to God. To Dante, art was "the grandchild of God." For Michelangelo, beauty "lifts to heaven hearts that truly know."

Artists sought to achieve the representation of beauty in a realistic way by using the proportions created by God in the universe. It was the

Stories of Saint John the Evangelist: Vision on the Island of Patmos, fresco by Giotti, Peruzzi Chapel in the Basilica of Santa Croce in Florence.

supreme compliment to say of a Renaissance painter that his work had surpassed nature in beauty. Leonardo put it this way: "Painting . . . compels the mind of the painter to transform itself into the mind of nature itself and to translate between nature and art." During the Renaissance, nature ceased to be mere background. Painters now faithfully depicted the beauty of mountains, rocks, and gardens for their own sake.

Objects of everyday life increasingly appeared in paintings, reflecting a greater preoccupation with realistic depiction. Take, for example, Raphael's painting of the pudgy Pope Leo X, staring off into space while fiddling with a magnifying glass with which he has been examining a book (see p. 64).

Beauty could be portrayed with extraordinary richness. The memorable figures of the frescoes of Giotto di Bondone (c. 1266–1337) in the chapels of Holy Cross Church in Florence, particularly their facial expressions, reflect humanity, deeply personal emotion, and naturalism, unseen since the classical age. The fame of Giotto, who is usually considered the first great painter of the Renaissance, spread rapidly throughout much of Italy, and his style greatly influenced his successors. Raphael, who admired and learned from Michelangelo, eight years his senior, wrote of trying to paint a beautiful woman, "I use as my guide a certain idea of the beautiful that I carry in my mind." Raphael's figures reflect a softness and inner beauty

Masaccio's *The Expulsion of Adam and Eve from Eden* (c. 1427).

that contrast with the powerful, stirring subjects of the tempestuous Michelangelo. Reflecting neo-Platonist influence, Titian early in the sixteenth century strove to bring the viewers of his paintings closer to the idea of the eternal form of female beauty that he sought to represent with his depictions of Venus.

The Greeks and Romans believed that the painter and sculptor understood and portrayed the soul when they reproduced the human face. Leonardo's famous *Mona Lisa* (1503–1507), with its mysterious, confident half-smile, is a compelling illustration of this undertaking. "Movements of the soul," wrote Alberti early in the fifteenth century, "are recognized in movements of the body." The artist had to be able to reveal the emotions and passions of the figures he depicted.

Renaissance artists used a large repertoire of stylized portrayals of emotion, the meanings of which were immediately recognized by virtually all viewers of their paintings. The Florentine Masaccio intended his extraordinary fresco *The Expulsion of Adam and Eve from Eden* (c. 1427) to represent the tortured souls, as well as bodies, of those biblical figures. Masaccio's Adam covers his eyes with his fingers in anguish in this truly gripping depiction of Adam and Eve's crushing grief as they leave the Garden of Eden. Although Renaissance artists generally avoided many of the routine associations of the medieval period (gold for piety, for example), certain colors were used for symbolic purposes. Violet was often a color of reverence, white that of charity, red of fire, and gray of earth. Clear colors, intense light, and ideal proportions were combined in representations of Christ. Deep coloring, more subtle and natural than the blues and golds of medieval painting, enriched the canvas.

Medieval and Byzantine artists typically painted rigid images on a flat space, thus their work often appeared two-dimensional and lifeless; linear forms were arranged in order of importance, accompanied by symbols easily identifiable to the viewer. The Renaissance development of perspective theory, in which parallel lines recede from the surface and seem to converge on the vanishing point, facilitated the realistic presentation of figures and movement. Renaissance artists believed that naturalism could only be achieved through the use of perspective. Masaccio first applied the mathematical laws of perspective to painting in his revolutionary *Trinity* (1425), which makes a two-dimensional surface seem to be three-dimensional. The mastery of light

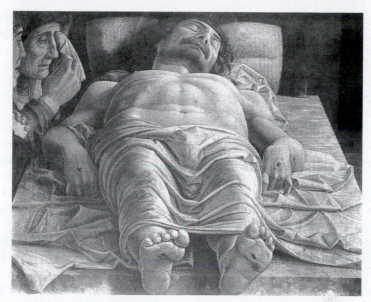

Andrea Mantegna's *The Dead Christ* (c. 1506), an example of Renaissance treatment of perspective.

also contributed to innovative uses of space; for example, through the technique of foreshortening, artists proportionally contracted depth so as to give the viewer the illusion of projection or extension into space. In his realistic *The Dead Christ* (c. 1506), Andrea Mantegna (c. 1430–1506) utilized this technique, which had been pioneered by Masaccio. This shortcut allowed the artist to create the visual impression of a three-dimensional body on a flat surface. Florentine artists, in particular, used perspective to develop high relief and silhouette, presenting rounded figures on the canvas surface by effective use of tones and shades.

This mastery of perspective by the naturalist painter Masaccio and, above all, the sculptor Donatello (c. 1386–1466) helped Renaissance painters choose difficult, complicated themes and treat them with a more complex realism. Donatello utilized perspective to achieve dramatic action through gradations of relief. In *The Feast of Herod* (c. 1417), sculpted in bronze for the stone basin in the Siena Baptistery, Donatello captures the shocked reaction of the king and guests as John the Baptist's head is presented to Herod. In Leonardo's painting *The Last Supper* (c. 1495–1498), Christ's disciples crowd around the table. The viewer's eye is drawn along the lines of perspective of the ceiling to the central figure of Christ, whose image stands out because it is framed by a large window. Leonardo identifies Judas, the betrayer of Christ, not by leaving him without a halo nor by placing him alone on the other side of the table from Christ, but by painting him as the only figure in shadow.

To Leonardo, painting was the highest form of science, based on "what has passed through our senses." He believed that "the scientific and true principles of painting first determine" the components of painting: "darkness, light, color, body, figure, position, distance, nearness, motion, and rest." The work of Michelangelo reflects a mastery of mathematics, anatomy, and optics. Animals, birds, and inanimate objects also took on a lifelike quality based upon artists' discovery of proper proportions.

The quest for the natural representation of beauty led some artists to depict the human body in nude form, which some took to be a more natural and expressive form borrowed from classical paganism. Michelangelo believed that the depiction of the human body in sculpture was the ultimate expression of mankind as a divine creation, made in God's image. In his sculptures and paintings of the nude figure, the muscles and sinews of the body are infused with the emotions and passions of humanity.

Religious, public, and private life overlapped, as the people of Renaissance Italy sought religious meanings in everything they saw. Art with religious subjects also served a teaching function for the Church. In many patrician houses, a religious image could be found in every room. Devotional images, known as *ex votos*, were often erected in public spaces to fulfill a vow made to a saint in times of danger or illness. Patricians commissioned paintings with religious themes to realize similar vows. Moreover, the splendid tombs sculpted for patricians and popes may have reflected a preoccupation with glorifying the individual, but they nonetheless also emphasized eternal salvation.

Religious themes continued to dominate painting, accounting for perhaps nine of every ten paintings; the Virgin Mary was the most popular figure, followed by Christ and the saints (above all, Saint John the Baptist, the patron saint of Florence). The visualization of certain episodes in the life of Christ or of the martyrdom of Saint Sebastian were intended to stimulate piety and encourage morality. Thus, artists took on a role similar to preachers, whose orations evoked a powerful emotional response.

Classical symbolism abounded in Renaissance painting and influenced the depiction of religious themes, incorporating images drawn from pagan Rome. Artists used details about history or mythology that patrons insisted grace their canvases. Some of the classical gods stood as Renaissance symbols of moral or physical qualities. Michelangelo modeled his Christ in *The Last Judgment* (1536–1541) on a classical portrayal of the god Apollo.

Yet, along with scenes from classical mythology, paintings with secular themes increased in number, notably portraits of famous men or of wealthy patricians, but also of more ordinary people as well. Aretino, who criticized everything, found fault with the democratization of the portrait, despite the fact that he was the son of a shoemaker, insisting, "It is the disgrace of our age that it tolerates the portraits even of tailors and butchers."

A section of Michelangelo's fresco, *The Creation of Man*, on the ceiling of the Sistine Chapel, the Vatican, showing God banishing Adam and Eve from the Garden of Eden.

High Renaissance Style

During the period of the High Renaissance (1490–1530), the city-states of Italy lost much of their economic and political vitality, confronting French invasion and then Spanish domination. In the midst of economic decline as well as internecine political warfare, artists no longer enjoyed the lavish patronage of wealthy patrician families. Instead, the Church became their patron.

The papacy inspired the monumentalism of the High Renaissance. Besieged in the first two decades of the sixteenth century by denunciations of the sale of indulgences—the purchase of the remission of some punishment in Purgatory for one's sins or for those of some family member—the papacy sought to assert its authority and image (see Chapter 3). Papal commissions in Rome were one attempt to recover public confidence and made possible the artistic achievements of the High Renaissance. Following excavations beginning in the 1470s that heightened interest in the ancient Roman Empire, Raphael himself oversaw the reconstruction of Rome and personally supervised excavations of the Roman Forum. Influenced by and more dependent on the Church, the canvases of the painters of the High Renaissance became even larger as they became less concerned with rational order and more with achieving a powerful visual response in their viewers.

Some humanists now began to claim that the papacy was the heir to the glories of classical Rome. Popes took names that echoed the Roman Empire. Julius II (pope 1503–1513) ordered a medal struck that read

Leonardo da Vinci's *The Last Supper* (c. 1495–1498).

"Julius Caeser Pont[ifex]. II," a term that meant "high priest" in classical Rome. Wide boulevards and spaces were forged to accommodate waves of pilgrims descending upon the city.

Leonardo's *The Last Supper* is perhaps the first example of the style of the High Renaissance, or what is sometimes called the Grand Manner. Mannerism (a term from the Italian word for style), which particularly characterized the 1520s, is marked by heightened scale, exaggerated drama, and the submersion of detail to a total emotional effect. Donato Bramante (1444–1514), who constructed St. Peter's Basilica in Rome in the "grand manner" of the High Renaissance, designed its grand Byzantine dome, which was completed by Michelangelo and a successor.

Painters of the High Renaissance increasingly presented large, ambitious, complex, and sometimes even bizarre canvases. Mannerism's imaginative distortions and sense of restlessness offered an unsettling vision in tune with new uncertainties. Mannerism marked something of a reaction against the Renaissance ideal of attaining classical perfection. Thus, some painters ignored the rules of perspective; emotionalism, as well as mysticism and illusionism, won out over classicism. Toward the end of his career, Michelangelo's work reflected this influence. His majestic marble *Moses* (1515), sculpted for the tomb of Pope Julius II, has an immensely prominent head, with an exaggerated facial expression. It reflects Michelangelo's tragic vision of human limitations, including his own. Raphael and Titian presented human figures who seem almost empowered by divine attributes but who nonetheless retain their humanity.

The End of the Renaissance

Late in the fifteenth century, the Italian city-states entered a period of economic and political decline, making the peninsula more vulnerable to foreign invasion. Subsequently, some of the battles between Spain and France, Europe's two dominant powers, were fought on the Italian peninsula. The exploration and gradual colonization of the Americas, first by Spain, and the increase in trade and manufacturing in northwestern Europe, helped move economic and cultural vigor toward the Atlantic Ocean, to Spain and northwestern Europe, most notably, England, France, and the Dutch Netherlands, and to the New World (see Chapter 5).

Economic Decline

The economic decline of the northern Italian city-states during the second half of the fifteenth century undermined the material base of Renaissance prosperity, indeed the economic primacy of the Mediterranean region. The Italian city-states lost most of their trading routes with Asia. The Turks conquered Genoese trading posts in the Black Sea, the traditional merchant route to Asia, and in the Aegean Sea. Turkish domination reduced Genoa's once mighty commercial network to trade centered on the Aegean island of Chios. Of the Italian city-states, Venice alone continued to prosper. After the Ottoman conquest of Constantinople in 1453, merchants in Venice concluded a deal with the Turks by which they received a monopoly on trade with the East, leaving the other city-states without access to their traditional Asian markets. Venice's economy soon diversified with small-scale manufacturing, however, particularly as the Turkish threat to its interests mounted in the eastern Mediterranean and Venetian galleys no longer could venture into the Black Sea.

Merchants of the Italian city-states sought alternatives. The Genoese established a trading post in the Muslim city of Málaga on the southern coast of Spain, although this made them dependent on local Muslim middlemen. Portuguese fleets began to monopolize the spice trade with India and beyond.

The Florentine silk and woolen industries, long prosperous, now faced stiff competition from French and Dutch producers and merchants in northwestern Europe. The dazzling prosperity of the great Italian merchant families ebbed. The economy of Europe—and even of world commerce itself—was changing. Portuguese, Spanish, English, and Dutch traders looked to the New World for new products and significant profits (see Chapter 1). The rapid growth of Portuguese and then Spanish trade accentuated the rise of the Atlantic economy. Competition from the larger sailing ships of England, Holland, and Portugal overwhelmed Florence and Genoa and then, more gradually, Venice.

Foreign Invasion

As long as the Italian peninsula remained free from the intervention of France and Spain or other powers, the city-states could continue to prosper while fighting each other and casting wary glances toward the Ottoman Empire as it expanded its influence in the Mediterranean. But the city-states, divided by economic interests and with a long tradition of quarreling among themselves, became increasingly vulnerable to the expansion of French interests.

France had adhered to an alliance of Milan and Florence against Venice, signed in 1451. But the three city-states recognized the threat the aggressive French monarchy posed to the peninsula. Furthermore, following the capture of Constantinople in 1453, Turkish ships now appeared more frequently in the Adriatic Sea. It seemed imperative to end the struggles between the city-states. The Peace of Lodi (1454), signed by Florence, Milan, and Venice, established a new political order. Helping discourage Turkish or French aggrandizement, the treaty brought four decades of relative peace, which saw some of the crowning artistic glories of the Renaissance.

The establishment of this Italian League formalized this balance of power—it was already called that—between the strongest city-states. Whenever one or two of the states became aggressive—as when Venice and the Papal States attacked Ferrara—the others joined together to restore the status quo. Such wars were fought for the most part by mercenaries, imported and organized by *condottieri* paid for the task. For the moment, Milan's strong army served as a barricade against French invasion.

Perhaps accentuated by the ebbing of prosperity, political life within the city-states deteriorated. In Florence, the Medici despotism faced opposition from republicans. In the 1480s, Perugia had become a warring camp, torn between two rival families. In 1491, 130 members of one faction were executed on a main square and hanged from poles for all to see. Then, in repentance, the oligarchs erected thirty-five altars on that same square, and ordered priests to say Mass for three days in atonement. In a number of the city-states, some patrician families tried to outdo each other in their violence, crushing their opponents with brutality, then praying over the bodies. The leading Florentine families faithfully attended church, even as they undertook murders of vengeance in defense of family honor. Considerable tension, then, remained between two parallel codes of conduct, one religious, the other defined by family loyalties.

The Italian peninsula then became a battleground for the dynastic ambitions and rivalries of the French kings and the Holy Roman emperors, powerful rulers who could mobilize considerably larger armies than those of the city-states. The absorption of the wealthy and strategically important duchy of Burgundy into the Holy Roman Empire accentuated the struggle between the Habsburg dynasty and Charles VIII (ruled 1483–1498) of

France. The latter decided to press his dubious claim to the throne of Naples, encouraged by the Sforza family of Milan, the enemy of Naples. In response, Naples allied with Florence and Pope Alexander VI (pope 1492–1503), himself a Florentine member of the Borgia family, against Milan.

In 1494, Charles VIII invaded the Italian peninsula with an army of 30,000 men. His French cavalry, Swiss mercenary infantry, and Scottish bowmen tore through northern Italy. In Florence, the Medici ruler handed over Pisa to France in exchange for leaving. This angered Florentine republicans. When the French army entered Florence, the Florentines drove the Medici from power (after sixty years of rule). The new Florentine government, establishing the Great Council as a legislative assembly, contributed to the city's artistic splendors by commissioning works of art that symbolized republican independence and ideals. Leonardo and Michelangelo painted scenes of Florentine military victories for the meeting hall of the Great Council. Seven years later, the city government commissioned Michelangelo's great statue *David*. Michelangelo's conscious imitation of a Donatello bust of the same name from early in the fifteenth century referred back to the republic's successful resistance to challenges at that time.

In the meantime, the army of Charles VIII moved toward Naples, devastating everything in its path. It marched into the city to cheers from Neapolitans who opposed the harsh taxes that had been levied by their rulers. But an anti-French coalition that included King Ferdinand of Aragon—whose dynastic territories included Sicily, Venice, and the Papal States—and the Holy Roman emperor rallied to defeat the French forces. Although the French army left the Italian peninsula, the city-states' troubles had only just begun.

In Florence, Girolamo Savonarola (1452–1498), a charismatic Dominican monk who had predicted the French invasion, opposed both the Medici in Florence and the papacy on the grounds that both were worldly and corrupt. He had welcomed Charles VIII of France as "an instrument in the hands of the Lord who has sent you to cure the ills of Italy," including the sinfulness of the Florentines. With the Medici driven from power, Savonarola took virtual control of the Florentine republic. His denunciation of abuses within the Church led to his excommunication by Pope Alexander VI. Savonarola also incurred the enmity of patrician families by appealing for support to all ranks of Florentine society. With the pope's blessing, Savonarola's enemies first hanged and then burned him—the penalty for heresy—in 1498.

The next year, Louis XII (ruled 1498–1515), the new king of France, invaded the Italian peninsula, intent on making good his claim on the duchy of Milan. He did so with the support of the corrupt Pope Alexander VI, who wanted French assistance as he tried to solidify papal territorial claims, as well as to look after the extended interests of his children. To encourage the French king, the pope annulled Louis's marriage, so that he could marry his

Girolamo Savonarola being burned at the stake in Florence, sixteenth-century painting.

predecessor's widow, thereby keeping Brittany within his domains. When Julius II, who had been a bitter enemy of Alexander VI, became pope in 1503, he drove the powerful Borgia family from Rome. Then the dissolute pope set about trying to restore territorial holdings taken from the Papal States by Venice and its allies, constructing an alliance against the Venetians and becoming the last pope to lead his troops into the field of battle. That year the Spanish army defeated the French army and the Habsburgs absorbed the kingdom of Naples. Milan remained a fief of Louis XII until French forces were driven from the city in 1512, the same year that a Spanish army defeated the Florentines and the Medici overthrew the republic. Three years later, French troops overwhelmed Swiss mercenaries and recaptured Milan. After the intervention of Emperor Charles V in 1522 and French defeats, the Lombardy city became a Spanish possession in 1535.

Machiavelli

A mood of vulnerability and insecurity spread through the Italian peninsula as the city-states battled each other. Peasants, crushed by taxes and hunger, ever more deeply resented the rich. In turn, wealthy people were increasingly suspicious of the poor, viewing them as dangerous monsters capable of threatening social order.

The devoted Florentine Niccolò Machiavelli was among those seeking to understand why the once proud and independent city-states of Italy now seemed virtually helpless before the invasion of foreign powers. Machiavelli's view of politics reflects his experience living in Florence during these tumultuous decades. The turmoil in Florence led him to write his *Histories* in 1494, which described the decline of

The pensive Niccolò Machiavelli.

the city-states. Influenced by his experience in government, Machiavelli, who had served as a Florentine diplomat at the court of the king of France and in Rome, believed himself to be a realist. He considered war a natural outlet for human aggression. But he also preferred the resolution of disputes by diplomacy. He believed that the absence of "civic virtue" accounted for the factionalism within and rivalries between the city-states. By civic virtue, Machiavelli meant the effective use of military force.

In 1512, the Medici overthrew the Florentine Republic, returning to power with the help of the papal army and that of Spain. Following the discovery of a plot, of which he was innocent, against the Medici patriarchs, Machiavelli was forced into exile on his country estate outside of the city. Florence had changed. A Medici supporter wrote one of the family heads: "Your forefathers, in maintaining their rule, employed skill rather than force; you must use force rather than skill."

A year later, Machiavelli wrote *The Prince* (1513). In it he reflected on the recent history of the Italian peninsula and offered a pessimistic assessment of human nature, marked by his belief that a strong leader—the prince—could arise out of strife. By making his subjects afraid of him, the prince could end political instability and bring about a moral regeneration that Machiavelli believed had characterized antiquity. Drawing on Cicero, he studied the cities of the Roman Republic and the Roman Empire. Machiavelli can be considered the first political scientist, because his works reflect a systematic attempt to draw general, realistic conclusions from his understanding of the recent history of the Italian city-states. This preoccupation with the past in itself reveals the influence of the Renaissance.

Machiavelli put his faith in political leadership. Regardless of whether the form was monarchical or republican, he believed that the goal of government should be to bring stability to the city. A sense of civic responsibility could only be reestablished through "good laws and institutions," but these, for Machiavelli, depended completely on military strength. He called on the Medici to drive away the new barbarians. Machiavelli's *The Art of War* (1521) expressed hope that the brutish mercenaries who had devastated the Italian peninsula would give way to soldier-citizens who would restore virtue. But for the Italian city-states, it was too late.

Machiavelli's invocation of "reasons of state" as sufficient justification for political action and as a political principle in itself, and his open admiration of ruthless rulers, would leave a chilling legacy, reflected by his belief that the "ends justify the means." While it is unlikely that Machiavelli had a sense of the state in the impersonal, modern sense of the term, he held that "good arms make good laws."

The Decline of the City-States

For much of the first thirty years of the sixteenth century, in Italy foreign armies fought against each other and against alliances formed by the city-states. The army of France in Italy reached 32,000 men by 1525, that of Spain 100,000 soldiers. Only Venice could resist the two great powers. In 1521, the first war broke out between Holy Roman Emperor Charles V (King Charles I of Spain) and King Francis I of France, who became the first Western ruler to ally with the Ottoman Turkish sultan. Charles V's armies decimated the French at Pavia, Italy, in 1525, carting the French king off to Madrid, where he remained until his family paid a ransom. In 1527, Charles V's mercenary army, angry over lack of pay, sacked Rome. By the Peace of Cambrai (1529), France gave up claims to Naples and Milan. But with the exception of Venice, the Italian city-states were now in one way or another dependent upon Charles V, the Holy Roman emperor, as the Spanish army repulsed new French invasions. In Rome, where Spanish merchants already had a significant presence, the pope increasingly depended on the Holy Roman emperor for defense against the Turks, as Charles added to his resources by taxing ecclesiastical revenues.

The long wars drained the city-states of financial resources and men, devastating some of the countryside. Nobles, whose political power had been diminished by the wealthy merchants of the fourteenth and fifteenth centuries, took advantage of the chaos to return to prominence in some cities. Patrician families struggled to maintain their authority against newcomers, including wealthy merchants who had married into poorer noble lines and who began to ape the styles of nobles. The Medici, after having once again been expelled by republicans, reconquered their city in 1530 after a siege of ten months. But in Florence, too, the Renaissance was over.

Artistic styles had already begun to reflect the loss of Renaissance self-confidence that accompanied the devastating impact of the French invasion. Botticelli seemed to abandon the serenity and cheerful optimism that characterized the Renaissance. To his painting *Mystical Nativity*, Botticelli added an anxious inscription: "I Sandro painted this picture at the end of the year 1500 in the troubles of Italy." Botticelli thereafter became preoccupied with suffering and the Passion of Christ, reflecting the fact that the High Renaissance was more closely tied to ecclesiastical influence. The deteriorating political situation, combined with the expansion of Spanish influence after 1530, made it more difficult for artists to find patronage in the Italian city-states.

Soon in Italy only Venice, the city of Titian, remained a center of artistic life. Machiavelli, who died in 1527, the year Charles V's troops pillaged Rome, sensed that the humiliation of the Italian city-states by foreign armies brought to a close a truly unique period in not only the history of Italy but in Western civilization. Of the great figures of the High Renaissance, only Michelangelo and Titian lived past 1530.

Impulses Elsewhere

The cultural glories of the Renaissance ebbed even as different kinds of discoveries by Europeans opened up new possibilities for mankind. Columbus's transatlantic voyages were signs that the economic and cultural vitality of Europe was shifting away from the Mediterranean to Spain and, to a lesser extent, England. The economic interests of these states would increasingly be across the Atlantic Ocean. The mood of optimism associated with the Renaissance seemed to have moved to central and northern Europe as Italy lapsed into a considerably less happy period. Many humanists and artists began to emigrate north of the Alps to lands considered by most cultured Italians to have been barbarian only a century earlier. Now new universities in northern Europe beckoned them.

Other dramatic changes had already begun to occur across the Alps. Relentless calls for reform of the Catholic Church led to a schism within Christendom: the Reformation. In northern Europe, the Dutch monk and humanist Erasmus expressed the exhilaration many men of learning felt when he wrote, "The world is coming to its senses as if awakening out of a deep Sleep."

CHAPTER **3**

THE TWO REFORMATIONS

After paying a handsome sum to Pope Leo X in 1515, Albert of Hohenzollern received a papal dispensation (exemption from canon law) that enabled him to become archbishop of Mainz, a lucrative and prestigious ecclesiastical post. Otherwise, under canon law, the twenty-three-year-old Albert would have been ineligible due to his age (archbishops were supposed to be at least thirty years old) and because he already drew income from two other ecclesiastical posts. As part of his payment to the pope and in order to repay the large sum of money loaned to him by the Fugger banking family, the new archbishop authorized the sale of the St. Peter's indulgence, which would release a sinner from punishment for his sins. Johann Tetzel, a Dominican friar who was in charge of the sale of papal indulgences in the archbishopric of Mainz, was commissioned to preach the indulgence. Half of the proceeds were to go to the papacy, and half to Albert and the Fuggers. In his tour of parishes, Tetzel emotionally depicted the wailing of dead parents in Purgatory, pleading with their children to put coins in the box so that they could be released from their suffering.

The sale of indulgences, particularly their commercial use to allow clergymen to obtain multiple posts, had drawn increasing criticism in some of the German states. Indeed, no other ecclesiastical financial abuse drew as much passionate opposition as did indulgences. More than this, the Roman papacy itself faced considerable opposition in the German states, as the pope had appointed foreigners to many key ecclesiastical posts and had attempted to force the German states to provide him with money for a war against the Turks. The young German monk Martin Luther was among those denouncing Tetzel, the sale of indulgences, and the role of the Roman papacy in the German states.

This opposition to the papacy created a schism that would tear Christendom apart beginning in the second decade of the sixteenth century. Origi-

(*Left*) The young Martin Luther by Lucas Cranach. (*Right*) The pope selling indulgences.

nating in the German states and Switzerland, a movement for religious reform began to spread across much of Europe, in part reflecting the influence of Renaissance humanism in northern Europe. Reformers rejected the pope's authority and some Church doctrine itself. The movement for reform, or of "protest," came to be called the "Reformation." It led to the establishment of many Protestant denominations within Christianity. The followers of the German priest Martin Luther became Lutherans, while those of the Frenchman Jean Calvin in Switzerland became known as Calvinists. King Henry VIII established the Church of England (Anglican Church). Under attack from many sides, the Roman Catholic Church undertook a Counter-Reformation, or Catholic Reformation, which sought to reform some aspects of ecclesiastic life, while reaffirming the basic tenets of Catholic theology and belief in the authority of the pope.

By 1600, the pattern of Christian religious adherence had largely been established in Europe. Catholicism remained the religion of the vast majority of people living in Spain, France, Austria, Poland, the Italian states, Bavaria, and other parts of the southern German states. Protestants dominated England and much of Switzerland, the Dutch Netherlands, Scandinavia, and the northern German states. Wars fought in the name of religion broke out within and between European states, beginning in the late sixteenth century and culminating in the Thirty Years' War (1618–1648). These conflicts shaped the next century of European history, with religious divisions affecting the lives of millions of people.

THE NORTHERN RENAISSANCE

Until the middle of the fifteenth century, the Renaissance had been limited to the Italian peninsula. Northern Europe enjoyed very little of the economic and cultural vitality of the Italian city-states, where wealthy merchant and banking families patronized humanists and artists. The country estates of noble families were rarely centers of learning. The future Pope Pius II claimed in the mid-fifteenth century that "literature flourishes in Italy and princes there are not ashamed to listen to, and themselves to know, poetry. But in Germany princes pay more attention to horses and dogs than to poets—and thus neglecting the arts they die unremembered like their own beasts."

In about 1460, Renaissance humanism began to influence scholars in northern Europe. As in Italy, humanism changed the way many people thought about the world. Humanists were interested in morality and ethics, as well as in subjecting texts to critical scrutiny. Therefore, debates over religion, and the Bible itself, attracted their attention. Humanists began to criticize Church venality and corruption, and the seeming idleness of monastic life. They also called into question scholasticism and its influence on religious theology, as well as criticizing parts of religious practice that they considered illogical and therefore superstitious. The spread of humanism in northern Europe was gradual, first influencing isolated scholars. In the beginning, it posed no immediate threat to the Church; humanists could not imagine organized religion beyond Roman Catholicism. But the cumulative effect of the Northern Renaissance, and humanism in particular, helped engender a critical spirit that by the first decades of the sixteenth century directly began to challenge Church practices and then doctrine.

Northern Art and Humanism

The Northern Renaissance that began in the late fifteenth century reflected considerable Italian influence. Italian ambassadors, envoys, and humanists brought Renaissance art and humanistic thought to northern Europe. Many of the Italian envoys to northern Europe had studied the classics. They carried on diplomacy with oratorical and writing skills learned by reading Cicero and other Roman authors. Yet, much of the artistic creativity in northern Europe, particularly Flanders, emerged independent of Italian influence. Like the Italian city-states, in the Dutch Netherlands, which had a well-developed network of trading towns, wealthy urban families patronized the arts. Lacking the patronage of the Church, which so benefited Florentine and other Italian painters, Flemish painters did few church frescoes (which, in any case, a wet climate also discouraged). They emphasized decorative detail, such as that found in illuminated manuscripts, more than the spatial harmonies of Italian art. Dutch and Flemish painters favored realism

more than Italian Renaissance idealism in their portrayal of the human
body. They broke away from religious subject matter and Gothic use
of dark, gloomy colors and tones. In
contrast to Italian painting, intense
religiosity remained an important
element in Flemish and German
painting, and it was relatively rare to
see a depiction of nudes.

Albrecht Dürer's visits to Italy
reflect the dissemination and influence of the Italian Renaissance
beyond the Alps. The son of a
Nuremberg goldsmith, Dürer was
apprenticed to a book engraver. As a
young man, he seemed irresistibly
drawn to Italy as he wrestled with
how to depict the human form.
During two visits to Venice—in

Albrecht Dürer's *Self-Portrait* (1500).

1494 and 1505–1506—he sought out Italian painters, studying their use
of mathematics in determining and representing proportion.

Literary societies, academies, and universities contributed to the diffusion of Renaissance ideals in northern Europe. Francis I established the Col-
lège de France in 1530 in Paris, which soon had chairs in Greek, Hebrew,
and classical Latin. Northern universities became centers of humanistic
study, gradually taking over the role royal and noble households had played
in the diffusion of education. In Poland, the University of Krakow, which
had its first printing press in 1476, emerged as a center of humanism in the
late fifteenth and early sixteenth centuries. But some universities were quite
slow to include humanists; only one humanist taught at the University of
Cambridge in the early sixteenth century.

Some nobles now sent their children to humanist schools or employed
humanists as tutors, as did a number of wealthy urban bourgeois. Some Italian artists and scholars found employment in northern courts. Leonardo da
Vinci, Renaissance artist and scientist, was employed by King Francis I of
France. Kings and princes also hired humanists to serve as secretaries and
diplomats.

Latin gradually became the language of scholarship beyond the Alps. German, French, Spanish, and English historians borrowed from the style of the
Roman historians to celebrate their own medieval past. Unlike Italian historians, they viewed the medieval period not as a sad interlude between two
glorious epochs but as a time when their own political institutions and customs had been established.

In England at the end of the sixteenth century, Latin remained the language of high culture. There Machiavelli's *The Prince* was widely read and debated in Latin. When continental scholars traveled to England, they could discuss common texts with their English counterparts. Sir Thomas More (1478–1535), English lawyer and statesman, reflected the influence of Renaissance humanism, writing poetry in Latin. In his *Utopia* (1516), a satire of contemporary political and social life, More asked readers to consider their own values in the context of their expanding knowledge of other societies, including those of the New World.

The spread of the cultural values of Renaissance humanism across the Alps into the German states and northern Europe helped prepare the way for the Reformation. Like the Renaissance, the Reformation was in some ways the work of humanists moving beyond what they considered to be the constraints of Church theology. Humanists, who had always been concerned with ethics, attacked not only the failings of some clerics but also some of the Church's teachings, especially its claim to be immune to criticism. They also condemned superstition in the guise of religiosity. Northern Renaissance humanists were the sworn enemies of scholasticism, the medieval system of ecclesiastical inquiry in which Church scholars used reason to prove the tenets of Christian doctrine within the context of assumed theological truths. By suggesting that individuals who were not priests could interpret the Bible for themselves, they threatened the monopoly of Church theologians over biblical interpretation.

Erasmus's Humanistic Critique of the Church

An energetic Dutch cleric contributed more than any other person to the growth of Renaissance humanism in northern Europe. Born to unmarried parents and orphaned in Rotterdam, Desiderius Erasmus (c. 1469–1536) spent seven years in a monastery. Ordained a priest in 1492, he taught at the universities of Cambridge and Louvain, and then worked as a tutor in Paris and in Italy. As a young man, Erasmus may have suffered some sort of trauma—perhaps a romantic attachment that was either unreciprocated or inopportunely discovered. Thereafter compulsively obsessed with cleanliness, he was determined to infuse the Church with a new moral purity influenced by the Renaissance.

The patronage of Holy Roman Emperor Charles V and several other statesmen permitted Erasmus to apply the scholarly techniques of humanism to biblical study. Erasmus's *In Praise of Folly* (1509) was a satirical survey of the world as he saw it but also a clear call for a pure Christian morality shorn of the corruption he beheld in the monastic system. Thus, he wrote that priests claimed "that they've properly performed their duty if they reel off perfunctorily their feeble prayers which I'd be greatly surprised if any god could hear or understand." He believed that the scholastics of the Middle Ages had, like the barbarians, overwhelmed the Church with empty, lifeless theology.

Erasmus's attacks on those who believed in the curing power of relics (remains of saints venerated by the faithful) reflected his Renaissance sense of the dignity of the individual. His *Handbook of the Christian Soldier* (1503), which called for a theology that de-emphasized the sacraments, provided a guide to living a moral life. The little book went through twenty Latin editions and was translated into ten other languages. Erasmus wrote at length on how a prince ought to be educated and how children should be raised. The most well-known intellectual figure of his time in Europe, Erasmus greatly expanded the knowledge and appreciation of the classics in northern Europe.

Portrait of Desiderius Erasmus by Hans Holbein the Younger.

He and other major Northern Renaissance figures forged a Christian humanism focused on the early Christian past. Following his lead, northern humanists turned their skills in editing texts in Greek and Latin to the large body of early Christian writings.

THE ROOTS OF THE REFORMATION

In principle, the pope governed the Church in all of Western Christendom. But in reality, the emergence of the monarchical states of France, England, and the kingdoms of Spain in the late Middle Ages had eroded papal authority. Gradually these rulers assumed more prerogatives over the Church in their states. This expansion of monarchical authority itself provided the impetus toward the development of churches that gradually took on a national character as monarchs bargained for authority over religious appointments and worked to bring ecclesiastical property under their fiscal control by imposing taxation.

In the Italian and German states and in Switzerland, where many smaller, independent states ruled by princes, urban oligarchs, or even bishops survived, the very complexity of territorial political arrangements served to limit the direct authority of the pope. For in these smaller states, too, the ability of the pope and his appointees to manage their own affairs depended on the cooperation of lay rulers. Furthermore, the territorial expanse of Western

Christendom and daunting problems of transportation and communication made it difficult for the papal bureaucracy to reform blatant financial abuses. That the papacy itself increasingly appeared to condone or even encourage corruption added to the calls for reform.

Yet Erasmus and other northern humanists, while sharply criticizing the Church, were unwilling to challenge papal authority. The papacy, however, had other, more vociferous critics. First, the monarchs of France, Spain, and England had repudiated the interference of the pope in temporal affairs, creating what were, for all intents and purposes, national churches. Second, religious movements deemed heretical by the Church rejected papal authority. Some people sought refuge from the turmoil in spiritualism. Others based their idea of religion on personal study of the Bible, turning away from not only papal authority but also the entire formal hierarchy of the Church. Third, within the Church, a reform movement known as conciliarism sought to subject the authority of the popes to councils of cardinals and other Church leaders. More and more calls echoed for the reform of clerical abuses. As the Church seemed determined to protect its authority, to critics it also seemed more venal, even corrupt, than ever before. By questioning fundamental Church doctrine and the nature of religious faith, the resulting reform movement, culminating in the Reformation, shattered the unity of Western Christendom.

The Great Schism (1378–1417)

In the fourteenth century, the struggle between the king of France and the pope put the authority of the papacy in jeopardy. The French and English kings had imposed taxes on ecclesiastical property. In response, Pope Boniface VIII's bull *Unam Sanctam* (1302) threw down the gauntlet to lay rulers, asserting that "it is absolutely necessary for salvation for everyone to be subject to the Roman pontiff." King Philip IV of France ordered Boniface's arrest, and the pope died a year later, shortly after his release from captivity. Philip then arranged the election of a pliant pope, Clement V (pope 1305–1314). In 1309, he installed him in the papal enclave of Avignon, a town on the Rhône River. During the "Avignon Papacy" (1309–1378), the popes remained under the direct influence of the kings of France. At the same time, the popes continued to build up their bureaucracies and, like the monarchs whose authority they sometimes contested, to extract ever greater revenues from the faithful.

In 1377, Pope Gregory XI (pope 1370–1378) returned to Rome, in the hope that his presence there might calm the political situation in the Italian states. When Gregory XI died a year later, a group of cardinals in Rome, most of whom were French, elected Pope Urban VI (pope 1378–1389), popularly believed to be faithful to the Avignon Papacy. After a Roman mob invaded the proceedings, the cardinals fled. Upon their return several months later, a smaller group of thirteen cardinals was vexed by the new pope's denunciation of their wealth and privileges. Furthermore, they now viewed him as temperamentally unstable, unfit to be pope. They elected another pope, Clement VII, who claimed to be pope between 1378 and 1394. He returned to set up shop in Avignon, leaving his rival, Urban VI, in Rome. The Great Schism (1378–1417) began with two men now claiming authority over the Church.

The two popes and their successors thereafter sought to win the allegiance of rulers. The Avignon popes, like their pre-Schism predecessors, were under the close scrutiny of the king of France, and the Roman pope was caught up in the morass of Italian and Roman politics. France, Castile, Navarre, and Scotland supported the Avignon popes; most of the Italian states, Portugal, the Holy Roman Empire, and England obeyed the Roman popes. In 1409, Church dignitaries gathered at the Council of Pisa to resolve the conflict, and they elected a third pope. However, neither of the other two would agree to resign. And, in the meantime, secular rulers forced the popes to make agreements that increased the authority of the former over the Church in their states. The Great Schism enabled lay rulers to construct virtual national churches at the expense of papal power.

Heretical and Spiritual Movements

The chaos of two and then three popes claiming authority over the Church, along with the ruthlessness and greed of the claimants, greatly increased dissatisfaction with the organization of the Church. From time to time, heresies (movements based on beliefs deemed contrary to the teaching of the Church) had denied the authority of the papacy and demanded reform. In the twelfth century, the Waldensians in the Alps and the Albigensians in the south of France had defied the papacy by withdrawing into strictly organized communities that, unlike monasteries and convents, recognized neither Church doctrine nor authority.

An undercurrent of mysticism persisted in Europe, based on a belief in the supremacy of individual piety in the quest for knowledge of God and eternal salvation. William of Occam (c. 1290–1349), an English monk and another critic of the papacy, rejected scholastic rationalism. Scholasticism had become increasingly linked to the theology of Thomas Aquinas (1225–1274), who had deduced the existence of God from what he considered rational proofs that moved from one premise to the next. Occam, in contrast, posited that the gulf between God and man was so great that scholastic proofs of God's existence, such as those of Aquinas, were pointless because mankind could not understand God through reason. "Nominalists," as Occam and his followers were known, believed that individual piety should be the cornerstone of religious life. Nominalists rejected papal authority and the hierarchical structure of the Church. Their views reflected and accentuated the turn of more clergy and laymen toward the Scriptures as a guide for the individual's relationship with God, emphasizing the importance of leading a good, simple life. The Great Schism may have increased the yearning for spirituality as well as for the institutional reform of the Church.

The English cleric and scholar John Wyclif (c. 1328–1384) also questioned the pope's authority and claimed that an unworthy pope did not have to be obeyed, views that drew papal censorship. For Wyclif, the Church consisted of the body of those God had chosen to be saved, and no more. Stressing the role of faith in reaching eternal salvation, he insisted that reading the Scriptures formed the basis of faith and the individual's relationship with God. Wyclif also put himself at odds with Church theology by rejecting transubstantiation (the doctrine that holds that during Mass the priest transforms ordinary bread and wine into the body and blood of Christ).

Wyclif's de-emphasis of rituals and his advocacy of a religion based on faith suggested the significantly reduced importance of the Church as intermediary between man and God. Wyclif, who had powerful English noble and clerical protectors, called for Church reform. But the Peasants' Revolt of 1381 in England, in which wealthy churchmen were targets of popular wrath, gave even Wyclif's powerful protectors pause by raising the specter of future social unrest. An English Church synod condemned Wyclif, but he was allowed to live out his remaining years in a monastery. Some of his English followers, poor folk known as the Lollards, carried on Wyclif's work after his death. They criticized the Church's landed wealth and espoused a simpler religion. Led by gentry known as "Lollard knights," the Lollards rose up in rebellion in 1414, but were brutally crushed by King Henry V.

In Bohemia in Central Europe, Jan Hus (c. 1369–1415), a theologian, had learned of Wyclif's teaching. He, too, loudly criticized the worldliness of some clerics, and called for a return to a more unadorned religion. Rejecting the authority of the papacy and denouncing popes as "anti-Christs," Hus held that ordinary people could reform the Church.

The Challenge of Conciliarism to Papal Authority

The doctrine of conciliarism arose not only in response to the Great Schism but also to growing demands from many churchmen that the Church must undertake reform. The Council of Constance (1414–1418) was called to resolve the Great Schism and to undertake a reform of the Church. Many of the ecclesiastical dignitaries who attended also wanted to limit and define the authority of the papacy.

There were at least four significant parties to conciliarism: the popes themselves; bishops who supported councils as a way of resolving Church problems; secular rulers, particularly French kings, but also Holy Roman emperors, intervening in the Great Schism; and heretics condemned at Constance, who were far more radical than the mainstream conciliarists in their challenge to papal authority.

The Council of Constance first turned its attention to Jan Hus. Holding a safe-conduct pass given to him by the king of Bohemia, Hus travelled to the Council of Constance in 1414 but was arrested and put on trial for heresy. Hus refused to recant Wyclif's views, defending his own belief that the faithful, like the priest saying Mass, ought to be able to receive communion, the Church's rite of unity, in the two forms of bread and wine. The council condemned Hus, turning him over to the Holy Roman emperor, who ordered him burned at the stake as a heretic. The Hussites, the only major fifteenth-century dissidents within the Church, fought off several papal armies. They finally won special papal dispensation for the faithful to take communion in both bread and wine; their "Utraquist" ("in both kinds") church lasted until 1620.

The Council of Constance resolved the ongoing conflicting claims to papal authority by deposing two of the claimants and accepting the resignation of the third. In 1417, the council elected Martin V (pope 1417–1431). But the Great Schism, with its multiple papal claimants, by delaying any serious attempts at reform, had reinforced the insistence of some prelates that councils of Church bishops ought to have more authority than the pope.

Convoked by the pope, at least in principle, councils brought together leading ecclesiastical dignitaries from throughout Europe. These councils deliberated on matters of faith, as well as on the organization of the Church. But some councils began to come together in defiance of papal authority. Those holding a "conciliar" view of the Church conceived of it as

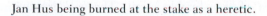

Jan Hus being burned at the stake as a heretic.

a corporation of cardinals that could override the pope. William of Occam had argued a century earlier that, when confronted by a heretical pope, a general council of the Church could stand as the repository of truth and authority. Some reformers wanted to impose a written constitution on the Church. At the Council of Basel, which began in 1431, exponents of unlimited papal authority and their counterparts favoring conciliarist positions both presented their views. In 1437, the pope ordered the council moved to Ferrara, and then the next year to Florence. Some participants, mostly conciliarists, continued to meet in Basel until 1445, although the pope declared that council schismatic. Fifteen years later, Pope Pius II (pope 1458–1464) declared the conciliar movement to be a heresy.

Clerical Abuses and Indulgences

The assertion by some churchmen that councils had authority over the papacy merged easily with those who called for the reform of blatant abuses within the Church. Some monasteries were mocked as hypocritical institutions no more saintly than the supposedly profane world monks and nuns sought to leave behind. Several new religious orders had been founded at least partially out of impatience with, if not disgust with, ecclesiastical worldliness.

Critics of the papacy attacked with particular energy ecclesiastical financial and moral abuses. They claimed that the papacy had become an investment trust run by the priests who administered the papacy's temporal affairs. No clerical financial abuse was more attacked than indulgences, which were based on the idea of transferable merit. Through granting indulgences, the Church supposedly reduced the time a soul would have to suffer punishment in Purgatory (that halfway house between Hell and Heaven that had emerged in Church belief early in the Middle Ages) for sins committed on earth. The practice of selling indulgences began during the Crusades as a means of raising revenue for churches and hospitals. Those seeking the salvation of their souls did not purchase God's forgiveness (which could only be received in the confessional) but rather cancelled or reduced the temporal punishment (such as the obligation to undertake pilgrimages, or give charity, or say so many prayers) required to atone for their sins. In 1457, the pope had announced that indulgences could be applied to the souls of family members or friends suffering in Purgatory. Some people had the impression that purchasing indulgences rather than offering real repentance brought immediate entry to Heaven for oneself or one's relatives. "The moment the money tinkles in the collecting box, a soul flies out of Purgatory," went one ditty. The implication was that wealthy families had a greater chance of opening the doors of Heaven for their loved ones than poor people. One papal critic interpreted all of this to mean that "the Lord desireth not the death of a sinner but rather that he may live and pay."

Another clerical practice that was much criticized was that of the sale of Church offices, known as simony. More than ever before, those who participated in—and benefited from—this practice were Italian clerics. Most popes appointed Italians as cardinals, many of whom lived in Rome while accumulating great wealth from ecclesiastical sees (areas of a bishops' jurisdiction) they rarely if ever visited. Some prominent families looked to the Church to provide lucrative sinecures—offices that generated income but that required little or no work—for their children. Reformers decried the appointment of unqualified bishops who had purchased their offices.

Many priests charged exorbitant fees for burial. Resentment also mounted, particularly in the German states, because clerics were immune from civil justice and paid no taxes. Indulgences and pardons, swapped for gold or services, had since 1300 become a papal monopoly. Commenting on Leo's death in 1521, one wag remarked, "His last moments come, he couldn't even have the [Last] Sacrament. By God, he's sold it!"

The papacy also came under attack for moral abuses. In the diocese of Trent in the early sixteenth century, about a fifth of all priests kept concubines. Nepotism, the awarding of posts to relatives or friends, seemed to reign supreme. In the fifteenth century, Pope Paul II was mocked as the "happy father," not revered as the Holy Father. Alexander VI (pope 1492–1503) looked after his own children with the care of any other father. Paul III (pope 1534–1549) made two of his grandsons cardinals, their expensive hats far bigger than the young heads upon which they rested.

The sacrament of penance also generated popular resentment against the clergy. Since 1215, the faithful were required to confess their sins at least once a year to a priest. This sacrament originated in the context of instruction to encourage good behavior. But for many people, penance had become the priest's interrogation of the faithful in the confessional, during which the confessor sought out details of misdeeds in order to determine one of the sixteen stated degrees of transgression. The Church's call for sinners to repent seemed particularly ironic in view of popularly perceived ecclesiastical abuses.

Given a boost by the conciliar movement, calls for reform echoed louder and louder. The representatives of the clergy who had gathered at the Estates-General of France in 1484 criticized the sale of Church offices. In 1510, the Augsburg Diet, an imperial institution of the Holy Roman Empire, refused to grant money to the pope for war against the Turks unless he first ordered an end to financial abuses. The imperial representative Assembly (Reichstag) had increasingly served as a forum for denunciations against the papacy. In 1511, King Louis XII of France, whose armies had backed up his territorial ambitions in northern Italy, called a council with the goal of reasserting the conciliar doctrine and ordered reforms in the monastic houses of his realm. The Fifth Lateran Council, which met from 1512 to 1517, urged more education for the clergy, sought to end some monastic financial abuses, and insisted that occupants of religious houses uphold their vows of chastity. The council also suggested missions to carry the Church's influence into the Americas. Pope Leo X, however, emphatically insisted that he alone could convoke Church councils, and the Fifth Lateran Council itself forbade sermons denouncing the moral state of the Church.

Martin Luther

Martin Luther (1483–1546) was born in the small town of Eisleben in central Germany. He was the son of a miner whose family had been prosperous peasants. His peasant background could be seen in the coarseness of his language, song, and humor. The stocky, pious, and determined Luther began his studies in 1501 at the University of Erfurt, where he took courses in philosophy and then began the study of law.

In July 1505, Luther was engulfed in a violent storm as he returned to Erfurt after a visit home. As a bolt of lightning struck not far from where he stood in terror, the young student cried out to the patron saint of travelers, "Help me, Saint Anne, I will become a monk." Returning safely to Erfurt, he gathered his friends together and told them, "Today you see me, henceforth, never more." They escorted him to the nearby monastery of the Augustinian monks, which he entered against his father's wishes. Luther prayed, fasted, and, outside the monastery, begged for charity. In 1507, he was ordained a priest and soon became a doctor of theology, administrator of eleven Augustinian monasteries, and dean of the theological seminary in the town of Wittenberg.

Luther had, for some time, been wracked with gnawing doubt concerning his personal unworthiness. Was he not a sinner? He had been saved from the storm, but would he be saved from damnation on Judgment Day? Was there really any connection between good works effected on earth and salvation? If mankind was so corrupted by sin, how could charity, fasting, or constant prayer and self-flagellation in the monastery earn one entry to Heaven? He later recalled, "I tried hard . . . to be contrite, and make a list of my sins. I confessed them again and again. I scrupulously carried out the penances that were allotted to me. And yet my conscience kept telling me: 'You fell short there.' 'You were not sorry enough.' 'You left that sin off your list.' I was trying to cure the doubts and scruples of the conscience with human remedies. . . . The more I tried these remedies, the more troubled and uneasy my conscience grew."

Luther's lonely study of theology in the tower library of the monastery did not resolve his doubts. Like other Augustinians, he had been influenced by the nominalism of William of Occam, which emphasized individual piety. This led Luther closer to his contention that faith, not good works, was the key to salvation. Indeed, the teachings of Saint Augustine himself also suggested to him that each person could be saved by faith alone through the grace of God. Believing man is saved "not by pieces, but in a heap," Luther became obsessed with a phrase from the Bible (Romans 1:17), "The just shall live by faith." Such a conclusion broke with the accepted teachings of the Church as defined by medieval scholasticism. But more than faith was troubling Luther. He was also especially troubled by the abuse of the ecclesiastical sale of indulgences.

On October 31, 1517, Luther tacked up on the door of the castle church of Wittenberg "Ninety-five Theses or Disputations on the Power and Efficacy of Indulgences." He denounced the theoretical underpinnings of the papal granting of indulgences out of the "treasury of merits" accumulated by Christ and the saints. He then had his theses printed and distributed in the region and invited those who might want to dispute his theses to present themselves to debate with him, as was the custom. In February 1518, Pope Leo X demanded that Luther's monastic superior order him to cease his small crusade. Luther refused, citing his right as a professor of theology to dispute formally the charges now leveled against him. And he found a protector, Frederick III, elector of Saxony, a religious ruler who turned to the Bible as he mulled over matters of state.

In April, as denunciations against Luther poured into Rome, he successfully defended his theses before his Augustinian superiors. Pope Leo was

An allegorical painting of the dream of Frederick the Wise wherein Martin Luther uses an enormous quill to tack his Ninety-Five Theses to the door of the castle church at Wittenberg.

trying to remain on good terms with Frederick III, a strong candidate for election as Holy Roman emperor. Instead of immediately summoning Luther to Rome, he therefore proposed that a papal legate travel to Augsburg to hear Luther out. At their meeting, the legate warned Luther to desist or face the consequences. Luther's friends, suspecting that the pope had ordered his arrest, whisked him away to safety.

Luther sought a negotiated solution. He agreed to write a treatise calling on the German people to honor the Church, and promised neither to preach nor publish anything else if his opponents would also keep silent. At this point Luther did not seek to create a new church, but merely to reform the old one. A papal representative sent to meet with Luther in Leipzig in June 1519 accused him of being a Hussite, that is, of denying the pope's authority. Luther admitted that he did not believe the pope to be infallible.

Luther crossed his Rubicon, but unlike Caesar moved not toward Rome but away from it. "Farewell, unhappy, hopeless, blasphemous Rome! The wrath of God come upon thee, as you deserve," he wrote a friend, "We have cared for Babylon and she is not healed; let us then leave her. . . ." Luther would not be silenced. "I am hot-blooded by temperament and my pen gets irritated easily," he proclaimed.

Three treatises published in 1520 marked Luther's final break with Rome. Here Luther developed his theology of reform, one that went far beyond the prohibition of indulgences and the sale of ecclesiastical offices. He argued his view that faith alone could bring salvation, that good works follow faith but do not in themselves save the soul. Nor, he argued, does the absence of good works condemn man to eternal damnation. Upon reading one of these tracts, Erasmus, loyal critic of the Church, stated emphatically, "The breach is irreparable."

Developing the theological concept of "freedom of a Christian," Luther's immediate goal was to free German communities from the strictures of religious beliefs and institutions that seemed increasingly foreign to their faith. He called on the princes of the German states to reform the Church in their states. In doing so, he argued that the Scriptures declared the Church itself to be a priestly body that was not subject to the pope's interpretation. Luther acknowledged only two of the seven sacraments, those instituted by Christ, not the papacy: baptism and communion. After first retaining penance, he dropped it, arguing that faith was sufficient to bring about a sinner's reconciliation with God. If this was true, the monastic life no longer seemed to Luther to provide any advantage in the quest for salvation. And he rejected what he called the "unnatural" demands of poverty, chastity, and obedience.

On June 15, 1520, Pope Leo X excommunicated Luther from the Church, accusing him of forty-one heresies. The papal bull of excommunication called Luther "the wild boar who has invaded the Lord's vineyard." In Wittenberg, a crowd burned papal bulls and documents. Luther defiantly tossed the writ of excommunication into the flames.

Charles V had been elected Holy Roman emperor following his father's death in 1519. He had promised before his election that no one would be excommunicated within the empire without a proper hearing. Through the influence of Frederick III of Saxony, Charles summoned Luther to the German town of Worms in April 1521 to confront the imperial Diet (assembly).

Before the Diet, Luther was asked if he had written the imposing number of treatises and books placed on the table. Acknowledging them all, Luther replied: "I am bound by the Scriptures I have quoted and my conscience is captive to the Word of God. I cannot and I will not retract anything, since it is neither safe nor right to go against conscience. I cannot do otherwise, here I stand, may God help me. Amen." The Diet condemned Luther's beliefs. Charles V, in agreement with the pope, signed the Edict of Worms in May 1521, placing Luther under the "ban of the empire." This forbade him from preaching and declared him a heretic. Several men loyal to Frederick III, Luther's protector, escorted him to safety.

By declaring Luther an outlaw and forbidding any changes in religion in the Holy Roman Empire, the Edict of Worms made religious reform an issue of state. But Luther could not have survived the ban of the empire if his influence had not already spread, convincing many that through Luther they had now discovered the true Gospel.

SOCIAL BACKGROUND OF THE REFORMATION IN THE GERMAN STATES

Challenging the ways people in Central Europe had thought about religion for centuries, the movement for reform, spread by preachers, found converts in the German states. During the early 1520s, the proponents of Martin Luther's reform convinced many clergy and lay people to reconsider their religious beliefs and to restructure their communities. Social and political unrest, perhaps encouraged by the quest for religious reform, began to stir in the central and southern German states as peasants rose up against their lords. This uprising, although roundly condemned by Luther, left no doubt that the Reformation would shake the foundations of the German states.

Urban Centers of Reform

At first the Reformation was overwhelmingly an urban phenomenon in the German states and then Switzerland. The decentralized political structure of the Holy Roman Empire and traditions of popular participation in urban government aided the movement for reform, for example in the free cities in the northern German states like the powerful Baltic trading city of Lübeck, leader of the Hanseatic League, and self-governing towns in the southern German states. Each German town had its own elite of prosperous burghers. Reformers found these communities fertile ground for Luther's ideas. Complaining of incompetent or lazy priests, members of some towns had endowed posts for preachers in order to attract vigorous, effective priests, a good many of whom now followed Luther.

German towns also had a particularly well-developed sense of civic solidarity that included a belief that all citizens of the town shared a common fate in the material world—vulnerability to bad times, and a certain degree of prosperity in good times—and that salvation itself was something of a group enterprise. Erasmus had asked, "What else is the city but a great monastery?" Luther sought to spark a more personal religion that would make people not only better Christians, but better citizens of their communities as well. In many towns, urban leaders and ordinary people may have accepted reform because it appeared more promising than unreformed Catholicism for the maintenance of local order.

Yet no simple formula could predict how the Reformation would fare in German towns. In the southern German states, urban nobles, merchants, and bankers remained staunchly Catholic. These property-owning groups were more conservative by instinct. Here the role of personality and the configuration of local social and political life came into play; so did pure chance, including such factors as whether preachers and reform literature arrived, how both were received, and by whom.

The Process of Reform

Social and political factors thus helped shape religious outcomes. While the embrace of the Reformation did not constitute a social revolution, in many cases clergy supporting religious reform were drawn from the middle and lower middle classes, groups with some possibility of social mobility. The "middling sort," in turn, brought reform to the lower classes. This process might be marked by the spontaneous singing of Lutheran hymns by those sitting in Mass, or by some other signs of a turn to reform. While archbishops and bishops in general opposed Luther, the lower clergy, particularly those of recent ordination, became influential converts in their towns. Communities accepted reformers by consensus, as local governments began to bow to the wishes of townspeople.

Thus, a crowd cheered in Basel when a priest carried the Bible instead of the communion host during the feast of Corpus Christi. Priests began to wear simpler clothes instead of rich robes. For the first time some of the Mass was said in German. Some reformed priests began to give the faithful both bread and wine during communion. Some crowds mocked Church rituals in angry ways: ringing cow bells to disrupt Mass; heckling priests trying to deliver sermons; smashing stained-glass windows, crucifixes, statues, and other images of the saints; and even destroying relics considered sacred. Such largely spontaneous actions bewildered Luther, who remained in most ways a very conservative man.

Luther and his followers denied the special status of the clergy as a group marked off from the rest of the population. In the early days of the Reformation, some reformers undertook expeditions to "rescue" nuns from convents. A number of former priests began to take wives, which at first shocked Luther, since this represented the end of clerical celibacy, which the Church had proclaimed in the eleventh century. Luther asserted in 1521, "Good Lord! Will our people at Wittenberg give wives even to monks? They will not push a wife on me!" But by 1525 he changed his mind, and married a former nun. The marriage of clerics further broke down the barrier between the priest and the people, symbolizing the "priesthood of all believers" by eliminating the clerical distinction of celibacy. Nonetheless, Luther limited the task of interpreting the Scriptures to professors of theology.

The Peasants' Revolt

In the southern German states, some burghers worried that law and order would collapse, and that the poor might rise up. Some lords and burghers expressed concern that the villagers might "turn Swiss," referring to the Swiss towns that lived without lords and were self-governing and independent. News of several strange and alarming prophecies circulated.

In 1524–1525, peasants rose up against their lords in parts of the central and southern German states (see Map 3.1). They demanded the return of rights (such as to hunt freely and to pasture their animals on the common lands) that lords had usurped. They also asked for the abolition of serfdom and the tithe, which they declared to be against God's will. Bands of poor people burned castles and monasteries.

The peasants' revolt spread into Austria and Carinthia, and up into Thuringia and Saxony. Pamphlets called for social as well as religious reform. Thomas Münzer (c. 1491–1525), a priest and theologian, merged religious reform with social revolution. He preached against the Church and Luther with equal fury, for he believed that both the Church and Luther had humbled themselves to lay authorities. Münzer led a peasant army in Thuringia, where Luther's reform movement had made many converts.

In the northwestern German states, also in 1525, some towns that had been won over to religious reform rose up against Catholic princes. Swabian peasants promulgated twelve articles against their lords, princes, and bishops, demanding that communities have the right to choose their own pastors. But here, too, the demands of the rebels had a social content. They asked for an end to double taxation by both lay and ecclesiastical lords and the "death tax" by which heirs had to give up the deceased's finest horse, cow, or garment. They demanded the end of serfdom, the return of common lands to their use, and free access to forests and streams.

Luther had some sympathy with the plight of the poor. Some of his followers began to see in his teaching a means of resistance against the powerful. But Luther rejected the idea that his central theological idea of

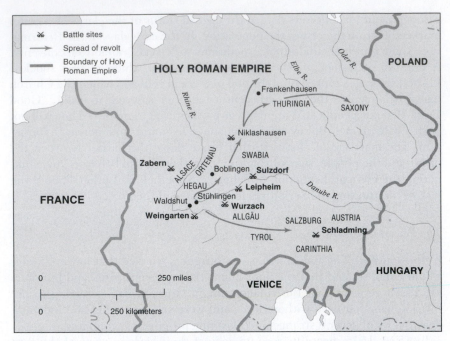

MAP 3.1 THE PEASANTS' REVOLT, 1525–1526   Sites of peasant uprisings in parts of the central and southern German states. The revolt began in Waldshut and Stühlingen in the southern German states and spread east to the Tyrol and Salzburg in Austria, and north to Thuringia and Saxony.

"Christian freedom," which he believed applied only to the spiritual realm, could be extended into the relationship between lord and peasant. Luther asked lords to "act rationally" and "try kindness" when confronted by peasant demands. As nobles and churchmen began to accuse him of fomenting insurrection, he denounced the peasants in extravagant language. In *Against the Murdering, Thieving Hordes of Peasants,* he advised the German princes to "brandish their swords. . . . You cannot meet a rebel with reason. Your best answer is to punch him in the face until he has a bloody nose." Catholic and reformed princes put aside their differences to crush the revolt, in which more than 100,000 peasants perished. Münzer was defeated, captured, tortured, and beheaded.

THE SPREAD OF THE REFORMATION

Because of the intertwining of religion and politics, what began as a movement for Church reform became entangled in princely rivalries in the German states. As the breach between Catholic and reformed princes widened, religion became a source of division rather than of unity.

Although Luther had never intended to bring about a permanent division within Christianity, his followers gradually created a new church in many of the German states. The Reformation then spread beyond the German states.

Divisions within Christendom

The Augsburg Confession, a summary of beliefs presented by Luther's friends to the Diet that gathered in that city in 1530, became the doctrinal basis of the Lutheran Church. It was implemented by princes and prelates in the reformed states and towns, and in some places by a council, known as a Consistory, of ministers and lawyers.

Some humanists influenced by the Renaissance were attracted by Luther's writing. In the tradition of their predecessors who had rediscovered the classics, they admired Luther's return to the Scriptures as an original source of knowledge. One of Luther's converts later wrote that his own excitement at the new teaching was so great that he studied the Bible at night with sand in his mouth so that he would not fall asleep. Humanists transformed some monasteries into schools. The first reformed university began in Marburg in 1527.

But as the gap between reformers and the Church grew larger, Erasmus was caught in the middle. His own criticism of ecclesiastical abuses did not go far enough for reformers, but it went too far for churchmen. Erasmus remained loyal to Church doctrine. Similarly, Luther and the humanists parted ways by 1525. For the latter, humanistic knowledge was an end in

The Augsburg Confession read before Charles V in 1530.

itself; for the reformers, rhetoric was a method for teaching the Scriptures and for arguing in favor of ecclesiastical reform. Many reformers were less committed than humanists to the belief that man is a rational and autonomous being. Luther himself did not share the humanists' Renaissance optimism about mankind. He was not interested in rediscovering mankind but was instead preoccupied with an individual's relationship to God. Furthermore, Luther opposed attempts by philosophers to intrude in theological questions. Nonetheless, a humanist curriculum continued to influence the training of reform ministers.

Luther's followers gained their first martyrs in 1523, when two former monks were executed in Brussels for their beliefs. German princes requested from Holy Roman Emperor Charles V that a "free general council or at least a national council" consider the growing religious division within the Holy Roman Empire. The Diet of Speyer (1526) proclaimed that each German prince was "to live, govern, and bear himself as he hopes and trusts to answer to God and his imperial majesty." This truce gave reformers time to win even more converts. In 1529, German princes again gathered in Speyer. Some of them prepared a "protest" against the policies of Charles V and the Catholic princes, who had declared themselves against Luther. The followers of Luther thus became known as "Protestants."

Luther's writings, translated into Latin, then spread beyond the German states, following trade routes east and west. The reformers easily revived the anti-papal Hussite traditions of Bohemia and Moravia and that of the Waldensians in the southwestern Alps. German merchants carried reform to the Baltic states and Scandinavia. In Denmark, King Christian II adopted Lutheranism for his state. When Lutheranism was declared its official religion in 1527, Sweden and its territory of Finland had the first national reformed church.

Charles V and the Protestants

Holy Roman Emperor Charles V, the pope's most powerful potential advocate, was a pious man who first denounced Luther with passion. But extensive Habsburg imperial interests kept him fighting a war in Western Europe against King Francis I of France, which prevented him from acting against those who supported Luther. The French king, for his part, was pleased that religion was dividing the German princes, thereby weakening the imperial crown that he had coveted. Charles V was away from his German states between 1521 and 1530, for the most part in Italy, crucial years during which the Reformation spread within the Holy Roman Empire. In 1524, the first Protestant leagues were formed between states. Protestant governments dissolved convents and monasteries, turning them to secular uses, such as hospices or schools.

The Christian crusade against the Turks in Eastern Europe and the Mediterranean preoccupied Charles and other Catholic princes as well. In

1526, the Turks defeated the Hungarian king at Mohács in Hungary. This left Lutheran missionaries an open field there, although Muslim Turks did not care about which version of Christianity their non-Muslim subjects practiced. A subsequent Turkish advance forced Charles to offer concessions to Lutheran princes in exchange for assistance against the Turks. (Luther's hymn "A Mighty Fortress Is Our God" began as a martial song to inspire soldiers against the Ottoman forces.)

To be sure, not all political and religious leaders and their followers were intolerant of other religions. But in a time of sharp religious contention, too few shared the toleration of a French traveler to Turkey in 1652, who reported, "There are many in Christendom who believe that the Turks are great devils, barbarians, and people without faith, but those who have known them and who have talked with them have quite a different opinion, since it is certain that the Turks are good people who follow very well the commandment given us by nature, only to do to others what we would have done to us."

For a time, Charles V held out hope for conciliation with the Protestants. In 1531, however, the princes of Hesse, Saxony, and other states and cities that had adopted religious reform formed the Schmalkaldic League. Although first and foremost a defensive alliance, the princes intended that the league would replace the Holy Roman Empire as the source of their political allegiance. Up until this time, Charles had accepted temporary truces, and thus toleration of Protestants. He had suspended the Edict of Worms (which had condemned Luther as a heretic) until a general council of the Church could be held. When the pope announced that it would be held in the Alpine town of Trent (see p. 116), the stage was set for confrontation with the Protestants. Meanwhile, however, Charles was still preoccupied by hostilities with Francis I of France, who shocked many Christians by allying with the Turks against the Habsburgs. After Charles forced an end to the wars by launching an invasion of France from the Netherlands, he was finally ready to move against Protestants, routing the Schmalkaldic League in battle in 1547. He then forced reconversion on the people in about thirty German cities. By that time, however, Protestantism had established itself definitively in much of Central Europe.

The Peace of Augsburg

Charles V now tried to bring more of the German princes and their people back into the Catholic fold. He tried without success to impose moderate Catholic reform in Central Europe to answer some of the criticism of the reformers. But several of the Catholic princes took up arms against him in a short war in 1551. The political complexity of the myriad German states militated against a general settlement. The Holy Roman emperor gave up the idea of restoring Catholicism in all of the German states.

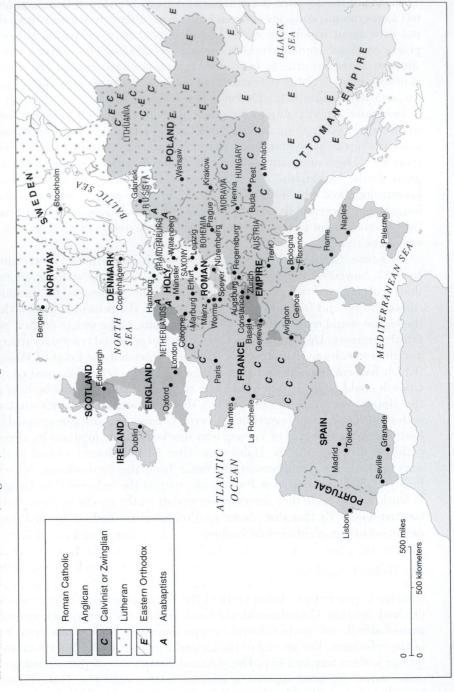

MAP 3.2 THE RELIGIOUS SITUATION IN EUROPE AFTER THE PEACE OF AUGSBURG, 1555 The Peace of Augsburg stipulated that the religion of the ruler of each of the Holy Roman Empire's states would be the religion of the state. The map indicates areas that were Roman Catholic, Anglican, Calvinist/Zwinglian, Lutheran, Eastern Orthodox, and Anabaptist.

The Peace of Augsburg of 1555 was a compromise. It was agreed upon by the imperial representative assembly after Charles, worn down by the complexity of imperial politics, refused to participate. It stipulated that the religion of the ruler of each of the empire's states would be the religion of the state (*cuius regio, eius religio*) (see Map 3.2). Protestants living in states with a Catholic ruler were free to emigrate, as were Catholics in the same situation. The Peace of Augsburg thus recognized that the institutions of the Holy Roman Empire could not provide a solution to what now appeared to be permanent religious divisions in Central Europe. It acknowledged that the Reformation in the German states was an accomplished fact. Thus, what had begun as a "squabble among monks" shaped the territorial and political history of Germany. Through the compromise that allowed each prince to determine the religion of his state, the Peace of Augsburg reaffirmed German particularism, the existence of many independent German states.

THE REFORMATION IN SWITZERLAND AND FRANCE

The next stage of the Reformation occurred in Switzerland, land of rugged peasants, craftsmen, and mercenary soldiers. The thirteen sparsely populated, independent cantons of Switzerland (then about a million people) were loosely joined in a federal Diet, closer in organization and in spirit to the Italian city-states than to the German states. Unlike the German states, where the conversion of a powerful prince could sway an entire state, there were no such territorial rulers in Switzerland. The Swiss reformers, then, would be even more closely tied to privileged residents of towns of relatively small size. Their movement would also soon spread to parts of France.

Zwingli and Reform

In Zurich, then a town of about 6,000, Huldrych Zwingli (1484–1531) preached salvation through faith alone. In 1522, several citizens of Zurich publicly munched sausages during Lent in defiance of the Lenten ban on eating meat. Zwingli published two tracts on their behalf in which he insisted that the Scriptures alone should be the basis of religious practice, and that as there was nothing in the Bible about sausages, they could be eaten at any time. This scriptural test also led Zwingli and his followers to iconoclasm, the stripping of images and altar decorations from churches because nothing about them could be found in the Bible. The Zurich municipal council then embraced reform. It ordered the canton's priests to preach only from the Bible, and two years later it forbade the saying of Mass. Zwingli convinced the town's magistrates that tithes should be used to aid the poor, whom he believed represented the real image of God.

A doctrinal conflict among reformers helped define the character of the Swiss Reformation. Luther maintained that communion represented the physical presence of Christ. In this he had not diverged far from the Catholic Church, which insisted that through the miracle of transubstantiation (which the pope formulated in 1215), the priest transformed bread and wine into the actual body and blood of Christ, the sacrament of the Holy Eucharist. But to Luther, who condemned Catholic worship of the Eucharist, the bodily presence of Christ in the Eucharist came from the fact that Christ and God were universally present. Zwingli, by contrast, believed that communion was only a symbol of Christ's real presence in the Eucharist and that Luther's refusal to abandon this idea demonstrated that he still stood with one foot in Rome. The "Sacramentarian Controversy" emerged as the first major doctrinal dispute among Protestants. The Augsburg Confession of 1530 sealed the rift by excluding reformers who rejected Lutheranism, such as Zwingli and his followers.

Between 1525 and 1530, some German-speaking parts of Switzerland and regions of the southern German states accepted Zwingli's reforms. In 1531, Catholic forces attacked Protestant cantons because Zwingli was actively espousing his version of reform there. Zwingli, carrying a sword and a Bible, led the Protestant forces into the Battle of Kappel and was killed in the fighting. Both Catholics and Lutherans claimed Zwingli's death to be divine judgment against his religious positions. The peace that followed, however, specified that each canton could choose its own religion.

(*Left*) Woodcut of Huldrych Zwingli. (*Right*) Burning church ornaments and religious statues in Zurich.

MAP 3.3 RADICAL RELIGIOUS MOVEMENTS   Areas in which there were Hussites, Utraquists, Anabaptists, and Mennonites.

Radical Reformers

The reforms of Zwingli were not the only kind spreading in southern Germany and Switzerland in the 1520s. Some groups had even more radical ideas in mind for changing religious morality and communal life. Radicals shared an impatience with the plans of more moderate reformers, although they sometimes had very different visions of what this would constitute. Some were Anti-Trinitarians who rejected the orthodox Christian teaching that God consisted of the Father, the Son, and the Holy Spirit. Many radicals believed that they had been called to form the communities in which they sought to implement "godly living" (see Map 3.3).

Most radical reformers in the 1520s held apocalyptic beliefs, convinced that the world would soon end with a victory of God's true faithful over the forces of evil, in which they included those who did not agree with them or tolerate their views. Some radical reformers who had broken with Zwingli in Zurich became known as Anabaptists—"anabaptism" means rebaptism in Greek. Believing that neither Luther nor Zwingli had sufficiently transformed religious morality and community life, they sought to implement "godly" living on the model of the New Testament. Because they could find no reference to infant baptism in the Bible, they began baptizing adults in 1525 against Zwingli's advice. They believed that only adults could manifest true faith and therefore be worthy of baptism.

Anabaptist groups sprung up in areas influenced by Protestant reform, including Zurich, the Netherlands, parts of Italy, and Poland. Anabaptists were a very diverse group. Many Anabaptists advocated a congregational form of organization, because for them membership was through free will or voluntary self-selection, rather than through territorial organization of churches as was true for Catholics, Lutherans, and Zwinglians. Yet there were major differences between groups. Some Anabaptists in Switzerland and southern Germany formed communities of believers seeking isolation— "separation from iniquity," as they put it—from the struggles and temptations of the sinful secular world. These Anabaptists did not accept temporal government and refused to take civil oaths, pay taxes, hold public office, or serve in armies. However, other Anabaptists did seek alliances with local rulers and sought to be loyal subjects.

Catholic and Protestant states moved to crush these communities of radicals, seeing them as seditious rebels against God-given authority in church and state. At the Diet of Speyer in 1529, Charles V, along with Catholic and Protestant rulers in the empire, declared Anabaptism a crime punishable by death, usually by—with intentional irony—drowning, "the third baptism." Some of these radical reformers sought refuge in the mountains of the Tyrol and Moravia, and in the Netherlands, while others accepted a martyr's death or spoke out against authorities who persecuted them.

In 1534, a radical group of Anabaptists led by a local preacher took over the town government of Münster by election. Those not sympathetic to Anabaptism left town willingly or were expelled. Soon several thousand Anabaptists from as far away as the Netherlands arrived in Münster, believing it to be the "New Jerusalem," where God's chosen people would be protected. The Anabaptists established a council of twelve that expropriated Catholic Church property, abolished private property, banned the use of money, and established communally held property and a system of barter.

Münster's territorial ruler and his allies laid siege to the town. Inside Münster, John of Leiden, a Dutchman, gained influence as a leader and prophet. He convinced the ministers and elders of Münster to abolish private property, which they justified on biblical grounds—upon Christ's return, believers would not need possessions. Moreover, sharing possessions helped them ration goods during the siege. They also began to practice polygamy, in part because there were four times as many women than men in town. John of Leiden, who became king of Münster, led the way by taking sixteen wives. He also ordered the burning of all books in Münster except the Bible. Forces sent by Lutheran and Catholic princes stormed the town in June 1535 and tortured to death John of Leiden and other lesser leaders, placing their mutilated corpses in iron cages that still hang in a church steeple in Münster.

After the fall of Münster, Dutch Anabaptists led by a former Catholic priest named Menno Simons (1496–1561) tried to save adult baptism by preaching disciplined, godly living and Christian pacifism. They became known as Mennonites, and some of them left for the Americas more than a century later in search of religious toleration. Other descendants of such radical reformers include the adult-baptizing Hutterites of Moravia, the forebears of a group who settled in the American Midwest and the Canadian prairies. Likewise, the Unitarian religion has roots in this period, deriving from the Anti-Trinitarian views of God as being one, not the trinity of Father, Son, and Holy Spirit.

Jean Calvin and Reform

France, too, provided fertile ground for reform. The French monarchy had traditionally maintained a stubborn independence from Rome. Pope Leo X had signed the Concordat of Bologna (1516) with King Francis I, giving the king the right to appoint bishops and abbots in France. Initially the Valois ruler was far more preoccupied with his wars against Charles V and the Habsburgs than with the stormy tracts of an obscure German monk. The threat of heresy, however, convinced him in 1521 to order Luther's writings confiscated and burned. Yet Protestant propaganda arrived in France from Germany. In 1534, reformers affixed placards in Paris denouncing the Mass and on the king's bedroom door in his château at Amboise. The "affair of the placards" convinced the king to combat reform in earnest.

Jean Calvin (1509–1564) embodied the second major current of the Reformation. He was born in the small town of Noyon in northern France, where his father worked as a secretary to the local bishop. Calvin's mother died when he was about five years old, and his father sent him to Paris to be trained as a priest. He then decided that his son should become a lawyer, because he might earn more money.

Late-Renaissance humanism and particularly the teachings of Erasmus helped stimulate in the pious young Calvin an interest in religious reform during his legal studies. In 1534, the Catholic hierarchy and the king himself moved to crush this movement. Finding exile in the Swiss town of Basel, Calvin probably still considered himself a follower of Erasmus within the Catholic Church. In Basel, he penned tracts denouncing the papacy and calling on the king of France to end religious persecution.

Throughout his life, Calvin was overwhelmed by anxiety and self-doubt, compounded by his virtual abandonment by his father and his forced exile. He was also terror-struck by the power of nature and, in particular, by storms as manifestations of God's power—rather like Luther. Humanity seemed to Calvin to be poised before an abyss, a metaphor he frequently used. He feared that oceans might rise and sweep humankind away. Around him Calvin saw only the absence of order.

Like other thinkers of the early sixteenth century, Calvin believed that he lived in a time of extraordinary moral crisis: "Luxury increases daily, lawless passions are inflamed, and human beings continue in their crimes and profligacy more shameless than ever." It seemed to Calvin that the sense of religious community that ought to bind people together was dissolving.

Calvin argued that the Catholic Church had made the faithful anxious by emphasizing the necessity of good works in achieving salvation. The anxiety of never knowing how many good works were enough had, Calvin insisted, turned Catholics to seek the intercession of saints. He attacked the sacrament of penance with particular vehemence: "The souls of those who have been affected with some awareness of God are most cruelly torn by this butchery . . . the sky and sea were on every side, there was no port of anchorage." Calvin also rejected the increasingly human-like images given God and Christ over the previous century. Unlike Luther, Calvin emphasized not reconciliation with God through faith, but rather obedience to his will. He sought to provide a doctrine that would reassure the faithful of God's grace and of their own salvation. There was hope in Calvin's thought, faith that the labyrinth—another of his frequent images—of life could be successfully navigated. The imposition of order, based upon the mo-

(*Left*) Jean Calvin. (*Right*) A Calvinist service. Note the austerity of the church.

rality dictated by the Bible, would put an end to some of life's haunting uncertainties.

With this in mind, Calvin developed in his *Institutes of the Christian Religion* (1536–1559) the doctrine of election or predestination: "God's eternal decree. . . . For all are not created in equal condition; rather, eternal life is foreordained for some, eternal damnation for others." The belief in predestination called into question the efficacy of good works. If one's fate were predestined and if good works in themselves (as the Catholic Church claimed) did not bring eternal salvation, why lead a righteous life? Calvin believed that good works were signs of having been chosen by God for eternal salvation, though they did not in themselves guarantee Heaven.

Whereas medieval theologians had condemned lending money for profit, Calvin, unlike Luther, distinguished between usury and productive loans that would raise capital and increase the well-being of the entire community. Replacing penance as a means of imposing individual discipline, Calvin preached collective, communal discipline in the pursuit of holiness. Validating economic activity, later Calvinists came to view prosperity, along with "sober living," as a sign of election by God. In the late nineteenth century, this came to be known as the "Protestant ethic."

Late in 1536, Calvin went to the Swiss lakeside city of Geneva, a town of about 13,000 people. With the first successes of the Reformation, word of which had originally been carried there by German merchants, Geneva broke away from the domination of the Catholic House of Savoy. Earlier that year, troops of the Swiss canton of Bern, which had embraced Zwinglian reform, occupied the city. Bern established a protectorate, with Geneva retaining its nominal independence. Citizens elected magistrates and members of two representative councils.

In 1537, Calvin persuaded the smaller and most powerful of the two councils to adopt a Confession of Faith, swearing that the people of Geneva "live according to the holy evangelical law and the Word of God." Residency in Geneva would be contingent on formal adherence to the document. The Mass was banned, and priests were informed that they had to convert to reformed religion or leave the city.

Calvin hoped to impose Christian discipline and asceticism on the city in order to construct a righteous society. His "Ecclesiastical Ordinances" would provide for the organization of religious life in reformed Geneva, but they threatened the powers of the councils. Calvin insisted that the Consistory, the judiciary of the reformed church made up of lay elders (called presbyters), would have the right to discipline all citizens and to dispense harsh penalties against those who transgressed Geneva's religious laws. These penalties would include excommunication from the church, exile, imprisonment, and even execution. Calvin wanted municipal supervisors to monitor the religious behavior of the people, but the councils hesitated to surrender their authority to Calvin, who was French, or to assume such a supervisory role. In 1538, the councils told Calvin to leave Geneva.

In 1540, the majority of citizens of Geneva, believing that the town's ties to Bern limited its sovereignty, elected new magistrates, who executed the leaders of the pro-Bern faction. The two councils then invited Calvin to return to oversee reform in Geneva, and they adopted his Ecclesiastical Ordinances. Calvin returned to the city he had called "a place so grossly immoral."

To John Knox, a Scottish reformer, Geneva seemed "the most perfect school of Christ that ever was on earth since the days of the Apostles." But many citizens of Geneva resisted the close scrutiny of the Consistory. One man named his dog "Calvin" in protest. Always on the alert for the "many ambushes and clandestine intrigues Satan daily directs against us," Calvin forced another man who had publicly criticized him to wear a hair shirt (a shirt made of coarse animal hair) and walk slowly through town, stopping at street corners to pray and acknowledge Calvin's authority. Calvin took it upon himself to decide whether future bridegrooms were free from venereal disease and could marry in Geneva. He determined the punishment of merchants who cheated their clients. Drinking establishments were permitted (indeed part of Calvin's salary was paid in barrels of wine) if no lewd songs were sung or cards played, a Bible was always available, and grace said before meals. The Consistory imposed penalties for laughing during a sermon, having one's fortune told, or praising the pope. Calvin's death in 1564 was brought on by a variety of illnesses that were probably compounded by his chronic state of exhaustion and his fretful anxiety about the possibility of reforming a fallen and sinful world.

Calvinist Conversions

Calvinism proved the most aggressive version of the reformed religions, finding converts in places as diverse as France, the Netherlands, a number of German states, Hungary, Transylvania, Poland, and Scotland, where, following the efforts of the fiery reformer John Knox, the Scottish Parliament accepted Calvinism in 1560 as the national religion. In France, Calvinism made some inroads among all social classes during the 1530s, following the flow of reform literature coming from Switzerland and the German states. People who could not read could nonetheless listen to the Bible being read aloud.

Henry II, who came to the throne of France in 1547, denounced the "common malady of this contagious pestilence which has infected many noble towns." The Parlement of Paris created a special chamber to hear heresy cases—"the Burning Chamber"—and tried about 500 people. The sadistic king attended many of the executions himself. A magistrate from Bordeaux described the courage of the Protestant martyrs:

> Fires were being kindled everywhere . . . the stubborn resolution of those who were carried off to the gallows . . . stupefied many people.

They saw innocent, weak women submit to torture so as to bear witness to their faith . . . men exulting upon seeing the dreadful and frightful preparations for and implements of death that were readied for them . . . half charred and roasted, they looked down from the stakes with invincible courage . . . they died smiling.

The judicial system could not keep up with the rapid pace of conversion, including the conversion of many nobles. By 1560, there were more than 2,000 Protestant, or Huguenot (so named after a leading French reformer in Geneva, Besançon Hugues), congregations in France.

Calvinism became the dominant religion of reform in the Netherlands. To root out Protestants there, Philip II of Spain expanded the Inquisition (which had been set up by the Spanish crown after the expulsion of the Moors and Jews from Spain in 1492 and later extended to the Spanish Empire in the Americas). When the Dutch declared independence from Spain in 1581, Calvinism quickly became part of the Dutch national movement during the long war of independence that followed (see Chapter 5).

THE ENGLISH REFORMATION

Unlike continental reform, the English Reformation began with a struggle between the king and the Church. But this dispute must also be placed in the context of discontentment with ecclesiastical venality, and the distant rule of Rome. Lollard influence persisted among the middle and lower classes, which resented the wealth of the high clergy and papal authority. Merchants and travelers returned to England from the continent with Lutheran tracts. Among Luther's small group of followers at the University of Cambridge was William Tyndale, who published the first English translation of the New Testament. Burned at the stake as a heretic in 1536, his last words were "Lord, open the eyes of the king of England."

Henry VIII and the Break with Rome

King Henry VIII of England (ruled 1509–1547) was a religious conservative who published a book in 1521 defending the Catholic view of the sacraments against Martin Luther, prompting the pope to grant him the title of "defender of the faith." The Catholic Church in England already enjoyed considerable autonomy, granted by the pope in the fourteenth century, and the king could appoint bishops.

The issue of royal divorce led to the English break with Rome. Henry's wife, Catherine of Aragon (1485–1536), had given birth five times, but only an extremely frail girl, Mary Tudor, survived. Henry not only urgently

(*Left*) Henry VIII. (*Right*) Anne Boleyn.

desired a male heir for the prestige of the dynasty but he also desired Anne Boleyn (1507–1536), a lady-in-waiting with long black hair and flashing eyes.

Henry had obtained a special papal dispensation to marry Catherine, who was his brother's widow, and now sought the annulment of this same marriage. Obtaining an annulment—which meant, from the point of view of the Church, that the marriage had never taken place—was not uncommon in sixteenth-century Europe, providing an escape clause for those of great wealth. Henry justified his efforts by invoking an Old Testament passage that placed the curse of childlessness on any man who married his brother's widow. He furthermore claimed that English ecclesiastical authorities, not the pope, had the authority to grant an annulment. Pope Clement VII (pope 1523–1534) was at this time a prisoner of Charles V, the Holy Roman emperor, whose armies had occupied Rome, and who happened to be Catherine of Aragon's nephew. In addition to these political circumstances, the pope opposed the annulment as a matter of conscience. At Henry's insistence, Lord Chancellor Thomas Wolsey (1475–1530), in his capacity as cardinal-legate, opened a formal church proceeding in London in 1529 to hear the king's case. But Pope Clement ordered the case transferred to Rome, where the English king had no chance of winning.

Furious, Henry blamed Wolsey for this defeat. Stripped of his post, Wolsey died a shattered man in 1530 on the way to his trial for treason and certain execution. The king had named Thomas More to be his lord chancellor in

1529. But More, a lawyer and a humanist, was a vigorous opponent of the reform movement. Although a layman, each Friday More whipped himself in memory of Christ's suffering. More balked at Henry's plan to have his marriage to Catherine of Aragon annulled. In 1533, Henry secretly married the pregnant Anne Boleyn. He then convoked Parliament, which dutifully passed a series of acts that cut the ties between the English church and Rome. The Act in Restraint of Appeals (1533) denied the pope's authority. Thomas Cranmer (1489–1556), archbishop of Canterbury, showed himself a loyal servant of the throne by simply declaring Henry's marriage to Catherine, who was sent to a convent, annulled. The Act of Suc-

Sir Thomas More, painted by Hans Holbein the Younger. More, who is here shown as lord chancellor, was later executed for his beliefs.

cession in 1534 required all of the king's subjects to take an oath of loyalty to the king as head of the Church of England. Thomas More refused to do so, and Henry ordered his execution. When Pope Clement named another cleric languishing in the Tower of London a cardinal, Henry scoffed, "Let the pope send him a [cardinal's] hat when he will, but I will provide that whensoever it cometh, he shall wear it on his shoulders, for his head he shall have none to set it on."

The Act of Supremacy, also passed in 1534, proclaimed the king "supreme head of the Church of England." Another law made possible the execution of anyone who denied the king's authority over the clergy, or who supported "the bishop of Rome or his pretended power." Parliament limited fees that the clergy could assess for burials and forbade bishops of the Church of England from living away from their sees. Reforms brought the clergy under civil law. The lack of resistance to Henry's usurpation of ecclesiastical authority reflected the pope's unpopularity, as well as the growing strength of the English monarchy.

After the Break with Rome

Henry VIII's nascent Church of England remained doctrinally conservative in contrast to some of the continental reform churches. Several dozen people were burned at the stake for heresy in the 1530s after Henry broke with Rome, including twenty-five Anabaptists. In 1536, in the Church of England's first doctrinal pronouncement, Ten Articles affirmed the essential tenets of Lutheran reform: salvation by faith alone (although good works were still advised), three sacraments, and rejection of the concept of Purgatory and the cult of saints. However, six more articles promulgated two years later reaffirmed some aspects of orthodox Catholic doctrine, including transubstantiation and clerical celibacy.

Thomas Cromwell (1485–1540), Wolsey's ambitious protégé, oversaw the dissolution of England's 600 monasteries, completed in 1538 despite a northern insurrection (the "Pilgrimage of Grace") in defense of the Roman Catholic Church. Two-thirds of the monasteries were sold within ten years, the largest transfer of land in England since the Norman Conquest of 1066. The appropriation of Church lands doubled royal revenue, allowing the construction of forts along the troublesome border with Scotland and on the Channel coast, and financing the purchase of new ships of war. Nobles, particularly those living in the more prosperous south, were the chief purchasers of monastic lands. Many turned their acquisitions into pastureland for sheep, or undertook more intensive agricultural production.

A few months after she married Henry, Anne Boleyn gave birth to a daughter, Elizabeth, a future queen of England. But Henry then had Anne tried on charges of adultery with one of his courtiers, claiming that she had coyly dropped her handkerchief in order to attract him. Anne was executed in 1536, insisting to the end that "a gentler nor a more merciful prince [than Henry] was there never." Next the king married Jane Seymour, who died shortly after giving birth to a son. Another Anne, this one from a small German state, was next in line, as Henry sought allies against Spain and the other Catholic powers. But this Anne did not please Henry—he claimed he had never consummated his marriage to this woman he disparaged as a "Flemish mare." He divorced her, too. Catherine Howard became Henry's fifth wife, but in 1542 he ordered her dispatched for "treasonable unchastity." Henry's sixth wife, a pious older woman named Catherine Parr, could have been excused for entering the marriage with considerable trepidation, but managed to outlive her husband.

THE CATHOLIC REFORMATION

The Catholic Church responded to the schism within Christendom by reasserting the pope's authority and strengthening its own organization. The Catholic Reformation (sometimes called the Counter-Reformation) was both a defensive response by the Church to the success of Protestantism and an aggressive attempt to undertake reform within the limits determined by Catholic theology.

Retreat to Dogmatism

In 1536, Pope Paul III (pope 1534–1549) designated a commission to report on possible reforms in the Church. This commission documented the lack of education of many clergy and the scandalous cases of bishops and priests earning benefices from sees and parishes they never visited. But the papacy held firm on matters of Catholic Church doctrine. Paul III rejected a last-ditch attempt in 1541 by one of his cardinals and several German bishops to reach agreement on the thorny theological issue of salvation by faith alone. Luther, too, vehemently refused to accept compromise. The papacy then went on the offensive. The next year, the pope ordered Cardinal Gian Pietro Carafa to establish an Inquisition in Rome to root out Protestantism in Italy.

Carafa became Pope Paul IV (pope 1555–1559) despite the opposition of Holy Roman Emperor Charles V. He once declared, "If our own father were a heretic, we would gladly carry the wood to burn him!" The new pope retreated into doctrinal orthodoxy and aggressive repression. He formalized pre-publication censorship, establishing a list—the Index—of forbidden books in 1559. Censors ordered other books altered, and refused to authorize the printing of publications they deemed controversial.

As part of the Catholic Reformation's efforts to combat, contain, and eliminate "error" in all forms, Paul IV invented the "ghetto," ordering Jews living in the Papal States to reside in specific neighborhoods, which they could leave only at certain times. In a 1555 bull, he stated that the Jews were guilty of killing Christ, and therefore ought to be slaves. In much of Catholic Europe, Jews had to wear yellow caps to identify themselves, could not own land, and were excluded from most professions.

Ignatius of Loyola and the Jesuits

Ignatius of Loyola (1491–1556), a dashing Basque noble, became one of the leading figures of the Catholic Reformation. While recovering from a grave injury suffered in battle, Loyola read an account of the life of Christ and a book on the lives of saints. He vowed to help rekindle Catholic orthodoxy throughout Europe. Loyola made a pilgrimage to a Spanish monastery, left his sword in a chapel, gave his rich robe to a poor man, put on a sackcloth, and traveled through Spain and Italy. Gradually Loyola attracted followers. The Inquisition came to suspect him because his claims to help people through "spiritual conversion" seemed dangerously close to heresy. He defended himself ably, however, receiving only a short prison sentence.

Loyola wanted to establish a new order that could inculcate the same kind of intense religious experience that he had undergone while lying wounded. He traveled to Rome, offered his services to the pope, and organized the Society of Jesus, which was officially approved by the pope in 1540. Under

Loyola's military-style leadership, the Jesuits, as the order's members became known, grew rapidly in number and influence as aggressive crusaders for the Catholic Reformation.

The Jesuit order provided a model for Church organization, orthodoxy, and discipline. Jesuits underwent a program of rigorous training and took a special oath of allegiance to the pope. They combined the study of Thomas à Kempis's mystical *Imitation of Christ* (1418) and Loyola's own intense devotional reflections.

When Loyola died in 1556, there were more than a thousand Jesuits. Counselors to kings and princes and educators of the Catholic elite, the Jesuit religious order contributed greatly to the success of the Catholic Reformation in Austria, Bavaria, and the Rhineland. Jesuits also contributed to the Church's reconquest of Poland, where religious toleration had been proclaimed in 1573 and some landowners had converted to Calvinism. In the service of the Catholic Reformation, Jesuits began to travel to North America, Latin America, and Asia, eventually establishing a presence even in the court of the Chinese emperors. They led "missions," delivering fire-and-brimstone sermons, which were aimed at rekindling loyalty to the Church.

The Council of Trent

In 1545, at the insistence of Holy Roman Emperor Charles V, Pope Paul III convoked the Council of Trent (1545–1563) to assess the condition of the Catholic Church and to define its doctrines. While such an internal reckoning had seemed inevitable for some time, the papacy had long viewed conciliarism as a potential threat to its authority and invoked every possible reason for delay. Once convened, the Council of Trent, which met off and on for eighteen years, made the split within Western Christendom irreparable. Most of the prelates who came to the Alpine town of Trent believed the central goal of the council was a blanket condemnation of what the Church viewed as heresy, as well as the reaffirmation of theological doctrine. Although the pope himself never went to Trent, the Italian delegates dominated the proceedings, coughing and sneezing during speeches with which they disagreed.

The council rejected point after point of reformed doctrine, declaring such positions "to be anathema." It reaffirmed the authority of the pope and of the bishops, the seven sacraments, and the presence of Christ in the Eucharist. It also unequivocally opposed the marriage of clerics and reaffirmed belief in Purgatory and in the redeeming power of indulgences, although the practice of selling them was abolished.

In 1562, Pope Pius IV (pope 1559–1565) convoked the last session of the Council of Trent. The council ordained the creation of seminaries in each diocese to increase the number and quality of priests. The priests were henceforth to keep parish registers listing the births, baptisms, and deaths of the faithful, which in recent times have provided historians with extraordinarily useful demographic information. Some monastic houses undertook reforms. The infusion of better educated clergy in the southern German states and Austria aided the Church's efforts to maintain its influence there.

The papacy emerged from the Council of Trent much more centralized, better organized and administered, and more aggressive, like the most powerful European states themselves. Gradually a series of more able popes helped restore the prestige of the papacy within the Church.

Putting Its House in Order

"The best way," one churchman advised, "to fight the heretics is not to deserve their criticisms." Some leaders within the Catholic Church reasoned that the Church should put its own house in order and seek to reconvert people who had joined the reformed religions. Pius V (pope 1566–1572) declared war on venality, luxury, and ostentation in Rome. But abuses still seemed rampant. In 1569, the Venetian ambassador to France reported that the French "deal in bishoprics and abbeys as merchants trade in pepper and cinnamon." Pius V sent some bishops living in Roman luxury packing to their sees, putting those who refused to leave in prison.

Reformers wanted to bring order and discipline to members of religious orders and the secular clergy. "No wonder the Church is as it is, when the religious live as they do [in monasteries and convents]," Teresa of Avila (1515–1582) exclaimed in response to the demeaning battles between religious houses in Spain, struggles that she tried to end. Some churchmen, however, now rejected monastic life as irrelevant to the activist missionary tasks of the Church, another sign of the influence of Protestant reform. New orders, such as the Capuchins—an offshoot of the Franciscans— and the female order of the Ursulines, worked to bring faith to the poor and the sick. The missionary work of Vincent de Paul (1581–1660) also helped restore faith among the poor. Seeing the success Reformation preachers had with mass-produced pamphlets, the Catholic Church also produced catechisms that spread Church teachings, along with accounts of the lives of the saints. The Catholic Reformation encouraged other new devotional confraternities (religious brotherhoods of people who heard Mass together), some bringing together laymen of various social classes. The cult of the Virgin Mary became more popular. The Protestant Reformation had emphasized the religious life of the individual and the development of his or her personal piety through Bible study and personal reflection. The Catholic Reformation, too, now encouraged individual forms of devotion and spirituality.

Culture during the Two Reformations

The Protestant Reformation began as a religious reaction against abuses within the Church. But it also reflected profound changes in European society. The Reformation followed not only the discovery of the printing press but also the expansion of commerce, the arteries of which became the conduits of reform. Both the Protestant and Catholic Reformations affected art, architecture, print culture, education, popular culture, and family life at a time when religious belief and practice had an enormous impact on daily life.

Print Culture

The printing press did not cause the Reformation, but it certainly helped expand it. A rapid expansion in the publication of pamphlets, books, and other printed material occurred at a time when reformers were challenging Church doctrine and papal authority. The printing of Luther's works facilitated their rapid diffusion, with perhaps a million copies circulating through the German states by the mid-1520s. The German reformer called the printing press "God's highest and ultimate gift of grace by which He would have His Gospel carried forward." Luther's Wartburg translation of the Bible went through fifty printings in two years. He wrote 450 treatises and delivered more than 3,000 sermons; his collected works fill more than 100 volumes and 60,000 pages. Luther also published a hymnal containing many hymns that are sung today. He directed many of his dialogues, poems, and sermons to ordinary Germans, and even to children, adopting popular religious themes and images.

Since about 1480, the diffusion of printing had contributed to the expansion of a lay culture in the German states. Much of what was printed was published in the vernacular, that is, German, as opposed to Latin. Although religious literature was the greatest output of early printing presses, other favored themes of books and pamphlets included nature, the discoveries of the explorers, the acquisition of technical skills (such as medical skills from self-help medical handbooks), manuals of self-instruction (such as how to

Private devotion: an old woman reading the Bible.

defend oneself in court, or how to make beer and wine), and everyday moral-ity. Visual, often satirical images such as woodcut illustrations and broad-sheets, directed at those who could not read, probably reached far more people than did printed tracts, however. Caricatures portrayed Luther as Hercules, as an evangelical saint doing battle with wretched animals repre-senting the Church, as a new Moses, as a miracle worker, and, in one popu-lar legend, as the inventor of bratwurst sausage.

Lay Education and Reading

The Reformation, drawing on printing, also profited from increased educa-tional opportunities for laypeople in Europe, which engendered a critical spirit among students and scholars. The number of universities rose steadily during the last half of the fifteenth century. More people could read than ever before—although in most places no more than 5 to 10 percent of the population. Lutherans and Calvinists stressed the importance of education as essential to individual and critical study of the Scriptures, and de-emphasized the clergy's role in religious instruction.

During the Reformation, princes and ecclesiastical leaders intensified their efforts to secure religious conformity by controlling what people read. The "blue library" (so called because small books or pamphlets were wrapped in blue paper) helped diffuse pamphlets deemed acceptable and sold at a low price by itinerant peddlers. Each Western European country had such a "literature of bits and pieces." Didactic stories were meant to instruct people about religious events, saints, and ideals approved by the Church, and to distance them from the "superstitions" of popular culture. Yet many people living in England probably still knew far more about Robin Hood than they did about the Bible. A chapbook (a small book of popular lit-erature) published in Augsburg in 1621 told the story of Saint George slay-ing the dragon. The Catholic hierarchy removed the dragon from the story, while Protestants left out Saint George.

Popular Rituals and Festivals

Protestant ministers, like their Catholic counterparts, tried to root out such rituals as baptizing a child by dunking her three times for good luck. Songs rife with pagan imagery had survived virtually unchanged since medieval times. Religion and magic remained closely intertwined; the Catholic Church had been unable to eradicate the difference in the popu-lar mind between prayer and good luck charms, for example.

Many a village became the site of an elaborate tug-of-war between state and ecclesiastical authorities and ordinary people. The clergy, often previ-ously active participants in festive occasions, were caught in the middle and moved away from what they considered "profane" amusements. The Catholic hierarchy tried to suppress some popular festivals and rein in

Pieter Brueghel the Elder's *Combat between Carnival and Lent* (1559). Note the contrast between the church on the left with the somewhat more pious-looking people near it, and the drinking place on the other side of the square. Revelry seems to be winning out.

others, returning them to the control of the clergy by imposing a religious purpose that seemed to have been lost in all the fun. A dance known as the "twirl" in southern France was banned in 1666 because boys tossed girls into the air "in such an infamous manner that what shame obliges us to hide most of all is uncovered naked to the eyes of those taking part and those passing by." Ecclesiastical and lay hierarchies, Catholic and Protestant, came to view popular festivity as immoral, or at least licentious. *Combat between Carnival and Lent* (1559), a painting by Pieter Brueghel the Elder (see above), depicts Carnival as a fat man and Lent as a thin woman. Under the twin assault of absolutism and ecclesiastic hierarchy, Lent won. The clergy also began a long and often unsuccessful struggle for control over lay confraternities, which had their origins in religious devotion, but they now were often fiercely independent and more like festive clubs, especially during Carnival. Carnival was largely eradicated in Protestant countries, but it survived in some Catholic ones, although often much transformed.

Social and political elites contrasted the "civility" of their beliefs, conduct, and manners with the "barbarity" or "savagery" of popular beliefs and customs. Didactic literature stressing polite comportment and etiquette became popular among people of wealth, further separating them from the poor. The Church tried to impose strict sexual mores on ordinary people, while encouraging gestures of deference toward social superiors.

The Role of Women

Although convents and nunneries were almost always abolished in a Protestant state, reformers nonetheless encouraged women to take an active role in the religious process of being saved. Protestant women, like men, were encouraged to read the Bible themselves, or, as most could not read, to have it read to them. In the case of Anabaptists, women appear to have made decisions about not baptizing their children; most Anabaptist martyrs were female. More women than men seem to have converted to Calvinism in France, perhaps attracted by special catechism classes, or by the fact that in Calvinist services, men and women sang psalms together.

Yet Protestant reformers still believed women were subordinate to men. Although a few women published religious pamphlets in the early 1520s and others undertook devotional writing and publishing later, women could not be ministers nor could they hold offices within the new churches. Calvin believed that the subjugation of women to their husbands was crucial for the maintenance of moral order. Protestant denominations provided a domestic vision of women, emphasizing their role in the Christian household.

The fact that a Protestant minister could now marry, however, reflected a more positive view not only of women but of the family as a foundation of organized religion. One pamphleteer admonished husbands that their wives were "no dish-clouts . . . nor no drudges, but fellow-heirs with them of everlasting life, and so dear to God as the men."

Because they no longer considered marriage a sacrament, Protestants also reluctantly accepted divorce in limited cases. Luther viewed adultery, impotence, and abandonment as reasons for divorce, but he condemned Henry VIII's effort to divorce Catherine of Aragon. Divorce remained quite rare and occurred only after a long, expensive legal process only the rich could afford.

In Catholic areas, women could still rise to positions of importance in convents, or in the new charitable religious orders. But the Council of Trent reaffirmed the Catholic Church's ideal of female chastity, reinforced by the widespread cult of the Virgin Mary. The chapbooks of the Catholic Reformation still taught that the female body was a source of sin, and therefore had to be controlled.

Witches came to reflect superstitious aspects of popular religion. Catholic and Protestant churchmen identified and persecuted witches as part of the campaign to acculturate the masses with "acceptable" beliefs. Witch hunts peaked during the first half of the seventeenth century. In the southwestern states of the Holy Roman Empire alone, more than 300 witch trials resulted in the execution of 2,500 people between 1570 and

1630, almost all women (in itself not surprising, as Church authorities and priests were all male).

Theologians and judges sought to demonstrate that accused witches embodied the kingdom of the devil. To some extent, the Catholic Reformation wanted to create the idea of a satanic realm of evil on earth with which to juxtapose orthodoxy. "Witches," identified by common reputation, sometimes stood accused of saying Latin prayers backward or performing "black Masses" while standing facing their "congregations," instead of facing the altar, defiantly inverting the kingdom of God. One woman was accused of "consuming" several husbands. Often "witches" were blamed for evil that had befallen villagers: a fire, the unexplained death of a cow, or a male suddenly smitten with impotence.

Most of those accused of being witches were rural, poor, and single women who were victims of other villagers, particularly small town officials and wealthy peasants (it was the opposite in 1692 in Salem, Massachusetts, where many of the women accused of witchcraft had just inherited property, and therefore were resented by the community). Some "witches" confessed under pain of torture, such as one woman in southern France, who was "scorched like a pig" and cooked alive, having been accused of spreading an "evil powder" while committing crimes.

Women stood out as targets because they were transmitters of the collective memory of popular culture. They were genealogists, storytellers, and healers, but almost always without formal education. Women were in many ways the guardians of tradition, although also regarded by the Catholic hierarchy as the source of sin. The social exclusion or even execution of women had a social value for those in power, affirming authorities' position and role as interpreters of beliefs and customs deemed appropriate.

After the persecution of witches ebbed, some lay authorities then turned their attention to outcasts, the socially marginal. In the Austrian Netherlands, a sign "useless to the world" was hung above the head of a beggar. Monarchies increasingly demonstrated their authority in carrying out sentences of royal justice and, therefore, the justice of God. Those found guilty of capital crimes—at least those of the lower classes—were tortured and then executed in public, their mutilated bodies exhibited for all to see.

The Baroque Style

The monumentalism, flamboyance, and theatrical religiosity of the baroque style complemented the Catholic Reformation. "Baroque" refers to a style of extravagant and irregularly shaped ornamentation (the term itself comes from Old French for "irregularly shaped pear"). As an architectural, artistic, and decorative style, the baroque triumphed in southern Germany, Austria, Flanders, Spain, and other Catholic regions during the first decades of the seventeenth century (but was also popular in Protestant England, where it merged with the classical style).

As in the Renaissance, in Rome the Church remained a major patron of the arts, expressing religious themes through visual representation. Its goal was to impress—indeed, to overwhelm—the emotions through awe-inspiring dimensions, opulence, movement, and, in painting, lurid color. The Baroque style sought to express the experience of the soul. Baroque palaces and churches featured exuberant curves and ornate decoration and were cluttered with lustrous marble altars, ornate statues, golden cherubs, and intensely colorful murals and ceiling paintings. The baroque merged easily with neoclassicism—the revival of an architectural design dominated by Greek and Roman forms. The

Gianlorenzo Bernini's *The Ecstasy of Saint Theresa* (1645–1652).

Gesú Church of the Jesuits in Rome is a masterpiece of baroque style. With its vast ceilings and enormous paintings of the ascension of Christ and the assumption of the Virgin Mary, it symbolizes the spirit of the Catholic Reformation. The baroque style used optical illusions such as Gesú's false cupola to achieve the impression that the viewer is reaching for Heaven.

The monumental fountains in Rome of the Venetian sculptor Gianlorenzo Bernini (1598–1680) best represent the period of high baroque of the Catholic Reformation. He also sculpted the magnificent canopy over the high altar of St. Peter's. Bernini sought to communicate the intensity of religious experience. In the altarpiece *The Ecstasy of Saint Theresa* (1645–1652), Bernini depicted the saint's convulsions of joy when an angel stabs her with a spear as beams of sunlight engulf the scene. Bernini wrote, "It pleased the Lord that I should see this angel in [this] way. . . . In his hands I saw a long golden spear and at the end of the iron tip I seemed to see a point of fire. With this he seemed to pierce my heart several times so that it penetrated to my entrails." This highly sexual description stands in marked contrast with the puritanical impulse that had seen Renaissance popes order the painting of fig leaves on nudes.

THE LEGACY OF THE TWO REFORMATIONS

In 1600, more than half of Europe remained primarily Catholic, including Spain, France, and Habsburg Austria, three of the four most powerful states in Europe. The fourth was England, and it was overwhelmingly Protestant. The Dutch Netherlands, at war with its Spanish overlords, was largely Protestant as well. Unlike the case of the German states, where the religion of the princes determined the religion of the state, the Reformations in France, the Netherlands, and Scotland were to a great extent movements from below. The Reformation generated a strong missionary impulse among Protestants and Catholics alike. With the gradual opening up of the world to European commerce and colonization, the Jesuits, particularly, ranged far and wide. In the burgeoning Spanish Empire, conquest and the quest for religious conversion, which was remarkably successful, went hand in hand. More than a few missionaries, however, found martyrdom, for example in Asia.

In Central Europe, the complexity of the state system facilitated reform. The Peace of Augsburg of 1555, as we have seen, reinforced German particularism, the persistence of small, independent states. In contrast, the larger, centralized, and more powerful states like Spain and France most successfully resisted the reform movement, despite the wars of religion that lay ahead in the latter. Yet, in both states, the Catholic Church remained subordinate to the monarchy, with both the French and Spanish kings retaining considerable authority over ecclesiastical appointments.

Protestant reformers accepted a separation of functions within the community, what Luther called the "realm of the spirit" and the "realm of the world." Henceforth, the political institutions of the Protestant states remained relatively secularized. In the German states and in Scandinavia, Lutheranism was introduced as a state church, in part because reformers originally needed the protection of princes against Catholic rulers, notably Charles V, the Holy Roman emperor. In England, Anglicanism also took on the status of a state religion. Both Lutheran and Anglican reforms rigorously subordinated the church to the state, separating the spiritual and temporal realms. Whereas Zwingli had called for the complete fusion of church and state, Calvinism alone provided for the institutional separation of both; after Calvin's death the magistrates of Geneva restricted the church's autonomy. Anabaptist sectarians, in contrast, wanted their communities to have nothing at all to do with the state.

The Lutheran and Calvinist states were not necessarily any more tolerant of religious dissent than those that remained Catholic. Following the Peace of Augsburg, German princes used their control of the reformed churches to consolidate their political authority. Lutheranism remained wedded to a patriarchal structure of society, which appealed to property owners at all social levels.

In an attempt to obtain religious adherence, some princes declared that church attendance would be mandatory and those who were absent would be punished. Nonetheless, compelling people to attend Sunday services did not guarantee what or even if they believed. One can never know how typical were the thoughts of one girl who related that the sermon she had just sat through was "such a deale of bible babble that I am weary to heare yt and I can then sitt downe in my seat and take a good napp." In one English parish in 1547, it was reported that "when the vicar goeth into the pulpit to read what [he] himself hath written, then the multitude of the parish goeth straight out of the church, home to drink."

In some places, to be sure, ordinary Protestants and Catholics coexisted and even shared churches. In Saxony, Catholics heard Mass in the lavishly decorated front part of a church and Lutherans used the end of the nave, which had little adornment, for their own services, by common accord. The division of the church was marked by a painting of the Last Supper, the importance of which both sides agreed upon. In some towns in the Netherlands in the late sixteenth century, dissenters from the Dutch Reformed religion, including Catholics, could worship in churches that were deliberately hidden from public view. Ordinary people thus greatly contributed to the religious peace that emerged in the immediate post-Reformation period, sometimes defying tyrannical rulers who insisted on religious orthodoxy.

The Peace of Augsburg and the Council of Trent did not end the rivalry between Catholics and Protestants, nor, for that matter, the rivalry between different Protestant denominations. Religious intolerance and conflict would, to a great extent, help define the first half of the seventeenth century, the age of the wars of religion.

CHAPTER 4

THE WARS OF RELIGION

On May 23, 1618, a crowd of protesters carried a petition to Prague's Hradcany Palace, where representatives of the royal government of Bohemia were gathered. The crowd stormed into the council chamber, engaged Catholic officials in a heated debate, organized an impromptu trial, and hurled two royal delegates from the window. The crowd below roared its approval of this "defenestration" (an elegant term for throwing someone out a window), angered only that neither man was killed by the fall. Catholic partisans construed their good fortune as a miracle, as the rumor spread that guardian angels had swooped down to pluck the falling dignitaries from the air. Protestants liked to claim that the men had been saved because they fell on large dung heaps in the moat below.

The different reactions to the Defenestration of Prague illustrate how the Reformation left some of Europe, particularly the German states, a veritable patchwork of religious allegiances. Religious affiliation, like ethnicity, frequently did not correspond to the borders of states. The Peace of Augsburg in 1555 ended the fighting between German Protestant and Catholic princes. It stated that the religion of each state would henceforth be that of its ruler. Hundreds of thousands of families left home and crossed frontiers in order to relocate to a state where the prince was of their religious denomination.

The German states entered a period of relative religious peace, but in France in 1572, the Huguenots (the popular name for the French Protestants) rebelled against Catholic domination, setting off a civil war. Moreover, after years of mounting religious and political tension, Dutch Protestants led the revolt against Spanish Catholic authority in 1572, beginning a bitter struggle that lasted until the middle of the next century.

Then in 1618, religious wars broke out again in the German states with unparalleled intensity. The Thirty Years' War (1618–1648) devastated Central Europe, bringing into the conflict, in one way or another, almost all of the powers of Europe. Armies reached unprecedented size, and fought with a cruelty that may also have been unprecedented.

The wars of religion in France and the Thirty Years' War began because of religious antagonisms, but the dynastic ambitions of French princes lay not far behind the rivalry between Protestants and Catholics. In the Thirty Years' War, the dynastic rivalry between the Bourbons of France and the Habsburgs of Austria—both Catholic dynasties—came to the fore, eventually dominating religious considerations.

The wars of religion resulted in the strengthening of the monarchies of France, Austria, and the smaller German states as well. Kings and princes further extended their administrative, judicial, and fiscal reach over their subjects in the interest of maintaining control over their populations and waging war. In France, a stronger monarchy emerged out of the trauma of religious struggles and competing claimants to the throne. Germany, in contrast, remained divided into several strong states and many smaller ones. Competing religious allegiances reinforced German particularism, that is, the multiplicity of independent German states.

THE WARS OF RELIGION IN SIXTEENTH-CENTURY FRANCE

Early in the sixteenth century, France was divided by law, customs, languages, and traditions. Under King Francis I (ruled 1515–1547), the Valois monarchy effectively extended its authority. Of Francis I, it was said, "If the king endures bodily fatigues unflinchingly, he finds mental preoccupations more difficult to bear." Yet, the French monarch ruled with an authority unequaled in Europe, however much he was still dependent on the good will of nobles. When the king sought loans to continue a war, a Parisian noble assured him that "we do not wish to dispute or minimize your power; that would be a sacrilege, and we know very well that you are above the law."

When the Reformation reached France in the 1540s and 1550s, Calvinism won many converts (see Chapter 3). At a time when nobles were resisting the expansion of the king's judicial prerogatives and the proliferation of his officials, religious division precipitated a crisis of the French state and brought civil war.

A Strengthened Monarchy

Francis I and his successors became more insistent on their authority to assess taxes on the towns of the kingdom, many of which had held privileged exemptions granted in exchange for loyalty. Raising an army or royal revenue depended on the willingness of the most powerful nobles to answer the king's call. The monarchs had justified such requests with an appeal to the common good in tactful language that also held out the possibility of the use of force. Now the French king wished to tax the towns even when there was no war.

Francis reduced the authority of the Catholic Church in France. The Concordat of Bologna (1516), signed between Francis and Pope Leo X, despite

King Francis I of France, looking very regal and proud of his increased authority, despite not being painted wearing his crown.

the resistance of the French clergy, established royal control over ecclesiastical appointments. Many more royal officials now represented and enforced the royal will in the provinces than ever before. One sign of the growing power of the monarchy was that nobles lost some privileges of local jurisdiction to the royal law courts. Francis confirmed and enhanced Paris's identity as the seat and emerging symbol of royal power. The sale of offices originated in the king's desire for the allegiance of nobles and for the revenue they could provide the monarchy. His successors would depend increasingly on the sale of offices and titles for raising revenue. Finding nobles unwilling to provide all the funds the king desired, the monarchy, in turn, put the squeeze on peasants, extracting more resources through taxation.

The political and religious crises in the middle decades of the sixteenth century threatened monarchical stability in France. They pushed the country into a period of chaos brought by the lengthy, savage war of religion during which the four Valois kings who succeeded Francis I proved unable to rule effectively.

Economic Crisis

The end of a period of economic expansion provided a backdrop for the political and religious struggles of the French monarchy. The population of France had risen rapidly between the late fifteenth century and about 1570, reversing the decline in population resulting from plagues and natural disasters in the fourteenth and fifteenth centuries. Land under cultivation increased, particularly near the Mediterranean, where landowners planted olive trees on hills and terraces. But by 1570, the increase in cultivable land slowed down in much of France. The European population, which had risen to about 100 million people during the sixteenth century, outstripped available resources. Prices rose rapidly in France, as in most of Europe, pushed upward relentlessly by population increase. Beginning in the late 1550s, the purchasing power of the laborer declined dramatically, whereas that of landowners remained stable, fed by high prices. As agricultural income fell, nobles demanded vexing services from peasants, such as repairing roads and paths on their estates. Many wealthy nobles rented out land to tenant farmers, then took the proceeds back to their luxurious urban residences. Nobles of lesser means, however, did not do as well as the owners of great estates, because the rents they drew from their land failed to keep pace with rising prices.

As the price of profitable land soared, peasant families tried to protect their children by subdividing land among male offspring. Many peasants with small parcels of land became sharecroppers at highly disadvantageous terms—working someone else's land for a return of roughly half of what was produced. Both trends worked against increased agricultural efficiency, reducing land yields. Landless laborers were barely able to sustain themselves.

Taxes and tithes (payments owed the Catholic Church—in principle, 10 percent of income) weighed heavily on the poor. Peasants, particularly in the southwest, sporadically revolted against taxes, and against their landlords, during the period from 1560 to 1660. The popular nicknames of some of the groups of rebels reflect their abject poverty and desperation: the "poor wretches," who rose up against the nobles in central and southern France in 1594–1595, and the "bare feet." Many of the rebels espoused the popular belief that their violence might restore an imagined world of social justice in which wise rulers looked after the needs of their people.

French Calvinists and the Crisis of the French State

Followers of John Calvin arriving in France from nearby Geneva attracted converts in the 1540s and 1550s. Henry II (ruled 1547–1559), who succeeded his father Francis I, began a religious repression that created Calvinist martyrs, perhaps further encouraging Protestant dissent. The spread of Calvinism led the king to sign the Treaty of Cateau-Cambrésis in 1559, ending the protracted struggle between France and Spain. After decades of reckless invasions, Henry II agreed to respect Habsburg primacy in Italy and control over Flanders. King Philip II (ruled 1556–1598) of Spain, in return, promised that Spain would desist in its attempts to weaken the Valois kings. These two most powerful kings in Europe ended their struggle for supremacy not only because their resources were nearly exhausted, but also because as Catholic rulers they viewed with alarm the spread of Calvinism in Western Europe, both within the Netherlands (a rich territory of the Spanish Habsburgs) and within France itself. After signing the treaty, Henry II and Philip II could now turn their attention to combating Protestantism.

Some nobles in France, wary of the extending reach of the Valois monarchy and tired of providing funds for wars, resisted the monarchy. The conflict between the monarchy and the nobility compounded growing religious division in the last half of the sixteenth century. Perhaps as many as 40 percent of French nobles converted to Calvinism, some of them nobles of relatively modest means squeezed by economic setbacks.

In 1559, King Henry II was accidentally killed by an errant lance during a jousting tournament celebrating peace with Spain. He was succeeded by his fifteen-year-old son, who became Francis II (ruled 1559–1560). Catherine de' Medici (1519–1589), Henry II's talented, manipulative, and domineering widow, served as regent to the first of her three sickly and incapable sons. Catherine was reviled as a "shopkeeper's daughter," as her Florentine ancestors had been merchants, bankers, and money changers, all things incompatible with the French concept of nobility (but not with the Italian one). That she was the daughter of the man to whom Machiavelli had dedicated *The Prince* added to the "legend of the wicked Italian queen" in France.

The throne immediately faced challenges to its authority by three powerful noble families, each dominating large parts of France. Religious differences sharpened the rivalry between them. The Catholic Guise family, the strongest, concentrated its influence in northern and eastern France. In the south, the Catholic Montmorency family, one of the oldest and wealthiest in the kingdom, held through marriage alliances the allegiance of some of the population there. The influence of the Huguenot Bourbon family extended into central France and also reached the far southwestern corner.

In 1560, Louis, prince of Condé (1530–1569), a member of the Huguenot Bourbon family, conspired to kidnap Francis II and remove him from the clutches of the House of Guise, who were related to Francis's wife, Mary Stuart, queen of Scotland. The Guise clan, who discovered the plot, killed some of the Bourbon conspirators. Francis died after a stormy reign of only eighteen months, succeeded by his ten-year-old brother Charles IX (ruled 1560–1574), under the regency of their mother.

The rivalry between the Guise, Montmorency, and Bourbon families undermined royal authority. Henry II's lengthy war with Spain had drained the royal coffers, and the economic downturn made it extremely difficult to fill them again. Catherine's efforts to bring some of the nobles who had converted to Protestantism to the royal court and to bring about a rapprochement

Catherine de' Medici, widow of Henry II, served as regent to Francis II.

between the two denominations failed utterly. Such attempts only infuriated the House of Guise, several of whose members held important positions within the Catholic Church hierarchy. For their part, Philip II of
Spain and the Jesuit religious order backed the Guise family. The political
crisis of France, then, became increasingly tied to the struggle of the
Church with Protestants.

Taking advantage of the confusion surrounding the throne, French
Calvinists became bolder in practicing their religion. Religious festivals
occasioned brawls between Catholics and Huguenots. Calvinists seized
control of Lyon in 1562, forcing the rest of the population to attend their
services. Where they were a majority, Calvinists desecrated Catholic cemeteries, smashed ornate stained-glass windows, shattered altar rails of
churches, and covered statues of saints with mud. Catholics replied by
slaughtering Calvinists, more than once forcing them to wear crowns of
thorns, like Christ, to their death. Both sides burned the "heretical" books
of the other denomination. The violence of a holy war was accentuated by
rumors that the Huguenots indulged in orgies, while Protestants accused
Catholics of idolatry and of doing the devil's work.

Yet in France—as in other parts of Europe where the Reformation had
taken hold—some brave souls urged religion toleration. For example, an
abbot warned in 1561:

> I am well aware of the fact that many think it wrong to tolerate two
> religions in one kingdom, and in truth it could be wished that there
> were only one, provided it were the true religion. . . . there is indeed
> no sense in wanting to use force in matters of conscience and religion,
> because conscience is like the palm of the hand, the more it is
> pressed, the more it resists, and lets itself be ordered only by reason
> and good advice.

In 1562, the first full-scale religious war broke out in France. It began
when Francis, the duke of Guise (1519–1563), ordered the execution of
Huguenots who had been found worshipping on his land. In the southwestern town of Toulouse, more than 3,000 people were killed in the fighting; the bodies of Protestants were tossed into the river, and their
neighborhoods were burned as part of a "purification." Members of the
Catholic lay confraternities took oaths to protect France against "heresy"
and erected crosses in public places as a sign of religious commitment.
Catholics won back control of several major cities.

This first stage of the war, during which a Huguenot assassinated Francis, the duke of Guise, ended in 1563. A royal edict granted Huguenots the
right to worship in one designated town in each region, as well as in places
where Calvinist congregations had already been established. Intensifying
the eagerness of the powerful quarreling noble families to impose their
will on the monarchy was the fact that Francis had died childless and

young King Charles IX and his younger brother had no sons. There was no clear heir to the throne of France.

In 1567, war between French Protestants and Catholics broke out again. It dragged on to an inconclusive halt three years later in a peace settlement that pleased neither side. In 1572, Charles and Catherine, though Catholics, at first agreed to provide military support to the Dutch Protestants, who had rebelled against Spanish authority. The goal was to help weaken France's principal rival. But pressured by his mother and fearful of upsetting the more radical Catholics, as well as the pope, Charles soon renounced assistance to the Dutch and agreed to accept instead the guidance of the Catholic House of Guise. With or without the king's knowledge or connivance, the Guise family tried but failed to assassinate the Protestant leader Admiral Gaspard de Coligny (1519–1572), a Montmorency who had converted to Protestantism and whom they blamed for the earlier murder of the Catholic Francis, duke of Guise.

The marriage between Charles's sister, Margaret, a Catholic Valois, and Henry of Navarre, a Bourbon Huguenot, was to be, in principle, one of religious reconciliation. The negotiations for the wedding had specified that the Huguenots in Paris come to the wedding unarmed. But the king's Guise advisers, and perhaps his mother as well, convinced him that the only way of preventing a Protestant uprising against the throne was to strike brutally against the Huguenots. Therefore, early in the morning on August 24, 1572, Catholic assassins hunted down and murdered Huguenot leaders. During what became known as the Saint Bartholomew's Day Massacre, the (new) duke of Guise killed Admiral Gaspard de Coligny, whose battered corpse was thrown through a window, castrated, and then dragged through the dusty streets of Paris by children. For six days Catholic mobs stormed through the streets, killing more than 2,000 Protestants. Outside of Paris, another 10,000 Protestants perished. The Parlement of Toulouse, one of the twelve judicial courts of medieval origin that combined judicial and administrative functions, made it legal to kill any "heretic." The pope had a special Mass sung in celebration of the slaughter. Thousands of Huguenots emigrated or moved to safer places, including fortified towns they still held in the southwest.

Charles IX died in 1574 and was succeeded by his ailing brother, Henry III (ruled 1574–1589). At his coronation, the crown twice slipped from Henry's head, a bad omen in a superstitious age. The new king was a picture of contradictions. He seemed pious, undertook religious pilgrimages, and hoped to bring about a revival of faith in his kingdom. He also spent money with abandon and enjoyed dressing up as a woman, while lavishing every attention on the handsome young men he gathered around him.

Henry III also had to confront a worsening fiscal crisis compounded by a series of meager harvests. But when he asked the provincial Estates (regional assemblies dominated by nobles) for more taxes, the king found that his promises of financial reform and of an end to fiscal abuses by royal revenue

The Saint Bartholomew's Day Massacre, 1572, in which more than 2,000 Huguenots perished in Paris.

agents were not enough to bring forth more revenue. The Estates deeply resented the influence of Italian financiers at court, the luxurious life of the court itself, and the nobles who had bought royal favor.

The Catholic forces around the king were not themselves united. A group of moderate Catholics, known as the *politiques,* pushed for conciliation. Tired of anarchy and bloodshed, they were ready to put politics ahead of religion. The *politiques* therefore sought to win the support of the moderate Huguenots, and thereby to bring religious toleration and peace to France.

In 1576, Henry III signed an agreement that liberalized the conditions under which Protestants could practice their religion. Concessions, however, only further infuriated the intransigent Catholics, who became known as the "fanatics" (*dévots*). Angered by these concessions to Huguenots, a nobleman in the northern province of Picardy organized a Catholic League, which because of its size posed a threat not only to Huguenots but also to the monarchy. It was led by the dashing Henry, duke of Guise (1550–1588), who was subsidized by Philip II of Spain, and vowed to fight until Protestantism was completely driven from France. But another military campaign against Protestants led to nothing more than a restatement of the conditions under which they could worship.

Henry III's reconciliation with the House of Guise did not last long. The death of the last of the king's brothers, Francis, duke of Anjou, in 1584 made Henry of Navarre, a Protestant, heir to the throne. This was the Catholics' worst nightmare. The Catholic League threw its full support behind the aged, ambitious Catholic Cardinal de Bourbon, who was next in line after Henry of Navarre.

Henry of Navarre

Henry of Navarre (1553–1610) was born in the town of Pau on the edge of the Pyrenees Mountains in southwestern France. The son of Antoine of Bourbon, patriarch of the powerful Bourbon family, and Jeanne d'Albret, Henry inherited the keen intelligence of his mother and his father's indecisiveness. His mother was a committed Huguenot and raised Henry in that faith. When his father, who was notoriously unfaithful to his wife, sent her back to the southwest in 1562, Henry converted to Catholicism, his father's religion. After his father's death in battle, Henry reembraced Protestantism. Taken to the royal court as a hostage by Catherine de' Medici, he was permitted to have Huguenot tutors. Among his friends at court were the future Henry III and Henry, duke of Guise. It was after Henry of Navarre's wedding in Paris in August 1572 to Margaret, Catherine de' Medici's daughter, that the Saint Bartholomew's Day Massacre occurred. Henry then was given the choice of embracing Catholicism or being executed. He chose the former. When the fighting temporarily ended, Henry had more time for his favorite pursuits—pursuing women and hunting.

The Huguenots had every reason to be wary of a young man who seemed to change faiths with such ease. Furthermore, he seemed to have reconciled himself to the Saint Bartholomew's Day Massacre, still counted the duke of Guise among his friends, had accompanied the Catholic army, albeit under guard, and had written the pope begging forgiveness for past misdeeds.

But having left Paris and the watchful eye of the Catholic dukes, Henry then formally abjured Catholicism and took up residence as royal governor in the southwest, where Protestantism was strong. There he tried to steer a path between militant Catholics and Huguenots. His endorsement of mutual religious toleration won wide approval. After Henry of Navarre became heir to the throne in 1584, the Catholic League rallied its forces, drawing its muscle from the artisans of Paris and other northern towns. In defiance of the king, it forced the Parlement of Paris to withdraw the toleration afforded the Huguenots. The Catholic League's goal was to put the Cardinal de Bourbon on the throne, although the duke of Guise wanted it for himself.

The struggle between the "three Henrys" now began in earnest. Henry (Valois) III first allied with Henry (Bourbon) of Navarre and with the duke of Montmorency against Henry, duke of Guise. The Guise family provocatively accused the king in 1585 of destroying the kingdom through inept rule and called for a rebellion that would bring the duke of Guise to the throne and drive Protestantism from the kingdom.

Henry III then switched partners, joining the duke of Guise against Henry of Navarre. The Treaty of Nemours (1585) between Catherine de' Medici and Henry, duke of Guise, abrogated all edicts of religious toleration and turned over a number of towns to the Catholic League. Now the odd man out, Henry of Navarre prepared for a new war. He denounced Spanish meddling and in a quintessentially *politique* statement, called on soldiers "to rally around me . . . all true Frenchmen without regard to religion." Although he increasingly depended on German and Swiss mercenaries for his army and benefited from the intervention of a German Protestant force, Henry's denunciation of foreign influence was a shrewd piece of political propaganda aimed at moderate Catholics—the *politiques*—and the Catholic clergy.

In 1587, Henry of Navarre defeated the combined forces of the king and the Catholic League at Coutras, near Bordeaux. Here his defensive position and use of artillery and cavalry proved decisive. But instead of following up his surprising victory by pursuing the Catholic army, Henry went back to hunting and making love. As a contemporary put it, "All the advantage of so famous a victory floated away like smoke in the wind."

That year, 1587, Queen Elizabeth I of England put to death Mary Stuart, the Catholic queen of Scots and the niece of the duke of Guise (see Chapter 5). Angered by Henry III's inability to prevent the execution of his niece, Guise, at the urging of the king of Spain, marched the next year to Paris, where he and the Catholic League enjoyed support. The Spanish king hoped to keep the French king from contemplating any possible assistance to England as the Spanish Armada sailed toward the English Channel. When Henry III sent troops to Paris to oppose the duke of Guise, the Parisian population rose in rebellion on May 12, 1588, stretching barricades throughout the city center. The king ordered his troops to withdraw. The "Day of Barricades" marked the victory of a council led by clergymen known as the Sixteen, then the number of neighborhoods in Paris.

For several years, the Sixteen had been energetically supporting the League, while denouncing the king, the Catholic *politiques,* and Huguenots with equal fervor. The hostility of the population of Paris convinced the king to accept Cardinal de Bourbon (1523–1590) as his heir, the duke of Guise as his lieutenant-general, and to convoke the Estates-General (representatives of the provincial Estates, which the monarch could summon in times of great crisis).

Then in 1588, the delegates to the Estates-General, many of them members of the Catholic League, gathered in the Loire Valley town of Blois. Scathing written grievances were submitted to the delegation, including one from Paris that denounced the king as a "cancer . . . filled with filth and infectious putrefaction" and called for "all heretics, whatever their quality, condition or estate, [to] be imprisoned and punished by being burned alive." By now, however, the English fleet had defeated Philip II's Armada in the Channel (see Chapter 5), and the nobles found Henry III

Assassination of Henry, duke of Guise.

less intimidated than they had anticipated. When the duke of Guise heard a rumor that the king was planning his assassination, he replied, "He does not dare." But Henry III's bodyguards murdered Henry, duke of Guise, shortly before Christmas 1588 in the Château of Blois, as Catherine de' Medici lay dying in a room beneath the bloody struggle. The Valois king had the Cardinal de Bourbon and other prominent members of the Catholic League arrested.

The duke of Guise's assassination drove the Catholic League to full-fledged revolt against Henry III. More than 300 towns, most of them in the north, now joined the "Holy Union" against the king. As Catholics prepared to fight Catholics, Henry of Navarre (again Protestant) appealed for peace: "We have been mad, senseless and furious for four years. Is that not enough?"

Henry III was then forced to make an alliance of convenience with Henry of Navarre against the Catholic League. As their combined armies besieged Paris, a monk assassinated Henry III in August 1589. The king's Swiss guards, who had not done a terribly good job protecting their king, threw themselves at the feet of Henry of Navarre, telling him, "Sire, you are now our king and master."

The Catholic League, however, had proclaimed five years earlier that Cardinal de Bourbon would become king upon Henry III's death. Henry imprisoned his potential rival. Henry of Navarre's forces defeated Catholic League armies twice in Normandy, in 1589 and in 1590. But once again

Henry failed to take advantage of the situation his shrewd generalship had made possible. He dawdled before finally laying siege to starving Paris.

The arrival of a Spanish army from Flanders to provision Paris helped win Henry further support from moderate Catholics, who resented Spanish intervention that might prolong the siege. Fatigue began to overcome religious conviction. Henry also played on resentment at the involvement of the pope in French affairs (Henry had been excommunicated in 1585 and, for good measure, a second time six years later). As Henry's army besieged Paris, Spanish troops defeated forces loyal to him in several provinces. The death of Cardinal de Bourbon in 1590 led Philip II to proclaim the candidacy of the late Henry II's Spanish granddaughter as heir to the throne of France, and then to suggest that he might claim it himself. In the meantime, Henry's continued successes on the battlefield and conciliatory proclamations furthered his popularity.

Henry of Navarre, a man of changing colors, had another major surprise up his sleeve. In 1593, he astonished friend and foe alike by announcing that he would now again renounce Protestantism. This move, however, reflected his shrewd sense of politics. Paris, as he put it, was worth a Mass, the price of the capital's obedience. Following his coronation as Henry IV at Chartres the following year, Paris surrendered after very little fighting. Henry's entry into his capital was a carefully orchestrated series of ceremonies that included the "cure" of hundreds of people afflicted with scrofula (a tuberculous condition) by the royal touch, a monarchical tradition in France and England that went back centuries. Henry nodded enthusiastically to the women who came to their windows to catch a glimpse of the first Bourbon king of France.

Catholic League forces gradually dispersed, one town after another pledging its loyalty to Henry, usually in return for payments. Henry's declaration of war on Spain in 1595 helped rally people to the monarchy. The pope lifted Henry's excommunication from the Church. Henry invaded Philip's territory of Burgundy, defeating his army. In 1598, the last Catholic League soldiers capitulated. Henry, having secured the frontiers of his kingdom, signed the Treaty of Vervins with Philip II to end the war that neither side could afford to continue. However, bringing stability to France would be no easy matter. The wars of religion had worsened the plight of the poor. Disastrous harvests and epidemics in the 1590s compounded the misery. The wars of the Catholic League caused great damage and dislocated the economy in many parts of France. The indiscriminate minting of coins by both sides worsened inflation.

Henry's emissaries gradually restored order by promising that "the Well-Loved," as the king became known, would end injustices and provide "a chicken in every pot." He did slightly reduce the direct tax, of which the peasants bore the brunt. Henry also rooted out some of the corruption in the farming of taxes, whereby government officials allowed ambitious middlemen to collect taxes in exchange for a share. But, in all, even more of the tax burden fell upon the poor.

Gradually Henry succeeded in putting the finances of the monarchy on a firmer footing. In 1596, he convinced an Assembly of Notables to approve a supplementary tax. A new imposition (the *paulette*) permitted officeholders, through an annual payment to the throne, to assure that their office would remain in the hands of their heirs. The *paulette* gave the wealthiest nobles of the realm a greater stake in the monarchy. But while increasing royal revenue, it intensified the phenomenon of the venality of office: the purchase of offices and the noble titles that went with them.

Henry could rarely rest at ease. In 1602 and again two years later, he uncovered plots against him by nobles in connivance with the Spanish monarchy. He survived nine assassination attempts. Indeed, Jesuit pamphleteers called for his assassination. Small wonder that he carried two loaded pistols in his belt and that some nervous soul tasted his food and drink before he did.

In 1598, Henry's Edict of Nantes made Catholicism the official religion of France. But it also granted the nation's 2 million Protestants (in a population of about 18.5 million) the right to worship at home, hold religious services and establish schools in specified towns—almost all in the southwest and west—and to maintain a number of fortified towns. The Edict of Nantes also established chambers in the provincial parlements, or law courts dominated by nobles, to judge the cases of Protestants (see Map 4.1).

But careful to placate powerful sources of Catholic opposition, a series of secret decrees also promised Paris, Toulouse, and other staunchly Catholic towns that Protestant worship would be forbidden within their walls. The Edict of Nantes thus left the Protestants as something of a separate estate with specified privileges and rights, but still on the margin of French life. "What I have done is for the sake of peace," Henry stated emphatically. Yet former Catholic Leaguers howled in protest. By registering royal edicts, the parlements gave them the status of law. In this case, they only gradually and grudgingly registered the edict, which provided the Huguenots with arguably more secure status than any other religious minority in Europe.

Henry's foreign policy, which appeared pro-Protestant, supporting the Dutch rebels against Spain and certain German states against the Catholic Habsburgs, was based on dynastic interests. This support of Protestant rebels and princes made it impossible for Henry to consider further concessions to the Huguenots.

At the same time, the Catholic Reformation bore fruit in France. The Church benefited from a revival in organizational zeal and popularity. Henry allowed the Jesuits to return to France in 1604, a sign that religious tensions were ebbing, and he admitted several Italian religious orders.

With various would-be assassins lurking, Henry had to think about an heir. He sought a papal annulment of his marriage to Margaret of Valois, whom he had not seen in eighteen years. While waiting, he prepared to marry one of his mistresses, but she died miscarrying their child. With the

MAP 4.1 WARS OF RELIGION IN FRANCE IN THE SIXTEENTH CENTURY France at the time of the Edict of Nantes, 1598. The map indicates neutral provinces, Huguenot provinces, and Catholic League provinces during the wars of religion, as well as Huguenot and Catholic League towns and battle sites during the wars.

blessing of the Church, he then arranged to marry Marie de' Medici (1573–1642), a distant relative of Catherine de' Medici. This second marriage of convenience brought a sizable dowry that Henry used, in part, to pay off more international debts.

Intelligent and well organized, Henry kept abreast of events throughout his vast kingdom. But he had little sense of protocol, often rushing out of the Louvre palace by himself as his guards scurried to catch up. His wit was well known: when formally welcomed by a long-winded representative of the town of Amiens, who began "O most benign, greatest and most clement of kings," Henry interjected, "Add as well, the most tired of kings!" When a second spokesman began his official greeting, "Agesilaus, king of Sparta, Sire," Henry cut him short, "I too have heard of that Agesilaus, but he had eaten, and I have not."

Henry had a charismatic and somewhat contradictory personality. In contrast to the portraits he encouraged depicting him as Hercules or Apollo, or arrayed in a splendid white plume and a warrior's helmet, the king of France was extremely slovenly, sometimes wearing torn or ragged clothes. He became renowned for his physical vigor on the battlefield and gambled large sums, with a notorious lack of success. Marie de' Medici bore the constant burden of her husband's various infidelities and occasional bouts of gonorrhea. Henry produced six illegitimate children by three mistresses, along with the three born to the queen. His nine offspring made up what he proudly referred to as his "herd."

Although he knew nothing of music or poetry, and regularly fell asleep at the theater, Henry IV nonetheless was a patron of new architectural projects that added to the beauty of the city of Paris and imprinted his rule upon it. He ordered the construction of four quays facilitating the docking of boats along the Seine River, and had built the splendid Place Dauphine, ringed by elegant buildings on the western end of the island of Cité, where his equestrian statue now stands. And he orchestrated the construction of the Place Royale, with pavilions of symmetrical arcades, brick construction, and steeply inclining roofs in the northern architectural style.

Statemaking

Restoring monarchical prestige and authority in France, Henry IV laid the foundations for what would become the strongest power in seventeenth-

The Place Dauphine, seen here from Pont-Neuf, was one of Henry IV's grand architectural projects.

century Europe. His reign was an exercise in early modern European statemaking as he reimposed royal authority throughout the realm. Henry was suspicious of any representative institutions, which he believed threatened the exercise of royal authority: he never convoked the Estates-General, and he ignored the provincial parlements.

Henry IV made the monarchy more powerful by dispensing privilege, favors, and, above all, money with judiciousness that earned loyalty. The difficulties of extracting resources were complicated by the division of the provinces into more peripheral "state provinces" like Languedoc, Burgundy, and Provence, which had been recently added to the realm and retained some of their traditional privileges, and the "election provinces." In the former, the noble Estates assessed and collected taxation; in the latter, royal officials assumed these functions. Provincial governors represented the interests of the monarchy in the face of the privileges and resistance to taxes maintained by the provincial parlements and Estates. Conciliatory royal language began to disappear when it came to asking for money. The governors strengthened the monarchy at the expense of towns that prided themselves on their ancient privileges, further eroding their fiscal independence.

The royal privy council, some of whose members were chosen, like Sully, from the ranks of lesser nobles known for their competence and dedication, strengthened the effectiveness of state administration and foreign relations. The king personally oversaw this council, excluding troublesome nobles. Henry monitored the activities of his ambassadors and his court, whose 1,500 residents included the purveyors of perfume, of which he might have made greater use.

Much of Henry's success in achieving the political reconstruction of France can be credited to his arrogant minister of finance, Maximilien de Béthune, the baron and, as of 1604, the duke of Sully (1560–1641). Sully was the son of a prosperous Protestant family whose great wealth had earned ennoblement. He established budgets and systematic bookkeeping, which helped eliminate some needless expenses.

The monarchy gradually began to pay off some international debts, including those owed to the English crown, and the Swiss cantons, whose good will Henry needed to counter Spanish influence in the Alps. These repayments allowed Henry to contrast his honor in the realm of finances with that of the Spanish monarchy, whose periodic declarations of bankruptcy left creditors grasping at air.

Meanwhile, the nobles reaffirmed their own economic and social domination over their provinces. In 1609, Charles Loyseau, a lawyer, published a *Treatise on Orders and Plain Dignities* that portrayed French society as a hierarchy of orders, or three estates: the clergy, the nobility, and everyone else. He portrayed the king as the guarantor of this organic society. Henry restored the hierarchy of social orders based upon rank and privilege. But the boundaries between and within these estates were fairly fluid. A few

A FAUT ESPERER Q'EU SE JEU LA FINIRA BENTOT

At the time of the Estates-General in 1789, an image of an
impoverished, elderly peasant carrying on his back a noble
and a priest while scratching out a living from the soil.

newcomers ascended into the highest rank of dukes and peers who stood
above even the "nobles of the sword," the oldest and most powerful nobles
traditionally called on by the monarchy to provide military support. The
"nobles of the robe," while not a coherent or self-conscious group, were
men who claimed noble status on the basis of high administrative and judicial office, for example, in the parlements. Henry strengthened the social
hierarchy by bolstering established institutions, including the parlements,
the treasury, the universities, and, ultimately, the Catholic Church.

   Henry also took an interest in encouraging French manufacturing, particularly silk and the production of tapestries. To promote internal trade, he
encouraged investment in the construction of several canals linking navigable rivers. He was the first king to take an active interest in supporting a permanent French settlement in the New World, thereby increasing the
prospects of French fishermen and trappers following Jacques Cartier's

exploration of the St. Lawrence River in 1534. Samuel de Champlain founded the colony of Quebec in 1608. Two years later, the first two French Jesuit missionaries arrived in what became known as New France.

On May 14, 1610, Henry's carriage became ensnared in traffic in central Paris. When some of his guards dashed forward to try to clear the way, a crazed monk named François Ravaillac jumped up to take revenge for the king's protection of Protestants. He stabbed the king three times, fatally.

Louis XIII and the Origins of Absolute Rule

Henry's sudden death left Marie de' Medici, his widow, as regent for his young son, Louis XIII (ruled 1610–1643), who was eight years old at the time. Neither Philip III (ruled 1598–1621) of Spain nor James I of England, nor any of the princes of the German states, were in a position to try to intervene in France on behalf of either Huguenots or Catholics. Marie put aside Henry's planned campaign against the Habsburgs and adopted a policy that considered Catholic powers to be friends.

Marie foiled several nobles' plots against her in 1614–1616. The convocation of the Estates-General in 1614 accentuated the eagerness of noble rivals to gain influence with the young king. One of them convinced Louis to impose his own rule. The king ordered the murder of one of his mother's confidants; Louis then exiled his unpopular mother, hoping to restore calm. When a group of nobles took this as occasion to raise the standard of revolt, the young king's army defeated them at Ponts-de-Cé near Angers in 1620. The royal army then defeated a revolt by Huguenot nobles in the southwest and west.

Emotionally, the stubborn and high-strung boy-king Louis XIII never really grew up. Throughout his life, he demonstrated the psychological burdens of having been regularly whipped as punishment on his father's orders. His father's murder when he was young also marked him. Louis XIII's marriage to an Austrian princess began with a wedding-night fiasco that, whatever happened between the precocious young couple, led to a six-month period in which they did not even share a meal. Finally, things went better. After suffering several miscarriages, the queen produced an heir in 1638, but the royal couple was otherwise unhappy.

Louis XIII was intelligent and liked to sketch and listen to music, the latter calming him when he fell into a rage. He enjoyed hunting and winning at chess, once hurling the offending pieces at the head of a courtier who had the bad grace to checkmate him. Louis was a pious man who attended church every day. But he was also invariably willful, ruthless, and cruel, lashing out savagely at his enemies; indeed, no other ruler of France ordered as many executions as Louis XIII. Among those executed were a number of nobles convicted of dueling, a practice that the king detested because it represented to him the possibility that nobles could raise private armies against the throne.

During Louis XIII's reign, Cardinal Armand Jean du Plessis de Richelieu (1585–1642) expanded the administrative authority and fiscal reach of the crown, dramatically increasing tax revenues. Richelieu's family, solidly entrenched in the west of France, had long served the monarchy in court, army, and church. The gaunt, clever Richelieu staked his future on and won the patronage of the queen mother. He perfected the art of political survival during the court struggles of the next few years. Richelieu was a realist. His foreign and domestic policies reflected his *politique* approach to both.

In 1629, Richelieu prepared a long memorandum for his king. "If the King wants to make himself the most powerful monarch and the most highly esteemed prince in the world," he advised that "[The Estates and the parlements] which oppose the welfare of the kingdom by their pretended sovereignty must be humbled and disciplined. Absolute obedience to the King must be enforced upon great and small alike." Richelieu divided France into thirty-two districts (*généralités*), organizing and extending the king's authority. Officials called intendants governed each district, overseen by the king's council and ultimately responsible to the king himself.

In order to enhance the authority of the monarchy and the Church, Richelieu turned his attention to the Huguenots. After forcing the surrender of insurgent Protestant forces at La Rochelle in 1628, he ordered the destruction of the Huguenot fortresses in the south and southwest, as well as the châteaux of other nobles whose loyalty he had reason to doubt.

During the Thirty Years' War (1618–1648, see p. 145), Louis XIII, influenced by Richelieu, reversed his mother's pro-Spanish foreign policy, returning to the traditional French position of opposition to the Habsburgs. The dynastic rivalry between the two powers proved greater than the fact that both kings were Catholic. Louis XIII thus surprised and outraged the Spanish king by joining England and the Dutch Republic, both Protestant powers, against the powerful Catholic Austrian Habsburgs during the Thirty Years' War. And in 1635, France declared war against Spain itself.

Richelieu's successes, however, did not stand well with his resentful enemies within France. His toleration of Huguenot worship drew the wrath of some Catholic nobles, as did continuing costly wars against the Catholic Habsburgs, which led to French subsidies to Protestant Sweden. Revolts occurred in Dijon and Aix, both seats of provincial parlements, where local notables resented having to bow to the authority of royal officials.

One of the most conservative Catholic nobles, a royal minister, briefly turned the king against Richelieu. Marie de' Medici, returned from brief disgrace, tried to convince her son to dismiss the cagey cardinal. The "Day of Dupes" (November 10, 1630) followed, which amounted to little more than a high-stakes family shouting match between Marie de' Medici, Louis XIII, and Richelieu. Marie left thinking she had won the day, but awoke the next morning to find that the king had ordered her exile. The king's own brother led a second plot against Richelieu from 1641 to 1642, backed by the king of Spain.

Philippe de Champagne's portrait of the sad-eyed Louis XIII.

After decades of religious wars, the assassination of Henry IV, and a fragile, temperamental young monarch around whom plots swirled, the monarchy of France had nonetheless been greatly strengthened, building upon the accomplishments of his predecessor. Louis XIII's sometimes decisive and brutal actions enhanced the reputation of the king who was known to many of his subjects as "The Just," whether fitting or not. A hypochondriac whose health was even worse than he feared, Louis XIII died of tuberculosis in 1643 at the age of forty-two. But the man-child monarch had, with Richelieu, laid the foundations for absolute monarchical rule in France.

THE THIRTY YEARS' WAR (1618–1648)

In Central Europe, religious divisions and intolerance led to the Thirty Years' War, a brutal conflict during which the largely mercenary armies of Catholic and Protestant states laid waste to the German states. Dynastic rivalries were never far from the stage, bringing the continental Great Powers into the fray. When the war finally ended, the Treaty of Westphalia (1648) established a territorial and religious settlement that lasted until the French Revolution.

Factionalism in the Holy Roman Empire

The Holy Roman Empire was a loose confederation of approximately 1,000 German autonomous or semi-autonomous states. These states ranged in size from powerful Habsburg Austria to Hamburg, Lübeck, and other free cities in the north, and even smaller territories no more than a few square kilometers in size run by bishops. It would have been almost impossible for a traveler to determine where one state stopped and another began had it not been for the frequent toll stations, which provided revenue for each. The southwestern German state of Swabia, for example, was divided among sixty-eight secular and forty ecclesiastical lords and included thirty-two free cities.

Geographic factors further complicated the political life of the German states. A few of the largest states included territories that were not contiguous. The Upper Palatinate lay squeezed between Bohemia and Bavaria; the Lower Palatinate lay far away in the Rhineland. The former was predominantly Lutheran, the latter Calvinist.

Since 1356, when the constitutional law of the Holy Roman Empire had been established, seven electors (four electoral princes and three archbishops) selected each new Holy Roman emperor. The empire's loose federal structure had a chancery to carry out foreign policy and negotiations with the various German princes. But only in confronting the threat of the Turks from the southeast did the German princes mount a consistent and relatively unified foreign policy.

Other institutions of the Holy Roman Empire also reflected the political complexity of Central Europe. An imperial Diet brought princes, nobles, and representatives of the towns together when the emperor summoned them. An Imperial Court of Justice ruled on matters of importance to the empire. The Holy Roman Empire, once the most powerful force in Europe, had been weakened by its battles with the papacy in the thirteenth century. Yet for some states the empire offered a balance between the desire for a figure of authority who could maintain law and order and their continued political independence.

The Peace of Augsburg (1555), which ended the war between the Holy Roman Emperor Charles V and the Protestant German states, had stated that, with the exception of ecclesiastical states and the free cities, the religion of the ruler would be the religion of the land (*cuius regio, eius religio*) (see Chapter 3). This formula, however, did not end religious rivalries or the demands of religious minorities that rulers tolerate their beliefs. The Peace of Augsburg, in fact, reinforced German particularism. It also helped secularize the institutions of the Holy Roman emperor by recognizing the right of the German princes to determine the religion of their states. This also served to end the hope of Charles V to establish an empire that would bring together all of the Habsburg territories in the German states, Spain, and the Netherlands.

The Origins of the Thirty Years' War

Rudolf II (1557–1612), king of Bohemia and Holy Roman emperor (he succeeded his father Maximilian II as Holy Roman emperor in 1576), wanted to launch a religious crusade against Protestantism. He closed Lutheran churches in 1578, reneging on an earlier promise to Bohemian nobles that he would tolerate the religion to which a good many of them had converted.

Moreover, Rudolf's cousin Archduke Ferdinand II (1578–1637) withdrew the religious toleration Maximilian II had granted in Inner Austria.

Rudolf's imperial army, which had been fighting the Turks on and off since 1593, had annexed Transylvania. The emperor moved against Protestants both there and in Hungary. But in 1605, when Rudolf's army undertook a campaign against the Turks in the Balkans, Protestants rebelled in both places. A Protestant army invaded Moravia, which lies east of Bohemia and north of Austria, close to the Habsburg capital of Vienna. In the meantime, Emperor Rudolf, only marginally competent on his best days (he was subject to depression and later to fits of insanity), lived as a recluse in his castle in Prague. His family convinced his brother Matthias (1557–1619) to act on Rudolf's behalf by making peace with the Hungarian and Transylvanian Protestants, and with the Turks. This Peace of Vienna (1606) guaranteed religious freedom in Hungary. Matthias was then recognized as head of the Habsburgs and Rudolf's heir.

Most everyone seemed pleased with the peace except Rudolf, who concluded that a plague that was ravaging Bohemia was proof that God was displeased with the concessions he had granted Protestants. He denounced Matthias and Ferdinand for their accommodation with the Protestants and with the Turkish "infidels." Matthias allied with the Protestant Hungarian noble Estates and marched against Rudolf, who surrendered. Rudolf ceded Hungary, Austria, and Moravia to Matthias in 1608, and Bohemia in 1611. Rudolf was forced to sign a "Letter of Majesty" in 1609 that granted Bohemians the right to choose between Catholicism, Lutheranism, or one of two groups of Hussites (see Chapter 3). Protestant churches, schools, and cemeteries were to be tolerated.

The decline in the effective authority of the Holy Roman emperor contributed to the end of a period of relative peace in the German states. In the last decades of the sixteenth century, these states had become increasingly quarrelsome and militarized. "The dear old Holy Roman Empire," went one song, "How does it stay together?" Rulers of some member states began to undermine imperial political institutions by refusing to accept rulings by the Imperial Supreme Court and even to attend the occasional convocations of the Diet. "Imperial Military Circles," which were inter-state alliances responsible for defense of a number of states within the empire, had become moribund because of religious antagonisms between the member states.

For a time, the Catholic Reformation profited from acrimonious debates and even small wars between Lutherans and Calvinists. But increasingly Protestants put aside their differences, however substantial, in the face of the continued determination of some Catholic rulers to win back territories lost to Protestantism.

Acts of intolerance heated up religious rivalries. In 1606, in Donauwörth, a southern German imperial free city in which Lutherans held the upper hand and Catholics enjoyed toleration, a riot began when Lutherans tried to prevent Catholics from holding a procession. The following year, Duke Maximilian of Bavaria sent troops to assure Catholic domination. This angered Calvinist princes in the region, as well as some Lutheran sovereigns. The imperial Diet, convoked two years later, broke up in chaos when Holy Roman Emperor Rudolf II refused to increase Protestant representation in the Diet. The political crisis now spread further when some of the German Catholic states sought Spanish intervention in a dispute over princely succession in the small northern Rhineland Catholic territories of Cleves-Jülich, which Henry IV of France threatened to invade. In 1609, Catholic German princes organized a Catholic League, headed by Maximilian of Bavaria. Six Protestant princes then signed a defensive alliance, the Protestant Union, against the Catholic League.

Matthias, who had been elected Holy Roman emperor in 1612, wanted to make the Catholic League an institution of Habsburg will. He also hoped to woo Lutherans from the Protestant Union, which was dominated by the Calvinists. But Matthias's obsession with Habsburg dynastic ambitions, his history of having fought with the Protestant Dutch rebels against Spain (see Chapter 5), and his opportunistic toleration of Lutheranism cost him the confidence of some Catholic princes. Archduke Ferdinand, ruler of Inner Austria, waited in the wings to lead a Catholic crusade against Protestantism. Ferdinand, who had inherited the throne of Hungary in 1617 and that of Bohemia the following year, became Holy Roman emperor upon his uncle Matthias's death in 1619. Ferdinand was a pious man whose confessor convinced him that he could only save his soul by launching a war of religion. In the meantime, Protestant resistance in Bohemia mobilized, seeking Protestant assistance from Transylvania and the Palatinate.

Conflict in Bohemia

In Bohemia, Ferdinand imposed significant limitations on Protestant worship. In Prague, Calvinists and Lutherans began to look outside of Bohemia for potential support from Protestant princes. Protestant leaders convoked

FERDINAND II PAR LA GRACE DE DIEV EMPERVR DES ROMAINS.

Ferdinand II, Holy Roman Emperor and King of Bohemia.

MAP 4.2 THE THIRTY YEARS' WAR, 1618–1648 Protestant and Catholic armies clashed in battles that ranged back and forth across Europe.

an assembly of the Estates of Bohemia, citing rights specified by Rudolf's "Letter of Majesty" of 1609. Ferdinand ordered the assembly to disband.

Following the Defenestration of Prague in 1618, Protestant leaders established a provisional government in Bohemia. "This business of Bohemia is likely to put all Christendom in combustion," predicted the English ambassador to the Dutch capital of Amsterdam. Indeed it began a destructive war between Catholic and Protestant forces that would last thirty years, lay waste to many of the German states, and finally bring a religious and territorial settlement that would last for two centuries.

Bohemia rose in full revolt against not only the Church but the Habsburg dynasty as well. With almost no assistance from the nobles, the rebels turned to the Protestant Union, promising the Bohemian crown to Frederick, the young Calvinist elector of the Palatinate and the most important

Protestant prince in Central Europe. In 1619, the Estates offered Frederick the crown, and he accepted.

The Protestant cause, like that of the Catholics, became increasingly internationalized and tied to dynastic considerations (see Map 4.2). Now Holy Roman Emperor Ferdinand II learned that Protestant rebels had refused to recognize his authority in Bohemia and had offered his throne to Frederick. Even more determined to drive Protestants from his realm but lacking an army, Ferdinand turned to outside help. The Catholic king of Spain agreed to send troops he could ill afford; the price of his intervention was the promise of the cession of the Rhineland state of the Lower Palatinate to Spain. The Catholic Maximilian I of Bavaria also sent an army, expecting to be rewarded for his trouble with the Upper Palatinate and with Frederick's title of elector in the Holy Roman Empire.

The Expansion of the Conflict

Protestant armies besieged Vienna, the Habsburg capital, until the arrival of Catholic armies in 1619. The Dutch could not provide assistance to the Protestants, as they were fighting for independence from Spain. Several of the German Protestant states also declined, fearing Catholic rebellions in their own lands. However, with Spanish armies and monies already on the way, the internationalization of the Bohemian crisis had reached the point of no return.

In 1620 the Catholic League raised a largely Bavarian army of 30,000 troops. Count Johannes von Tilly (1559–1632) commanded the Catholic forces. The depressed, indecisive count from Flanders managed to subdue Upper Austria and then defeated the main Protestant Union army at the Battle of White Mountain, near Prague, in November. With the Catholic forces now holding Bohemia, Tilly's army then overran Silesia, Moravia, Austria, and part of the Upper Palatinate. The extent of the Catholic victory expanded the war, increasing the determination of the Catholic League to crush all Protestant resistance and, at the same time, of the Protestant forces to resist at all costs.

Frederick's Protestant forces fought on, counting on help from France and other states who had reason to fear an expansion of Habsburg power in Central Europe. Frederick also hoped to convince James I of England that a victory of the Catholic League would threaten Protestantism. But the English king had placed his hopes on the marriage of his son, Charles, to the sister of Philip IV of Spain (see Chapter 5). Again dynastic rivalries outweighed those of religion.

The war went on, and Tilly's army won a series of small victories. In 1622, the Spanish army defeated Dutch forces at Jülich in the Rhineland, eliminating any possibility of English armed assistance to Frederick through Holland. For the moment, Frederick's only effective force was a plundering mercenary horde in northeastern Germany. Tilly's victory over a Protestant army in 1623 and conquest of most of the Palatinate forced Frederick to abandon his claims to Bohemia's throne after having been king for all of one winter. But encouraged by the renewed possibility of English assistance after James's plans for the marriage of his son to the Spanish princess fell through, Frederick turned north to Scandinavia for assistance.

The Danish Period

Christian IV (ruled 1588–1648), the Protestant king of Denmark, had ambition and money, but not a great deal of sense. Also duke of the northern German state of Holstein, the gambling, hard-drinking Dane wanted to extend his influence and perhaps even add territories in the northern German states. Frederick's difficulties seemed to offer the Danish sovereign the opportunity of a lifetime. In 1625, he led his troops into the northern German states, assuming that the English and the Dutch, and perhaps the French as well, would rush to follow his leadership against the Habsburgs.

But King James I of England had died and was succeeded by Charles I, whose provocative policies generated increasing opposition from Parliament (see Chapter 6), leaving him little time to consider intervening on behalf of the Protestant cause on the continent. England and the Netherlands sent only some money and a few thousand soldiers to help the Danish king. Moreover, Louis XIII of France, who was besieging Protestants at La Rochelle, provided the Danes with only a modest subsidy to aid the fight against the Habsburgs. Christian, essentially left to his own devices, was unaware of the approach of a large imperial army commanded by one of the most intriguing figures in the age of religious wars.

Albrecht Wallenstein (1583–1634) was a Bohemian noble who, after marrying a wealthy widow, had risen to even greater fortune as a supplier of armies. Raised a Lutheran, he converted to Catholicism at age twenty and became the most powerful of the Catholic generals. The fact that a convert could rise to such a powerful position again reveals how a religious war evolved into not only a dynastic struggle between the rulers of France, Spain, and Austria, as well as Sweden and Denmark, but also into an unprincipled free-for-all in which mercenary soldiers of fortune played a major part. Wallenstein, an ardent student of astrology, was ambitious, ruthless, and possessed a violent temper. His abhorrence of noise was obsessive—and odd, for a military person. Because he detested the sound of barking or meowing, he sometimes ordered all dogs and cats killed upon arriving in a town, and forbade the townspeople and his soldiers from wearing heavy boots or spurs or anything else that would make noise. He alternated between extreme generosity and horrible cruelty, and was always accompanied by an executioner awaiting his master's command. Wallenstein, entrusted by Ferdinand with raising and commanding an army drawn from states for the Catholic cause, marched north with 30,000 men.

The Catholic army defeated the Danes in 1626, and then marched to the Baltic coast, crossed into Denmark, and devastated the peninsula of Jutland. But Wallenstein's successes engendered nervous opposition within the Catholic states. Furthermore, his troops devastated the lands of friend and foe alike, extracting money and food, plundering, and selling military leadership positions to any buyer, including criminals.

Christian, who had bankrupted his kingdom during this ill-fated excursion, signed the Treaty of Lübeck in 1629, whereby he withdrew from the war and gave up his claims in northern Germany. The treaty was less draconian than it might have been because the seemingly endless war was wearing heavily on some of the Catholic German states. They feared an expansion of Habsburg power, and some of them did not want to add Protestants to their domains.

Ferdinand II now implemented measures against Protestants without convoking the imperial Diet. He expelled from Bohemia Calvinist and Lutheran ministers and nobles who refused to convert to Catholicism and ennobled new men, including foreigners, as a means of assuring Catholic domination. He confiscated the property of nobles suspected of participating in any phase of the Protestant rebellion. With Frederick's electorship now transferred to Maximilian I of Bavaria, the Habsburgs could count on the fact that a majority of the electors were Catholic princes. Captured Habsburg dispatches in 1628 made clear that Ferdinand sought to destroy the freedom of the Protestant German cities of the Hanseatic League in the north in the interest of expanding the Habsburg domains. These revelations alarmed Louis XIII of France.

Ferdinand found that it was not easy to impose Catholicism in territories where it had not been practiced for decades. In the Upper Palatinate, the first priests who came to celebrate Mass there were unable to find a chalice. Half of the parishes in Bohemia were without clergy. Italian priests brought to Upper Austria could not be understood by their parishioners. The Edict of Restitution (1629) allowed Lutherans—but not Calvinists, who were few in number in the German states except in the Palatinate—to practice their religion in certain cities, but ordered them to return to the Catholic Church all monasteries and convents acquired since 1552, when signatories of the Peace of Augsburg had first gathered. Because the Edict of Restitution also gave rulers the right to enforce the practice of their religion within their territories, the war went on.

The Swedish Interlude

In the meantime, England, the Dutch Republic, the northern German state of Brandenburg, and the Palatinate asked the Lutheran king Gustavus Adolphus (ruled 1611–1632) of Sweden to intervene on the Protestant side. The possibility of expanding Swedish territory, a kingdom of

King Gustavus Adolphus of Sweden in battle.

barely a million inhabitants, was more than Gustavus, with an adventurer's disposition, could resist.

Gustavus, the "Lion of the North," who survived a shipwreck at the age of five, had been tutored in the art of war by mercenary soldiers. He also played the flute, composed poetry, and conversed in ten languages. Gustavus retained, as did a disproportionate number of rulers in his century, a violent temper. Once, coming upon two stolen cows outside an officer's tent, he dragged the thief by the ear to the executioner. His courage was legendary—he barely paused as cannonballs exploded nearby and as his horses were shot out from under him or fell through the ice.

Gustavus, influenced by an appreciation of Roman military tactics, formed his battle lines thinner—about six men deep—than those of rival commanders. This allowed his lines to be more widely spread out. Gustavus organized his army into brigades of four squadrons with nine cannon to protect them, sending the unit into battle in an arrow-shaped formation. Superior artillery served his cause well, hurling larger shot farther and more accurately than the cannon of his enemies.

The dashing young Swedish king subdued Catholic Poland with his army of about 70,000 men. Swedish intervention and the continuing woes of Spain, now at war in the Alps, Italy, and the Netherlands, gave Protestants reason for hope. After defeating a combined Polish and Habsburg army in 1629, Swedish troops occupied Pomerania along the Baltic Sea.

In 1630, sure of a Catholic majority, Emperor Ferdinand convoked the imperial electors to recognize his son as his heir. He also wanted them to support his promise to aid Spain against the Dutch in exchange for Spanish assistance against the Protestant armies. But the Protestant electors of Saxony and Brandenburg refused even to attend the gathering. Catholic electors demanded that the powerful Wallenstein be dismissed; even the king of Spain feared the general's powerful ragtag army. Ferdinand thereby dismissed the one man whose accomplishments and influence might have enabled the Habsburg monarchy to master all of the German states.

Despite a sizable subsidy from the king of France, Gustavus Adolphus enjoyed the support of only several tiny Protestant states. Some Lutheran German states still hoped to receive territorial concessions from the Habsburgs. The Catholic dynasty preferred Lutherans to Calvinists, viewing the latter as more radical reformers. Ferdinand now sent Tilly to stop the invading Swedes. He besieged the Protestant city of Magdeburg in Brandenburg, forcing its surrender in 1631. The subsequent massacre of the population and accompanying pillage had an effect similar to that of the Defenestration of Prague; the story of the atrocities spread across Protestant Europe. Brandenburg and Saxony now allied with Sweden. The combined Protestant forces under Gustavus Adolphus defeated Tilly's imperial Catholic army at Breitenfeld near Leipzig. The Swedish army, swollen by German mercenaries, then marched through the northern German states, easily reversing Habsburg gains over the previous twelve years.

The expansion of Swedish power generated anxiety among both Protestant and Catholic states, including France, although Louis XIII had helped finance Gustavus Adolphus. In Bavaria, the Swedes defeated Tilly, who was killed in battle in 1632. The rout of the Catholic imperial forces seemed complete. Spain, its interests spread too far afield in Europe and the Americas, could not then afford to help. The plague prevented another Catholic army from being raised in Italy; even the pope begged off a request for help by complaining that the eruption of Mount Vesuvius was preventing the collection of taxes.

In April 1632, Ferdinand turned once again to Wallenstein to save the Catholic cause, the latter agreeing to raise a new imperial army in return for almost unlimited authority over it. Wallenstein reconquered Silesia and Bohemia. Against him, Gustavus led the largest army (175,000) that had ever been under a single command in Europe. Although reason dictated that the Swedish army should dig in for the winter of 1632, Gustavus took a chance by attacking Wallenstein in the fog at Lützen in Saxony in November. The two sides fought to a bloody draw, but a draw amounted to a Catholic victory. Gustavus Adolphus fell dead in the battle, facedown in the mud.

Wallenstein's days were also numbered. His new army was now living off the land in Central Europe, engendering peasant resistance. Furthermore, Wallenstein, who was ill, demanded command of a Spanish army that had subsequently arrived to help the Catholic forces. In the meantime, it became known that Wallenstein had considered joining Gustavus after the Battle of Breitenfeld in 1631, and that he was offering his services to both France and the German Protestants. Ferdinand dismissed Wallenstein for the final time, and then ordered his murder. In February 1634, an Irish mercenary crept into Wallenstein's room, and killed him with a spear.

With the aid of the remnants of Wallenstein's forces, the Spanish army defeated the combined Swedish and German Protestant army in 1634 in Swabia. The elector of Saxony abandoned the Protestant struggle, making peace in 1635 with Ferdinand. One by one, other Protestant princes also left the war. The Catholic forces now held the upper hand.

The Armies of the Thirty Years' War

The Thirty Years' War was certainly one of the cruelest episodes in the history of warfare. A contemporary described the horror of the seemingly endless brutalities that afflicted Central Europe:

> [The soldiers] stretched out a hired man flat on the ground, stuck a wooden wedge in his mouth to keep it open, and emptied a milk bucket full of stinking manure droppings down his throat—they called it a Swedish cocktail. . . . Then they used thumb-screws . . . to torture the peasants. . . . They put one of the captured bumpkins in the bakeoven and lighted a fire in it. . . . I can't say much about the captured wives, hired girls, and daughters because the soldiers did not let me watch their doings. But I do remember hearing pitiful screams in various dark corners.

Several factors may have contributed to the barbarity of soldiers during the Thirty Years' War. Mercenaries and volunteers were usually fighting far

Soldiers pillaging a farmhouse during the Thirty Years' War, some torturing the farmer over his hearth while others rape the women and steal the food.

from home, living off the land to survive. Strident propaganda against other religions may have contributed to the brutality. In response, however, Gustavus Adolphus and other leaders imposed harsh penalties, including execution, for atrocities, not wanting to so frighten the local population that ordinary channels of provisioning the army would disappear.

During the Thirty Years' War, at least a million men took arms. The armies were enormous for the time. Even Sweden, where there was no fighting, felt the impact of the death of at least 50,000 soldiers between 1621 and 1632 from battle wounds and, more often, disease. Yet, considering the number of troops engaged in the long war, relatively few soldiers perished in battle, particularly when compared to those who succumbed to illness and to civilians who died at the hands of marauding troops. Armies rampaged through the German states, Catholic and Protestant, speaking many languages, taking what they wanted, burning and looting. Marburg was occupied eleven different times. Atrocity followed atrocity.

The armies themselves remained ragtag forces, lacking discipline and accompanied by, in some cases, the families of soldiers. The presence of large numbers of women (including many prostitutes) and children as camp followers may have contributed to the length of the war, making life in the army seem more normal for soldiers.

Soldiers, for the most part, wore what they could find. Some, if they were lucky, had leather clothes, carried rain cloaks against the damp German climate, and wore felt hats. Some Habsburg troops sported uniforms of pale gray, at least at the beginning of a campaign. As the months passed and uniforms disintegrated, soldiers were forced to disrobe the dead, friend and foe alike, or to steal from civilians. At best, soldiers wore symbols indicating their regiment and fought behind banners bearing the colors of the army—thus the expression "show your colors." The Swedes wore a yellow band around their hats. The imperial forces placed red symbols in their hats, plumes, or sashes if they could find them.

Most armies also lacked a common language. The Habsburg army included Saxons, Bavarians, Westphalians, and Austrians; Maximilian's Bavarian army counted various other Germans, Italians, Poles, Slovenes, Croats, Greeks, Hungarians, Burgundians, French, Czechs, Spaniards, Scots, Irish, and Turks.

Some soldiers may have joined regiments because they were searching for adventure; others joined out of religious conviction. Yet a multitude of soldiers fought against armies of their own religion, changing sides when a better opportunity arose. Army recruiters gave religion not the slightest thought in their search for soldiers to fill quotas for which they were being handsomely paid. In any case, recruits on both sides were attracted by the strong possibility that they would be better clothed and fed—bread, meat, lots of beer, and occasionally some butter and cheese—than they were when they joined up.

The Wars of Religion and Dynastic Struggles (1635–1648)

Between 1635 and 1648, what had begun as a religious war became a dynastic struggle between two Catholic states, France and Habsburg Austria, the former allied with Sweden, the latter with Spain. France declared war on Philip IV of Spain in 1635. Richelieu hoped to force Habsburg armies away from the borders of France. He took as a pretext the Spanish arrest of a French ally, the elector of Trier. Alliances with the Dutch Republic and Sweden had prepared the way, as did reassurances given by neighboring Savoy and Lorraine, and by French protectorates in Alsace.

The French incursions into the Netherlands and the southern German states did not go well. Louis XIII's army was short on capable commanders and battle-experienced troops, largely because France was already fighting in Italy, the Pyrenees, and the northern German states. But France's involvement, like that of Sweden before it, did provide the Protestant states with some breathing room. French forces joined the Swedish army, helping defeat the imperial army in Saxony.

The wars went on. When the pope called for representatives of the Catholic and Protestant states to assemble in Cologne for a peace congress in 1636, no one showed up. Four years later, another combined French and Swedish force defeated the Habsburg army. Maximilian I of Bavaria then sought a separate peace with France. Devastating Spanish defeats in northern France in 1643, as well as in the Netherlands and the Pyrenees, and the outbreak of rebellions inside Spain, left the Austrian Habsburgs with no choice but to make peace.

At the same time, unrest in France, including plots against Richelieu, and the English Civil War, which began in 1642, served to warn other rulers of the dangers that continued instability could bring. The Swedish population was tiring of distant battles that brought home nothing but news of casualties. In the German states, calls for peace echoed in music and plays. Lutheran ministers inveighed against the war from the pulpit. Among the rulers of the great powers, only Louis XIII wanted the war to go on, at the expense of the Austrian Habsburgs. He helped subsidize an invasion of Hungary by Transylvanian Protestants in 1644. As Swedish and Transylvanian forces prepared to besiege the imperial capital of Vienna, Holy Roman Emperor Ferdinand III (ruled 1637–1657), who had succeeded his father, concluded a peace treaty with the prince of Transylvania, promising to tolerate Protestantism in Hungary. After Habsburg armies suffered further defeats in 1645, Ferdinand III realized that he had to make peace, and offered an amnesty to princes within the empire who had fought against him.

The preliminaries for a general peace agreement had begun in 1643 and dragged on even as a Franco-Swedish army drove the imperial army out of the Rhineland and Bavaria in 1647. Following another French victory early in 1648, only the outbreak of the Fronde, a rebellion of nobles against the king's authority in France (see Chapter 7), forced the young Louis XIV to seek peace.

The Treaty of Westphalia (1648)

The Treaty of Westphalia was unlike any previous peace settlement in history, which had invariably been between two or three states, rarely more. Its framers believed that they could restore international stability and diplomatic process in a Europe torn by anarchy by eliminating religious divisions as a cause of conflict. The treaty proved almost as complicated as the Thirty Years' War itself. Two hundred rulers converged on Westphalia. Thousands of diplomats and other officials shuttled back and forth between two towns. Letters took ten to twelve days to reach the courts of Paris and Vienna, at least twenty to Stockholm, and a month to arrive in Madrid. In the meantime, the French tried to delay any treaty, hoping to force Spain to surrender. In the summer of 1648, the Swedes reoccupied Bohemia, hoping to win a larger indemnity and toleration for the Lutherans. When, by the separate Treaty of Münster, Spain finally formally recognized the *fait accompli* of Dutch independence, the Spanish Army of Flanders fought against France in a last-ditch effort to help Ferdinand III. In August 1648, the French defeated a Spanish force a month after the Swedes had captured part of Prague. His back to the wall, Ferdinand signed the peace treaty, finally concluded on October 24, 1648.

The Treaty of Westphalia redrew the map of Europe, confirming the existence of the Dutch United Provinces and Switzerland. The treaty did not end the war between Spain and France, but it did end the wars of the German states and in doing so put an end to one of the most brutal, ghastly periods in European history. Sweden absorbed West Pomerania and the bishoprics of Verden and Bremen on the North Sea (see Map 4.3). France, by an agreement signed two years earlier, annexed the frontier towns of Metz, Toul, and Verdun, and parts of Alsace. Maximilian I of Bavaria kept the Upper Palatinate, and therefore the status of elector. Frederick's Protestant son ended up with the Lower, or Rhine Palatinate. With this addition of an elector, eight votes would now be necessary to elect the Holy Roman emperor.

With minor exceptions, the territorial settlement reached in Westphalia remained in place until the French Revolution of 1789. For the most part, the treaty ended wars of religion in early modern Europe. It encouraged religious toleration, finally rewarding those people who had worked for and advocated religious toleration, or suffered intolerance and repression, during the long, bloody conflicts. The philosopher Baruch Spinoza (1632–1677), who had been forced to flee intolerance in Portugal, undoubtedly spoke for many when he wrote, "As for rebellions which are aroused under the pretext of religion . . . opinions are regarded as wicked and condemned

MAP 4.3 EUROPE AFTER THE TREATY OF WESTPHALIA, 1648 The treaty ended the Thirty Years' War.

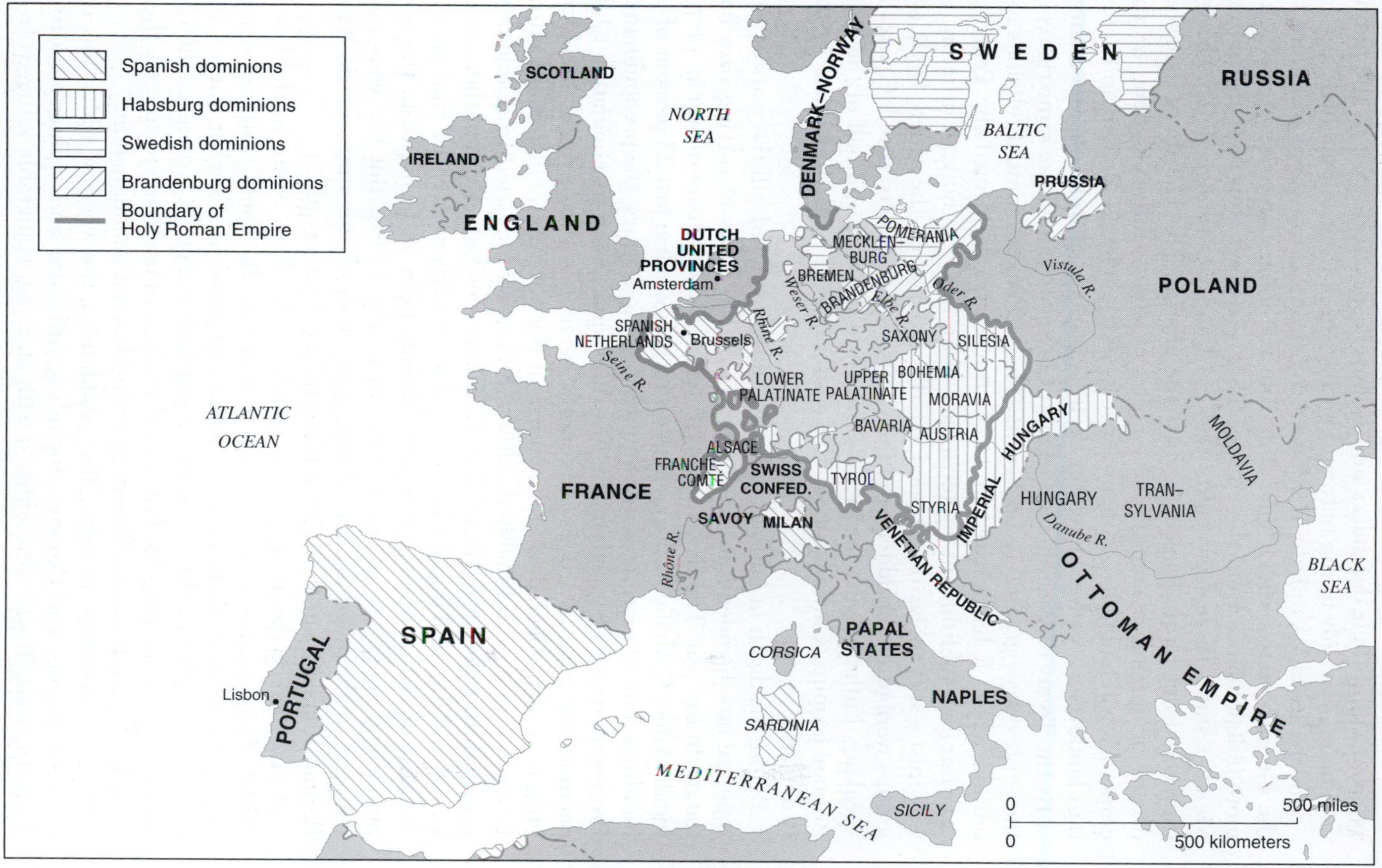

as crimes, and their defenders and followers sacrificed. Not to the public well-being, but only to the hate and barbarism of their opponents."

The Treaty of Westphalia reinforced the strong autonomous traditions of the German states, which emerged from the long nightmare of war with more independence from the considerably weakened Holy Roman Empire. Member states thereafter could carry out their own foreign policy, though they could not form alliances against the empire. The Habsburg dynasty's dream of forging a centralized empire of states fully obedient to the emperor's will had failed. Bohemia lost its independence. Bohemian Protestant landowners recovered neither their lands nor their religious freedom.

By the Treaty of Westphalia, German Calvinists gained the same rights as those previously granted to Lutherans. The settlement granted religious toleration where it had existed in 1624. But it also confirmed the Peace of Augsburg's establishment of territorial churches—Catholic, Lutheran, or Calvinist—still to be determined by the religion of the ruler. Dissident groups were often forbidden, and their followers were persecuted. Generally speaking, Lutheranism remained dominant in the northern half of the Holy Roman Empire, Catholicism in the southern half, with Calvinists in the Rhineland.

Before his death in battle, Gustavus Adolphus noted "all the wars of Europe are now blended into one." More than 200 states of varying sizes had fought in the war. The devastation brought by thirty years of war is simply incalculable. Catholic Mainz, occupied by the Swedes, lost 25 percent of its buildings and 40 percent of its population. In four years, the predominantly Protestant duchy of Württemberg lost three-quarters of its population while occupied by imperial troops. Almost 90 percent of the farms of Mecklenburg were abandoned during the course of the war. Many villages in Central Europe were now uninhabited. Although devastation varied from region to region during the Thirty Years' War, German cities lost a third of their population, and the rural population declined by 40 percent. Central Europe, like the rest of the continent, may have already been suffering from the economic and social crisis that had begun in the 1590s. But the wars contributed to the huge decline of the population of the states of the Holy Roman Empire from about 20 million to 16 million people.

A year before the Treaty of Westphalia, a Swabian wrote in the family Bible: "They say that the terrible war is now over. But there is still no sign of peace. Everywhere there is envy, hatred and greed; that's what the war has taught us. . . . We live like animals, eating bark and grass. No one could have imagined that anything like this would happen to us. Many people say there is no God . . . but we still believe that God has not abandoned us."

War was not alone in taking lives: epidemics, the worst of which was the bubonic plague, and diseases, including influenza and typhus, also took fearsome tolls. Towns were clogged with starving, vulnerable refugees from the fighting and marauding. The flight of peasants from their lands reduced agricultural productivity. It would be decades before the German states recovered from the Thirty Years' War.

Although much of the religious settlement of the Treaty of Westphalia would endure, dynastic rivalries still raged. France had emerged from its religious wars with a stronger monarchy; Louis XIII had made his state more centralized and powerful. France's rivals, too, would extend their authority within their own states. In the mid-seventeenth century, Europe would enter the era of monarchical absolutism. The most powerful European states—above all, Louis XIV's France—would enter a period of aggressive territorial expansion. Dynastic wars would help shape the European experience from the mid-seventeenth century to the French Revolution of 1789.

PART TWO

STATEMAKING

During the last half of the fifteenth century, the balance of economic and political power in Europe began to shift away from the Mediterranean region and the Italian city-states. The discovery and then colonization of the Americas contributed greatly to the development of the Atlantic economy, adding to the strength of Spain and then, beginning a century later, of England, transporting their rivalry across the Atlantic Ocean. The surprising English naval victory over the Spanish Armada in 1588 symbolized the subsequent shift in power from southern to northern Europe, even if Spain remained militarily stronger until the 1630s.

In the seventeenth century, when aggressive European monarchs were running roughshod over noble prerogatives and town privileges, England and the Dutch Republic both maintained their representative governments. The English Civil War led to the defeat and execution of the king in 1649, the fall of the monarchy, and in 1688, to the "Glorious Revolution," which affirmed the civil liberties of the English people and the rights of Parliament. In the largely Protestant Netherlands, which earned its independence after a protracted struggle against Catholic Spain, the prosperous merchants retained a republican form of government and helped generate the golden age of Dutch culture. In contrast, many European rulers relentlessly extended their power between 1650 and 1750, becoming absolute rulers. In principle, they were above all challenge from within the state itself, affecting the lives of more people than ever before through taxation, military service, and the royal quest for religious orthodoxy as Europe entered the era of absolutism.

CHAPTER **5**

THE RISE OF THE ATLANTIC ECONOMY: SPAIN AND ENGLAND

In 1585, Protestant England went to war with Catholic Spain. On July 30, 1588, English observers on the cliffs above the English Channel first caught sight of the supposedly invincible Spanish Armada, a force of 130 ships. On the night of August 7, the English fleet attacked King Philip II's Armada along the English coast. After the Armada anchored near Calais, the English sent ships set on fire against the Armada, which caused the Spanish ships to break their tight tactical formation. With the help of strong winds, the English then pinned the Spanish ships against the shore, and destroyed six of them, in the longest and most intense naval artillery battle, much of it at such close range that the sailors could hurl insults at each other. Superior English cannon, shot, and gunners took their toll on the Armada. More than 1,000 Spaniards died during the long battle that day. The captain of one Spanish ship that had failed to answer the flagship's call for help was hanged from a yardarm, his body hauled from ship to ship to reestablish discipline.

The English ships failed to follow up their advantage, however, letting the Spanish galleons escape. The rough winds of the Channel carried the Spanish ships away from the dangerous Flemish shoals toward the North Sea and then on a long, northern voyage up to the straits between the Orkney and Shetland Islands. This was decidedly the long way to reach the safety of Spanish ports. More than thirty Spanish ships sank in gales off the western coasts of Scotland and Ireland. When some of the ships of the Armada limped into port in Spain, the fleet's captain wrote King Philip II, "I am unable to describe to Your Majesty the misfortunes and miseries that have befallen us, because they are the worst that have been known on any voyage; and some of the ships that put into this port have spent the last fourteen days without a single drop of water." Of the 130 ships that had sailed against

165

English vessels attack the Spanish Armada off Calais in the English Channel in 1588.

England, only 60 could now be accounted for. At least a third had been sunk or wrecked, and many others were severely damaged.

Victory over the Spanish Armada accentuated England's rise to international dominance. English armies then crushed an Irish rebellion in 1603, ending fears of an effective Irish alliance with Catholic Spain. Despite the defeat of the Spanish Armada, however, Philip did not make peace with England, and the war between the two nations dragged on until 1604.

ECONOMIC EXPANSION

The rise of Spain, England, and the Netherlands must be seen in the context of the sixteenth-century expansion of the European economy. By 1450, the European population had begun to recover slowly from the Black Death, the disastrous plague that had swept the continent a century earlier. In general, the population continued to rise until the mid-seventeenth century, when religious and dynastic wars and new plagues led to such devastation that the period has become known as "the age of crisis." These cataclysms particularly struck Central Europe. But the Mediterranean region, too, suffered population decline, and the European population of the Turkish Ottoman Empire remained extremely sparse, about half that of France and Italy in 1600.

During the sixteenth century, the commercial and manufacturing center of Europe shifted from the Mediterranean to northwestern Europe. England and France established colonies in North America, and English and

Dutch traders ventured beyond the coast of India to the East Indies. By 1700, Venice—which, alone among the Italian city-states, had managed to retain significant trade links with Asia—had become a virtual backwater because it had failed to adapt to the global economy that was expanding across the Atlantic Ocean to the Americas. Spain, France, England, and the Dutch United Provinces emerged as burgeoning colonial powers in the late sixteenth century, developing trade routes to Asia and gradually establishing empires.

Spain's preeminence did not survive the end of the seventeenth-century economic crisis. Its merchants lacked the flexibility shown by the English and Dutch to adjust to the varying demand for colonial products and to create new trading opportunities. The extraction and importation of silver dominated their efforts. Furthermore, merchants in Amsterdam and London, not those in the Spanish city of Seville, expanded trade by using innovative commercial techniques. Spanish merchants proved less able than their northern rivals to lower costs of transportation from the New World. In contrast, English textile merchants found new markets in Spain and the Mediterranean for their cloth.

Increased Agricultural Productivity

Populations cannot grow unless the rural economy can produce enough additional food to feed more people. During the sixteenth century, farmers brought more land into cultivation at the expense of forests and fens (marsh lands). Dutch reclamation of land from the sea in the Netherlands in the sixteenth and seventeenth centuries provides the most spectacular example of the expansion of farm land; the Dutch reclaimed more than 36,000 acres between 1590 and 1615 alone. Modest agricultural progress was, however, limited to Western Europe, in villages with access to urban merchants, markets, and trade routes. In Russia and Eastern Europe, hundreds of thousands of serfs who were legally bound to the land labored to produce enough grain to feed the population and to generate a surplus that their lords could sell to Western European traders.

Population growth generated an expansion of small-scale manufacturing, particularly handicrafts, textiles, and metallurgy in England, Flanders, parts of northern Italy, the southwestern German states, and in parts of Spain. Only iron smelting and mining required marshaling a significant amount of capital. Rural industry was an intrinsic part of the expansion of industry. Woolens and textile manufacturers, in particular, utilized rural cottage (domestic) production, which took advantage of cheap and plentiful rural labor. Members of poor peasant families spun or wove cloth and linens at home for scant remuneration in an attempt to supplement meager family income.

Expansion of Trade

Extended trading networks developed the European economy. Improved banking and other financial services contributed to the expansion of trade. By the middle of the sixteenth century, financiers and traders commonly accepted bills of exchange in place of gold or silver or other goods. Bills of exchange, which had their origins in medieval Italy, were promissory notes that could be sold to third parties, and in this way they provided credit. At mid-century, an Antwerp financier only slightly exaggerated when he claimed, "One can no more trade without bills of exchange than sail without water." Merchants no longer had to carry gold and silver over long, dangerous journeys, nor did they have to identify and assess the approximate value of a variety of coins issued by mints here and there. Thus, an Amsterdam merchant purchasing soap from a counterpart in Marseille could go to an exchanger and pay him the equivalent sum in guilders, the Dutch currency. The exchanger would then send a bill of exchange to a colleague in Marseille, authorizing him to pay the Marseille merchant in his own currency after the actual exchange of goods had taken place. Bills of exchange contributed to the development of banking, as exchangers began to provide loans, profiting from the interest attached to them.

The rapid expansion in international trade increased the role of merchant capitalists, particularly in northern Europe, in the emerging global economy. The infusion of capital stemmed largely from gold and silver brought by

The money changer's office.

Spanish vessels from the Americas. This capital financed the production of goods, storage, trade, and even credit across Europe and overseas. Moreover, an increased credit supply was generated by investments and loans by bankers and wealthy merchants to states and by joint-stock partnerships, an English innovation (the first major company began in 1600). Unlike short-term financial cooperation between investors for a single commercial under-taking, joint-stock companies provided capital by drawing on the investments of merchants and other investors who purchased shares in the company.

Amsterdam and then London emerged as the banking and trading cen-ters of Europe. (Not until the eighteenth century, however, did the Bank of Amsterdam and the Bank of England begin to provide capital for business investment.) Merchant towns in Castile, Catalonia, Italy, Holland, and England, as well as the Hanseatic cities of northern Germany, each had their own merchant dynasties.

The Global Economy

Trade with the Americas and Asia provided new outlets for European goods. It also brought from the New World products such as tomatoes, corn, bell peppers, rum, and spices to those who could afford them. The construction of larger ships, weighing as much as eighty tons, a size that would not be sur-passed until the middle of the nineteenth century, facilitated oceangoing trade. From seaports, trade followed the major rivers—principally the Rhine, which flows from Switzerland to the North Sea; the Danube, which flows from Central Europe to the Black Sea; the Seine, which links Paris to the English Channel; and the Rhône, which carries boat traffic from Lyon to the Mediterranean. The Scheldt River estuary led from the North Sea to the powerful trading and manufacturing city of Antwerp, which already had a population of more than 100,000 people. There, vast quantities of English and Flemish goods and, increasingly, colonial products were traded for goods from the German and Italian states. Land trade routes also remained important—for example, the route from Marseille to northern France and the Netherlands, that from Valencia on the Mediterranean to Madrid and Toledo in the heart of Castile, and that from Piedmont to the western Ger-man states and the Netherlands.

Specially chartered East Indian trading companies helped mobilize investment capital in England and the Netherlands and, enjoying monopo-lies issued to them by each state, set out to make money. When Hugo Grotius published his treatise on the freedom of the seas in 1609, he subti-tled it *The Right which Belongs to the Dutch to Take Part in the East India Trade*. Although officially independent of each government, trade companies represented the interests of the state. Above all, in England colonial trade played a major role in the development of the national economy, principally because England's manufactured goods increasingly found markets in its developing settlement colonies in North America.

Overseas trading remained a risky business, however; storms, wars, and pirates all posed considerable risks. England, Spain, Portugal, and France spent fortunes maintaining fortresses and trading ports in colonies and along trading routes. Funds available to finance global treks could quickly disappear in times of political crisis or international conflict, and distant markets for European goods, never very certain, could quickly dry up. Appropriately enough, the first English company to receive royal authorization for a monopoly on colonial trade was called the London Merchant Adventurers. Spanish kings, in particular, were notorious for declaring bankruptcy and thus repudiating all debts after borrowing money from wealthy subjects based on the expectation—sometimes in vain—of the arrival of valued colonial goods or bullion.

The major European powers had only limited means of exerting authority over their merchants and other subjects in distant places. Trading strategies followed negotiations and, often, angry confrontations between royal officials and aggressive trading lobbies. This, in addition to the daunting problems of distance, discouraged early attempts to establish the kind of full-fledged colonies in Asia and Africa that Spain and then England had in the Americas. Moreover, diseases indigenous to regions to which Europeans traveled as well as those they carried with them made life not only dangerous but often short, particularly in tropical climates.

Price Revolution and Depression

The rise in population and the economic boom of the sixteenth century brought a considerable rise in prices, particularly during the last few decades of the century. It seemed to one Spaniard that "a pound of mutton now costs as much as a whole sheep used to." Between 1500 and 1600, the price of wheat rose by 425 percent in England, 650 percent in France, and 400 percent in Poland. Prices rose dramatically even before the arrival of silver from Latin America, a cause of continued inflation during the second half of the century. The cost of living far outdistanced wage increases as real income fell for ordinary people. Among those who suffered were small landholders in England, relatively poor nobles in France and Italy whose tenants had long-term leases, and landless laborers and wage earners in city and country alike.

Those affected adversely by the price revolution were quick to blame rapacious landlords, greedy merchants, hoarders of grain, selfish masters in the crafts, usurers, and the spirit of acquisition engendered, some believed, by the Reformation. Basic long-term causes included the infusion of gold and particularly silver brought principally by the Spanish from the Americas, currency debasement undertaken by monarchs to help finance wars, and the population increase itself, which placed more pressure on scarce resources.

A long depression followed the economic expansion of the sixteenth century. This in itself reflected the relative decline of Mediterranean trade, symbolized by the end of Venetian supremacy by 1600. The Thirty Years' War (1618–1648) also disrupted trade and manufacturing. International trade fell off dramatically. Furthermore, Spaniards had begun to exhaust the gold and silver mines of Latin America, disrupting the money supply. A leveling off of the population probably compounded the saturation of European markets. Urban growth slowed, and many of Europe's old ecclesiastical, administrative, and commercial centers stagnated. In sharp contrast, ports such as Amsterdam, Hamburg, and Liverpool grew with the expansion of the Atlantic trading system.

THE RISE OF SPAIN

Sixteenth-century Spain, the most powerful state of its time, was not one kingdom but two: Castile and Aragon. Castile was by far the larger and wealthier; its vast stretch of mountainous land across much of the center of the Iberian Peninsula contained a population of about six million

MAP 5.1 SPAIN IN THE LATE FIFTEENTH CENTURY

people, five-sixths of the population of Spain as a whole. Aragon, lying in northern Spain, had prospered during the Middle Ages because of its flourishing Mediterranean trade. It became a federation of dominions, including Catalonia and Valencia, greatly influenced by Mediterranean peoples and cultures (see Map 5.1). In contrast, Portugal was a relatively poor Atlantic state of mariners lying on the western edge of Iberia, despite its precocious development of trade routes along the West African coast and as far as the Indian Ocean and beyond. It had a population of about 1 million people (roughly equivalent to that of Aragon). Following the death of the Portuguese king without a male heir, Philip II of Spain claimed the Portuguese throne by virtue of being the only son of Isabella of Portugal, daughter of King Manuel I. Portugal was merged into the Spanish kingdom in 1580. (Portugal did not regain its independence until 1640.)

Centralization and the Spanish Monarchy

In 1469, Isabella of Castile (1451–1504) married Ferdinand (1452–1516), heir to the throne of Aragon. Castilian policies were successfully implemented to create a relatively centralized monarchy. The Castilian dialect gradually emerged as the language of Spain, giving some truth to the old saying that "a language is a dialect with an army." In 1492, Spanish armies captured Granada, which was the last part of the Iberian Peninsula controlled by the Moors.

(*Left*) King Ferdinand II of Aragon was devoted to the Catholic Church. (*Right*) Isabella, Queen of Castile.

Ferdinand and Isabella and their successors were known as the Catholic monarchs because of their devotion to the Church. But like other monarchs, they brought the Church, its privileges, and some of its income from tithes and the sale of indulgences under royal control. While the Reformation shook the foundations of the Church in much of Europe, it barely challenged Spanish religious orthodoxy. The Spanish Inquisition, whose original purpose had been to enforce the conversion of Islamic Moors and Jews in the late fifteenth century, served the Catholic Reformation in the late sixteenth century. The tribunal of the Inquisition interrogated and punished those accused of questioning Church doctrine. Housed in Castile, the Inquisition became a respected agent of royal as well as Church authority in some parts of Spain. Elsewhere—in Sicily and the Dutch Netherlands, above all—local people resisted the Inquisition, seeing it as another aspect of Spanish domination.

In Castile, Ferdinand and Isabella centralized the system of justice and made towns more subservient to the royal will. They stripped the Castilian nobles of some of their privileges while dispensing titles and positions. In Catalonia and Valencia, on the other hand, nobles resisted, maintaining most of their noble prerogatives. Nonetheless, because they feared a revolt of the lower classes, the Catalan and Valencian nobles became willing allies with the crown in maintaining social hierarchy and order.

Parliamentary traditions in the Spanish principalities to some extent limited the reach of the Castilian monarchy. The rulers of Spain were not able to tamper with Catalonia's traditionally less centralized constitutional traditions, which dated from the late thirteenth and fourteenth centuries, when Catalonia itself had been a Mediterranean power. Thus, the territories of Catalonia and Valencia maintained their political institutions, principally their *Cortes* (assembly), which continued to limit the authority of the monarchy and which had to be consulted in order to achieve compliance with royal edicts. The Spanish monarchy therefore was less a "new monarchy"—at least outside of Castile—than that of France, because particularly strong institutional limits on its effective authority remained.

In Castile, disagreements between the monarchy and the Cortes there were frequent during the middle decades of the sixteenth century. The Cortes excluded nobles and included only representatives from the eighteen most important cities and towns of Castile. The Castilian Cortes, which maintained the right to approve special taxes, refused taxes to subsidize the monarchy for thirty-five years (1541–1575), obviously hampering the royal fiscal apparatus. The long reign of Philip II began (1556) and ended (1598) with a declaration of royal bankruptcy.

The Spanish Economy

Although income from its colonies never accounted for more than about 10 percent of the crown's total income, Spain's colonial empire in the Americas contributed to its expanding economy. During the first years of the Spanish colonial period, Mexican gold helped finance the next wave of conquests. In 1545, Spaniards discovered the rich silver mines of Potosí (then in Peru, now in Bolivia), and a year later they uncovered more deposits in Mexico. A new refining process helped Spain triple the silver resources of Europe to its own profit. Mules carried silver extracted at Potosí on a fifteen-day journey down 12,000 feet and many miles to the port of Arica in northern Chile; then the sea voyage of several months by convoy began. Among other things, the silver paid for slaves brought from the coast of Africa. The Spanish Empire contributed considerably to the sixteenth-century European trading boom. Spain shipped colonial products and Spanish woolens to France and the Italian city-states. Spanish ships also supplied the colonies with wine, oil, European grain, shoes, and clothing.

The Castilian economy developed rapidly. The mountain ranges and central plateaus of Castile were divided between land for agricultural production and for raising sheep. The wool trade formed the basis of the Castilian export economy. The mining of silver, lead, iron, and mercury also developed in sixteenth-century Castile. Agricultural production was closely linked to manufacturing, as were sheep to the production of woolen goods. Nonetheless, 85 percent of the land of Spain could not be plowed because it was too mountainous or rocky, or could not be irrigated because of the high elevation.

Spanish royal revenue came from peasant obligations owed on royal domains as well as from taxes on commerce and manufacturing, import and export taxes, levies assessed for moving sheep through specific mountain passes, and payment from the Church for collecting tithes (the ecclesiastical tax of 10 percent of revenue). The crown imposed protectionist measures against foreign goods, banned the export of gold and silver, and attracted Italian and Flemish craftsmen to Spain.

In northern Spain, the mountains and valleys of the rainy Cantabrian coast were populated by farmers and fishermen. To the south, the Castilian provinces of Andalusia and Granada produced wheat, olives, and wine. Castilian farmers expanded production by terracing hillsides and planting them in perennials, including grapevines and olive trees. Demand for textiles increased, and farmers planted flax and hemp. Farm towns built irrigation works and processing facilities such as wine and olive presses, flax-soaking ponds, and grist and fulling mills to turn these crops into market commodities.

Spanish nobles incurred no social stigma by engaging in wholesale or international commerce until the eighteenth century. Many nobles capitalized on their revenues from farm products by building facilities to store and process the products—including flour mills, tanneries, and wine cellars, which often doubled as taverns. Several wealthy dukes became shipping magnates. They owned the tuna fishing rights on Castile's Mediterranean shore, exporting fish preserved in salt or olive oil all over Europe.

The Expansion of the Spanish Empire

Through marriage and inheritance, Spain's territorial interests reached far and wide. The Spanish throne passed to the Austrian branch of the Habsburg dynasty in 1496, with Ferdinand and Isabella's daughter, Princess Joanna, marrying Philip the Fair, the Habsburg duke of Burgundy, the son of Maximilian, the Holy Roman emperor. A year after Isabella's death in 1504, Ferdinand, hoping to produce an heir to the Spanish throne, married a niece of King Louis XII of France. But their infant son died three years later—royal families were also subject to the harsh demographic realities of the age. In 1516, the Flanders-born son of Joanna and Philip the Fair inherited the throne of Castile and Aragon as Charles I of Spain. In

Charles V was the grandson of Ferdinand and Isabella. This portrait is by Titian (1548).

1519, he became Holy Roman Emperor Charles V (ruled 1519–1558) upon the death of his grandfather, Maximilian I. Along with Spain's American territories, he inherited Aragon's Italian possessions. The emperor only briefly resided in Catalonia and rarely visited Castile. But with far-flung dynastic interests, he demanded extraordinary taxes from his Spanish subjects to pay for his wars abroad, including the defense of the Spanish-Italian possessions of Naples, Sicily, and Sardinia against France during the 1520s.

The king's departure from Spain in 1520 was followed by open revolt against royal taxation. The revolt of the *Comuneros* (urban communities) began in Toledo and spread to other towns in northern Castile. Bourgeois and artisans opposed the royal officials Charles had imported from Flanders, but the revolt was also directed against Castilian nobles. After royal forces burned the arsenal and town of Medina del Campo in north-central Castile in August 1520, the young king suddenly switched tactics. He suspended supplementary tax collections and agreed not to appoint any more foreigners to office in Spain. When uprisings continued, Charles's army gradually restored order, brutally executing the leaders of the rebellion.

With an eye toward his succession, Charles V arranged the marriage of his son, Philip, to the English princess Mary Tudor of England in 1554. Charles

MAP 5.2 HABSBURG LANDS AT THE ABDICATION OF CHARLES V, 1558   The division of the Habsburg lands between Philip II (who had already begun to rule Spain in 1556) and Ferdinand I.

formally abdicated as Holy Roman emperor in 1558, dividing the Habsburg domains between his son Philip and his brother Ferdinand (see Map 5.2). Philip II (ruled 1556–1598) inherited Spain, the Netherlands, the Spanish colonies in the Americas, and parts of Italy. Ferdinand I (ruled 1558–1564), who was elected Holy Roman emperor, inherited the Habsburg ancestral domains, including Austria. This ended the period when one ruler held all Habsburg territories and also eliminated any possibility that a single Catholic monarch would rule all of Europe. It did not, however, end the cooperation and strong family ties between the two branches of the Habsburg dynasty. Mary Tudor's death in 1558 eliminated the intriguing prospect that England might have become part of the Spanish Empire.

Philip II inherited the problem of ruling a vast empire. Like its rivals France and England, the Spanish state developed a large, centralized bureaucracy, including royal councils, essential to the operations of the empire. The council of state and the council of war offered the king advice on matters of internal and colonial policy. Royal secretaries handled correspondence and busied themselves with the operations of the royal household. Most such officials were commoners, for whom such positions provided financial and social advantages.

The Council of the Indies oversaw the administration of Spain's vast empire, sending viceroys and other officials to enforce the royal will and assure the extraction of precious metals for the royal coffers. The monarchy sent officials, many trained in law, to the Americas. It could take two years for administrative instructions or correspondence to reach distant officials in Latin America and for their response to arrive in Spain. One official awaiting instructions put it this way, "If death came from Madrid, we should all live to a very old age."

The Age of Philip II

Spanish power peaked during the reign of Philip II. Madrid, in the center of Castile, became a capital city of nobles and bureaucrats, many of whom, in one way or another, lived off the court. The city grew from a town of about 30,000 people in the 1540s to well over 150,000 inhabitants in the 1620s. Madrid survived through a "command economy"; royal commissioners paid government-fixed prices for what they wanted from the capital's hinterland. As Spain's capital grew, it had to import supplies, which were transported from distant regions by countless mule trains that traversed rough mountain ranges and deep valleys.

Philip decided that he needed a permanent royal residence that would provide an elegant symbol of his power. Outside of Madrid, Philip built the magnificent Escorial Palace. Virtually the king's only public appearances after he became crippled by gout were elaborate religious ceremonies at the palace, carefully orchestrated to uphold the sanctity of the throne. Rituals of court etiquette affirmed a sense of authority, social hierarchy, and order that were supposed to radiate from the Escorial through Spain and to the far reaches of the empire.

Philip II led a tragic life marred by the premature deaths of four wives and a number of children. Perhaps because of sadness, he wore only black. The king himself may have contributed to the misfortunes of his offspring. In 1568, he ordered Don Carlos, his bad-tempered and irresponsible twenty-three-year-old son by his first marriage, placed under lock and key. Don Carlos seemed unfit to rule; furthermore, detesting

Philip II of Spain ruled during the height of Spanish power.

The Ottoman Empire of Suleiman the Magnificent threatened Spanish rule during the sixteenth century.

his father, he may have even entered into contact with Dutch leaders who had begun to denounce Spanish policies in their land. Don Carlos's death six months later haunted Philip, inevitably generating stories that he had ordered him murdered. The introverted king thereafter lived among the whispers of intrigue and storms of aristocratic rivalries of the noble families and factions.

With Habsburg domination of Italy secured by the 1559 Peace of Cateau-Cambrésis with France, Philip turned his attention to fighting the Turks. The Ottoman Empire had expanded into Europe following the conquest of Constantinople in 1453 (see Chapter 1), taking advantage of dynastic and religious wars between its European rivals. Suleiman the Magnificent (ruled 1520–1566) expanded his territories in the Balkans, where some of the Ottoman cultural heritage endures today, and into the rich plains of Hungary. The Turks also became bolder in their attacks on Spanish ships in the central and western Mediterranean. When the Turks took the Venetian island of Cyprus in 1571, the pope helped initiate the Holy League, in which Venice and Spain allied. The long naval war against the Ottoman Empire lasted from 1559 to 1577. With southern Spain virtually undefended and with the Moriscos (Moors who had been forced to convert to Christianity) rebelling (1568–1570) against taxes, the Turks might well have captured Granada. But a Spanish-Austrian Habsburg fleet defeated the sultan's larger navy in the Adriatic Sea at the Battle of Lepanto (1571), a monumental struggle in which more than 200 galleys fought, taking the lives of thousands of combatants. The Turkish threat in the western Mediterranean ended, although the possibility of the further expansion of the Ottoman Empire in southeastern and central Europe remained. In the meantime, overexpansion had already planted the seeds of Spanish imperial decline.

THE RISE OF ENGLAND

The consolidation and then the extension of the authority of the Tudor monarchy facilitated England's emergence as a power late in the sixteenth century. From the reign of Henry VII to that of Elizabeth I, the Tudor monarchs held in check the great landed magnates, putting down rebellions and extending the reach and prestige of royal government. During the same period, the English state expanded its control over Wales and Ireland while holding at bay Scottish threats to the Tudor dynasty.

The House of Tudor

Victorious in the long War of the Roses between the Lancaster and York families, Henry Tudor, the last claimant to the throne of the Lancasters, became the first Tudor monarch as Henry VII (ruled 1485–1509). Like Isabella of Castile and Ferdinand of Aragon, the ambitious Henry VII set out to make the Tudor state so powerful that it could resist any challenge from noble factions and "overmighty subjects."

Thomas Wolsey, who was archbishop of York and adviser to the king, brought to the King's Council loyal officials drawn from the ranks of the nobility and high clergy. These men met in a room known as the Star Chamber because its blue ceiling, like the night sky, was spangled with stars. The Star Chamber became one of the highest courts in the land.

Henry VII strengthened royal authority in England. He imposed tariffs protecting the cloth and wool industries, decreed acts unifying weights and measures, and put forth edicts punishing vagabondage and begging. He reduced expenses by disbanding his army, while filling royal coffers by selling monopolies (the exclusive right to import and market foodstuffs or commodities). Monopolies were extremely unpopular, however, among the middle and lower classes because they kept the prices of some products artificially high.

The king won the loyalty of most nobles. When selling offices failed as a means of assuring compliance, he resorted to the sheer coercive power of the throne. The Star Chamber enforced compliance, exacting fines and sometimes arresting the recalcitrant for real or imagined offenses. Henry obtained from Parliament writs of attainder and forfeiture, by which he could declare anyone guilty of treason, order their execution, and seize their property.

Henry VII depended not only upon the personal loyalty of local elites but also on the efficiency and prestige of about 600 unpaid justices of the peace. These men, largely drawn from prosperous landed families, dispensed justice, collected taxes, enforced troop levies, and maintained order. Their judicial authority covered every criminal offense except treason. While maintaining a strong tradition of decentralized government in England, the justices of the peace also strengthened the efficiency and prestige of the monarchy. Gradually, the royal Assize Courts took responsibility for felony cases. Charged with enforcing parliamentary statutes and the orders of the Privy Council, which administered the Tudor state, the Assize Courts also helped extend the state's effective authority.

Henry VIII became king upon his father's death in 1509 and married Catherine of Aragon, who was Ferdinand and Isabella's daughter, as well as his brother's widow. Beneath Henry's proud and impetuous character lay a deep-seated inferiority complex that he tried to overcome with grand deeds. The single-minded Henry dreamed of standing at the head of an empire. The new king spent vast sums fighting against France for more than a decade, beginning in 1512. Cardinal Wolsey, who had been his father's trusted adviser, sought to restrain Henry's ambition. But when the House of Commons refused to provide the king with more funds, Henry simply debased the currency, giving the state more spending power at the cost of higher inflation.

Foreign wars devastated royal finances. To raise money, the spendthrift monarch heaped more financial obligations on the backs of the poor. Wolsey utilized the cynically named "amicable grant," a royal assessment first imposed in 1525 on lay and ecclesiastical revenues. Peasants in southeastern England rebelled against these new levies. They were sometimes led by rural "gentlemen." Henry responded to the threat by forcing landowners to loan money to the crown, imprisoning some of the wealthiest and confiscating their estates, and further debasing the currency, adding to inflation.

To make his monarchy more efficient, Henry shifted royal government, including control of the state's finances, from the royal household of the king's servants to a small but able bureaucracy of officials, who were loyal to both the king and Parliament. He reduced the size of the king's advisory council and formalized its structure. The Privy Council assumed oversight functions and routinely communicated with the local justices of the peace. The king appointed new administrative officials and established new revenue courts. At the same time, the general acceptance of the "king's law"—common law—gradually helped generate a sense of national unity.

Henry extended the power of his monarchy by breaking with Rome in the 1530s over his divorce of Catherine of Aragon. He established the Church of England (see Chapter 3), which kept some of the ritual and doctrine of the Catholic Church. Henry became head of the Church of England, dissolving monasteries and confiscating and selling ecclesiastical lands. Henry planted the seeds for future conflicts between Protestants and Catholics in England.

Fearing that the Welsh or Irish might assist Holy Roman Emperor Charles V in an attempt to invade England to restore Catholicism, Henry established English domination over Wales and direct rule over Ireland. Since the late twelfth century, English lords had gradually increased their military colonization of Ireland, pushing back the Gaelic tribes and claiming the finest land by virtue of ancient titles. The English kings delegated authority to

English nobles. Yet effective English authority remained fragile in Ireland as long as the crown's continental interests took precedence. After the English Reformation, the crown selected English Protestants for all posts in Ireland. And after a minor rebellion against royal authority, which was put down with great cruelty, in 1541 Henry proclaimed himself king of Ireland and head of the Irish Church. In exchange for the Gaelic chieftains' recognition of Henry as their king and acceptance of English law, the crown recognized them as Irish lords. Thereafter, however, the costs of administering Ireland increased rapidly, requiring more troops, as the Irish chafed at English rule. Queen Elizabeth's policy of English settlement in Ulster during the 1590s generated Gaelic resistance in the Nine Years' War (1594–1603). Resistance was led by Hugh O'Neill (1540–1616), Earl of Tyrone. English forces defeated a combined Irish and Spanish force at the Battle of Kinsale in 1601. This completed the English conquest of Gaelic Ireland. O'Neill left Ireland and ended up in Rome, where he was welcomed by the pope. Religious persecution frequently forced Catholics to hear Masses in secret in the countryside, with priests using rock slabs as altars, or "Mass rocks."

Scotland also proved to be a thorny problem for England. Although in 1503 the Scottish King James IV had married Henry VII's daughter, Margaret Tudor, relations between Scotland and England deteriorated when Henry VIII became king. When James invaded England in 1513 in support of France, Henry VIII undertook a major military campaign against the Scots. This ended with a bloody English victory at the Battle of Flodden, where James IV was killed. Nonetheless, Catholic Scotland remained an ally of Catholic France. In 1542, an English army again invaded Scotland, defeating the Scots at Solway Moss. Following James V's sudden death a month after the battle, Mary Stuart (James's six-day-old daughter) became queen of the Scots. In 1546, after Henry's war with France dragged to a halt, another English army laid waste to Scotland, sacking the capital and university town of Edinburgh.

Henry VIII died in 1547. On his deathbed, the king, whose insistence on divorce began the English Reformation, hedged his bets, leaving money to pay for Catholic Masses to be said for the eternal repose of his soul. The nine-year-old son of Henry and Jane Seymour became King Edward VI (ruled 1547–1553), governing under the tutelage of his uncle, the duke of Somerset, who served as Lord Protector. While seeking accommodation with Protestant dissenters, the young Edward undertook an aggressive campaign on behalf of the Reformed Church of England.

Wars against Catholic Scotland and France continued. The Lord Protector was intent on destroying Catholicism in Scotland. After English troops defeated a French force sent to help the Catholic cause there, the young Catholic queen of Scots, Mary Stuart (1542–1587), fled to safety, marrying Francis, the son of Henry II, the king of France. Tensions between Protestants and Catholics worsened in England. Moreover, landowners resisted

Mary Tudor, later queen of England.

paying more taxes to finance new wars. Allied with fearful Catholic nobles, the earl of Warwick overthrew Somerset in 1549. Warwick assumed the role of Lord Protector and took the title of duke of Northumberland.

Northumberland quickly betrayed the Catholic lords who had supported him. He tightened the crown's control over the Church of England and undertook a repressive campaign against Catholicism. Northumberland's influence over the sickly young king whetted his desire for power. He plotted for Lady Jane Grey (1537–1554; Henry VIII's niece and third in line to the monarchy) to ascend the throne after she married his son. After Edward's death, Northumberland proclaimed his daughter-in-law queen of England. But most nobles rallied to the cause of Mary Tudor (ruled 1553–1558), the daughter of Henry VIII and Catherine of Aragon. She seemed to them the rightful heir to the throne, despite the fact that she was Catholic.

Mary Tudor succeeded her half brother and attempted to return England to Catholicism. She restored all rituals and doctrines of the Catholic Church and she acknowledged the primacy of the pope over the Church of England. The queen abrogated Henry VIII's reforms and began to persecute Protestants, some of whom fled to France. "Bloody Mary" embellished the macabre heritage of the Tower of London with the heads of Northumberland, his son, and Lady Jane Grey, who had ruled for only nine days. Mary married Philip II, who ascended the Spanish throne in 1556. England joined Spain in its war against France, which had long rivaled the Habsburgs in Italy. Calais, the last English outpost in France, was soon lost. Sparked by widespread opposition to her Catholicism, which was popularly identified with France and Spain, a rebellion broke out against the queen. When Mary died in 1558, few in England grieved.

Elizabeth I (ruled 1558–1603), Anne Boleyn's daughter, restored Protestant rule to England when she became queen at age twenty-five, succeeding Mary, her half sister. Elizabeth's throne was threatened by religious division, which was compounded by the antagonism of Catholic France and Spain. Not many people could have expected the young queen to succeed.

Elizabeth was a woman of intelligence, vanity, sporadic fickleness, and an occasional flash of temper. She enjoyed music, dancing, hunting, and the company of men. Tall, with reddish hair and an olive complexion, she was cautious, even suspicious, having been raised in a world of conspiracy. The queen preferred to wait out many pressing problems in the hope that they would just go away. Educated in the tradition of Italian humanism, Elizabeth learned French, German, and Italian, as well as Latin, and enjoyed translating texts from these languages into English.

Elizabeth never married. It was not uncommon for women to remain unmarried in early modern Europe—in England, about 10 percent of all women remained single throughout their lives—but it was unusual for a monarch not to marry. The question of whether Elizabeth would ever take a husband preoccupied the other rulers of Europe, as well as her subjects.

In response to a parliamentary petition that she marry and produce a direct heir, Elizabeth responded that she trusted God to ensure that "the realm shall not remain destitute of an heir." As for her, it would be enough that at the end of her life "a marble stone shall declare that a queen, having reigned such a time, lived and died a virgin." Elizabeth rejected one continental hopeful after another, beginning with the handsome but dull Philip II of Spain, Catholic widower of Mary Tudor. Nor was marriage the outcome of a two-year romance with the handsome Lord Robert Dudley, the death of whose wife in 1560 from a suspicious fall down a flight of stairs understandably fueled rumors for some years.

Queen Elizabeth dancing with Robert Dudley.

Religious Settlement and Conflict under Elizabeth I

Elizabeth was determined to find a means to resolve religious conflict within England, which might one day threaten her reign. Elizabeth had been raised a Protestant, but she did not hold particularly strong religious convictions and rarely attended church. Although she was thought to favor some Catholic rituals, when she first encountered a procession of monks with candles and incense at Westminster Abbey, she cried out, "Away with these torches, we see very well." She dismissed many Catholic advisers.

In 1559, Parliament passed the Act of Uniformity and the Act of Supremacy, which established the lasting foundations of the Church of England, reorganizing it to have Protestant dogma but essentially Catholic structure. The Uniformity Bill imposed the *Book of Common Prayer* (1550) on religious services of the Church of England and required attendance at public worship and imposed fines for not attending services. The bill barely passed the House of Lords (which was primarily composed of Catholics), and probably would not have passed at all had two bishops not been imprisoned in the Tower of London and thus been unable to vote. The Act of Supremacy required all officials, clergy, and candidates for university degrees to take an oath acknowledging the queen as "governor" of the English Church. This title replaced that of "head" of the Church and suggested that the queen would not interfere in matters of doctrine. The Thirty-Nine Articles, enacted in 1563, provided an institutional framework for subsequent relations between state and church in England. The landed elite, strengthening its control of Parliament during Elizabeth's reign, generally supported the Church of England.

Some English Protestants wanted to carry the reforms farther than Elizabeth's religious settlement. They sought to eliminate from the Church of England what some members considered vestiges of elaborate Catholic ceremonies, such as baptismal crosses, altar rails before which the faithful knelt while receiving communion, elaborate priestly garb, and stained-glass windows.

Puritanism, the English version of Calvinism, first emerged in the late 1550s as a dissident force within the Church of England. Puritans were drawn primarily from the middle and lower classes. They insisted on a simplified but more intense religion based on individual conscience, the direct authority of the Holy Scriptures, and a community of belief in which preaching played a preeminent role. Although a few Puritans served as bishops in the Church of England, others wanted the Church of England to be separate from the English monarchy. The Tudor monarchy, on the other hand, wanted to make the Church serve its secular goals of national glory, prosperity, and public order.

A modest Catholic revival, aided by the arrival of Catholic Jesuit missionaries from the continent, accentuated religious divisions in England. Royal religious policies became harsher. Dissident Protestants suffered persecution along with Catholics. A Jesuit missionary was tortured to death on the rack in 1581, and six years later the first Puritan was executed for having spoken in Parliament on behalf of free speech in the name of his religion.

Since Elizabeth had no heirs, the Catholic Mary Stuart stood next in line for succession to the English throne. After her husband King Francis II of France died in 1560, Mary returned to her native Scotland to assume the power that her mother wielded as regent until her death that same year. The Scottish Reformation had begun in earnest when the theologian John Knox (c. 1505–1572) returned home from Geneva to preach reform. Soon after coming to the throne of England, Eliza-

Mary, Queen of Scots.

beth had made peace with Scotland and France. But Elizabeth and Protestants worried that if Mary became queen of England, she would restore Catholicism to England. When Protestants forced Mary to abdicate the Scottish throne in 1568, she fled to England. Elizabeth kept her potential rival under virtual house arrest.

In 1569, Catholics in the moors and bogs of the isolated English north rebelled in the hope of putting Mary Stuart on the English throne, precipitating Elizabeth's order for her rival's imprisonment. The Catholic force marched southward, but hastily retreated upon learning that sizable English forces loyal to Elizabeth awaited them. English troops defeated a second Scottish army near the border between the two countries. Elizabeth ordered the execution of over 500 of the rebels. This "Northern Rising" ended in complete failure, and the Catholic Church's hopes for a successful Counter-Reformation in England were finally dashed. Pope Pius V excommunicated Elizabeth in 1570 from the Church to which she did not wish to belong, removing the queen's Catholic subjects from the obligation of obedience to her and encouraging several more plots against her. Two years later, French Catholics undertook the Saint Bartholomew's Day Massacre of Protestants in Paris (see Chapter 4), the horror of which firmed Elizabeth's resolve to resist Mary's claims to the throne at all costs. She then vowed to support the Dutch, most of whom were Protestant, in their rebellion against Catholic Spain. In 1583, she foiled a plot, which involved the Spanish and French embassies, to depose her in favor of Mary Stuart.

Four years later, under pressure from Parliament, Elizabeth ordered Mary Stuart's execution.

Elizabeth's Statemaking

The reach and efficiency of the English state increased under Elizabeth's guidance. Lords and other wealthy gentlemen served on the Privy Council, which consisted of between twelve and eighteen members drawn from the nobility, landed elite, and officers in the royal household. It oversaw the lord-lieutenants, a new office that gave noblemen control of local militia. England's queen, like her predecessors, used patronage to foster loyalty to the crown. The most desirable posts were at court, including those in the royal household. Some of these carried life tenures and a few were hereditary. In Elizabethan England, unlike France, churchmen did not serve in the highest offices of the realm. The most powerful officials at court, such as the Lord Chancellor, dispensed patronage by selecting officials and filling local positions in the counties. Closely tied to the satisfaction of the private interests of the landed elite, the office of the Exchequer resembled similar offices created by continental monarchs who did not have to contend with a representative body as powerful as the English Parliament, divided into the House of Lords and the House of Commons. Although it met during only three of the forty-five years of Elizabeth's reign, Parliament retained an important role in government because the crown needed its assent for new laws and new taxes.

Upon ascending the throne, Elizabeth found the crown's financial situation bleak. Revenues raised through taxation and customs dues were inadequate to finance the war against Spain and campaigns in Ireland. The sale of some royal lands, forced loans, the occasional seizure of a Spanish ship laden with silver or gold, and purveyance (the right of agents of the monarchy to buy food at below-market prices) could only be temporary expedients. The collection of "ship money" (a tax on ports, which the crown with dubious logic extended to inland towns as well) was extremely unpopular and generated resistance during the hard times of the 1590s. But by exercising frugality in the expenses of government and increasing taxation, the crown managed to replenish its coffers, another sign of a stronger and more efficient state, despite a decade and a half of expensive warfare against Spain. The English monarchy in the Elizabethan Age was relatively more efficient than that of Spain or France.

English nobles by the 1590s no longer had full-fledged private armies that could threaten the throne's monopoly on force. This contrasted with the situation in France during the same period, when the Guise and Bourbon families, among others, maintained their own armies in the wars of religion.

Foreign wars also served to increase the reach of central government in England. The second half of the sixteenth century brought regular training for the militia, which provided the bulk of troops as needed, along with gentlemen volunteers and cavalrymen still recruited by summons. During the last eighteen years of Elizabeth's reign, more than 100,000 soldiers were impressed into service for wars on the continent and to maintain English hegemony in Ireland. Lord-lieutenants assumed responsibility for troop levies in the counties. The vast majority who were conscripted as soldiers were the poorest of the poor—unfortunate men who happened to be at the wrong place at the wrong time when the press-gangs turned up to roll them out of taverns or even out of church and into the queen's service.

The monarchy imposed English law on northern England, Wales (which Henry VIII had absorbed into England), and Ireland. The emergence of a national market economy increasingly linked to London also played an important part in the nationalization of English political institutions. Within England, the sense of belonging to a nationality was certainly more advanced than anywhere on the continent. With the exception of part of Cornwall in southwestern England (where the Cornish language was spoken), the people of England spoke English, however great the variation in dialect and accents. A somewhat Anglicized Welsh elite began to send their sons to Oxford and Cambridge Universities.

The fact that Britain is an island may have made the English more xenophobic and precociously nationalistic than their continental counterparts. Strong traditions of local government and loyalties persisted in England, however, fueled by social differences and the overwhelming influence of wealthy local landed families. The county and parish remained the economic, social, and political universe of most people in England. The state still remained an abstraction until the tax collector or the press-gang arrived.

Demographic and Economic Expansion

In the last half of the sixteenth century, England emerged as a commercial and manufacturing power. The population of England and Wales grew rapidly, from about 2.5 million in the 1520s to more than 3.5 million in 1580, reaching about 4.5 million in 1610. Reduced mortality rates and increased fertility, the latter probably generated by expanding work opportunities in manufacturing and farming (leading to earlier marriage and more children), help explain this rapid rise in population. While epidemics and plague occasionally took their toll, the people in England still suffered them less often than did those on the continent. Furthermore, despite the wrenching effects of the English Reformation, the country had been spared the protracted wars of religion that occurred in France and Central Europe.

English towns grew as migrants arrived in sufficient numbers to overcome high mortality rates caused by catastrophic health conditions stemming from poor sanitation. London became the second largest city in the world, its population rising from about 50,000 in the 1520s to 200,000 in 1600, and jumping its walls to 375,000 in 1650 (only Edo [Tokyo] was larger). The next biggest towns in England lagged far behind: Norwich, Newcastle, and

Bristol boasted only about 25,000 people each. About 8 percent of the population of England lived in London by the mid-seventeenth century.

England provides the primary example of the expansion of agricultural production well before the "agricultural revolution" of the eighteenth and nineteenth centuries. A larger population stimulated increased demand for food, as well as for manufactured goods. Through crop specialization, English agriculture became more efficient and market oriented than almost anywhere on the continent. Between 1450 and 1650, the yield of grain per acre increased by at least 30 percent. In sharp contrast with farming in Spain, English landowners brought more dense marshes and woodlands into cultivation.

The great estates of the English nobility largely remained intact, and many wealthy landowners aggressively increased the size of their holdings. Timely marriages also increased the size of landed estates. Primogeniture (the full inheritance of land by the eldest son) helped keep land from being subdivided. Younger sons of independent landowners left behind the family land to find other respectable occupations, often in the church or in urban trades. Larger farms were conducive to more commercialized farming at a time when an expanding population pushed up demand and prices. Some landowners turned a part of their land into pastureland for sheep in order to supply the developing woolens trade.

Some of the great landlords, as well as yeomen (farmers whose holdings and security of land tenure guaranteed their prosperity and status), reorganized their holdings in the interest of efficiency. Open-field farmers selected crops in response to the growing London market. Between 1580 and 1620, in a quest for greater profits, landlords raised rents and altered conditions of land tenure in their favor, preferring shorter leases and forcing tenants to pay an "entry fee" before they would agree to rent them land. They evicted those who could not afford their new, more onerous terms. They also pushed tenants toward more productive farming methods, including crop rotation. During hard years, the peasants might be forced to sell their land, while wealthy neighbors could survive with relative ease.

Many landowners utilized "enclosure" to expand their holdings. Parliamentary acts of enclosure aided landowners by allowing them to buy wastelands, consolidate arable strips of land, and divide up common lands and pasture areas. The enclosure of common lands, sold by villages to the highest bidders, over the long run would spell the end of the common rights of villagers to use the land, and the removal of tenants in order to consolidate estates marked a push toward "agrarian individualism." Enclosure drew considerable resistance, for it left many of the rural poor fenced out of common land on which they had depended for firewood, gleaning, and pasturing. Thomas More's *Utopia* (1516), which describes an imaginary island where all people live in peace and harmony, blamed England's economic inequities on enclosure. Riots against enclosure were widespread in the

In this seventeenth-century woodcut, a country wife engages in domestic industry, part of the expansion of textile manufacturing that transformed England's economy.

1590s, a decade in which popular tax rebellions shook France, Spain, Austria, and Ukraine, among other places, and again in the 1620s and 1630s.

England's exceptional economic development drew upon the country's natural resources, including iron, timber, and, above all, coal, extracted in far greater quantities than anywhere on the continent. New industrial methods expanded the production of iron, brass, and pewter in and around Birmingham. But, primarily, textile manufacturing developed the English economy. Woolens (which accounted for about 80 percent of exports), worsteds (sturdy yarn spun from combed wool fibers), and cloth found eager buyers in England as well as on the continent. Moreover, late in the sixteenth century, as English merchants began making forays across the Atlantic, these textiles were also sold in the New World. Cloth manufacturers undercut production by urban craftsmen by "putting out" work to the villages and farms of the countryside. In such domestic industry, poor rural women and girls could do spinning and carding (combing fibers in preparation for spinning) of wool in their homes.

The English textile trade was closely tied to Antwerp, where workers dyed English cloth. Sir Thomas Gresham, a sixteenth-century entrepreneur, became England's representative in the bustling river port. Wining and dining the city's merchants and serving as a royal ambassador, he so enhanced the reputation of English merchants that they could operate on credit, no small achievement in the sixteenth century. At home, he convinced the government to end special privileges accorded the Hanseatic cities of northern Germany and to authorize lucrative English trading monopolies. Gresham's shrewd sense of finance saved the relatively meager royal coffers from bankruptcy on several occasions through the negotiation of timely loans.

Gresham advised the crown to explore the economic possibilities of the Americas. This led to the first concerted English efforts at colonization. Far more than Spanish colonialism, English overseas ventures were undertaken with commercial profits in mind. When the Spanish, hoping to crush the Dutch rebellion that began against their rule in 1566, closed the Scheldt River, English merchants responded by seeking new, more distant outlets for trade across the oceans. From 1577 to 1580, Sir Francis Drake (1540–1596), an explorer and privateer, sailed around Cape Horn in his search for a passage that would permit commercial ties with Asia. Sir Walter Raleigh (1554–1618), a Renaissance scholar, poet, historian, and explorer, said of Drake, "A single purpose animates all his exploits and the chart of his movements is like a cord laced and knotted round the throat of the Spanish monarchy."

English Society in the Tudor Period

English society under the Tudors reflected what a churchman writing in 1577 called "degrees of people," that is, sharply defined social groups. Contemporaries sometimes simplified English social structure by dividing people into the ranks of "gentlemen," "the middling sort," and "the poor." Ownership of land in the form of estates—inherited or acquired—conferred status, or "gentility," in England. All nobles (that is, with a noble title passed on by inheritance) were gentry, but the vast majority of gentry were not titled nobles or peers in the House of Lords. Gentry status came from the ownership of land, and gentry dominated the House of Commons. In exchange for military service, the crown granted titles that were inherited by the eldest son.

The nobility and gentry dominated England for more than the next three centuries from their country manors that commanded the surrounding countryside. Ordinary people addressed the nobleman as "your lordship" and the wealthy gentleman as "sir"; poor women curtsied to them as a mark of respect. Village bells were rung in their honor when they passed through. Wealthy landowners mediated in village disputes and provided some charity in exchange for deference. (One man of means chatted with "his people" in the street: "I asked a poor woman how many children she had. She answered 'Six.' 'Here,' I said, 'is a sixpence for them.' 'No, sir,' she said proudly, not realizing the gentleman was offering a gift, 'I will not sell my children.'") The education of gentlemen at Oxford and Cambridge Universities or through private tutoring helped shape common cultural values and social homogeneity among what was increasingly becoming a national elite.

An Elizabethan country house, late sixteenth century.

Yeomen stood beneath the gentry on the social ladder, but they could move up if they were able to purchase and maintain large estates, and they could vote in parliamentary elections.

Within the upper reaches of the "middling sort" were men considered "of sufficiency," even if they were not lords or gentlemen. They were believed by virtue of steady income to be worthy of assuming some kind of public responsibility. England's precocious economic boom in the sixteenth century increased the wealth and status of merchants and manufacturers. Wealthy merchants and artisans from the guilds served on town councils, perpetuating their influence from generation to generation.

Lower on the social scale were smallholders, farmers who owned just enough land to get by ("husbandmen"), poor clergymen depending for survival upon small fees rendered for their services, and ordinary craftsmen. The majority of the population owned neither land nor skills, and thus lay at the bottom of the social hierarchy. Most laboring families lived in rented one-room cottages. Cottagers, employed as farmhands but also often employed as spinners, weavers, carders, or nail makers, lived on bread, cheese, lard, soup, beer, and garden greens, occasionally supplemented by harvest-time feasts provided by their employers. Farm servants lived in Spartan accommodations. In London and smaller towns, the urban poor struggled to survive as common laborers, porters, and sweepers, or in other menial occupations, living in squalor in whatever pitiful lodgings they could afford, or, for many, living without shelter.

During the sixteenth century, the rich got richer—and lived that way, dressing and eating differently from the poor. Responding to complaints that "a Babylon of confusion" might blur class lines because anyone with money could purchase the most elegant clothing, Parliament had earlier in the century decreed that only dukes, earls, and barons could wear sable cloth woven of gold and embroidered with gold and silver. Ben Jonson (1572–1637), author of scurrilous satires on London life, wrote that to become recognized as a gentleman, a man had to go to London, "where at your first appearance 'twere good you turned four or five hundred acres of your best land into two or three trunks of apparel."

Cardinal Wolsey had earlier attempted to moderate the dietary excesses of wealthy people, including the high clergy. Copying sumptuary regulations that could be found throughout Europe since the Middle Ages, he specified the number of separate dinner courses that people of various ranks might consume, with the largest number—nine—reserved for cardinals like himself. The poor, however, ate no such meals. Soaring food and lodging prices sapped the meager earnings of craftsmen, landless cottagers, rural laborers, and unskilled workers.

There was, to be sure, some degree of social mobility in Tudor England as new economic opportunities brought greater prosperity to gentry, yeomen, merchants, and manufacturers. Some yeomen achieved gentry status. The interests and lifestyles of the middling sort gradually moved closer to those of gentlemen and their families. Some apprentices became independent masters within their trades. But social advancement remained relatively rare among the poor, whose numbers were rapidly expanding along with their impoverishment.

The Quest for Public Order

After almost a century of inflation accentuated by a rising population, harvest failures in the 1590s brought the period of economic expansion to an abrupt halt in England. Never had there seemed to be so many poor and hungry people on the roads, dressed in rags, sleeping in fields, searching for wild berries or edible roots, and begging, just trying to get by. "They lie in the streets," one man of means observed, "and are permitted to die like dogs or beasts without any mercy or compassion showed them at all."

Ordinary people sometimes took matters into their own hands. Food riots spread throughout much of England, as the poor seized grain and sold it at what they considered a reasonable price. Women usually made up the majority of participants in the food riots because it fell to them to try to make ends meet at the market. Such disturbances increased the resolve of the state to maintain order at all costs.

Punishing a man by exposing him at a pillory, sixteenth-century England.

The prosecution of serious crimes increased rapidly during Elizabeth's reign, peaking between 1590 and 1620. Vagrancy was the most prevalent of these offenses, as people took to the road in search of food. Vagrants were arrested and placed in stocks for three days, before being sent home. Thefts rose in number and audacity. A contemporary estimated that there were twenty-three different categories of thieves and swindlers, including "hookers," who snatched linen and clothes with a long pole from windows, "priggers of prancers" (horse thieves), and "Abraham men," who "feign themselves to be mad." The theft of goods worth more than twelve shillings could bring the death penalty, but more often offenders were publicly whipped, branded, mutilated by having an ear cut off, or sent to serve as oarsmen in the galley ships. Women were often treated more harshly than men, unless they were pregnant. Although only about 10 percent of those convicted of capital crimes were actually executed, such punishment was particularly brutal, including slow strangulation by hanging and being slowly crushed to death by weights.

The English upper classes, convinced that most crimes went unpunished, became obsessed with maintaining order, a fact reflected in several of Shakespeare's plays, in which ordinary people appear as potential threats to social order. Many Elizabethans believed that social order depended on the maintenance of social hierarchy and the securing of obedience to the moral authority of government. Thus, the Tudors formulated a doctrine of obedience to authority, basing their arguments on religious teaching.

Elizabethan literature and drama constantly returned to the theme of a moral law based upon the necessity of social order. In Shakespeare's *The History of Troilus and Cressida*, Ulysses proclaims:

> The heavens themselves, the planets, and this centre
> Observe degree, priority, and place,
> [. . .]But when the planets
> In evil mixture to disorder wander,
> What plagues and what portents, what mutiny!
> [. . .]And hark what discord follows. . . .

Many in the middle and upper classes believed that the slightest offense against the monarchy contained the seeds of rebellion; in 1576, a woman was burned at the stake for saying that Elizabeth was "baseborn and not born to the crown." Fear of disturbances and challenges to authority contributed to the development of a sense of national consciousness of England's elite, just as the defeat of Spain's Armada in 1588 led to pride in being both Protestant and English.

In 1598, Parliament passed the first "poor law," followed by another in 1601. These laws recognized for the first time the principle that the needy ought to receive some sort of assistance from the community in which they live. Justices of the peace, under the supervision of the clergy, were to oversee the distribution of assistance to the poor. The poor laws also specified the establishment of poor houses for the incarceration of the poor who would not or could not work (including the aged, sick, and insane).

The Elizabethan Theater

In 1576, two theaters opened in London, followed by others in a number of provincial towns. Putting aside the repertory of religious allegories and miracle and morality plays that had been staged in royal castles, country manor houses, or entire towns, they staked their survival on their ability to attract audiences that would pay to see actors perform. More than 2,000 different plays were staged in London between 1580 and 1640, mainly romances and dramas. During that period, more than 300 playwrights produced enough work to keep 100 acting companies working in London or touring provincial towns.

The plays of William Shakespeare (1564–1616) reflected uncertainty, ambivalence, and even disillusionment about contemporary English society. He was born in Stratford-on-Avon, where his father made gloves and was able to provide him with a primary school education. Shakespeare moved with his wife to London to become an actor, and in the late 1580s he began to write plays. He found first patronage and then unparalleled

(*Left*) William Shakespeare (*Right*) The Globe Theater, London, 1616.

success, angering rivals. Shakespeare became part owner and actor in the Lord Chamberlain's Men, an acting company of the Globe theater, which held an audience of 3,000 and hence was the largest of London's six private theaters. Seats at such theaters cost at least six times more than the cheapest tickets at the public theaters, which included places for the "penny stinkards" who stood in the uncovered pit below the stage.

Audiences shouted for what they liked and hooted at what they did not. Fights were not infrequent, both inside and outside of the theater. The playwright Christopher Marlowe (1564–1593) died in a brawl in an inn under mysterious circumstances; the actor and playwright Ben Jonson killed another actor in a duel. Because of their rowdy reputations, most London theaters stood outside the city walls. London officials sometimes tried to close down the public theaters because they thought that disease spread easily among assembled crowds and because of complaints about profanity and lewdness on stage.

An Emerging Empire of Trade

During the later years of Elizabeth's reign, bitter battles for influence and power within Elizabeth's inner circle belied the appearance of relative harmony. Elizabeth died in 1603, the forty-fifth year of her reign, leaving England a substantially more unified, effectively ruled, and powerful state that had begun to look across the oceans in the interest of expanding trade. Over the next few decades, England slowly began to develop a trading and then settlement empire in North America—as did France—while gradually extending its influence across other oceans, as well. This increasingly brought England into competition with France, which began to colonize Nouvelle France (now Quebec).

The development of English overseas trade allowed London to replace Antwerp as Europe's leading center of trade. London's Merchant Adventurers competed with Spanish and Portuguese rivals for spices and other products that fetched increasingly handsome prices at home. They traded textiles and other manufactured goods for slaves, gold, and ivory from the African and Brazilian coasts. Above all, West Indian sugar from Barbados entered the English domestic market in lucrative quantities. English merchants traded in India and Indonesia. In 1600, Queen Elizabeth chartered the East India Company with the goal of competing with Dutch traders.

To compete with the Spanish, who already had a colonial empire that stretched several thousand miles from what is now the southern United States to Tierra del Fuego at the southern tip of South America, Raleigh sought to establish a colony in Virginia between 1584 and 1587. Despite the failure of a first settlement on Roanoke Island, a permanent colony finally succeeded at Jamestown in Virginia, a full century after Spain took possession of its colonies in Mexico and Latin America. Tobacco began to reach England in the first decades of the seventeenth century. Tobacco was, to an extent, the equivalent of what silver was to the Spanish Empire, because of its great role in the economic development of the English colonies. Whereas the Spanish arrived in the Americas as conquerors, the English came intent on developing trade. Gradually, the English began to arrive in North America as permanent settlers. The Virginia Company, a joint-stock company, received in 1606 a royal charter to settle the region of Chesapeake Bay. The Virginia Company brought the first slaves to North America ten years later, although it was not until late in the century that a full slave system emerged. In 1625 the English throne proclaimed Virginia part of "Our Royal Empire." The Puritan settlement in Plymouth followed in 1620, and the Massachusetts Bay Company received its charter in 1629. Unlike the case of Spain, where colonization followed the impulse of a strongly centralized state and the Roman Catholic Church, English colonies reflected the Reformation, as Protestants, including Protestant dissidents like the Puritans, led the way as they sought religious freedom for themselves. In contrast to the Spanish Empire, English America remained extremely rural, despite the slow growth of Boston and New York (6,000 residents and 4,500, respectively, in 1692, at a time when Mexico City already boasted more than 100,000 people). The rising English population encouraged more emigrants to the New World, despite the high cost of the difficult trip across the Atlantic. In the developing colonies, settlers moved westward to take available land, pushing Native Americans farther back. Disease, along with guns, helped them. John Winthrop, the governor of Massachusetts, noted in 1634, "For the natives, they are all near dead of the smallpox, so as the Lord hath cleared our title to what we possess."

The English arrive in what would become Virginia.

Unlike that of the Spanish Empire's colonies in the Americas, the absorption of the emerging colonies of North America into what became an English and then a British Empire (following England's formal union with Scotland as Great Britain in 1707) proceeded at a much slower and unpredictable pace, following the vicissitudes of trans-Atlantic trade instead of conquest and tight incorporation into England. The number of ships that went back and forth between England and the American colonies doubled to more than 1,000 per year between the 1680s and the 1730s, a round-trip voyage of 100 days under the best of circumstances. There was no English equivalent of the Council of the Indies, which oversaw the Spanish Empire in the Americas. In England's North American colonies, administrative institutions, representative assemblies—eight of which had been established by 1640—and judicial systems developed at their own pace without a phalanx of royal officials. The local administration of the English colonies continued to be influenced by regional differences, without the centralized distribution of resources that characterized the Spanish Empire. A sense of political participation developed in the English colonies, at least among men of property. With this went the growing sense that the colonies were a place of liberty, as many colonists arrived seeking religious freedom. Tensions were almost inevitable between the colonies, with their emerging sense of liberty and separateness, and Britain, which tried to extract more revenues from the colonies (see Chapter 11).

Again in contrast to Spain, which developed an empire marked by the firm alliance of Church altar and an authoritarian throne, the English felt less of a mission to bring Christianity to indigenous peoples. Moreover, unlike Catholicism in the case of the Spanish Empire, the established English religion, Anglicanism, was just one religion among others in the English colonies. By 1675, only an estimated 2,500 Native Americans had been converted to Christianity. In the Spanish Empire, many colonists undertook inter-ethnic marriages and thus helped bring about a considerable mixed population, allowing social mobility for a select few. In contrast, English settlers from the beginning sought to exclude and push back the indigenous population. Fearful of cultural mixing and of those they continued to consider "savages," most of whom showed no interest in assimilation, the settlers drove them farther west.

THE DECLINE OF SPAIN

The "decline" of the overstretched Spanish Empire was first noted in 1600. Had the Spain of the Catholic kings fallen from God's favor? Castilians themselves still regarded Spain as a haven of peace and prosperity compared to the rest of Europe, which was wracked by religious wars.

The Dutch Revolt

The decline of Spanish power began with the Dutch revolt. In the Netherlands, Dutch nobles and officials resented higher taxes imposed by the Spanish crown. Above all, many Dutch were angered by the Spanish king's attempt to promote the Catholic Reformation by imposing the Inquisition in a land where most people were now Calvinists. In the early 1560s, resistance first began against the presence of Spanish garrisons.

In 1567, Philip II appointed the duke of Alba (1507–1582) to restore order in the north with 10,000 Spanish troops. The ruthless Castilian ordered the execution of prominent Calvinist nobles on the central square of Brussels, established military courts, imposed heavy new taxes, and virtually destroyed self-government in the Netherlands. But Alba's reign of terror as governor also helped transform the resistance of Dutch nobles and officials, led by William of Orange (1533–1584), into a national revolt.

In the Southern Netherlands (Belgium), Alba's Council of Troubles, known to the Dutch as the "Council of Blood," executed thousands of people from 1567 to 1573. In 1572, rebellion became full-fledged insurrection. Spanish troops dominated on land, but Dutch ships controlled the seas. When a Spanish army undertook a siege of Leiden, southwest of Amsterdam, the people of the town opened the dikes, and Dutch ships sailed over the rushing waters to drive the Spaniards away. But Spanish victories

Prince William of Orange leading the revolt in the Netherlands against higher taxes from the Spanish crown. The Dutch revolt signified the decline of Spanish power.

in the Southern Netherlands followed. There Catholic nobles began to have second thoughts about continuing a struggle launched by Dutch Protestants. They detached the southern provinces from the rebellious federation. In 1579, the Dutch provinces formed the Union of Utrecht, and two years later they declared their independence from Spain as the Dutch United Provinces.

For the moment, Spain, which was also at war against France, could supply its armies because Alba's armies had recaptured some of the Southern Netherlands, while Philip II maintained peace with England. As the Dutch revolt wore on, however, the problems of fighting a war a thousand miles away plagued the Spanish king. Military contractors or entrepreneurs recruited mercenaries; Italians, Burgundians, Germans, and Walloons made up much of the Spanish army.

Spanish routes for troops, supplies, and bullion to the Netherlands had to be maintained through a combination of diplomatic charm, cunning, and coercion. As allegiances and the fortunes of war eliminated first the Palatinate and then Alsace and Lorraine as routes through which armies could pass, the Spanish forged the "Spanish Road" as a military corridor (see Map 5.3). It began in Genoa, went overland across the Alps, and then passed through Lombardy and Piedmont, Geneva, Franche-Comté, Lorraine and,

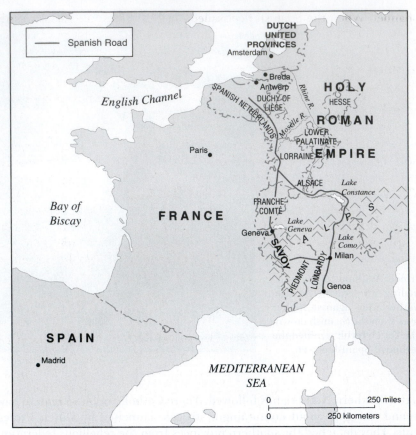

MAP 5.3 THE SPANISH ROAD   The route taken by the Spanish armies, supplies, and money to the Netherlands was long and difficult, as it passed through mountainous terrain and many states.

finally, the duchy of Liège, with Spanish agents assuring supplies along the way.

Spain's acute problems of recruiting and supply were exacerbated by dubious efforts to save money—for instance, charging sharpshooters for powder and shot. The army's guarantee to carry out the written wills made by soldiers also seems to have been a curiously self-defeating approach to inspiring confidence. Desertions and mutinies—the largest involving non-Spanish troops—occurred with ever more frequency as troops demanded payment of back wages, better and more regular food, and decent medical care. By 1577, the Spanish army in the Netherlands, unpaid for months, had dwindled in size from 60,000 to no more than 8,000 men.

Throughout the long war, the superior Dutch fleet kept the Spanish ships in port. The ships of "sea beggars," as they were called, harassed Spanish ships. The English navy, allied with the Dutch in 1586, controlled the English

Channel. When the Spanish fleet sailed north in 1588, the result was the disastrous defeat of the Armada. At the beginning of the seventeenth century, the Dutch gradually fell back behind protective town fortifications and natural barriers formed by rivers. The war became a series of long Spanish sieges against frontier towns defended by brick fortifications, bastions, and moats—a defensive system that had its origins with the Italian city-states. With the defense having a marked advantage, towns could be conquered only by being starved out.

France withdrew from the war in 1598, and England withdrew six years later. A truce between the Spanish and the Dutch, signed in 1609, lapsed in 1621. In Holland the "war party" won the upper hand. Led by Maurice of Nassau (1567–1625), the son of William of Orange, who had been assassinated in 1584, the war party appealed to Calvinist religious orthodoxy by calling for a crusade against Catholicism that would also free the Southern Netherlands from Spanish rule. Army officers and merchant traders wanted to keep the struggle against Spain going as long as possible. It dragged on, draining the Spanish economy.

Economic Decline

Economic decline—above all, that of Castile in the middle decades of the seventeenth century—underlay Spain's fall from a position of European domination. But decline is, of course, relative. Spain remained an important state. Yet its population, which had risen to well over 6 million people during the last half of the sixteenth century, fell by almost a quarter to about 5.2 million by the middle of the seventeenth century, as harvest failures, plague, smallpox, war, and emigration took their tolls.

The "price revolution," the sharp rise in inflation during the sixteenth century in Europe, may well have affected Spain less than some parts of northern Europe, but it still had adverse effects on the Spanish monarchy. Gold and silver from the Americas accelerated inflation by increasing the supply of money, as did royal monetary policies of currency debasement. The monarchy, which had declared bankruptcy in 1557, suspended payments in 1575, and again in 1596, renegotiating loans at more favorable rates. From 1568 to 1598, Spain had five times the military expenditures of the Dutch, English, and French combined. The economy slipped into stagnation. To one noble it already seemed that "the ship is sinking."

Forced to borrow money from foreign bankers at disadvantageous interest rates, the Spanish state attempted to find new sources of revenue. To raise funds, the crown imposed a tithe, or assessment of a tenth of the most valuable piece of real estate in each parish, and in 1590 the Castilian Cortes agreed to an extraordinary tax assessed on towns. An excise (sales) tax was imposed on consumption. This undermined the economy by encouraging the middle class to abandon business in favor of the acquisition of perpetual privileges—and thus tax exemptions—as they obtained noble status.

The monarchy's massive expulsion of the Moriscos in 1609 proved counter-productive. The king succumbed to pressure from the Catholic Church and from wealthy families eager to seize Moorish land. The region of Valencia lost one-third of its population, including many skilled craftsmen and farmers.

Nobles added the lands of indebted peasants to their large estates (*latifundia*), but they showed little interest in increasing the productivity of their land, in contrast to their English counterparts. They turned fields into pastureland or simply left them untended. Farmers were hampered by a state-imposed fixed maximum for grain prices, which discouraged ambitious agricultural initiatives. Spain became dependent on imported grain. Royal policies also favored sheepherding over farming—because it was easier to collect taxes on sheep than on agricultural produce. But fine woolens manufacturing suffered from competition with foreign textile imports, especially lighter cloth brought from France and the Netherlands.

"Conquered by you, the New World has conquered you in turn, and has weakened and exhausted your ancient vigor," a Flemish scholar wrote a friend in Spain. The Spanish colonies themselves became a financial drain on the crown because of the cost of administering and defending them. The flow of Latin American silver, which had paid less than a quarter of the crown's colonial and military expenses, slowed to a trickle beginning in the 1620s. Spain had never really developed commerce with the empire to the same extent as the English, who had made trade the basis of their maritime empire, enormously developing the colonial market. In the Spanish Empire, the market for Spanish goods, already limited by the poverty of the colonies, shrank with the precipitous decline in the Indian population (caused, above all, by disease; see Chapter 1). Unlike in the English colonies, emigration to the New World from Spain had slowed to a trickle by the early eighteenth century, in part because economic opportunities in Spanish-held territories were relatively limited. This was compounded by the prohibition of non-Spanish migration to Spain's American colonies. The colonies had also developed their own basic agricultural and artisanal production and relied far less on Spanish goods. The Atlantic ports of northern Castile suffered competition not only from Seville and Cádiz, but from Spain's own colonies, and above all, from England and the Netherlands.

Although the burden of taxes in Castile increased by four times between 1570 and 1670, the Spanish crown proved less efficient in collecting taxes than the monarchs of France and England. Increased taxes on the poor generated more discontent than income. Spain's Italian subjects resisted contributing money for distant wars that did not concern them. No more tax income came to Spain from the Netherlands.

Contemporary Spaniards lapsed into a morose acceptance of decline. The novelist Miguel de Cervantes (1547–1616) had fought and been wounded

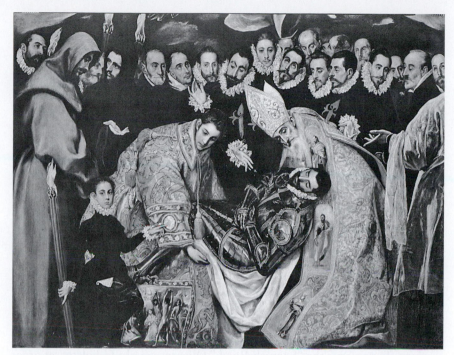

El Greco's *Burial of the Count Orgaz*, 1586.

with the king's armies at the Battle of Lepanto (1571). Several years later, he was captured by Turkish pirates and spent five years as a slave before managing to return to Spain. *Don Quixote* (1605–1615) is on one level a humorous tale of a zany noble intent on bringing true chivalry back to Spain, accompanied by his sensible, subservient squire, Sancho Panza. On a deeper level, however, it is the story of national disillusionment in the face of perceived national decline. The dramatist Pedro Calderón de la Barca (1600–1681) portrayed in his plays the floundering Spanish aristocracy struggling to preserve its honor. Nobles and churchmen, the two pillars of Spain, purchased the paintings of the increasingly gloomy Greek-born artist El Greco (1541–1614). His *Burial of the Count Orgaz* (1586) shows figures gazing up at a vision of celestial glory, the splendor of which is heightened by the dismal scenes below them on earth.

An Empire Spread Too Thin

Spain's mounting economic problems were exacerbated by the fact that the empire's interests were spread so widely, not only in Europe, but across the seas. Philip IV (1605–1665), who succeeded to the throne in 1621, was intelligent and had a keen interest in the arts, but he was stubborn. He chose as his chief adviser Gaspar de Guzmán, the duke of Olivares (1587–1645), an Andalusian noble whose family had, like Spain itself, suffered reverses. The short, fiery, and increasingly obese Olivares sketched ambitious plans to shape the rebirth of Spanish might. Confronted with the economic strength of the Dutch rebels, as well as that of the English, Olivares sensed that Spain could not remain a power without a marked economic resurgence. "We must devote all our efforts," he had written, "to turning Spaniards into merchants," like the English. The Count Duke, as he was called, mastered his master, convincing the indolent king that only hard work and reform could restore the glories of the not-so-distant past. He would tutor the king, whose chamber pot he once ceremoniously kissed, in the fine art of monarchy.

The Count Duke espoused the growth of monarchical power and state centralization. His motto "one king, one law, one money" generated resistance, in the latter case because of the by then notorious instability of the Castilian currency. Olivares sought to subject all of Spain to the laws and royal administration of Castile, promising the king that, if he did so, he would become the most powerful prince in the world.

Olivares wanted to force Dutch capitulation to restore the monarchy's reputation, afraid that the Dutch rebellion might begin a chain reaction that would destroy the empire. He persuaded the king to allow the truce with the Dutch to lapse in 1621, thus necessitating massive expenses for land and sea warfare. To preserve the "Spanish Road," Olivares sought to bolster, at great expense, Spanish interests in northern Italy and in Austria. But France cut the Spanish supply routes in Savoy in 1622 and then in Alsace nine years later. Intermittent hostilities with France lasted from 1628 to 1631.

Spain could now ill afford such conflicts. In 1628, Dutch pirates captured a Spanish fleet loaded with silver. This enormous loss made it imperative that the crown find new resources with which to wage war. But for the first time, Castile's monarchs could not establish credit with foreign investors. Increased taxation, the flotation of short-term loans through bonds, the sale of yet more privileges, and the imposition of new financial obligations on Aragon and the Italian territories all proved inadequate to the task of financing expensive wars.

Its interests gravely overextended, Spain's position weakened. English ships began to nip at its imperial interests in the Americas. Dutch warships took on the proud Spanish galleons in the West Indies. Three decades of intermittent warfare with France began in 1635, as the Thirty Years' War (see Chapter 4) became a struggle between competing dynasties. As more and more bullion from the Americas had to be diverted to pay military expenses in the Netherlands and Italy, the monarchy demanded new contributions from Catalonia and Portugal (which had been merged with Spain in 1580), as Spain had assumed the expensive and ultimately extremely damaging responsibility for protecting Portuguese shipping around the world. Tumultuous tax riots broke out in Portugal, where the upper classes resisted Spanish authority.

Olivares's decision to demand more taxes from Catalonia proved fateful. Faced with resistance, he ordered the arrest of several Catalan leaders. Catalan nobles put aside their differences, and a full-scale revolt against Castilian rule began in 1640. Catalan and French forces together defeated the Spanish army. A year later, Andalusian nobles were foiled in a plot to create an independent kingdom there. Nobles in Madrid hatched plots against Olivares. Portugal reasserted its independence in 1640. Three years later, Philip packed off the despondent Olivares into exile.

However, the illusion of Don Quixote was maintained—that the restoration of traditional aristocratic and ecclesiastical values would restore Spanish power and prestige. Olivares established two court academies intended to train young nobles in the art of government. Heeding the advice of churchmen, he censored the theater and books, prohibiting certain kinds of fancy clothing and long hair. Over the long run, Spanish rulers weakened parliamentary traditions. Soon the Cortes was convoked only on ceremonial occasions. The crown continued to extend its reach and solidify its authority against possible provincial rebellions. In Catalonia, Barcelona surrendered to royal troops in 1652. Catalan nobles accepted the supremacy of the crown in exchange for an affirmation of social hierarchy and royal protection against ordinary Catalans who resented their privileges. The Aragonese nobles, too, accepted this compromise.

Ironically, given the intense perception of Spanish decline, the last years of Philip IV and the reign of his pathetic successor, Charles II (ruled 1665–1700), sustained a period of great cultural accomplishment in the arts and literature. But this, too, may have been generated by the prevailing mood of introspection. Olivares put dramatists and a small host of other writers to work in the name of glorifying the monarchy and imparting a sense of purpose that he hoped would revive Spain. Philip IV added more than 2,000 canvases to what already was a rich royal art collection, including many by Italian masters. He covered the palace walls with grandiose paintings of battle scenes. Diego Velázquez (1599–1660), the court painter, undertook forty somber portraits of the vain king, a commentary on the monarchy's fading glory and disillusionment.

King Philip IV of Spain.

In the meantime, the Dutch rebels, aided by increased commercial prosperity, had fought the Spanish armies to a draw. The Treaty of Münster, which was part of the Westphalia settlement of 1648 that ended the Thirty Years' War, officially recognized Dutch independence after a struggle that had lasted three-quarters of a century. The provinces of the Southern Netherlands, which were overwhelmingly Catholic, remained a Habsburg possession.

The Spanish monarchy, overstretched by its vast empire in the Americas, had not learned that it could not fight effectively on a variety of fronts. In contrast, the French monarchy was concentrating its efforts in Italy, for the moment realizing the wisdom of fighting on one front at a time. Thus, subsequent Spanish victories in the north against French armies were not enough, for when the French turned their attention to Spain, they held their own. The Treaty of the Pyrenees, signed between France and Spain in 1659, established the border between these countries that has lasted, with only a few minor changes, until this day. Spain also gave up Milan to Austria, and Naples and Sicily to the Italian Bourbon dynasty. The Portuguese, aided by the English, turned back several halfhearted invasions by Spanish armies, and in 1668 Spain recognized Portugal's independence. Ten years later, France occupied the Franche-Comté, the last major Spanish holding in northern Europe. By 1680, when the depression that had lasted almost a century ended, Spain was no longer a great power. This was because of agricultural and manufacturing decline, to be sure, but, above all, because the Spanish crown had overreached its ability to maintain its vast and distant empire.

CONCLUSION

The development of trade across the Atlantic Ocean to the Americas was part of European economic expansion during the sixteenth century. Following the union of the crowns of Castile and Aragon, Spain grew into a great power. Philip II expanded the Spanish Empire, which, in the Americas stretched from what is now the southwestern United States to the southern tip of Latin America, and in Europe included the Netherlands and several Italian states. In England, the Tudor monarchy overcame the country's religious divisions in the wake of the English Reformation to strengthen its authority. In this, it resembled the ruling Valois dynasty of France, another "new monarchy" that had enhanced its reach, efficiency, and prestige. Burgeoning trade, manufacturing, and agriculture in the Elizabethan Age underlay England's growing prosperity, even as social polarization, reflected in the crises of the 1590s, became more apparent.

The surprising English naval defeat of the Spanish Armada in 1588 symbolized not only the rise of England but in some ways anticipated the decline of Spanish power. Spain's rulers had expanded their vast empire and imperial interests beyond the ability of the state to sustain them. When silver from the Americas slowed to a trickle, Spain's own limited natural resources and inability to collect taxes efficiently, combined with demographic stagnation that began early in the seventeenth century, as well as, arguably, resistance from Aragon and Catalonia, prevented a revival of Spanish preeminence. The long revolt of the Netherlands ended with recognition of Dutch independence in 1648. That the Dutch Republic and England, two trading nations, had emerged as European powers reflected the shift of economic primacy to northwestern Europe.

CHAPTER 6

ENGLAND AND THE DUTCH REPUBLIC IN THE SEVENTEENTH CENTURY

England and the Dutch Republic were anomalies in the seventeenth century. At a time when aggressive European monarchs were forging absolute states (see Chapter 7), these two seafaring, trading nations maintained representative governments.

The Stuart monarchs' flirtation with absolutism in England brought bitter discord, resistance, and civil war. In the Dutch Republic, which had earned its independence in 1648 after a long war against Spanish absolute rule, the prosperous merchants who dominated the economic and political life of the country brushed aside the absolutist challenge of the House of Orange, which wanted to establish a hereditary monarchy.

In both England and the Netherlands, religious divisions accentuated the struggle between absolutism and constitutionalism. Both the protracted revolt of the largely Protestant Dutch against Catholic Spain and the English Civil War echoed the religious struggles between Catholics and Protestants during the Thirty Years' War (1618–1648) in Central Europe (see Chapter 4). The Dutch had risen up in open rebellion in 1566 in part because the Spanish Habsburgs attempted to impose the Catholic Inquisition on what had become a Protestant country. In England, Kings James I and Charles I attempted to return the English Church to the elaborate rituals that many people associated with Catholicism, thereby pitting the monarchy against Parliament. This constitutional crisis led to the defeat and execution of Charles I in 1649, the fall of the monarchy, and in 1688, to the "Glorious Revolution," which brought King William III and Queen Mary to the throne. Parliament, which historically represented landed interests, succeeded in balancing and constraining royal authority. By virtue of Parliament's victory in the English Civil War, England remained a constitutional monarchy. England's new monarchs agreed to a Bill of Rights, which affirmed the civil liberties of English people and the rights of Parliament.

The emergence of England and the Dutch Republic, both predominantly Protestant states, as great powers reflected the vitality of the middle classes in both nations, the relative unity of the two states, and the location of both rising powers on the Atlantic. England's international commerce developed rapidly. And as Amsterdam emerged as a banking center and first port of call for international trade, the Dutch Republic enjoyed the golden age of its culture.

CONFLICTS IN STUART ENGLAND

Conflicts between the Stuart kings and Parliament, in which religious conflict played an important part, led to the English Civil War, which helped define the constitutional and political institutions of modern Britain. The monarchy tried to enhance its authority at the expense of Parliament by attempting to impose extralegal taxes without the consent of Parliament. But the English gentry, whose status and influence came from ownership of land, emerged from the period with their parliamentary prerogatives intact.

Conflicts between James I and Parliament

King James I (1566–1625) succeeded his cousin Queen Elizabeth to the English throne in 1603. As King James VI of Scotland, he had overcome court factionalism and challenges from dissident Presbyterians. After he also became king of England, the two countries were joined in a personal union. The first Stuart king of England, James was lazy, frivolous, and slovenly, particularly enjoying hurling jelly at his courtiers. But there was more to him than that. He was an intelligent and well-read blunderer, once described as "the wisest fool in Christendom." Before coming to the throne, James had sketched out a theory of divine right monarchy. And in a speech to Parliament in 1609 the king had called "the state of monarchie . . . the supremest thing upon earth: for Kings are not only God's Lieutenants upon earth, and sit upon throne, but even by God himselfe they are called Gods." James described Parliament as nothing but "cries, shouts, and confusion." Relations between the monarch and Parliament degenerated rapidly.

The English monarchy found itself in a precarious financial position, with Queen Elizabeth's war debts at least partially to blame. James brought to court like-minded dandies, most of whom proved not only unpopular with Parliament but incompetent as well. In the last years of his reign, James became increasingly dependent on his young, handsome favorite, George Villiers, the duke of Buckingham (1592–1628). A relative newcomer to court circles, Buckingham convinced the king to sell peerages and titles, offices, monopolies, and other privileges to the highest bidder. Opposition to the monarch's attempts to raise money in such ways mounted within Parliament.

Although it met only sporadically and at the king's pleasure, Parliament transformed itself from a debating society into an institution that saw itself as defending the rights of the English people. The House of Commons, lashing out at the beneficiaries of royal monopolies, impeached on charges of bribery Lord Chancellor Francis Bacon (1561–1626), philosopher of science and once the king's friend. Here, too, there was a principle at stake: the accountability of ministers to Parliament.

English foreign policy contributed both to the monarchy's mounting debt and to the emerging political crisis. Queen Elizabeth had denied that Parliament had the right to discuss matters of foreign policy unless invited by the monarch to do so. Parliament still insisted on that right. Thus, James favored peace with Spain, but Parliament clamored for war because Catholic Bavaria, an ally of Habsburg Spain, had invaded the Protestant Upper Palatinate. And in 1621, asserting its right to influence foreign policy, Parliament refused to provide more funds for the conflict, setting the stage for the greatest constitutional crisis in English history.

Parliament denounced the monarch's attempt to arrange a marriage between his son, Charles, the heir to the throne, and the daughter of Philip IV of Spain. As dynastic marriages were an essential part of foreign policy, cementing or building alliances, members of Parliament objected to a royal foreign policy that seemed pro-Spanish and therefore pro-Catholic. Parliament declared its right to discuss the proposed marriage, and thus foreign affairs. But James defied Parliament by stating that it could not discuss matters of foreign policy, denying that the privileges of Parliament were "your ancient and undoubted birthright and inheritance." Rather he described them as "derived from the grace and permission of our ancestors and us."

James's wedding plans for his son fell through in 1623, however, when the Spanish king refused to allow Charles, who had gone to Madrid, even to set eyes on his daughter. But two years later, James then arranged Charles's marriage to another devout Catholic, Henrietta Maria of France, the daughter of Henry IV and Maria de' Medici. The secret price of this liaison included the king's promise that he would one day allow English Catholics, who numbered 2 or 3 percent of the population, to practice their religion freely. In a country in which anti-Catholicism had been endemic since the English Reformation of the mid-sixteenth century, James seemed to be taking steps to favor Catholicism.

James was succeeded upon his death by his son, Charles I (ruled 1625–1649). The young king was indecisive and painfully shy, traits compounded by a stammer. Even more than his father, Charles rejected the view that his appointments to ministries and other important offices should represent a wide spectrum of political and religious views. He stubbornly refused to oust the duke of Buckingham.

(Left) King James I. *(Right)* The young Charles, heir to the throne and later Charles I.

RELIGIOUS DIVISIONS

King Charles I once claimed, "People are governed by the pulpit more than the sword in time of peace." In the seventeenth century, no other realm of life so bitterly divided Europeans as religion. In England, religious divisions helped accentuate and define the political crisis. The Established or Anglican Church faced a challenge from the Puritans, a dissident religious group of Calvinists that had emerged during Elizabeth's reign.

Many Puritans were more sure of what they were against than what they were for. Puritans were strongly attracted by the Calvinist idea that each individual was predestined by God through His grace to be saved or not to be saved. They emphasized preaching and the individual's personal understanding of the Bible, spiritual devotion, discipline, and sacrifice as the basis of religion. Because they emphasized the personal worth of the individual minister, not the value of an ecclesiastical title, Puritans opposed the role of bishops in the Church of England. They wanted authority to be taken away from bishops and given to local synods (ecclesiastical councils made up of clerical and lay leaders). They de-emphasized the sacraments and wanted worship to be simpler than the contemporary Anglican Church services. Relentlessly hostile to Catholicism, Puritans held that elaborate church accoutrements in the Church of England—such as stained-glass windows and ornate altar rails—smacked of the Roman papacy.

Puritans did not choose the name by which they came to be known in the late sixteenth century, which was originally intended as a term of abuse. Considering themselves "the godly," they believed that they represented the true Church of England. They constituted not more than 10 percent of the population, and perhaps a third of all gentry, but their influence grew. University graduates who had embraced Puritanism formed "a godly preaching ministry" in many parishes, providing opportunities for Puritans to preach and win converts.

The Puritans were increasingly hostile to those who espoused a kind of Protestantism known as Arminianism. At first no more than a handful of ecclesiastics with the king's ear, Arminians soon came to wield considerable power. Charles I became an Arminian, and so did the duke of Buckingham. English Arminians, like their Dutch counterparts, rejected the Calvinist idea of predestination, which Puritans accepted, and, unlike the latter, believed that an individual could achieve salvation through free will. Arminians also accepted rituals that to the Puritans seemed to replicate those of the Catholic Church, and they emphasized the authority and ceremonial role of bishops, which Puritans opposed with particular vehemence. The Arminians emphasized royal authority over the Church of England. Increasingly they seemed to be proponents of royal absolutism.

The king's aggressive espousal of Arminianism enhanced the influence of William Laud (1573–1645), bishop of London. In 1633, Charles named Laud to be the head of the Church of England as Primate of England (archbishop of Canterbury). The pious, hard-working, and stubborn son of a draper, Laud warned Charles that the religious extremes of Catholicism and radical Puritanism both posed threats to the Established Church. An Arminian, Laud espoused High Church rituals, and because of this, the Puritans thought that he was secretly working to make Catholicism the established religion of England. Under Elizabeth I and James I, Catholics had remained a force in some sectors of English life. Fear of a "popish plot" to restore Catholicism as the religion of the English state existed at all levels of English society. Landowners whose families had purchased ecclesiastical lands during the Reformation now worried that Laud might return them to the Catholic Church. Catholicism and "popery" was popularly identified with the Spanish Inquisition, the Saint Bartholomew's Day Massacre in France, and the duke of Alba's "Council of Blood" in the Netherlands.

Charles I and Parliament Clash

Charles's fiscal policies deepened popular dissatisfaction with his reign. In 1625, the king decreed a forced loan on landowners, which he levied without Parliament's consent and which he insisted be paid within three months, an unprecedented short period of time. The next year, he ordered the imprisonment of seventy-six gentlemen who refused to meet the royal demand. Parliament refused to consent to the levies unless Charles met its demands for fiscal reform. The king convoked three Parliaments in four years, but dissolved each when it refused to provide him with funds. Parliament continued to demand that Charles appoint ministers it could trust and began impeachment proceedings against the duke of Buckingham. However, Buckingham disappeared as a source of irritation to Parliament when a disgruntled naval officer who had not been paid assassinated him in 1628.

Charles again asked Parliament to provide him with more funds. In response, Parliament promulgated the Petition of Right, which it forced Charles to accept in return for the granting of a tax. This constrained the king to agree that in the future he would not attempt to impose "loans" without Parliament's consent, and that no "gentlemen" who refused to pay up would be arrested—nor would anyone else be imprisoned without a show of just cause. The Petition of Right, which was initially put forward in 1628 by Sir Thomas Wentworth (1593–1641), then an opponent of the crown and one of the men imprisoned for refusing to pay the forced loan, was a significant document in the constitutional evolution of England. It defined the rights of Parliament as inalienable and condemned arbitrary arrest, martial law, and taxes imposed without its consent.

Angered by the Petition of Right and by Parliament's insistence that customs duties were a violation of the Petition, Charles ordered Parliament's dissolution in 1629. Because it was the role of the speaker of the house to communicate with the king on behalf of Parliament, members of the Commons physically held the speaker in his chair so he could not leave. They proceeded to declare that anyone who attempted to collect funds not levied with the approval of Parliament would be considered "a capital enemy to the kingdom and commonwealth," as would anyone who sponsored "innovation of religion," which is what Puritans considered Laud's espousal of elaborate High Church ceremonies. A defiant Parliament then disbanded.

For the next eleven years, Charles ruled without Parliament and tried to raise monies in new and controversial ways. Inflation had increased not only the royal debt but also the cost of ships and arms for waging war. The monarchy had exhausted its credit. Unlike James, Charles had some scruples about peddling privileges, but none at all about other means of raising funds. He fined gentlemen who did not attend his coronation. Most controversially, Charles ordered that "ship money" again be imposed without Parliament's consent on inland towns beginning in 1634.

Charles's high-handed royal policies led to a rebellion in Scotland. The king had seized lands from Scottish nobles, and, at Laud's instigation, in 1637 he ordered the imposition of the Anglican Book of Common Prayer on the Scottish Presbyterian Church (established as the Scottish national church in the 1560s). The Scots had never been pleased with the union with England that had been weakly forged in 1603 when James VI of Scotland ascended the English throne as James I. They demanded that Charles allow a general church assembly to consider the prayer book. In 1638, some Scottish leaders signed the *National Covenant,* attacking the pope and the prayer book and swearing to defend their religion and liberties. Faced with the resolution of Scots to maintain the Presbyterian Church, Charles convoked the

Riot in St. Giles' Cathedral, Edinburgh, when the bishop begins to read from the Anglican Book of Common Prayer.

church assembly in Scotland, but he also began to prepare for an invasion of Scotland. In the meantime, Scottish nobles and landowners began evicting Anglican bishops and taking over churches. The Scots rose up in arms.

This was a turning point in the dramatic reign of King Charles I. Desperately needing funds to defeat the Scots, in 1639 the king demanded that the city of London help pay for the war. After several small allocations, London finally consented to lend the crown a large sum, but only on the condition that Charles convene Parliament and allow it to sit for a reasonable period of time.

Nobles and gentry led resistance to royal policies from the beginning; some were already in touch with the rebellious Scots, who in 1640 occupied the northeastern English port of Newcastle without resistance. Running short of cash and facing mutinies in the royal army, in April 1640 the king summoned Parliament for the first time in eleven years. But when it refused to allocate money for the war against Scotland until Charles agreed to consider a list of grievances, the king dissolved this "Short Parliament" after less than two months. Charles I's defiance of Parliament initiated a full-fledged constitutional crisis.

THE ENGLISH CIVIL WAR

The political crisis of the Stuart monarchy became a constitutional conflict about how England was to be governed. To the king's opponents, Parliament existed to protect fundamental English liberties that had been established under the Magna Carta in 1215. By this reasoning the king did not have the right to dispense with its counsel and its traditional authority to allocate royal finances, nor did he have the right to impose taxes without historical precedent. While Parliament, led by Puritans, was not yet claiming sovereignty, it was clearly asserting its traditional role as a balance to royal authority.

Defenders of Parliament believed Laudian religious reforms and the collection of ship money to be the work of power-crazed men perhaps manipulated by the pope. Justices of the peace resented the usurpation of their authority by various decrees of martial law and by royal courts that impinged on regional courts. Local officials believed that the king's lieutenants were exceeding their traditional authority over military affairs by bypassing established routines of local approval of military levies. London merchants felt aggrieved that they were not able to export cloth because of royal control over cloth exports through the monopoly of the Merchant Adventurers (see Chapter 5). The monarchy alienated other Londoners by allowing some craftsmen to operate outside the structure of the London guilds and by attempting to force the city to provide more money for the war with Scotland. The sale of the right to collect royal customs generated controversy as well, particularly as the government sold more privileges to pay off those who "farmed" taxes.

In the meantime, Charles surrounded himself with confidants, advisers, artists, and musicians, whose sense of royal decorum and aesthetic tastes seemed to suggest the influence of continental Catholicism. The queen brought to the court Flemish artists who emphasized the religious themes of the Catholic Reformation, leading critics to believe that a plot was afloat "to seduce the King himself with Pictures, Antiquities, Images & other vanities brought from *Rome*."

Those who consistently supported Parliament became known as the supporters of "Country," while those who supported virtually unlimited monarchical prerogatives were identified with "Court." Titled nobles, of whom there were about 1,200, generally supported Charles. Gentry formed the core of the political opposition to the king. During the previous century, many gentry had extended their landholdings, and men enriched by commerce or service in the law or army had become part of the gentry through the purchase of land. The roots of confrontation may have come from the struggle of these economically dynamic gentry to obtain political power commensurate with their rising station in English life. Some gentry of lesser means who had fallen upon hard times may have blamed the monarchy for their plight and hence supported Parliament.

The English Civil War has been called the "Puritan Revolution," even though its causes extended beyond the question of religion and Puritans were not alone in resisting the monarchy. There were indeed many Puritans in Parliament, including the body's leader, John Pym (1584–1643). A brilliant speaker and debater, Pym was a zealot, an impetuous and perhaps even paranoid man whose strong convictions were in part defined by an obsession that a "popish plot" existed to restore Catholicism to England. Puritans were

PYM.

John Pym.

numerous among the lesser gentry in eastern England, areas that took the side of Parliament during the Civil War.

As the political crisis grew in the 1630s, the authority of Anglican bishops, their appointment as state officials, and their right to nominate ministers also smacked of "popery." Charles I echoed the famous statement of his father, James I, "No bishops, no king!"—an assertion that would come back to haunt him. Laud expanded the power of ecclesiastical courts, which tried people accused of offenses against the Church of England. This reminded some people of the Spanish Inquisition.

Moving toward Conflict

Having dissolved the "Short Parliament" in May 1640, Charles again convoked a newly elected Parliament the following October. The crown's strengthening of the army with Catholic Irish regiments, commanded by Wentworth, who was now a supporter and adviser of the king and had been named the earl of Strafford, confirmed to credulous ears that a "popish plot" was in the works. Ordinary people smashed altar rails and shattered stained-glass windows. The English army suffered defeat in Scotland; the war required yet more funds. Led by Pym, Parliament turned its wrath upon Charles's advisers. It indicted Strafford, who was tried and executed in London before a rejoicing throng. Parliament denounced as illegal the most unpopular royal acts during the previous eleven years and abolished some of the courts controlled by the monarchy. Parliament proclaimed that it could only dissolve itself, and that in the future the king would have to summon it every three years. In the meantime, Irish peasants rose up against the English in 1641 and killed many Protestant landlords. The Irish rebellion highlighted the rights of Parliament by making urgent the issue of who controlled the militia.

In November 1641, Parliament passed the Grand Remonstrance. Presenting what Parliament considered a history of royal misdeeds, the document denounced "a malignant and pernicious design of subverting the fundamental laws and principles" of English government. It called for religious and administrative reforms. Its passage by a narrow margin indicated that Parliament remained divided over how far to carry its opposition to royal policies.

Puritans, who narrowly controlled the House of Commons, wanted to reform both church and state. Wealthy nobles began to form a solid bloc around the cause of the king, fearing that reform might weaken their influence. Shortly after the passage of the Grand Remonstrance, the high sheriff of Lancashire called upon "gentlemen" to take arms with their tenants and servants on behalf of the king "for the securing of our own lives and estates, which are now ready to be surprised by a heady multitude." In some places, fighting began that month, as both sides fought for control of the militias.

The king attempted a bold coup against Parliament in January 1642. He personally led several hundred armed soldiers into Parliament and ordered the arrest of Pym. Forewarned by someone, Pym and other leaders had left the House of Commons before Charles arrived, but they remained in London where they were protected by artisans and craftsmen. The latter opposed the crown's support of monopolies and for religious reasons supported Laud. Charles, fearing for his safety in London, where people had become more forceful in their support of Parliament, headed north with his family to more friendly country, and his supporters left Parliament. In June, Parliament's "Nineteen Propositions" denounced the confrontational royal policy. In August 1642, Charles mobilized his forces at Nottingham.

Taking Sides

As civil war spread, Parliament's soldiers came to be known as "Roundheads" for the short, bowl-shaped haircuts many of them wore. The king's "Cavaliers" liked to think of themselves as fighting the good fight for God and king against those who would shatter social harmony by making "subjects princes and princes slaves." But so far as civil wars go, there was little actual fighting. Winter interrupted relatively short "campaign seasons." There were only four major battles (see Map 6.1). The two sides fought to a draw on October 23, 1642, at Edgehill, south of Birmingham. When a royal military advance on London was turned back, Charles set up headquarters in Oxford, fifty miles northwest of London. In February 1643, the king rejected Parliament's terms for a settlement. When a second royal march on London failed, both sides intensified massive propaganda campaigns to win support. The war became a war of words, among the first in history. More than 22,000 newspapers, newsletters, pamphlets, broadsides, sermons, and speeches were published between 1640 and 1661.

Yet life in thousands of villages was disrupted by requisitions, plundering, and general hardship. About 10 percent of the English population was forced to leave home during the war. Many counties—perhaps most—were neutral, as local leaders struggled to maintain control and keep their counties free of fighting and devastation.

Without London's credit institutions, Charles financed the war with gifts and loans from nobles, selling more titles, and forced levies. The Roundheads, in keeping with Parliament's resistance to monarchical centralization,

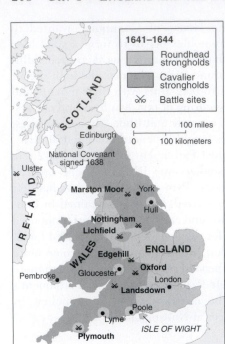

MAP 6.1 THE ENGLISH CIVIL WAR   Major battles during the English Civil War, as well as Cavalier and Roundhead strongholds.

kept civil, fiscal, and military authority relatively decentralized in regions under its control. Parliament raised funds through heavy excise and property taxes, and confiscated the property of some prominent families supporting the king's cause. A regional military structure developed, based on associations of counties pledging mutual assistance to the parliamentary cause.

Parliament drew considerable support from the most economically advanced regions where commercialized agriculture had developed through deforestation, the draining of marshland, and acts of enclosure, and where cloth manufacturing had brought prosperity, particularly in the south and east. Charles I retained the allegiance of most of northern and western England, regions of more traditional agriculture and social hierarchy. In some places, villages became sites for religious and political struggle. For example, in regions where traditional festive rituals had survived the assault of Puritans, who considered them frivolous, disruptive, and ungodly spectacles that brought drinking, dancing, and sexual freedom, support was strong for the king, whose supporters—wealthy country gentlemen—encouraged such merriment.

Oliver Cromwell and the New Model Army

In 1643, Parliament allied with the Scots, many of whom were Presbyterians. John Pym's sudden death at the end of the year did not lessen Parliament's resolve to force the king to capitulate. In July 1644, the Roundheads and Scots defeated the Cavaliers at Marston Moor, near York. About 45,000 men fought in this battle, the largest of the English Civil War. This gave Parliament control of northern England. Scottish participation only added to the determination of the "war party" to whom Charles listened.

Oliver Cromwell.

Oliver Cromwell (1599–1658), who led the Roundheads to victory at Marston Moor, emerged as the leader of Parliament. Cromwell, born into a modest gentry family, never lost what more well-heeled gentry considered his rough edges. Several years before being elected to Parliament in 1640, he had undergone—perhaps during serious illness—a deep spiritual conversion, becoming convinced that God had chosen him to be one of the Puritan elect. Cromwell displayed idealism as well as the stubbornness of someone who is convinced that he is always right.

Combining three armies, Parliament formed the New Model Army in 1645. Cromwell instilled strict discipline, and the Roundhead soldiers' morale improved with regular wages. Unlike its predecessors, the New Model Army won grudging good will in the counties by paying for supplies and not plundering, in contrast to the king's army.

Divisions within Parliament

Two political groups emerged in Parliament: Presbyterians and Independents. Presbyterians, a majority within Parliament, were moderates. Originally a pro-Scottish group that had rallied behind John Pym, most (despite the name "Presbyterians") were Puritans. Opposed to the bishops' authority, they rejected religious toleration and wanted an established national Calvinist Church. They were ready to accept a negotiated settlement with the king.

The Independents were militant Puritans who desired more drastic changes than the Presbyterians. They wanted the church to be a loose alliance of congregations that would choose their own ministers, a more radical position than that of the Presbyterians. The Independents were less willing to compromise with the king on the issue of parliamentary prerogatives.

Crowds watch Puritan soldiers leaving London, c. 1647. Note the "roundheads" and the armed preacher urging them on.

They opposed the creation of a new established church and favored toleration of some religious dissent. Some of them even desired more far-reaching political reforms that would protect individual rights. Cromwell's rise to leadership reflected the ascendancy of the Independents in Parliament.

Cromwell purged Presbyterian commanders within the New Model Army, replacing them with Independents loyal to him. Singing psalms as they rushed fearlessly into battle, Cromwell's "Ironsides," as his troops were called, maintained an air of invincibility. In June 1645, the New Model Army routed the royalists. Charles surrendered to the Scots a year later, hoping to obtain a less draconian peace than if he capitulated directly to Parliament. But the Scottish army soon withdrew from England and left the king in the custody of Parliament in February 1647.

Radicals

As the war dragged on, England fell into virtual anarchy amid growing resentment over the billeting of soldiers, food shortages, and rising prices. The English Civil War unleashed forces that seemed to challenge the foundation of social and political order. During the siege of royalist Oxford, a hungry sentry called down to the besieging forces, "Roundhead, fling me up half a mutton and I will fling thee down a lord!" At times the Roundheads appeared to hold back as if wary of the consequences of victory. Even some gentry who had taken the side of Parliament feared that a crushing victory might unleash "turbulent spirits, backed by rude and tumultuous mechanic persons [i.e., ordinary people]" and attacks against property by the mob, "that many headed monster."

In such an uncertain climate, new religious groups proliferated. Baptists did not believe that children should be baptized, reasoning that only adults were old enough to choose a congregation and hence be baptized. Some Baptists permitted couples to marry by simply making a declaration before the congregation.

"Levellers" were far more radical. They called for new laws that would protect the poor as well as the wealthy. Levellers, many of whom had been Baptists or Puritans, found adherents among small property owners, London artisans, and the ranks of the New Model Army "wherein there is not one lord." Yet, while the Levellers proposed a new English constitution and demanded sweeping political reforms that would greatly broaden the electoral franchise, they still based these rights on property ownership, which they defined as men having "a permanent fixed interest in this kingdom," excluding wage laborers and servants. Women were also prominent in Leveller petition campaigns, but calls for female enfranchisement were extremely rare.

Smaller groups of radicals soon went even farther. The "Diggers," who called themselves the "True Levellers," denied the claim of Parliament to speak for Englishmen and opposed the private ownership of land. They espoused agrarian reform and began a brief colony that began to share wasteland with the poor and the landless. The "Ranters" rejected the idea of heaven, hell, and sin, and postulated that true salvation could be found only in drink and sex.

To some people in mid-seventeenth-century England, the world indeed seemed "turned upside down." Some radicals opposed not only hierarchical authority, but also paternal authority within the family. The assumption that the king ruled his nation as a husband and father directed his wife and children had been prominent in early modern political theory. Now some pamphlets denounced the subjugation of women to their husbands.

Parliament's Victory

Pressured by the Presbyterians, who feared the radicals of the New Model Army, Parliament ordered the disbandment of part of it without paying the soldiers. The army, however, refused to disband, and instead it set up a general council, some of whose members were drawn from the lower officer corps and even the rank and file, perhaps reflecting Leveller influence.

The New Model Army considered Parliament's attempts to disband it to be part of a plot against the Independents. A few regiments mutinied and prepared a political platform, the *Agreement of the People,* written by

London Levellers. This text anticipated later theorists by claiming that all "freeborn Englishmen," not just property owners, were the source of political authority and that "the poorest man in England is not at all bound in a strict sense to that government that he hath not had a voice to put himself under." Cromwell ruthlessly restored order in the New Model Army, subduing mutinous Leveller regiments and ordering several leaders shot.

In November 1647, King Charles escaped the custody of Parliament and fled to the Isle of Wight. Against the opposition of Presbyterians who hoped that some compromise could still be reached with the king, the House of Commons passed a motion that no further addresses should be made to King Charles. The implication was that Parliament alone should proceed to establish a new government without Charles's participation or consent, probably indicating that Cromwell and many other members of Parliament had already decided that Charles I should be put to death and a republic declared.

In May 1648, Presbyterian moderates joined Cavalier uprisings in southern Wales and southern England. Charles had been secretly negotiating with the Presbyterian Scots, hoping that they now would join an alliance of Anglicans and members of Parliament who had become disillusioned with Cromwell's radicalism. But the New Model Army turned back a Scottish invasion in August, and besieged royalist forces in Wales surrendered. The king was placed under guard on the Isle of Wight, "more a Prisoner," as an observer put it, "than ever . . . and could not goe to pisse without a guarde nor to Goffe [play golf]."

A detachment of the New Model Army, under Colonel Thomas Pride, then surrounded the Parliament house and refused to let Presbyterians— and some Independents as well—join the other members. "Pride's Purge," which took place without Cromwell's consent or knowledge, left a "Rump Parliament" of about a fifth of the members sitting.

The Rump Parliament, dominated by Independents, appointed a High Court to try the king on charges of high treason. Charles refused to defend himself and was found guilty. Charles I was executed at Whitehall on January 30, 1649, the first monarch to be tried and executed by his own subjects. Charles's beheading had immediate international repercussions; one power after another severed diplomatic relations with England.

The Puritan Republic and Restoration

The Rump Parliament abolished the monarchy and the House of Lords. It established a Puritan republic, the Commonwealth of England, with Cromwell as its leader. In 1649, Cromwell brutally put down the Irish uprising that had gone on for eight years. The Act of Settlement in 1652 expropriated the land of two-thirds of the Catholic property owners in Ireland, assuring the ascendancy of English Protestants in that strife-torn land for

Eyewitness depiction of Charles I's execution, January 30, 1649.

the next 300 years. The Scottish Protestants did not fare any better for having supported Charles, however belatedly, as Cromwell then conquered Scotland in 1650–1651. Having defeated both the Irish and the Scots, Cromwell then fought wars against the Dutch Republic from 1652 to 1654 and Spain from 1655 to 1659, with an eye toward reducing the power of both of these economic rivals.

The Rump Parliament met until 1653. It would not dissolve itself and so Cromwell, torn between his determination to assure a "godly reformation" in England and a mistrust of political assemblies, dissolved it in a military coup. The Long Parliament (if the Rump session is counted) had lasted since 1640. Cromwell now picked 140 men to serve as a new Parliament. This body came to be called the Barebones Parliament, named after one of its members, a certain "Praise-God Barbon," a leather merchant.

England became a military dictatorship. The army council dissolved the Barebones Parliament six months later and proclaimed a Protectorate under a new constitution, the Instrument of Government. Cromwell took the title "Lord Protector" and held almost unlimited power. The contention of the philosopher Thomas Hobbes (1588–1679), who had supported Charles I against Parliament, that the natural state of mankind is one of war, "everyone against everyone," seemed now to apply to England.

The Puritan republic turned out to be as oppressive as the monarchy of the Stuart kings. Cromwell imposed taxes without parliamentary approval and purged Parliament when it disagreed with him. When Parliament produced its own constitution, Cromwell sent its members packing in 1655.

But, like Charles I before him, he was obliged to recall Parliament the following year to vote money for war, this time against Spain.

Although Cromwell granted *de facto* religious freedom to all Puritan sects (including the Presbyterians, Independents, and Baptists), he continued to deny such freedom to Anglicans and Catholics. He did, however, allow Jews, who had not been allowed in England since 1290, to return in 1655. But Cromwell lost support as a result of financial impositions necessary to fight wars and supply an army of 50,000 men in England. The Lord Protector proved to be a better military administrator than a civilian one. Cromwell also alienated people through his exhortations that people behave in "godly" Puritan ways, as set forth in a code enforced by the army. Cromwell began to wear armor under his clothes and took circuitous routes in order to foil assassins who might be stalking him.

In the meantime, Cromwell claimed to be a humble caretaker of government who would keep order until godly righteousness prevailed. In 1657, a newly elected Parliament produced another constitution and offered Cromwell the throne of England. He refused, perhaps because he believed God had spoken to him against this and because a monarchy would alienate elements in the army. But he accepted the terms of the "Humble Petition and Advice," introducing a second house of Parliament (a nominated House of Lords) and a quasi-monarchical position for the Lord Protector, including the right to name his successor. Cromwell then dissolved Parliament because republicans in it were hostile to an evident monarchical direction. A year later, Cromwell died, succeeded by his considerably less able son, Richard (1626–1712), the New Protector. After Richard, several military successors stumbled on, backed by remnants of the New Model Army.

Increasingly, however, it seemed to the upper classes that only the restoration of the Stuart monarchy could restore order in England. Charles (1630–1685), heir to the throne of his executed father, lived in exile in The Netherlands. Armed force would still play a deciding role in this tumultuous time. General George Monck (1608–1670), a former royalist officer who now commanded the army in Scotland, had shrewdly kept Scottish tax money to pay his soldiers. His army became the only reliable force in England. After Parliament tried to assert control over the army, Monck marched with his forces on London and dissolved Parliament. New elections returned an alliance of royalists and Presbyterians, giving Parliament a moderate majority inclined to accept a restoration. When Charles issued a conciliatory proclamation, Parliament invited him to assume the throne of England. Eleven years after his father's execution, he crossed the English Channel in May 1660 and was crowned King Charles II on April 23, 1661.

Charles II, who disbanded the New Model Army, manifested considerable charm, energy, courage, unfailing good humor, and loyalty to those who had remained loyal to him (with the notable exception of the queen, to whom he was anything but faithful). He could also lash out vindictively when he believed himself betrayed. He earned the affection of most of his subjects

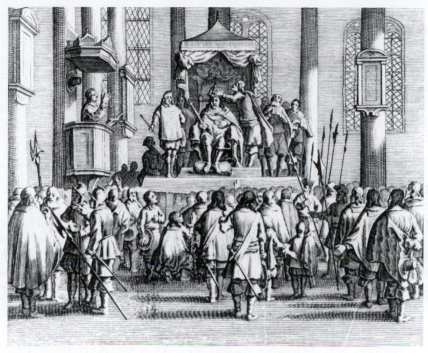

The coronation of King Charles II in 1661.

because the return of monarchy seemed to end the extended period of division and chaos. He used grand royal ceremonies to help restore faith in the monarchy, even attempting to cure sufferers of scrofula with the "royal touch" of his hand, as had his predecessors centuries earlier.

Although the English Civil War was a victory for parliamentary rule, in some ways the Restoration turned the clock back to before the conflict. The Church of England again became the Established Church. The crown refused to extend official toleration to other religions, and the Church of England expelled Presbyterian ministers. Once again the king, chronically short of money, depended on Parliament for funds.

The way now seemed clear for England to continue to expand its commerce and influence in a climate of social and political peace. Between 1660 and 1688, the tonnage hauled by English ships more than doubled, as the merchant fleet established regular trade routes to Newfoundland, Virginia, and the Caribbean. In 1664, a small English force seized the Dutch colony of New Amsterdam, which became New York City. Tobacco, calico, furs, sugar, chocolate, and rum brought from the New World changed habits of consumption. London became a booming port, and the East India Company emerged as a powerful force in shaping royal policy. Lloyd's of London began to insure vessels sailing to the New World in 1688. By then almost half of

England's ships were trading with India or America. Exports and imports increased by a third by 1700.

England's foreign policy entered a new, aggressive period in support of English manufacture and commerce. To undermine Dutch commercial competition, Parliament passed a series of Navigation Acts between 1651 and 1673, requiring that all goods brought to England be transported either in English ships or in those belonging to the country of their origin. This led to three wars with the Netherlands, in 1652–1654 (undertaken by Cromwell), 1665–1667, and 1672–1674.

The Glorious Revolution

The highly charged issues of royal authority and Catholicism, which had sparked the English Civil War, led to another constitutional crisis and planted the seeds for the Glorious Revolution of 1688, when Parliament summoned a new king to rule England. Then the following year Parliament passed the Bill of Rights, which enshrined the rights of Parliament and the English people, and above all, men who owned property.

Stuart Religious Designs

After the return of the Stuarts to power, religion once again surfaced as a divisive issue in England, threatening to shatter the political unity seemingly achieved with the Restoration. Charles II had returned if not with strong Catholic sympathies at least with the conviction that he owed toleration to Catholics, some of whom had supported his father. Again, a Stuart king's seemingly provocative policies generated determined opposition from Parliament, which asserted its prerogatives.

Charles favored Catholics among his ministers and seemed to be trying to appeal to Dissenters in order to build a coalition against the Church of England. In response, Parliament passed a series of laws against Dissenters (1661–1665), known as the Clarendon Code. The Act of Corporation (1661) required all holders of office in incorporated municipalities to receive communion in the Anglican Church. The Act of Uniformity (1662) stated that all ministers had to use the Anglican Book of Common Prayer. Nonconformists had to take an oath that they would not try to alter the established order of church and state in England. Hundreds of Quakers, members of a pacifist group formed in 1649, refused to pay tithes or take oaths and were incarcerated, left to die in prison.

In 1670, Charles II signed a secret treaty of alliance with Louis XIV of France. He promised the king of France that he would declare himself a Catholic when the political circumstances in England were favorable. In return, he received subsidies from the French monarch. Charles ended restrictions on religious worship and laws that had been directed at

Catholics and Dissident Protestant groups. The hostile reaction to his decision, however, forced the king to reinstate the restrictive measures. In 1673, Parliament passed the Test Act, which largely superseded the Clarendon Code and excluded non-Anglicans from military and civil office.

Many people in England suspected that there were plots afoot to restore Catholicism as the state religion. Although Charles II's agreement with Louis XIV remained secret, in 1678 a strange man named Titus Oates loudly claimed the existence of a plot by the Catholic Church against England. Oates claimed that the Jesuits were preparing to assassinate the king and slaughter all English Protestants. They then would proclaim James, Charles's devout Catholic brother, king. (James was heir to the throne since Charles had no legitimate children, although he had a good many who were not.) Oates had made it all up, as the king knew perfectly well. But the monarch could not speak up because of his own secret promise to Louis XIV of France to restore Catholicism to England.

In the 1670s, two factions had emerged in Parliament that in some ways echoed the split between "Court" and "Country" before the Civil War. Members of Parliament who supported the full prerogatives of the monarchy, some of them trumpeting the theories of divine-right monarchy, became known as Tories, corresponding to the old "Court" faction. Those members of Parliament who espoused parliamentary supremacy and religious toleration became known as Whigs (corresponding to "Country"). Whig leaders orchestrated a plan to exclude James from the royal succession because of his Catholicism. During the ensuing Exclusion Crisis (1678–1681), the Tories defended James as the legitimate heir to the throne of England. When in 1679 some members of Parliament tried to make Charles's illegitimate son heir to the throne, Charles dissolved Parliament. In three subsequent parliamentary elections, Whigs profited from the mood of anti-Catholicism to take a majority of seats.

Parliament's passage in 1679 of the Habeas Corpus Act reflected Whig ascendancy. This act forced the government to provide a quick trial for those arrested. By establishing the legal rights of individuals accused of crimes, it further limited monarchical authority. The Habeas Corpus Act was thus part of the century-long struggle of the House of Commons for the maintenance of its constitutional role in England's governance.

In 1681, Charles II attempted, like his father before him, to rule without Parliament. Two years later, a number of Whigs were charged with plotting to kill both the king and his brother, and the king had them executed. On his deathbed two years later, Charles proclaimed his Catholicism.

Thus, in 1685, Charles II's brother assumed the throne as James II (1633–1701). In Scotland and in western England, royal armies crushed the small insurrections that rose up in favor of Charles's illegitimate son (who was executed). Naive as he was devout, James forgot the lessons of recent history and began to dismiss advisers who were not Catholics.

The prince regent riding a horse along a street strewn with the
heads of members of the opposition placed on large stones.

In 1687, James made Catholics eligible for office. The Dissenters also benefited from toleration, because the new king needed them as allies. The king
did not denounce Louis XIV's revocation of the Edict of Nantes in 1685,
which ended toleration for Huguenots (French Protestants, see Chapter 7).
This made English Protestants even more anxious. When it became apparent
that the queen was pregnant, James boldly predicted the birth of a son and
Catholic heir to the throne. For the enemies of the king, the timing of the
birth of a son and the fact that the only witnesses were Catholics inevitably
sparked rumors that the newborn was not really the king's son but a surro-
gate baby.

Royal prerogative thus remained the central constitutional issue. James
may have entertained visions of implanting monarchical absolutism, a tide
that approached from the continent. Certainly he sought to restore
Catholicism as the state religion. In April 1688, he issued a declaration of
toleration and ordered the Anglican clergy to read it from the pulpit. When
seven bishops protested, James put them in prison. However, when the
bishops were tried in court, a jury declared them not guilty.

The "Protestant Wind"

One of James's Protestant daughters by a previous marriage, Mary (1662–
1694), had married the Protestant Dutchman William of Orange (1650–
1702), the stadholder (chief official) of the Netherlands. A group of Tories
and Whigs, the "immortal seven"—six nobles and a bishop—invited William
to restore Protestantism and, from their point of view, the English constitution. William, eager that England assist the Dutch in resisting Louis XIV's
aggressive designs, prepared to invade England from the Netherlands. His
followers flooded England with propaganda on behalf of his cause.

The context of European international politics seemed favorable to William. Louis XIV's revocation of the Edict of Nantes had outraged the Dutch, who worried that James's successful restoration of Catholicism in England might make the Dutch Republic more vulnerable to Catholic France. They believed that England was an indispensable partner in helping resist Louis XIV's grand ambitions. A friendly Protestant monarch on the throne of England might even reduce tensions stemming from the trade rivalry between the Dutch Republic and England.

The Catholic continental monarchs would not aid James II. Louis XIV's principal interest remained continental territorial expansion. Despite declaring war on the Dutch Republic, Louis limited his attacks to verbal bluster and the seizure of several Dutch ships in French ports. Emperor Leopold of Austria, another powerful Catholic monarch, was tied up fighting the Turks in the east.

James did little to prepare military defenses except to appoint Catholic officers in his new regiments and to bring more troops from Ireland. He relied on his navy to protect his throne. Hoping for a last-minute compromise, he promised to summon a "free" Parliament. But it was too late.

In a declaration promulgated early in October 1688, William accused James of arbitrary acts against the nation, Parliament, and the Church of England. Aided by a munificent wind—later dubbed the "Protestant wind"—that blew his ships to the southwestern coast of England but pinned James's loyal fleet farther away in the Channel or kept them in port, William landed at Torbay on the English Channel with a force of 15,000 men on November 5,

William III of England and Queen Mary, joint rulers of England.

1688. William marched cautiously to London, encouraged by defections from James's cause. Uprisings on William's behalf in several northern towns further isolated the king. James was in a state of virtual physical and psychological collapse. At the end of November, he promised to summon Parliament and allow William's supporters to sit. But riots broke out against his rule and against Catholics. In December, James left England for exile in France. Parliament, victorious again, declared the throne vacant by abdication and invited William and Mary to occupy a double throne.

The Bill of Rights

This "Glorious Revolution" of 1688, less dramatic than the English Civil War, was arguably of more lasting importance in the constitutional evolution of England. Parliament passed a Bill of Rights in 1689 that ratified the Revolution of 1688, ending decades of constitutional battles. Accepted by William and Mary, it became a milestone in English history. It was passed at a time when the rights and influence of representative bodies lay in shambles throughout much of the continent as absolute monarchs consolidated their power (see Chapter 7). The Bill of Rights reaffirmed the rights of Parliament and guaranteed the rights of property owners to self-government and of the accused to the rule of law. In particular, it reasserted Parliament's financial authority over government by enumerating what a monarch should not do and by reducing royal control over the army. The Toleration Act (1689) stipulated that Protestant Dissenters could hold public services in licensed meeting houses and could maintain preachers. Anglicanism, however, remained the Established Church of England, and only Anglicans could hold office. Catholics could not occupy the throne and, like Dissenters, they were excluded from government positions.

The Glorious Revolution pleased the English philosopher John Locke (1632–1704), friend of some of the wealthy landowners who sent James II into exile. Locke was specific about the ways in which the power of monarchs ought to be limited. "The end of government," he wrote, should be "the good of mankind." Locke argued that the rights of individuals and, above all, the ownership of property found protection when Parliament's rights limited monarchical prerogatives. Knowing of the bloody chaos of the Thirty Years' War (1618–1648) on the continent, Locke also advocated religious toleration and espoused the right of subjects to rise up against tyranny, as the English supporters of Parliament had against Charles I.

The Glorious Revolution reaffirmed the political domination of the gentry, whose interests Parliament represented above all. English monarchs named nobles to hereditary seats in the House of Lords, but wealthy landowners elected members to the House of Commons. The gentry's economic and social position was more secure than during the inflationary years of the first half of the century. Order and social hierarchy reigned, and the fear of popular disorder ebbed. Benefiting from the consensus of 1688, the elite of wealthy landowners, increasingly more open to newcomers than their continental counterparts, would continue to shape British political life in the eighteenth century. The English Civil War and the Glorious Revolution affirmed the principle of representation not only in England, but also in the North American colonies, an important legacy for the future.

THE GOLDEN AGE OF THE DUTCH REPUBLIC

The Dutch Republic of the United Provinces (usually known today as the Netherlands, or sometimes simply—and erroneously—as Holland, its most populated and prosperous province) was the other European power (besides

MAP 6.2 THE NETHERLANDS, 1648   At the conclusion of the Thirty Years' War, the Dutch war of independence also ended, with the northern United Provinces becoming the Dutch Republic and the southern provinces remaining under Spain as the Spanish Netherlands.

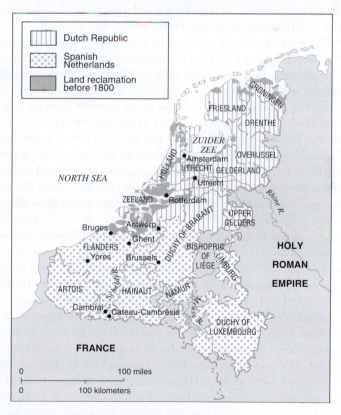

Poland) that defied the pattern of absolute and increasingly centralized rule that characterized seventeenth-century Europe. Spain ruled the Netherlands from 1516, when Holy Roman Emperor Charles V, who had inherited the territories of the dukes of Burgundy, became king of Spain. After a long, intermittent war that had begun in 1566 against Spanish rule (Chapter 5), the Dutch Republic officially became independent in 1648 (see Map 6.2 and pp. 98–202). The United Provinces, a confederation of republics, had been federalist in structure since the Union of Utrecht in 1579, when the provinces and cities of the Dutch Netherlands came together to form a defensive alliance against the advancing Spanish army. The Dutch Republic, from which William of Orange had launched his successful invasion of England in 1688, resisted the aspirations of the House of Orange for a centralized government dominated by a hereditary monarchy. Like their English counterparts, most people in the Netherlands did not want absolute rule, which they identified with the arbitrary acts of the Catholic Spanish monarchy.

The Structure of the Dutch State

The States General served as a federal legislative body of delegations from each of the seven provinces of the Dutch Republic. Each of the provinces held to traditions of autonomy, provincial sovereignty, and, since the Reformation, religious pluralism. Nobles received automatic representation in the States General. But their economic and political role in the Republic was relatively weak, except in the overwhelmingly agricultural eastern provinces.

The Dutch Republic was in some ways less a republic than an oligarchy of wealthy families who monopolized political power. No republican ideology existed until at least the second half of the seventeenth century. But Dutch citizens enjoyed some basic rights unavailable in most other states at the time. Provincial courts protected the Dutch against occasional arbitrary acts of both the central government and town governments. Solid fiscal institutions generated international confidence, permitting the Republic to raise sizable loans as needed.

The princes of the House of Orange served as *stadholder* of the Republic. A stadholder was at first appointed, and served as a political broker. He had influence, but not authority. He was not a ruler, and could not declare war, legislate, or even participate in the important decisions of the Republic. Many of the Orangist stadholders chafed under the restrictions on their authority, although they dominated some high federal appointments and named the sons of nobles to important positions in the army and navy. The Orangist stadholders dreamed of establishing a powerful hereditary monarchy. In 1650, William II (1626–1650), stadholder of five of the seven provinces, arrested six leaders of Holland and sent an army to besiege Amsterdam. A compromise reinforced the stadholders' power. But with William's sudden death several months later, the balance of power swung back to the regents (wealthy merchants and bankers) of the provinces. Any possibility of the Netherlands becoming an absolute state ended.

Expanding Economy

The Dutch economy developed more rapidly during the first two-thirds of the seventeenth century than did the economies of its competitors, England and France. The increased affluence brought by foreign trade helped the Dutch carry on the war against Spain. In 1609, following the signing of a truce with Spain, the Amsterdam Public Bank opened its offices in the town hall. The bank's principal function was to facilitate Amsterdam's burgeoning foreign trade by encouraging merchants to make payments in bills drawn on the bank. Foreign merchants were attracted to Amsterdam, particularly after mid-century, when bills of exchange became acceptable as currency.

Amsterdam's banking, credit, and warehousing facilities were soon unmatched in Europe. Although an ordinance in 1581 had included bankers among those occupations considered disreputable—along with actors, jugglers, and brothel keepers—and therefore excluded them from receiving communion in the Dutch Reformed Church, bankers came to be respected by the beginning of the seventeenth century. Good credit allowed the United Provinces to raise loans by selling negotiable bonds at low interest rates.

The Amsterdam Bourse in the seventeenth century. Merchants had fixed places at the Stock Exchange where they met to arrange various financial matters.

Canals and rivers expedited internal trade in the Dutch Republic. These boats along the Spaarne at Haarlem carried goods to the port, where they were loaded for distant trade.

The Dutch Republic, small in territory and population, expanded its agricultural resources during the first half of the seventeenth century. Workers and horses reclaimed much of the country's most fertile land from the sea. Increased productivity generated an agricultural surplus that was invested in commerce or manufacturing; an increased food supply sustained a larger population. Commercial livestock raising and capital-intensive farming became lucrative.

The Dutch Republic's population rose by a third between 1550 and 1650, to almost 2 million people, which made it Europe's most densely populated country after several of the Italian states. More than half of the population lived in towns. As Amsterdam became a major international port of trade and London's primary rival, its population rose from about 50,000 in 1600 to about 200,000 by 1670.

Early in the seventeenth century, construction of three large canals expanded Amsterdam's area by almost four times. These canals permitted boats to dock outside merchants' warehouses, where they were loaded with goods, which they then carried to the large ships of the port. Handsome townhouses reached skyward above new tree-lined streets along the canals. Built for bankers and merchants, the townhouses had narrow and increasingly ornamented facades, dauntingly steep staircases, and drains and sewers. The city spread out from the port along the semi-radial canals. The Dutch Republic benefited not only from relatively good roads, which expedited internal trade, but also from 500 miles of canals dug during the middle decades of the century.

Dutch traders steadily expanded their range and the variety of goods they bartered. They specialized in bulk goods carried by specially designed long, flat vessels that could be cheaply built and operated. The Dutch Republic's merchant fleet tripled during the first half of the century. Dutch shipbuilding boomed, aided by wind-powered sawmills. The Dutch Republic's 2,500 ships in the 1630s accounted for about half of Europe's shipping. Amsterdam became the principal supplier of grain and fish in Europe as the Dutch dominated the lucrative Baltic trade. Dutch ships hauled most of the iron produced in Sweden, and carried wheat and rye from Poland and East Prussia, dropping off what was needed for local consumption and then carrying what was left to France, Spain, and the Mediterranean. Capital investment and shrewd knowledge of markets made the herring trade a crucial part of Dutch prosperity. Dutch fishing boats were omnipresent in the rich North Sea fishing grounds. In 500 ships solid enough to stand up to the storms of the North Sea, Dutch fishermen worked in waters as far away as northern Scotland, the Shetland Islands, and Iceland. As many as 200 million herring a year were salted and packed in wooden casks, then exchanged for grain, salt, wine, and other commodities.

In 1602, a group of investors founded a private trading company, the Dutch East India Company, to which the government of the Dutch Republic granted a monopoly for trade in East Asia. When the Thirty Years' War and a Spanish embargo on Dutch commerce reduced continental trade, Dutch traders successfully developed trade overseas with India, Ceylon, Indonesia, and Japan. The Dutch East India Company proved to be stiff competition for the English company of the same name.

Tolerance and Prosperity

In contrast to England, where religious division led to civil war, the Dutch Republic remained a relative haven of toleration in an era of religious hatred. During the last decades of the sixteenth century, perhaps 60,000 Huguenots fled to the Dutch Republic to escape persecution in France and the Spanish Netherlands. Published works circulated throughout the Netherlands defending the rights of religious dissidents, including Mennonites, Lutherans, Quakers fleeing England, and Dutch Collegiants (a dissident Protestant group). Amsterdam's Jewish community numbered 7,500. Most were immigrants from the German states, and they spoke Yiddish among themselves, as well as German and Dutch; others had originally left persecution in Spain and Portugal. The municipal government rejected a request by Christian merchants that their Jewish competitors be restricted, as in many European cities, to a specific neighborhood, or ghetto. The

Amsterdam regents built 1,000 dwellings for refugees. Refugees from religious persecution in other countries contributed to the prosperity of the Dutch Republic.

Nonetheless, despite the religious toleration generally accorded in the Dutch Republic, the Dutch Reformed Church, a strict Calvinist religion, did persecute and discriminate against some religious groups. Dutch Arminians asked for protection from persecution in a Remonstrance (which gave them their most common name, the Remonstrants). Catholics, most of whom lived in the eastern provinces, also faced Calvinist hostility, although many had fought for Dutch independence. Jews were excluded from most guilds, and gypsies were routinely hounded and persecuted. Overall, however, toleration seemed less divisive to the Dutch than intolerance, and it seemed to make economic sense as well.

The Dutch Republic blossomed like the famous tulips that were so popular in Holland (the craze over this flower, originally imported from Turkey, reached such a fever pitch that a single tulip bulb could cost as much as the equivalent of three years' wages for a master artisan). To the eyes of a French visitor, Amsterdam was "swollen with people, chock-full of goods, and filled with gold and silver." The Dutch in the middle decades of the seventeenth century reached a level of prosperity unmatched in Europe at the time. Real wages rose during the last half of the seventeenth century while falling elsewhere. Dutch families enjoyed a relatively varied diet, consuming more meat and cheese—as well as, of course, fish—than households elsewhere in Europe. Amsterdam's market offered a plethora of colonial goods, such as coffee, tea, cocoa, ginger, and other spices; dried and pickled herring and other fish; a wide range of grains; finished cloth from Antwerp and Florence; Silesian linens; and English woolens. Dutch manufacturers, with windmills providing power, found lucrative outlets for draperies, worsteds, papers, books, and jewels. Even at the beginning of the century, Amsterdam had almost 200 breweries and more than 500 taverns.

Although prosperity reached far down the social ladder, the Dutch Republic also had its poor, who lived in the narrow streets around the Bourse (Stock Exchange), in poor farmhouses in the eastern flatlands, and in the huts of ethnic Frisian fishermen exposed to the onslaught of the waves and wind of the North Sea. The urban poor occasionally rioted and sometimes stole in order to survive. The proliferation of charitable institutions demonstrated Dutch compassion but also the desire to confine vagrants and beggars, as well as a capacity to lash out in brutal repression when patience with the poor grew thin. Beatings, floggings, branding, and even death remained common forms of punishment, and gallows stood at the main gates of large cities.

Yet despite prosperity, a sense of precariousness and vulnerability permeated the Republic. The armies of the ambitious king of France camped across the low-lying Southern Netherlands (now Belgium). The Republic had almost no natural resources and was subject to sudden calamities

Dike breach at Caevarden. Because so much land had been reclaimed from the sea, many of the Dutch lived in chronic fear of flooding.

brought by weather. A good part of the Dutch Netherlands would have been under water were it not for the famous dikes. These occasionally broke with catastrophic consequences long remembered (a flood in 1421 had claimed over 100,000 lives). A sense that disaster might be looming was reflected by the popularity in the Republic of novels and histories about disasters. This may explain the sense of solidarity and patriotic duty that brought people of various classes together against Spanish rule.

Seventeenth-Century Dutch Culture

Dutch painting in the golden age of the seventeenth century reflected not only the Republic's commercial wealth, but also its toleration and openness to secular styles and subject matter. The Dutch press enjoyed relative freedom; books were printed in the Republic that could not have been printed elsewhere. The first English and French newspapers were published in 1620, not in London and Paris, but in Amsterdam. Dutch publishers diffused knowledge of the Scientific Revolution (see Chapter 8). Dutch writers and poets discovered their own language, translated Latin authors, and popularized Dutch accounts of the revolt against Spain.

Dutch painting reflected the prosperity and taste of the middle class. Like the artists of the Renaissance, Dutch painters depended on the patronage of people of means, particularly wealthy Amsterdam merchants. Although Delft and several other towns each claimed their own style, the great port of Amsterdam dominated the art market. Some shopkeepers and craftsmen were prosperous enough to buy a painting or two, and some well-off peasants did as well.

Holland's regents, in particular, patronized Dutch painting. In contrast, the princes of Orange and some nobles patronized French and other foreign artists whose work reflected baroque themes associated with the Catholic Reformation found in the Southern Netherlands. Flanders became a northern outpost of the Catholic Reformation, encouraging religious themes with emotional appeal. In the Dutch Republic, by contrast, ecclesiastical artistic patronage was generally absent. Indeed, the Dutch Reformed Church ordered the removal of paintings from its churches.

Dutch painters looked to picturesque urban and rural scenes within their own country for inspiration. The Dutch school retained much of its cultural unity at least through the first half of the seventeenth century. Until 1650, the Republic remained relatively isolated from outside cultural influences, despite the arrival of refugees and immigrants. Very few Dutch artists and writers had the resources to travel as far as Italy or even France; even those who earned a comfortable living showed little inclination to go abroad. The group paintings of merchants or regents and municipal governments were usually commissioned by the subjects themselves, as in the case of Rembrandt van Rijn's *The Night Watch* (1642), a theatrically staged masterpiece presenting a group of city officials in uniform.

Rembrandt (1606–1669) was the son of a miller from Leiden. He was one of a handful of Dutch painters who amassed a fortune. Certainly, few artists have so successfully portrayed human emotions through the use of color, light, and shadow. Despite his posthumous fame, in his own time the brooding Rembrandt was a loner isolated from other painters. He bickered with his patrons and squandered most of what he made. Rembrandt increasingly became his own favorite subject, and he did at least eighty self-portraits, some of which reveal a thinly disguised sadness.

Dutch painters depicted everyday life. The prolific Jacob van Ruisdael (c. 1628–1682) mastered the visual effects of light on figures, trees, and household objects. The remarkable ability of Delft-born Jan Vermeer (1632–1675) to place simple scenes of ordinary people in astonishing light exemplifies the Golden Age of Dutch painting. Within the Dutch school of the seventeenth century, only Rembrandt frequently turned to the classical biblical themes that were so predominant in Flemish art. Although seascapes and naval scenes proliferated in Dutch painting, there were few canvases depicting battles, a favorite subject in absolute states, and those took their place on the large walls of noble châteaux in the distant countryside, not in the narrow houses of Amsterdam.

The Dutch considered the household a place of refuge and safety from the struggles of the outside world, as well as the basis of economic, social, and political order, and therefore worthy of artistic representation. Frans Hals (1580–1666) brought middle-class subjects and militia companies to life in remarkably composed individual and collective portraits. Paintings of fami-

A peasant family pausing to pray before mealtime.

lies at work, at play, or eating were particularly popular. Jan Steen (1626–1679) portrayed boisterous revelers of different means. Still lifes of platters of food became staples for Dutch artists, with titles such as *Still Life with Herring* and *Jug Still Life with Lobster*. The banquet became a favorite subject, with all of its accoutrements, such as oak table and chairs, iron cooking pans, elegant plates and drinking vessels, and its rituals, such as the prayer, the careful carving of the meat, and rounds of toasts.

The relationship between parents and children emerged as another familiar domestic theme. The Dutch painters also frequently portrayed servants, furniture and other household goods, and domestic pets. However, women on Dutch canvases appear more equal to men than they were in reality.

THE DECLINE OF THE DUTCH REPUBLIC

The relative decline of Dutch power is perhaps not surprising, given the greater economic resources and populations of France and England. England emerged in the second half of the century as the world's dominant commercial power, although the decline of Dutch trade was not complete until early in the eighteenth century.

The Dutch Republic tried to steer a course between England (its greatest commercial rival) and France, but this proved impossible. Wars against England in defense of Dutch commercial interests drained resources. Furthermore, Louis XIV of France had designs on the Netherlands. In 1667, France imposed damaging tariffs on Dutch goods and also forced the Dutch out of the cinnamon-producing island of Ceylon (now Sri Lanka) in the Indian Ocean. In Brazil, the Dutch West India Company failed to dislodge the Portuguese. Few Dutch demonstrated much enthusiasm for these distant places, and the Republic's colonial empire lagged behind those of England and Spain, to be sure, but also behind that of France.

With Spain weakened, Louis XIV coveted the Southern Netherlands, the conquest of which would place the Dutch in direct danger. Should France be able to open the Scheldt River (closed by the Spanish in 1585 with the goal of breaking the Dutch rebellion) to international trade, Antwerp's return to its former prosperity would be at Amsterdam's expense. In 1672, Louis XIV invaded the Dutch Republic, having signed a secret treaty with King Charles II of England (see Chapter 7). French armies quickly occupied all of the Republic except for two provinces, one of which was Holland. But the Dutch successfully defended the Republic, defeating the English fleet and pushing back the French army.

Taking advantage of the invasion, William of Orange (King William III of England in 1688) forced the States General to name him stadholder in 1672. He ordered the dikes opened, literally flooding the French into retreat. Royalist mobs murdered the leading official of the Republic and several influential regents of Holland who had dedicated themselves to keeping the stadholders in place. Supporters of the House of Orange eased into important political positions in that province. The Orangists controlled the Republic's foreign policy until the end of the century, but they still could not impose a monarchy on the provinces. With William's death in 1702, the main Orange dynastic line ended.

After the Glorious Revolution in England in 1688, the United Provinces allied with England and Sweden, fearing that Louis XIV of France might again invade. The alliance helped stave off the French threat in the last decades of the century, but at the same time it dragged the small country into a series of wars with France that lasted until the mid-eighteenth century, necessitating considerable spending on armies and southern fortifications.

The relative decline of Dutch influence in Europe could be first seen by about 1670 or 1680. Some luxury products, such as linen and Delft porcelain, continued to sell abroad, but Holland's textile industry and shipbuilding failed to keep pace with those of its rivals, above all England. Higher production costs (particularly wages) and a lack of technological innovation were at least partially to blame. Rivals imposed tariffs, which kept out many Dutch products. Dutch ships lost control of the Baltic trade. The Dutch faced competition in the herring market from England, France, and Sweden. The protectionist policies of Britain and Sweden protected their own fishermen while cutting off their domestic markets to Dutch herring. English warships destroyed Dutch ships in the wars fought between the two rivals. Furthermore, some Dutch entrepreneurs lent money abroad or invested in the colonies, land, government stocks, and even in English manufacturing, not in Dutch businesses. Investment in agriculture and land reclamation fell off.

Spain's golden age of art coincided with its decline as a great power. In contrast, Dutch painting languished with the nation's decline. Painters began looking abroad for inspiration and, in doing so, lost some originality. In the 1650s, the Amsterdam regents ignored the Dutch school when planning the construction and decoration of the new town hall, which combines Italian classicism and the Flemish baroque flamboyance. Some Dutch leaders now took pride in speaking French, believing it the language of good taste. French classicism overwhelmed Dutch literature and poetry. Although the French military invasion of 1672 failed, a cultural invasion succeeded. Dutch artists began to offer pale imitations of French works. There were fewer paintings of attentive and hardworking municipal and provincial officials.

The originality of Dutch political life also waned with relative economic decline. The great merchant families maintained increasingly tight control over the position of regent and other influential posts. A form of municipal corruption ("contracts of correspondence") allowed them to divide up or even purchase lucrative government positions. More regents were now major landowners and had little in common with merchants, who had vital interests in government policies.

Government became more rigid, more distant from the Dutch people, and less tolerant, persecuting religious dissenters and undertaking a witch hunt against homosexuals. The Dutch army became increasingly one of mercenaries, not citizens. The Dutch Republic's loss of vitality and economic primacy was accompanied by its decline in international affairs.

CONCLUSION

At the dawn of the eighteenth century, England and the Netherlands remained non-absolutist states. The victory of Parliament in the English Civil War, the Glorious Revolution of 1688, and the Bill of Rights of 1689, accepted by the monarchy, guaranteed the rights of Parliament and the rule of law. While the Netherlands entered a period of decline, as had Spain, Great Britain (as England became known in 1707 after the formal union with Scotland) would remain a great power in the eighteenth century, enriched by commerce and empire. In the meantime, the kings of Spain and the rulers of France, Prussia, Austria, Russia, and Sweden increased their authority over their subjects as continental Europe entered the age of absolutism.

CHAPTER **7**

THE AGE OF ABSOLUTISM, 1650–1720

In Louis XIV's France, architects and artists were paid to glorify the monarch. In 1662, the king chose the sun as his emblem; he declared himself *nec pluribus impar*—without equal. To Louis, the sun embodied virtues that he associated with the ideal monarch: firmness, benevolence, and equity. Henceforth, Louis XIV would frequently be depicted as Apollo, the Greek and Roman sun god.

The rulers of continental Europe, including Louis XIV (ruled 1643–1715), relentlessly extended their power between 1650 and 1750. The sovereigns of France, Prussia, Russia, Austria, and Sweden, in particular, became absolute rulers, in principle above all challenge from within the state itself. To the east, the power of the Turkish sultan of the Ottoman Empire was itself already in principle absolute. Rulers extended their dynastic domains and prestige, making their personal rule absolute, based on loyalty to them as individuals, not to the state as an abstraction. But at the same time, they helped lay the foundations for the modern centralized state. Absolute rulers asserted their supreme right to proclaim laws and levy taxes, appointing more officials to carry out the details of governance and multiplying fiscal demands on their subjects. They ended most of the long-standing privileges of towns, which had survived longer in Western Europe than in Eastern Europe, such as freedom from taxation, or the right to maintain independent courts.

The absolute state affected the lives of more people than ever before through taxation, military service, and the royal quest for religious orthodoxy. Absolute rule thus impinged directly on the lives of subjects, who felt the extended reach of state power through, for example, more efficient tax collection. A Prussian recalled that in school no child would question "that the king could cut off the noses and ears of all his subjects if he wished to

242

do so, and that we owed it to his goodness and his gentle disposition that he had left us in possession of these necessary organs."

Absolutism was at least in part an attempt to reassert public order and coercive state authority after almost seventy years of wars that had brought economic, social, and political chaos. England and Spain had been at war in the last decades of the sixteenth century. Wars of religion had raged through much of Europe on and off for more than a century—above all, during the Thirty Years' War (1618–1648). The Dutch war of independence against Spain began in 1566 and did not officially end until 1648. The tumultuous decade of the 1640s was particularly marked by political crises. Wars had led to often dramatic increases in taxes, which quadrupled in Spain under Philip II, and jumped fivefold in France between 1609 and 1648. During the 1640s, the English Civil War led to the execution of King Charles I in 1649 (see Chapter 6). In France, the period of mid-century rebellion known as the Fronde included a noble uprising against the crown and determined, violent peasant resistance against increased taxation. The multiplicity and seemingly interrelated character of these crises engendered great anxiety among social elites: "These are days of shaking, and this shaking is universal," a preacher warned the English Parliament.

THEORIES OF ABSOLUTISM

The doctrine of absolutism originated with French jurists late in the sixteenth century. The emergence of theories of absolutism reflected contemporary attempts to conceptualize the significance of the rise of larger territorial states whose rulers enjoyed more power than their predecessors. France was a prime example of this trend. The legal theorist Jean Bodin (1530–1596) had lived through the wars of religion. "Seeing that nothing upon earth is greater or higher, next unto God, than the majesty of kings and sovereign princes," he wrote in the *Six Books of the Republic* (1576), the "principal point of sovereign majesty and absolute power [is] to consist principally in giving laws unto the subjects in general, without their consent." The ruler became the father, a stern but supposedly benevolent figure. Bodin, who like many other people in France longed for peace and order, helped establish the political theory legitimizing French absolute rule.

Almost a century later, the political philosopher Thomas Hobbes (1588–1679) emerged as the thundering theorist of absolutism. Hobbes had experienced the turmoil of the English Civil War (see Chapter 6). In *Leviathan* (1651), he argued that absolutism alone could prevent society from lapsing into the "state of nature," a constant "war of every man against every man" that made life "solitary, poor, nasty, brutish, and short." People would only obey, Hobbes insisted, when they were afraid of the consequences of not doing so. Seeking individual security, individuals would enter into a type of social contract with their ruler, surrendering their rights in exchange for

Non est potestas Super Terram quæ Comparetur ei Iob. 41. 24.

The illustration for the cover of the Englishman Thomas Hobbes's *Leviathan* (1651) depicts the absolute state. Note how the ruler's body is made up of the masses over whom he rules. England and then Great Britain, however, remained an exception to the absolutist wave that swept across continental Europe.

protection. A ruler's will thus became for Hobbes the almost sacred embodiment of the state. In France, Jacques Bossuet (1627–1704), bishop and tutor to Louis XIV, postulated that kings ruled by "divine right," that is, by virtue of the will of God. Unlike Hobbes's notion of authority based on a social contract, Bossuet held that the ruler's authority stemmed from God alone.

Yet theorists of absolutism recognized the difference between absolute and arbitrary or despotic rule. Inherent in their theories was the idea that the absolute ruler was responsible for looking after the needs of his people. Bossuet summed up: "It is one thing for a government to be absolute, and quite another for it to be arbitrary. It is absolute in that it is not liable to constraint, there being no other power capable of coercing the sovereign, who is in this sense independent of all human authority." But he went on, "it does not follow from this that the government is arbitrary, for besides the fact that all is subject to the judgment of God . . . there are also laws, in states, so that whatever is done contrary to them is null in a legal sense; moreover, there is always an opportunity for redress, either at other times or in other conditions." Thus, even according to one of the most determined proponents of absolutism, the monarch, whose legitimacy came from God, nonetheless was subject to limits imposed by reason through laws and traditions. Western monarchs recognized, at least in theory, the necessity of consulting with institutions considered to be representative of interests such as the Church and nobility: parlements (noble law courts), Estates, the Cortes in Spain, and Parliament, which had been victorious in the English Civil War in non-absolutist England, where the law remained separated from the will of the monarch.

CHARACTERIZING ABSOLUTE RULE

Absolute states were characterized by strong, ambitious dynasties, which through advantageous marriages, inheritance, warfare, and treaties added to their dynastic domains and prestige. Their states had nobilities that accepted monarchical authority in exchange for a guarantee of their status, ownership of land, and privileges within the state and over the peasantry, whether peasants were legally free, as in Western Europe, or serfs, as in Prussia, Austria, Poland, and Russia. The absolute states of Central and Eastern Europe—Prussia, Austria, and Russia—shared similar social structures: a strong nobility with ties to rulers who granted privileges in exchange for cooperation; a subservient peasantry in the process of losing remaining rights to rulers and landlords, including—by becoming serfs attached to the land they worked—that of personal freedom; and a relatively weak and politically powerless middle class. Unlike England and the Dutch United Provinces, these states had no representative institutions and few towns of sufficient importance to stand in the way of absolute rule.

The Commonwealth of Poland-Lithuania was an exception and thus did not fit the Russian or Prussian model. In 1386 the Kingdom of Poland and the Grand Duchy of Lithuania had been joined in a personal union (Warsaw became the capital in 1595). The Commonwealth of Poland-Lithuania was created in 1569 by virtue of the Union of Lublin. In the Commonwealth, the authority of the king was limited by the strength of the landed nobility—the *szlachta*, who dominated the Parliament (the Sejm). Particularly in northern Poland around the port city of Gdańsk, a concept of sovereignty emerged that paralleled similar important transformations in England and the Netherlands. The Commonwealth of Poland-Lithuania is thus sometimes referred to as a "gentry democracy." Here the parliamentary system, which had been founded in the fifteenth century, protected the personal freedom of the citizens of the monarchy.

Although some Western sovereigns were somewhat limited by representative bodies—diets, parlements, Estates—absolute monarchies nonetheless created an unprecedented concentration of governing power. Between 1614 and 1788, no king of France convoked the Estates-General, an assembly of

representatives from the three estates—clergy, nobility, and commoners—
that had been created early in the fourteenth century as an advisory council
to the king. To take another example, the Portuguese assembly of nobles did
not meet at all during the eighteenth century.

Monarchs and Nobles

In each absolute state, the relationship between ruler and nobles determined the specific character of absolutism. This delicate balance is reflected
in the oath of loyalty sworn to the king of Spain by the Aragonese nobility:
"We who are as good as you swear to you who are no better than we to accept
you as our king and sovereign lord, provided you observe all our liberties and
laws; but if not, not." Monarchs negotiated compromises with nobles,
awarding titles and confirming privileges for obedience, or at least compliance. In some cases, nobles asserted independence vis-à-vis royal authority.
But emphatic assertions of royal authority reduced nobles to the role of junior ruling partners in governance, dominating state and local government.
Nobles frightened by the social and political turmoil that shook Europe during the first half of the century now more willingly served rulers as royal officials and military commanders.

"Tables of ranks" dividing nobles into distinct grades or ranks were established at the turn of the century by the kings of Sweden, Denmark, Prussia,
and Russia, making it clear that noble privileges were bestowed by monarchs. Louis XIV of France asserted the right to monitor the legitimacy of all
titles and even to confiscate noble estates. In 1668, he ordered the investigation of "false" nobles holding dubious titles. These measures helped the king
maintain the loyalty of nobles, some of whom resented those who held titles
they considered suspect. The great noble families thereafter enjoyed an
even greater monopoly over the most lucrative and prestigious royal and
ecclesiastical posts. Using the augmented power of the state, rulers also pla-
cated nobles by ending a turbulent period of peasant uprisings against taxes,
obligations to lords, and the high price of grain. Insurrections occurred less
frequently and were savagely repressed.

The gradual centralization of authority in Eastern Europe left nobles with
even more autonomy than they had in the West, allowing Russian lords, Polish nobles, and Prussian nobles (*Junkers*) the possibility of further increasing their wealth and power through the extension of their estates, which
were worked by serfs. Beginning in the late sixteenth century, such
seigneurs made fortunes shipping grain to the West, where prices of cereal
and food had risen dramatically in response to population growth. Royal
decrees in Prussia and Russia and assembly legislation in Poland progressively limited the right of peasants to move from the land they worked, or
even to inherit property. Ravaged by hard times, peasant proprietors had to
sell their land to nobles. Impoverished and virtually powerless to resist, peasants lost their personal freedom, a process most marked in Russia. Thus, as

feudalism disappeared in Western Europe, it became more prevalent in the East as lords dispossessed peasants from their land and the latter became serfs. The economic crises of the seventeenth century, including the Thirty Years' War and the decline in Western demand for grain imported from the East because of increased production in the West, only made conditions of life harder for serfs.

In the Ottoman Empire, absolutism was even more despotic. All lands were considered the sultan's private imperial possessions. He granted landed estates to those who served him, but because the sultan recognized no rights of property, no hereditary nobility could develop to challenge his authority. No representative institutions existed. Towns in the overwhelmingly rural empire had neither autonomy nor rights.

Expanding State Structures

Absolute monarchs extended their authority within their territories by expanding the structure of the state. The Renaissance city-states of Italy had created relatively efficient civil administrations and had set up the first permanent diplomatic corps. During the seventeenth century, the apparatus of administration, taxation, and military conscription gradually became part of the structure of the absolute states, which were increasingly centralized. The result was that in Europe as a whole, the number of government officials grew about fourfold. To fill the most prestigious offices, monarchs chose nobles for their influence more than for their competence. But some absolute rulers also began to employ commoners as officials to collect vital information—for example, to project revenues or to anticipate the number of soldiers available for war.

One result of these expanding ranks of officials was the tripling of tax revenues between 1520 and 1670 in France and Spain, and in England as well. To raise money, absolute rulers sold monopolies (which permitted only the holder of the monopoly to produce and sell particular goods) on the production and sale of salt, tobacco, and other commodities, and imposed taxes on trading towns. The rulers of France, Spain, and Austria also filled the state coffers by selling hereditary offices. James I of England doubled the number of knights during the first four months of his reign. Queen Christina of Sweden doubled the number of noble families in ten years. In addition, as royal power and prestige rose, the monarchs more easily found wealthy families to loan them money, usually in exchange for tax exemptions, titles, or other privileges.

Absolutism and Warfare

The regular collection of taxes and the expansion of sources of revenue increased the capacity of absolute rulers to maintain standing armies and fortifications, and to wage war. Absolute states were characterized by the

Table 7.1. The Size of European Armies, 1690–1814

	1690	1710	1756/60	1789	1812/14
Britain	70,000	75,000	200,000	40,000*	250,000
France	400,000	350,000	330,000	180,000	600,000
Habsburg Emp.	50,000	100,000	200,000	300,000	250,000
Prussia	30,000	39,000	195,000	190,000	270,000
Spain	na	30,000	na	50,000	na
Sweden	na	110,000	na	na	na
United Prov.	73,000	130,000	40,000*	na	na

*Drop reflects peacetime and non-absolutist character of the state.
na: Figures not available.
Source: Paul Kennedy, *The Rise and Fall of the Great Powers* (New York: Vintage, 1989), p. 99.

deployment of a large standing army capable of maintaining order at home and maintaining or expanding dynastic interests and territories. Absolutist statemaking and warfare had direct and indirect consequences for most of the European population. Kings no longer depended on troops provided by nobles or military contractors, thereby avoiding the risk that private armies might challenge royal power. Standing armies continued to grow in size during the eighteenth century (see Table 7.1). During the 1500s, the peacetime armies of the continental powers had included about 10,000 to 20,000 soldiers; by the 1690s, they reached about 150,000 soldiers. For the first time, uniforms became standard equipment for every soldier. The French army, which soon stood at about 180,000 men in peacetime, rose to 350,000 soldiers during the War of the Spanish Succession (1701–1714). The Russian army grew from 130,000 in 1731 to 458,000 in 1796. In contrast, England and the Dutch Republic, two non-absolutist powers, had relatively small armies, and, as sea powers, both depended on their navies.

As absolute monarchs consolidated their power, the reasons for waging international wars changed. The wars of the previous century had been fought, in principle, over the rivalry between the Catholic and Protestant religions, even if dynastic interests were never far from the surface. Now, although religious rivalries still constituted an important factor in international conflict (as in the case of the long struggle between the Muslim Ottoman Empire and the Catholic Habsburg Empire), "reasons of state" became a prevalent justification for the rulers of France, Prussia, and Russia to make war on their neighbors.

Warfare both encouraged and drew upon the development of credit institutions. But as the British and Dutch cases demonstrated, a state did not have to be absolutist to marshal sufficient resources to fight sustained wars. English colonial trade generated excise and customs taxes, permitting the expansion of the Royal Navy. The crown's reputation for repayment facilitated raising money through loans at home and abroad. Amsterdam's stature as a great banking center contributed to the ability of the Dutch government to fight extended wars. In contrast, the French monarchy lacked the confidence of wary investors, and despite the sale of privileges found itself in an increasingly perilous financial situation. Moreover, the French monarchy often had to pay higher rates of interest than private investors because it was a bad credit risk.

Even in peacetime, military expenditures now took up almost half of the budget of the European state. In times of war, the percentage rose to 80 percent, or even more. By the end of the sixteenth century, Philip II of Spain had allocated three-quarters of state expenditures to pay for past wars or to wage new ones. Appropriately enough, the bureau in Prussia that a century later would oversee tax collection itself evolved from the General War Office, making explicit the close connection between the extraction of state revenue and the waging of dynastic wars. Inevitably, there came a point even in absolute states when noble and other wealthy families upon which monarchies depended for financial support began to grumble.

Absolutism and Religion

An alliance with established churches helped monarchs achieve and maintain absolute rule. Absolute monarchs lent their authority and prestige to the established churches, the support of which, in turn, seemed to legitimize absolute monarchical power. In Catholic states in particular, the Church's quest for uniformity of belief and practice went hand in hand with the absolutist monarch's desire to eliminate challenges to his authority. The Church helped create an image of the king as a sacred figure who must be obeyed because he served God's interests on earth. In turn, absolute monarchs obliged the Church by persecuting religious minorities.

Absolute rulers also reduced ecclesiastical autonomy in their realms. The Catholic Church lost authority to their absolute monarchs. Yet the Church owned as much as two-thirds of the land in Portugal, at least one-tenth of the land in Spain, Austria, and France, half the land in Bavaria and Flanders, and considerable holdings in every Italian state. Moreover, the Church claimed the right to the tithe, the tax of 10 percent on annual resources. But absolute monarchs maintained authority over ecclesiastical appointments, in effect creating national churches, much to the consternation of the papacy in Rome. Signs of the victory of absolute rulers over the Catholic Church included eliminating the Inquisition in France and Spain, closing monasteries and expelling religious orders in France and Austria, assuming control over censorship, reducing ecclesiastical authority over marriage, and establishing the principle of state supervision over education.

The siege of Constantinople by the Turks in 1453 from a French manuscript illumination.

In France, the very existence of the French, or Gallican Church, defied papal claims to complete authority over the Church. By the Concordat of Bologna in 1516, the pope had given the kings of France virtual control (subject to papal confirmation) over the appointment of bishops in France and the right to over-rule the judgments of ecclesi-astical courts. This irritated French "ultramontane" clergy, who recognized only the authority of the pope "beyond the mountains," that is, over the Alps in distant Rome. The provincial parlements, or noble law courts, by contrast, remained defiantly Gallican. The Gallican Church itself was far more likely to remain loyal to the monarchy that defended its prerogatives, even if Gallicans themselves insisted that the pope and bishops retain spiritual authority, with the king having a monopoly only on temporal power.

Recognizing no distinction between church and state, the Turkish Ottoman Empire remained a theocracy. The sultan's subjects believed his despotic authority to be divine. The Muslim religious hierarchy, which included judges, theologians, and teachers, provided officials for the imperial administration. The supreme religious dignitary occasionally invoked religious law, of which he was the main interpreter, to counter orders of the sultan, but the latter's political authority remained absolute.

The expansion of the Ottoman Empire had been based upon the concept of the crusading "Holy War" against infidels, that is, non-Muslims. As the Turks destroyed the Byzantine Empire, capturing Constantinople in 1453, they confiscated many of the resources of the Orthodox Church and other Christian denominations. The Ottoman Turks enslaved prisoners of war, purchased slaves abroad, and imposed slave levies upon the Christians of the empire. Many Christian children had been trained as officials or soldiers and had converted to Islam. The empire also depended on the contri-butions of nonslave Christians, including skilled Greek sailors who made

Turkish galleys feared in the Mediterranean. Some joined the "janissary" infantry, a military corps that assumed police duties in periods of peace.

Yet the Ottoman Empire tolerated religious diversity. As long as non-Muslims did not resist Turkish authority, they were free to practice their religion and to become officials within the empire. In Albania (where alone conversions seemed to have been forced), Bosnia, and Herzegovina, many people, including some nobles, converted to the Muslim faith. Young Christians captured by Turkish fleets could convert to Islam to escape a life chained to benches as galley slaves. In contrast, Muslims captured by Christian powers remained galley slaves, even if they converted.

Monumentalism in Architecture and Art

Absolute monarchs utilized the extravagant emotional appeal of monumental architecture. They designed their capitals to reflect the imperatives of monarchical authority. Madrid, Berlin, Saint Petersburg, and Versailles were planned, shaped, and invested with symbols of absolute rule. These cities were laid out according to geometric principles. In contrast to the narrow, winding streets of cities that had evolved organically from medieval times, straight, wide boulevards were created in one fell swoop. These symmetrical boulevards symbolized the organized and far-reaching power of absolutism and the growth of the modern state. Royal armies paraded down boulevards to squares or royal palaces, around which were grouped government buildings and noble residences. Barracks housing standing armies also became a prominent feature of the new urban landscape.

Monarchs paid artists and architects to combine baroque elements with a more restrained, balanced classicism, influenced by the early sixteenth-century Roman style of the High Renaissance. This became known as the Louis XIV style. Thus, the facade completing the Louvre palace in Paris, the work of Gianlorenzo Bernini (1598–1680), drew on the architectural style of Roman temples, thereby linking Louis to the glories of Julius Caesar. Hyacinthe Rigaud's full-length

Hyacinthe Rigaud's *Louis XIV* (1701).

portrait of Louis XIV in 1701 shows a supremely confident and powerful king standing in a regal pose, wearing luxurious coronation robes, clutching his staff of authority, and looking with condescension at the viewer—his subject.

Absolutism in France

Absolutist France became the strongest state in early modern Europe. Francis I and Henry IV had extended the effective reach of monarchical authority (see Chapter 4). Louis XIII's invaluable minister Cardinal Richelieu had used provincial "intendants" to centralize and further extend monarchical authority. Richelieu's policies led to the doubling of taxes between 1630 and 1650, sparking four major waves of peasant resistance, including one uprising in the southwest in 1636 in which about 60,000 peasants took up arms, some shouting the impossible demand, "Long live the king without taxes!" Upon Louis XIII's death in 1643, the stage was set for Louis XIV to rule as a divine-right king of an absolute state. But before the young Louis could take control of the government, France would first experience the regency of his mother and the revolt known as the Fronde.

The Fronde: Taming "Overmighty Subjects"

Louis XIV was four years old at the time of his accession to the throne. His mother, Anne of Austria (1601–1666), served as regent. She depended on Cardinal Jules Mazarin (1602–1661) for advice. Mazarin, a worldly, charming, and witty Italian, always dressed in the finest red silk and was well known for his love of money. A master of intrigue, rumor had it that he and Anne had secretly married.

During the Regency period, Anne and Mazarin kept French armies in the field, prolonging the Thirty Years' War, which had become a struggle pitting the dynastic interests of France against the Austrian and Spanish Habsburgs (see Chapter 4). Most nobles, with much to lose from civil disturbances, remained loyal to the monarchy. But Mazarin's prolongation of the victorious struggle against Spain generated a political crisis.

Resistance to royal authority culminated in a revolt that shook the Bourbon monarchy at mid-century. Between 1648 and 1653, powerful "nobles of the sword" (those nobles who held ancient titles and whose forebears had gathered retainers to fight for the king) tried to regain the influence lost during the reign of Louis XIII. Ordinary people entered the fray, demanding lower taxes because of deteriorating economic conditions. The revolt became known as the Fronde—named for a slingshot boys in Paris used to hurl rocks.

Mazarin, whom many nobles considered a "foreign plotter" and an outsider like Anne of Austria, had borrowed money for the state from financiers. He did so against expected revenue from new taxes or the sale of offices.

Nobles were willing to suffer extraordinary levies in times of war. But now they complained bitterly that since the wars had ended supplementary impositions were needless. Furthermore, some of the oldest noble families had claimed for some time that they had been systematically excluded from the highest and most lucrative and prestigious offices. In fact, there was some truth in this claim, as the king feared the power of disloyal "overmighty subjects," preferring lesser nobles for military offices and skilled bureaucrats for some civil posts. Now nobles of the sword denounced Mazarin, his system of patronage, and his financier friends, some of whom had made fortunes supplying the royal armies.

In 1648, Mazarin attempted to secure the approval of the Parlement of Paris for increased taxes. The Parlement of Paris, the chief law court in France, was made up of nobles who had purchased their positions from the crown. Wanting to safeguard their privileges and power, the Parlement of Paris defied the Regency by calling for an assembly of the four sovereign courts of Paris to consider the financial crisis. Meeting without royal permission, the assembly proposed that the courts elect delegates to consider financial reforms in the realm. The provincial parlements joined the protest against what seemed to be unchecked royal authority. Financiers who had earlier purchased titles from the crown now refused to loan the state any more money.

When Mazarin ordered the arrest of some of the defiant members of the parlement in August 1648, barricades went up in Paris in support of the parlement. From inside the Louvre palace, Louis XIV, now nine years of age, heard the angry shouts of the crowds. Popular discontent forced the royal court to flee Paris in January 1649.

The role of the prince of Condé (Louis de Bourbon, 1621–1686), head of the junior branch of the Bourbon family, was crucial in the Fronde. Condé's great victory in 1643 over the Spanish at the battle of Rocroi in northern France, which ended any possibility of a successful Spanish invasion of the country, earned him the name of "the Great Condé." But as long as Mazarin had met Condé's demands for money and offices, the latter remained loyal to the young king and in 1648 marched to Paris with his army to defend him. Short-lived tax reforms bought time. But major uprisings against taxes, which had doubled in two decades as Richelieu and Mazarin had in turn raised money to wage war, broke out in several provinces. Relatively poor nobles, who resented that wealthy commoners were able to purchase titles, led other revolts. Condé himself changed sides in 1649 and supported the *frondeurs*.

Fearing Condé's influence, a Spanish invasion, and further insurrections, Anne and Mazarin found noble allies against Condé and early in 1650 ordered him imprisoned. Condé's arrest further mobilized opposition to Mazarin, whose enemies forced the minister to flee the country early the next year. A year later, Condé was released from prison at the demand of the Parlement of Paris. In September 1651, Louis XIV declared his majority and right to rule, although he was only thirteen. But he faced an immediate challenge from Condé, who marched to Paris in 1652 with the goals of reestablishing the great nobles' political influence and of getting rid of Mazarin (who continued to sway royal policy from his exile in Germany). However, finding insufficient support from the parlement, the municipal government, or ordinary Parisians, Condé fled to Spain. The boy-king recalled Mazarin to Paris.

Louis XIV restored monarchical authority by ending the nobles' rebellion and putting down peasant resistance against taxation. Louis made clear that henceforth the Parlement of Paris could not meddle in the king's business. And in 1673 the king deprived the twelve parlements of their right to issue remonstrances (formal objections to the registration of new royal ordinances, edicts, or declarations, which could be overridden by the king) before they registered an edict. The king also disbanded the private armies of headstrong nobles and tightened royal control over provincial governors.

Unlike the English Parliament's successful rebellion against the crown in defense of constitutional rule (see Chapter 6), royal victory in the Fronde broke French noble resistance to absolute rule. The king's predecessors had frequently consulted with prominent nobles about important matters. Louis XIV felt no obligation to do so. Yet the Fronde also demonstrated that the crown had to rule more subtly with respect to noble interests.

Mercantilism under Louis XIV

Following Mazarin's death in 1661, Louis XIV, now twenty-two years of age, assumed more personal responsibility. The state's firmer financial footing owed much to the cool calculations of Jean-Baptiste Colbert (1619–1683), controller-general of the realm, who directed administration, taxation, and public works. The grandson of a provincial merchant of modest standing, Colbert endured the hostility of the old noble families. His frosty personality led him to be dubbed "the North." He employed surveyors and mapmakers to assess the economic resources of the provinces. Whereas formerly only about a quarter of revenues reached royal coffers, now as much as four-fifths of what was collected poured into the royal treasury. Even though the direct royal tax on land (the *taille*) had been reduced, state revenues doubled, despite abuses and privileged exemptions (nobles and clergy did not pay the land tax).

Mercantilism underlay the economy of absolutist France, as it did royal economic policies in Europe. Mercantilists posited that all resources should be put into the service of the state and that a state's wealth was measured by its ability to import more gold and silver than it exported. Jealous of English and Dutch prosperity, Colbert became the chief proponent of French mercantilist policies, which emphasized economic self-sufficiency. He founded commercial trading companies to which the king granted monopolies on colonial trade, and levied high protective tariffs on Dutch and English imports. Louis XIV established the royal Gobelins tapestry manufacture on the edge of Paris and encouraged the textile industry and the manufacture of other goods that could be exported. He improved roads and oversaw the extension of France's network of canals, including the Languedoc Canal (Canal du Midi), which links the Mediterranean to the Garonne River and thus to the Atlantic Ocean.

Yet despite the growth of the French merchant fleet and navy, the French East India Company, established by Colbert in 1664, could not effectively compete with its more efficient and adventurous Dutch and English rivals in the quest for global trade. The monarchy had to bail out the company and later took away its trading monopoly. Moreover, trade within France remained hamstrung by a bewildering variety of restrictions and internal tariffs that in some places were not much different from those that characterized the hodgepodge of German states.

At the same time, while the king was a master of extracting revenue from his subjects, his greatest talent was for emptying the royal coffers with dizzying speed. Louis XIV and his successors plunged the monarchy into an ever-deepening and eventually disastrous financial crisis.

The Absolute Louis XIV

As Louis XIV grew into manhood, he looked the part of a great king and played it superbly. Handsome, proud, energetic, and decisive, the king's love of gambling, hunting, and women sometimes took precedence over matters of state. But he also supervised the work of the high council of his prominent officials, and, although a spendthrift, he closely monitored the accounts of his realm.

The king became a shrewd judge of character, surrounding himself with men of talent. He consciously avoided being dependent on any single person, the way Louis XIII had been on Richelieu, or his mother on Mazarin. During a visit to the château of Vaux-le-Vicomte, built by the unpopular minister of finance Nicolas Fouquet, Louis was served with solid gold tableware and viewed large pools filled with seawater and even saltwater fish. The king promptly ordered Fouquet arrested and took the magnificent château for himself.

Having affirmed his authority over Paris, Louis dissolved any remaining pretensions of autonomy held by the elites in the major provincial towns. One result of the Fronde was that the monarchy expanded the narrow social base on which state power had previously rested. Louis selected governors, intendants, and bishops who would be loyal to him. Mayors became officials of the state who had to purchase their titles in exchange for fidelity to the king. Wealthy merchants now preferred to seek ennoblement rather than try to maintain municipal privileges that seemed increasingly archaic. The presence of royal garrisons, which towns once resisted, not only affirmed the sovereign's authority but were welcomed by local elites as protection against plebeian insurrection. Troops were also good for local business. In 1667, Louis took another important step in affirming his authority by appointing a lieutenant-general of police for Paris, who was given extensive authority ranging from powers of arrest to responsibility for street cleaning and fire fighting. Paris soon had street lighting—thousands of glass-enclosed candles—during the early evening hours.

Louis XIV portrayed himself as God's representative, charged with maintaining earthly order. "*L'état, c'est moi*" ("I am the state"), he is said to have remarked. The royal propaganda machine provided ideological legitimacy by cranking out images of the king as a glorious monarch. At the same time, royal censors suppressed publications, prohibited imported books, and limited the number of printers. The goal of censorship was to protect the honor and reputation of the king and religion.

Louis XIV created the first French ministry of war and shaped it into an effective bureaucracy. The king and his ministers brought the noble-dominated officer corps under royal control, making seniority the determinant of rank and charging wealthy nobles handsome sums for the privilege of commanding their own regiments or companies. The ministry of war ordered the construction of military academies, barracks, and drilling grounds, and ordered the brilliant military engineer Sébastien le Prestre de Vauban (1633–1707) to fortify key border towns.

Louis XIV described himself as first seigneur of the realm. Nobles still insisted more than ever—though more quietly than at the time of the Fronde—that institutionalized noble privileges were necessary to counter the excesses of absolute authority. Nobles were almost completely immune from royal taxes (basically paying only indirect taxes) until Louis made them subject to two additional taxes (the *capitation,* a head tax, and the *vingtième,* a tax of 5 percent, usually only on land). They benefited from the economic development the monarchy encouraged, such as the construction of better roads and networks of canals that were largely underwritten by the state.

Since the time of Henry IV, offices had effectively become forms of hereditary property. Louis XIV's lavish sale of offices and titles—500 sold with a single edict in 1696—expanded the nobility. As one minister put it, "as soon as the crown creates an office God creates a fool willing to buy it." Few noble families now could trace their titles back more than several generations. This accentuated differences between nobles of the sword and nobles of the robe (many of whom had purchased their offices). The nobles of the sword dominated court life, but the king did not hesitate to dip into the ranks of commoners to find efficient, loyal officials, exempting them from taxation and providing lucrative posts for their offspring. A noble of the sword denounced the "reign of the vile bourgeoisie," that is, nobles of recent title and other relative upstarts he viewed as unworthy of prominent posts.

The château of Versailles, built by Louis XIV between 1669 and 1686.

Louis XIV at Versailles

Louis XIV never forgot hearing the howling Parisian mob from his room in the royal palace. Resolving to move his court to Versailles, twelve miles west of Paris, he visited Paris only four times during the seventy-two years of his reign. Realizing that an adequately fed population would be less likely to riot, Louis XIV and his successors worked to assure the sufficient provisioning of the capital.

The Sun King followed Colbert's admonition that "nothing marks the greatness of princes better than the buildings that compel the people to look on them with awe, and all posterity judges them by the superb palaces they have built during their lifetime." The staging ground for royal ceremonies was the monumental château of Versailles (constructed 1669–1686), surrounded by geometrically arranged formal gardens, interspersed by 1,400 fountains supplied by the largest hydraulic pumps in the Western world. Sculptures in the gardens made clear the identification of Louis XIV with the Greek and Roman sun god Apollo. In the vast château, the royal dining room was so far from the kitchen that the king's food often arrived at his table cold and, during one particularly cold winter, the wine froze before Louis could taste it. The château's corridors were so long that some nobles used them as urinals, instead of continuing the lengthy trek to a more appropriate place.

Louis summoned the greatest nobles of the realm to Versailles to share in his glory. There they could be honored, but none could become too powerful. More than 10,000 nobles, officials, and servants lived in or near the château. Each day began with the elaborate routine of dressing the king in the company of the richest and most powerful nobles. The ultimate reward for a loyal noble was to be named to a post within the royal household. Louis XIV allowed the nobles to form cabals and conspire, but only against each other.

For nobles at Versailles there was little else to do except eat, drink, hunt— in the company of the king, if they were favored—gamble, and chase around each other's wives and mistresses. Nobles also attended the expensive theatrical and operatic productions put on at royal expense. These included the works of Jean-Baptiste Molière (1622–1673) and Jean Racine (1639–1699), master of the tragic dramatic style, who drew themes from the classical Greek poets. Both Molière and Racine wrote effusive praise for the king into some of their plays, the latter dedicating his first great success, *Alexander the Great,* to Louis XIV.

Social struggles mark the plays of Molière. The son of an upholsterer, the playwright started a traveling theatrical company before settling in Paris. The lonely, unhappy Molière poked fun at the pretensions of aristocratic and ecclesiastical society, depicting the private, cruel dramas of upper-class family life. But his popular works also helped reaffirm the boundaries between social classes. He ridiculed burghers, whose wealth could purchase titles but not teach them how to behave as nobles. In *The Bourgeois Gentilhomme* (1670), the parvenu gives himself away with a social gaffe. Molière also detested hypocrisy, which he depicted in *Tartuffe* (1664), a tale of the unfortunate effects of unrestrained religious enthusiasm on a family. *Tartuffe* brought Molière the wrath of the Church, but he had an even more powerful protector in the king.

Louis XIV believed that his court stood as the center and apex of civilization. Indeed, French arts and literature had an enormous influence in Europe. Foreign monarchs, nobles, and writers still considered French the language of high culture. The château of Versailles encouraged imitation. Philip V of Spain, among others, ordered a similar palace built. The duke of Saxony rebuilt his capital of Dresden along neoclassical lines. The château of Versailles also served as a model for noble estates and townhouses built in the classical style.

Louis XIV's Persecution of Religious Minorities

One of the most salient results of the victory of absolute rule in Catholic states was the persecution of religious minorities. Such campaigns in part served to placate the papacy and the Church hierarchy in each Catholic state. Louis XIV had little interest in theology, although he was relatively pious. But as he grew older, the king brought into his inner circle a number

(Left) The symbol of the sun used to glorify the absolute ruler, Louis XIV. *(Right)* This caricature shows Louis XIV, the Sun King, as the exterminator of Protestantism.

of extremely devout advisers, and into his bedroom a fervently religious mistress.

Reversing the tolerant policies of Henry IV and Louis XIII, Louis XIV launched a vigorous campaign of persecution against Huguenots, closing most Protestant churches and initiating attempts to force conversions to Catholicism. In 1685, he revoked the Edict of Nantes, by which Henry IV in 1598 had extended religious tolerance to Protestants. This pleased the provincial estates in regions where Protestants were a forceful minority and memories of the wars of religion were still fresh. But the economic cost to France was considerable in the long run. Although the king forbade Huguenots from leaving France, many merchants and skilled craftsmen were among the 200,000 Huguenots who emigrated during the next forty years. Many went to England, Prussia, the Dutch United Provinces, and even South Africa.

With the motto "one king, one law, one faith," Louis XIV also persecuted Jansenists in his quest for religious orthodoxy. Jansenists were followers of Cornelis Jansen, bishop of Ypres in the Southern Netherlands (Belgium), who died in 1638. They could be found in France, the Netherlands, Austria, and several Italian states. Seeking reforms within the Church, Jansenists emphasized the role of faith and divine grace in the pursuit of salvation. Believing mankind to be fallen and hapless, incapable of understanding the will of God, Jansenists came close to accepting a Calvinist doctrine of pre-destination. Their enemies called them "Calvinists who go to Mass." However, Jansenists believed that one should completely withdraw from the world, given the certainty of sin and mankind's ignorance of God's will.

Notoriously ascetic, they criticized the Church for encouraging a lax morality by holding out the possibility of repeated penance and deathbed conversion.

The pope had condemned Jansenism in 1653, perhaps at the insistence of the Jesuits, the Jansenists' most determined enemy. Louis XIV began to persecute them in the name of "one faith" in 1709; he ordered the Jansenist community at Port-Royal outside of Paris evicted and its abbey burned to the ground. He convinced Pope Clement XI to issue a papal bull, *Unigenitus* (1713), which condemned Jansenism. The Parlement of Paris, however, refused to register the edict. Louis was still trying to force compliance two years later when he died. The king's attempt to impose religious orthodoxy in France fell short, indicating that absolute rule had its limits.

The Limits of French Absolutism

France, like other countries, was far from being a nation-state in which most people thought of themselves as French, as well as or instead of Norman, Breton, or Provençal, or from other regions with their own traditions. More than half the population did not speak French. Inadequate roads isolated mountain regions, in particular, limiting the effective reach of absolute rule.

The absolute monarchy stood at the top of a complex network of patronage based on personal ties that reached into every province and every town. But Louis XIV's intendants still had to take local networks of influence into consideration, using intimidation, cajoling, and negotiation to gain their ends in what was then Western Europe's most populous state.

The king played off against one another the jurisdictions and interests of the Estates, parlements, and other provincial institutions dominated by nobles. The provincial Estates were assemblies of nobles of the *pays d'état* (regions more recently integrated into France and retaining a degree of fiscal autonomy, including Brittany, Provence, Burgundy, and Languedoc), which represented each province. The Estates oversaw the collection of taxes and tended to the details of provincial administration and spending. They met annually amid great pageantry and carefully orchestrated ceremony that, like those at Versailles, reaffirmed social hierarchy. In principle, the Estates could refuse to provide the crown with the annual "free grant" (a subsidy provided by each region to the monarch), which was hardly "free," since the king informed the Estates of the amount of money he wanted. Louis XIV abolished the custom of allowing the Estates to express grievances before voting the amount of their "gift" to the monarchy.

The interests of the nobles also prevailed in the parlements, the sovereign law courts that registered, publicized, and carried out royal laws. The parlements, most of whose members were nobles, claimed to speak for their province in legal matters, asserting the right to issue binding commands in cases of emergencies. But, unlike the English Parliament, no national representative political institution existed in France. The Estates-General, which had met four times between 1560 and 1593, had not been convoked since 1614.

Even the king of France was not as omnipotent or omniscient as he would have liked to think. Jean Bodin had expressed his view that a ruler would be wise to avoid exercising full power—for example, to avoid interfering with his subjects' property. This seeming paradox is perhaps best symbolized by the king's phrase to the Estates of a province: "We entreat you but we also command you. . . ." Even the powerful Bourbons were bound by the so-called fundamental laws of the realm, as well as by those they believed God had established.

THE BALANCE OF POWER

During the century beginning about 1650, the concept of a balance of power between states gradually took hold in many of the courts of Europe. Like the evolving European state system itself, the emergence of the concept arose in part out of the decline of religious antagonisms as a dominant cause of warfare. The quest of absolute rulers to add to their dynastic territories and the growing global commercial rivalry between the great powers increasingly shaped European warfare.

A diplomatic concept dating from the time of the Renaissance city-states of fifteenth-century Italy, the balance of power principle held that great powers should be in equilibrium, and that one power should not be allowed to become too powerful. The decline of one power could threaten the balance of power if, as a result, another power considerably enhanced its strength. Now the main threat to peace ceased to be religious division but rather the power of Louis XIV of France.

The Origins of International Law

Horrified by the Thirty Years' War, two northern European political theorists systematically analyzed questions of international relations, drawing on the recent history of Europe. They helped lay the foundations for the evolution of modern diplomacy. In 1625, the Dutch jurist Hugo Grotius (1583–1645) sought to establish the foundations of international law by arguing that laws to which nations were subject followed from nature and not from God. Samuel von Pufendorf (1632–1694), a German Protestant, found himself under arrest for eight months when he was caught up in the war between Sweden and Denmark. Pufendorf's *Of the Law of Nature and Nations* (1672) postulated legal principles for times of peace—which he argued should be the natural state—and for times of war. He claimed that only a defensive war was justified, pending international arbitration to resolve crises. The problem was, of course, that unless there existed some powerful, impartial body to adjudicate disputes between nations, each side in any conflict invariably claimed that its cause was just. European power politics swept away such theoretical considerations.

THE HABSBURG MONARCHY

The eighteenth-century French Enlightenment philosophe Voltaire only somewhat exaggerated when he dismissed the Holy Roman Empire, that cumbersome federal structure of Central European states that once served as a powerful protector of the papacy, as having ceased to be holy, Roman, or an empire. The Holy Roman Empire included almost 300 German states. Seven, and then in 1648, eight electors (princes and archbishops) selected the Holy Roman emperor, invariably the Habsburg ruler. But in a Europe increasingly dominated by absolute monarchs, the Holy Roman Empire seemed an anomaly.

In principle, the Holy Roman emperor still commanded the allegiance of the states of the empire. These included sizable states such as Austria, Bavaria, and Saxony, whose rulers oversaw elaborate courts, maintained standing armies, and paid for all this by levying taxes on their subjects and customs duties and tolls on merchandise being carried through their territories. The Holy Roman Empire also included many small principalities, duchies, and even archbishoprics barely extending beyond the walls of towns like Mainz and Trier. But in reality the empire had increasingly only a shadow existence, despite its mystique as the defender of Catholicism. The Treaty of Westphalia (1648), which concluded the Thirty Years' War (see Chapter 4), reflected the inability of the Holy Roman Empire to enforce its will, conduct foreign policy, or effectively maintain an army. During the long war, some German princes with powerful allies outside the empire had gone their own way. Indeed, the Treaty of Westphalia specifically empowered each member state to carry out its own foreign policy. The imperial Assembly of the Holy Roman Empire (the Reichstag) thus had virtually no authority to conduct foreign policy with other states. The imperial army was too small and difficult to mobilize to be effective, and the imperial court of law was powerless to enforce its decisions, depending entirely on the good will of the individual states.

The strongest state within the Holy Roman Empire, Habsburg Austria, extended beyond the boundaries of the empire itself. The Habsburgs had ruled Austria without interruption since the thirteenth century. The old Habsburg principle was "Let others wage war. You, happy Austria, marry [to prosper]." Advantageous marriages brought the dynasty the wealthy territories of Burgundy and the Netherlands in the fifteenth century. Charles V, who became Holy Roman emperor in 1519, added Hungary and Bohemia. Counting Spain and its far-flung possessions, he reigned over perhaps a quarter of the population of the European continent, as well as the Spanish Empire in the Americas.

When Charles V abdicated as emperor in 1558, he divided the Habsburg domains into two parts. His brother Ferdinand I inherited the Austrian Habsburg lands (including Austria, Hungary, and Bohemia) and succeeded him as the elected Holy Roman emperor. Charles's son Philip II became king of Spain. His empire included the Netherlands, dependencies in Italy, and colonies in the Americas. The Spanish and Austrian branches of the Habsburgs were henceforth two separate dynasties, although the interests of both as Catholic states and dynastic rivals of France sometimes converged.

The Austrian Habsburg monarchy exercised foreign policy and directed the army, but had less effective authority within its territories than the kings of France had within their realm. Nobles oversaw the court system and policing. When confronted with threats to their traditional prerogatives, nobles put aside differences, such as those between the great landowners and the lower nobility, and formed a common front to preserve their privileges against monarchical erosion.

Austria was the only power able to exercise its influence equally in both Western and Eastern Europe. The Austrian Habsburgs successfully implemented an effective state administration, expanded educational opportunities for the upper classes, and brought resistant or even rebellious nobles under dynastic control. But timely marriages were no longer enough. Throughout the sixteenth century and during the first half of the seventeenth century, the Habsburgs had been almost constantly preoccupied with politics within the German states. During the Thirty Years' War, however, the Habsburgs were unable to expand their domination throughout Central Europe. The Habsburgs remained vulnerable to French expansionism and to Turkish incursions, forcing the monarchy to address threats on two fronts.

That the Habsburg empire contained territories of different nationalities was a source of weakness. Leopold I, elected Holy Roman emperor in 1658 (ruled 1658–1705; Louis XIV was the opposing candidate), was simultaneously Holy Roman emperor, duke of Upper and Lower Silesia, count of Tyrol, archduke of Upper and Lower Austria, king of Bohemia, prince of Transylvania, king of Hungary, Slavonia, Dalmatia, and Croatia, and titular ruler of Lombardy, Styria, and Moravia (see Map 7.1). The monarch necessarily had to consider local political institutions. The Hungarian and Croatian provincial diets, or noble Estates, impeded Habsburg absolutism. Hungarians also resented German-speaking administrators and tax collectors, as well as the Habsburg armies stationed in Hungary to protect the empire from the Turks. In Bohemia, the scars of the religious conflicts between Catholics and Protestants during the Thirty Years' War healed very slowly. Bohemia and Moravia remained centers of Protestant intellectual ferment, despite Catholic domination. Bohemian nobles resented the fact that a decree in 1627 had abolished the elective monarchy, made the Bohemian crown a hereditary Habsburg possession, and brought the confiscation of their lands.

Hungary had been part of the Habsburg domains since the sixteenth century. The Hungarian crown included Hungary, Transylvania, and Croatia.

The Hungarian nobles, proud of their defense of the Habsburg empire against Turkish incursions, seized every opportunity to extract concessions from the Habsburgs. Unlike their Austrian counterparts, most of the Hungarian, or Magyar, nobles had become Protestant during the Reformation. Habsburg persecution of Hungarian Protestants helped spark an insurrection in 1679 that spread into Moravia, Slavonia, and Silesia. This led Leopold to promise the Hungarian Estates to restore some privileges of landowners that had been suppressed. But dissatisfied Protestants then called for Turkish assistance at a time when the Turks were preparing to attack Habsburg territories. The Ottoman army besieged Vienna, the Habsburg capital, in 1683. It was saved after two months by the arrival of a combined relief army of Austrians, Germans, and Poles under the command of the crusading King John Sobieski (ruled 1674–1696), Catholic ruler of Poland. Pope Innocent XI succeeded in convincing Emperor Leopold I, who saw himself as a prince of the Catholic Reformation, to lead a "Holy League" in 1684 against the Ottoman Turks. In the War of the Holy League (1686–1687), and in subsequent fighting, Habsburg armies recaptured most of Hungary and the eastern province of Transylvania from the Turks, as well as

Map 7.1 The Holy Roman Empire under Leopold I, 1658   The Holy Roman Empire was a polyglot state, made up of territories of different nationalities.

much of Croatia. The Peace of Karlowitz (1699) confirmed the Habsburg victory over the Turks. Although Ottoman garrisons remained in Belgrade and Turkish galleys still roamed the Mediterranean, the Ottoman threat to Central Europe had passed.

The Habsburg victory over the Turks consolidated the dynasty's authority over Hungary. In 1687, the Hungarian Estates were forced to declare that the Hungarian throne (the crown of Saint Stephen, named after Hungary's patron saint) would henceforth be a hereditary possession of the Habsburgs and no longer elective. Hungary thereby recognized the sovereignty of the Habsburg dynasty in exchange for several promises: the Hungarian Diet would be convened at regular intervals; Hungary would have its own administration; and Magyar nobles would continue to be exempt from royal taxation. Thus, although he consolidated Habsburg authority within the dynasty's domains, Leopold failed to impose centralized rule on Hungary. Hungary's special position within the monarchy revealed the limits of Habsburg absolutism and Austrian power.

The Habsburg monarchy, the least absolute of Europe's absolute states, was less successful than France in maintaining its power. In 1700, Austria's Habsburg dynasty lost its long-standing ties to Spain when that country passed from the Habsburg dynasty to the Bourbon dynasty with the death of the childless Charles II (ruled 1665–1700). France's defeat in the War of the Spanish Succession (1701–1714), which had been fought to determine who would inherit the Spanish Habsburg territories, enabled the Austrian Habsburgs to pick up some of the remaining pieces of the decimated Spanish Empire in Europe. However, during the eighteenth century Austria ceded its preeminence in Central Europe to Prussia.

THE RISE OF PRUSSIA

The presence of all the essential components of absolutism explain Prussia's rise as a major European power: a proud, ambitious dynasty, the Hohenzollern family of Brandenburg; privileged but loyal nobles, whose estates formed the base of the economy and who dominated a downtrodden peasantry devoid of rights; an increasingly centralized and efficient bureaucracy; and the emergence of a large standing army. Austrian defeats in the Thirty Years' War and vulnerability to French and Turkish challenges left the way open for a rival to emerge among the German states. Bavaria and Saxony were not strong claimants for primacy among the German states, with weak nobilities and lacking effective bureaucracies or large armies. The Catholic clergy undermined the authority of the Bavarian dukes. The attention of Saxony, subject to Swedish influence, was often turned away from German affairs eastward toward the volatile world of Polish politics.

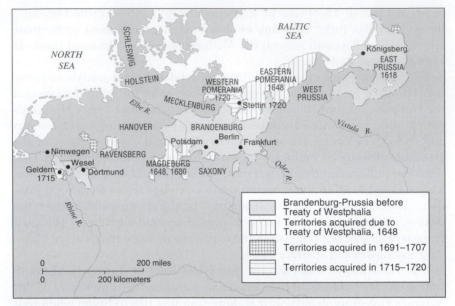

MAP 7.2 THE RISE OF PRUSSIA, 1648–1720   Territories acquired by Brandenburg-Prussia.

The small north-central German state of Brandenburg-Prussia, stretching across the sandy marshes between the Elbe and Oder Rivers, seemed an unlikely candidate to rival Austria and to grow into a powerful absolute state. In 1618, Brandenburg's ruling Hohenzollern dynasty inherited East Prussia, which lay 100 miles to the east of Brandenburg along the Baltic Sea, bordered by Poland. It then absorbed several smaller territories in the Rhineland, more than 100 miles to the west (see Map 7.2). Consisting of three diverse, noncontiguous realms, Brandenburg-Prussia lacked not only defensible frontiers but also the network of prosperous trading towns of other states in Germany. During the Thirty Years' War, Swedish and Austrian armies took turns ravaging Prussia. But with the Treaty of Westphalia (1648), Prussia absorbed much of Pomerania on the coast of the Baltic Sea.

In one of the typical trade-offs that built absolute states in early modern Europe, Prussian nobles accepted Hohenzollern authority as a guarantee of their privileges. At the same time that Junkers were securing their privileges, Prussian peasants were losing their freedom, including their rights to free movement and often even to inheritance. During the late fifteenth and the sixteenth centuries, they became serfs, legally bound to a lord's estate, and could be sold with the land on which they worked. A burgher in a Prussian town in 1614 described serfdom as "this barbaric and Egyptian servitude . . . in our territory serfdom did not exist fifty or a hundred years ago, but lately, it has been brought in on a large scale, with the help of the authorities." The authority of the Hohenzollerns, however, stopped at the gate of the manor: Junkers retained rights of seigneurial justice over their peasants. Burghers, including merchants and skilled craftsmen, also stood powerless before nobles, in contrast to the middle class in England and the Dutch United Provinces, where they presented an imposing obstacle to the growth of absolutism.

Frederick William (ruled 1640–1688), the "Great Elector" of Brandenburg (so named because the ruler of Brandenburg had the right to cast a ballot in the election of the Holy Roman emperor), initially had neither a standing army nor the resources to raise one. Prussian nobles at first resisted the creation of a standing army, fearful that it might aid Frederick William in reducing their privileges. In 1653, Frederick William convinced the Junkers to grant him funds with which to build an army in exchange for royal confirmation of their privileges over the peasantry and their right to import goods without paying duties. Furthermore, the king agreed to consult the nobles on matters of foreign policy.

Then Frederick William turned to the business of augmenting state authority in his three fragmented territories. He extracted concessions from each of them, including more taxes and the right to recruit soldiers. The Hohenzollern family owned more than half of East Prussia, which provided considerable state revenue. The Great Elector established a centralized administrative bureaucracy, arguably the first modern efficient civil service in Europe. The Prussian bureaucracy was coordinated by an office with the suitably imposing name of "General Directory Over Finance, War, and Royal Domains." Prussian towns, which paid a disproportionate percentage of taxes, lost their representation in the provincial Estates. In 1701, the Great Elector's son Frederick III (his title as elector of Brandenburg) took the title of King Frederick I of Prussia (ruled 1688–1713).

Frederick William I (ruled 1713–1740), grandson of the Great Elector, succeeded Frederick III as elector of Brandenburg and king in Prussia. As a boy, Frederick William could not count to ten without his tutor's assistance, but upon his succession to the throne he continued the centralizing policies of his grandfather and father. The bad-tempered "Sergeant-King" wore his officer's uniform around the house and turned the royal gardens into a military training ground. Frederick William I was known for fits of screaming rage, calling everyone in sight "blockhead," sometimes beating officials with a stick, and knocking out the teeth of several judges whose sentences displeased him. Officials known as "fiscals" went around to ensure that the king's representatives served him well. But the king was astute enough to break with tradition by employing some commoners, many of whom served with uncommon loyalty and efficiency.

A Prussian official described, with some exaggeration, the feature that defined his country's absolutism and the emergence of Brandenburg-Prussia as a power: "What distinguishes the Prussians from other people is that theirs is not a country with an army. They have an army and a country that serves it." Military expenditures accounted for half of Prussia's state budget.

King Frederick William I increased the Prussian army from about 39,000 to 80,000 soldiers. He engaged only tall soldiers for his royal guard, those standing more than six feet in height, virtual giants at the time. One of his first royal acts was to abolish the luxury industries in Berlin, the capital, that catered to court and nobles, and to replace them with workshops that turned out military uniforms. The king ordered all young men in Prussia to register for military service and organized a procedure by which each regiment was assigned a specific region from which to recruit or conscript soldiers. Prussia established the first system of military reserves in Europe: soldiers drilled in the summer for two months. This meant that far more men in Prussia experienced military life than in any other country.

THE RUSSIAN AND SWEDISH EMPIRES

Two other empires rose in eastern and northern Europe. Early in the sixteenth century, Muscovy was a relatively small state. It stood vulnerable to invasions by the Mongols, who had conquered what is now Russia in the thirteenth century, the Tatars of Crimea on the edge of the Black Sea, and by the kingdom of Poland-Lithuania. That kingdom and grand duchy had been joined in an enormous confederation in 1386, becoming the Commonwealth of Poland-Lithuania in 1569, with Warsaw becoming the capital in 1595. Twice the size of France, the confederation had only about 8 million inhabitants. Gradually, the duchy of Muscovy, where Orthodox Christianity had taken hold, emerged as the strongest of the states of Russia, absorbing Novgorod and other rivals and principalities late in the fifteenth century. By the early sixteenth century, the Russian Orthodox Church had become centered in Moscow, which now claimed the title of the third Rome (the second was Constantinople). Muscovy's ruler Ivan III (ruled 1462–1505) began using the title "lord of all Russia," a title that offended the more powerful state of Poland-Lithuania. In 1500 and again twelve years later, Ivan brazenly attacked Poland-Lithuania, capturing the fortress town of Smolensk, which guarded the upper Dnieper River.

The Expansion of Muscovy

The rise of Russia as an absolute state and empire began with the further expansion of Muscovy in the late sixteenth century. Tsar Ivan IV (ruled 1533–1584) became in 1547 the first to be crowned tsar of Russia. Muscovy conquered the Volga basin, driving back the nomadic Muslim Tatars, conquered the Don and Volga river basins to the south before they could be taken by either the Ottoman Empire or the Safavid rulers of Iran, absorbed parts of the Mongol states to the east, and unsuccessfully battled Poland-Lithuania for control of the Baltic territory of Livonia. Peasants, hunters, and fur traders expanded the domination of Muscovy into the cold and

Ivan the Terrible watching the beggars of Novgorod being tortured to death.

sparsely populated forest reaches of Siberia. Muscovy annexed the steppe khanates of Astrakhan and Kazan at mid-century, reaching the borderlands of China.

Ivan IV truly earned his sobriquet "the Terrible." He was raised in a world of violence marked by the bloody feuds of the Muscovite nobles, some of whom poisoned his mother when he was eight years old. Five years later, Ivan ordered a noble ripped apart by fierce dogs; as an adult, he had an archbishop sewn into a bearskin and thrown to hungry wolves. His goal was to assure himself a reliable military force and revenue. His means was to create a "service state" in which Muscovite nobles, the *boyars*, held their estates in exchange for agreeing to serve in an administrative or military capacity, thus receiving protection against peasant insurrections or other nobles. Allying with a group of military retainers, Ivan decimated noble families he viewed as too powerful or too slow to obey. Ivan alternated between moods of religious fervor, drunken passion, and stormy brutality. After being defeated in Lithuania in 1564, Ivan subjected his people to an eight-year reign of terror. He killed his own son with a massive blow to the skull and routinely ordered anyone who displeased him tortured to death.

Ivan's death in 1584 led, almost unimaginably, to an even worse period for Muscovy. The "Time of Troubles" (1598–1613) was a period of intermittent anarchy. Weak successors allowed nobles to regain control of the now sprawling country. Polish armies took Moscow in 1605 and again five years later. In 1613, the Assembly of Nobles elected the first tsar from the

Romanov family. The next two tsars restored order, regaining some of the lands lost to Poland-Lithuania and Sweden.

For most peasants, life itself was an endless "time of troubles" in the face of state taxation and brutalization at the hands of their lords. Revolts seemed endemic, some led by men who claimed to be the "true" tsar who would restore justice. One of the latter led a huge force of peasants, which captured several cities before being decimated in 1670.

Serfdom emerged as one of the fundamental characteristics of Russia. In times of dearth or crisis, many peasants traditionally had fled the region of Moscow to settle on the frontier lands of Siberia in the east or in Ukraine, standing between Russia, Poland-Lithuania, and a Tatar state on the Crimean peninsula—the word Ukraine itself means "border region." The resulting chronic shortage of rural labor, and the need to provide landed estates to loyal nobles, led the state in 1649 officially to establish serfdom, which had already become widespread in the late sixteenth century. The chronically indebted Russian peasants gave up their freedom in exchange for loans from the crown and from landlords. The Orthodox Church, a major landowner, also contributed to the expansion of serfdom. Nearly 90 percent of peasants in Russia were now bound to the land, assuring the state and nobles of a relatively immobile labor supply. In exchange for the tsar's support of this system, Russian nobles, like their counterparts in Prussia, pledged their service to the state.

In the meantime, the Commonwealth of Poland and Lithuania to the west, Swedish territories to the north, and the Ottoman Turks to the south blocked Russia's further expansion. The northern port of Archangel on the White Sea, its harbor frozen solid much of the year, offered Muscovy its only access to the sea. Polish territories included much of today's Belarus and Ukraine. Most landowners in Ukraine were Polish Catholics. Most Ukrainian peasants were, like Russians, Orthodox Christians and spoke a language similar to Russian. Peasant revolts rocked Ukraine in the late 1640s, and, after an uprising that drove back the Polish army, Ukraine accepted Russian sovereignty in 1654. Under the Treaty of Andrussovo (1667), which concluded a war with Poland, Russia absorbed Ukraine east of the Dnieper River. To the south, several peoples resisted incorporation into Russia as well as into Poland-Lithuania. These included Turks, Crimean Tatars (an ethnic Turkic group), and Cossacks, a warrior people living on the steppes of southern Russia and Ukraine.

The Rival Swedish Empire

In the 1640s and 1650s, Swedish kings added to their dynastic holdings the regions of Denmark and Norway, Estonia and Lithuania, and West Pomerania in northern Germany. Like the Habsburg empire, the kingdom of Sweden encompassed a farraginous set of languages, including Swedish, Finnish, Latvian, Estonian, and German, the language of administration. Sweden was a relatively poor state, but revenues from lucrative copper mines, the sale of Swedish iron and steel—the finest in Europe—and trade with Muscovy and then Russia and the West generated enough revenue to finance expansion. But expansion had its costs: Queen Christina (ruled 1632–1654) raised money by selling almost two-thirds of the royal lands, with Swedish nobles becoming the main beneficiaries. Swedish peasants, who had their own Estate in the Swedish Diet (assembly), demanded in vain the return of all alienated lands to the throne. The lower Estates did not dare challenge royal prerogatives: "We esteem Your Majesty's royal power as the buttress of our liberties, the one being bound up in the other, and both standing or falling together."

Emboldened by his fledgling empire, King Charles XI (ruled 1660–1697) in the 1680s established absolute rule in Sweden. He overcame the resistance of the wealthiest nobles by winning the support of their jealous colleagues of lesser means, as well as that of the burghers, clergy, and peasants, who increasingly sought royal protection against the most powerful nobles. His son Charles XII (ruled 1697–1718) became king at the age of fifteen. He snatched the crown during his coronation and placed it on his own head, and never convoked the Estates. Having been instructed only in warfare as a youth, he remained a headstrong military man who acted by impulse, not reflection, relying on military force to achieve Swedish ends. Instead of turning Sweden's full military attention toward Denmark, which sought to recapture lost provinces from Sweden, he spent five years campaigning against Russia (see p. 277), a quest that took him into the Ottoman Empire, where he sought assistance against Russia. But during Charles XII's reign, the crown added to its wealth by reclaiming land that had been sold to nobles in the previous decades. Gradually the Swedish monarchy established a bureaucracy and increased state revenue. But when Charles XII was killed in a war in Norway, leaving no heir, the Swedish nobility succeeded in imposing a parliamentary regime based on the prerogatives of the Estates and marked by complicated political struggles. In 1772, however, King Gustavus III (ruled 1771–1792) overthrew the parliamentary system, supported by some nobles, and reimposed absolute rule, albeit with a new constitution that reduced the power of the Senate and the Diet. Gustavus III portrayed himself as a "patriot king" protecting peasants from avaricious nobles. By then, however, Sweden's empire was a fading memory and Gustavus's aristocratic enemies organized his assassination in 1792.

Peter the Great Turns Westward

In Western Europe so little was known about "barbaric" Russia that Louis XIV sent a letter to a tsar who had been dead for twelve years. Peter the Great (ruled 1682–1725) first imposed order on a state torn by bloody uprisings; then he created an enormous inland Russian Empire. Whereas Ivan the Terrible and several of his successors had been turned back by

Poland and Turkey, Peter's wars brought territorial acquisitions at the expense of Sweden, Poland, and the Turks. No European state more dramatically increased its territory than Russia, which expanded its frontiers at a rapid pace between the 1620s and 1740s. During the seventeenth century, Russian territory increased from 2.1 to 5.9 million square miles, even if in the distant reaches of north Asia this included little more than a series of trade routes.

As a boy growing up in the violent world of Russian court politics, Peter was schooled in all manner of guns, ballistics, and fortifications, and he was fascinated by sailing. Wearing a military uniform, he became tsar at the age of ten after a bloody struggle, which he witnessed firsthand, between the clans of his father's two widows. Seven years later, Peter killed members of his own family whom he perceived to be a threat to his rule.

Tsar Peter, who wore shabby clothes, worn-out boots, socks he had darned himself, a battered hat, and very long hair, stood close to seven feet tall and suffered from chronic back problems compounded by frenetic energy. Facial tics became most apparent when he was anxious or angry, which seemed to be most of the time, as he lashed out with clubs or fists. On several occasions he carried out public executions himself with an axe.

When he was twenty-five, Peter visited Western Europe incognito, dressed as a humble, giant workman. He preferred the company of ordinary people (his second wife was a Latvian peasant), enjoyed wood turning and fire fighting, and was most comfortable in simple Russian wooden houses. In the West, he shocked statesmen and nobles with his dress and coarse manners, snatching meat from dining tables. In London, Peter and his entourage virtually destroyed a rented house with wild parties—the tsar loved to dance and drink—leading an English bishop to worry aloud that this "furious man had been raised up to so absolute an authority over so great a part of the world."

Peter was not an uncritical admirer of the West, but he borrowed Western technical knowledge as he sought to copy absolutism. In London he became fascinated by the use of mathematics in shipbuilding, and four months on the Dutch docks taught him ship carpentry. Impressed with the military strength and administrative efficiency of the Western powers, Peter emulated what he considered to be more "rational" organization. His turn toward the West represented a monumental cultural change that was secular in character. He ordered nobles to become educated, told his guards and officials to shave off their beards, encouraged the use of glasses, bowls, and napkins at meals, and ordered a Western book of etiquette translated into Russian. Furthermore, he ordered nobles to build Western-style palaces, and he demanded that women wear bonnets, petticoats, and skirts. German and, to a lesser extent, French became the language of court. Purchasing German and Italian paintings and statues, Peter began the royal collection that would later become the renowned Hermitage Museum in St. Petersburg, and he also created the Russian Academy of Science and the Moscow School of Mathematics and Navigation.

Peter the Great trimming the long sleeves of the boyars, symbolically reducing noble power in the Russian Empire.

Peter retained a marked ambivalence about the role of tsar, maintaining a "Drunken Assembly," a kind of mock parallel government of people he trusted with strange statutes and rituals. Presided over by a pretend "prince-pope," the "All Jesting Assembly" undertook boisterous, bawdy farces that mocked religious ceremonies. Yet Peter the Great's reforms reflected the influence of Western absolutism on the Russian state. He believed that it was his role to help his people achieve the best living conditions possible. He thus came to a conception of the common good that he closely identified with Russian patriotism. At the time Peter became tsar, only three books considering nonreligious themes had been translated into Russian—a grammar book, a law code, and a military manual. Translations of Western books followed at Peter's instigation, including works by John Locke. The tsar sent Russian students abroad to learn and, in doing so, helped move Russia away from a uniquely religious culture.

Fearing the military superiority of his rivals, Sweden and Poland-Lithuania, Peter now raised the first Russian standing army, gradually replacing Western mercenary soldiers with Russian troops by implementing military conscription in 1705 in order to have an infantry to complement Cossack cavalrymen. Thereafter, one recruit—who would serve for life—had to be provided for every twenty peasant households. Peter brought in Western commanders to train his army and provided soldiers with uniforms and Western flintlock muskets with socket bayonets.

The bustling docks of Amsterdam and London had inspired Peter's interest in building first a river navy and eventually an oceangoing fleet. Skilled workers from Prussia and the Dutch Republic were hired to build warships, and Russian craftsmen were sent abroad to learn new skills. Russians gradually replaced Western Europeans as designers, builders, and ship commanders. By the end of the century, Russia had a naval fleet.

Military might, then, also underlay Russian absolutism. Even in peacetime, at least two-thirds of state revenue went to the army and navy. Peter forced nobles to send their sons to new military and engineering schools by decreeing they could not marry unless they did so. To pay for his army, the tsar tripled state revenues, imposing a direct tax on each male serf, or "soul." Landlords became responsible for the collection of these taxes. He established state monopolies on the production and sale of salt, oil, tobacco, rhubarb, and even dice, awarding the profitable right to collect these revenues to his favorite nobles, to "official" merchants, or to foreigners. The acquisition of new territories helped increase state tax revenues by three times. Hoping to expand Russian industry and attract gold and silver payments from abroad, Peter oversaw the exploitation of mines and the establishment of a metal industry in the Ural Mountains. But even absolute authority could not overcome a primitive transportation system, the lack of capital, and the absence of a sizable merchant class.

Peter succeeded in managing the often volatile politics of the court and the boyars, the 200 to 300 noble families (some of whom had as many as 40,000 serfs on their lands). While remaining an autocrat, Peter was nonetheless the first tsar to distinguish between his person as ruler and the state itself. Indeed, he made officials take two oaths, one to him and one to the state whose power he enhanced.

Tsar Peter reorganized the civil administration, dividing his domains into fifty administrative districts, each with a governor, although the effective reach of the state over such vast lands remained quite weak. He created a Senate, an administrative body charged with ruling in his absence during wartime and with overseeing state administration in times of peace. He experimented with councils, or committees, whose members could—if they dared—give him advice, representing the equivalent of government ministries. The tsar also put towns under the direct control of provincial governors, although they retained some measure of self-government. The Table of Ranks (1722) required all male nobles to enter state service and serve in the army, navy, or bureaucracy, and allowed commoners who rose through the bureaucracy or military to assume noble titles. Thus, the nobility also became an instrument of the state, and in Moscow nobles sought places on the boyar council (Duma), which met in the throne room of the palace.

The tsar's turn toward the West angered the old noble families of Moscow and the traditional Orthodox Church leaders, despite the fact that Peter himself remained quite pious. In particular, Peter faced the hostility of the Old Believers, dissidents who claimed authority over the tsars and resented that Peter subordinated the church to his state. They also opposed Greek and Byzantine liturgical forms, as well as the growing influence of baroque art and religious architecture imported to Russia from Central Europe. They considered such reforms, which constituted a "Russian reformation," sacrilegious. For example, they believed that the beards the tsar had ordered shaved had distinguished Russians from people in the West. Peter placed the Orthodox Church fully under state control, first by not naming a new patriarch (the head of the Russian Orthodox Church) upon the death of the incumbent in 1700 and later by simply abolishing the patriarchate. Peter overcame four uprisings and several conspiracies directed against him. In 1716–1718, he suspected his son Alexei, who was influenced by churchmen and boyars who did not support the tsar's wars, of being involved in a plot with the Habsburg monarchy against him. Peter ordered him tortured to reveal his accomplices, who were executed, and Alexei died in a prison cell.

MAP 7.3 THE EXPANSION OF RUSSIA The state of Muscovy was expanded through the acquisitions of Ivan III, Ivan IV (the Terrible), and Peter the Great.

In the meantime, Peter the Great pushed back the neighbors who had blocked Muscovy's expansion: Sweden, Poland, and the Ottoman Turks. He added territory beyond the Ural Mountains, and along the Caspian Sea at the expense of the Turks (see Map 7.3). Peter dreamed of conquering the Turkish capital of Constantinople, which would give him control over its straits, the crucial passage between Europe and Asia leading to the Black Sea. Peter's new fleet sailed down the Don River in 1696, taking the Turkish port of Azov on the Sea of Azov, which gives access to the Black Sea. However, he was forced to surrender Azov back to the Turks after an unsuccessful war against them (1710–1711), thus remaining without access to the Black Sea.

Russia's role in European affairs, however, had remained minimal, despite its participation, with Habsburg Austria, Poland, and Venice, in the long series of wars against the Turks in the last decades of the seventeenth century. Russia joined Denmark and Saxony in attacking Sweden in the Great Northern War (1700–1721). The Russian ambassador in Vienna reported that once the news of Peter's victory arrived, "people begin to fear the tsar as formerly they feared Sweden." Peter's goal was to win a "window on the Baltic Sea" at Sweden's expense. The Swedes turned back the assault of a much larger Russian army at Narva (1700) in Estonia. But after Charles XII of Sweden passed up the opportunity to pursue the Russian army in order to invade Poland and Saxony, the Russian army conquered the mouth of the Neva River in 1703.

There Peter ordered the construction of a new capital city, where he forced nobles and wealthy merchants to build elegant townhouses. Saint

St. Petersburg, Peter the Great's new capital of the Russian Empire.

Petersburg offered a striking contrast to the chaos of tangled streets and shabby wooden buildings of Moscow, then by far the largest city in Russia. Built on coastal marshlands, Saint Petersburg reflected architectural ideas borrowed from the West, particularly Amsterdam. State offices, including army and military headquarters, occupied the centrally located islands. Symmetrical facades rose along the Neva River's south bank, near the shipyards, admiralty, and fortresses. Unlike Moscow, churches did not dominate the skyline of Saint Petersburg. Geometrically arranged boulevards, squares, gardens, and baroque palaces completed the tsar's capital, which itself became a reflection of absolute rule.

Russia supplanted Sweden as the Baltic region's dominant power. In 1709 at the Battle of Poltava, Peter's army turned back an invading Swedish army in Ukraine, a battle that marked the end of Sweden's status as a great power and its domination of northern Europe, allowing Peter to annex eastern Ukraine and bringing the Black Sea into sight. Five years later Russian troops raided Sweden for the first time. After losing its German and Polish territories, Sweden then entered a period of constitutional struggles, as the nobility tried to reassert economic and social prerogatives lost to the monarchy (see p. 271). This allowed Russia to solidify its expansion. The Treaty of Nystadt (1721) confirmed Russian primacy in the Baltic region, adding Estonia and Livonia (the southeastern part of modern Finland) to Peter's empire and bringing Russia ever closer to European affairs.

By the time of Peter's death in 1725, the territory controlled by absolutist Russia had increased sixfold since the time of Ivan the Terrible. The Russian Empire, thirty times bigger than France, had joined the European state system.

Louis XIV's Dynastic Wars

As rulers of Russia, Sweden, Prussia, Austria, Turkey, and France sought to expand their territories, dynastic interests determined the choice of allies. Yet strong states were also likely to switch sides to gain the most beneficial terms from new allies. For example, in order to expand its influence in Central Europe, France needed an alliance with either Austria or Prussia. But inevitably such a coalition pushed the other German power into opposition, forcing it to look for allies against France. Usually this partner was England (Great Britain after the union of England and Scotland in 1707), France's rival in North America. Following the conclusion of hostilities that reworked borders, alliances frequently shifted, as rulers anticipated their next opportunity to conquer new lands.

Louis XIV was determined that territorial gain and prestige should be the measure of his greatness (see Map 7.4). France was the continent's richest, strongest, and most populous state. The king of France sought to expand his kingdom's borders to what he considered to be France's "natural" frontiers, that is, the Pyrenees Mountains to the south and the Rhine River to the east.

MAP 7.4 EXTENSION OF FRANCE'S FRONTIERS UNDER LOUIS XIV   Louis XIV sought to expand his dynastic territories through wars fought between 1643 and 1715.

International conditions seemed conducive to such grandiose plans. England had been divided by civil war in the 1640s, and its restored monarch, Charles II, faced mounting political opposition at home (see Chapter 6). To the north, Sweden confronted a Danish threat to its control of the Baltic Sea. In Central Europe, the Austrian Habsburgs confronted other German princes, as well as threats from Poland-Lithuania and the Turks.

Louis XIV's "grand strategy" was to contain the two Habsburg powers, Spain and Austria, by initiating a series of wars. Each conflict followed the king's violation of a previous agreement or formal treaty, and was accompanied by the claim that French aggression was "just." Each war was to pay for itself: French armies would force local populations to offer "contributions." The Treaty of the Pyrenees (1659), ending essentially a quarter of a century of hostilities with Spain, established the lasting frontier between the two states and confirmed France's status as the preeminent European power.

France again went to war against Spain in 1667. Louis wanted to annex Spain's French-speaking Franche-Comté to the east and the Spanish Netherlands (Belgium) to the north. When French armies invaded the Spanish Netherlands, England, fearful that Flanders and its Channel ports would fall to France, joined the Dutch Republic, Sweden, and Spain to turn back Louis XIV's armies. By the Treaty of Aix-la-Chapelle (Aachen) in 1668, France annexed Lille and part of Flanders. Four years later, Louis XIV invaded the Dutch Republic after assuring English neutrality by making secret payments to King Charles II. The Dutch fended off the French by opening up the dikes to create a barrier of water (see Chapter 6). After several more years of indecisive fighting and negotiations, France absorbed Franche-Comté and tiny parcels of the Southern Netherlands. Still the king of France was not satisfied. He conquered Alsace and Lorraine beyond his eastern frontier. Despite the opposition of a wary alliance of Habsburg Austria, Spain, Sweden, and Saxony, Louis XIV ordered the invasion of the Palatinate, intending to secure the Rhine River. This initiated the War of the League of Augsburg (1688–1697). England and the Dutch Republic (an alliance solidified by the fact that William III of Orange now was king of England) and a number of other German states joined the coalition against France.

After hesitating, in 1692 Louis made a foolish attempt to invade England. Dutch and English ships drove the French fleet onto rocks off the coast of Normandy; the two sea powers then enforced an economic blockade of France. Louis XIV retaliated by turning French privateers loose on his enemies' ships. French defeats as well as rising opposition in the Dutch Republic and England to the cost of the war forced both sides to negotiate. The Treaty of Ryswick of 1697 confirmed French gains in Alsace, but also made clear that the other European powers would ally again if necessary to keep France from further territorial acquisitions in the Southern Netherlands and the German states in order to preserve the balance of power.

The question of the succession to the throne of Spain soon presented Louis XIV with the greatest temptation of all. The Habsburg King Charles II of Spain had no direct heir. Louis opposed the candidacy of the Habsburg archduke Charles of Austria (son of Holy Roman Emperor Leopold I), hoping to end the virtual encirclement of France by Habsburg powers. Then Louis XIV, whose wife was the daughter of the late Philip IV of Spain, put forth his own claim to the throne.

When Charles II died in 1700, he left a will expressing his desire that his diminished empire remain intact, and that Louis XIV's grandson Philip of Anjou succeed him, but renounce any claim to the throne of France. However, on ascending the Spanish throne, Philip V (ruled 1700–1746) made clear that he favored the interests of his imposing grandfather. The Austrian Habsburg ruler Leopold I refused to accept Charles II's will as valid and invaded the Italian territories of the Spanish Habsburgs.

Louis XIV refused to rule Philip V out of the line of succession to the French throne, so that if Philip's elder brother, the duke of Bourgogne, died without male issue, Philip would then inherit the throne of France, and the kingdoms of France and Spain would be joined. The matter became pressing in 1712, when smallpox struck the French royal family, leaving only Bourgogne's youngest son as heir to the French throne. If the future Louis XV had died then, Philip would have become heir to both kingdoms.

The French king's obvious interest in the possibility of the two thrones being brought together drew Great Britain into the war. The Dutch Republic again had reason to fear French occupation of the Spanish Netherlands. If the French opened up the Scheldt River to trade, Antwerp would reemerge as a commercial rival to Amsterdam. This vital link to the English Channel had been closed since the Dutch formally received independence from Spain in 1648, thus preventing ships from reaching Antwerp. The alliance against France also included Austria, Prussia, and Portugal. The War of the Spanish Succession reflected the fact that European wars were taking on a global dimension (see Chapter 6), as the powers fought for markets as well as prestige. As in the War of the League of Augsburg, British and French forces also battled in North America.

The Rock of Gibraltar being captured by the English fleet during the War of Spanish Succession.

France fought with Bavaria and Spain as allies. The English commander, the duke of Marlborough (1650–1722), raised an army of English, Dutch, and mercenary troops. In 1704, at Blenheim in southern Germany, the allied armies, aided by Habsburg Austrian troops, crushed a combined French and Bavarian force. Louis XIV's armies retreated behind the Rhine River. Winning victories in the Spanish Netherlands in 1708 and 1709, the allied armies also drove the French from the Spanish Netherlands and out of the Italian peninsula. The English fleet captured Gibraltar (1704), which guards the entrance to the Mediterranean Sea. During the terrible winter of 1709–1710, France suffered military defeat and famine. The great kingdom of Louis XIV seemed on the verge of collapse.

But the French and Spanish armies revived their fortunes. Dynastic changes, too, helped Louis XIV's cause. In 1711, Archduke Charles of Austria became Holy Roman Emperor Charles VI (ruled 1711–1740). Should France and Philip V of Spain be defeated, the British and Dutch now confronted the possibility that Charles might one day become king of Spain, reviving the dynastic union that had made the Habsburg dynasty Europe's strongest power during the first half of the seventeenth century. It was now in the interests of Great Britain and the Dutch Republic to bring the war to an honorable conclusion. Louis XIV, weakened by age and illness and suffering the financial burdens of the war, agreed to negotiate.

Under the 1713 Treaty of Utrecht (confirmed by the Treaty of Rastatt in 1714, when Emperor Charles VI accepted peace), Habsburg Austria received the Southern Netherlands as security against future French ambitions and annexed Lombardy and Naples, replacing Spain as the paramount power on the Italian peninsula (see Map 7.5). The decline of Spain, which had now lost all of its European possessions beyond the Pyrenees Mountains, continued unabated. In North America, France ceded Newfoundland, Nova Scotia, and Hudson Bay to Great Britain.

Louis XIV had reigned so long that on his death in 1715 the throne passed to his great-grandson, young Louis XV (ruled 1715–1774), with affairs of state in the hands of a regent. Philip V kept the throne of Spain, but the monarchies of Spain and France would remain separate. Louis XIV was defeated by more than powerful alliances mounted against him. Britain had proved better able to sustain long wars; its more developed commerce and manufactures provided greater tax revenues. The non-absolutist British state collected taxes more efficiently than the absolute monarchy of France, where tax farmers kept part of the take. Britain's interests remained overseas, dominated by lucrative commercial concerns that were protected by the Royal Navy. France's foreign policy had led to costly wars on the continent.

France had been the preeminent power in Europe at the time of the accession of Louis XIV; this was no longer true at his death. The king's reputation had fallen victim to unrestrained ambition. Perhaps a lingering sense of failure explains why Louis XIV tried to burn his memoirs shortly before his

MAP 7.5 EUROPE IN 1721 Territorial realignments in Europe after the Treaty of Utrecht (1713), the Treaty of Rastatt (1714), and the Treaty of Nystadt (1721).

Europe in 1721

- Austrian Habsburg lands
- Spanish House of Bourbon lands

Treaty Lands 1714–1721

- To Russia
- To Savoy
- To Prussia
- To France

RUSSIA

Moscow

BLACK SEA

OTTOMAN EMPIRE

Constantinople

AEGEAN SEA

Neva R.

Gulf of Finland

FINLAND

ESTONIA

LIVONIA

LITHUANIA

POLAND

Dnieper R.

Dniester R.

MOLDAVIA

WALLACHIA

TRANSYLVANIA

HUNGARY

Vistula R.

Danube R.

SWEDEN

NORWAY

BALTIC SEA

DENMARK

PRUSSIA

BRANDENBURG

HANOVER

SAXONY

HOLY
ROMAN
EMPIRE

BOHEMIA

MORAVIA

AUSTRIA

BAVARIA

Blenheim 1704

Rastatt

TYROL

SWITZ.

MILAN

VENICE

PAPAL
STATES

NAPLES

SICILY
Savoy 1714
Austria 1720

NORTH
SEA

DUTCH
REPUBLIC

Utrecht

Ryswick

Oudenaarde 1708

SOUTHERN
NETHERLANDS

Aix-la-Chapelle

Schledt R.

Rhine R.

LORRAINE

ALSACE

Seine R.

Paris

Loire R.

FRANCE

SAVOY

Rhône R.

to France

CORSICA

SARDINIA
Austria 1714
Savoy 1720

MINORCA

MEDITERRANEAN SEA

GREAT
BRITAIN

London

SPAIN

Madrid

Ebro R.

PORTUGAL

Lisbon

Tagus R.

Guadalquivir R.

Gibraltar

ATLANTIC OCEAN

200 miles

200 kilometers

death (although they were rescued from the fire). On his deathbed, Louis confessed with uncharacteristic insight that perhaps he had "loved glory too much."

THE MODERN STATE

As they established absolute rule, the sovereigns of continental Europe constructed the modern state. While extending authority over their subjects and expanding their dynastic territories, they developed state bureaucracies and established large standing armies. They broke noble resistance to absolute rule, confirming their privileges in exchange for loyalty to the throne. This relationship between rulers and nobles thus remained essential to the functioning of most European states in the eighteenth century.

Following a period of relative stability, the structure of Western European society then began to change as the European economy entered a remarkable period of dynamic growth, particularly during the second half of the eighteenth century. This was the case above all in Britain, where the expansion of capital-intensive agricultural techniques, population growth, and a boom in manufacturing combined to begin the Industrial Revolution. The changing structure of society, in turn, would affect states by encouraging demands for political reform that began in the 1760s and 1770s and challenged the monopoly on political power by oligarchies and absolute rule itself. Traditional assumptions about science also came under attack. The methodology, discoveries, and culture of the Scientific Revolution helped create modern science.

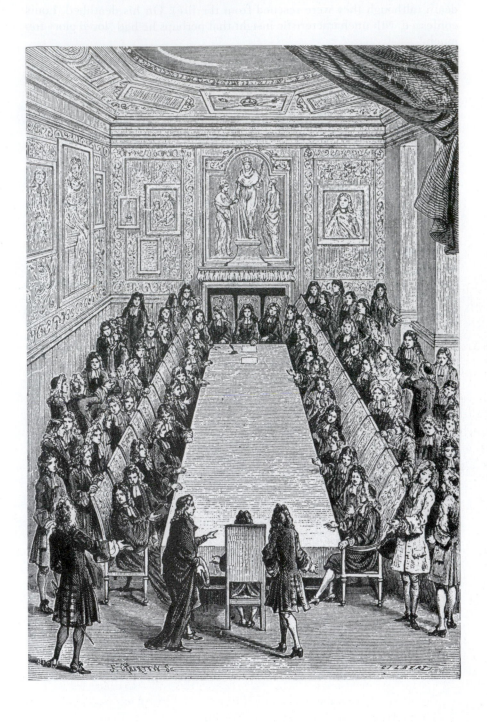

PART THREE

NEW CULTURAL AND POLITICAL HORIZONS

During the late seventeenth century and the eighteenth century, Europe entered a period of remarkable intellectual and political ferment. Rejecting the weight of tradition, men and women of science developed the scientific method, a means of understanding based on systematic observation of natural phenomena and experimentation regarding causes and effects. Their successors, the philosophes—the thinkers and writers of the Enlightenment—believed their role was to bring progress to the world through the application of reason to their reflections on the nature of mankind. Influenced by growing religious skepticism and increased knowledge of the New World brought through overseas trade and the establishment of European empires, and drawing on expanding literacy, the philosophes espoused views of nature, mankind, society, and government that challenged some of the fundamental tenets most Europeans shared.

During this exciting period, Europe also entered a remarkable time of economic and social change. Increased agricultural productivity supported a larger population that, in turn, raised the demand for food and permitted the development of large-scale manufacturing in and around northern English towns.

Changes also came in the realm of political life. The public political sphere was transformed by the emergence of newspapers and learned associations, which facilitated political interest and discussion. Reform-minded people began to denounce unwarranted privilege and "despotism," and they celebrated the British model of constitutional monarchy and the successful rebellion of the American colonists against British rule. In a time of economic and social change, new cultural and political innovations began to transform Europe.

CHAPTER **8**

THE NEW PHILOSOPHY OF SCIENCE

In 1633, ecclesiastical authorities summoned the astronomer and physicist Galileo Galilei (1564–1642) to Rome to face the Inquisition. The stakes were high. In the first year of the new century, the Italian Giordano Bruno (1548–1600), a Dominican friar accused of heresy who loudly proclaimed the virtues of scientific investigation, had been burned along with his books in Rome. Many Church fathers vehemently objected to Galileo's work on physics, for he, like Bruno, espoused an atomistic theory of matter that seemed to challenge the Catholic Church's view that during communion bread and wine become the body and blood of Christ. The Church also opposed Galileo's contention that the earth revolves around the sun. The papacy's political situation forced the Church's hand. Protestant armies had recaptured some of the lands in which the Catholic Reformation had appeared victorious. The papacy, its influence weakened by the Protestant Reformation and eclipsed by powerful dynastic rulers, could ill afford another defeat.

Pope Urban VIII, who before his elevation to the pontificate had been Galileo's friend, accused the astronomer only of supporting the views of the Polish scientist Copernicus, not of heresy. This would save Galileo from death but might also put the pope in a bad light for protecting the scientist. Although Galileo agreed to renounce these "errors" as heresies in order to avoid a death sentence, in 1633 he was still sentenced to a lifetime of house arrest. When guards returned him to his house, however, he cast a glance to the heavens and proclaimed of the earth, "See, it's still moving!"

The origins of modern science date to the seventeenth century, a period so marked by innovative thinking that it has been called the "century of genius." In several different corners of Europe, a few people struggled to understand the workings of the cosmos in a new way. Their own observations of the skies seemed to contradict explanations of the universe that had originated with Aristotle in the fourth century B.C. and, having acquired the authority of the Church, had been passed down for centuries. Breaking

287

free of the bonds of tradition, these seventeenth-century thinkers developed the scientific method, a means of understanding based on systematic observation of natural phenomena and experimentation regarding causes and effects. But what we now know as the Scientific Revolution owed its impact less to new technology and inventions than to new ways of thinking about the universe.

Changing Views of the Universe

The writings of the Greek philosopher Aristotle (384–322 B.C.) dominated European science for centuries. Then, in the sixteenth century, the Polish astronomer Copernicus observed the heavens and concluded that ancient and medieval science could not explain what he saw with his own eyes. Later in the century, his successors—above all, Galileo—made systematic mathematical calculations to explain celestial motion. In doing so, they created scientific methodology, which would also be applied to reach an understanding of the workings of the human body.

Ancient and Medieval Science

Aristotle believed that the earth was located at or near the center of the universe. He envisioned a hierarchical order of the cosmos comprised of a series of spheres that became progressively purer. Aristotle also believed that terrestrial bodies naturally moved toward the earth, the center of the universe, unless they were propelled in another direction. In this view, impetus imparted motion through contact with an object; when the contact ceased, the object simply stopped moving or fell back to earth. The natural tendency of all matter, then, was toward rest, regarded as a nobler state than motion. Because all motion had to be explained, a "mover" therefore had to be found for every motion.

In the second century A.D., the Greek astronomer Claudius Ptolemy (c. 85–165) published a massive work that became known as *Almagest* (from the Arabic for "greatest"), which summarized the conclusions of Greek astronomers and presented his own theories and observations. He described instruments such as the quadrant, invented by the Arabs, with which he tried to measure the orbits (which he believed to be spherical) of the sun, moon, and planets in the sky. Ptolemy accepted Aristotle's contentions, asserting that the earth was encased by a series of clear spheres—about eighty—revolving around it. The most distant sphere contained the farthest stars, which he believed were fixed points of light. Within those spheres, the moon was closest to the earth; next came the planets Mars, Venus, Jupiter, and Saturn. With minor variations, medieval thinkers still held Ptolemy's views.

Within the context of Christian theology, people of learning in the Middle Ages believed that scientific inquiry should serve theological ends through the study of nature to explain the mysterious ways of God. Church savants never raised the possibility that mankind could, with understanding, alter or master nature.

Aristotle's belief that the heavens and earth displayed two different kinds of motion—one toward the center of the earth, which seemed the natural state, but also an unnatural violent motion away from it—nicely fit the medieval Church's view that the universe consisted of good and evil. The earth, standing at the center, was heavy, corrupted not only by its weight but also by original sin and earthly misdeeds. Angels therefore were placed far off in a weightless existence in Heaven. The goal of human beings was to achieve the lightness of Heaven, God's domain, on the exterior edge of the universe.

The writings of the medieval poet Dante (1265–1321) reflected the prevailing influence of Aristotle's physics and Ptolemy's astronomy. Dante held that the universe comprised ten spheres surrounding the spherical, motionless earth. In his *Inferno,* Dante and the Roman poet Virgil travel to the core of the earth, then climb out to the other side, the Southern Hemisphere, where they find Purgatory. Hell lay at the earth's center, with Heaven in the distant tenth sphere. Dante and his contemporaries believed that the earth consisted of four elements: earth, water, air, and fire, the first two of which had a natural tendency to fall toward the center of the stationary earth.

Medieval European scholars seemed little interested in astronomy. Yet, to be sure, some medieval thinkers took significant steps toward modern science by embracing the study of natural phenomena and revering the

Virgil, Cicero, and the Three Giants in the Lost Circle, from Dante's *Devine Comedy (The Inferno),* 1313.

scholars who studied such problems. Medieval scientists made lasting contributions in such fields as optics—inventing eyeglasses—and biology. They classified objects for study and espoused experimentation based on scientific procedures and the use of mathematics to verify theories. But even the contributions of the most brilliant medieval thinkers remained only in the realm of theory.

As the Renaissance drew on the discovery of classical prose, poetry, art, and architecture, Italian scholars of the period also turned to classical Greek scientific texts that had been recovered, edited, and printed. The Arabs had come into contact with classical learning centuries earlier, when they conquered the eastern reaches of the Byzantine Empire. Arab scholars, who also made significant original contributions in astronomy, mathematics, and medicine, preserved many ancient Greek and Roman texts, translating them into Arabic. Some of the manuscripts brought by Greek scholars to the West from Constantinople after its conquest by the Turks in 1453 suggested that mathematics could be applied in the quest for knowledge about the universe. Arab scholars had raised troubling questions challenging age-old views of the earth as they observed and even began to measure the heavenly phenomena they beheld. In this way, the texts of Ptolemy became subjects of renewed interest and study.

Ptolemy's view of the cosmos reflected the domination of Aristotle's theory of motion. Yet there had earlier been at least one dissenting voice. Archimedes of Syracuse (c. 287–212 B.C.) had challenged Aristotle's contention that rest was a natural state for all objects and that only the presence of an "active mover" could generate motion. This view was picked up again in the fourteenth century by thinkers at Paris and Oxford Universities. They observed that falling bodies move at an accelerating speed and that the accompanying presence of a "mover" simply could not be observed. A few scholars also rejected Aristotle's explanation that air itself served as a natural propellant. They observed that an arrow shot from a bow clearly was not continually propelled by air or anything else, but sooner or later simply fell to earth. The gradual development of a theory of motion, based on an understanding of the role of the mass of the moving object, along with the advances in the field of mathematics itself, provided the basis for new discoveries in astronomy and mechanics.

Copernicus Challenges the Aristotelian View of the Universe

The revolution in scientific thinking moved forward because of a cleric who kept his eyes toward the heavens, but not necessarily in pious contemplation. Nicolaus Copernicus (1473–1543) launched the strongest attack yet on the Aristotelian view of the universe. He was born near the Baltic coast in Poland. After the death of his father, Copernicus's uncle (a wealthy bishop) assumed responsibility for his education. From the University of Krakow, Copernicus went to Italy to study medicine and law. After learning Greek, he read medieval scientific and humanist texts. Also trained as a doctor and portrait painter, he devoted his life to observation and discovery.

Copernicus's *Concerning the Revolutions of the Celestial Spheres* was not published until he lay dying in 1543, the same year the work of Archimedes was first translated into Latin. Paradoxically, in view of the intense theological debate it would generate, Copernicus dedicated his study to the pope. Copernicus was troubled by the inability of the Ptolemaic system (itself a refraction of the Aristotelian view of the universe) to account for what his own observations, made with the naked eye, told him: that the planets, the moon, and the stars obviously did not move around the earth at the same speed. Nor did they seem to be in the spherical orbits Ptolemy had assigned them. That Mars seemed to vary in brightness particularly perplexed him. What Copernicus observed, in short, contradicted the fundamental assumptions of the Aristotelian and Ptolemaic universe.

Even before Copernicus, some thinkers questioned Aristotelian physics and the Ptolemaic cosmos, but they generally did not venture out of the realm of mere speculation. Nicholas of Cusa (1401–1464), a German bishop and theologian who wrote on astronomy, believed the earth might be in motion, but neither he nor anyone else in the period tried to make mathematical calculations that might prove or reject this bold theory. He suggested the possibility that the sun stands at the center of the universe and, by implication, that the universe is infinite and nonhierarchical in nature, unlimited by Aristotelian layers of spheres. The extraordinary Renaissance artist and humanist Leonardo da Vinci (see Chapter 2), who called wisdom "the daughter of experiment," had also suggested that the earth might move around the sun.

Copernicus concluded that the sun, not the earth, lies at the center of the universe and that the earth rotates on its axis once a day and revolves around the sun once every 365 days. "In the middle of all sits the Sun enthroned," he wrote. "How could we place this luminary in any better position in this most beautiful temple from which to illuminate the whole at once?" Copernicus's postulation was, like his critique of some of Ptolemy's conclusions, not totally original. But his assertions were bold, explicit, and, for many, convincing. Furthermore, they suggested that mathematics could verify astronomical theories.

The notion that the earth was just one of many planets rotating in circular orbit around the sun raised shocking questions about the earth's status. This perplexed and angered Catholic, Protestant, and Jewish theologians by seeming to reduce the standing of mankind. It seemed unbelievable that mere mortals peering into the heavens were themselves moving rapidly through the universe. Martin Luther, himself not given to accepting inherited wisdom without skepticism, said of Copernicus, "This fool wants to turn the whole of astronomy upside down!"

Copernicus did just that. Yet he seemed uninterested in carrying out his own systematic observations and made serious errors in some of his calculations. He could not explain why there was no constant wind from the east, which might be expected based on the assumption that the earth moved in that direction around the sun. Copernicus sometimes sought to answer his own doubts by turning to the teachings of the ancients and did not completely abandon the system of celestial spheres postulated by Ptolemy. Copernicus also continued to accept the notion that the spherical universe was finite, and that it perhaps was limited by the stars fixed in the heavens.

The Universal Laws of the Human Body

As scientists began to chart movements in the heavens, some scholars now began to question old assumptions about the human body. They contended that it is subject to the same universal laws that govern celestial and terrestrial motion. The Renaissance had generated interest in human anatomy. Most assumptions about how the body works had been passed down for centuries from the ancient world. Galen (129–c. 210), a Greek contemporary of Ptolemy, was the first person to develop theories about medicine based on scientific experiments. He carried out a number of experiments

Dissecting a cadaver at the University of Montpellier, 1363.

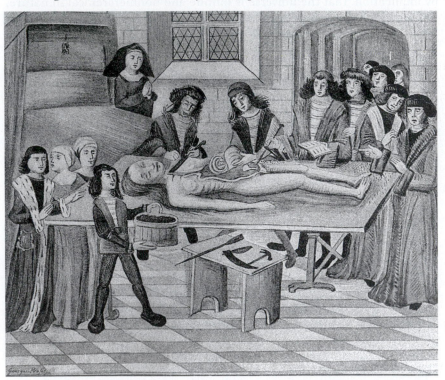

on apes, assuming that animal and human bodies were essentially the same in the arrangement of bodily organs. Like Aristotle, Galen believed that disease followed from an imbalance in the four bodily humors—blood, phlegm, yellow bile, and black bile. He held that two kinds of blood initiated muscle movement and digestion, respectively: bright red blood, which flowed up and down through the arteries, and dark red blood, which could be found in the veins. Doubting Galen's view of anatomy, Andreas Vesalius (1514–1564) published *On the Fabric of the Human Body* (1543). Arguably the founder of modern biological science, Vesalius rejected old explanations for the circulation of blood and began to dissect and study cadavers—in the Middle Ages, the Church had considered this to be sinful—and was the first to assemble human skeletons.

The English scientist William Harvey (1578–1657) largely solved the riddle of how blood circulates. Like the astronomers, he adopted a scientific methodology: "I profess," he wrote, "to learn and teach anatomy not from books but from dissections, not from the tenets of philosophers but from the fabric of nature." Harvey's accomplishment was in the realm of thought and owed virtually nothing to prior inventions. Indeed, he made his discoveries before the invention of the microscope, and he referred only twice in his experiments to a magnifying glass.

Harvey's theory of blood circulation pictured the heart and its valves functioning as a mechanical pump. Yet Harvey, like medieval thinkers, retained a belief that "vital spirits" were to be found in the blood. The long-term consequence of Harvey's work was, as in the case of Vesalius, to undermine further Aristotelian philosophy and medieval science and to help establish a basis for the development of modern biology and medicine in later centuries.

Brahe and Kepler Explore the Heavens

Tycho Brahe (1546–1601), a Danish astronomer, and Johannes Kepler (1571–1630), his German assistant, carried the search for an understanding of the way the universe works to a new stage of scientific knowledge. While studying philosophy at the University of Copenhagen, Brahe became fascinated with the heavens after observing a partial eclipse of the sun. Brahe, an odd-looking nobleman who had lost part of his nose in a duel and had replaced it with a construction of silver and gold alloy perched above his handlebar moustache, built an astronomical observatory on a Danish island.

Brahe rejected Copernicus's contention that the earth rotated around the sun. He claimed that if this were true, a cannonball fired from west to east (the direction Copernicus thought the earth moved) would travel farther in that direction, and a weight dropped from a tall tower would strike earth to the west of the tower because of the earth's movement. Brahe came up with a cumbersome compromise explanation that had the five known planets rotating around the sun, which in turn moved around the stationary earth.

In 1572, Brahe observed a bright exploding star. This and a comet sighted five years later irrevocably compromised the Aristotelian view of the universe as unchanging. Brahe compiled extensive data based upon his own observations, systematically charting what he could see of the planetary orbits and using mathematics to locate the position of the planets and stars. At the same time, his rejection of the Copernican view that the sun was the center of the universe and the fact that his calculations were often inaccurate remind us that the Scientific Revolution did not develop in a linear fashion. False turns and setbacks were part of the story.

Johannes Kepler, Brahe's assistant, was the son of a German mercenary soldier and an herb dealer with an interest in astrology (his mother would later be condemned to be burned at the stake for her dabblings in astrology; Kepler saved her life by undertaking a lengthy legal process). Kepler was a dazzling but strange individual: a rigorous astronomer and mathematician as well as a religious mystic and astrologer, who took credit for predicting not only a particularly harsh winter but also peasant uprisings in Germany.

Facing persecution from Lutheran theologians in 1596 because of his Copernican beliefs, Kepler briefly found protection from the Jesuits. But four years later, he was forced to leave a teaching position in Austria because he refused to convert from Lutheranism to Catholicism. Kepler moved to Prague and began to work with Brahe in 1600. On his deathbed, Brahe implored Kepler to complete his observation tables. Holy Roman Emperor Rudolph II, whose interest in science outweighed any concern

(*Left*) Tycho Brahe's system of planetary rotation, about 1560, (*Right*) Kepler's concept of an attractive force from the sun, early sixteenth century.

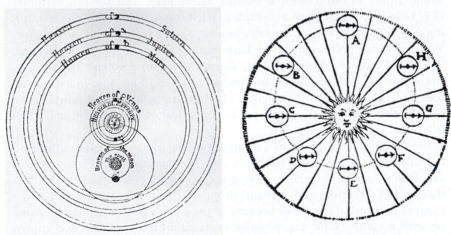

that Kepler was Protestant, appointed him to succeed Brahe as imperial mathematician.

Kepler shared Copernicus's belief that observers on earth were moving while the sun stood still. After carefully plotting the orbit of Mars, Kepler concluded that the orbits of the planets were "imperfect"—not circular, but rather elliptical. He also concluded that the planets were affected by some sort of force emanating from the sun. William Gilbert (1544–1603), an English scientist, had published a book on the magnet in 1600, the first study written by a university scholar and informed by laboratory experimentation. Gilbert's investigations of magnetic force provided a model for the development of a modern theory of gravitation. Kepler now decided that it was perhaps magnetic force that attracted the earth and sun to each other. He also determined that tides were the result of the magnetic attraction of the earth and the moon.

Based upon his mathematical calculations, Kepler postulated three laws of planetary motion, which he assumed were determined by the power, or specific magnetic attraction, of the sun. He used observation and mathematical calculations to demonstrate that the planets were a separate grouping with different properties from those of the fixed stars, and that Aristotle's crystalline spheres simply did not exist.

Kepler's discoveries, blows to Aristotelian and medieval science, also suggested that the hand of the prime mover—God—was not required to govern the movement of the planets. Even more than Copernicus's placing of the sun at the center of the universe, Kepler's conclusions challenged the theological assumptions of the Catholic Church. Nonetheless, the Scientific Revolution still occurred within the system of Christian belief. Kepler himself sought to glorify God by demonstrating the consistency, harmony, and order of divine creation as expressed in the working of the universe.

Francis Bacon and the Scientific Method

From England, Sir Francis Bacon (1561–1626), lawyer, statesman, and philosopher, launched a frontal assault on ancient and medieval metaphysics and science. Calling himself "a bellringer who is first up to call others to church," Bacon helped detach science from philosophy. Medieval scholasticism had focused, he argued, on abstract problems that were without practical consequences, such as the question of how many angels could stand on the head of a pin. So, too, had Renaissance humanism. Bacon rejected outright all arguments based on the weight of traditional authority, calling for "a total reconstruction of sciences, arts and all human knowledge."

Bacon carried out few experiments and made no discoveries that could have been considered significant by his own standards (he died after catching a bad cold while carrying out an experiment of marginal value: stuffing snow into a dead chicken). But Bacon announced the dawn of a new era in which humans would gradually begin to understand and then perhaps

even overcome their physical environment. Through inductive reasoning—
that is, proceeding from observation and experimentation to conclusions
or generalizations—the truths of the universe would be revealed by discovery and scientific experiment, not by religion. "Arts and sciences," Bacon
wrote in 1620, "should be like mines, where the noise of new works and
further advances is heard on every side." Scientists should divide up the toil
by specializing and working in cooperation to "overcome the necessities and
miseries of humanity." Bacon's renown—he served for three years as King
James I of England's Lord Chancellor (before being dismissed for accepting
bribes)—helped create interest in science in England, although for the
moment this was limited to a small number of people.

Galileo and Science on Trial

On the Italian peninsula, Galileo emerged as the dominant figure of the
early stage of the Scientific Revolution. The scion of a wealthy family, he
studied medicine and mathematics. Like Copernicus, he taught at the University of Padua, the leading center of scientific learning in Europe, at a
time when virtually every other university showed little interest in scientific observation. That Padua was under the protection of Venice, which
was hostile to the pope, facilitated its university's precocious role in the
development of scientific methodology. Scholars in Padua hotly debated

(*Left*) Sir Francis Bacon. (*Right*) The feisty Galileo at age sixty.

Aristotelian explanations of motion as well as the question of the relationship between the natural sciences and metaphysics, or the nature of being. The latter debate was especially crucial, because on it hinged the question of whether scientific investigation could be independent of the Catholic Church, which considered revealed religion the only source of true knowledge.

New ways of thinking about the heavens, systematic observation, and scientific measurement had played a more significant role in the early stages of the Scientific Revolution than did the development of new technology. The invention of the telescope, however, led to further advances. Upon learning in 1609 that a man in the Netherlands had invented a "spy glass" that could magnify objects many times, Galileo constructed one of his own. This telescope enabled him to study Jupiter's moons, Saturn's spectacular rings, some of the innumerable stars of the Milky Way, and craters on the moon. His observation of spots that seemed to move on the surface of the sun led Galileo to conclude that the sun, too, rotated. That sunspots seemed to change also challenged the traditional view of the static nature of the universe.

Galileo undermined the Aristotelian theories of motion. He demonstrated that the earth was in perpetual rotation and that balls of varying weights will pick up speed at the same rate as they fall, so therefore their speed is not determined by their mass. From such experiments, he developed a theory of inertia: a body moving at a constant speed in a straight line will continue to move until encountering another force. He demonstrated that air and clouds move with the earth as it rotates around the sun, while appearing immobile to an observer also moving with the earth. The rooms in his house that he set aside for experimentation served as the first university laboratory.

Unlike other scholars, Galileo did not disdain seeking practical information from craftsmen and artisans. He consulted workers who built cannons, soldiers who fired them, and people who made compasses, astrolabes, quadrants, and other scientific instruments for navigation. He began to investigate water pumps and other means of regulating rivers, as well as planning the construction of stronger military fortresses. Nonetheless, Galileo did not care whether or not his discoveries reached ordinary people. Moreover, he claimed that "the mobility of the earth is a proposition far beyond the comprehension of the common people." And he believed that the "all-too-numerous vulgar" ought to be kept in darkness, lest they "become confused, obstinate, and contumacious."

At first, Galileo tried to reconcile his findings and those of Copernicus with early Church texts. But the feisty Galileo's insistence that the universe was mathematical in its very structure and subject to laws of mechanics that could be discovered left him open to attacks by ecclesiastical authorities. In 1610, he wrote Kepler, "Here at Padua is the principal professor of theology, whom I have repeatedly and urgently requested to look at the moon and planets through my glass, which he obstinately refused to do. Why are you not here? What shouts of laughter we should have at this glorious folly!" In 1616, the pope condemned Galileo's proposition that the sun is the center of the universe and warned him not to teach it. Undaunted, Galileo published his *Dialogue Concerning Two World Systems—Ptolemaic and Copernican,* in which he taunted Aristotelians by presenting a lengthy dialogue between those espousing the respective systems of Ptolemy and Copernicus. A certain Simplicio took the side of Ptolemy in the dialogues; the character's very name outraged the Church by intimating that a farcical character symbolized the pope. This led to Galileo's condemnation by the Inquisition in 1633. But from house arrest in his villa in the hills above Florence, Galileo continued to observe, experiment, and write, publishing his texts in the Netherlands. When he went blind in 1638, the pope refused to allow him to go to Florence to see a doctor. Despite his blindness, he continued his scientific investigations until his death four years later.

Descartes and Newton: Competing Theories of Scientific Knowledge

Two brilliant thinkers, one French and the other English, accepted Galileo's revision of classical and medieval systems of knowledge. But they offered contrasting theories of scientific knowledge. René Descartes sought to discover the truth through deductive reasoning. Across the English Channel, Isaac Newton followed his countryman Bacon's insistence that the way to knowledge was through scientific experiment. One amazing discovery after another added to the foundations of the "new philosophy" of science. Science played a major part in the quest for demonstrable truth and authority during and following the period of intense social and political turmoil that lasted from the 1590s until the mid-seventeenth century (see Chapter 4).

Descartes and Deductive Reasoning

The reclusive French philosopher René Descartes (1596–1650) shared Bacon's and Galileo's critiques of ancient and medieval learning. But he offered a different methodology for understanding the universe, espousing deductive reasoning, that is, deducing a conclusion from a set of premises, not from scientific observation.

In 1637, Descartes published *Discourse on Method.* In this deeply personal account, he discussed his rejection of the scientific teaching he had encountered as a young man. Too much of what he had learned had been handed down from tradition without critical commentary. He defiantly "resolved no longer to seek any other science than the knowledge of myself, or of the great book of the world."

Any person, Descartes claimed, has to begin as a blank slate in order to understand the world through deductive reasoning. "I think, therefore I am" (*Cogito, ergo sum*) was his starting point, the postulation of a self-evident truth and the assertion that the ability to think is the basis of human existence. Then each problem has to be separated, he argued, into "as many parts as may be necessary for its adequate solution," moving from the simplest idea to the most difficult, in the same way as a mathematical proof is formulated. Cartesianism (the philosophy of Descartes and his followers) held that the world could be reduced to two substances:

René Descartes.

mind and matter, "thinking substance" and "extended substance." Matter—defined as an infinite number of particles that fill all space, leaving neither void nor vacuum—could be discovered and described mathematically, as could the laws of motion. Beginning with the certainty of his own existence, Descartes argued that the existence of the material universe and God could be deduced. "Begin with the smallest object, the easiest to understand," he insisted, "and gradually move to a knowledge of those that are the most complex."

This materialist approach to knowledge left little or no room for ancient or medieval learning. As a sign of this break, Descartes published his works in French, identifying Latin with scholasticism and ecclesiastical doctrine. Like Kepler, Descartes viewed God as a benevolent, infinitely powerful clockmaker, who created the universe according to rules that the human mind could discover with proper reasoning. God then stepped back, according to this view, forever absent from the actual workings of what He had created.

Mathematics, Descartes argued, demonstrates "the certainty and self-evidence of its reasonings." It therefore stood as the foundation of all science. Eventually a rule for every phenomenon could be discovered. Descartes thus subordinated experimentation to reason in the quest for truth. One of the stream of savants who went to meet Descartes recalled that "many of them would desire him to shew them his Instruments . . . he would drawe out a little Drawer under his Table, and shew them a paire of Compasses with one of the Legges broken; and then, for his Ruler, he used a sheet of paper folded double."

The Newtonian Synthesis

Sir Isaac Newton (1642–1727) built upon the thought of Kepler, Galileo, and Descartes to effect a bold synthesis of the Scientific Revolution, to which he added his own extraordinary discoveries. Newton's *Principia, The Mathematical Principles of Natural Philosophy* (1687) was the first synthesis of scientific principles. Newton synthesized the empiricism of Galileo and others with the theoretical rigor and logic of Descartes, thereby laying the foundations for modern science, which is based on both theory and experimentation.

Newton conducted some of his experiments while living on his prosperous family's farm. There, sitting under a tree, ruminating about celestial motion, Newton observed a falling apple, which led him to recognize that the force that caused objects to fall to earth was related to planetary motion. Newton demonstrated that earthly and celestial motion are subject to laws that could be described by mathematical formulas, the science of mechanics. Going beyond Kepler's three laws of planetary motion, Newton postulated a theory of universal gravitation, the existence of forces of attraction and repulsion operating between objects. Newton concluded that Kepler's laws of planetary motion would be correct if the planets were being pulled toward the sun by a force whose strength was in inverse proportion to their distance from it. The moon, too, seemed to be drawn to the earth in the same way, while the pull that it exerted determined the ocean tides. Every particle of matter, Newton concluded, attracts every other particle with a force proportional to the product of the two masses, and inversely proportional to the square of the distance that separates them.

Newton combined the insights of his predecessors with his own brilliant discoveries. He correctly calculated that the average density of the earth is about five and a half times that of water, suggested that electrical messages activate the nervous system, and anticipated some of the ideas that two centuries later would form the basis of thermodynamics and quantum theory. Newton was the first to understand that all colors are composed of a mixture of the primary colors of the spectrum. He explained the phenomenon of the rainbow, calculated sound waves, and invented calculus (with Gottfried Leibniz, concurrently but separately). In the late 1660s, he also constructed the first reflecting telescope (previous

Sir Isaac Newton.

telescopes had used a refracting lens). Newton's first paper on optics, published in 1671, proposed that light could be mathematically described and
analyzed. Some scientists still consider this paper as the beginning of theoretical physics.

Unlike his predecessors in the development of science, Newton became
wealthy and a hero in his own time. He was elected to Parliament in 1689
representing the University of Cambridge, (where he was a professor),
became warden of the Royal Mint, and was knighted by the king. However,
Newton remained a remote, chaste, humorless figure who published his
discoveries with reluctance and initially only when it seemed that rivals
might first take the credit for a discovery. He brazenly accused those working on similar problems of copying him, and was ungenerous in acknowledging what he had learned from others. Newton's fame marked the victory
of the scientific method, however, over ancient and medieval thought. The
eighteenth-century English poet Alexander Pope went so far as to compare
Newton's accomplishments with those of God on the first day of creation:
"Nature and Nature's laws lay hid in night; God said, Let Newton be! and
all was light!" Newton was given a state funeral and buried in London's
Westminster Abbey.

The Newtonian synthesis of scientific thinking and discovery spread
rapidly from England to the continent. Newton's followers clashed with
Cartesians, the followers of Descartes. Newton rejected Descartes's materialism, at least partially because it seemed to leave open the possibility
that the world was made up totally of matter and that God did not exist,
although the French philosopher never made such an assertion. For his
part, Newton believed that God had to intervene from time to time to keep
the great clock of creation running, lest it run down. That Newton continued to produce manuscripts on theological questions reflected his own
belief that there seemed to be no necessary contradiction between science
and religious faith.

Like Descartes, Newton insisted on the explanatory power of abstract
reasoning. But despite his postulation of theories that could not be demonstrated by the scientific method, such as his description of gravity as a force
that operates between two objects in space, where possible Newton sought
to confirm them experimentally. Until at least 1720, some tension remained
between the English scientific groups (who insisted on the necessity of
experimentation) and their French and German Cartesian counterparts. Yet
this was a creative tension, based on a common acceptance of the primacy
of scientific inquiry.

The Cartesians found an ally in the Spanish-born Dutch philosopher
and mathematician Baruch Spinoza (1632–1677), who also believed that
thought and matter formed the two categories of reality. While making his
living grinding lenses for glasses, he found both a philosopher's introspec-
tive isolation—arguing in a Cartesian manner that human understanding
advances through inner reflection—and stimulation from the new physics.

Expelled from the Jewish community of Amsterdam in 1656 for refusing to participate in religious ceremonies, Spinoza, a proponent of human liberation, called for toleration of all beliefs.

The northern German philosopher and mathematician Gottfried Leibniz (1646–1716) agreed with Descartes and rejected Newton's suggestion that God had to intervene from time to time in the operations of the universe, believing this idea to be demeaning to the Creator's divinity. For Leibniz, the universe was, like God, infinite in space and time. The bodies of humans and animals ran like clocks, set in motion, like the universe itself, by God. Leibniz's popularity helped perpetuate the Cartesian challenge to Newton, notably in France. His deductive postulation of the infinite nature of the universe and his Cartesian insistence that God created the universe to run without further divine intervention according to the mathematical laws Newton had discovered became the hallmarks of the "new philosophy."

The Culture of Science

A "culture of science" developed in Western Europe and gradually spread eastward. By the 1660s, letters, newsletters, and periodicals linked Europeans interested in science. Gradually a "republic of science" took shape, spawning meetings, lectures, visits by traveling scholars, correspondence, book purchases, personal libraries, and public experiments. Above all, the formation of learned associations provided a focal point for the exchange of scientific information and vigorous debates over methodology and findings, expanding the ranks of people interested in science. Only a few decades after Galileo's condemnation, Louis XIV of France and Charles II of England granted patronage to institutions founded to propagate scientific learning. Attracted by scientific discoveries, rulers realized that science could be put to use in the interest of their states.

The Diffusion of the Scientific Method

Although most scientific exchange still occurred by correspondence, savants of science also traveled widely seeking to exchange ideas and learn from each other. For example, the Czech scholar Comenius (Jan Komensky, 1592–1670), a member of the Protestant Unity of Czech Brethren, left his native Moravia in the wake of religious persecution during the Thirty Years' War. After more than a decade in Poland, he began to visit scholars in many countries. For seven years, he traveled in the German states, the Netherlands, England, Sweden, and Hungary. Publishing hundreds of works, he proposed that one day scientific knowledge should be brought together in a collaborative form.

Learned associations and scientific societies had already begun to appear in a number of cities, including Rome and Paris, in the 1620s. In

London, a bequest made possible the establishment of Gresham College, which became a center for scientific discussion and research. In Paris, Marin Mersenne (1588–1637), a monk who had translated Galileo's writings into French, stood at the center of a network of vigorous scientific exchange that cut across national boundaries of states. He organized informal gatherings, attended by, among others, Blaise Pascal (1623–1662), a gloomy young physicist and mathematician who originated the science of probability.

In England, above all, the culture of science became part of public life during the period from 1640 to 1660, with the vocabulary of science joining the discourse of the English upper classes. Newton's prestige further spurred interest in scientific method. In several London coffeehouses, Newtonians offered "a course of Philosophical Lectures on Mechanics, Hydrostatis, Pneumatics [and] Opticks." Exchanges, debates, and even acrimonious disputes reached an ever wider scholarly audience. In England, pamphlets and books on scientific subjects were published in unprecedented numbers.

The Royal Society of London for Improving Natural Knowledge was formed in 1662 under the patronage of Charles II. Its diverse membership, which included merchants, naval officers, and craftsmen, reflected the growing interest in science in England. Members included Edmund Halley (1656–1742), an astronomer who catalogued and discovered the actual movement of the stars and who also discovered the comet that bears his name; the philosopher John Locke (1632–1704), founder of British empiricism, who held that laws of society, like those of science, could be discovered; and Christopher Wren (1632–1723), a versatile architect who rebuilt some of London's churches (including St. Paul's Cathedral) in the wake of the fire of 1666, but who was also a mathematician and professor of astronomy.

The Royal Society, to which Newton dedicated *Principia* and of which he served as president, took its motto from one of the letters of the Roman writer Horace: "The words are the words of a master, but we are not forced to swear by them. Instead we are to be borne wherever experiment drives us." The Royal Society's hundred original members doubled in number by 1670, its weekly meetings attracting visiting scholars. The *Philosophical Transactions of the Royal Society* published some of the most important work of members and foreign correspondents, especially in the field of mathematics.

The natural philosopher Margaret Cavendish, the duchess of Newcastle (1623–1673), participated in debates about matter and motion, the vacuum, magnetism, and the components of color and fire. The author of books on natural philosophy, as well as a number of plays and poems, Cavendish also hosted the "Newcastle circle," an informal gathering of distinguished scientists that received Descartes. But she worked in isolation, which she attributed not only to the fact that she was shy, but to her sex. Despite the

The Newcastle circle hosted by the duke and duchess of Newcastle. Margaret Cavendish, the duchess, is seated on the far right crowned with laurels.

evidence of her own achievements, she accepted, at least in her early years, the contemporary assumptions that women had smaller and softer brains than men, and thus were somehow unfit for science and philosophy. Few men of science would have agreed with the assertion in 1673 by one of Descartes's disciples in France that "the mind has no sex." This bold statement reflected Descartes's belief that thought transcended gender differences—and, therefore, having sense organs equal to men's, women should be recognized as their equals. But although Cavendish was permitted to attend one session, women were formally banned from the Royal Society—this would last until 1945—and they were excluded from English universities.

Yet as an interest in scientific theories and discoveries became influential among the educated upper classes, women also wanted to be informed about science. Several women assisted their husbands in scientific experiments. In Italy, it was more common for women to participate in the scientific life of their cities. Laura Bassi Veratti (1711–1778) studied philosophy at the University of Bologna and was elected to the Academy of Sciences, where she regularly presented her work—although she published very little. She received the title of university lecturer, but because of her gender she was not allowed to teach in public, only at home (which was very common in Italy). Later, however, after having studied mathematics, Bassi was named professor of experimental physics, experimented with fluid mechanics and electricity (perhaps even before Benjamin Franklin conducted his

Testelin's tapestry of the establishment of the French Royal Academy of Science, 1666, and the Foundation of the Observatory, 1667.

studies), was allowed in the last years of her life to teach in public, and thanks to surprising patronage from prelates in Rome was even able to gain access to the scientific studies that the pope had placed on the Index of Forbidden Ideas or Books. Laura Bassi remained an active participant in the scientific community.

In 1666, the French Royal Academy of Science held its first formal meeting in Paris. Like the English Royal Society, the French Academy enjoyed the patronage of the monarchy, which even provided the Academy with an astronomical observatory. Branches of the Academy began in several provincial cities. Unlike members of its English counterpart, those in the French Academy spent much time eating and drinking—one of them complained that too much time was wasted at the fancy dinners that preceded scholarly discussion.

Although some writers deliberately had used Latin because they believed that knowledge ought to remain the preserve of the educated few, with the gradual ebbing of Latin as the language of science, language barriers became a greater obstacle to the diffusion of ideas and research. Galileo had written in Italian to attract a wider audience among the elite, but also to remove science from Latin, the language of religious discourse. Newton wrote *Principia* in Latin, in part because only then could his work be read by most continental scholars. Newton's *Optics,* by contrast, appeared first in English, then in Latin and French translations. Gradually during the eighteenth century, each country's vernacular became the language of its scientists.

By the end of the seventeenth century, the ideas of Descartes had over-come Calvinist opposition to find their way into Dutch university curricula. But the further east one went in Europe, the weaker was the impact of the Scientific Revolution. Scientific inquiry lagged in Poland, in part because of the success of the Catholic Reformation, which restricted the free flow of scholarly thought. Several printing houses in Gdańsk owned by Protestants began publishing scientific works in the second half of the seventeenth century. Leibniz enjoyed popularity in the Habsburg domains, at least partially because he served several German rulers in a diplomatic capacity, and perhaps also because his contagious optimism and belief that God had preordained harmony found resonance in the diverse and scattered kingdom. Nonetheless, theological and devotional literature still dominated the shelves of university, monastic, and imperial libraries. The few publications on science remained strongly Aristotelian.

Some savants in the East did become aware of the debates in the West on the scientific method. Protestant thinkers in Hungary and Silesia, for example, were gradually exposed to the ideas of Bacon and Descartes by traveling scholars from Western Europe, and a few Hungarians and Silesians learned of the new ideas by visiting Dutch universities. Some Bohemian and Polish nobles began to include books on the new science in their private libraries, one of which eventually comprised over 300,000 volumes and 10,000 manuscripts. Theoretical and practical astronomical work spread in the Habsburg lands, carried on in some cases by Jesuits. Mathematics, optics, and problems of atmospheric pressure, too, were the focus of debate. Holy Roman Emperor Ferdinand III (ruled 1637–1657) studied military geometry, constructing arithmetic toys for his children.

Russia's distant isolation from Western culture was compounded by the Orthodox Church's antipathy toward the West and, therefore, opposition to scientific experimentation. There was, to be sure, acceptance of some practical knowledge from the West, for example relating to the military, mining, or metallurgy, which largely arrived with foreign merchants and adventurous craftsmen. Seventeenth-century Russia had no gifted scientists and no scientific societies. Until the reign of Peter the Great, virtually all books published in Russia were devotional in character, and Russian culture was essentially that of a monastery. Foreign books began to appear at court only after about 1650, many arriving from Poland and Ukraine. At that point, however, the Orthodox Church, having suffered a schism, launched another campaign against Western ideas, denouncing secular knowledge as heresy and science as the work of the Antichrist. But gradually some nobles began to be exposed to ideas from the natural sciences. These were the Russian nobles who were dissatisfied with Church learning and eager to know more, for example, about the geography of their own expanding state. The literate classes in Russia would thereafter in many ways remain divided between those interested in ideas coming from the West (most of what was known in the West was available in Russia by

1725) and those who rejected them in the name of preserving what they considered Russia's uniqueness as the most dominant Slavic state.

The Uses of Science

The seventeenth-century Scientific Revolution was above all a revolution in thought. Technological inventions that would change the way people lived lay for the most part in the future. But during the second half of the seventeenth century, scientific experimentation led to the practical application of some discoveries. Thanks to Newton, longitude could now be easily established and ocean tides accurately charted. Voyages of discovery, commerce, and conquest to the Americas increased the demand for new navigational instruments. Dutch scientists and craftsmen led the way in producing telescopes, microscopes, binoculars, and other scientific instruments.

But gradually, too, physicians, engineers, mariners, instrument makers, opticians, pharmacists, and surveyors, many of them self-educated, began to apply the new discoveries to daily life. Robert Hooke (1635–1703), another member of the Royal Society, improved the barometer, which measures atmospheric pressure, and augmented the power of the microscope by adding multiple lenses. This allowed him to study the cellular structure of plants. Biologists began to collect, categorize, dissect, and describe fossils, birds, and exotic fish, adding to contemporary understanding of the richness and complexity of the world around them.

As Francis Bacon had predicted, governments began to tap science in the service of the state. Absolute monarchs on the continent sought out scientists to produce inventions that would give them commercial and military advantages over their rivals. In France, Jean-Baptiste Colbert, Louis XIV's minister of finance, sought to steer the Royal Academy of Science toward the study of what he considered useful subjects that might benefit French commerce and industry, ordered the collection of statistics, and commissioned people to make reliable maps of the provinces and colonies. English government officials also began to apply statistics to administrative and social problems.

Tsar Peter the Great (see Chapter 7) was convinced by his trip to Western Europe that Russia would have to borrow from the West. He corresponded with Leibniz, who convinced him that empirical science, along with the creation of a system of education, would bring progress. The tsar wanted to refute the Western view that "[Russians] are barbarians who disregard science." Peter's campaign of westernization, which included opening his country to Western scientific ideas, made Russia a great power. The sciences that interested Peter were those that were useful in statemaking: mechanics, chemistry, and mathematics all aided in building ships and improving artillery. Peter established the Russian Academy of Sciences and the Moscow School of Mathematics and Navigation, which produced the first generation of Russian explorers, cartographers, and astronomers.

Science and Religion

As scientific discoveries led more people to doubt religious authority that was based on faith alone, points of tension not surprisingly continued to emerge between science and religion. This was particularly the case with the Catholic and Orthodox Churches. There seemed to be a close association between Protestant countries and advances in science, given the precocious role of England and, to a lesser extent, the Netherlands in the emergence of a culture of science. This contributed to the debate over whether Protestantism itself was more conducive to scientific inquiry.

Theological concerns still dominated the curricula at most universities, despite the role of science at the University of Padua, and the University of Cambridge, where by the 1690s both Newton's theories and those of Descartes were taught. Universities contributed relatively little to the diffusion of the scientific method. During the seventeenth century as a whole, their enrollments declined as the European population stagnated. In Catholic countries, canon law, and in Protestant states, civil law predominated in universities, which trained Church and state officials, respectively. The number of German universities more than doubled to about forty during the seventeenth century. The impetus for their creation came from Lutheranism and Calvinism, however, not from an interest in science.

The University of Padua in Italy, pictured at about the time Galileo taught there.

Catholic universities continued to be the most traditional. Following Descartes's death in 1650, the University of Paris, which had about 30,000 students and was the largest university on the continent, forbade a funeral oration for him. Almost three decades later, the archbishop of Paris declared that "in physics it is forbidden to deviate from the principles of the physics of Aristotle . . . and to attach oneself to the new doctrines of Descartes." The University of Paris continued to exclude the new philosophy until the 1730s. Experimental physics as well as botany and chemistry were absent from university study throughout Europe.

The salient role of Protestants in the diffusion of scientific method reflected differences between the theological stance of the Catholic Church and the more liberal ethos of the Protestant Reformation. Catholic theologians left little room for innovation or experimentation. The Protestant belief that an individual should seek truth and salvation in his or her own religious experience through a personal interpretation of the Bible encouraged skepticism about doctrinal theology. The emphasis on individual discovery seemed to lead naturally to empiricism. While Protestant theologians also could be rigid and unyielding, there was no Protestant equivalent to the papal Index of Forbidden Ideas or Books or the mechanism of the Inquisition.

Scientists in Catholic states, confronted by ecclesiastical denunciations or by reports of miracles that seemed to fly in the face of logic, found support in Protestant lands. The Protestant Dutch Republic, fighting a long civil war against Spanish rule, emerged as a center of toleration, where most books could be published. When Descartes learned of the condemnation of Galileo's work, he fled France for the Netherlands, where he published *Discourse on Method*. Francis Bacon had been among the first to associate the Scientific Revolution with the Protestant Reformation. Indeed, many Protestants believed that scientific discovery would lead to a better world and that the wonders of nature were there to be discovered and to give greater glory to God. Yet Jesuits in Bohemia protected Kepler (who had faced persecution from Protestant theologians), provided he limited himself to speculation about astronomy and mathematics and avoided what they considered to be theological questions.

The development of a scientific view of the world in England may be better understood in the context of decades of social, intellectual, and political crisis during the mid-seventeenth century. The campaigns of Parliament and of Puritanism against Charles I's seeming moves toward absolutism and Catholicism attracted political and religious reformers (see Chapter 6). Many who considered the Catholic Church an obstacle to scientific inquiry opposed Charles I as they sought a climate of freedom. The reformers' triumph in the English Civil War may have emboldened Newton and other proponents of the new philosophy. Moderate Anglicans, like the Puritans before them, insisted that science could bring progress. They encouraged the creation of the Royal Observatory, founded by Charles II

Astronomers using a telescope at the Royal Observatory of London.

at Greenwich in 1675. Newton and other members of the Royal Society almost unanimously supported the exile of the Catholic King James II to France and the Glorious Revolution of 1688. Censorship was relatively rare in England, where political and ecclesiastical authority was not so centralized.

By way of contrast, state censorship, encouraged by the Catholic Church, had formally begun in France in 1623, five years after the sovereign law court of Toulouse had ordered a defrocked monk burned at the stake for denouncing belief in miracles after studying at the University of Padua. Thereafter, each new manuscript had to be submitted to a royal office for authorization to be published. Six years later, separate offices were established for literature, science, and politics, with ecclesiastics having veto power over books treating religious subjects.

Yet, to be sure, not all churchmen in France adamantly waged a war on science. Some French Jesuits were open-minded about the scientific method. Jansenists, forming a dissident movement within the Church, also favored scientific discovery, discussion, and debate (see Chapter 7).

CONSEQUENCES OF THE SCIENTIFIC REVOLUTION

The Scientific Revolution seemed to push theology into the background. Even though the earliest exponents of scientific method never doubted

God's creation of the universe, the idea that mankind might one day master nature shocked many Church officials. Descartes's materialism seemed to suggest that humanity could live independently of God. Faith in the scientific method indeed had distinct philosophical consequences: "If natural Philosophy, in all its parts, by pursuing this method, shall at length be perfected," Newton reasoned, "the bounds of moral philosophy will also be enlarged." The English poet John Donne had already come to the same conclusion in 1612. "The new philosophy," he wrote prophetically, "calls all in doubt."

The men and women of science espoused the application of the scientific method to the study of nature and the universe. It was but a short step to subjecting society, government, and political thought to similar critical scrutiny. The English philosopher John Locke claimed that society was, as much as astronomy, a discipline subject to the rigors of the scientific method. Moreover, the Scientific Revolution would ultimately help call absolutism into doubt by influencing the philosophes, the thinkers and writers of the eighteenth-century Enlightenment. The philosophes' belief in the intrinsic value of freedom and their assertion that people should be ruled by law, not rulers, would challenge the very foundations of absolutism.

CHAPTER 9

ENLIGHTENED THOUGHT AND THE REPUBLIC OF LETTERS

"What is the Enlightenment?" wrote the German philosopher Immanuel Kant. His response was *"Dare to know!* Have the courage to make use of your own understanding," as exciting a challenge today as in the eighteenth century. During that period of contagious intellectual energy and enthusiastic quest for knowledge, the philosophes, the thinkers and writers of the Enlightenment, espoused intellectual freedom and the use of reason in the search for progress. Unlike most scientists of the preceding period, they wanted their ideas to reach the general reading public. Education therefore loomed large in this view of their mission. Their approach to education was not limited to formal schooling, but instead took in the development of the individual and the continued application of critical inquiry throughout one's life.

The Enlightenment began in Paris but extended to much of Western Europe, including the German states, the Dutch Republic, Great Britain, and as far as North America. The works of the philosophes reached Poland and Russia. Orthodox Christian intellectuals carried the Enlightenment's celebration of science and humanism into the Balkans. The philosophes' writings helped confirm French as the language of high culture in eighteenth-century Europe. Indeed, it was reported from Potsdam that at the court of Frederick the Great of Prussia "the language least spoken is German." But French was hardly the only language of philosophic discourse. In Italy, those influenced by the new thinking used the ideas of the philosophes to attack clerical and particularly papal influence in political life. In Britain, the philosopher David Hume and economist Adam Smith, father of free-market liberalism, represented the thought of the "Scottish Enlightenment."

The Enlightenment can be roughly divided into three stages. The first covers the first half of the eighteenth century and most directly reflects the influence of the Scientific Revolution; the second, the "high Enlightenment," begins with the publication of *The Spirit of Laws* (1748) by Charles-Louis de Montesquieu and ends in 1778 with the deaths of François-Marie Voltaire and Jean-Jacques Rousseau; and the third, the late Enlightenment, influenced by Rousseau's work, marks a shift from an emphasis on human reason to a greater preoccupation with the emotions and passions of mankind. This final stage also features new ideas relating the concept of freedom to the working of economies, best represented by the thought of Adam Smith. At this time, too, several monarchs applied the philosophes' principle that rulers should work for the good of their subjects. But these experiments in "enlightened absolutism" were most noteworthy for rulers' organizing their states more effectively, further enhancing their authority. This third period also brought the popular diffusion of the lesser works of would-be philosophes seeking to capitalize on an expanding literary market. These works, too, were influential in undermining respect for the authority of the monarchy of France and thus indirectly contributed to the French Revolution.

ENLIGHTENED IDEAS

The philosophes espoused views of nature, mankind, society, government, and the intrinsic value of freedom that challenged some of the most fundamental tenets Europeans had held for centuries. Slavery, for example, violated the principle of human freedom. The implications of Enlightenment thought were revolutionary, because the philosophes argued that progress had been constrained by social and political institutions that did not reflect humanity's natural goodness and capacity for material and moral improvement. Although many philosophes saw no or little incompatibility between science and religion, they were skeptical of received truths passed down from generation to generation. Thus, they challenged the doctrinal authority of the established churches and launched a crusade for the secularization of political institutions.

It is to the Enlightenment that we trace the origins of many of our modern political beliefs: the idea that people should be ruled by law, not rulers; the belief that a separation of powers ought to exist within government to prevent the accumulation of too much power in a few hands; the concept of popular sovereignty (legal authority should be wholly or at least partly based in the people, reflecting their interests, if not their consent); and the assumption that it is the responsibility of rulers to look after the welfare of the people. The consequences of such modern views of sovereignty, political rights, and the organization of states would be seen in the French Revolution and the era of liberalism in the nineteenth century.

Intellectual Influences on Enlightened Thought

Like all intellectual and cultural movements, the Enlightenment did not emerge spontaneously. Creating what David Hume (1711–1776) called "the science of man," the philosophes reflected the influence of the Scientific Revolution, whose proponents had espoused the scientific method in the study of nature and the universe. Sir Isaac Newton, the brilliant English scientist and theoretician (see Chapter 8), emphasized that science—reason and experimentation—holds the key to understanding nature, and that mankind discovers knowledge not through religious teaching but through "observation, analysis, and experiment."

Two thinkers linked the Scientific Revolution and Enlightenment thought: John Locke and Georges-Louis Buffon. Locke (1632–1704) claimed that philosophy was, as much as astronomy, a discipline subject to the rigors of the scientific method and critical inquiry. The son of a landowner and a member of the British Royal Society, Locke maintained a strong interest in medicine. After returning from Holland, where he had gone into self-imposed exile during the political crisis swirling around the throne of King James II, Locke remained close to the government of King William and Queen Mary (see Chapter 6).

Locke believed that the scientific method could be applied to the study of society. In *An Essay Concerning Human Understanding* (1690), Locke postulated that each individual is a *tabula rasa*, or blank slate, at birth. Believing that all knowledge is sensory, Locke denied the existence of

John Locke (*left*) and Georges-Louis Buffon (*right*), who both linked the Scientific Revolution and Enlightenment thought.

inherited abilities and rejected the idea that humanity is stained by original sin, a view held by the Catholic Church. He anticipated that the discovery of more laws of nature would be the basis of secular laws on which society should be based. He was confident that humanity might thereby be able to improve social conditions.

Locke had asserted the dignity of the individual in contending that every person has the right to life, liberty, and property (though he excluded slaves in the Americas from such innate rights). He argued that monarchies were based on a social contract between rulers and the ruled. People had to relinquish some of their liberty in exchange for security. But, unlike Thomas Hobbes, who famously believed that individuals should surrender their rights to the absolute state of unlimited sovereignty in exchange for protection from the "state of nature," Locke insisted that mankind's liberty and rights stemmed from the laws of nature. He became a leading proponent of educational reform, freedom of the press, religious toleration, and the separation of political powers.

Locke's interest in the relationship between nature and the social order led him to consider issues of gender. The assumption that the king ruled his nation as a husband and father ruled his wife and children had been prominent in early modern political theory, only briefly challenged by a handful of radicals during the English Civil War in the mid-seventeenth century. Locke argued against the contemporary vision of the state in which "all power on earth is either derived from or usurped from the fatherly power." He denied the appropriateness of the analogy between the family and the state as patriarchal institutions. Rejecting the contemporary view that Adam held supremacy over Eve, he viewed marriage, like government, to be organized by social contract. However, Locke went no further than that, and his espousal of equality within marriage remained only an ideal. In everyday life, he believed that women should defer to men. But Locke's analysis of the family as an institution nonetheless helped stimulate intellectual interest in the social role of women.

Georges-Louis Buffon (1707–1788) linked the Scientific Revolution to the Enlightenment. Buffon, whose initial presentation to the French Royal Academy of Science was a study of probability theory applied to gambling on hopscotch, became the curator of the Royal Gardens. Surrounded by monkeys and badgers in his laboratory, he carried out experiments, some of which worked, such as his study of the burning effect of the sun through glass, and some of which did not, including his study of the emotional life of birds. Buffon's experiments with cooling metals led him to build a large forge near his home in Burgundy.

The philosophes acknowledged their debt to the late-seventeenth-century proponents of the scientific method. Voltaire saluted Newton for having called on scientists and philosophers "to examine, weigh, calculate, and measure, but never conjecture." Hume insisted that all knowledge came from critical inquiry and scientific discovery and that the ability to reason distinguished mankind from other animals. Many philosophes, reflecting the influence of the Scientific Revolution, considered religion, the origins of which they found not in reason but in faith and custom, to be a social phenomenon, like any other to be studied scientifically. Hume blasted away at the idea of religious truths revealed through the Bible.

The very universality of their principles led some of the philosophes to suggest that a sense of morality—of what is right and wrong—might vary across cultures because it emerged from the nature of mankind, not from religious teaching. Denis Diderot, influenced by Locke, argued that sensory stimulation—or in the case of people who are blind, sensory deprivation—shapes individual moral responses, and that moral principles for a blind man might be somewhat different from those of someone who could see. He described the people of distant Tahiti as forming a rational social order without the benefit of any ecclesiastical doctrine. Hume called for a "science of morals" to serve the interests of Christians.

The Republic of Ideas

The philosophes' calls for reform were sometimes subtle, sometimes boldly forceful. Yet they did not lead insurrections. Their pens and pencils were their only weapons as they sought to change the way people thought. They communicated their ideas in letters, unpublished manuscripts, books, pamphlets, brochures, and through writing novels, poetry, drama, literary and art criticism, and political philosophy.

The philosophes glorified the collegiality and interdependence of writers within the "republic of letters," what the men and women of the Enlightenment sometimes called the informal international community of philosophes. By the mid-eighteenth century, Voltaire claimed with some exaggeration that the professional writer stood at the top of the social summit. He, Montesquieu, and Diderot accepted election to the prestigious French Royal Academy, revealing their ambivalence toward the monarchy that they attacked, however subtly, in their work. The most famous of the philosophes gained money as well as prestige, although Voltaire and Montesquieu were among the few who could support themselves by writing.

The philosophes may have shared the fundamental ideas of the Enlightenment, but significant differences existed among them. They came from different social classes, generations, and nations. And they often disagreed, like people in any republic, arguing in person, by letter, and in their published work. They could not agree, for example, whether the ideal state was an enlightened, benevolent monarchy, a monarchy balanced by a parliamentary body representing the nobility, or a kind of direct democracy. Their views on religion also varied. Montesquieu, Voltaire, and Rousseau were deists. Because scientific inquiry seemed to have demonstrated that the persistent intervention of God was unnecessary to keep the world in motion, they viewed God as a clockmaker who set the world in motion according to the

Voltaire presiding (with his arm raised) over a dinner gathering of philosophes, including Denis Diderot, who is sitting at the far left.

laws of nature and then left knowledge and human progress to the discovery and action of mankind. In contrast, Diderot became an atheist.

For all the variety and richness of the republic of letters, four philosophes dominated Enlightenment discourse with startling ideas about society, religion, and politics: Montesquieu, Voltaire, Diderot, and Rousseau. Each is well worth considering separately.

Montesquieu

Montesquieu (Charles-Louis de Secondat; 1689–1755) inherited a feudal château near Bordeaux and a small income upon the death of his father. He studied law and later inherited from a wealthy relative more property and the title of baron de Montesquieu, as well as the presidency of the noble parlement, or provincial sovereign law court, seated at Bordeaux.

In 1721, after moving to Paris, Montesquieu published *Persian Letters*. In the form of reports sent home by two Persian visitors to Paris, his work detailed the political and social injustices of life in the West. By casting this critique of eighteenth-century France in the form of a travelogue, Montesquieu was able to dodge royal censorship. The work irritated ecclesiastics who resented its insinuation that the pope was a "magician." As for the king of France, the Persians reported that he "is the most powerful of European potentates. He has no mines of gold like his neighbor, the king of Spain: but he is much wealthier than that prince, because his riches are drawn from a more inexhaustible source, the vanity of his subjects. He has undertaken and carried on great wars, without any other supplies than those derived from the sale of titles of honors." But beneath the satire of the *Persian Letters*, Montesquieu was arguing the point that nature reveals a universal standard of justice that applies for all people in all places at all times, in Islamic Persia as in Christian France.

Montesquieu's ideas reflected the increased contact between Europeans and much of the rest of the world. Merchants, soldiers, missionaries, and colonists had followed the first European explorers to, among other places, the Americas and Asia. Published accounts of travel stirred the imagination of upper-class Europeans who were interested in societies and cultures that lay on the fringes of or beyond their continent. America and China, in particular, fascinated Europeans who had read about them. Yet in *Persian Letters*, Montesquieu manifested doubts about the quest for colonies: "empires were like the branches of a tree that sapped all the strength from the trunk." He also offered the first critical examination of the institution of slavery by a philosophe. He rejected slavery as an extension of despotism, concluding that "slavery is against natural law, by which all men are born free and independent" because "the liberty of each citizen is part of public liberty." Thus slavery compromised "the general good of men [and] that of particular societies."

The Spirit of Laws (1748) inaugurated the high Enlightenment. Montesquieu applied the principles of observation, experimentation, and analysis, which lie at the heart of scientific inquiry, to the social and political foundations of states. He described the relationship between climate, religion, and tradition, and the historical evolution of a nation's political life. Laws, he argued, are subject to critical inquiry and historical study because they develop over time. Historians, freeing themselves from the influence of the Church, could now study "general causes, whether moral or physical."

The British political system fascinated Montesquieu, who spent two years in England. He was impressed by the historical role of Parliament, a representative body unlike French parlements (law courts), despite the similarity of their names. The English Parliament seemed an "intermediate power" that had during the English Civil War prevented Britain from becoming either a monarchical despotism or a republic, which Montesquieu identified with chaos. His point was that each political system and legal tradition evolved differently. He feared that the French monarchy was showing signs of becoming despotic because it lacked the separation of powers found in England. Only constitutionalism could combine the guarantees for order (offered by monarchy) with those of freedom. Montesquieu believed that noble rights and municipal privileges, which had been eroded by royal absolutism in France, could stave off monarchical despotism. Montesquieu held that the sovereignty of the king came not from God, but from the people.

Voltaire

Brilliant, witty, and sarcastic, Voltaire (François-Marie Arouet, 1694–1778) was the most widely read, cited, and lionized of the philosophes. He was the son of a notary who had enhanced his family's position through a favorable marriage. Voltaire's parents, who wanted him to be a lawyer, sent him to Paris to be educated by the Jesuits. Instead, the brash, ambitious young man made a name for himself as a dramatist and poet—though many of these early works are quite forgettable. Voltaire developed a pen as quick and cutting as a sword. Some of his early works were banned in France; everything he ever wrote was forbidden in Spain.

Like Montesquieu, Voltaire reflected the Anglophilia of the philosophes of the early and high Enlightenment. He extolled Britain, its commercial empire, relative religious toleration, and freedom of the press. Voltaire believed that the only representative body that might guarantee the natural rights of the king's subjects in France would be the equivalent of the British House of Commons. Whereas Montesquieu looked to the nobility to protect people from monarchical despotism, Voltaire counted on the enlightened monarchs of centralized states to protect their people against the self-interest of nobles.

Voltaire claimed that the political organization of each state was at least partially determined by its specific history and circumstances. As science should study the world of nature, so should the philosophe trace the separate development of nations. This line of reasoning convinced him that Montesquieu was wrong to think that the British political system could be successfully transplanted to France.

Voltaire reserved his most scathing attacks for the Church, an institution, like the parlements, which seemed to block the development of freedom in his own country. His motto was an impassioned cry against the teaching of the Church—"*Écrasez l'infâme!*" ("Crush the horrible thing!"). Of monks, he once said, "They sing, they eat, they digest." The pope and the Parlement of Paris both condemned his polemical *Philosophical Dictionary* (1764). His attacks were clever and devastating; for example, his pithy description of the Chinese as having "an admirable religion free from superstition and the rage to persecute" was read by virtually everyone as suggesting that in France the opposite was true. Voltaire believed that God created the universe and then let it operate according to scientific laws. He espoused a natural religion based upon reason.

Voltaire intended *Candide* (1759) to be an indictment of fanaticism and superstition. In the short tale, the cheerful optimist Candide bumbles from disaster to disaster. Here Voltaire confronts the seeming contradiction between the goodness of God and the evil in the world. He writes about the earthquake that ravaged Lisbon in 1755, killing thousands of people and destroying much of the Portuguese capital. If God is all good and omniscient, why, Voltaire reasoned, would He allow such an event to occur? But Voltaire nonetheless believed that religion was beneficial because it offered people hope, and therefore made their lives more bearable. It also kept them in line: "If God did not exist, one would have to invent him. I want my attorney, my tailor, my servants, even my wife to believe in God, and I think that I shall then be robbed and cuckholded less often."

Voltaire's fame spread when he took up the cause of a man who seemed wrongly accused of murder. In 1761, Jean Calas, a Protestant from Toulouse, stood accused of killing his son, who had been found hanging in the family basement. The young Calas had intended to convert to Catholicism. Convicted by the Parlement of Toulouse, the father was tortured to death, though it seemed likely that his son had committed suicide. Several years later, the parlement reversed its earlier decision—too late, alas, for Jean Calas. But the Calas Affair helped put the philosophes' critique of religious intolerance into the limelight of public opinion.

Voltaire's energetic interest in the Calas Affair reflected his insistence that progress is somehow inevitable without human action. He concludes *Candide* with the famous, though seemingly ambiguous, advice that "one must cultivate one's own garden," as he did at his rural retreat. But Voltaire was counseling anything but a withdrawal into the sanctuary of introspection. He called for each person to follow the path of light and do battle with those institutions that seemed to stand in the way of humanity's potential. In 1764 he predicted, "Everything I see scatters the seeds of a revolution which will definitely come. . . . Enlightenment has gradually spread so widely that it will burst into full light at the first right opportunity, and then there will be a fine uproar. Lucky are the young, for they will see great things."

Diderot

Denis Diderot's monumental *Encyclopedia* best reflected the collaborative nature of the Enlightenment, as well as its wide influence. Diderot (1713–1784), the son of an artisan, was something of a jack-of-all-trades, a man of letters who wrote plays, art criticism, history, theology, and philosophy. Educated by the Jesuits (like Voltaire), he flirted with the idea of becoming a priest, and for a time supported himself by writing sermons for bishops. Unlike Montesquieu and Voltaire, Diderot underwent a rugged apprenticeship in the "republic of letters." He penned a pornographic novel to earn enough to indulge the fancies of his mistress. But he also questioned how, through centuries of male domination, women, despite their capacity for reproduction, had come to be considered inferior to men. Diderot claimed that laws that limited the rights of women were counter to nature.

The *Encyclopedia*, on which Diderot worked for twenty-five years and to which he contributed 5,000 articles, stands as the greatest monument of the Enlightenment. At the heart of the project lay the philosophes' insistence that knowledge is rational and that it follows the laws of nature. Social and political institutions should be submitted to standards of rationality. All things, as Diderot put it, are equally subject to criticism. By elevating mankind to the center of human inquiry, the 140 authors of the *Encyclopedia*—including Rousseau, who penned 344 articles—sought to achieve Diderot's goal, "to change the general way of thinking," as well as to bring glory to France.

Voltaire had set a goal for the Enlightenment itself: to educate the literate and intellectually curious of the social elite, and perhaps people farther down the social scale as well. The *Encyclopedia* at least partially fulfilled that goal. Published over a period of more than twenty years beginning in 1751, it consisted of 60,000 articles and 2,885 illustrations in 28 volumes. Subtitled "A Classified Dictionary of the Sciences, Arts and

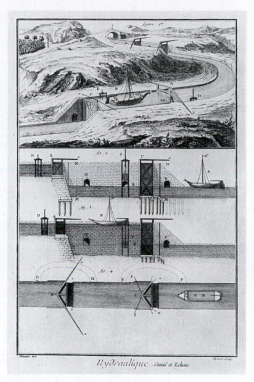

Depiction of an eighteenth-century canal with locks, from Denis Diderot's *Encyclopedia*.

Trades," this first such compilation in the West was a bold attempt to organize and classify all knowledge gathered from "over the face of the earth." Its authors insisted that by learning more about the universe, men and women could improve the world. This marked a departure from the assumption that mankind's ability to penetrate the secrets of the universe was limited. Montesquieu contributed sections on artistic taste, Rousseau on music, Voltaire on literature, and Buffon on nature. Diderot gave particular credit to the everyday contributions of artisans by describing how and why ingeniously simple tools and machines could make tasks easier.

The *Encyclopedia* generated sufficient excitement that advance sales alone financed its publication. It earned its publishers a handsome profit. After the first edition, subsequent editions with less expensive paper and fewer illustrations became available at about a sixth of the original price. Lawyers, officials, and *rentiers* (people living from property income) were more likely to own a copy than merchants or manufacturers, who could afford the volumes but seemed less interested. What began as a luxury product ended up on the shelves of the "middling sort."

The philosophes wanted the *Encyclopedia* to carry the Enlightenment far beyond the borders of France. Although only about one in ten volumes

MAP 9.1 DIFFUSION OF DIDEROT'S *ENCYCLOPEDIA* Subscriptions to Diderot's *Encyclopedia* throughout Europe.

Subscriptions
· 1-10
• 11-50
● 51-100
⬤ More than 100

0 ____ 400 miles
0 ____ 400 kilometers

Moscow
St. Petersburg
FINLAND
NORWAY
SWEDEN
RUSSIA
Warsaw
BALTIC SEA
Copenhagen
DENMARK
HOLY ROMAN EMPIRE
Prague
NORTH SEA
Amsterdam
Munich
OTTOMAN EMPIRE
DUTCH REPUBLIC
Brussels
Strasbourg
Basel
Geneva
Milan
Turin
Genoa
Naples
Lille
Arras
Reims
Amiens
Rouen
Paris
Dijon
Lyon
Avignon
Aix
Marseille
London
BRITAIN
Dublin
Angers
Tours
Poitiers
FRANCE
Grenoble
Nantes
La Rochelle
Bordeaux
Toulouse
MEDITERRANEAN SEA
ATLANTIC OCEAN
SPAIN
Madrid
PORTUGAL
Lisbon

traveled beyond the country, its pattern of distribution in the 1770s and 1780s reflected the success of the enterprise (see Map 9.1). The *Encyclopedia*'s prospectus and booksellers' advertisements assured potential buyers that ownership would proclaim one's standing as a person of knowledge, a philosophe. In northern Germany and Scandinavia, customers were described as "sovereign princes" and "Swedish seigneurs." A few copies reached African settlements, including the Cape of Good Hope. Thomas Jefferson helped promote the *Encyclopedia* in America, finding several subscribers, among them Benjamin Franklin. King Louis XVI of France owned a copy. There was an Italian edition, despite the opposition of the Church. However, in Spain, Inquisition censorship frightened booksellers and buyers alike, and in Portugal only a few copies got by the police.

The *Encyclopedia* implicitly challenged monarchical authority. Jean-Jacques Rousseau wrote enthusiastically about representative government and even popular sovereignty, and came close to espousing a republic. After initially tolerating the project, French royal censors banned Volume 7 in 1757, after an unsuccessful assassination attempt on Louis XV. Diderot, whose first serious philosophical work had been burned by the public executioner, was briefly imprisoned. In the 1770s, the French state again tolerated the *Encyclopedia*, which it now treated more as a commodity than as an ideological threat to monarchy or Church. The small subsequent skirmishes fought over the volumes had more to do with rivalries between publishers, between those privileged with official favor and those without. In this way, Diderot's grand project symbolized the ongoing political struggles within the French monarchy itself.

Rousseau

The place of Jean-Jacques Rousseau (1712–1778) in the Enlightenment is far more ambiguous than that of Diderot and his *Encyclopedia*. Rousseau embraced human freedom, but more than any other of the philosophes, Rousseau idealized emotion, instinct, and spontaneity, which he believed to be, along with reason, essential parts of human nature.

The son of a Geneva watchmaker, Rousseau, a Protestant, went to Paris as a young man in the hope of becoming a composer. The arrogant, self-righteous Rousseau received an introduction into several aristocratic Parisian salons, informal upper-class gatherings at which ideas were discussed, where he became friendly with Diderot. In 1749, the Academy of Dijon (an academy in France was a regular gathering of people to discuss ideas, and, as we shall see below, a way that enlightenment thought spread) sponsored an essay contest on the question of whether the progress of science had strengthened or weakened morality. Rousseau's first-prize essay concluded that primitive or natural humanity had embodied the essential goodness of mankind and that for humanity to be happy, new social and political institutions would be necessary.

Portrait of Jean-Jacques Rousseau.

Exiled by the Parlement of Paris because his writings offended monarchy and Church, Rousseau returned to Geneva. Following the condemnation of his writings there in the early 1770s, he abandoned his children in an orphanage—as his father had abandoned him—and set off to visit England. Rousseau remained a contentious loner, quarreling with other philosophes. He assumed that when his former friends disagreed with his ideas, they knew that he was right but simply refused to admit it. In his *Confessions* (the first volume of which appeared in 1782), he appealed to future generations to see how contemporary thinkers had misinterpreted or misrepresented him.

In *Discourse on the Arts and Sciences* (1750), Rousseau argued that civilization had corrupted the natural goodness of man, which he called the "fundamental principle" of political thought. The intemperate quest for property had disrupted the harmony that had once characterized mankind in its primitive state by creating a hierarchy of wealth. Rousseau's idealization of relatively primitive, uncomplicated, and, he thought, manageable social and political groupings led him to believe that a republic, such as his own Geneva, alone offered its citizens the possibility of freedom. As free people in primitive societies joined together for mutual protection, enlightened people could associate for their mutual development in a kind of direct democracy. However, Rousseau remained suspicious of representative government, believing that people might ultimately vote themselves into slavery by electing unworthy representatives. He remained vague on how people were to be organized and governed.

In *The Social Contract* (1762), Rousseau tried to resolve the question of how people could join together in society to find protection and justice and yet remain free individuals. Locke had described the relationship between a ruler and his people as a contractual one. Hobbes, in contrast, had argued that individuals could find refuge from the brutality of the state of nature only by surrendering their rights to an absolute ruler in exchange for safety. Rousseau imagined a social contract in which the individual surrenders his or her natural rights to the "general will" in order to find order and security. By "general will," Rousseau meant the consensus of a community of citizens with equal political rights. Citizens would live in peace because they would be ruled by other citizens, not by dynastic rulers eager to expand their territorial holdings.

Although *The Social Contract* remained largely unknown until after the French Revolution of 1789, it offered an unparalleled critique of contemporary society. Rousseau summed up his thinking with the stirring assertion that "men are born free yet everywhere they are in chains." Whereas Voltaire and other philosophes hoped that rulers would become enlightened, Rousseau insisted that sovereignty comes not from kings or oligarchies, or even from God, but through the collective search for freedom.

Rousseau thus helped shape the final period of the Enlightenment, which anticipated nineteenth-century romanticism by giving emotion more free play. "Everything is good as it comes from the hands of the Author of nature, but everything degenerates in the hands of man," Rousseau's novel *Émile* (1762) began. It described what he considered to be the ideal natural, secular education, as the young Émile is gradually exposed by his tutor to nature during walks to explore brooks and mills. Rousseau intended such wonders to stimulate Émile's emotions, which were to be developed before his sense of reason, "the one that develops last and with the greatest difficulty." Émile's primitive virtue needed to be preserved against the vices of culture, but also developed as an end in itself so that he would become an autonomous individual. Rousseau assigned Sophie, Émile's chosen "well-born" spouse, an education appropriate to what Rousseau considered a woman's lower status in life. Yet, even Rousseau's insistence on the capacity of women for intellectual development was ahead of its time. The novel became a literary sensation.

Voltaire ridiculed Rousseau's espousal of primitiveness as virtue: "I have received, Monsieur, your new book against the human race, and I thank you. No one has employed so much intelligence turning men into beasts. One starts wanting to walk on all fours after reading your book. However, in more than sixty years I have lost the habit."

THE DIFFUSION AND EXPANSION OF THE ENLIGHTENMENT

The groundwork for the Enlightenment lay not only in the realm of ideas, such as those of the Scientific Revolution and Locke, but also in gradual social changes that affected the climate of opinion. These changes, especially but not exclusively found in France, included challenges to and even the decline of organized religion in the eighteenth century, at least in some regions, and the emergence of a more broadly based culture.

Religious Enthusiasm and Skepticism

During the first half of the seventeenth century, the Catholic Reformation engendered a slow but steady religious revival in France, Spain, and the Habsburg domains. The founding of new religious orders and monasteries and the popularity of the cults and shrines of local saints reflected religious intensity. The established churches still retained formidable authority and prestige.

The development late in the seventeenth century of Pietism among Protestants in the northern German states, emphasizing preaching and the study of the Bible, reflected, however, growing dissatisfaction with established religions and the existence of considerable religious creativity. Disaffected by abstract theological debates and by the Lutheran Church's hierarchical structure, Pietists wanted to reaffirm Protestant belief in the primacy of the individual conscience. Like English Puritans and French Jansenists (a dissident group within the Catholic Church), they called for a more austere religion. Pietists wanted a revival of piety and good works, and asked that laymen take an active role in religious life. Bible reading and small discussion groups replaced the more elaborate, formal services of the Lutherans, helping expand interest in the German language and culture among the upper classes. But by the last quarter of the eighteenth century, Pietist influence had waned, reflecting not only the diffusion of Enlightenment thought but also the fact that Lutheranism remained the state religion in the northern German states, maintaining a hold on the universities.

In Britain, religious practice seems to have increased among all social classes during the seventeenth century. The Anglican Church of England was the Established Church, but Britain also had about half a million non-Anglican Protestants, or Dissenters, at the end of the eighteenth century. Some middle-class Presbyterians, Congregationalists, Unitarians, Baptists, and Quakers sent their sons to private academies. Oxford and Cambridge Universities admitted only Anglicans. Anti-Catholicism remained endemic in England, where there were about 70,000 Catholics in 1770, most in the lower classes.

Although many Baptists, Congregationalists, and Quakers, among other Dissenters, had traditionally been laborers, no one religion held the allegiance of many ordinary people in England in the eighteenth century until the ministry of John Wesley (1703–1791). An Anglican trained in theology at the Univer-

John Wesley, who preached Methodist evangelism to the ordinary people of England.

sity of Oxford, the brooding Wesley began to believe that his mission was to infuse ordinary people—who seemed ignored by the Established Church—with religious enthusiasm.

Wesley never formally broke with the Anglican Church nor claimed to be setting up a new denomination. Yet that was the effect of his lifetime of preaching directly to ordinary people on grassy hills and in open fields and of writing religious tracts directed at ordinary Britons. Wesley attracted about 100,000 followers to Methodism. Stressing personal conversion, Methodism suggested that all people were equal in God's eyes. This offended upper-class Englishmen and -women, not the least because Methodists shouted out their beliefs and sometimes publicly confessed sins that the upper classes thought best left unnamed. A duchess explained that she hated the Methodists because "it is monstrous to be told that you have a heart as sinful as the common wretches that crawl on the earth."

Methodist evangelism was both a dynamic and a stabilizing force in British society. There was little or nothing politically or socially radical about Wesley, as shown by his unwillingness to break formally with the Established Church. Far from preaching rebellion, Wesley encouraged work, self-discipline, and abstinence from dancing, drinking, and gambling.

The Anglican Church, in turn, began to seek more followers among the lower classes. It established the Society for the Promotion of Christian Knowledge and Anglican Sunday schools, which provided poor children with food and catechism. The evangelical Hannah More (1745–1833), the "bishop in petticoats," abandoned the material comforts of upper-class life for the challenges of bringing religion to the poor.

Despite all of the evangelistic efforts, by the middle of the eighteenth century religion seemed to play a significantly smaller role in the lives of people of all classes, particularly in regions with expanding economies and relatively high literacy rates. The numbers of men and women entering the clergy in France declined, and male and female monastic orders lost a third of their members between 1770 and 1790 alone. Fewer wills requested that Masses be said for the deceased or for souls in Purgatory. A Venetian theologian at mid-century claimed that the people of his state had become "de-christianized." In France, popular dislike of the exemption of the clergy from taxes increased, although the Church still provided the monarchy a sizable yearly contribution from its great wealth. Thus, the philosophes who challenged the role of the established churches in public life were addressing many readers who had lost interest in organized religion.

Expansion of the Cultural Base

The expanding influence of the middle classes in England and northwestern Europe also began slowly to transform cultural life, expanding interest in literature, music, and the arts. The increasing number of literary associations reflected this change. A rise in literacy expanded the size of the potential audience of the philosophes. By the end of the century, perhaps half of the men in England, France, the Netherlands, and the German states could read. A smaller proportion of women—between a third to a half of the female population of these countries—was literate. The rate was considerably lower in southern Europe, and relatively few people could read in Eastern Europe, Russia, and the Balkans. Opportunities for women, even those from noble families, to obtain more than a minimal education remained quite rare, although several German states began schools for girls. Even Marie Antoinette, queen of France and one of the wealthiest people in the world, made frequent grammatical and spelling errors.

Publishers fed the growing appetites of readers eager to know what events were taking place in their own country and abroad. Newspapers published one or two times a week summarized events transpiring in other countries. The number of English periodicals increased sixfold between 1700 and 1780. In the German states, the number of books and magazines published grew by three times during the last decades of the eighteenth century. Novels gained in popularity at the expense of books on theology and popular piety. Sentimental novels presented syrupy stories of domestic life and tender love. English female novelists gave women an unprecedented public voice in Britain, presenting their heroines as affectionate companions to their husbands and good mothers. Diderot and the German dramatist and critic Gotthold Lessing (1729–1781) called for the theater to portray the lives and passions of ordinary people, instead of only kings and queens, princes and princesses. However, traditional literature, such as religious tracts, popular almanacs, and folktales, remained the most widely read literature.

The Enlightenment had a direct influence on the growing popularity of history. Reflecting their interest in understanding human experience, the philosophes helped create history as a modern discipline. Since the classical Greeks, there had been relatively little interest in history in Europe. Church fathers espoused the primacy of theology and viewed the world as little more than a test to prepare Christians for the afterlife. But now all human experience, including non-Western cultures, emerged as suitable for historical inquiry. Edward Gibbon (1737–1794) was inspired to undertake his *History of the Decline and Fall of the Roman Empire* (published over a period of twelve years beginning in 1776) by visiting the coliseum in Rome. Natural science, too, developed a following.

The number of lending libraries, as well as reading circles or clubs, some organized by resourceful booksellers, increased. In Paris, London, Milan, Berlin, and other large cities, lending libraries rented books for as short a period as an hour. Small private libraries became more common. Reading, which heretofore had largely been a group activity in which a literate person read to others—in the same way that storytellers spun their yarns—became more of a private undertaking.

BIBLIOTHECÆ LUGDUNO-BATAVÆ CUM PULPITIS ET ARCIS VERA IXNOGRAPHIA.

The library of the University of Leyden in the Netherlands, 1610.

While some of the most significant works of the Enlightenment were virtually unknown outside the republic of letters, others became the bestsellers of the age. Montesquieu's *The Spirit of Laws* went through twenty-two printings—approximately 35,000 copies—in the first eighteen months after publication in 1748. Buffon's thirty-volume study, *The System of Nature* (1749–1804)—despite its bulk—also enjoyed prodigious success. Voltaire's *Candide* was reprinted eight times the year of its publication in 1759. Abbé Guillaume Raynal's *The Philosophical and Political History of European Colonies and Commerce in the Two Indies* (1770) was reprinted seventy times to supply an eager market. It described the colonization of the New World, Asia, and Africa, including the development of the slave trade, which Raynal denounced in no uncertain terms.

The Arts

The philosophes sought the same status and freedom for artists that they demanded for writers. They believed that the arts had to be not only unfettered by censorship but also subject to critical inquiry. Some philosophes worked toward a philosophy of art, but they did not espouse a single theory. The distinguished English portrait painter Joshua Reynolds (1723–1792) believed that classical rules preserved from antiquity had to be followed. But David Hume, among other Enlightenment figures, emphasized the aesthetic appreciation of art, rejecting formal rules or standards for art imposed by royal academies or ecclesiastical influence.

The secularization of culture could be seen in the development of rococo, a new and generally secular decorative style. It evolved from the highly ornamental baroque style that had characterized the art and architecture of the Catholic Reformation, particularly in Austria and Bavaria. Closely tied to noble taste, rococo's popularity in France reflected the fact that many nobles now spent more time in elegant townhouses. However spacious, such urban residences afforded them less room than they enjoyed in their countryside châteaux. They therefore lavished more attention on decoration.

The rococo style—sometimes called Louis XV style—began in France but also became quite popular in the German and Italian states. Like the baroque, it featured flowing curves, thus suggesting rocks and shells (*rocailles* and *coquilles*, thus its name). Rococo stressed smallness of scale, reducing baroque forms to elegant decorative style. It utilized different materials, including wood, metal, stucco, glass, and porcelain, brought for the first time from China during the eighteenth century and reflecting the growing interest in Asia. It combined texture and color with spirited and even erotic subject matter. Elements drawn from nature, such as birds and flowers, replaced religious objects as decorative elements.

Engraving depicting the grand rococo style that was popular in France in the eighteenth century.

Although Greek mythology and religious themes remained popular, eighteenth-century painters found new sources for artistic inspiration. The French painter Jean-Antoine Watteau (1684–1721) influenced the artistic move away from traditional religious subjects laden with didactic meaning toward lighter, more secular themes. Adopting a more realistic style than baroque painting, he depicted elegantly dressed noble subjects at leisure. Painters adopted the rococo style, emphasizing smallness of scale. As the market for painting widened, scenes of nature and everyday life also became popular, as they had a century earlier in the Netherlands.

William Hogarth's *Gin Lane* (1751) is a commentary on the deleterious impact of alcohol on the poor of eighteenth-century London.

In France, the Academy of Painting and Sculpture organized the first public art exhibition in Paris in 1737, bringing together viewers of different social classes. The expanding middle-class art market and the growing secularization of artistic taste was nowhere more apparent than in Britain. William Hogarth (1697–1764) portrayed everyday life in London with affection and satire. He was as adept at conveying the elegance of London's parks as the depravation of the city's notorious "Gin Lane." He poked fun at the hearty Englishman putting away pounds of roast beef (Hogarth himself died after eating a huge steak), the dishonest lawyer, the clergyman looking for a better post while ignoring his pastoral duties, and the laboring poor drowning their sorrows in cheap gin, a plague that led the government to raise the tax on alcohol.

Music

The taste for music moved beyond the constraints of court, ecclesiastical, and noble patronage. Opera's great popularity in the seventeenth century had been closely tied to ornate opera houses constructed at European courts. Composers and their music passed from court to court. Court composers were considered the equivalent of favored upper servants. The German composer George Frideric Handel (1685–1759) gratefully accepted the patronage of several English aristocrats as well as King George II. When someone asked Franz Joseph Haydn (1732–1809), who worked as *kapellmeister* (orchestra director) for the fabulously wealthy Esterházy family of Hungary, why he had never written any quintets, he replied, "Nobody has ordered any."

In the early 1750s, Rousseau penned stinging attacks on French opera. Readers understood his strident language as he intended—he was denouncing court and aristocratic taste itself. Rousseau compared the Royal Academy of Music's monopoly on French music to a ruthless Inquisition that stifled imagination. Rousseau's critique generated a storm of controversy because it seemed to be nothing less than a denunciation of the social and cultural foundations of contemporary French society. Like his philosophical works, Rousseau's operatic compositions extolled the simple, unpretentious life of rural people.

In England, concerts were held at court or in the homes of wealthy families; in Italy, they were sponsored by groups of educated people who gathered to discuss science and the arts; and in Switzerland, concerts were sponsored by societies of music lovers. The public concert also emerged in some German cities early in the eighteenth century. Gradually public concert halls were built in the capitals of Europe. Handel began to perform his operas and concerts in rented theaters, attracting large crowds. By the 1790s, Haydn was conducting his symphonies in public concerts in London.

The short, brilliant life of Wolfgang Amadeus Mozart (1756–1791) reflected the gradual evolution from dependence on court and aristocratic patronage to the emergence of the public concert. Mozart began playing the harpsichord at age three and composing at five. In 1763, his father took him and his sister on a tour of European courts that would last three years, hoping to make the family fortune, with mixed results. Mozart returned to Paris in 1778 at his father's insistence that he "get a job or at least make some money." The temperamental Mozart failed to make his way in the social world of Paris: "I would wish for his fortune," a contemporary wrote, "that he had half as much talent and twice as much tact."

Thereafter Mozart resided in his native Salzburg, where he served as unhappy court

The young Wolfgang Amadeus Mozart at a pianoforte.

musician of an unpleasant archbishop. Mozart wrote church music and light music, including a hunting symphony for strings, two horns, dogs, and a rifle, before resigning after quarreling with his patron. Mozart spent money as rapidly as he made it and was constantly in debt, unable to attract the lavish court, noble, or ecclesiastical patronage he desired. But his schedule increasingly included public concerts. Unlike Handel, Mozart died a poor man at age thirty-five and was buried in an unmarked pauper's grave in Vienna.

A prolific genius, Mozart moved away from the melodious regularity of his predecessors to more varied and freely articulated compositions. The operas *The Marriage of Figaro* (1786) and *Don Giovanni* (1787) demonstrated Mozart's capacity to present characters from many walks of life, revealing not only their shared humanity but their personal moods and expectations. *The Magic Flute* (1791), his last opera, expressed his belief in the ability of mankind to develop greater virtue and a capacity for love. Mozart thus shared the confident optimism of the philosophes.

The Spread of Enlightened Ideas

Salons, academies, and Masonic lodges helped spread Enlightenment thought. Salons, which brought together people of means, noble and bourgeois alike, in private homes for sociability and discussion, were concentrated in Paris, but they were also found in Berlin, London, and Vienna, as well as in some smaller provincial towns. The English historian Edward Gibbon claimed that in two weeks in Paris he had "heard more conversation worth remembering than I had done in two or three winters in London." The salons of Paris were organized and hosted mainly by women, who selected topics for discussion and presided over conversations. In Warsaw, Princess Sophia Czartoryska's salon played an important role in conveying Enlightenment ideas to Polish elites. In London, women hosted similar gatherings, some composed exclusively of women.

In Paris Madame Marie-Thérèse Geoffrin hosted artists on Monday and men of letters on Wednesday. "I well remember seeing all Europe standing three deep around her chair," recalled one of her visitors. Her husband sat silently at the other end of the table while his wife put the philosophes through their paces. One night, a regular guest noted that the place where the silent man usually sat was empty and asked where he was. "He was my husband," came the laconic reply, "and he's dead."

Salon guests could discuss the work of the philosophes without fear of police interference. By the middle of the century, political discussions increasingly captured intellectuals' attention. Not all ideas discussed, of course, were of equal merit. In the 1780s, a German scientist, Franz Mesmer (1734–1815), proclaimed the healing properties of electromagnetic treatments. "Mesmerism" attracted considerable interest in the salons of Paris, where the nature of the "universal fluid" that Mesmer and his disciples

An actor reading from a work of Voltaire at the salon of Madame Geoffrin. Note the bust of Voltaire, then in exile.

believed linked the human body to the universe, was debated. The French Academy of Science vigorously denounced Mesmerism as nothing more than resourceful charlatanism.

In France and in some Italian cities academies played a similar role to that of the salons. These were not "academies" in the sense of offering an organized curriculum, but rather formal gatherings taking place about every two weeks of people interested in science and philosophy. Meetings consisted of reading minutes and correspondence, followed by lectures and debates. The academies also helped spread Enlightenment ideas by bringing together people, including some clergymen, eager to discuss the works of the philosophes. Unlike the salons, women (with several exceptions) were not elected to the academies.

The French academies served two masters: the king and the public. They depended on royal intendants, governors, and other state officials for funding and meeting places. The monarchy believed that the academies served the public interest because members discussed questions of contemporary importance. Some academics sponsored essay competitions in the arts and sciences; during the decade of the 1780s, more than 600 such competitions were held. Topics increasingly reflected Enlightenment influence, such as "religious intolerance and the role of magistrates in the defense of liberty."

Many members of the provincial academies began by mid-century to think of themselves both as representing public opinion in their role as informal counselors to the monarchy, and interpreting the sciences and philosophy for a more general audience. Thus the academies contributed to the development of a sense that reforms in France were possible.

Masonic lodges, another medium for the ideas of the philosophes, had begun in Scotland, perhaps as early as the sixteenth century, as stonemasons' guilds. They now brought together freethinkers and others who opposed the influence of the established churches in public life. Masonic lodges proliferated in Europe during the middle years of the eighteenth century. Members took vows of secrecy, although their meetings, membership lists, and rituals were widely known. In some places women were admitted as affiliated or adopted members. Members held a variety of political opinions, but they shared a general faith in progress, toleration, and a critical view of institutionalized religion. In Scotland in particular, clubs, coffeehouses, and taverns also provided the setting for discussion of the new ideas.

Still, several obstacles limited the dissemination of Enlightenment ideas. Books and even pamphlets were expensive. Censorship, although erratic and varying greatly from place to place, also discouraged publication. In France and Spain, among other countries, censored books were burned, and those who published material officially considered blasphemous could be, at least in principle, sentenced to death. Far more frequently, officials closed printers' shops. Even the relatively tolerant Dutch Republic banned Diderot's

A gathering of a Masonic lodge in Vienna. Masonic rituals included the use of allegorical symbols, blindfolds, and swords.

Philosophic Thoughts as an attack on religion. In the face of a spate of publications critical of monarchy, aristocracy, and the Church, Louis XV (ruled 1715–1774) promulgated censorship laws in 1757 that were much harsher than those regulating the book trade in England. The French monarchy also controlled what was published through the licensing of printers, booksellers, and peddlers.

Enlightened Absolutism

The philosophes believed that the success of any state depended on the degree of freedom and happiness it was able to assure its people. As David Hume put it, a state is justified by the good that is done in its name. Voltaire and Diderot, in particular, believed in "enlightened absolutism." They wanted enlightened monarchs to impose reforms that would benefit their subjects. Leopold II of Tuscany (1747–1792), the most significant reformer of his era, went so far as to declare that "the sovereign, even if hereditary, is only the delegate of his people." Rousseau, however, warned that absolutism and enlightened thinking were incompatible. However, some rulers applied Enlightenment "rationality" to statecraft, with the goal, above all, of making their regimes more efficient.

Reform of Jurisprudence

Cesare Bonesana, the marquis of Beccaria (1738–1794), had the greatest influence on his era as a reformer influenced by the Enlightenment. A noble from Milan, Beccaria became a professor of political philosophy in Habsburg Austria and ended his career advising the state chancellory on such diverse topics as agriculture, mining, and trade. He made his reputation, however, with his ideas on crime and punishment.

In *On Crimes and Punishment* (1764), Beccaria, who had read Montesquieu, Buffon, Diderot, and Rousseau, applied their analysis to the issues at hand. He argued that the state's task was to protect society while respecting the dignity of all people. This meant that the rights of those accused of crimes, too, had to be protected. Beccaria wanted standard procedures to govern criminal trials, so that rich and poor would stand equal before the law. The Italian philosopher's assumption that the accused is innocent until proven guilty has remained, along with the tradition of English constitutional law and trial by jury, a cornerstone of Western judicial systems.

Beccaria argued that the punishment for a given crime should not be linked to the religious concept of sin, but rather rationally determined by an assessment of the damage done to society. He argued that "it is better to prevent crimes than to punish them." His principles reflected the origins of utilitarianism, the influential social theory of the first decades of the nineteenth century that held that laws should be judged by their social utility.

Beccaria opposed torture to extract confessions or render punishment. Barbarous punishment, instead of protecting society, seemed only to encourage disrespect for the law and more awful crimes. This led him to object to capital punishment, lamenting the enthusiastic crowds that were attracted to public executions. Leopold II of Tuscany (who admired Beccaria), Gustavus III of Sweden, and Frederick the Great of Prussia banned torture—clear examples of the influence of enlightened thought on contemporary rulers.

Educational Reform

Education in the widest sense was central to the program of the philosophes. The Empress Catherine the Great of Russia (ruled 1762–1796) admired and read Montesquieu and Voltaire, hosted Diderot, and purchased the latter's library for a handsome price. Born a German princess, she was contemptuous of Russian culture and preferred French. She seemed to heed the advice she had received from Diderot: "To instruct a nation is to civilize it." Catherine established a school for the daughters of nobles. Without eliminating censorship, she authorized the first private printing presses and encouraged the publication of more books.

A few other monarchs implemented educational reforms, but they did so at least partially to assure a supply of able civil servants. In 1774, Joseph II (1741–1790) established a structured, centralized system of education from primary school to university, which doubled the number of elementary schools in Bohemia. In Poland, the Seym created the Commission for National Education in 1773 to serve as a ministry for education, overseeing Poland's universities in Krakow and Vilnius, as well as all secondary and parish schools. During this period in Central and Eastern Europe, textbooks appeared in the Magyar, German, Croatian, Slovak, Ukrainian, and Romanian languages.

Religious Toleration

Although the eighteenth century was a period of relative religious peace, intolerance could still be intense. In England, Catholics, in particular, suffered legal discrimination (see

Empress Catherine the Great.

Chapter 11), and could not vote or be elected to the House of Commons. French Protestants had no civil rights; their births, baptisms, and marriages were considered not to have occurred unless registered by a Catholic priest. Protestants suffered discrimination in Hungary and the Catholic Rhineland. In Austria, in 1728 the bishop of Salzburg gave 20,000 Protestants three days to leave their homes, and royal edicts forced Protestants out of Upper Austria and Styria during the next decade.

Europe's 3 million Jews suffered intolerance and often persecution all across Europe—especially in Eastern Europe. Jews could not hold titles of nobility, join guilds, or hold municipal office. In many places, they could own land, although in some German states they needed special permission to buy houses. They were excluded from agricultural occupations and certain trades in France, Eastern Europe, and Russia. The Habsburg monarchy required Jews to stay inside until noon on Sundays, and in 1745 it suddenly ordered the thousands of Jews living in Prague to leave. In Vienna and Zurich, Jews were confined to ghettos, and in several German towns they were not allowed inside the city walls. Although the Swedish government allowed Jews to build synagogues beginning in 1782, they could reside only in certain cities, and were forbidden to marry anyone who was not Jewish, to purchase land, or to produce handicrafts.

Because moneylending had been one of the few professions Jews were allowed to practice, Polish, Russian, and Ukrainian Jews faced resentment from peasants who often owed them money. In Poland the Catholic Church often led the way in persecution; rumors that Jews were ritually sacrificing Christian children during Passover found credulous ears. In 1762, Ukrainian peasants killed at least 20,000 Jews in the bloodiest pogrom of the century. Yet, by about 1750, Western Europe seemed to be entering a more tolerant age. For one thing, intolerance generated periodic rebellions, which took state funds to put down. But a more humanitarian spirit could also be felt.

Some of the rulers who undertook religious reforms were inspired by a desire to strengthen their authority. This was the case in the expulsion of the Jesuits from several countries, which highlighted the struggle between the popes and Catholic monarchs. The Jesuits had been closely identified with the papacy since the inception of the order during the Catholic Reformation. They had gained great influence as tutors to powerful noble families and in the Spanish, French, and Portuguese colonies in the Americas. Catholic kings perceived the Jesuits as a threat to their authority.

In Portugal, King John V's strong-willed minister, Sebastião, the marquis of Pombal (1699–1782), enhanced the monarchy's authority at the expense of the great noble families and the Church. When Jesuits criticized the regime for, among other things, orchestrating anti-Semitism, Pombal accused them of exploiting the indigenous population of Paraguay, where they virtually ran the colonial state. After Pombal falsely accused the order of planning the king's assassination, the monarch expelled the Jesuits from

Jesuits being expelled from Spain, 1764.

Portugal in 1759. Ten years later, Pombal ended the Inquisition's status as an independent tribunal, making it a royal court. Other rulers followed suit, including Louis XV of France in 1764. The expulsion of the Jesuits from some of the most powerful Catholic states reflected the diminishing power of the papacy in the face of absolute monarchs determined to retain control over what they considered to be national churches.

In Spain, Charles III (ruled 1759–1788) ordered universities to include instruction in science and philosophy. In 1781, Spain carried out its last execution of a person accused of heretical religious beliefs. Charles then reduced the feared Spanish Inquisition to a series of legal hurdles governing publishing. Like the kings of Portugal and France, Charles III in 1776 expelled the Jesuits in part because their near-monopoly on education seemed to pose a threat to the monarchy's control over the Church. In Italy, Leopold II also reduced the authority of the Church in Tuscany, ending the tithe and crippling the Inquisition. Catherine the Great's enlightened approach to religion could be seen in her termination of official (or "government") persecution of Old Believers, the dissident sect within the Russian Orthodox Church. And when Jews came under tsarist rule for the first time after the first Partition of Poland in 1772 (see Chapter 11), she initially placed Jewish merchants and other townspeople on an equal basis with their Christian neighbors. However, protests brought Catherine to adopt more restrictive measures. In 1794 she introduced double taxation for Jews. Louis XVI granted French Protestants most civil rights in 1787. And in Great Britain the following year Parliament reduced some restrictions on

Catholics—although they still could not hold public office. Nonetheless, London crowds shouting "No popery!" attacked the property of Catholics during the "Gordon riots," in which almost 300 people were killed. In 1792, however, the first legal Catholic church in England since the sixteenth century opened its doors in London.

Protestant states seemed most receptive to religious toleration. In the northern German states and Swiss cantons, the ideals of the philosophes provided support for religious toleration that had grown out of the sixteenth-century Reformation. The quest for religious tolerance played an important part in German enlightened thought. In his drama *Nathan the Wise* (1779), Gotthold Lessing argued that people of all religions are members of the human family. In Catholic Austria, Joseph II's relaxation of censorship permitted a spate of pamphlets and brochures calling for toleration of Protestants. The king's Edict of Toleration (1781) extended some toleration to non-Catholics. The edict included Jews, who were now "free" to bear the burden of a "toleration tax" and to pay an assessment on kosher meat. Joseph also ennobled several Jews, incurring the wrath of other nobles. Moreover, for the first time, Protestants could enter the Habsburg civil service.

Frederick the Great

The German states appeared to be the most fertile ground for enlightened absolutism. German philosophes remained closely tied to the existing order, looking to the individual states and to religion for reforms. They were less critical of the state than their French counterparts. For Immanuel Kant (1724–1804), the Enlightenment meant the liberation of the individual intellectually and morally, but not politically or socially. The individual should think critically, but also obey.

Frederick II of Prussia (ruled 1740–1786 and known as Frederick the Great), wanted to be remembered as an enlightened ruler. A man of considerable intelligence, he turned his court into a center of learning for the nobility. "Sans Souci," his rococo château in Potsdam outside Berlin, had French formal gardens and was considered the height of civility. Frederick, a flute-playing "philosopher-king," made Voltaire the centerpiece of his palace for two years. Voltaire praised Frederick for having transformed "a sad Sparta into a brilliant Athens." But the French philosophe soon grew disenchanted with the cynical, manipulative Prussian king, who coolly invaded the Habsburg territory of Silesia in 1740, in the first year of his reign. Voltaire angered Frederick by lampooning a royal favorite, and when the king ordered his hangman to burn the offending tract publicly, Voltaire took the hint and left Potsdam in 1752.

But Frederick again borrowed Enlightenment discourse when he claimed that one of his major tasks was "to make people as happy as is compatible with human nature and the means at my disposal." He once

Frederick the Great playing the flute at Sans Souci.

claimed somewhat disingenuously that he was nothing more than the "first servant" of his people as king: "I well know that the rich have many advocates, but the poor have only one, and that is I." Frederick freed the serfs of the royal domains (1763) and ordered the abolition of the lords' right to punish their own serfs physically. Judicial reforms ended some flagrant abuses by magistrates. The Prussian king relaxed censorship and abolished capital punishment, except in the army. Yet he refused to emancipate Prussian Jews, while continuing to depend on loans from them. Nonetheless, the Prussian Code, finally completed and promulgated in 1794, eight years after Frederick's death, granted "every inhabitant of the state . . . complete freedom of religion and conscience."

Frederick the Great's "enlightened" reforms were, above all, intended to make the Prussian state more powerful, not more just (see Chapter 11). He made Prussia a more efficient absolutist state. Frederick intended his law code to enhance the reach of the state rather than to make his people equal before the law. When he freed the serfs of the royal domains, it was because he needed them in the army. Nobles (Junkers) dominated most of the plum positions as military officers and high officials. Yet some commoners did in fact rise to important posts, including some army officers, who were subsequently ennobled. Frederick improved the state bureaucracy by introducing an examination system to govern entry. In the courts of justice, candidates had to pass the most difficult examinations, and in Berlin only a third of all judges were nobles.

Prussian law reinforced the distinction between noble and commoner. The Prussian Code divided Prussian society into noble, bourgeois, and common estates. Frederick bolstered the position of Prussian nobles because he was determined to prevent any erosion of their status as the landowning class. He refused to ban serfdom on private estates, and he created institutions that would provide credit to nobles in financial difficulty. Nobles were not permitted to sell their lands to non-nobles, and marriages between nobles and commoners were not recognized.

The Prussian monarch's *Essay on the Forms of Government* (1781) offered a recipe for enhancing the efficiency of the absolute state. Frederick's view of the world bound the state and the individual subject together. When their mutual interests could not be reconciled, however, the Prussian state always took precedence. As Voltaire had discovered for himself, Frederick the Great's reign reflected the limitations of enlightened absolutism.

Rural Reforms

Several other European rulers tried to improve conditions of rural life. Leopold II, who promulgated a new code of laws in 1786 and established a new and more independent judiciary, ended some restrictions on the grain trade, freeing the price of grain. These moves were popular among merchants and wealthy peasants, but not among poor people, who depended upon bread to survive. Following the disastrous decade of the 1770s, marked by hunger and disease, Austrian Queen Maria Theresa banned the mistreatment of peasants by their lords and tried to limit seigneurial obligations. As she put it, sheep must be well fed if they are to yield more wool and milk. Her son Joseph II abolished serfdom in 1781, converting peasant labor obligations into an annual payment to the lord, and ended obligations of personal service to the lord. Henceforth a peasant could marry and/or leave the land without the lord's permission. Peasants, at least in principle, could also turn to the state for support against an oppressive lord; they could even take the lord to court. However, Joseph II's Serfdom Patent encountered resistance among landowners and regional powers in the eastern regions of the empire. The nobility of Bohemia simply refused to enact any of the provisions, while nobles in Transylvania neglected to inform the peasants of any changes in their condition. In Hungary, the estate owners insisted that their peasants were not actually serfs but simple tenants and therefore not covered by the law. In the German-speaking parts of the empire, the Serfdom Patent granted the serfs legal rights but left most of the financial obligations of the old system intact. And in Tuscany, as in the Habsburg domains, aristocrats and state officials sabotaged Leopold's reforms.

Reasons of state lay behind even these seemingly enlightened reforms. By restricting labor obligations in some parts of the empire, peasants now owed the state even more taxes and were subject to a longer term of military service. Peasants, though legally free, remained indebted to their lords. Thus, "enlightened" reforms had little effect on the lives of most peasants.

Joseph II announced that he wanted the Habsburg state to follow "uniform principles," which included a reorganization of the imperial bureaucracy. He taxed Church property, abolished some monastic orders, and forced a reorganization of the Church within the Habsburg domains. None of the "enlightened" rulers gave up any of his or her monarchical prerogatives.

Catherine the Great, influenced by Montesquieu's *The Spirit of Laws*, wanted the nobility to serve as an "intermediary body" standing between the crown and its subjects. Catherine hoped that by clarifying their rights, nobles might contribute to the functioning and glory of her state. The Charter of the Nobility of 1785 formalized the relationship between the autocratic state and the nobles, recognizing the nobility of blood as equal to that of service. It confirmed their security of property, the right to hold serfs, and immunity from arrest and confiscation of property by the state. For the first time, nobles could travel abroad without the permission of the emperor. Local elective councils of nobles could henceforth send petitions to the tsar or empress, but the latter had no obligation to respond. Catherine herself turned against Enlightenment thought, however, fearing that it might become a tool of those opposed to absolute rule. Like Voltaire's experience at the court of Frederick the Great, Diderot's confidence in Catherine ended in disappointment when, to his chagrin, he learned that the empress had imprisoned those with whom she disagreed.

CURRENTS OF THE LATE ENLIGHTENMENT

The late Enlightenment contained several currents. British economists applied the concept of freedom for the first time to the workings of the economy. Meanwhile, on the continent, philosophes turned away from the preoccupation with rationality and the laws of nature. The mark of human freedom was no longer the exercise of reason but the expression of the emotions. Rousseau himself had begun this turn toward what he called "reasoned sentimentality" by stressing the importance of emotional development and fulfillment. In a related development, a number of writers began to "discover" and embrace their own national cultures, seeking their origins in medieval poems and songs. And in France, when there were no more Voltaires or Rousseaus, a generation of would-be philosophes, mediocre writers who attacked the institutional structure of the French monarchy, influenced public opinion. All of these developments served to undermine the established order (see Chapter 11). The late Enlightenment's emphasis on the historical roots of national culture provided a way of conceptualizing national identity, a transformation that would, for example, have enormous consequences in Europe in the nineteenth century and beyond.

Enlightened Thought and Economic Freedom

The philosophes' quest to discover the laws of nature and society led several of them to try to establish a set of laws that could explain the working of the economy. This search led away from mercantilism, which had formed the basis of seventeenth- and early eighteenth-century economic theory, to the emergence of classical economic liberalism. Mercantilist theory held that states should protect their economies with restrictions and tariffs that would maintain a favorable balance of trade, with more gold and silver flowing into a nation than going out.

The "physiocrats" believed that land, not gold and silver, was the source of all wealth. They wanted to end state interference in agriculture and the commerce of farm products. Writing in Diderot's *Encyclopedia*, François Quesnay (1694–1774), a French doctor and economist, called on the monarchy to free the grain trade and end arbitrary controls on prices, which states sometimes imposed to preserve public order. He and other physiocrats insisted that higher prices for goods would encourage production, thereby bringing about lower prices over the long run. The physiocrats also encouraged wealthy landowners to put science to work to increase farm yields, and wanted enlightened rulers to free the agricultural economy from tolls and internal tariffs. In England, where commercial agriculture was already well developed, the physiocrats attracted an interested following.

Adam Smith admiring his book, *The Wealth of Nations*.

However, when the oddly named Anne-Robert Turgot (1727–1781), Louis XVI's controller-general, freed France's grain trade from controls in the early 1770s, disastrous shortages accompanied a series of bad harvests (see Chapter 11). Hoarding contributed to much higher prices; grain riots followed, and the experiment soon ended with the old strictures and controls back in place.

Adam Smith (1723–1790), a Scottish professor of moral philosophy at the University of Glasgow, argued against some of the hallmarks of mercantilism in his *An Inquiry into the Nature and Causes of the Wealth of Nations* (1776). In the name of freeing the economy from restraints, he opposed guild restrictions and monopolies, as well as trade barriers and other forms of protectionism. Such bold proposals flew in the face of contemporary economic thought, which held closely to regulated monopolies and remained suspicious of free-market competition. Merchants looked to the state to provide financial, political, and military protection. The Scottish philosopher's optimistic doctrine came to be known universally by its French name, *"laissez-faire,"* or "leave alone." Each person, Smith insisted, should be "free to pursue his own interest his own way." If "left alone," Smith argued, the British economy would thrive naturally, generating domestic and foreign markets. The "invisible hand" of the unfettered economy would over time cause the forces of supply and demand to meet, determining the price of goods. By overcoming that "wretched spirit of monopoly," which made people less energetic, the "virtue of the marketplace" would also enhance social happiness and civic virtue. This was a common theme in the Scottish Enlightenment—Scottish philosophes were particularly concerned with how civic virtue and public morality could be inculcated in a society being slowly transformed by commerce and manufacture.

German Idealism

While in England the late Enlightenment brought an emphasis on economic freedom, on the continent it was marked by subjectivism and a greater emphasis on emotion, a shift already reflected by Rousseau's "reasoned sentimentality." The basic tenet of German idealism was that we perceive and understand the world through the medium of our ideas, and not through the direct application of our senses. Kant was the foremost proponent of this school. Born an artisan's son in the Prussian town of Königsberg, Kant's *Critique of Pure Reason* (1781) affirmed that rational inquiry into nature leads to knowledge. In his memorable analogy, reason is like a judge who "compels the witness to answer questions which he himself has formulated." But for Kant, reason alone was not the basis for our knowledge of the world. Instead, each person understands the world through concepts that cannot be separated from his or her unique experience. This philosophy undermined faith in the rational objectivity and universalism that had characterized the high Enlightenment. German idealism invited the subjectivity and relativism of early nineteenth-century romanticism.

In the eighteenth century, writers became interested in discovering the roots of national cultures; Sweden, Denmark, Russia, and Poland all discovered their "national" literatures, written in their own languages. The first Czech national theater opened in Prague in 1737. Gotthold Lessing proudly wrote in German and called for a national theater. Scottish readers eagerly saluted the "discovery" by the poet James Macpherson (1736–1796) of the work of an imaginary Gaelic bard of the third century, Ossian. Macpherson's publication in the early 1760s of what he claimed were translations of the poet he called the Gaelic Homer set off a bitter debate, one that contributed to the emergence of Scottish romanticism.

Composers began to borrow from popular culture, especially from folk music not necessarily religious in inspiration. The first Jewish periodicals were published in Königsberg in the century's last decades, and the first Jewish school established in Berlin in 1778. The emotional search for and enthusiastic identification with national cultures contributed, as in the case of Scotland, to the development of romanticism, and very gradually of nationalism. Nationalism would help undermine the established order in several continental states, notably France, where the established order was based on allegiance to a monarchical dynasty and often to established religion as well, and not yet necessarily on national identity.

The Enlightenment and Public Opinion

Public opinion, a concept we take for granted, did not always exist. But it began to take shape in French, English, and several other European languages in the eighteenth century (see Chapter 11). During the 1770s, more people in France discussed the pressing political issues of the day than ever before. Lawyers helped establish the concept of public opinion when they sought a wide spectrum of support for the parlements. Louis XV had decided to replace these provincial noble law courts in 1768 with malleable institutions more directly under royal control. Public opinion forced the king to restore the parlements six years later. Public opinion, to which opponents of the monarchy and increasingly the court itself now appealed, provided a forum in which political ideas were increasingly discussed. These ideas were shaped by Enlightenment discourse on political sovereignty and the limits of absolute rule.

A number of the treatises published during the late Enlightenment dealt with contemporary political issues, in the tradition of Voltaire's broadsides at the time of the Calas Affair, which had exposed the consequences of intolerance and persecution to public opinion. As the financial crisis of the French monarchy worsened during the 1780s, such publications would help make the question of reform an increasingly national issue.

Forbidden Publications and the Undermining of Authority

Some of the fringe members of the republic of letters, whom Voltaire had dismissed as mere "scribblers," also undermined respect for the monarchy and the royal family. Whereas the milieu of the philosophes earlier in the century had been elegant salons, the would-be philosophes of the last period of the Enlightenment hung around cheap cafés, lived in rooms high above the street, and dodged creditors by frequently changing addresses. At the same time, they insisted that royal censorship blocked their ascent to better things. Some made a modest living peddling forbidden publications. While claiming common cause with the major philosophes against the unenlightened institutions of France, some wrote pornography or penned pieces slandering prominent people, including the royal family, and a few kept afloat by spying on other writers for the police. There had been such publications before the 1770s and 1780s, but never so many of them, and never had they been so widely read.

Banned books reached France through the efforts of resourceful shipping agents, transporters, bargemen, dockers, and peddlers, who smuggled books published in Switzerland or the Austrian Netherlands to French booksellers willing to circumvent the controls of the booksellers' guild and the state. In 1783, the crown redoubled its efforts to stem the tide of smuggled books and to still the clandestine presses within France. These publishers undercut the legitimate Parisian book trade because they published banned books and produced cheaper editions of acceptable works. Moreover, royal officials were concerned about the effects of these smuggled satires on public opinion.

Was there any connection between the high-minded philosophes and their "successors," who included the authors of *Venus in the Cloister, or the Nun in a Nightgown*; *Christianity Unveiled*; and *Margot the Campfollower*? In fact, the envious and mediocre descendants of the philosophes in some ways continued their predecessors' work by undermining respect for the authority of the Church, the aristocracy, and, above all, the monarchy.

Moreover, certain themes of the Enlightenment did find their way into their work. They joined their far more illustrious predecessors in attacking the foundations of the French monarchy. Frustrated authors attacked the privileges, for example, of the printing and booksellers' guild, which they blamed for keeping them from reaching the stature they desired. Their identification of censorship with despotism, though self-serving, was nonetheless effective, as they argued that only its abolition could permit the free exchange of ideas. Political events and scandals kept the presses of the literary underground turning, fanning popular critiques of the monarchy, Church, and nobility.

LEGACY OF THE ENLIGHTENMENT

The Enlightenment philosophes celebrated reason, while acknowledging the passions, and were suspicious of pure faith. Steeped in respect for science and reason and confident that humanity would discover the truths of nature, they were optimistic about human potential. The philosophes' belief in progress, which Kant insisted was a sign of modernity, separated them sharply from the Catholic Church, in particular. Yet, they were not as naive, uncritical, or foolish as Voltaire's Candide, who thought progress inevitable. The philosophes believed that the combination of thought, study, education, and action would lead to a better future. States, they thought, were not ordained by God but by mankind and, like other phenomena, should be subject to critical scrutiny.

The philosophes' belief in human dignity led them to oppose all forms of despotism. Most spoke out against religious intolerance, torture, and slavery. (Yet an effective campaign against slavery, launched by the English abolitionists of the Society for the Abolition of the Slave Trade in 1787, stood independent of the Enlightenment). Furthermore, some Enlightenment thinkers and writers recognized that contemporary assertions about the inequality of women contradicted their understanding of nature.

Some philosophes had strong reservations about the ability of individuals to develop equally. "As for the rabble," Voltaire once said, "I don't concern myself with it; they will always remain rabble." Those with power and influence first must be enlightened, they reasoned, so that eventually everyone could develop through education. However, Diderot, Montesquieu, and Voltaire supported the right to divorce, but also opposed equal status for women.

In their commitment to individual freedom the philosophes influenced the subsequent history of the Western world. Whereas most people in the eighteenth century still considered the monarchy to be the repository of the public good, the philosophes proclaimed that the public had rights of its own and that freedom was a good in itself. Enlightenment thought helped create a discourse of principled opposition that would shake the foundations of absolutism. If the philosophes themselves were not revolutionaries, many of their ideas in the context of eighteenth-century Europe were indeed revolutionary.

CHAPTER 10

EIGHTEENTH-CENTURY ECONOMIC AND SOCIAL CHANGE

The great English landowners did as they pleased in the eighteenth century. More than one gentleman had an entire village demolished or flooded because it stood in the way of his landscaping plans. Another wrote, "It is a melancholy thing to stand alone in one's own country. I look around, not a single house to be seen but for my own. I am Giant, of Giant's Castle, and have ate up all my neighbors." Fences and servants kept venturesome interlopers far away. Some men of great means gambled fantastic sums on horse races. Sir Robert Walpole's estate guests drank up £1,500 of wine a year, the combined annual wages of more than 100 laborers. English nobles seemed particularly vulnerable to overeating. A certain Parson Woodforde carefully entered in his diary the day of his death, "Very weak this morning, scarce able to put on my clothes and with great difficulty get downstairs with help. Dinner today, roast beef, etc."

At about the same time, in Switzerland, a peasant lived a very different and arguably more productive life. Jakob Gujer, who was called Kleinjogg (Little Jake) by his friends, inherited an indebted small farm and transformed it into something of a model enterprise, where he grew vegetables and new crops and raised cattle. It is said that when the duke of Württemberg came to see the famous peasant, Kleinjogg told him how flattered he was that a prince should pay a visit to a humble peasant. The prince, teary eyed, replied, "I do not come down to you, I rise up to you, for you are better than I." To which Kleinjogg is alleged to have answered with tactful deference, "We are both good if each of us does what he should. You lords and princes must order us peasants what to do, for you have the time to decide what is best for the state, and it is for we peasants to obey you and work with diligence and loyalty." But there were few peasants with the means and initiative of Kleinjogg on the continent. In England, there were relatively few peasants left at all.

Although in some ways society remained the same as in earlier centuries, economic, social, and political developments transformed Europe during the last half of the eighteenth century. To be sure, these transformations were uneven and regionally specific, affecting England and northwestern Europe the most, while bypassing much of Central and Eastern Europe. In economically advanced regions, some of the traditional checks on population growth became less imposing. Increased agricultural productivity supported a larger population that, in turn, expanded the demand for food. Manufacturing developed in and around northern English towns, leading to the beginning of what we know as the Industrial Revolution.

In a related change, distinctions within the highest social estates or orders were becoming less marked in Western Europe. Moreover, increased wealth generated some fluidity between social groups, contributing, in particular, to the dynamism that made Britain the most powerful state in the world. In France, too, wealth increasingly blurred lines of social class without, however, eliminating them entirely. Distinctions in title no longer necessarily corresponded to patterns of wealth distribution. By contrast, social barriers remained much more rigidly defined in Central and Eastern Europe.

The Social Order

In much of early modern Europe, social structure was marked by birth into particular estates, or orders, which conferred collective identities and privileges. Each order was legally defined, with specific functions and rights conferred to it by virtue of being part of the order, not through individual rights. The nobility was a privileged order, with special rights accorded by rulers and law, such as exemption from taxation. Noble titles were hereditary, and stemmed in principle from birth, although in reality many families during the century were able to purchase titles. The clergy was also a privileged order and, like the nobility, generally exempt from taxation. In France, the "third estate" was simply everyone who was neither noble nor a member of the clergy, and included peasants and townspeople, all of whom were subject to taxation. Within and between these estates, or orders, some degree of social movement was possible, particularly in Western Europe. The extent of social mobility that existed within the "societies of orders" was debated by contemporaries, as it has been subsequently by historians.

Nobles

In most of the continental European states (with the exception of the Dutch Republic and Switzerland), nobles dominated political life during the eighteenth century, although in most of these states they numbered no more than 2 to 3 percent of the population. They accounted for a much larger percentage in Russia, Spain, Poland, and Hungary, which together probably accounted for almost two-thirds of the nobles in Europe. In Spain's northern provinces and in Poland, more than 10 percent of the male population held noble titles. In Hungary, what may have been the first accurate census in European history in 1784 counted more than 400,000 people claiming to be nobles, about 5 percent of the population. In France, by contrast, there were only somewhere between 25,000 and 55,000 noble families.

The vast majority of nobles drew their wealth and status from land they owned but that other people worked ("I am idle, therefore I am," went a Hungarian saying about Magyar nobles, spoofing the words of the French philosopher Descartes). Noble landlords owned between 15 and 40

Hungarian noblemen in the eighteenth century.

percent of the land, depending on the country, and an even higher percentage of productive land. In Prussia, only nobles could own land that was exempt from taxes; in Poland, commoners could not own any land at all. Russian commoners lost the right to own property to which serfs were legally bound. Austrian nobles held half of the arable land in the Habsburg domains, hiring agents to collect what peasants owed them. Nine thousand nobles owned a third of all Swedish land. In the Italian states, the nobility's share of the wealth was even more than that of the Catholic Church.

Many continental nobles retained specific rights, often called seigneurial rights, over the peasantry. Nobles drew income in rent (cash), kind (crops), and dues (often labor) owed them by virtue of their social status and ownership of land. Some dispensed justice in their own courts. Peasants were obligated to pay to have their grain ground in the lord's mill, to bake bread in his oven, and to squeeze grapes in his press. The burden of seigneurial dues and debts left peasants with little or sometimes nothing left to pay state taxes and church taxes (tithes), or to feed their families, which might well include parents and unmarried sisters, brothers, and children.

Nobles proved remarkably adept at maintaining their privileges while adapting to the challenges and possibilities resulting from the growth of the centralized state. Such privileges included being exempt from virtually all taxation, as were nobles in Prussia, Poland, Hungary, and Russia, or exempt from the direct tax on land. Other noble privileges included the nobles' right to bear a family coat of arms, to wear certain clothing and jewelry, to occupy special church pews near the altar (in some places Mass could not start until the local nobles had taken their accustomed places), to receive communion before anyone else, and to sit in specially reserved sections at concerts and on special benches at universities. Commoners were expected to bow, curtsy, or tip their hats when a noble walked by, gestures upon which nobles increasingly insisted. The right to duel over family "honor" in some states and the right to wear a sword were honorific privileges that served to distinguish nobles from their social inferiors.

There were significant differences in the wealth and status of European nobles, however. The wealthiest, most powerful nobles considered themselves "aristocrats," although this was not a legal category. They were proud possessors of the most ancient titles (in France, they were the nobles of the sword, whose titles originated in military service to the king), and many of them were members of the court nobility. Aristocrats viewed themselves as the epitome of integrity, honor, and personal courage, and the embodiment of elite culture. The *grands seigneurs* in France and the *grandees* in Spain were identified by their great wealth and ownership of very large estates. But the wealthiest nobles may have been the great landed magnates of East Central Europe. Prince Charles Radziwill of Poland was served by 10,000 retainers and a private army of 6,000 soldiers. Another Polish nobleman's property included 25,000 square kilometers of land, territory about four-fifths the size of today's Belgium. A single Russian prince owned 9,000 peasant households.

On the other hand, in every country there were also nobles of modest means who eagerly, even desperately, sought advantageous marriages for their daughters, and state, military, and church posts to provide a living for their sons. Demographic factors put pressure on poorer nobles, because now more noble children survived birth and childhood. Many Sicilian, Polish, and Spanish nobles owned little more than their titles. About 120,000 Polish nobles were landless, many so poor that they were referred to as the "barefoot nobility." The *hobereaux* were the threadbare nobles of France. Spanish *hidalgos* depended on modest state pensions, and some were so poor that it was said that they "ate black bread under the genealogical tree." In Spain, these impoverished nobles retained the right to display their coat of arms and to be called "Don" ("Sir"), and freedom from arrest for debt. But until 1773 they were not permitted to engage in manual work, and hence they had few ways to emerge from poverty.

Nobles who could afford to do so tried to maintain an aristocratic lifestyle, keeping up châteaux (manor houses) on their rural estates, some also owning elegant townhouses with gardens designed to recreate the illusion of a rural manor. Some nobles of lesser means attempted to keep an aristocratic lifestyle, going into debt as a result.

The British Landed Elite

In Britain, there were only about 200 families that claimed noble title. Yet the percentage of English land owned by nobles rose from about 15 to 25 percent, a far larger percentage than in either France or the German states. Unlike their continental counterparts, British nobles had to pay property taxes, and the only special privileges that peers retained (besides their vast wealth) were the rights to sit in the House of Lords and, if accused of a crime, to be tried there by a jury of their equals. Because in Britain only the eldest son inherited his father's title and land, younger sons had to find other sources of income. One such source was the Anglican Church and its twenty-six bishoprics, the plums of which were reserved for the younger sons of peers and which offered considerable revenue and prestige. Whereas in the previous century about a quarter of Anglican bishops had been common-ers, by 1760 only a few were not the sons of nobles.

Although only nobles could sit in the House of Lords, the British ruling elite of great landowners was considerably broader. British landowners became even more prosperous during the eighteenth century, particularly after about 1750, when they raised rents on their estates and amassed fortunes selling agricultural products. Wealthy newcomers who owned large chunks of land also joined the elite. The ownership of landed estates conferred "gentry" status, which a broad range of families claimed. At the time of the Glorious Revolution of 1688, the landed elite numbered about 4,000 gentry families.

The wives of gentlemen oversaw governesses and domestic servants while instructing their children in the responsibilities of family, religion, and social status—to behave politely, but confidently. It was considered poor form to show too much emotion, to be too enthusiastic, and, above all, to be overly passionate, sensual or, worse, licentious. One did not seek openly to convert the lower classes to better manners and virtue, but rather to set a good example. The writer Horace Walpole (1717–1797) once claimed he attended church only to set a good example for the servants.

Young gentlemen were tutored at home, or they attended secondary schools, such as Westminster and Eton, boarding schools that character-ized a gradual shift to out-of-home education throughout Europe for elites. Oxford and Cambridge Universities then beckoned some, although few actually graduated. Scottish universities, in contrast, offered more dynamic thought and research. Young gentlemen were expected to know something about the classics and contemporary poets. Yet, to many if not most wealthy families, academic knowledge seemed superfluous, even suspect. When Edward Gibbon (1737–1794), the historian of ancient Rome, pre-sented one of his books to a duke, the latter exclaimed, "Another damned thick square book! Scribble, scribble, scribble, eh Mister Gibbon?" A wealthy dowager offered her grandnephew and heir a handsome annual stipend if he would "chuse to travel" and thus forsake "one of the Schools of Vice, the Universities." The goal of the "grand tour" of the continent, servants in tow, was to achieve some knowledge of culture and painting. Such trips further enhanced the popularity in Britain of the classical style of architecture, so called because it emulated classical Greek and Roman edifices.

The Clergy

Although in France, Prussia, and Sweden the clergy was technically the first order or estate, the clergy did not really form a separate corporate entity, but rather reflected the social divisions between rich and poor that characterized European life. Most village priests and ministers had prestige and local influence, but they shared the poverty of their parishioners. Yet in many places, the material advantages of being a priest (including exclusion from some taxes) attracted the sons of peasant families. On the continent, the members of the French clergy were likely to be the most literate, Russian Orthodox priests the least.

The lower clergy, drawn from the lower middle class, artisans, or the relatively prosperous peasantry, resented the undisguised ambition, greed, and arrogance of the bishops. Wealth and rank, not piety, usually determined such selections, as in the Italian states, where bishops were invariably drawn from the families of the great landowners. Even so, few monarchs were as brazen as King Philip V of Spain, who named his eight-year-old son to be archbishop of Toledo. Many bishops did not take their responsibilities seriously. In the 1760s at least forty bishops resided in Paris, only one of whom was, in principle, supposed to live there.

A baptism performed in Italy, a religious ritual that maintained its importance in most Catholic places.

Although some parts of Europe, especially regions in France, had already become "de-christianized," meaning that religious practice and presumably belief had declined (see Chapter 9), in most places religion still played an important part in village life. The clergy baptized children, registered their births, married couples, and buried the dead. Priests and ministers supervised charitable activities and provided certificates of good behavior for those leaving to search for work elsewhere. Religion offered consolation to many impoverished people: everyone could go to church, even if the poor were restricted as to where they could sit or stand. In general, the quality of the parish clergy seems to have been quite high in the eighteenth century (when compared to the next century), due in part to efforts to improve clerical training. Nonetheless, many parish priests were still caught between liturgical demands and the persistence of popular superstitions shared by all social groups—for example, the duchess of Alba in Spain tried to cure her son's illness by having him ingest powder from the mummified finger of a saint.

The "Middling Sort"

Most of those people who engaged in commerce, trade, and manufacturing were known as the "middling sort" by the English and the "bourgeoisie" by the French. The term "bourgeois" evolved from the medieval sense of "privileged townsmen" (in earlier times they had been exempt from having to pay taxes to territorial rulers; see Chapter 1).

The middle classes ranged from wealthy entrepreneurs, who had developed the economies of trading and manufacturing cities, to struggling retail merchants, craftsmen, and innkeepers, who made barely enough to hang on to their businesses. Purchasing land and titles when they could, the wealthiest commoners owned about a quarter of the land in France and most of the land in Switzerland. Great Britain had already become the proverbial "nation of shopkeepers," with one shop for every thirty or forty people.

In Western Europe, the middle decades of the eighteenth century brought an expansion of the liberal professions, particularly in the number of lawyers. Men trained in law took positions in state bureaucracies and law courts. In England and France, some of the best students, or at least the best connected, became barristers; this gave them the right to plead in court, which attorneys (solicitors), their subordinates, could not do. Distinguished medical schools produced few physicians, not yet a profession viewed with great respect. Beneath them were surgeons, some of whom were former barbers. Military surgeons tended to be a cut above the others, their skills honed in the heat of battle. Despite the fact that some universities taught anatomy, surgical techniques were learned on the job.

To some nobles, "bourgeois" was an expression of contempt, seen in the sense of a seventeenth-century play in which a protagonist is jeered by a young nobleman: "Bourgeois is the insult given by these hooligans to anybody they deem slow-witted or out of touch with the court." In the eighteenth century, the term had not lost the sense provided by a seventeenth-century dictionary: "Lacking in court grace, not altogether polite, overfamiliar, insufficiently respectful."

Triumphant merchants at table. Note that one of the merchants is smoking tobacco, a new fad. Note also the aristocratic wig on the dog on the right.

Peasants

In 1787, the peripatetic Englishman Arthur Young was traveling in Champagne in northern France when he encountered a peasant woman who looked to be about sixty or seventy years of age. To his astonishment, she gave her age as twenty-eight, a mother of seven children who survived by virtue of "a morsel of land, one cow and a poor little horse." Each year her husband owed 42 pounds of wheat to one noble, and 168 pounds of oats, one chicken, and a cash payment to another noble. He also owed taxes to the state. The woman, old before her time, stated simply that the "taxes and seigneurial obligations" were a crushing burden, one that seemed to be getting worse.

Peasants still formed the vast majority of the population on the continent: from about 75 percent (Prussia and France) to more than 90 percent (Russia). Peasants were the source of the wealth that sustained the incomes of crown, nobility, and church. Peasants stood at the bottom of society, condemned as "a hybrid between animal and human" in the words of a Bavarian official. An upper-class Moldavian called peasants "strangers to any discipline, order, economy or cleanliness . . . thoroughly lazy, mendacious . . . people who are accustomed to do the little work that they do only under invectives or blows." Such cruel images were particularly prevalent in regions where lords dominated peasants of another ethnic group, as in Bohemia, where German landowners drew on the labor of Czech peasants.

The village was the center of the peasant's universe. Village solidarities helped them pull through as best they could in hard times, through harvest failures, epidemics, and wars. Villagers viewed outsiders with suspicion. Folk songs celebrated peasant wisdom and wiliness, as humble rural people outfoxed naive and bumbling outsiders, whose wealth could not impart common sense.

All peasants were vulnerable to powerful outsiders in the overlapping and interdependent systems of domination that characterized early modern Europe. The state, nobles, and churchmen extracted taxes, produce, labor, and cash. The proportion of peasant revenue in kind or cash that disappeared into the pockets of nobles, officials, and clergy ranged from about 30 percent (France) to 70 percent (Bohemia). Rulers extracted money, commodities, and labor payments, imposing additional taxes when they were at war.

The peasantry was not, however, a homogeneous mass. In Western Europe, where almost all peasants were free, a peasant's status depended upon the amount of land, if any, owned or controlled through leases. In northern France, Flanders, southwestern Germany, Switzerland, and Sweden, many peasants owned or rented plots of sufficient size and productivity to do well enough in most years. Swedish peasants owned about a third of the cultivable land in their country. Recognized formally as a fourth estate, the Swedish peasantry maintained a degree of independence perhaps unique in Europe. Charles XII of Sweden bragged that he would rather be the most miserable Swedish peasant than a Russian noble unprotected by law from the whims of the tsar. Rural industry—for example, linens—provided supplementary income for peasant families in parts of France, Switzerland, and in German states. In Zurich's hinterland in the 1780s, about a quarter of the population spun or wove at home for the cotton and silk industries.

Many landowning peasants were constantly in debt, borrowing against the often empty hope of the next harvest. Sharecroppers worked land owned by landlords in exchange for one-third to one-half of what was produced. Landless laborers scraped by, if they were lucky, working on rural estates. All over Europe, some peasants took to the road as peddlers. Seasonal migrants left their homes in the Alps, Pyrenees, and other mountain regions each year for construction work in Milan, Lyon, Barcelona, or other large cities, or to work in the grain fields in the summer or in the vineyards in the fall.

Serfdom had largely died out in Western Europe. Yet many free peasants continued to be subject to some kind of seigneurial justice. In France, thousands of manorial courts still existed in 1789, providing lords with additional income by virtue of legal fees and fines assessed on peasants. Most of these courts, presided over by nobles, occupied themselves with minor offenses such as poaching and trespassing, civil suits for debt, and family matters such as inheritances and guardianships.

In addition to taxes on land and salt, peasants also owed obligatory labor service, usually work on roads, in France, Denmark, Sweden, Switzerland, Poland, Russia, and some German states. Obligations varied from only a couple of days in parts of France to as much as 200 days per year in Denmark. In Eastern Europe, peasant children were sometimes required to work in the service of the lord. Other obligations included the duty to provide the lord's household with a certain amount of food—for example, a chicken or goose on a holiday, or even just a few eggs—to provide food for the lord's dogs, or to spin or weave cloth for the lord's household. To these were added mandatory payments to the seigneur upon transfer of land held by peasants with hereditary tenure. When a peasant with such tenure died, the lord claimed both money and the best animals the peasant owned.

The conditions of peasant life became worse the farther east one traveled. Peasants in Russia and Eastern Europe lived in hovels made of earth, clay mixed with straw, branches, twigs, and sometimes caked manure. Floors were of mud and beds of straw. Only well-off peasants could afford wood as building material.

The farther east one went, too, the more authority lords wielded over peasants. Most peasants east of the Elbe River were serfs, some of whom had to take an oath of loyalty to their seigneur, as during the Middle Ages. There were some free peasants in the Habsburg domains and in Poland, but very few in Russia. The number of people who lost their freedom by becoming serfs had increased so much in eastern Prussia and Brandenburg that the German term for serfdom had become the same word for slavery.

Gallows stood near some Prussian manor houses, symbolizing the judicial prerogatives nobles held over serfs, including the right to dispense corporal punishment. In Poland, nobles could have their serfs executed until late in the eighteenth century. Russian lords could torture serfs, as long as they did not die immediately from such treatment, or they could send them into exile in Siberia. In Poland, a noble convicted of murdering a peasant paid only a small fine.

In Russia, proprietary serfs remained personally bound to the land of the nobles and, after Catherine the Great's Charter of 1785, to the nobles themselves. Lords could sell serfs, give them away—for example, as part of a dowry—or lose title to them through gambling. Serfs could be sold individually or as a family to another noble, or be exchanged for animals. Lords could refuse permission for their serfs to marry or to choose a certain occupation. A good number of serfs took their chances in setting out to seek their freedom in the vast expanses of Siberia. In Russia, as well as in Central and Eastern Europe, a few serfs managed to put together enough money to purchase their freedom.

In Russia, a poll tax on males (called "souls"), from which only nobles were excluded, added to the dependence of the "bonded people" to the

A family of serfs paying homage to their lord. Note the wife kissing the noble's hand.

state. Villages were collectively responsible for the payment of taxes. Moreover, all male peasants could be conscripted into army service for terms of twenty-five years, a life sentence for most soldiers.

Possibilities for peasant resistance were limited; yet the "weapons of the weak" were not insignificant. These ranged from sullen resentment and foot-dragging to arson, or even insurrection. All nobles in an idle moment— and there were many—pondered the possibility of a massive uprising of "the dark masses." As the legal and material conditions of the serfs deteriorated, rebellions were endemic in eighteenth-century Russia. During the reign of Catherine the Great, the Cossack Emelian Pugachev appeared on the Siberian frontier claiming to be "Tsar Peter III" (the real Peter III had spoken of reforms but had been dethroned and then murdered). He led several million peasants against their lords in 1773 and 1774. Pugachev's followers included Cossacks, Old Believers (dissidents persecuted by the Orthodox Church and doubly taxed), miners from the Ural Mountains, and desperate serfs. About 3,000 landowners perished in the Pugachev rebellion before it was crushed.

In Bohemia and Moravia, 40,000 royal soldiers were required to put down peasant uprisings in 1775. And in the middle of the next decade, about

30,000 Transylvanian peasants rose up after a false rumor spread that those enlisting in the Habsburg army would gain freedom from serfdom. They demanded the abolition of the nobility and burned several hundred manor houses to make their point. The uprising ended with the torture of several of the leaders, parts of whose bodies were nailed to the gates of towns.

The Beginnings of the Industrial Revolution

The Industrial Revolution began in England during the eighteenth century. For the most part, its early stages brought an intensification of forms of production that already existed: small workshops and cottage-industry manufacturing, the production of goods at home. Technological innovation played a part, but in the beginning its role was not as large as has sometimes been assumed. Ultimately, however, a new source of power, the steam engine, would replace animal and human power, and in the nineteenth century manufacturing increasingly would be characterized by factory production.

The growth in manufacturing itself depended on two interrelated factors: agricultural productivity, then the principal source of wealth, and population growth. The two were so closely linked that it is sometimes difficult to know which followed which. An increase in agricultural productivity permitted the European population to increase during the century. At the same time, greater demand for food encouraged capital-intensive farming, including specialization of cash crops (such as olives, grapes, and raw silk) and the raising of cattle and poultry for the market. Greater profits from agriculture generated a surplus of funds that could be invested in manufacturing. In turn, a larger population, with some of the growth concentrated in and around cities and towns, increased the demand for manufactured goods and provided a labor supply for town-based and rural industry.

Stagnation and Growth in Agriculture

New agricultural methods, first applied in the middle of the seventeenth century, helped raise farm yields, in England above all, aided by the application of natural and artificial fertilizers. Gradually the practice of leaving part of the land fallow every other or every third year gave way to crop rotation, which helped regenerate the soil. Landowners planted fodder and root crops such as clover and turnips. This provided food for animals as well as for human beings, in addition to enriching the soil by helping it absorb and retain nitrogen.

By 1750, English agricultural yields had increased to the point that almost 15 percent of what was produced could be exported abroad (although about a third of the British population still did not have enough to eat). On average, at the end of the seventeenth century an acre of agricultural land yielded perhaps 2.5 times more food in England than in France. Agriculture's contribu-

Measuring land in preparation for enclosure.

tion to the British gross national product reached a peak of 45 percent in 1770, and then only slowly was overtaken by English manufacturing as its place in the economy rose remarkably. Increased farm profits provided capital not only for further investment in agriculture but also in manufacturing (although landowners were still more likely to invest in government bonds than in speculative ventures).

One of the impediments to the expansion of agricultural production in England had been the widespread existence of open fields or common lands, which made up about half of the arable land in 1700. Beginning in the sixteenth century, on request from landowners, acts of Parliament permitted the "enclosure" of common land, transforming open fields or land that was communally owned into privately owned, fenced-in fields that could be more intensively and profitably farmed by individual owners (see Chapter 5). Between 1760 and 1815, 3,600 separate parliamentary acts enclosed more than 7 million acres of land, more than one-fourth of the farmland of England. Over two centuries, enclosure acts forced perhaps half of English small landholders from the land, swelling the ranks of agricultural laborers. Small tenant farmers, too, suffered, as many could not afford to pay rents that rose rapidly after about 1760. The poorest members of the rural community lost their age-old access to lands on which they had gleaned firewood, gathered nuts and berries, and grazed animals. Before enclosure, it was said, a "cottager" was a laborer with land; after enclosure, he was a laborer without land. The Irish-born writer Oliver Goldsmith commented with playful, bitter irony:

> The law locks up both man and woman
> Who steals the goose from off the common,
> But lets the greater felon loose
> Who steals the common from the goose.

Agricultural change came far more slowly on the continent. Most producers remained at the subsistence level, farming small plots without an agricultural surplus that they might have used to expand their holdings or improve farming techniques. Primitive farming techniques (including wooden plows that barely scratched the surface of rocky terrain) characterized the mountainous and arid land of southern Italy and Sicily, the Dalmatian coast, southern France, much of Spain, and the Balkans. Peasants lacked farm and draft animals and therefore fertilizer, meat, and milk. Markets and transportation networks remained inadequate to the task of agricultural modernization.

On the continent, a bewildering variety of land tenures and agricultural practices under which they were held seemed to set rural poverty in stone. Most continental farmland remained divided into small strips, and each year more than one-third of arable land may have lain fallow, with crops rotated between fields. Traditional peasant agricultural methods also blocked a major expansion of production. "Slash and burn" tillage survived in some parts of Europe where peasants simply burned the stubble on their land once the harvest had been taken in, replenishing the soil with ash.

The studied attention many English country gentlemen gave to their lands may be contrasted with the approach of many French, Spanish, and Prussian nobles, content to sit back and live from revenue extracted from peasants. While the state had an interest in increasing farm output to generate additional tax revenue, most royal officials, seigneurs, and churchmen looked first to better ways of extracting peasant surpluses, not to improving yields. Nobles resisted occasional royal attempts to reduce the peasants' obligations, or to change them, such as by commuting labor service to payments in cash or in kind. Furthermore, much of what peasants managed to produce they owed to landlords, the state, and to a lesser extent, the Church. "Why should I build a better house," asked a Bavarian peasant, "so that my seigneur can line his pockets with the requisite fees to be paid?"

Serfs had even less interest than other peasants in innovation. In Central and Eastern Europe, an old adage went "there is no land without a lord" because in most places only a noble, the crown, or the Church could own land. The absence of independent peasant proprietors left a formidable obstacle to agricultural development.

Changes on the continent comparable to those taking place in England were mainly confined to northwestern Europe. In northern France, Flanders, the Dutch Republic, Schleswig-Holstein, parts of northern Italy, and Spanish Catalonia, the fertile land and sufficient capital facilitated investment in commercial agriculture. Moreover, these were regions generally farmed by people who owned the lands on which they worked, and who therefore had more incentive to augment production. But even in the less densely populated countryside of Eastern and southern Europe, more land was brought into cultivation, as in Russia where the population pushed into the steppes of the eastern frontier lands.

Other factors, too, contributed to improvements in Western European agriculture. During the eighteenth century, Europe as a whole experienced warmer, drier weather, particularly in the summers, in stark contrast to the unusually cold and damp seventeenth century. This had a salutary effect on population, agricultural yields, and commerce. Land reclamation projects helped expand the amount of land under cultivation. The Dutch continued to reclaim land from the sea, and land reclamation added significantly to the amount of land under cultivation in the Southern Netherlands (Belgium) and Brandenburg.

Though not to the same extent as in England, the enclosure of separate strips of land and the sale or consolidation of common lands in northwestern Europe permitted the development of "agricultural individualism," as more land passed to peasant-owners. Beginning in the 1760s, state policies created small farms owned by peasants, helping transform Danish agriculture from the stagnation of serfdom to relative prosperity. Royal decrees encouraged enclosure and forced the commutation of labor obligations to rent payments.

Gradually some techniques that characterized agricultural improvements in England reached the continent. Innovative landowners and tenant farmers began to implement crop rotation (growing foliage crops to improve the fertility of fields), replacing the old three-field system so that little or no land lay fallow. As in England, turnips, potatoes, and rice enhanced dietary nutrition. Yet many peasants remained prisoners of tradition, refusing to plant or eat potatoes (Russian peasants called them "apples of the devil"), despite the fact that they can grow almost anywhere under any conditions. The cultivation of sugar beets (from which sugar can be made), the tomato (despite the fact that some peasants believed it to be poisonous), and chestnuts (the "bread of the poor") also spread, sustaining population growth.

Animal husbandry also benefited from improved techniques. Oxen, mules, and especially horses could pull plows more easily than peasants. More cattle provided manure for fertilizer, and meat and milk for nutrition. Sheep-raising developed rapidly, providing both food and wool.

Some landowners formed societies to discuss agriculture, and a handful began model farms. Such groups included nobles, wealthy bourgeois, and clergy. French physiocrats, who believed that land was the source of all wealth, urged landowners to make their property more profitable and encouraged state policies to free the price of grain. Publications on agriculture dramatically increased in number.

A few continental rulers took steps to intervene in the interest of agricultural progress. The elector of Bavaria in 1762 offered farmers an exemption from taxes for ten years in the hope that they would plant foliage crops in their fallow fields. Several princes in the German Rhineland encouraged the selective breeding of cattle. In 1768, Queen Maria Theresa of Austria ordered the division of common pasturelands in some parts of the Habsburg territories and the establishment of agricultural societies.

Population Growth

The European population rose from about 120 million to about 190 million people during the eighteenth century (see Table 10.1). Historians have long debated the causes and consequences of this demographic revolution, studying parish registers of births, marriages, and deaths. Europe's birthrate increased, particularly after about 1740, and the number of deaths each year—the mortality rate—declined even more rapidly. These changes came first and foremost in densely settled regions of soaring agricultural productivity: England, the Netherlands, Flanders, northern Italy, and northern France (see Map 10.1). This suggests that an increase in agricultural production was the most important factor in explaining why the European population began to rise.

Plagues and epidemics, as well as chronic malnourishment, still intervened periodically to check population growth. Many monarchs ascended the throne because elder siblings had died young, as did Frederick II of Prussia, who came to the throne because his two elder brothers did not live past their first birthdays. Poor people were particularly vulnerable to infection, and rates of infant mortality remained high. Epidemics such as influenza, typhus, smallpox, and the plague occasionally ravaged populations. In 1719, 14,000 people in Paris died of smallpox. Malaria epidemics occurred frequently in Spain during the 1780s and 1790s. During the plagues of 1781–1783 in Salonika (Thessalonika) in the Ottoman Empire, more than 300 people died every day. Whooping cough alone killed at least 40,000 children in Sweden during a period of fifteen years in the middle of the century, and more than 100,000 people died of bacillary dysentery in Brittany in one year. In Moscow, half the population died of disease early in the 1770s. Some states tried to close their frontiers and ports to prevent the arrival of disease, or to put those arriving into quarantine, but

Table 10.1. European Population, 1700–1800 (millions)

	1700	1750	1800
Great Britain	9.0	10.5	16.5
France	19.0	21.5	28.0
Habsburg Empire	8.0	18.0	28.0
Prussia	2.0	6.0	9.5
Russia	17.5	20.0	37.0
Spain	6.0	9.0	11.0
Sweden	1.5*	1.7	2.3
United Provinces	1.8	1.9	2.0

*Data for Sweden is from Franklin D. Scott, *Sweden: The Nation's History* (Carbondale, Ill.: University of Southern Illinois Press, 1988), p. 260.
Source: Paul Kennedy, *The Rise and Fall of the Great Powers.* (New York: Vintage, 1989), p. 99.

MAP 10.1 POPULATION IN 1780 Distribution of the European population in 1780.

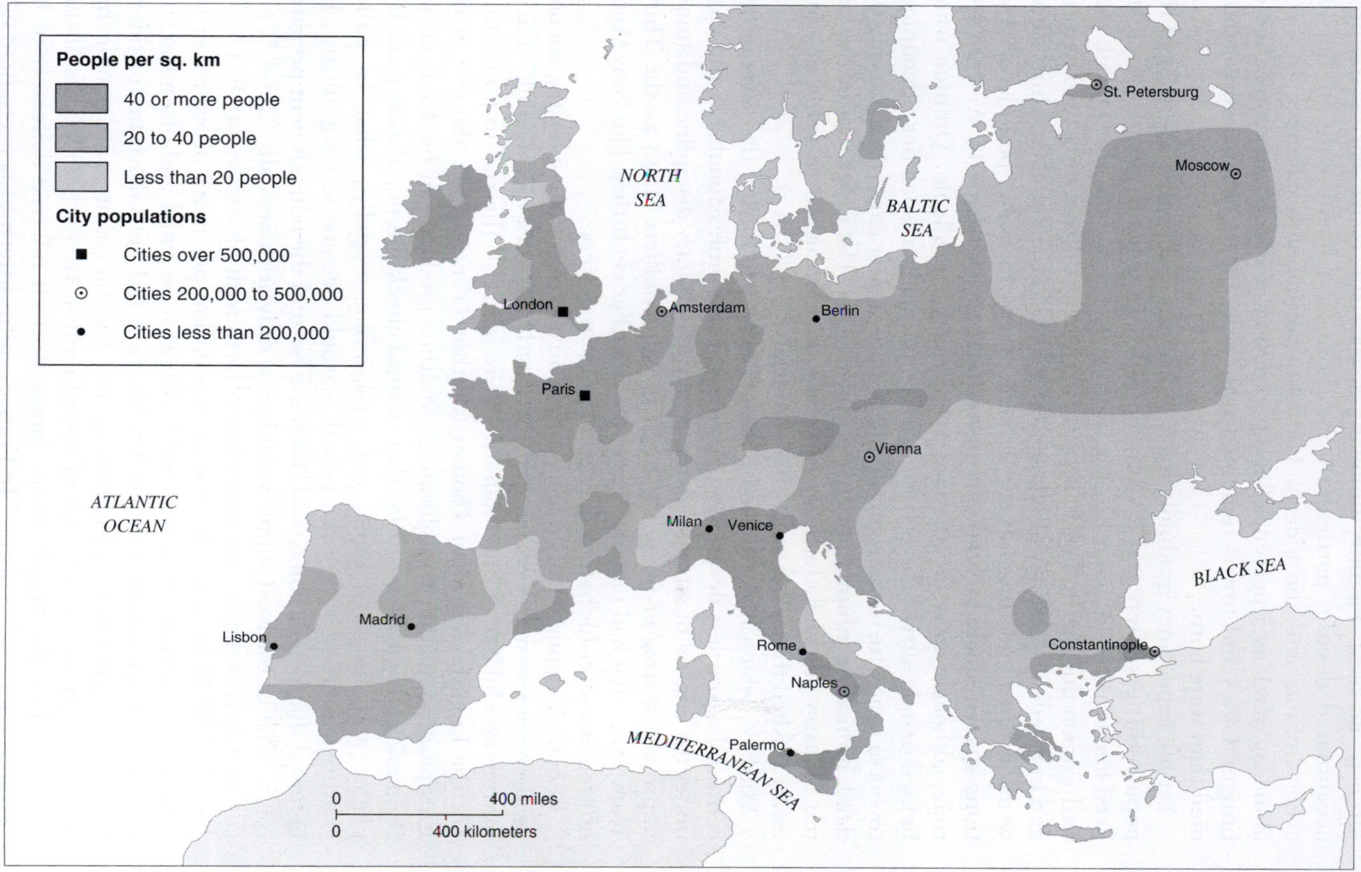

often to no avail. Famine, following several successive harvest failures, accentuated disease, particularly for those at opposite ends of the life cycle—infants and the elderly. Hardship turned into calamity. In 1769 alone, as much as 5 percent of the population of France may have died of hunger. Cities and towns remained unhealthy places where more people died than were born.

Yet life expectancy gradually rose as diseases and epidemics ravaged the population less often and less murderously. In general, people of means lived longer than the poor. But the average life expectancy for French men and women during the last half of the century still was only twenty-nine, and in Sweden, a country of relative longevity, it stood at about thirty-three years for men and thirty-six for women during the same period. Vaccinations against smallpox gradually proved effective, at least in Western Europe, although mass inoculations were not yet available. Quinine water helped people survive fevers. Scientific and medical societies encouraged towns to supervise waste removal and to take greater care when burying the dead, forbidding inhumations within town walls. The expansion of the cotton industry provided clothing, especially underwear, which could be more easily washed than wool and other materials.

Warfare, which had checked population growth during the seventeenth century, became less devastating. Armies became professionalized, and more under the control of stronger dynastic states. Military discipline and supply improved, sparing civilians the long, bloody conflicts (such as the Thirty Years' War) that had taken a heavy toll in earlier centuries. The New World offered new sites for battles between the great powers.

Economic opportunity, such as the expansion of cottage industry, encouraged couples to marry earlier—in their early twenties in England—and to have more children. Contemporaries were aware of the rise in population. For the English clergyman Thomas Malthus (1766–1834), the rise of the European population was alarming. Malthus predicted in his *Essay on the Principle of Population* (1798) that natural checks on population growth— plague and disease, famine, war, and infant mortality, what he called "nature's auditing with a red pencil"—would become less significant. He believed that population would "increase beyond the nourishment prepared for it," that is, the food supply would grow only arithmetically (2-3-4-5, and so on), whereas population would henceforth multiply exponentially (2-4-8-16-32 . . .). To be sure, the rise in population put more pressure on the land, particularly where most land holdings were small and often too subdivided to be profitably farmed. Yet Malthus did not take into consideration rising agricultural productivity, nor the fact that some people had already begun to limit the size of their families. We have only hints of this, such as when the British writer James Boswell referred delicately to his sexual encounters "in armor." In France, coitus interruptus is credited with bringing about a small decline in the birthrate after 1770. But birth control was unreliable, to say the least.

Manufacturing: Guilds and Domestic Industry

The workshop remained the basis of manufacturing in eighteenth-century Europe. In most countries, merchants and artisans were organized into corporate guilds by the goods they sold or produced. Guilds conferred a type of privilege, because rulers awarded them monopolies over the production or sale of certain products, particularly luxury goods. Masters' guilds and associations of journeymen gave rights and status to craftsmen; they limited and oversaw the training of boys as apprentices, beginning at the age of twelve or thirteen. In France, journeymen perfected their skills while completing a "tour of France," the origin of the modern bicycle race. A journeyman stopped in a number of cities over a period of several years; he was housed in the craft association's "mother house" before returning home with skills acquired from serving many masters, and with hope of one day becoming a master himself.

It was, however, becoming increasingly difficult for a journeyman to become a master, particularly if he did not have a father or other male relative to smooth the way with money. By the 1770s, Spanish and French skilled trades, in particular, had become glutted. Parisian guilds faced competition from outsiders who escaped corporate controls, such as craftsmen who lived on the outskirts of the city and produced cabinets and other goods more cheaply than their Parisian rivals, whose goods were taxed.

Since at least the sixteenth century in England, partially to circumvent the guilds, some merchant-manufacturers had looked to the countryside for workers to produce goods. This shift to domestic industry (also known as proto-industrialization, the cottage industry, or the putting-out system) contributed to what would eventually become a worldwide revolution in manufacturing. The early stages of the Industrial Revolution showed an increase in domestic industry rather than a shift to new forms of production. New technology would only gradually lead to mechanization and the standardization of tasks previously done by hand.

Britain's manufacturing base expanded early in the eighteenth century. Indeed, if in 1500 about a quarter of the people of England worked in non-agricultural occupations, by 1750 the proportion had increased to about half. The quest for profit was considered perfectly respectable, the manufacturer worthy of emulation. Daniel Defoe (1680–1731) described the Yorkshire countryside in 1720 as "one continuous village" in which were "scattered an infinite number of cottages or small dwellings, in which dwell the workmen which are employed, the women and children of whom are always busy carding and spinning." Home workers carded, spun, or wove with equipment (spinning wheels and looms) that they either owned or, in most cases, rented. Hand spinning continued throughout the century to be the largest source of female employment. Master clothiers, or merchant-manufacturers, provided domestic workers with raw materials, such as wool or Indian cotton purchased at a cloth hall, later coming back

Carding and spinning at home.

to collect and pay for the goods that had been completed. They would then transport the goods to the next stage in the production process, for example, to a dyer. Low pay rates in the countryside encouraged the persistence of rural industry. At the end of the eighteenth century, hand-knitted stockings produced by rural Scottish families still cost less than those knitted on a power loom.

As the cottage industry was organized by household, women had a major, even determining, role in the organization of the household economy, including training young children. There were both male and female wool spinners. One man, later a successful inventor of textile machinery, recalled, "my mother taught me to earn my bread by carding and spinning cotton, winding linen or cotton weft for my father and elder brothers at the loom, until I became of sufficient age and strength for my father to put me into a loom." Many families of home spinners, weavers, glove-makers, and shirt-buttoners also worked the land—theirs or someone else's—part time. Rural industry paused at harvest time.

Inventions

Technological change contributed to the Industrial Revolution. Between 1660 and 1760, 210 new inventions were patented in England; during the next twenty-nine years, there were 976. But inventions at first had little to do with increased productivity. They were probably less important than the infusion of investment capital into manufacturing and the expansion of the number of workers in the textile industry, the leading edge of the Industrial Revolution. Some inventions were only gradually diffused, or their importance not recognized until later. No invention, however, was of greater long-term significance than the steam engine, invented by James Watt (1736–1819), a Scot who made musical instruments. Watt added a separate condenser to a primitive steam engine, resulting in a more powerful engine, which he patented in 1769. Yet, like its predecessor, Watt's costly invention was first used only to drain mines, making it possible to dig deeper shafts and to rapidly increase coal production, so essential to the Industrial Revolution. Slowly, the steam engine was put to use in manufacturing.

In 1709, Abraham Darby, a foundry man, came up with a process to smelt iron ore into cast iron by using coke (coal residue) instead of charcoal. This process spread only slowly; in 1775, there were still only thirty-one blast furnaces in Britain. Moreover, charcoal smelting continued to be important, further depleting Britain's forests. In 1784, Henry Cort (1740–1800), an ironmaster, invented the "puddling and rolling" process in iron casting. Molten metal in a furnace was raked to remove carbon and other impurities, producing wrought iron, which was far stronger than cast iron. Iron bridges replaced their flimsy predecessors. Iron made new buildings sturdier and basically fire-resistant. Cast-iron railings and gates began to appear on landed estates and in elegant townhouses. Low-cost iron made possible sturdier plows and other farm implements that, in turn, significantly increased the demand for iron.

Improvements in the spinning wheel and basic looms had already accelerated textile production in the late seventeenth and early eighteenth centuries. The stocking frame produced lighter and more fashionable cotton and silk stockings that replaced the heavier woolen hose of the upper classes. John Kay (1704–1764) invented the "flying shuttle" (patented in 1733 but

(*Left*) James Watt. (*Right*) The steam engine.

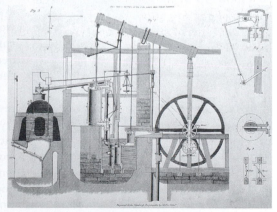

not diffused for more than twenty years), which ultimately made it possible to weave at a much greater speed, doubling productivity. But Kay's invention, too, has to be seen in the context of traditional manufacturing: its principal effect was to increase the productivity of hand-loom weavers.

Gradually machines powered by water and then by steam eliminated bottlenecks in textile production. In about 1764, James Hargreaves (c. 1720–1778), a carpenter and weaver, invented an apparatus known as the spinning jenny, which wrapped fibers around a spindle (a long, slender pin). Drawing on medieval technology, Hargreaves multiplied the number of thread spindles a worker could operate from one to eight, and then soon to eighty spindles. In 1769, Richard Arkwright (1732–1792), a former barber turned entrepreneur, borrowed some money from a publican and patented a mechanized "water frame," which, combining spindles and rollers, became the first spinning mill. The water frame turned out a strong, coarse yarn of quality that transformed the cotton industry and increased production of wool worsteds (combed wool). With the exception of its water-powered rollers, Arkwright built his power spinning machine out of the same components as the ordinary spinning wheel that had been found in Europe since medieval times. He had his portrait painted with his hand touching his famous spinning machine, as the same painter might have formerly depicted a country gentleman standing with his hand resting on a fence, his hunting dogs sitting at his feet.

Cottage industry, artisanal workshops, and factory production often coexisted within the same industry. With the gradual mechanization of spinning, weaving could only keep pace with the rapid expansion of the number of hand-loom weavers. Even a rudimentary power loom, invented in 1784, was too expensive to compete with domestic industry, which continued to be based on the availability of an inexpensive workforce. Hand-loom weavers survived well into the middle decades of the nineteenth century.

Richard Arkwright with his famous water frame at his fingertips.

The inventions that slowly revolutionized the textile industry did not inevitably lead to factory production. Like framework knitting, the first spinning jennys and mules were small enough to be adaptable to workshops and even some houses, where skilled workers and their apprentices used stronger, more reliable hand-operated machinery or tools.

The factory, however, slowly became the symbol of the new industrial age in England. One of Arkwright's textile mills in the early 1770s had 200 workers, and ten years later it had four times that number. An ironworks employed more than 1,000 workers by 1770, a concentration previously seen only in great shipyards. In 1774, Watt and Matthew Boulton (1728–1809), a toymaker, went into business in Birmingham producing engines and machine parts in the largest factory in the world. It was not a single structure but rather a number of adjacent workshops, which drew on the work of about 20,000 men, women, and children in the countryside around Birmingham.

The development of the factory at first had relatively little to do with technological imperatives. Manufacturers preferred bringing workers under one roof so that they could more easily supervise them, imposing the discipline of factory work on people used to having their schedule defined by the rising and setting of the sun and the passing of the seasons. When a defective piece of pottery emerged from the kilns, the pottery manufacturer Josiah Wedgwood (1730–1795) would storm over and stomp on it with his wooden leg, chiding his workers. "Thou shalt not be idle" was Wedgwood's eleventh commandment; "Everything gives way to experiment" his favorite maxim. His goal was to train his workers so thoroughly as "to make such machines of the men as cannot err." Putting workers in factories facilitated such a goal. By the middle of the eighteenth century, factory manufacturing had begun to alter the northern English landscape. "From the Establishment of Manufacturers, we see Hamlets swell into Villages, and Villages into Towns," exclaimed a gentleman in the 1770s.

Expanding British Economy

The production of manufactured goods doubled during the last half of the eighteenth century in Britain. Cotton made up 40 percent of British exports by the end of the century. India's domination of the world market for textiles ended. The production of iron followed in importance, along with wool and worsteds, linen, silk, copper, paper, cutlery, and the booming building trades.

Despite its relatively small size, Britain's significant economic advantages over the nations of the continent help explain why the manufacturing revolution first began there. Unlike the German or Italian states, Britain was unified politically. People living in England spoke basically the same language. France and the Italian and German states still had internal tariffs that made trade more costly, whereas in Britain there were no internal tariffs once the union between England and Scotland had been achieved in 1707. Weights and measures in Britain had largely been standardized.

Great Britain was by far the wealthiest nation in the world. Its colonies provided raw materials for manufacturing and markets for goods produced by the mother country. English merchants supplied slaves snatched from the west coast of Africa for the plantations of the West Indies in exchange for cotton. The amount of raw cotton imported from India increased by twenty times between 1750 and 1800. Beginning in the 1790s the United States provided Lancashire manufacturers with cotton picked by southern slaves.

England's stable banking and credit arrangements facilitated the reinvestment of agricultural and commercial profits in manufacturing. London's banks, particularly the giant Bank of England, were profitable and respected. Merchants and manufacturers accepted paper money and bills of exchange with confidence. Gentry invested in overseas trade expeditions and in manufacturing without the reticence of continental landowners. London's financial market could provide information twice a week on what investments were worth in Amsterdam and Paris. Joint-stock companies, which had begun in the late seventeenth century, offered limited personal liability, which meant that in the case of a company's financial disaster, individual investors would be liable only to the extent of their investments.

Expanded demand for manufactured goods led to a dramatic improvement in Britain's roads. A new process of road surfacing—macadamization—improved travel on the main routes. Turnpikes were extended and improved; investors formed "turnpike trusts," repairing the highways and turning a profit by charging a toll. In 1700, it took fifty hours to travel from Norwich to London by coach; by 1800, the journey could be achieved in nineteen hours. The daunting trek to the Scottish city of Edinburgh from London had been reduced to a mere sixty hours of travel.

England's water transportation was also unmatched in Europe, a gift of nature. Rich coal and iron ore deposits lay near water transportation. By 1800, Britain was extracting about 90 percent of the world's coal. No part of England stands more than seventy miles from the sea. Navigable rivers facilitated the transportation of raw materials and manufactured goods; so did canals built in the middle decades of the century, including a ninety-mile-long canal linking Manchester to the Mersey River and the Irish Sea.

The British government offered businessmen more assistance than any continental rivals could anticipate from their own governments. The Royal Navy protected the merchant fleet, which tripled in size during the first three-quarters of the century. Navigation Acts forced foreign merchants to ship export goods to Britain in British ships. Bowing to pressure from woolens producers, the British government in 1700 had imposed protective tariffs on imported silk and calico, undercutting imports from India. Agreements with the Dutch Republic and France in the late 1780s reduced trade tariffs with those states, which helped British exports. Political influence kept taxes low on business. Other British strategies were even more imaginative: a law dating from the late seventeenth century required that all corpses be dressed in woolens for burial, a clever way of helping woolens manufacturers.

Yet the British government rarely interfered in operations of the economy in ways that businessmen might have considered intrusive. Adam Smith (1723–1790) emerged as the first economic theorist of capitalism (see Chapter 9). Smith rejected the prevailing theory of mercantilism and extolled economic liberalism. He also observed that the greater division of labor was increasing productivity. Taking a famous example, he argued that a single worker could probably not make a single common pin in one day, but that ten workers, each repeating the same task, such as straightening the wire, or grinding its point, could make hundreds of pins in a workday. Smith's logic anticipated the age of factory manufacturing.

Expanding Continental Economies

On the continent, too, particularly in the West, manufacturing expanded rapidly in cities, towns, and the countryside. Continental European manufacturing was characterized by small-scale production and cottage industry (taking advantage of an almost endless supply of laborers). France did not lag far behind Britain in the production of manufactured goods, and it remained the principal supplier of Spain and its empire. Despite bewildering differences in, for example, weights and measures, currencies (even within large states), and calendars (Russia's was eleven days behind that of the West), European commerce developed rapidly during the eighteenth century.

Global trade also contributed to the economies of the Italian and German states, and to those of Spain, Portugal, and France (see Map 10.2). Increased trade with the wider world brought new products—Chinese silk and porcelain, Indian cotton, West Indian sugar and rum, East Indian tea, South Seas spices, and much more. In the chancy sweepstakes of the globalization of colonial trade, traders and their investors could make considerable fortunes, but they could also easily be ruined when a sudden storm or pirate attack destroyed a ship and its cargo.

Bankers, investors, shipbuilders, wholesale and retail merchants, insurance underwriters, transporters, and notaries profited from the marked increase in international trade. Some of the prosperity trickled down to more ordinary folk as well, providing work, for example in prosperous port towns, for carpenters, dockers, haulers, and artisans, who supplied luxuries for wealthy merchants.

Considerable obstacles remained, however, to further economic development on the continent. Traditional suspicion of paper money, the problems of obtaining credit and raising investment capital, and periodic government debasing of currencies created hurdles for those undertaking long-distance commerce. London and Amsterdam were alone in having respected banks, credit facilities, relatively low interest rates, and insurance companies.

MAP 10.2 TRADE FROM COLONIES TO EUROPE, c. 1775 Exports from the colonies to Europe, including the value of the trade.

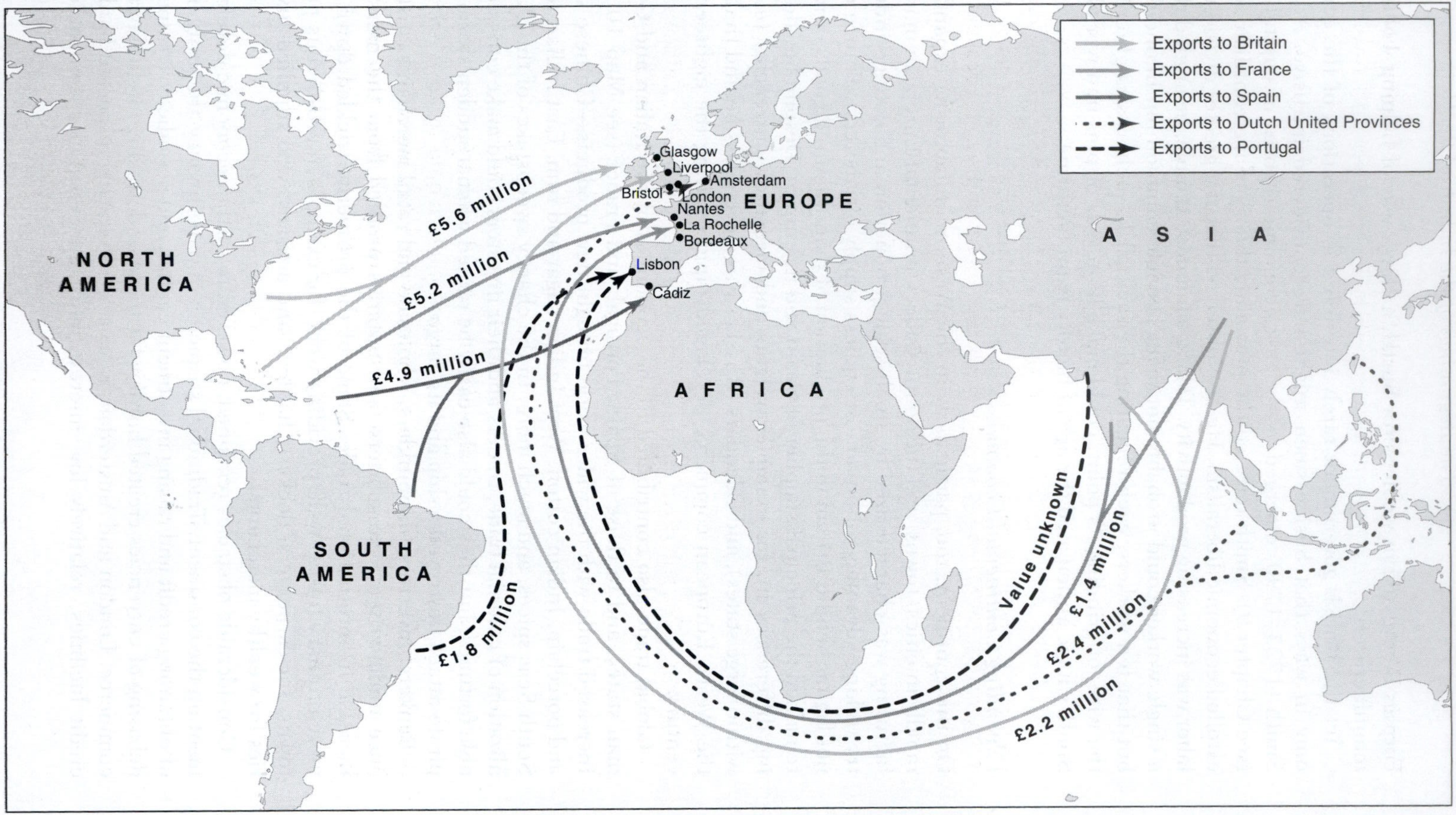

Legend:
- Exports to Britain
- Exports to France
- Exports to Spain
- Exports to Dutch United Provinces
- Exports to Portugal

£2.2 million
£1.4 million
£2.4 million
Value unknown
£5.6 million
£5.2 million
£4.9 million
£1.8 million

Glasgow
Liverpool
Amsterdam
Bristol
London
Nantes
La Rochelle
Bordeaux
Lisbon
Cádiz

EUROPE
ASIA
AFRICA
NORTH AMERICA
SOUTH AMERICA

Even in Western Europe, Britain's South Sea Bubble (see Chapter 11) and the collapse in 1720 of John Law's bank in France scared off investors. Capital remained for the most part in the hands of wealthy families and small groups of associates who loaned money to states, pushing up the cost of credit. The absence of investment capital led the Prussian and Austrian monarchies to supply capital for some manufacturing enterprises. Guilds held monopolies on the trade and production of certain products; international tariffs and tolls complicated trade between the many small states in Central Europe. Furthermore, as we have seen, relatively few nobles took an active interest in manufacturing, although exceptions were to be found in France, the Austrian Netherlands, and Russia, where some nobles developed coal mines and invested in the iron industry. Despite the development of the copper and iron industry of the Ural Mountains, in the Russian Empire the possibilities for increased manufacturing were limited by the monumental distances between population centers and natural resources, as well as an inadequate transportation network that had barely changed since the time of Ivan the Terrible in the sixteenth century.

SOCIAL CHANGES

Urban growth, particularly after 1750, was one of the most visible changes engendered by the rise in population and the expansion of trade and manufacturing, as well as the continuing centralization of state power. Other changes included the rise of the "middling sort" and the greater vulnerability of the laborer who was displaced by enclosure and forced to move from place to place in search of work.

The Growth of Towns and Cities

Although Europe remained overwhelmingly rural, cities and towns grew faster than the population as a whole, meaning that Europe, particularly the West, slowly urbanized. Cities grew as people moved to areas where there was work, or for the poorest of the poor, where they might find charity. New manufacturing centers served as magnets to which those who had no land or prospects were drawn. By the end of the century, Europe had twenty-two cities with more than 100,000 people (see Table 10.2).

The British urban population (any settlement of more than 2,500 people qualified as "urban") grew from slightly less than 20 percent of the population in 1700 to more than 30 percent in 1800, when London's population reached nearly a million people, nearly twice that of Paris. London was the world's largest port, the center of banking, finance, insurance, manufacturing, exports, and empire. In the eighteenth century, a fifth of the British population spent part of their lives in London. Two-thirds of the residents of London had been born outside of the city, migrants who had come to the

TABLE 10.2. EUROPE'S LARGEST CITIES AT THE END OF THE EIGHTEENTH CENTURY

City	Population	City	Population
London	950,000	St. Petersburg	270,000
Paris	550,000	Vienna	230,000
Naples	430,000	Amsterdam	220,000
Constantinople	300,000	Lisbon	180,000
Moscow	300,000	Berlin	170,000

capital in search of opportunity. Indians and blacks had also begun to appear in the imperial capital.

Some contemporaries believed that wickedness and crime increased almost inevitably with larger cities and towns. In the case of London, the book *Hell Upon Earth, or the Town in an Uproar* (1729) was subtitled "The Late Horrible Scenes of Forgery, Perjury, Street-Robbery, Murder, Sodomy, and Other Shocking Impieties." It denounced "this great, wicked, unwieldy, over-grown Town, one continued hurry of Vice and Pleasure, where nothing dwells but *Absurdities, Abuses, Accidents, Accusations.*"

London's emerging social geography reflected the paradox that Britain was both an aristocratic and commercial society. Bloomsbury Square and Bedford Square, elite districts in West London, near Westminster, the seat of Parliament, were largely aristocratic creations, as nobles developed some of their land. At the same time, commercial London also expanded rapidly along with the British Empire. Near the burgeoning docks of the East End on the River Thames, dilapidated buildings housed the poor.

As England's economic dynamism began to shift northward with increased manufacturing, Liverpool, a teeming port on the Irish Sea, "the emporium of the western world," and Manchester, a northern industrial town, developed rapidly. By 1800, Manchester had become the "metropolis of manufactures," with 75,000 inhabitants and growing industrial suburbs.

Continental cities, too, added population. In France, the growth of Paris, above all, but also Lyon, Lille, Bordeaux, and other cities was deceptive, as only about 10 percent of the population lived in towns of more than 5,000 people in 1789, compared to 25 percent in England. In the German states, there had been but twenty-four towns with more than 10,000 people in 1500; by 1800, there were sixty of them. In Berlin, royal officials, lawyers, and soldiers accounted for about 40 percent of the Prussian capital's 140,000 inhabitants in 1783. In southern Italy, Naples was barely able to support its impoverished population of more than 400,000 people. No other town in southern Italy had 10,000 inhabitants. In Rome, the clergy constituted about half the population of 160,000 people. East Central and Eastern Europe and the Balkans had relatively few cities. In the middle of the eighteenth century, only three cities within the vast Russian Empire had more than 30,000 inhabitants: Moscow, Saint Petersburg, and Kiev. Yet the Polish capital, Warsaw, which had only 7,000 inhabitants in the mid-sixteenth century, had grown to 150,000 a century later.

As cities developed, those with money and leisure time found more to do. The largest English towns sported theaters and concert halls, gentlemen's clubs, scientific societies, and racetracks. Towns took pride in their development, publishing guides for visitors and directories listing the names of shops. Elegant buildings of brick and stone replaced tottering wood-beamed medieval structures. Streets were widened, paved, and cleaned, at least in wealthy neighborhoods. Dublin, Boston, and Calcutta offered smaller versions of English urban society, sporting private clubs and municipal pride, at least for British residents.

Wealthy merchants and bankers lived in elegant townhouses near the docks in Hamburg, Nantes, and Genoa, bustling port cities of international trade. Expanded trade and urban growth engendered consumerism. Paris became the European capital of luxury goods, as French nobles continually raised the standards of conspicuous consumption. Polish lords traded grain for luxury goods from Western Europe. In Sweden, such luxury reached court, aristocrats, and wealthy bourgeois, but a diplomat in 1778 estimated the market for such goods in Sweden to be only 70,000 people of a population of 2.5 million. Thomas Jefferson, who espoused simplicity in life, nonetheless paid for a stream of luxury goods from London and Paris to be shipped to Virginia.

Noble and wealthy bourgeois alike insisted on personal prerogatives of taste, for example, in decoration and food. It became a compliment to say

Elegant shops on Capel Street in Dublin.

that someone or something reflected "urbanity." Three-cornered hats, along with wigs, which wealthy commoners as well as nobles increasingly favored, and stockings emerged as symbols of respectability. Cafés took their name from the coffee served there, a drink only people of means could afford. Upper-class men and women became concerned as never before with modesty; "water closets" became more common. A code of conduct served—with income and private space itself—as a barrier between wealthy and ordinary people.

The eighteenth-century consumer revolution extended to the poor, as well. By the mid-seventeenth century, resourceful households in northwestern Europe were finding ways to purchase consumer goods that would make their lives somewhat more comfortable. Families drew upon the labor of women and children, as well as longer working hours by husbands. Now the number of ordinary families able to acquire household utensils and even books and cheap prints increased dramatically. Different kinds of apparel were available even to the very poor. Many mill hands now had a change of clothes. Some servant girls wore silk kerchiefs, and an occasional laborer sported a watch, for which he paid the wages of several weeks. Even some infants deposited at foundling homes had been dressed in printed cottons. For very ordinary people with a little money or some credit, taverns and bars provided cheap liquor and sociability. For people with neither, there was the street.

Social Movement within the Elite

With the growth of manufacturing, trade, and cities came concomitant social changes, including mobility of the "middling sort." Bankers and wealthy merchants aspired to social distinction and an aristocratic lifestyle. In Paris, wealthy merchants purchased elegant townhouses and mingled with nobles. In Barcelona, members of the trading oligarchy earned the right to carry swords like nobles. The bourgeoisie of the Austrian Netherlands demanded the same privileges Habsburg rulers had granted to Belgian nobles. Noble titles could be purchased in most European states, providing a relatively easily obtained means of social ascension, without eliminating the distinctions between nobles and commoners. As the rising cost of warfare (larger armies to equip, train, and send into battle, and expensive fortifications to maintain) and reduced tax revenue during hard economic times weighed heavily on royal coffers, the sale of titles and offices swept more commoners into the nobility in France, Austria, and Castile. The number of French nobles doubled between 1715 and 1789, and relatively few noble families could trace their origins back more than a couple of generations.

In Britain, on the other hand, it was rare for commoners to move into the nobility. The sale of offices had never been as widespread in England as on the continent, at least not since the English Civil War in the mid-

Notice the marked contrast between the poor worker and the elegant member of the gentry in this English etching from the eighteenth century.

seventeenth century, and the purchase of noble titles was nonexistent. Yet the crown occasionally elevated spectacularly successful, wealthy commoners into the peerage with hereditary noble titles (baron, viscount, earl, marquis, and duke), which carried with them a seat in the House of Lords. The monarchy rewarded other landed gentlemen with various titles, including knight (a nonhereditary title) and baronet (a hereditary title, granted less frequently), both of which carried the title of "Sir." Very few people, however, ever rose from trade into a peerage, or even to the upper gentry.

Entry into the British elite, however, was generally more open than into its continental counterparts. Gradual shifts in social structure in English society, beginning in the seventeenth century, contributed to the nation's social stability. No legal or cultural barriers in Britain prevented bankers, manufacturers, merchants, and urban professionals from ascending through wealth to social and political predominance as "country gentlemen" through the purchase of landed estates that made them gentry.

Daniel Defoe, who wrote *Robinson Crusoe* and other novels for an expanding middle-class readership, claimed that "men are every day starting up from obscurity to wealth." Trade and manufacturing in England were honored occupations. Unlike on the continent, where second and third sons often were automatically relegated by their fathers into Church or military posts, many of these sons marched proudly into business. A Manchester cobbler wrote in 1756:

See, as the Owners of old Family Estates in your Neighborhood are selling off their patrimonies, how your townsmen are constantly purchasing; and thereby laying the Foundation of a new Race of Gentry! Not adorn'd, its true, with Coats of Arms and a long Parchment

Pedigree of useless Members of Society, but deck'd with Virtue and Frugality.

In France, Denmark, and Sweden, tensions remained between old noble families and those more recently ennobled, whom the former viewed as boorish newcomers. The number of ennobled commoners in the eighteenth century may not have been significantly greater than that in the previous century, but those who were ennobled were wealthier. However, the older noble families still controlled the most important and lucrative offices in the royal bureaucracy, the Church, and the army.

The French army began to phase out the purchase of commissions in the late 1770s, and early in the next decade nobles demanded and received royal assurance that the crown would respect their monopoly on the most prestigious military titles. Directed against newcomer nobles, the Ségur Law of 1782 asserted that no one could be appointed to a high post in the army who could not demonstrate at least four generations of nobility on his father's side. However, barriers between the bourgeois and nobles in many states were starting to break down. In some places, a small number of nobles entered commerce or manufacturing. The expansion of trade and manufacturing led more continental nobles to seek new sources of wealth. French and Russian nobles were principal owners of mines. Swedish nobles contributed to the modest expansion of manufacturing in their country. In eighteenth-century Spain, little stigma was attached to noble commercial ventures, perhaps because there were so many nobles. In contrast, in Prussia, Poland, and Hungary most nobles still considered participation in commercial activity (above all, retail commerce) or manufacturing to bring derogation, implying a loss of status and honor.

This painting depicts a socially mobile French merchant and banker receiving envoys from Joseph II, the Holy Roman Emperor, requesting a loan.

The Changing Condition of the Poor

For millions of people, only a thin line stood between having enough to eat and hunger or starvation, between occasional employment and begging, and between relatively good health and sudden illness and death. If both partners were young, healthy, and could occasionally find work, marriage increased the odds of survival in "an economy of makeshifts." But economic crisis often pulled a couple apart, as one partner might be forced to leave to look for work elsewhere.

At the end of the eighteenth century, almost 30 percent of the British population depended on some sort of poor relief; more than a million people were classified as "paupers" in England and Wales. Laborers, some of whom had been chased from village common lands by parliamentary acts of enclosure, wandered in search of work. Yet residents of a given village or neighborhood were far more likely to benefit from local charity than outsiders, often feared as thieves or worse. Beggars in Austrian law were referred to as "push people," because authorities sought to push them away.

Meager harvests and bitter winters periodically took terrible tolls on the poor, with indigents found frozen to death in church doorways, barns, or fields. When food shortages occurred or the police expelled beggars from large cities, country roads swarmed with young children who had been abandoned, told by their parents to make their way as best they could. The elderly, particularly widows, were often the poorest of the poor, unable to move elsewhere, depending on neighbors little better off than themselves.

The poor were perpetually undernourished. Bread remained the basis of the diet of the vast majority of Europeans—white bread for people of means; black bread, porridge or gruel made from rye, potatoes, or buckwheat for everybody else. Vegetables—peas and beans, and cabbage in Central and Eastern Europe—were prized as occasional additions to soup or porridge. Poor people rarely consumed meat, except for heavily salted meat that could be preserved. The orphanage of Amsterdam, a prosperous city, served meat and fish twice a week and vegetables once a week. But dried peas, beans, porridge, or gruel comprised most meals there. Fish and shellfish were common only at the sea's edge for ordinary people (especially because they were not allowed to fish in most rivers and ponds). Water, often not very clean, was the drink of necessity; wine and beer were beyond the budget of most people. Swiss peasants prosperous enough to drink coffee and eat chocolate were the exception in Europe. Yet overall, ordinary people experienced a modest improvement in diet and health during the eighteenth century.

Charity, however impressive, fell far short of relieving the crushing poverty, particularly in France, where it provided only about 5 percent of what was needed. During the Catholic Reformation, the Church had emphasized the importance of charitable works in the quest for eternal salvation. Most Protestants, too, believed in the importance of good works—after all, Christ had washed a beggar's feet. Parishes and, in Catholic countries, monasteries and convents regularly provided what relief they could afford to the poor, particularly around Christmas and during Lent. Hospices and other charitable institutions cared for the sick, invalids, and the elderly as best they could. But during hard times the number of abandoned infants increased dramatically, far beyond the capacity of institutions to care for them.

Social Control

By the middle of the eighteenth century, many upper-class Europeans believed that they had entered an age of clamoring crowds and even riots. In the 1770s and 1780s, particularly, the lower orders seemed increasingly less deferential. The poor protested the purchase and removal of grain from their markets at prices they could not afford. They stopped wagons, seized grain, and sold it at what they considered to be the "just price," a sum that would permit even the poor to buy enough to survive.

Work stoppages by craftsmen became more widespread. Following a London strike by journeymen tailors protesting cuts in their pay, the British Parliament passed the first Combination Act in 1721. The law established wages and working conditions for tailors and allowed the jailing of striking workers without benefit of a trial. Seeing that many craftsmen and skilled workers were leaving Britain, some for the colonies, Parliament then passed legislation forbidding their emigration.

Protecting Property in Britain

The British Parliament represented the interests of wealthy landowners, who consolidated their property during the eighteenth century and alone could elect members of the House of Commons. Thus, in 1723, Parliament passed without discussion a law that added fifty capital offenses against property.

Hunting was a badge of living nobly. It was a domesticated, usually non-lethal—at least for the hunters—version of warfare. The exclusive right to hunt was a vigilantly guarded prerogative of any and all who could claim noble status. But acts against poaching were invoked more often to protect property rights. Wealthy English landowners set brutal mantraps—including trap-guns—and snares that maimed poachers who snuck onto their property, including in the "deer parks" established on land that had once been common land. The felonies listed under the Black Act, among them the blackening of one's face as a form of disguise—hence the law's name—included poaching game or fish, chopping down trees, or gleaning branches blown down in storms. Henry Fielding (1707–1754) called attention to such a felony in his novel *The Adventures of Joseph Andrews*: "Jesu!" said the Squire, "would you commit two persons to Bridewell [prison] for a twig?" "Yes," said the Lawyer, "and with great leniency too; for if we had called it a young tree they would have been both hanged."

The concern for protecting property could be seen in the Marriage Act (1753), which forbade clandestine marriages. It specifically sought to protect property against ambitious men who might be tempted to try to elope with the daughters of wealthy property owners. Parliament also passed a law permitting divorce by parliamentary act—which none but the very wealthy and well-placed could seek—at least partially because gentlemen wanted to be free to divorce wives who shamed them with adultery or who could not produce heirs to inherit their estates.

A gamekeeper snags a poacher.

Subordination and Social Control

People of means debated strategies of social control with increasing urgency as economic crises widened the gap between rich and poor. During 1724–1733, the French state undertook a "great confinement" of paupers, beggars, and vagrants in workhouses, where they were to learn menial trades under conditions of strict discipline. The subsequent reorganization and expansion of royal efforts at policing the poor represented an increase in the reach of the state. Yet temporary programs of poor relief were common on the continent, as were periodic repressive campaigns against beggars and vagrants. Since the beginning of the seventeenth century, English parishes or townships provided charity to those wearing the requisite "P" for pauper. In order to keep indigents off the road, towns established workhouses, where the poor would be forced to work in exchange for subsistence. A 1782 English law replaced workhouses with somewhat more humane "poorhouses." In 1795, the Speenhamland system, so called after the parish in which it was conceived, provided for a sliding scale of assistance, determined by the current price of bread and wage rates. But such programs merely scratched the surface as the problem of poverty entered public discourse to an unprecedented degree.

Britain did not undertake the kind of largely successful campaign found in some places on the continent to limit the number of capital crimes to those that threatened life or the state. Parliament added almost two hundred capital offenses to the law between 1688 and 1810, sixty-three of

A public hanging at Tyburn in London.

them between 1760 and 1810. About mid-century, two young men were arrested for poaching. Their wives went to the landlord's estate to beg his merciful intercession. The lord, moved to tears, said that their husbands would be returned to them. True to his word, he sent the two corpses to the wives. But English juries, in particular, hesitated to convict those accused; only about two hundred criminals were executed each year. Executions drew huge throngs at London's Tyburn. Corporal punishment, such as branding or being exhibited in stocks to public contempt, was far more common. Children were worked and punished as adults, though not all as harshly as the seven-year-old girl who was hanged in Norwich for stealing a petticoat. England was relatively under-policed, particularly when compared to France (Paris had four times more policemen than London, which was twice its size).

Authorities everywhere tended to lump the poor into one of two broad categories—"deserving" and "undeserving," that is, whether they were considered worthy of pity and charity. Among the latter were "false beggars" who simulated horrifying wounds or injuries with the skill of a makeup artist and, clutching at the clothes of the wealthy passing by, received a few cents as his benefactors scurried away as rapidly as possible. These categories reflected the belief that many, if not most, of the poor were destitute because they were lazy and that stiff punishment would be enough to end begging.

In small bourgs, villages, and the countryside, people feared bands of thieves, whose threat of arson could intimidate, as a fire would destroy a harvest or a farm in a matter of minutes. Brigandage was rampant in southern Italy and in Sicily. In the grain-rich Beauce region south of Paris, some bandits were known as *chauffeurs* because they held their victims' feet to the fire to force them to reveal the hiding place of their valuables. Yet many poor people considered some bandits as heroic Robin Hoods, who stole from the rich to give to the poor.

A CENTURY OF CONTRASTS

The eighteenth century was a period of contrasts. Musical performances at court and in châteaux and elegant townhouses took place while peasants and rural day laborers struggled to survive, toiling in fields they rarely owned or working as dock or market porters, chimney sweeps, or common laborers in town. The well-heeled financier, wholesale merchant, manufacturer, or lawyer in Paris, Amsterdam, Barcelona, or Vienna lived in a vastly more cosmopolitan world, increasingly shaped by consumerism, than did their counterparts in the relatively few cities and towns in Prussia, Russia, and the Balkans. In many ways a century still dominated politically by nobles, the eighteenth century also was a dynamic period of economic and social transformation, beginning with the Industrial Revolution in England. Commerce and manufacturing increased on the continent, as well. Developing trade across oceans changed patterns of consumption in Europe. Trade remained the basis of the British Empire, which stretched across the world. Rivals Spain and France, too, were colonial powers.

Economic and social changes brought remarkable political consequences during the 1760s and 1770s. English country gentlemen who invariably supported court policies and those who sometimes opposed them began to look and act like political parties. And the domination of political life by an oligarchy of landowners came under challenge from ordinary people without the right to vote. In the North American colonies, the king's subjects protested the fact that they were taxed without representation, and they rebelled against British rule.

On the continent, denunciations of unwarranted privilege began to be heard, including calls for reform of the French absolute monarchy. Public opinion gradually began to see parlements as blocks against absolute rule and defenders of the rights of the "nation," a term that increasingly came into use. Elsewhere on the continent, too, opposition to entrenched privilege became more insistent.

CHAPTER 11

EIGHTEENTH-CENTURY DYNASTIC RIVALRIES AND POLITICS

King George III (ruled 1760–1820) proclaimed that he "gloried in the name of Britain." Indeed during his reign, despite his personal failings, a nationalist cult developed around the British monarchy, significantly after the empire suffered its biggest loss, that of the thirteen American colonies.

The king projected the image of an ordinary family man, surrounded by his homely wife and fifteen children. Less interested in goings-on in Hanover, his family's dynastic home, than his predecessors, he won popular affection in Britain. "This young man," assessed the writer Horace Walpole, "don't stand in one spot with his eyes fixed royally on the ground, and dropping bits of German news; he walks about and speaks to everybody." The king's domesticity also made him a target for the gentle spoofs of caricaturists. His nervousness led him to bombard almost everyone he encountered with questions, ending with "hey, hey?" By the last decade of the century, symptoms of a hereditary disease made George III appear to be quite mad.

Early in his reign, King George III held strongly to royal prerogatives, even within the context of the British constitutional monarchy. Yet not only did British nationalism develop rapidly with him on the throne, but the idea developed in and beyond Parliament that a party of opposition formed an essential part of the parliamentary system of representation.

The nature of the European state system itself also underwent fundamental change in the eighteenth century as the rivalries between Great Britain, France, Spain, and the Dutch Republic (the United Provinces) broadened to a global scale. Whereas Europe in the period of Louis XIV had been marked by frenetic war-making—much of it at his instigation—and the pursuit of alliances against France, Europe's dominant state, the wars fought between the great powers in the middle of the eighteenth century reflected a more even distribution of power. This balance of power was increasingly affected not only by events overseas but also by those in Eastern Europe. There, Russia expanded its empire at the expense of the Ottoman Empire, and Russia, Prussia, and Austria dismembered Poland in a series of Partitions, the last in 1795.

The increasingly global nature of conflicts between empires put strains on the structures of states in Europe. They were forced to reorganize themselves to become more efficient. In Britain, as the role of the House of Commons expanded and political parties emerged, newspapers and organizations in which politics was discussed created public opinion, transforming the public sphere as more people demanded political reform. A precocious sense of British national identity and patriotism developed.

Reform movements and even uprisings in Europe alarmed rulers and intrigued intellectuals, who in increasing numbers denounced unwarranted privilege and despotism. American colonists rose up against British rule. Public opinion on the continent demanded reform; in France, the parlements began to defend the "nation" against monarchical despotism. As contemporaries sought explanations for movements that sought to limit monarchical authority, the Bavarian envoy in Vienna went so far as to claim in 1775 that "the spirit of revolt has become universal."

THE EIGHTEENTH-CENTURY STATE SYSTEM

In eighteenth-century Europe, the powers danced together in temporary partnership until the music changed and old partners were deserted and new ones embraced. The eighteenth-century state system was a pattern of rivalry and alliance in which powerful states vied for dynastic and global power. Few borders or thrones were secure from challenge by other rulers coveting more territory. Rulers sought to expand their power through marriage, inheritance, alliances, or warfare. Other states sought to maintain the balance of power, so that one state did not grow more powerful at the expense of the others. Spain, France, the Dutch Republic, Sweden, Poland-Lithuania, the Holy Roman Empire, and the Ottoman Empire found themselves with less power than in the seventeenth century, while Britain, Russia, and Prussia continued to extend their reach.

The emergence of a global economy increasingly linked to colonial trade engendered rivalries as Britain, France, Spain, and the Dutch Republic battled for commercial and colonial advantage, preparing the way for European expansion in the nineteenth century. The wars between the great powers spilled into the Americas and India. The powers were motivated by the hope of economic gain and reflected the primacy of the economic theory of mercantilism, which assumed that there was a finite amount of wealth available in the world, and that the might of any state depended on its success in bringing in more gold than it paid out.

In the meantime, dynastic rivalries remained a major source of conflict. George I from the German state of Hanover succeeded to the throne of England in 1714, but his German origins and interests complicated British foreign policy and led to unsuccessful attempts by the Catholic Stuart pretenders to take back the British throne. On the continent, Frederick the Great of Prussia and Maria Theresa of Austria locked horns in a battle of expansion for the former and survival for the latter. The other great powers lined up in alliances on the side of each.

Global Rivalries

As voyages of discovery opened up new horizons to Europeans, the stakes of colonial rivalry between the great powers rose. During the seventeenth century, England, the Dutch Republic, France, Spain, and Portugal had gradually expanded their trading routes across the seas. Coffee, tea, molasses, ginger, indigo, Indian calicoes, tobacco, and other colonial products—for the most part luxury goods—fetched high prices at home. The discovery of gold in Brazil in 1694 and 1719 further whetted the appetites of commercial companies. By the end of the seventeenth century, Dutch and French traders began to sail to China in greater numbers. There the K'ang-hsi emperor and the Ch'ing dynasty had expanded toward the south even while affirming Chinese cultural unity, even within the context of a vast and varied land. The Chinese rulers manifested little interest in the traders from the West. (When a diplomat representing King George III of Britain arrived in China to try to convince the emperor to begin diplomatic relations with his country and brought presents from England, the emperor's message to him said "I set no value on objects strange and ingenious.") Ambitious European merchant-traders still brought back spices and fine silks from Asia, but sea routes had largely supplanted the old land trade routes that had stretched through the Middle East and Central Asia. Chinese prints, porcelain, silk, and rugs became popular in Western Europe.

In the eighteenth century, the British East India Company established new posts in South India and Bengal. Parliament licensed the company to operate as a military force. Ships of the British East India Company carried Chinese porcelain, silks, spices, and tea to England in exchange for silver and, increasingly, opium grown in India. British traders exchanged slaves taken from West Africa and textiles and other manufactured goods for colonial products. If at the middle of the eighteenth century there were about 3 to 4 million Europeans living in British, French, Spanish, and Portuguese colonies in America, several times that number of slaves had been carried there by European ships from Africa.

Spain still had the largest empire. It included the largest Caribbean islands, the Philippines in the Pacific, and most of South America except for

The trading post established by the British East India Company in Surat, India, late eighteenth century.

Brazil, which belonged to Portugal. The Dutch had bases on the northern coast of South America, West Africa, South Africa (their colony at the Cape of Good Hope was the only permanent European settlement at the time in South Africa), the island of Mauritius in the Indian Ocean, the Indian sub-continent, and Southeast Asia, where they conquered three Islamic states in the late seventeenth century. The Dutch were also in Japan, which in the late sixteenth and early seventeenth century had expanded trade in East Asia and Southeast Asia. The Dutch presence in Japan during the 1630s and 1640s had been limited to the port of Nagasaki, as Japan rejected more than superficial contacts with foreigners. As in the case of China, the Japanese exhibited little knowledge of or interest in other cultures.

French forts and settlements dotted the North American colony of Nou-velle (New) France. French trappers established posts on the Mississippi River, with the port of New Orleans at its mouth far to the south. The ter-ritories claimed by the French, on which they had only scattered military and trading posts, almost tripled in size by the middle of the eighteenth century, but by the 1760s the French population of Nouvelle France stood at only about 80,000 people.

Global rivalries led to conflicts between the great powers. French and British armies and navies battled in North America, the West Indies, and India, believing that the loss of Canadian furs, Caribbean spices, or Indian jewels might be a damaging blow to prosperity and prestige. Spanish colonial rivalry with Britain led to the only war ever fought over an ear. Both Spain and Britain insisted that their colonies ship goods only on vessels flying their flag. Since 1713 the Spanish had granted the right to Britain to supply its colonies with 4,800 slaves each year; in exchange for this sale, a single English ship each year could trade at one Spanish colonial port. Illegal trade, however, continued as before. The Spanish navy sank several British ships, and in 1731 one of its vessels accosted an English frigate suspected of smuggling. A Spanish sword cut off one of the ears of the captain, Jenkins. The incident led to the "War of Jenkins's Ear" in 1739 after a member of Parliament whipped up anti-Spanish sentiment by waving the severed ear in the air during a speech. The war, highlighted by the successful Spanish defense of the port of Cartagena in what now is Columbia, went on with neither side claiming victory, a settlement coming only with the conclusion of the War of the Austrian Succession (see pp. 394–396).

The Hanoverians and the Stuarts in Great Britain

In 1702, Queen Anne (1665–1714), the Protestant daughter of James II, succeeded her brother-in-law, William III, to the throne of England. Despite eighteen pregnancies and five live births, Anne had no surviving children. The House of Commons had passed the Act of Succession in 1701 to prevent any future restoration of the Catholic Stuart line to the throne. By this act, which broke strict rules of dynastic succession, the Protestant ruling dynasty of Hanover, related by blood to the English royal family, would become the English royal line upon Anne's death.

In 1707, the Act of Union created the Kingdom of Great Britain, which took the Union Jack as its flag, and linked Scotland to England and Wales. Scotland received seats in the House of Commons, but fewer than its population should have warranted. Parliament's goal in formalizing the dynastic union was fear that Scotland might seek to summon Queen Anne's exiled Catholic half-brother (James III; the Stuart son of James II) to be king of Scotland, instead of going along with England and Wales's awarding of the throne to the house of Hanover. Ireland, in which English Protestants owned seven-eighths of the land, continued to pay dearly for having supported the Catholic monarch James II after the Glorious Revolution of 1688 had evicted him from the throne. Legal restrictions prevented Irish Catholics from being merchants, lawyers, or members of the Irish Parliament, the powers of which were strictly limited. In England itself, Parliament had not extended the Toleration Act of 1689 to Catholics. British Catholics could not vote, be elected to Parliament, or hold state offices; they also were subject to special taxes, could not possess weapons,

George I, the Hanoverian king of Great Britain who never learned English.

be admitted to Oxford or Cambridge Universities, or worship freely, at a time when Protestant Dissenters—that is, Protestants not belonging to the Church of England—were able to rise to respectable positions within the British state.

The Hanoverian George I (1660–1727), a distant cousin of Queen Anne, became king in 1714. He never learned English, brought some of his own advisers from Hanover, was stubborn and obese (some of his subjects referred to their monarch as "King Log"), and may have ordered the murder of his wife's lover in Hanover. All of this was more easily forgiven by wealthy Englishmen than his apparent indifference toward the crown he wore, seemingly demonstrated by the fact that he spent long periods in his beloved Hanover.

The Hanoverian dynasty's accession to the throne complicated British foreign policy. The Treaty of Utrecht (1713), the first of two treaties that concluded the War of the Spanish Succession (1701–1714, see Chapter 7), confirmed Britain's colonial supremacy, adding Newfoundland, Nova Scotia, the Hudson Bay territory, and New Brunswick, as well as Gibraltar and the island of Minorca to the empire, and it also granted the right to trade in Spanish colonial ports. But George I looked with disfavor on the treaty because it had not advanced the interests of Hanover. Furthermore, some in Parliament considered the compromise treaty as too much of a compromise and thus humiliating for Britain. It was ratified by the House of Lords only because Queen Anne had created enough new peers to assure passage.

The new Hanoverian dynasty was threatened by remaining support for the Catholic Stuart dynasty. In 1715, the intransigent supporters (Jacobites) of James III rose up in Scotland. Although by the Treaty of Utrecht the king of France had officially renounced support for James, Catholic France still wanted him on the British throne. But troops loyal to George I quickly quelled the rebellion.

George II (1683–1760) became king in 1727. Like his father, he was courageous and had led troops into battle in the German states. But unlike his father, he took the time to learn English (although it remained decidedly his second language). He spoke it with a strong accent that his subjects mocked ("I hate bainting and boetry!" he once announced). He had a stiff, tedious personality, displaying impatience and a bad temper. On one occasion he bellowed, "I am sick to death of all this foolish stuff, and wish with all my heart that the devil may take all your bishops, ministers, Parliament, and the devil take the whole island—provided I can get out of it and go to Hanover!"

In 1745, the dreamy pretender Charles Edward Stuart (1720–1788) planned an invasion of England, similar to the one his father had undertaken thirty years earlier. "Bonnie Prince Charlie" landed in Scotland with a small army of enthusiasts. Adding Scottish clansmen from the Highlands to his force, he then marched into England with about 9,000 men. The threat to the throne was serious enough to give birth to the British anthem "God Save the King," which dates from this time.

But Charles Edward found in England almost no support for his cause. The young pretender hesitated a hundred miles from London and then retreated to Scotland. Many highlanders deserted his ranks as English troops ravaged their country, defeating Bonnie Prince Charlie at Culloden Moor near Inverness in April 1746. It was the last battle fought on British soil to this day. The pretender hightailed it back to France. The government ordered the execution of two Scottish peers who had thrown their support to the pretender, and forbade the wearing of kilts or tartans, symbols of the highlanders. Thereafter, a handful of Jacobites continued to celebrate Stuart birthdays. They toasted "the king over the water" living in French exile by holding their glasses of spirits over another glass filled with water.

The Prussian-Austrian Dynastic Rivalry in Central Europe

Prussia threatened Habsburg interests in Central Europe. Charles VI (ruled 1711–1740), the decent but mediocre Holy Roman emperor, had never recovered from the Habsburg loss of Spain in the War of the Spanish Succession. He remained obsessed with keeping the remaining Habsburg lands together. As Charles had no son, he spent years during his reign trying to bribe or otherwise convince the other European powers to recognize the integrity of the Habsburg inheritance upon his death. In 1713, he tried to get them to recognize the Pragmatic Sanction, which asserted the indivisibility of the Habsburg domains and recognized the right of female as well as male succession, should Charles have no sons.

When Charles VI died without a male heir, his twenty-three-year-old daughter Maria Theresa (ruled 1740–1780) assumed the Habsburg throne. While Maria Theresa could, as a woman, be archduchess of Austria and queen of Hungary and Bohemia, she was barred from becoming Holy Roman empress, thus opening up the question of imperial succession. The young queen had little money, no army, almost no bureaucracy, and bad advisers, and hence was in a poor position to defend her throne against aggressive hostile powers. France and Prussia, despite having pledged to uphold the Pragmatic Sanction, were each preparing to dismember the Habsburg Empire.

Frederick the Great, King of Prussia.

The immediate threat to Maria Theresa came from the Prussian King Frederick II (ruled 1740–1786). As a young man, Frederick had little in common with his raging father, Frederick William I. The royal son was intelligent, played the flute, enjoyed reading, preferred French to his native German, and as a boy expressed little interest in the army. At the age of eighteen, he tried to run off to England to catch a glimpse of his intended English bride. When young Frederick's scheme, planned by his best friend—and perhaps his lover—was foiled, the furious Frederick William decided to have his son executed. When dissuaded by his officials, Frederick William made the young prince watch from a prison cell the decapitation of his friend. Forced by his father to serve in the royal bureaucracy and as an army officer, Frederick became an aggressive absolute monarch.

Frederick, called "the Great" by his subjects, worked twelve hours a day lovingly overseeing minute details of army administration. His own physical courage was legendary—six times horses were killed beneath him in battle. At the same time, he eschewed an extravagant court life.

Frederick the Great's "enlightened" reforms (see Chapter 9) made Prussia a more efficient absolutist state. He improved the state bureaucracy by introducing an examination system. Talented commoners could be awarded positions in the courts of law. "Old Fritz" strengthened the Prussian economy by establishing state-operated iron- and steelworks, ordering the construction of more canals to haul goods, and encouraging the establishment of workshops in Berlin to produce textiles, glass, clocks, and porcelain. Because he ordered officials to accumulate stocks of grain in good times,

Prussia never suffered the desperate periods of dearth that occurred in France. With careful budgeting, Frederick the Great managed to pay for his wars, closely monitoring state tax revenues and expenses. He refused to undertake expensive loans, sell noble titles and privileges, or impose new levies on the peasantry, policies that were wreaking financial and social havoc in France.

Frederick continued the exemptions of the Junkers from many taxes and preserved their domination of the bureaucracy and army. He personally planned educational reforms with an eye to improving the performance of his officials. Nobles oversaw regional government, as well as the collection of taxes. But Frederick also wanted to keep the Junkers in a position of subordination to the crown. Noble army officers could not marry or travel abroad without the king's authority. He tolerated no appeal of royal decisions. In a society with a relatively rigid social structure, aristocratic and military virtues were henceforth inseparable in Prussia, a fact fraught with significance for modern German history.

Conflicts between the Great Powers

The rise of Prussia and Russia (see Chapter 7) carried European dynastic rivalries and warfare into Central Europe. The War of the Austrian Succession (1740–1748) revealed the fundamental principle in eighteenth-century power politics: the balance of power. The unchecked success of any one power seeking to expand its territory inevitably brought a combined response from the other powers to maintain a rough balance between the states. The expansion of Prussian power engendered the "Diplomatic Revolution" of 1756, when Austria and France put their long-standing rivalry aside to join forces against Prussia and Britain in the Seven Years' War (1756–1763). The long, costly war between France and Britain was truly global in extent, as both powers battled in North America (where the war became known as the French and Indian War), the Caribbean, and in India. The armies that fought in the war were larger and better drilled than ever before. At the same time, the French and British navies played a greater role in transporting troops and supplies, as well as guarding commercial vessels in the global struggle.

The War of the Austrian Succession

The War of the Austrian Succession reflected naked absolutist aggression. Frederick the Great coveted Silesia (now part of Poland), a Habsburg territory south of Prussia and then squeezed between Saxony, Poland, and Austria. With its textile, mining, and metallurgical industries, Silesia was a relatively wealthy province within the Habsburg domains. Frederick II had come to the throne in the same year as Maria Theresa and quickly sought to take advantage of the lone queen in a world of kings. Confident that the recent death of the Russian empress would preclude Russian assistance to Austria, Frederick sent his army into Silesia.

Frederick the Great was the latest in the line of aggressive Prussian kings who identified the interests of the state with a powerful army complemented by a centralized bureaucracy able to raise money through taxes. The Habsburg monarchy embodied, by contrast, the complexity of Central Europe. Austrian Germans dominated the administrative structure of the empire of many different peoples and languages. The multiplicity of privileges (particularly those of Magyar and Croatian nobles), traditions, and cultures undermined the authority, resources, and efficiency of the state. The Habsburg Empire also lacked the trading and manufacturing base of Great Britain and the Dutch Republic, foremost among the non-absolutist states, or of France or even Prussia. Mercantilists in Austria hoped that foreign trade would add to the coffers of the state, but the overwhelmingly rural Habsburg lands had little to export.

Maria Theresa's troubles were not limited to Silesia. The nobles of Bohemia, the richest Habsburg province, rebelled against Habsburg rule, offering the throne to the ruler of Bavaria, Austria's rival in southern Germany. Dependent on the good will of the provincial Diets, no Habsburg monarch could be sure of having either sufficient support from the Estates or money with which to raise an effective army.

Now, with Prussian troops occupying Silesia, Maria Theresa traveled to Hungary to ask for the support of the Hungarian Diet, which had agreed to the Pragmatic Sanction in exchange for recognition of Hungary's status as a separate kingdom within the Habsburg Empire. Dressed in mourning clothes following the recent death of an infant daughter and clutching one of her sixteen children to her, Maria Theresa convinced the Diet to provide an army of 40,000 men. The Magyar nobles held out their swords to her, shouting their promise to give "life and blood" for her. The gesture could not restore Silesia to the Habsburgs, but it may have saved the Habsburg monarchy. Aided by Hungarian troops, imperial forces put down the Bohemian revolt.

Fearing a disproportionate expansion of Prussian power in Central Europe, other states now joined an alliance against Frederick the Great. Yet, confronted by Austria, Russia, Sweden, Piedmont-Sardinia, and Denmark, states with a combined population twenty times that of Prussia, the Prussian army more than held its own, with the help of France as well as Spain and Bavaria, each hoping to help bring about the disintegration of the Habsburg Empire. France joined the anti-Austrian coalition because it coveted the Austrian Netherlands (Belgium); Spain participated because it wanted to recapture influence in Italy at Habsburg expense; and the king of Piedmont-Sardinia cooperated because he coveted Milan. Frederick, satisfied for the moment with the acquisition of Silesia, withdrew from the war in 1745 after the Peace of Dresden. But Britain was drawn into the

Aristocratic officers safely above the carnage at the Battle of Fontenoy, 1745.

conflict by its need to protect the dynastic territory of Hanover from Prussia and France. Indeed, at Dettingen in 1743, King George II became the last British monarch to fight in battle. His horse was spooked and rode off with its frightened royal rider still astride. In North America, a British force captured the French fort of Louisbourg, which guarded access to the Saint Lawrence River. France's army defeated the combined Dutch and British forces in the Battle of Fontenoy in what is now Belgium in 1745, the bloodiest battle of the century until the French Revolution. Fifteen thousand soldiers were dead or wounded among the 95,000 soldiers who fought at Fontenoy. In 1748, the inconclusive Treaty of Aix-la-Chapelle ended the War of the Austrian Succession (see Map 11.1). French forces withdrew from the Austrian Netherlands in return for the English abandoning the captured fort of Louisbourg. The northern Italian city of Parma passed to a branch of the Spanish Bourbons, and Piedmont-Sardinia absorbed parts of the duchy of Milan.

The Seven Years' War

The Seven Years' War (1756–1763) was remarkable for several reasons. First, it was arguably the first truly global conflict. The commercial interests of France and Britain clashed in North America (where the two powers claimed large reaches of the American interior as far as the Mississippi River

MAP 11.1 THE WAR OF THE AUSTRIAN SUCCESSION, 1740–1748   Major battles and territorial changes at the end of the war.

and had been at war since 1754), the Caribbean, and India (see Map 11.2). Second, for the first time we can speak of a war not just of kings but self-consciously of nations, at least in the cases of Britain and France. Both states underwent a surge of patriotic enthusiasm, marked, for example, in the case of France by calls for "patriotic gifts" to support the war. In Britain, the sense of being "Briton" developed among all classes, accentuated by an overwhelmingly popular war against Catholic France. In both countries there were calls for the more efficient management of the war, seen as part of pursuing national interests, arguably for the first time.

    Prussia's gains in the War of the Austrian Succession engendered the Diplomatic Revolution of 1756. France had previously undertaken alliances with Prussia and the Ottoman Empire to counter the threat of Austrian

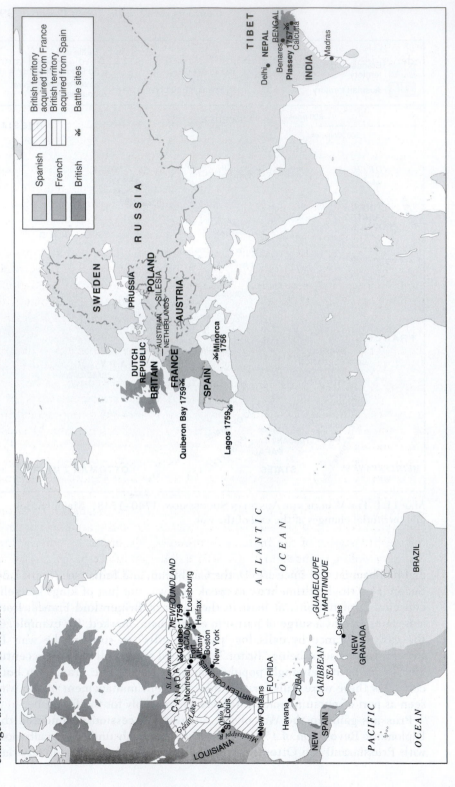

MAP 11.2 THE SEVEN YEARS' WAR, 1756–1763 Areas of conflict, including battle sites, during the Seven Years' War, as well as territorial changes at the end of the war.

and Russian expansion and was thus determined that Poland survive as an independent state. The Diplomatic Revolution of 1756 now ended more than a century of intermittent warfare between France and the Austrian Habsburgs. Alarmed by the expansion of Prussian power, Austria now allied with France, and then Russia, with the goal of recapturing Silesia. The cost of France's support would be its future annexation of the Austrian Netherlands and Austrian neutrality in the war between Britain and France (which in 1756 had been going on in North America for two years). Frederick the Great, determined to keep Silesia, turned to Britain, France's enemy. To France and Russia, Britain's sudden and shocking alliance with Prussia seemed a betrayal, even as France reversed its century-old opposition to Habsburg interests. Having changed partners, the great powers went to war again.

In 1757, Frederick defeated a large French army and then a Habsburg force. But a Russian army attacked from the north, occupying Berlin, while more Austrian troops marched on Prussia from the south. Prussia's situation seemed desperate, leading the king to compare his state to "a man with many wounds who has lost so much blood that he is on the point of death." But as luck would have it, Peter III became tsar of Russia in 1762, succeeding Empress Elizabeth, Frederick's determined enemy. The new tsar admired the Prussian king and called the Russian troops home. At the cost of perhaps 300,000 soldiers, Prussia preserved its full independence.

The rivalry between the European powers in India took the shape of a struggle between the British and French East India Companies against the background of intrigues and warfare among Indian rulers. The Mughals had conquered most of the subcontinent in the seventeenth century, but along the southern coast, where Mughal control was limited, the European trading network had continued to expand. In the meantime, India became the largest producer of textiles in the world, threatening the production of English cloth. The Mughal Empire collapsed during the first half of the eighteenth century following invasions from Iran and Afghanistan. Bengal, the wealthiest part of the Indian subcontinent, became autonomous. The resulting political chaos in the 1740s aided the subjection of India by Britain, even if in 1750 there were only about 5,000 British residents (and 20,000 soldiers) in the subcontinent.

Robert Clive (1725–1774), the son of a provincial gentleman and lawyer, led troops of the East India Company and Indian mercenaries into Bengal. There the prince preferred French to British traders and in 1757 had incarcerated more than a hundred British subjects in a room so small and stuffy that most of them died—the "Black Hole of Calcutta." That same year, Clive's force defeated the prince's army at Plassey, north of Calcutta. After putting a pliant puppet on the Bengali throne, Clive continued to use British troops to further not only the interests of the British East India Company, but himself as well. He became very rich through imperial acquisitions and secured a British peerage. By 1761, the stage was set for

General Wolfe's forces scale the heights of the Plains of Abraham in Quebec.

British control of most of the Indian subcontinent, with the British navy preventing French traders and soldiers from receiving sufficient supplies. The East India Company's great successes opened up new trade between Britain, India, and South China, a vast new market.

In what became Canada, there was much more at stake because Britain and France were fighting for control of a vast territory. In this struggle, France had a decided disadvantage. Even after more than a hundred years as a colony, at mid-century "New France" had a French population of only about 80,000 people, for the most part clustered in three towns along the St. Lawrence River—Montreal, Quebec, and Trois-Rivières. By contrast, the thirteen British colonies already had more than 2 million residents. British incursions into their territory led Native Americans to ally informally with the French. During the French and Indian War (1754–1763), British troops forced over 10,000 French-speaking Acadians living in Nova Scotia and New Brunswick to emigrate. Many of them settled in the French colony of New Orleans, where the word "Cajun" emerged as a corruption of the French "*acadien*."

The British navy accentuated its advantage on the seas by seizing 300 French merchant ships and capturing 8,000 sailors even before hostilities formally began. Despite the capture by French troops of several forts in the Great Lakes region, British ships reduced French reinforcements and supplies to a trickle, also besting a French fleet at Quiberon Bay off the coast of Brittany in 1759.

In 1759, General James Wolfe (1727–1759) led an audacious, successful British attack on the French near Quebec, his forces climbing up the cliffs from the St. Lawrence River to surprise their enemy. British forces captured Fort Duquesne in 1758, driving the French from the Ohio River Valley, and in 1760 took Montreal. In the Caribbean, the British picked off French islands and their small garrisons one by one.

War left all the combatants exhausted. The British national debt had doubled. The French monarchy entered a period of financial crisis. The Seven Years' War ended the domination of France on the continent and cleared the way for the expansion of the British Empire. By the Treaty of Paris of 1763, Austria recognized Prussia's absorption of Silesia in 1740 in exchange for Saxony's retention of independence. The Southern Netherlands, however, remained an Austrian Habsburg territory. The settlement in North America and the Caribbean was much more far-reaching. Canada became British. France retained fishing rights on the Grand Banks off Newfoundland, but accepted British claims to territory east of the Mississippi River, and those of Spain to all territory west of the Mississippi. This enormous western region, known as the Louisiana Territory, stretched from the almost tropical climate of New Orleans to the freezing plains of central Canada. France retained the Caribbean islands of Martinique and Guadeloupe, only because English colonists feared competition from sugar produced on those islands if they became British. Spain ceded Florida to Britain (though only, as it turned out, until 1783).

Britain then tried to mend fences in Europe, where the balance of power had been preserved. However, Austrian troops occupied Bavaria, leading to the brief War of Bavarian Succession (1778–1779). The resistance of Prussia and Saxony foiled the Habsburg plan. Like Franco-British enmity, Austro-Prussian rivalry for domination of German-speaking Central Europe continued unabated.

Armies and Their Tactics in the Eighteenth Century

Long after monarchs succeeded in putting an end to private noble armies, warfare remained part of noble culture. Military schools in France, Russia, and several German states trained the sons of nobles in the skills of war. In Prussia, Frederick William I believed that any attempt to allow commoners to become officers would be "the first step toward the decline and fall of the army." Noble officers had much more in common with the officers of the enemy than with their own troops, who were conscripted or impressed from the lower classes. Indeed, the Habsburgs often appointed foreign nobles as officers in its army. Officers captured during a war were treated to a nice glass of wine and a good meal, and then exchanged for their own officers who had fallen into enemy hands. War was fought over territory. In some ways, it seemed like a game of chess played between aristocrats in a manor house parlor. It is said that the French officers at the Battle of Fontenoy in 1745 gallantly shouted to their British counterparts, "Fire first, *messieurs les anglais!*" before the slaughter began.

Recruitment practices differed in the various European states. The Prussian army's military recruitment system was the most comprehensive. Each of its regiments was assigned a district from which to draw recruits. In France, military recruitment was placed directly under the control of the state bureaucracy, which relieved officers of the responsibility for filling a quota of recruits. In Russia, each commune (*mir*) had to provide at least one soldier. Throughout Europe, certain categories of the population were exempt from service, including prosperous farmers, the servants of French nobles, Russian merchants, and, in some countries, men with families. England was alone among the major powers in not having a standing army, at least in principle.

Yet mercenaries still sometimes provided the bulk of eighteenth-century European armies, the notable exception being France. Military service provided those who joined up with regular meals, shelter, and adventure. Swiss guards served the French royal family as well as the popes in Rome, and their countrymen fought with a variety of armies. The Dutch army included a brigade of Scottish highlanders. Military service could still provide respectability. Criminals and other men with something unpleasant in their past often turned up as soldiers. Non-military officials, servants, wives, children, and prostitutes accompanied armies: "We are a marching brothel," assessed one British commander.

Desertion remained widespread, affecting up to 35 percent of an army, despite threats of mutilation for those caught leaving. During the Seven Years' War, about 62,000 soldiers deserted the Habsburg army, 70,000 left the army of France behind, and 80,000 Russian soldiers disappeared into the night. Tightly packed formations served to discourage desertions, as they were intended to do, because soldiers were under more constant control. Harsh, even brutal, discipline in army camps complemented that in the field. Frederick the Great was not alone in believing that "[the soldier] must be more afraid of his officers than of the dangers to which he is exposed." Although strategies for supplying troops improved during the century, armies rarely moved far from their supply camps. The lack of commitment and unreliability of mercenary and levied troops often helped end fighting.

Military technology had evolved slowly since the invention of gunpowder. In the seventeenth century, the soldier wielding a bayonet, a musket topped with a razor-sharp knife, had pushed the pike man, a foot soldier armed with only a spear-like weapon, off the battlefield. Other significant changes in warfare in the seventeenth century included improved flintlock muskets, with cartridges and iron ramrods that permitted riflemen to fire three times per minute and increased their range. Handheld firearms became practical weapons for the first time. Artillery pieces were also lighter and more mobile, with somewhat greater range. The training of artillery officers improved.

Soldiers in the eighteenth century were now far better trained and disciplined than in the previous century; armies were far larger than ever before. The discipline and efficiency of troops in formation won or lost battles. Muskets, inaccurate beyond a short distance, were fired in deadly volleys by rows of soldiers taking turns reloading. Cavalry charges, which generally took place on the flanks of battle with the goal of neutralizing the enemy's cavalry, usually were over quickly.

New tactics had brought greater maneuverability in the sixteenth and seventeenth centuries, including linear formations involving coordinated movements that required well-trained and disciplined troops. In the eighteenth century, even greater troop mobility was achieved by combining line and column formations in a "mixed order." Moreover, the British and Prussian armies were the first to create a light infantry division that could engage the enemy more rapidly, often fighting with bayonets. Yet defense still dominated in battle, as symbolized by the impregnable fortresses along the northern frontier of France built in the late seventeenth century. Line formations were more conducive to defense than offense.

Following the unrestrained carnage of the Thirty Years' War (1618–1648), warfare became somewhat more civilized, or at least somewhat more predictable, with fewer civilian casualties. Prisoners of war, even commoners, were kept in relatively decent conditions and were sometimes exchanged for their counterparts. The development of logistical support and professionalized, well-drilled armies meant that soldiers no longer had to live off the land. The goals of warfare were now generally restrained by traditions of monarchical and aristocratic civility. Once victory was achieved, there seemed no reason to pursue one's enemy to finish him off. Civilians were now generally spared in times of war.

Navies

British statesmen knew that to maintain superiority over France on the seas, their enemy had to be kept busy on the continent, whether by direct military operations or by large subsidies paid to France's enemies among the German states. The Royal Navy had begun to grow in size during the second half of the seventeenth century. As its role in protecting commerce increased, it expanded further, from 105 ships in 1750 to 195 in 1790, while the smaller French navy increased only modestly in size to 81 warships, 9 more than those of the Spanish navy.

Building on earlier improvements in sails, rigging, charts, and navigational techniques, the size and quality of ships improved. Shipbuilding drew on scientific assistance from experts in mathematics and navigation. The British first added copper to hulls, which made their ships sturdier. Short-barreled cannon of greater caliber proved deadly in close combat.

Navies were also beset by problems of desertion, at least when ships were in port. Almost one-fourth of the men who joined the British navy between 1776 and 1780 deserted—many of whom had been dragged to the docks by press-gangs. Shipboard disease killed many sailors, despite the use of lemon juice to counter scurvy, an illness caused by a vitamin C deficiency.

As the British naval supremacy established the basis for the expansion of commerce and empire, there were few decisive naval confrontations in the eighteenth century. "Do you know what a naval battle is?" asked a French minister. "The fleets maneuver, come to grips, fire a few shots, and then each retreats . . . and the sea remains as salty as it was before." The cost of full-fledged battles seemed too high; ships were enormously expensive to build and maintain. Fifteen times more British sailors died of disease between 1774 and 1780 than succumbed to battle wounds.

POLITICAL CHANGE IN GREAT BRITAIN

In England, the Glorious Revolution of 1688 had put an end to fifty years of social and political turmoil. The Bill of Rights of 1689 guaranteed Parliament's right to approve taxation and prohibited the monarch from suspending or dispensing with laws. Parliament also maintained control of military funding and the size of the army. Only with the consent of Parliament could a standing army be raised in peacetime (even though this in itself was technically unconstitutional and the House of Commons had to annually approve funding). Thus, the political struggles of the seventeenth century had demonstrated that the king had to work with Parliament in governing the nation. In turn, the state served as a guarantor of rights of property and patronage. The rights of Parliament and the elective nature of the House of Commons, even if based on an extremely narrow electoral franchise, distinguished British political life from that of its continental rivals.

The period of "aristocratic consensus" that followed the Glorious Revolution was not as free from political contention as the term suggests. But it brought major changes in British political life. The interests of wealthy property owners were represented in the House of Commons, which gradually became a far more important political forum than the House of Lords, which only represented peers. It also became more difficult for the king to manage the House of Commons.

Political differences between Tories and Whigs (see Chapter 6) became more consistent. The former were now clearly identified with the prerogatives of the throne, the latter with the rights of Parliament. Whigs believed that the role of Parliament was to defend liberty, property, and the rule of law and thereby preserve the British constitution against possible abuses of power by the throne. In the words of the Irish-born political theorist Edmund Burke (1729–1797), the British "mixed constitution" (which balanced the institutions of monarchy, the House of Lords, and the House of Commons), stood as an "isthmus between arbitrary power and anarchy." During this period, there emerged a sense that opposition within Parliament to government policies was an intrinsic part of a political process in which competing interests were struggling for primacy. Moreover, during the eighteenth century, political life began to spill beyond the narrow confines of the British political elite as ordinary people demanded a voice in political life with increasing insistence. In Britain's North American colonies, a similar and in some ways parallel struggle for liberty began, leading to the American War of Independence (1775–1782).

Expanding Central Government in Britain

Britain was justly renowned for its political preoccupation with liberty. An essential part of eighteenth-century British identity included the victory of Parliament during the English Civil War in the mid-seventeenth century in defense of constitutional monarchy. Yet, as with the continental powers France, Spain, Austria, and Russia, in non-absolutist Great Britain, too, the powers of central government expanded, creating what has been called a "British version of the fiscal-military state, complete with large armies and navies, industrious administrators, high taxes and huge debts." By the end of the eighteenth century, the British state had perhaps ten times more revenues than a century earlier. At the same time, the increasingly global nature of trade and warfare made greater demands on the state's administrative abilities. The growth, greater centralization, professionalization, and efficiency of military and civilian administration permitted Britain to replace France as the strongest power on the globe. British landed, financial, commercial, and manufacturing interests followed British military engagements across the globe with rapt attention. Britain's financial community, centered in what would become called "The City"—London's financial district—became ever more tied to and financially dependent on Britain's wars in Europe and abroad. The British Empire became closely linked not only to British prosperity but also identity.

Between 1680 and 1780, Britain built and consolidated its empire. The British army and navy tripled in size. The power and reach of the treasury also increased, along with its capacity to raise money for foreign wars and imperial conquest. As the economy grew rapidly, the British state raised and efficiently collected taxes, including land taxes, excise taxes (on commodities), and customs taxes, which provided an increasing share of revenue. The government borrowed as never before, increasing the national debt. Britain's bureaucracy also grew in size and complexity. Government officials became more professional, technical expertise more important, and government offices more clearly defined. Civil service posts offered educated men chances for social advancement.

The British government, like its continental rivals, continued to confront the problem of paying off the massive national debt amassed by loans that financed dynastic and trade wars. The government spent more than three-quarters of its expenditures on the army, navy, or paying back debts from previous wars. In 1719, the government had awarded the South Sea

Company the right to take over the national debt. The South Sea Company had been founded in 1711. Two years later, the government had awarded it a monopoly over the slave trade with Latin America and favorable conditions for European trade. But because of the intermittent fighting with Spain during the War of the Spanish Succession, any profits from such trade seemed in the distant future. Needing a rapid infusion of capital, the directors of the company offered stock for sale on attractive terms. They bribed some potential purchasers and developed ties with high government officials.

With the help of unscrupulous investors, many of whom were holders of part of the national debt who wanted to get their money back, the company converted the debt owed them by the state into company shares. The directors parlayed the price of the stock higher. The scam worked as long as there were enough investors whose funds could be used to pay dividends to those who had bought shares earlier. But the profits were all based on the sale of the stock rather than on real commercial gains.

A fever of speculation seized England. Smaller companies started up overnight, most of them insolvent or strangely organized, such as one literally limited to women dressed in calico. One joint-stock company (made up of shareholders who would divide profits according to the amount of their investments) was created for "a purpose to be announced." The speculative craze ended with a jolt in 1720. With no gains of any kind forthcoming, the "South Sea Bubble" burst in September of that year. It was the

1720 cartoon showing how speculation caused shares in the South Sea Company to rise, which would eventually lead to the South Sea Bubble.

first great financial crash (and coincided with the bursting of smaller speculative "bubbles" in Amsterdam and Paris).

The financial scandal hung over political life when Robert Walpole
(1676–1745) became chancellor of the exchequer in 1721, a post he
would hold for more than twenty years. The son of a gentry landowner of
relatively modest means, the short, ruddy-cheeked Walpole was energetic
and ambitious, making himself quite rich at state expense. In office, he
was determined to restore political confidence to Britain. Parliament
passed a law that allowed only companies chartered by the government to
sell stock shares to the public. Walpole created a sinking fund (intended to
retire the debt by paying off, or "sinking," part of it each year). This helped
restore confidence. George II trusted Walpole's judgment, and the latter
survived the wrath of some members of Parliament (MPs) who disliked his
unpopular financial reforms, including greater taxes on imports and on
salt, and his goal of keeping Britain out of war.

Walpole perfected the system of political patronage, virtually managing
the House of Commons and making the Anglican Church part of a state
structure that would last more than a century. He placed MPs loyal to
him—"placemen"—in well-paying governmental positions, some of which
were veritable sinecures. In return, they voted with the government. On the
local level, the bigger fish became county lord-lieutenants and the smaller
fry justices of the peace. One tombstone epitaph flaunted the harvest of political patronage reaped by a well-connected lady lying therein: "By means
of her alliance with the illustrious family of Stanhope, she had the merit to
obtain for her husband and children twelve appointments in church and
state," not a bad haul. Walpole also worked to isolate Jacobites, smoothing
the Hanoverian succession to the British throne.

However, Walpole's support in Parliament eventually began to crumble.
His attempt to extend the excise tax to wine and tobacco failed in 1733,
after generating riots. William Pitt the Elder (1708–1778) led a coalition
of "boy patriots" against Walpole. Specifically, they objected to his inaction
against Spain, whose ships were harassing British ships in the Atlantic.
After being forced by public outcry to declare war on Spain in 1739—the
War of Jenkins's Ear—Walpole resigned two years later.

The duke of Newcastle (Thomas Pelham-Holles, 1693–1768), whose
notorious incoherence led him to be known as "Hubble-Bubble," succeeded
Walpole and ably manipulated the patronage of his position. Then Pitt
became prime minister. The "Great Commoner" Pitt was a lonely, unstable
man who alternated between feverish excitement and dark depression. He
was demagogic, arrogant, and ruthless, commanding respect through fear.

The Role of the House of Commons

The British monarch could declare war or make peace, call or dissolve
Parliament, and appoint whomever he or she wanted to serve as cabinet

minister, officer, bishop, general, or admiral. The cabinet and government officials carried out the functions of state. But they did so against the backdrop of ongoing practical compromises between Parliament and the monarch.

During the early decades of the eighteenth century, the House of Commons gradually emerged as an epicenter of political life. Unlike the House of Lords, all of whose members were nobles, members of the House of Commons were elected by Britain's narrow electoral franchise based on landed wealth. Although still dominated by "gentle," or landed, interests, the number of merchants elected to the Commons increased, for families that had made fortunes in business, whether they were titled nobles, nontitled gentry, or commoners, invested their money in land. Wealthy MPs could easily control blocs of votes in their countries through patronage. In 1776, only 5,700 men in Britain elected half of the members of Commons, most of whose members were routinely reelected every seven years. In only three boroughs did more than 4,000 men have the right to vote, and in several others, fewer than 15 men could cast ballots. Thus, one lord confidently assured his son in 1754, "Your seat in the new Parliament is at last absolutely secured and that without opposition or the least necessity of your personal trouble or appearance." Some MPs were returned from "rotten" and "pocket" boroughs. Rotten boroughs ranged from the infamous "Old Sarum," which had no inhabitants but two representatives in Commons, and another that had been under water for centuries, to those with several hundred voters almost as easily managed. Pocket boroughs were in the pocket of the MP because his election was uncontested.

Some of England's growing industrial towns were not represented in Parliament. Many urban elites no longer bought the idea that their interests were "virtually represented" by MPs from districts represented in the House of Commons. Furthermore, emerging political discontent reflected alarm that the role of the House of Commons as the defender of the constitution against possible tyrannical abuse was being compromised by institutionalized patronage and outright corruption, symbolized by rotten and pocket boroughs.

The Development of Party Politics in the 1760s: Whigs and Tories

Whigs and Tories had governed in reasonable harmony during the Robert Walpole era. But after Walpole, many Whigs came to believe that ministers ought to be acceptable to Parliament as well as to the king. In contrast, Tories traditionally took the view that the prerogatives of king and Church had to be maintained at all costs.

After coming to the throne in 1760, George III gave the impression that he intended to rule without Parliament. When the king refused to declare war on Spain in 1761 during the Seven Years' War, Pitt resigned as prime minister. Subsequently, the king appointed his former tutor, the aristocratic, aloof Scotsman John Stuart, the earl of Bute (1713–1792), as secretary of state and then as prime minister. But Bute was an unpopular choice because he was not an MP, had little political experience and even less influence, and did not want Britain to undertake hostilities against Spain.

The king's appointment of his "dearest friend" seemed to Whigs to violate the unwritten agreement that the king act with Parliament's consent. Determined opposition merely served to strengthen the king's resolve. The press castigated Bute, and crowds in the street howled against him. Rumor insisted that he owed his controversial appointment to having been the lover of the king's mother. On the verge of a nervous breakdown, Bute resigned in 1763.

Bute's appointment, raising the question of ministerial responsibility, divided Commons along ideological lines. George III turned against the Whig country gentlemen who no longer could be counted upon to support him on all matters. The king insisted on the monarchy's independence and particularly on his right to choose whomever he wished as minister.

MPs representing the interests of the "country gentlemen" began to use the term "party," but without the trappings of formal organization that would come late in the next century. Although they traditionally upheld the rights of Parliament, Whigs, to be sure, remained loyal to the throne, even if King George accused them of being otherwise. While the issues dividing Tories and Whigs remained in some ways the same as those that had characterized the Walpole period, or even the English Civil War, the emerging notion of political parties was probably of more lasting significance than the political groupings themselves.

The term "party" had existed since the time of the Glorious Revolution of 1688; it had the sense of a group of people sharing a belief on a specific matter of political controversy. It had been somewhat synonymous with "faction," which since the 1670s had the negative connotation of a cabal of individuals working for their own interests. With the exception of the Jacobite Tories, however, the differences between Whigs and Tories were vague and uncertain during the reign of the first two Georges. George III's seeming determination to create a government above parties revived the solidarity of the old Whigs. The idea developed that a party of parliamentary opposition formed an essential part of the parliamentary system of representation.

George III insisted that it was his duty to defeat the forces of "faction." Burke, for one, rejected the king's efforts to discredit the concept of "party." In *Thoughts on the Cause of the Present Discontents* (1770), he defined a party as "a body of men united for promoting by their joint endeavors *the national interest* upon some particular principle in which they are all agreed." He believed that political parties stood as the basis of representative government and therefore of political order. A newspaper article in 1770 went even further: "Opposition, in parliament, to the measures of government, is so far from being in itself an evil, that it has been often productive of good to the state." Parties alone could ensure the preservation "of responsible government," specifically, the notion that ministers ought to be acceptable to Parliament. This concept of a loyal parliamentary opposition did not exist in France or anywhere else on the continent. Nor, for that matter, did it exist in all constituencies in Britain; in many places, politics, dominated by family ties and outright patronage, went on as before.

George III could count on about a third of the members of Commons for unconditional support, at least partially because they held court-appointed posts. Unfailing voters for "court" became increasingly known as Tories, particularly to the Whig opposition. Supporters of the government rejected the term, as they did all labels, but at the same time they lent credence to the concept by cohesively defending a patriarchal society based on the prerogatives of monarchy, aristocracy, and the Anglican Church.

In 1766, George III turned to Pitt, who was immensely popular, again to serve as prime minister; he hoped to split the Whigs, because the "Great Commoner" was alienated from aristocratic Whigs. Pitt lost support even among his political friends by accepting a peerage, becoming duke of Chatham. Vigorous debates among Whigs, principally between the imperious Pitt and the duke of Newcastle and his followers, however, did not diminish the emerging notion of "party" that most Whigs now accepted. For Whigs, the most significant issue remained the extent to which the king could act without the support of Parliament.

The Rise of British Nationalism

Although king and Parliament had been bitterly divided during the crises that led to the English Civil War and the Glorious Revolution, they were thereafter unified in the quest for British commercial and international predominance. During the eighteenth century, a strong sense of nationalism developed in Great Britain. This included pride in the nation's high degree of freedom and reverence for Parliament as the Protestant institution that had turned back the threat of Catholicism and prevented absolute rule.

The fear of Catholicism, endemic in England since the Reformation, fired British nationalism. Faced with the threat of French invasion during the Anglo-French wars, British patriots across the social spectrum embraced the British Isles as the chosen land of God. They boasted of Britain's prosperity and social stability while belittling France and Spain, Catholic powers.

William Pitt the Elder was an empire builder. Believing that the throne's Hanoverian interests were dominating foreign policy, and having made his reputation accusing Walpole of indifference to British interests abroad, Pitt turned his attention to expanding the colonies. "Who will laugh at sugar, now?" he thundered in 1759 to nobles who had scorned colonial trade. Horace Walpole (1717–1797), Robert Walpole's youngest son, a novelist and the beneficiary of lucrative posts that left him plenty of time to write, was among the few who had some doubts about all of this. "No man ever went to the East Indies with good intentions," the younger Walpole said, adding sarcastically that "it really looks as if we intended to finish the conquest of the world during the next campaign."

The lure of commercial profit and empire thus helped define British nationalism. As we have seen, the financial community of investors in London closely followed not only the vicissitudes of the economy but the ups and downs of British warfare. A good many financiers had, after all, loaned money to their state and therefore eagerly watched what was done with it. Foreign and colonial trade often depended on naval protection, further linking their interests to the Union Jack, the flag of Great Britain. The state itself depended on expanding commercial activity for tax revenue. Representatives of economic interest groups and lobbies made contacts in the London financial community and in government circles to put forward their views, for example, on excise and customs taxes. New patriotic societies, some of them drawing ordinary people into the wave of nationalist enthusiasm, sprang up.

The generally harmonious relationship between the landed elite and the commercial community was a source of social and political stability and of rising British nationalism. They joined together in the pursuit of empire. Nobles and gentry benefited from the expansion of state activity, diversifying their investments with loans to the crown. Unlike the continental powers, in Britain all subjects paid taxes. This afforded all social groups the sense of being Britons. At the same time (in contrast to the case in France), improved communications and the development of a national market aided the process of national integration in Britain.

Their commitment to the nation also enabled the British elite, proud of their freedoms and their country's more decentralized form of government, to accept a stronger state apparatus without complaining about infringements on their liberty. Thus, they did not feel the need for constitutional guarantees (based upon equality before the law) against arbitrary tyranny. The stronger state did not diminish the status of British landowners, and it in no way infringed on their personal freedoms within civil society.

Anglo-Irish, Scottish, and Welsh landowners became more integrated into a national British elite, as the increasing intermarriage among these groups indicated. Many Scots, though hardly all, began to see themselves as British, just as fewer English people considered Scots or Welsh to be outsiders who were potentially disloyal to the crown, views they continued to hold, however, of the Catholic Irish. The prerogatives of Parliament notwithstanding, the British monarchy and its army and navy became increasingly revered and celebrated as a rallying point for the nation.

CHALLENGES TO ESTABLISHED AUTHORITY

In the 1760s and 1770s, movements for reform emerged in several countries. In Britain, "liberty" became the watchword of political opposition to the government. In a parallel struggle on the other side of the Atlantic Ocean, the American colonists of Britain's thirteen colonies demanded "no taxation without representation," and then, when rebuffed, these "Patriots" rebelled against British rule in the War of American Independence. Elsewhere, similar reform movements on the European continent sought to reduce absolute rule (as in Denmark), prevent it from lapsing into despotism (as in France), or wanted to prevent the imposition of a stronger centralized authority (as in the Dutch Republic). Other movements for reform challenged what seemed to be unwarranted privileges, again most notably in France. In every Western country, more information about political events in other states was available through newspapers and gazettes, as well as from merchants, travelers, and diplomats. In Britain and parts of Western Europe, political clubs also reflected greater preoccupation with politics. These reform movements, then, influenced each other, however indirectly.

British Radicals

In the 1760s in Britain, ordinary people demanded electoral reform, and some even called for universal male suffrage. Reformers asked that constituencies be redrawn so that rapidly growing industrial regions in the north of England be appropriately represented in Parliament, and that London, which was grossly underrepresented, elect more MPs. Moreover, shouts for more liberties came from ordinary people without the right to vote.

John Wilkes (1727–1797), the son of a successful London malt distiller, was an MP of modest means and a Protestant Dissenter. Charming, witty, and reckless, Wilkes leapt into the public eye in 1763 with the publication of his newspaper, the *North Briton*. Issue number 45 attacked the government—and the king himself directly—for signing the compromise Treaty of Paris with France that year, ending the Seven Years' War. The king ordered "that Devil Wilkes, a trumpet of sedition," arrested for libel. Wilkes announced that he considered his arrest a blow against liberty and the constitution by the unjust, arbitrary power of government; it was "a question of such importance," as he declared at his trial, "as to determine at once, whether English Liberty be a reality or a shadow." The court freed Wilkes after a week in jail on the basis of parliamentary immunity. Wilkes triumphantly boasted that his fate was tied to "that of the middling and inferior set of people" in Britain.

Fearing prosecution for pornography—the government had dug up a bawdy old poem he had written—since the House of Commons had lifted parliamentary immunity, Wilkes left for France in 1764. Upon his return four years later, he was arrested, tried, and convicted, and then freed after thousands of people demonstrated on his behalf. Wilkes then stood for election in Middlesex, the county making up most of metropolitan London north of the Thames and outside of "The City." With the support of merchants and small manufacturers wealthy enough to be eligible to vote, Wilkes was reelected to Parliament. Four times he was elected, and four times Parliament refused to seat him because of his previous conviction. Cloaking himself in a patriot's garb, he became a rallying symbol for the campaign for the rights of the unrepresented in a time of economic hardship, grain riots, and work stoppages.

The phrase "Wilkes and Liberty" echoed in speeches, conversation, and song. In 1769, the Society of the Supporters of the Bill of Rights invoked the name of Wilkes as it called for the government to "restore the constitution." The number 45—the libelous issue of the *North Briton*—became a rallying cry. Wilkes's rather misshapen face appeared on posters, handbills, verses, cartoons, tea mugs, and dinner plates. He was elected sheriff of London in 1771 and even lord mayor three years later, though he was not allowed to occupy either position.

More "respectable" reformers now began to demand greater freedom of the press, specifically a redefinition of libel laws, so that the government could be criticized, and the right to publish parliamentary debates. They further demanded that Parliament meet each year and that MPs be required to live in the districts they represented. However, most Whigs now

(*Left*) John Wilkes, in an etching by William Hogarth. (*Right*) Wilkes's supporters take to the streets.

disassociated themselves clearly from Wilkes, in part because of his rather unsavory reputation and identification in upper-class eyes with "the mob." They were wary of demonstrations for universal male suffrage. Few Whigs were willing to go beyond insisting on the principle of ministerial responsibility.

Literary and "philosophical" societies, which had sprung up in most large towns, facilitated the emergence of an even wider political culture than that which had developed during the political crises of the seventeenth century. Inns and coffeehouses added special reading rooms to accommodate their clientele. By 1760, London printing presses, the number of which had increased from seventy-five in 1724 to about two hundred at the time of Wilkes's first arrest, churned out eighty-nine newspapers, four of which were dailies. Another thirty-five newspapers were published outside London. By 1790, there were fourteen daily London newspapers, and the number of provincial papers had multiplied by four times. Political pamphlets, handbills, and caricatures inundated the capital and the larger provincial towns. By the 1760s, artists stopped omitting the names of the targets of their satirical wit. Like its Whig opponents and the extra-parliamentary radicals, the government found itself obliged to utilize newspapers, pamphlets, brochures, and handbills to argue its case before public opinion.

American Revolutionaries

During the 1760s, another challenge to the British crown was smoldering far across the Atlantic Ocean in North America. The thirteen American colonies, many times the size of England, had become ever more difficult for the British government to administer. The population of the colonies, which took in 20 percent of British exports and supplied 30 percent of its imports, had grown by tenfold in just seventy years, from about 250,000 in 1700 to more than 2.5 million in 1775, compared to about 6.4 million people in England at the same time. Those arriving in the colonies found a land of opportunity. Many were able to purchase land that would have been beyond their means at home. Artisans and even common laborers commanded relatively high wages because of the shortage of labor in the colonies.

Over the decades in the eighteenth century, the residents of the colonies had developed a sense of living in a British-American society with its own distinct culture. The North American colonies had developed without the kind of centralized organization for economic exploitation and determination to conquer that had characterized the Spanish Empire. The English settlement colonies had been founded in the quest for trade and economic opportunity, as well as religious freedom, as in the case of Massachusetts Puritans, and religious toleration, as in the case of Maryland Catholics. Thus, the colonies' insistence on the liberty of "freeborn Englishmen" (and, after 1707, British subjects) was easily transferred into a demand for a more encompassing liberty that included rejection of the idea that British sovereignty could not be challenged. Merchants, lawyers, and wealthy landowners, like the Virginians George Washington (1732–1799) and Thomas Jefferson (1743–1826), who stood on top of the social hierarchy, led the colonists. They resented the continued presence of the British army and the attempt of British officers to try to impose on colonial forces the same standards of discipline that applied in Britain. The American colonists believed that they had the right to resist unjust laws in the name of liberty.

The quest of George Grenville (1712–1770), who had succeeded Pitt in 1763 as prime minister, for supplementary revenue aggravated the strained relations between the colonists and the mother country. In 1765, Parliament passed the Stamp Act, which forced Americans to purchase stamps for virtually anything printed. A year later, Benjamin Franklin (1706–1790) of Philadelphia made the colonists' case to the House of Commons. He argued that the act represented the unfair domination of England over another part of the empire. The House of Commons repealed the Stamp Act, but the government then initiated other taxes. Furthermore, Parliament proclaimed a Declaratory Act in 1766, which asserted its right to tax the colonies as it pleased. A year later, the Townshend Acts levied duties on colonial imports of paper, tea, and other products.

Some British Whigs began to identify themselves with the colonists, who took the name Whigs themselves, claiming that corruption was threatening Britain's constitutional balance between monarchy and Parliament. They saw the two movements as parallel struggles for freedom. For radicals in Britain, rotten boroughs symbolized the threat to liberty; for the American colonists, as expressed by John Adams, "liberty can no more exist without virtue and independence than the body can live and move without a soul." The colonists' claim that they were being taxed without having the right to representation played nicely into the hands of political radicals in Britain. American political pamphlets and brochures found an eager audience among British merchants, manufacturers, artisans, and others eager for representation in Parliament. Colonists lobbied in Britain, claiming that "the cause of America is the common cause of the realm . . . both countries have the same complaint, and therefore claim the same friends."

The British government was at first divided and uncertain in the face of an upsurge of demonstrations at home and agitation in the colonies. Popular protest quickly revealed the limits of the hold Britain had on its thirteen American colonies. In March 1770 in Boston, British soldiers fired on a crowd that was vociferously protesting the quartering of British troops in that city. The "Boston Massacre," which took five lives, outraged colonists. That year, George III appointed Frederick Lord North (1732–1792) as prime minister. North, an amiable, sensible man who got along well with the king, was skilled at putting together political coalitions and was a brilliant debater in the House of Commons. He sponsored the Tea Act of 1773. North hoped to aid the East India Company by allowing the company to

Paul Revere's depiction of the Boston Massacre.

ship a surplus of tea to the colonies, with the British government collecting its tariff when the tea arrived in American ports. The move would reduce the price colonists paid for tea but would maintain the British government's assertion that it could tax goods imported into the colonies. It would also threaten the interests of American smuggling, a widespread money-making operation.

On December 16, 1773, colonists dressed as Native Americans forced their way aboard British merchant ships docked in Boston and dumped the cargo of tea into the harbor. Parliament responded to the Boston Tea Party by passing the "Intolerable Acts," which announced that the port of Boston be blocked until the colonists had reimbursed the merchants and government for the tea dumped into the harbor. In September 1774, representatives from the colonies met in the First Continental Congress. Benjamin Franklin drew a distinction between "uncorrupted new states," by which he meant the colonies, and "corrupted old ones," one of which seemed to be waging war on liberty. More troops arrived from England. In April 1775, in the first open fighting between colonists and British regulars, the colonial militia held its own against British troops searching for weapons at Concord and Lexington, Massachusetts, and then in the pitched battle at Bunker Hill near Boston.

In his pamphlet *Common Sense* (1776), 100,000 copies of which circulated in the colonies, Thomas Paine (1737–1809) launched a devastating attack on the king. *Common Sense* reflected the influence of the Enlightenment, particularly Rousseau's notion of the "social contract." Paine reiterated Locke's argument that governments received "their just powers from the consent of the people." He helped convince delegates to the Second Continental Congress to adopt Thomas Jefferson's Declaration of Independence on July 4, 1776. It declared the equality of all people, based on "inalienable rights," and it asserted that the authority of government stems from the consent of the governed. It also stated that when governments violate the "unalienable rights" to "life, liberty, and the pursuit of happiness" of their people, they had the right to rebel.

American resistance became a war for independence. The Continental Congress appointed George Washington to command its troops. The British government hoped to recover the colonies at the lowest possible cost; military campaigns were therefore compromised by halfhearted and often inept leadership by the British commanders. The initial British policy of isolating and punishing the rebels quickly failed. There were too few British troops to fight a war on unfamiliar territory against an increasingly determined foe. Next, the British undertook conventional military operations. But the colonial troops simply scattered. In 1776, Washington's army managed to cross the Hudson River into New Jersey. By the time Admiral Richard Howe (1726–1799) tried to negotiate with the rebels at the end of 1776, the colonists refused to listen because they had no reason to negotiate. Washington captured Trenton that December.

In contrast to British soldiers, the colonial army was virtually self-sufficient and broadly supported by the colonists. It became far more than what a loyalist (someone who supported the British cause) dismissed as "a vagabond Army of Ragamuffins, with Paper Pay, bad Cloathes, and worse Spirits." The most significant battles of the war were fought in the classic European style of confrontations, not as engagements between hit-and-run patriots and British regulars. The brutality of the British soldiers in requisitioning goods and maintaining order in the territories they controlled was self-defeating. In the meantime, during the war more than 60,000 American loyalists left the United States, many resettling—some taking their slaves with them—in distant reaches of the British Empire, including Canada, the Caribbean, and Africa.

France signed an alliance with the American rebels in February 1778, agreeing to provide substantial loans in gold. The French monarchy realized that favorable commercial treaties with an independent United States might more than compensate for having lost all rights to territory east of the Mississippi River in 1763. Thereafter, the French navy harassed British supply routes. In 1779, Spain joined the war on the American side, hoping to recapture Gibraltar and the island of Minorca, off the east coast of Spain. Seeking to prevent the North American colonies from purchasing

Benjamin Franklin was a favorite of the French, a relationship that was representative of the alliance between America and France against the British.

Dutch supplies, the British also fought the Dutch Republic. Britain confronted the refusal of Russia, Sweden, Prussia, Portugal, and Denmark to
curtail trade with the rebellious Americans.

Great Britain had overextended its capacity to wage war. Its naval advantage, the basis of its strength in modern times, had been eroded. Despite
swelling the army to 190,000 men, campaigns on land went badly. On
October 19, 1781, Lord Cornwallis surrendered his outnumbered army at
Yorktown, Virginia, to a combined force of American and French troops.
Britain officially recognized the independence of the American colonies by
signing the Treaty of Versailles in 1783.

Having lost its richest colony, Great Britain did not want to lose any others. In 1774, as the resistance in the thirteen colonies became more determined, Parliament had passed the Quebec Act, in an effort to prevent
tensions between the British Anglican conquerors and the Catholic population of Quebec from boiling over. The Test Act, which required all officials to
take communion in the Anglican Church, was abolished in Quebec, and the
Catholic Church was given the status of an established church. The British
government also strengthened its control over its other colonies. The India
Act (1784) created a board responsible to Parliament to which the East India
Company had to report. Another parliamentary act in 1791 created more
centralized administration in Canada, with a governor-general exercising far
more authority than two colonial assemblies elected by restricted suffrage.

The British government looked to extend the empire further, ordering the systematic charting of the oceans and their winds and currents. James Cook (1728–1779) sailed around New Zealand and along the eastern coast of Australia in 1770, claiming half of the continent for Britain. He was killed by indigenous people upon arriving in Hawaii, showing the dangers of venturing into unfamiliar waters. In 1788 the African Institution was established in London to encourage the exploration of Australia, only some coastal regions of which were known. At the same time, British Evangelicals imagined the conversion of the peoples with whom commerce and empire brought the British into contact.

British sea power and growing commercial empire expanded global trade beyond the luxury goods that had dominated it, particularly with the beginning of the Industrial Revolution in England (see Chapter 10). English textile production began to outproduce India by many times. Mercantilism's hold on the economic thinking of states disappeared forever. Britain became the world's major supplier of capital.

In the meantime, the advent to power in 1784 of William Pitt the Younger (1759–1806) restored political stability in Britain. The next year, Pitt introduced a wide-ranging bill for political reform. It proposed to reduce the minimum tax required for the electoral franchise and to abolish thirty-six rotten boroughs, awarding their representation to manufacturing regions and cities. Opposition among the country gentlemen, as well as that of the king himself, however, led to the bill's defeat. But Pitt did manage to eliminate useless offices that had become sinecures, introduce more accurate accounting methods into government, and facilitated the collection of excise taxes. Despite the personal failings of George III, Britain emerged from the turbulent decades of the 1760s and 1770s with its constitutional monarchy strengthened.

The Parlements and the French Monarchy

In France, two interrelated struggles in the early 1770s challenged the nature of absolute rule. The first was against privileges held by nobles and other corporate groups. The second opposed royal policies and pretensions that seemed to verge on despotism. In a way, this debate somewhat paralleled political issues in Britain.

In France, reformers seeking to limit royal authority had a daunting task because of the absolute nature of monarchical rule. The kings of France nonetheless depended on the support of the parlements. These law courts were made up primarily of nobles, seated in Paris and in twelve provinces. Their principal function was to give royal edicts the force of law by registering them. By refusing to register them, the parlements could impede the functioning of the absolute state. Thus, when the king's edicts had to do with increased or new taxation, political opposition to royal policies sometimes emerged in the parlements.

The increased centralization of the French state had in itself helped create contact between more people and the officials of the king. The concept of a "public" emerged, to which the monarch was in some sense considered responsible and before which the layers of privilege in French society no longer seemed to some acceptable. The crises that embroiled the king and the parlements from the 1750s to the 1780s helped shift public opinion toward the view that the parlements represented the rights of the "nation," threatened by a monarchy that seemed to be ruling in a despotic way.

The issue of Jansenism set the parlements against royal absolutism by raising the constitutional issue of the right of the monarch to circumscribe the parlements' traditional prerogatives. The Jansenists (see Chapter 7) were a dissident group within the Catholic Church. The pope had condemned Jansenism in 1713 with the papal bull *Unigenitus*, which Louis XV supported. But Jansenists, with a considerable following in Paris, found support within some of the parlements, which identified with Jansenist resistance against what they considered the papacy's undue interference in French affairs.

The period of conflict between the parlements and the crown really began in 1749. The controller-general attempted to make the *vingtième* tax (a tax applying to both nobles and commoners) permanent, drawing heated opposition from the parlements. And the Church again sought, without success, to force the French clergy to accept the papal bull *Unigenitus*. Many bishops threatened that sacraments would be refused to laymen who did not have a certificate signed by a priest attesting that the person had made his or her confession to a priest who had accepted the papal bull. Seven years later, the pope tried to defuse the crisis by banning these certificates.

But this concession did not placate the Parlement of Paris. Many of the parlements were manipulated by a handful of Jansenist magistrates and lawyers who managed to convince their colleagues that French acceptance of the papal edict amounted to an abandonment of French sovereignty over the temporal affairs of the Church. The king, refusing to hear the parlements' grievances, made clear that he considered the parlements nothing more than rubber stamps, a means of promulgating his will. When the Jesuit order continued to crusade against Jansenism, the Parlement of Paris responded by ordering Jesuit schools closed in 1761, citing the fact that members of the order took a vow of obedience to the pope.

The successive crises over Jansenism may have weakened the authority of the French monarchy by allowing the Parlement of Paris, and several provincial parlements as well, to claim they were defending constitutional liberties and the independence of the Gallican (French) Church—since Jansenists saw themselves as part of it—against royal encroachment and against Rome. By weakening the authority of the Catholic Church in France, the crisis over Jansenism also eroded the prestige of the absolute monarchy. Jansenism ceased being a political issue after 1758, when the

Parlement of Paris won judicial authority over many ecclesiastical matters. But the self-proclaimed role of magistrates as representatives of public opinion and protectors of the sovereign political will of the nation against abuses of power was a legacy of the Jansenist crisis.

The layers of economic privilege in France had proliferated with the extension of state power, as each monarch sought revenues with increased desperation. Despite increasing calls for reform, even critics who vociferously challenged monopolies (for example, those maintained by guilds) did not intend to end privileges per se. Rather, many of them wanted a share of the privileges and wanted to eliminate "unjust" monopolies that seemed to benefit others unfairly. Wealthy commoners, enriched by the economic changes, sought the kind of privileges nobles enjoyed—above all, exemption from many kinds of taxation. Thus, the issue of taxation would mobilize some of the parlements against the monarchy because it raised questions about the layers of privilege within the French state and about the limits of absolute authority.

In 1771, Chancellor René-Nicolas de Maupeou (1714–1792) provoked the parlements by attempting to make the *vingtième* tax permanent. Many nobles feared that general tax increases might lead to peasant uprisings, in which nobles stood to lose the most. Facing mounting resistance, Louis XV abolished the parlements. He then created new, more docile law courts that would not resist royal authority, staffed by magistrates who did not own their offices.

Both sides in the conflict between the parlements and Chancellor Maupeou appealed to public opinion. A declaration of high-ranking nobles stated that the king had abused "the constitution of the government and the rights of the people" by trying to establish "a despotism without bounds, without limits, and consequently without rights." The nobility asserted its "right of assembly," recalling that "the nation, in its assemblies, had charged the parlements with defending its rights." Influenced by the ideas of the Enlightenment, lawyers called for judicial reform, religious toleration, and the end to the abuse of privilege. When the monarchy tried to silence the lawyers, the latter turned courtrooms into forums for political opposition. Lawyers explored notions of national sovereignty while putting forward the case of the parlements against the crown.

As the idea of the nation gradually entered political discourse, the possibility emerged that when the interests of the monarchy and the nation clashed, popular allegiance could ultimately pass exclusively to the nation. Some degree of popular identification with parlements as defenders of the nation against despotism would not be effaced. The Maupeou "coup" lasted only three and a half years, but it had far-reaching effects on the nature of the opposition to the monarchy. It demonstrated that the parlements were not powerful enough to protect "the nation" against royal despotism, suggesting to some that only a body such as the Estates-General, which had not been convoked since 1614, could do so.

Chancellor René-Nicolas de Maupeou (*left*) and his supporter, Anne-Robert Turgot (*right*).

Louis XV was no stranger to unpopularity. He was held to be lazy and indifferent, and rumor had him obediently following the orders of his favorite mistress. The Seven Years' War had exhausted the treasury. Furthermore, France had lost Canada and several Caribbean islands to Britain. This loss of prestige, as well as income, increased the number of the king's critics. The structures of absolute rule seemed inadequate to the task of managing and paying for the cumbersome French state.

Louis XV's death in 1774 did not resolve the crisis. Following demonstrations and a spate of publications in support of the parlements, the twenty-year-old Louis XVI (ruled 1774–1793) dismissed Maupeou and reinstated the parlements. Public opinion seemed to have helped turn back what was popularly conceived to be a despotic assault on restraints on absolute rule.

Convinced that the financial difficulties of the monarchy stemmed from the stifling effect of privileges on the economy, a new minister, Anne-Robert Turgot, undertook ambitious reforms (see Chapter 9). His goal was to cut away some of the web of privileges, thus making the monarchy more efficient. Turgot convinced the young king to issue royal edicts, despite the opposition of the Parlement of Paris. These ended noble and clerical tax exemptions, abolished the guilds, freed the internal commerce of grain (the price of which had been first set free in the 1760s), and exempted peasants from having to work a certain number of days each year repairing roads. Economic liberalization would, he hoped, increase agricultural production and manufacturing, thereby augmenting tax revenue.

But like Louis XV's attempts to override the traditional role of the parlements, Turgot's reforms aroused vociferous opposition. Nobles—with
some significant exceptions—rallied against the proposed financial reforms.
The parlements, still smoldering over their treatment by Maupeou and
Louis XV several years earlier, refused to register—and thereby give the status of law to—the reforms of Turgot, who had supported Maupeou. Grain
merchants and guilds voiced strident opposition. Ordinary people rose up
in protest, blaming the freeing of the grain trade for the higher prices of
flour and bread in a period of dearth. Accusations of hoarding abounded.
Grain riots, in which women played the leading roles, swept across the
country during the spring "flour war" of 1775. Lawyers once again insisted
on the difference between absolute and despotic rule.

The king ended the most significant reform effort on the continent by
dismissing Turgot in 1776. When the American colonists declared their independence from Britain, France allied with them, forcing Louis XVI to
borrow ever more money at high interest rates and to sell more offices and
titles (about 3,700 venal offices conferred noble title). This helped shift
power within the nobility from the embittered "nobles of the sword" to
"nobles of the robe," ennobled through the purchase of office or title. The latter had a different way of looking at the world, even as they embraced aristocratic privilege. The more recently ennobled families remained in some ways
outsiders, their titles the result of worldly achievements, thus undercutting
the very essence of noble status passed down by heredity. In the meantime,
the French monarchy slid into an even deeper financial crisis.

Other Movements for Reform

In other cases, movements for reform came from below. In the Swiss Republic of Geneva, native-born artisans during 1765–1768 demanded equality
with the citizens possessing political rights. They were rebuffed by wealthy
Genevans, who tried to placate them with reductions in their taxes. An
uprising in 1782 unseated the ruling oligarchy before the intervention of
France, Sardinia, and the Swiss canton of Bern put an end to it.

In 1761, an uprising on the Mediterranean island of Corsica in the name
of "fatherland and liberty" ended rule by the northern Italian port city of
Genoa. France occupied Corsica seven years later. In 1770, the Greeks, with
Russian assistance, rose up against Turkish domination. Russia was eager to
enter the world of Mediterranean politics because it desired ultimately to
conquer Constantinople. The accession of Catherine the Great in 1762 had
ended a long succession crisis, palace plots, and assassinations, bringing stability to the Russian Empire. She sent an army and a small fleet in the hope
that Greek success might encourage other peoples to rise up against
Ottoman rule. Turkish troops crushed the revolt, but the Greek movement
for independence, by virtue of the special place of classical Greece in the
development of Western civilization, helped ignite Panhellenism.

In Denmark, where the king had imposed absolute rule in 1660 by suppressing the parliament and refusing to consult with the estates, a current of reform emerged early in the 1770s. In part, it was the inspiration of Johann Struensee (1737–1772), a German doctor, who convinced King Christian VII (ruled 1766–1808) to undertake reforms to strengthen the state economically so that, with Russian support, Sweden's residual Baltic ambitions could be thwarted. The king abolished censorship and the death penalty for thieves, extended religious toleration, and promised to undertake more agricultural reforms in the interests of creating a free peasantry. But the king's widowed mother and some nobles conspired against the reforms. Struensee was tried and convicted of, among other things, living "without religion or morality," and was executed in 1772. A decade later, however, the reforms Struensee had encouraged became part of a program for the future, a sign of the times.

Political struggles in the Dutch Republic—like the struggles between Whigs and the crown in Britain—were followed by the emergence of extra-parliamentary demands by ordinary people for political reform. The regents of the Dutch cities, defending the republic's federalism embodied in the Estates-General, opposed the policies of the bumbling William V of Orange (stadholder 1751–1795). The regents declared war on Britain in 1780 in the hope of weakening their commercial rival. As the war dragged on, they also sought to undercut the monarchical pretensions of William V.

In 1785, in the midst of political crisis, the Dutch Republic allied with France. The immediate goal was to counter the Austrian plan to reopen the Scheldt River and restore Antwerp to some of its former commercial glory, which would have undercut Amsterdam's prosperity. The possibility that France might annex the Southern Netherlands made the British government uneasy, further irritating the pro-British stadholder William V.

In the meantime, a radical "Patriot Party," primarily drawn from the middle class and artisans, put forward democratic reforms. Influenced by the success of the American revolutionaries, they demanded more democratic representation in the Estates. These Dutch reformers unseated the stadholder. Prussian King Frederick William II (ruled 1786–1797), whose sister was the stadholder's wife, sent an army in 1787, occupying Amsterdam and ending the challenge to William V's authority as stadholder. France seemed on the verge of offering the Patriots assistance, but distracted by a mounting political crisis, it backed down against the opposition of Prussia and Britain, powers that supported William V. The balance of power had once again been preserved. Dutch Patriot refugees poured into the Austrian Southern Netherlands and France.

The Austrian Netherlands, too, experienced political turmoil. Powerful nobles opposed to Austrian King Joseph II's enlightened reforms, which threatened their privileges, drove out Austrian troops in 1789. In the Austrian Netherlands, too, a movement for democratic reform emerged, calling for the transformation of the Estates into a representative assembly.

The Dutch (and, as we will see, French) mood seemed to be catching. Dutch Patriots invaded the Southern Netherlands in October 1789, driving away the Austrians. But a popular movement appealed to the nobles even less than did Austrian rule. Backed by the clergy and with the tacit support of most peasants, the nobles wrested control of the short-lived state from the urban-based reformers. The return of Austrian troops in 1790 occurred without resistance.

DECLINING POWER, DISAPPEARING STATE: THE OTTOMAN EMPIRE AND POLAND

The structure of international power in eighteenth-century Europe was not fundamentally changed by the quest for reform during the 1760s and 1770s. But in the new, more competitive European environment of the late eighteenth century, two other states that did not have access to the fruits of international trade and that were unwilling to restructure themselves lost their power in Europe: the Turkish Ottoman Empire and Poland. The Ottoman Empire, its power overextended and lacking a centralized structure of government, began to decline slowly but surely as its territories in the Balkans and Caucasus were eaten away by Austria and Russia. Poland, in which reforms had arguably come too late, fell prey to its aggressive absolutist neighbors: Russia, Prussia, and Austria, which divided up the state in three partitions in 1772, 1793, and 1795.

The Decline of Ottoman Turkish Power in Europe

In contrast to other absolute sovereigns, the Ottoman Turkish sultans ruled indirectly, governing through Islamic or village officials. Indeed, indirect rule itself may ultimately have hastened the decline of Ottoman absolutism. Like the Spanish Empire at its peak, the Ottoman domains were so extensive that they defied effective control. Insurrections, including some by the janissaries, the once-loyal court militia now increasingly subject to the influence of local elites, challenged the authority of the sultans— whose government in Constantinople became known as the Porte. Imperial officials, Muslim and Christian Orthodox alike, became notoriously corrupt, including the Greek-educated Phanariots, who served the sultans by collecting taxes, while making their families very wealthy. As the system of indirect rule declined in effectiveness, some local Christian and Muslim leaders commanded their own military forces, virtually independent of the sultan's authority in Constantinople. Sultans awarded large estates to those who served them well. This was precisely the same phenomenon that the absolute monarchs of France, Prussia, Russia, and Austria had overcome. However, the Ottoman Empire did not have a hereditary aristocracy. And unlike Russia and parts of Central and Eastern Europe, peasants within the

Sultan Selim III in his palace in Istanbul, with a line of followers stretching in front of him. The Turkish sultans ruled indirectly over a vast network of domains, a tactic that may have hastened the decline of Ottoman absolutism.

empire were free. But Turkish authority virtually collapsed in mountainous Montenegro and Bosnia, where the Turks battled Habsburg and Venetian forces. The government began to run out of money. Stop-gap measures, such as the debasement of the currency, failed to provide sufficient revenue.

Incapable sultans unwilling or unable to impose reforms further weakened the Ottoman Empire. As boys they lived in virtual isolation in a world of uncertainty among court eunuchs and palace intrigue. No regular pattern of succession had ever been established. Whereas Peter the Great of Russia undertook Western military reforms, the sultans did not. The Turkish economy, army, and navy could not keep pace with the Western powers. Turkish cavalrymen, with curved swords and magnificent horses, fell before Western artillery. The advice of officials who had been sent to Vienna and Paris to study methods of state went unheeded in Constantinople. Long wars fought against Persia in the east made it more difficult to repress disturbances in the Balkans. In some parts of the empire, a system of land inheritance replaced the old system, and new landowners began to force peasants into serfdom. European merchants took over Ottoman sea trade. The haphazard and inefficient collection of taxes, increasingly by dishonest tax farmers, engendered peasant resistance. As in the cases of China and Japan, Ottomans and the scholar class (*ulama*) showed little interest in Western ideas or technology. The single printing press in the empire, which dated only from the 1720s, was shut down sixty years later; no newspaper was published until 1828, and that in Cairo, not Istanbul. The classical literary tradition, as in China and Japan, continued to hold sway. The long decline of Ottoman power in Europe began when the Turks were turned back at the gates of Vienna in 1683. Austria's subsequent conquest of Hungary and Transylvania was confirmed by the Treaty of Carlowitz in 1699. However, the Turks continued to control the Black Sea by virtue of holding Constantinople and the straits. Major Ottoman defeats left the way open for continued Russian expansion. Although the Ottomans took advantage of inter-European wars to maintain their peripheral territories, in the 1760s this began to change. In 1774, following the destruction of the Turkish fleet in the Black Sea, the Ottoman Turks granted Russia the right to oversee Turkish authority in the Danubian principalities and to serve as the official protector of Christians living within its empire. In the meantime, in Morocco, Algiers, Tripoli, and Tunis, which remained nominally part of the Ottoman Empire, local dynasties set up shop. Yet we should not exaggerate the decline of the Ottoman Empire, which remained a power capable of effectively defending its interests well into the nineteenth century.

The Partitions of Poland

While the Ottoman Empire survived, Poland did not endure as an independent state (at least until the end of World War I). Poland was, for all intents and purposes, a republic. It had a king who was elected by citizens, a Senate (which included bishops and other important personages), and an elected Chamber of Deputies (the Sejm). The Sejm, which met every two years but which the king could convene in an emergency, elected the king for life and retained the right to pass laws, approve taxes, and ratify treaties. The king could not travel out of the country without the approval of the Sejm. Moreover, the "liberum veto" ("I freely forbid") accentuated the influence of the wealthiest nobles, who sometimes combined forces to block legislation. The rise of even more powerful aristocrats who owned vast estates exacerbated the impact of the "liberum veto" within the Sejm, preventing reforms that might have strengthened Poland.

During the first decades of the eighteenth century, the kingdom, its population reduced by wars and bubonic plague to only 6 million people, became increasingly dependent on Russia. Indeed, Poland's eclipse made possible Russia's gains in Ukraine. The War of Polish Succession (1733–1735) began when Russia attempted to impose its candidate on the Polish throne over the opposition of the Polish nobles. Because of France's interest in maintaining Sweden, the Ottoman Empire, and Poland as checks against

Austrian Habsburg domination of Central Europe, Louis XV proposed a candidate for the throne, his father-in-law, Stanislas Lesczinski, who had reigned as king of Poland from 1704 to 1709 and now had the support of most Polish nobles. But a Russian army forced the election of Augustus III of Saxony (ruled 1733–1763), the Austro-Russian candidate.

In 1763, the Polish throne again fell vacant with the death of Augustus III. A long period of legislative stagnation that accompanied the conflict between the Sejm and the Saxon kings ended the following year when the Sejm, reflecting Russian influence, elected as king the cultured, cosmopolitan Stanislas Poniatowski (ruled 1764–1795), one of the many lovers of the insatiable Russian Empress Catherine the Great ("many were called, and many were chosen," as one wag put it). Stanislas was somewhat influenced by Enlightenment thought. Sensing the necessity of reform, he hoped to advance manufacturing in Poland and looked to Britain as a model. He tried to end the liberum veto and to curtail the right of seigneurial courts to impose death sentences. He also established a number of schools. Only by such measures, he believed, could Poland escape poverty and backwardness. But some of the more powerful Polish nobles, who resented Russian influence, now opposed Stanislas and his reforms. They hoped that the French monarch or the Ottoman sultan might intervene on their behalf.

Catherine, like the Prussian king, feared that Stanislas's reforms might lead to a stronger, less subservient neighbor. Since 1764, Russia and Prussia had worked against an expansion of French influence in the Baltic, while preventing Poland from reviving its fortunes. Furthermore, Polish nobles had begun to persecute non-Catholics. Catherine, in the interest of the Orthodox Church, demanded that all non-Catholics be granted toleration in Poland. When Polish nobles formed an anti-Russian and anti-Orthodox confederation, Catherine sent troops into Poland. Ukrainian peasants took advantage of the chaos to rise up against their Polish lords. When they burned a Turkish town while chasing out Poles, Turkey entered the war against Russia (1768–74). Catherine annexed Wallachia and achieved Russia's dream since Peter the Great by reaching the Black Sea, annexing several territories at Turkish expense. In 1783, the Crimean peninsula, too, became part of the Russian Empire.

Alarmed by the expansion of the Russian Empire, Austria and Prussia demanded territorial compensation. Catherine suggested that the three powers might help themselves to parts of Poland. The First Partition in 1772 reduced Poland by about a third (see Map 11.3). Maria Theresa of Austria "wept and then took her share," the large province of Galicia, which lay between Russian Ukraine and Austria. Prussia absorbed West Prussia, which had formed a corridor separating East Prussia from the rest of the kingdom. Russia snatched large chunks of territory of eastern Poland.

The Polish Diet in 1791 voted what arguably was the first written constitution in Europe, a liberal document that established a hereditary monar-

MAP 11.3 THE PARTITIONS OF POLAND   Poland at its greatest extent in 1660–1667, and the loss of territory to Austria, Prussia, and Russia during the Partitions of 1772, 1793, and 1795.

chy, abolished the system of noble veto, and proclaimed that all authority stemmed from the nation. Reflecting the influence of the French Revolution (see Chapter 12), Poland became a constitutional monarchy, with the king naming ministers but with the parliament and Poland's major towns retaining privileges.

But Poland's days were numbered as an independent state, particularly given the fact that its old protector, France, was in the throes of revolution and had lost influence in East Central Europe. When Poles rose up in 1792 against Russian authority in the part of Poland that had been absorbed by Russia twenty years earlier, Russian troops intervened. They were backed by Polish nobles who opposed the liberal constitution. Prussia refused to come to Poland's aid, receiving in exchange for looking the other way annexation of more Polish territory in the Second Partition in 1793. With the Third Partition in 1795, Prussia and Russia ended Poland's independence for more than a century. The Constitution of 1791, perhaps the most progressive constitution of the century, was torn to shreds. Russia's new gains drew its interests farther into Central Europe, and it now shared a border with the Habsburg monarchy. Poles were now subject to the authority of three different states. In the lands acquired by Prussia, serfs gained some protection against abuses by landlords, but, as in the case of lands absorbed into the Habsburg Empire, the Polish secondary-school system was ended, imposing the German language.

Conclusion

Some historians have argued that movements against absolutism and against privilege, such as the political unrest in Great Britain and the successful rebellion of its North American colonies, constituted a general Western "democratic revolution." But despite the quest for political change in several Western states, demands for universal male suffrage were rare, and calls for the extension of political rights to women even more so (an exception being Geneva in the early 1780s). Even in Britain, after a contentious decade marked by demonstrations for political reform, the most widespread riots of the 1780s were the anti-Catholic Gordon riots. In France, calls for reform were less an attack on the nobles, per se, than on privilege. The institutions of the Old Regime in continental Europe demonstrated not only resiliency, but also some capacity to undertake reform.

Nonetheless, denunciations in France against privilege, shaped in part by Enlightenment thought, would be revived in the late 1780s. The Seven Years' War and assistance to the Americans worsened the financial crisis of the French monarchy, as the increasingly global dynastic rivalries and wars placed further strains on European states. France entered a serious political crisis when critics of the monarchy accused the king of ruling despotically and attacked the layers of economic and social privilege that seemed to constrain effective government and constrict freedom. Demands for sweeping reform led to the French Revolution of 1789, which proclaimed the principle of the sovereignty of the nation. Once again, the eyes of Europe turned toward France.

PART FOUR
REVOLUTIONARY
EUROPE, 1789–1850

The French Revolution of 1789 struck the first solid
blow in continental Western Europe against monarchical absolutism on behalf of popular sovereignty. The roots of revolution
extend back to the second half of the seventeenth century, an era
of hitherto unparalleled absolute monarchical authority. The
monarchs of France, Russia, Prussia, Austria, Spain, and Sweden
had reinforced their authority to the extent that they stood clearly
above any internal challenge to their power. Compliant nobles
served as junior partners in absolutism, acknowledging the ruler's
absolute power to proclaim laws, assess taxes, and raise armies, in
exchange for royal recognition of their noble standing and protection against popular revolts. The governments of Great Britain
and the Dutch United Provinces stood in sharp contrast to
absolute states. In the English Civil War in the 1640s, Parliament
had successfully turned aside the possibility of absolute monarchy in England, leading to the execution of King Charles II, followed after some years of turmoil by the Restoration of constitutional monarchy. In the Netherlands, the Dutch revolt against
absolutist Spain led to the establishment of the Dutch Republic.
The theory of popular sovereignty developed not only as an alternative to absolute rule but also as an extension of constitutional
rule. In the dramatic events of the French Revolution that began
in 1789, the theory of popular sovereignty became reality as ordinary people helped bring about the downfall of absolute rule and
then, three years later, the monarchy itself.

True popular sovereignty was a short-lived experiment, however, as counter-revolution and foreign intervention led to the
dramatic centralization of state authority. In 1799, Napoleon
Bonaparte helped overthrow the Directory, the last regime of

the revolutionary era in France. An admirer of the Enlightenment, Napoleon claimed that he was the heir of the French Revolution. But while Napoleon saw himself as a savior who carried "liberty, equality, and fraternity" abroad, his conquest of much of Europe before his final defeat left a mixed legacy for the future. More than a fifth of all the significant battles that took place in Europe from 1490 to 1815 occurred between the coming of the French Revolution and Napoleon's final defeat in 1815.

Following Napoleon's defeat in 1815 at the Battle of Waterloo, the Congress of Vienna created the Concert of Europe, the international basis of Restoration Europe, in the hope of preventing further liberal and nationalist insurrections in Europe. But liberal and nationalist movements could not so easily be swept away. During the subsequent three decades, "liberty" became the watchword for more and more people, particularly among the middle classes, who came to the forefront of economic, political, and cultural life. Liberal movements were in many places closely tied to the emergence of nationalism, the belief in the primacy of nationality as a source of allegiance and sovereignty.

In the meantime, during the first half of the nineteenth century, the Industrial Revolution slowly but surely transformed the way many Europeans lived. Dramatic improvements in transportation, notably the development of the railroad but also road improvements, expanded the market for manufactured and other goods. Rising agricultural production, increasingly commercialized in Western Europe, fed a larger population. Migrants poured into Europe's cities, which grew as never before. Contemporaries, particularly in Western Europe, sensed profound economic, social, political, and cultural changes.

CHAPTER **12**

THE FRENCH REVOLUTION

In 1791, King Louis XVI decided to flee Paris and the French Revolution. A virtual prisoner in the Tuileries Palace by the first months of the year, he had secretly negotiated for possible intervention on his behalf by the Austrian king and other European monarchs. The royal family furtively left the Tuileries Palace late at night on June 20, 1791, disguised as the family and entourage of a Russian baroness riding in a large black coach with yellow trim. But in an eastern town, the postmaster recognized the king, whose image he had seen on a coin. He rode rapidly to the town of Varennes, where the National Guard prevented the king's coach from going on. Three representatives of the National Assembly brought the royal family back to Paris. Near the capital, the crowds became threatening, and national guardsmen stood by the roadside with their rifles upside down, a sign of contempt or mourning.

The French Revolution mounted the first effective challenge to monarchical absolutism on behalf of popular sovereignty. The creation of a republican government in France and the diffusion of republican ideals in other European countries influenced the evolution of European political life long after the Revolution ended. Issues of the rights of the people, the role of the state in society, the values of democratic society, notions of "left" and "right" in political life, the concept of the "nation at arms," the place of religion in modern society and politics, and the question of economic freedom and the sanctity of property came to dominate the political agenda. They occupied the attention of much of France during the revolutionary decade of 1789–1799. The political violence of that decade would also be a legacy for the future.

The revolutionaries sought to make the French state more centralized and efficient, as well as more just. Napoleon Bonaparte, whom some historians consider the heir to the Revolution and others believe to be its betrayer, continued this process after his ascent to power in 1799.

Modern nationalism, too, has its roots in the French Revolution. The revolutionaries enthusiastically proclaimed principles they held to be universal. Among these were the sovereignty of the nation and the rights and duties of citizenship. The revolutionaries celebrated the fact that the Revolution had occurred in France. But wars intended to free European peoples from monarchical and noble domination turned into wars of French conquest. The revolutionary wars, pitting France against the other great powers, contributed to the emergence or extension of nationalism in other countries as well, ranging from Great Britain, where the sense of being British flourished in response to the French threat, to central and southern Europe, where some educated Germans and Italians began to espouse nationalism in response to the invading French armies.

THE OLD REGIME IN CRISIS

The French Revolution was not inevitable. Yet difficult economic conditions in the preceding two decades, combined with the growing popularity of a discourse that stressed freedom in the face of entrenched economic and social privileges, made some sort of change seem possible, perhaps even likely. When a financial crisis occurred in the 1780s and the king was forced to call the Estates-General, the stage was set for the confrontation that would culminate in the French Revolution.

Long-Term Causes of the French Revolution

The increasing prevalence of the language of the Enlightenment, stressing equality before the law and differentiating between absolute and despotic rule, placed the monarchy and its government under the closer scrutiny of public opinion. Adopting Enlightenment discourse, opponents accused Louis XV of acting despotically when he exiled the Parlement of Paris in 1771 and tried to establish new law courts that were likely to be more subservient than the *parlements*, the sovereign law courts, had been. Opponents believed that the king was trying to subvert long-accepted privileges. Following Louis XV's death in 1774, the young Louis XVI reinstated the parlements, which retained their right to register royal edicts.

As complaints mounted about noble privileges, guild monopolies, and corrupt royal officials, the implications of Enlightenment thought led to political action. In 1774, Controller-General of Finances Anne-Robert Turgot drew up a program to eliminate some monopolies and privileges that fettered the economy (see Chapter 11). However, the decree abolishing the guilds, among other decrees, generated immediate hostility from nobles, the Parlement of Paris, and from ordinary people, who rioted in Paris in 1775 because the freeing of the grain trade had brought higher prices in hard times. Two years later, Turgot's experiment ended. But some writers now began to contrast the freedoms Turgot had in mind with the corporate privileges that characterized the economy and society of eighteenth-century France.

France remained a state of overlapping layers of privileges, rights, traditions, and jurisdictions. Nobles and professional groups such as guilds and tax farmers (who generally had bought their offices and could pocket some of the taxes they collected) contested any plan to eliminate privileges. At the same time, the social lines of demarcation between nobles and wealthy commoners had become less fixed over the course of the eighteenth century. Despite increasing opposition from the oldest noble families who believed their ranks were being swamped by newcomers, in the fifteen years before 1789 almost 2,500 families bought their way into the nobility. Yet many people of means, too, resented noble privileges, above all the exemption of nobles from most kinds of taxes. Disgruntled commoners did not make the French Revolution, but their dissatisfaction helped create a litany of demands for reform. The monarchy's worsening financial crisis accentuated these calls.

The sharpest resistance to reform came from the poorer nobility. Among the "nobles of the sword," the oldest noble families whose ancestors had proudly taken arms to serve the king, some had fallen on hard times and clung frantically to any and all privileges as a way of maintaining their status. They resented the fact that the provincial parlements, in particular, had filled up with new nobles who had purchased offices—the "nobles of the robe"—and that power had shifted within the nobility from the oldest noble families to those recently ennobled.

The monarchy depended upon the sale of titles, offices, and economic monopolies for revenue and long-term credit. But by creating more offices— there were more than 50,000 offices in 1789—it risked destroying public confidence and driving down the value of offices already held.

Economic hardship compounded the monarchy's financial problems by decreasing revenue while exacerbating social tensions. Rising prices and rents darkened the 1770s and 1780s. A series of bad harvests—the worst of which occurred in 1775—made conditions of life even more difficult for poor people. The harvests of 1787 and 1788, which would be key years in the French political drama, were also very poor. Such crises were by no means unusual—indeed they were cyclical and would continue until the middle of the next century. Meager harvests generated popular resistance to taxation and protests against the high price of grain (and therefore bread). A growing population put more pressure on scarce resources.

Many peasants believed that their hardship was being increased by landowners. Something of a "seigneurial reaction" was under way as smaller agricultural yields diminished noble revenues, while inflation raised the costs of noble life. Noble landowners hired estate agents, lawyers, and surveyors to maximize income from their lands, and reasserted old rights over common lands, on which many poor peasants depended for pasturing animals and gathering wood for fuel. Many landlords raised rents and tried to force share-cropping arrangements on peasants who had previously rented land.

Although the feudal system of the Middle Ages had long since passed, remnants remained. Peasants were still vexed by seigneurial dues and cash owed to their lords. Many nobles still held some rights of justice over their peasants, which meant that they could determine guilt and assess penalties for alleged transgressions. Seigneurial courts were often used to enforce the landlord's rights over forests, lakes, and streams, and his exclusive rights to hunt and fish on his estate. The political crisis that led to the French Revolution would provide ordinary people with an opportunity to redress some of these mounting grievances.

The Financial Crisis

The serious financial crisis that confronted the monarchy in the 1780s was the short-term cause of the French Revolution. France had been at war with Britain, as well as with other European powers, off and on for more than a century. The financial support France had provided the rebel colonists in the American War of Independence against Britain had been underwritten by loans arranged by the king's Swiss minister of finance, Jacques Necker (1732–1804). Almost three-fourths of state expenses went to maintaining the army and navy, and to paying off debts accumulated from the War of the Austrian Succession (1740–1748) and the Seven Years' War (1756–1763), as well as from the American War of Independence. The monarchy was living beyond its means.

Where were more funds to be found? Nobles had traditionally enjoyed the privilege of being exempt from most, and the clergy from all, taxation. There was a limit to how many taxes could be imposed on peasants, by far the largest social group in France. In short, the financial crisis of the monarchy was closely tied to the very nature of its fiscal system.

The absolute monarchy in France collected taxes less efficiently than did the British government. In Britain, the Bank of England facilitated the government's borrowing of money at relatively low interest through the national debt. In France, there was no central bank, and the monarchy depended more than ever on private interests and suffered from a cumbersome assessment of fiscal obligations and inadequate accounting. French public debt already was much higher than that of Britain and continued to rise as the monarchy sought financial expedients.

The hesitant and naive Louis XVI was still in his twenties when he became king in 1774. Louis knew little of his kingdom, venturing beyond the region of Paris and Versailles only once during his reign. He preferred puttering around the palace, taking clocks and watches apart and putting them back together. He excelled at hunting. The unpopularity of Louis's elegant, haughty wife, Marie-Antoinette (1755–1793), accentuated the public's lack of confidence in the throne (whether or not she really snarled "Let them eat

(*Left*) Louis XVI. (*Right*) Marie-Antoinette.

cake!" when told that the people had no bread). The daughter of the Austrian queen Maria Theresa, Marie-Antoinette was married to Louis to
strengthen dynastic ties between Austria and France. She never felt really at
home in France. Unhappy in her marriage, Marie-Antoinette lived extrava-
gantly and was embroiled in controversy. In 1785, she became entangled in a
seamy scandal when a cardinal offered her a fabulous diamond necklace in
the hope of winning favor. The necklace and some of the prelate's money
were then deftly stolen by plotters, a strange scenario that included a prosti-
tute posing as the queen. The "diamond necklace affair," as it was called,
seemed to augment the public image of the king as a weak man, a cuckold.
The queen's reputed indiscretions and infidelities seemed to undercut the
authority of the monarchy itself. Her detractors indelicately dubbed her the
"Austrian whore."

In the meantime, Necker continued to float more loans. But in 1781,
some ministers and noble hangers-on convinced the king to dismiss Necker.
Necker produced a fanciful account of the royal finances that purported to
demonstrate that more revenue was coming to the state than was being
spent. Necker hoped to reassure creditors that reform was unnecessary.
Bankers, however, did not believe Necker's figures and some refused to loan
the monarchy any more money until the state enacted financial reforms. The
new finance minister, Charles-Alexandre de Calonne (1734–1802), demonstrated that Necker's calculations of royal finances were far-fetched. Yet
Calonne spent even more money and put the royal treasury deeper in debt
by borrowing from venal officeholders to pay off creditors now gathered at
the royal door.

The parlements were certain to oppose fiscal reform, which they believed
would lead to an increase in taxation through a general tax on land. They
distrusted Calonne, whom they identified with fiscal irresponsibility and
governmental arrogance that some believed bordered on despotism.

To sidestep the parlements, Calonne asked the king in February 1787 to convoke an Assembly of Notables consisting of handpicked representatives from each of the three estates: clergy, nobility, and the third estate (everybody else). The crown expected the Assembly to endorse its reform proposals, including new land taxes from which nobles would not be exempt. Calonne suggested that France's financial problems were systemic, resulting from a chaotic administrative organization, including the confusing regional differences in tax obligations. The monarchy's practice of selling the lucrative rights to collect, or "farm," taxes worsened the inefficiency. Calonne knew that the crown's contract with the tax farmers would soon have to be renegotiated, and that many short-term loans contracted by the monarchy would soon come due.

Denouncing "the dominance of custom" that had for so long prevented reform and encumbered commerce, Calonne proposed to overhaul the entire financial system. The Assembly of Notables, however, rejected Calonne's proposals for tax reform and refused to countenance the idea that nobles should be assessed land taxes. Moreover, the high clergy of the first estate, some of whom were nobles, also vociferously opposed Calonne's reforms. They, too, feared losing their exemption from taxation. The privilege-based nature of French society was at stake.

Nobles convinced the king to sack Calonne, which he did on April 8, 1788. Louis XVI replaced Calonne with the powerful archbishop of Toulouse, Étienne-Charles de Loménie de Brienne (1727–1794). Like his predecessor, Loménie de Brienne asked the provincial parlements to register—and thus approve—several edicts of financial reform, promising that the government would keep more accurate accounts. But the Parlement of Paris refused to register some of the edicts, including a new land tax and a stamp tax, which evoked the origins of the American Revolution.

THE FIRST STAGES OF THE REVOLUTION

Some members of the Assembly of Notables had been willing to accept fiscal reform and to pay more taxes, but only with accompanying institutional reforms that would guarantee their privileges. They wanted the king to convoke regular assemblies of the Estates-General—made up of representatives of the three estates—which had not been convoked since 1614. The king was in a difficult position. He needed to reduce the privileges of the nobles to solve the financial crisis, but to do so without their approval would lead to accusations of despotism, or even tyranny, the sometimes violent implementation of the structures of despotic authority. On the other hand, capitulating to the demands of the privileged classes in return for new taxes would compromise his absolute authority and suggest that his word was subject to the approval of the nation, or at least the nobility. The resolution of this dilemma would lead to the events that constituted the first stages of the French Revolution.

Convoking the Estates-General

The "noble revolt" began the French Revolution. In response to the refusal of the Parlement of Paris to register the land and stamp taxes, in August 1787 Louis XVI exiled its members to Troyes, a town east of Paris. Nobles and high clergymen protested vigorously. The provincial parlements backed up the Parlement of Paris. The Parlement of Grenoble refused to register the new stamp and land taxes and convoked its provincial estates (the assembly of nobles that represented the interests of the region) without royal authorization. The "revolt of the nobility" against the monarchy's attempt to force nobles to pay taxes spread. Provincial parlements demanded that the Estates-General be convoked. This revolt was not directed against the institution of the monarchy itself, but against what the nobles considered abuses of the rights and privileges of the nation committed by an increasingly despotic crown.

The monarchy sought compromise. Loménie de Brienne agreed to withdraw the new land and stamp taxes in exchange for maintaining the tax on income (the *vingtième* tax), which nobles and other privileged people had first been assessed in the late 1750s to pay for the Seven Years' War. He made clear, however, that the crown would be forced to settle its debts in paper money backed by royal decree. Louis XVI recalled the Parlement of Paris from exile in November 1787. But the king ordered new loan edicts registered without giving the parlement a chance to be heard. When the duke of Orléans, the king's cousin, interjected that such a procedure was illegal, Louis replied, "That is of no importance to me . . . it is legal because I will it." Louis XVI thus seemed to cross the line between absolutism and despotism.

In May 1788, the king ordered the arrest of two of the most radical members of the Parlement of Paris. He then suspended the parlements, establishing new provincial courts to take their place and creating a single plenary court that would register royal edicts. Resistance to the king's acts against the parlements came quickly. The Assembly of the Clergy, which had been summoned to decide on the amount of its annual gift to the crown, protested the abolition of the parlements. Riots in support of the parlements occurred in several towns, including Grenoble, where crowds expressed support for their parlement by pelting soldiers with stones and roof tiles.

On August 8, 1788, Louis XVI announced that he would convoke the Estates-General on May 1 of the following year. He hoped that he could avert royal bankruptcy if the Estates-General would agree to the imposition of the new taxes. Two weeks later, he reappointed Necker as minister of finance, a measure he believed would appease nobles, investors, and holders of government bonds, who had never objected to unrestrained borrowing.

But the convocation of the Estates-General helped unify public opinion against the king. That the nobles forced the crown to convoke the Estates-General became the first act of the French Revolution. Many people believed that the Estates-General, more than the parlements, would represent their interests and check royal despotism.

The question of how voting was to take place when the Estates-General met assumed increasing importance. Would each of the three estates—clergy, nobles, and the third estate—have a single vote (which would almost certainly quash any reform since the majority of nobles and clergymen were against reform), or would each member of the Estates-General be entitled to his own vote?

On September 25, 1788, the Parlement of Paris, which had been reinstated amid great celebration, ruled that voting within the Estates-General would take place by estate, as had been the case when the Estates-General had last met in 1614. Thus each of the three estates would have the same number of representatives and be seated separately. Henceforth, the parlements would be seen by many people as defending the prerogatives of their privileged members against the interests of the third estate, losing their claim to defend the nation against the king's despotism for having registered the royal decree that voting would be by estate.

Popular political writers now began to salute the third estate (which made up 95 percent of the population) as the true representative of liberty and of the nation against royal despotism. Others asked for some sort of representative assembly that would reflect "public opinion." The "patriot party," a coalition of bourgeois members and some liberal nobles, began to oppose royal policies, which they contrasted with the rights of the "nation." "Patriots" denounced the vested interests of the court and the nobles close to it. Political publications transformed these debates into national political issues. The Society of the Thirty, a group that included liberal nobles from very old families—for example, the Marquis de Lafayette (1757–1834), French hero of the American War of Independence—as well as a number of commoner lawyers, met to discuss, debate, and distribute liberal political pamphlets. They proposed that the third estate be entitled to twice as many representatives in the Estates-General as the nobility and clergy.

In January 1789, Emmanuel Joseph Sieyès (1748–1836), an obscure priest, offered the most radical expression of a crucial shift in political opinion. "We have three questions to ask and answer," he wrote. "First, What is the Third Estate? Everything. Second, What has it been heretofore in the political order? Nothing. Third, What does it demand? To become something therein." He contrasted the "nation" against royal absolutism and noble prerogative, demanding a predominant role for the third estate in political life.

The vast majority of the men elected to the Estates-General were residents of cities and towns, and two-thirds of these had some training in the law. Two-thirds of those elected to the first estate were parish priests, many of whom were of humble origin and resented the privileges of the bishops

(*Left*) The Marquis de Lafayette. (*Right*) The Abbé Sieyès.

and monastic orders. Some of the younger noble representatives elected to the second estate were relatively liberal. They wanted institutional reforms in the organization of the French monarchy that would permit them to check the power of the king, in much the same way as the Parliament in England served as a check on the English crown. In December 1788, the king agreed to double the number of representatives of the third estate but declined to give all members an individual vote.

The king asked the local assemblies, along with the first two estates, to draw up lists of grievances (*cahiers de doléances*), which the Estates-General would discuss. Thousands of grievances offered the monarchy a wide variety of opinions, ranging from concrete suggestions for reform to the considered opinion that the foul breath of sheep was ruining pastureland in Lorraine. More important, *cahiers* criticized monarchical absolutism and the intransigence of seigneurs, asked for a more consistent and equitable tax structure, and called for the creation of a new national representative body. A few of the *cahiers* denounced as an abuse of royal power the so-called *lettres de cachet,* documents issued in the name of the king that allowed a person to be arrested for any reason and imprisoned indefinitely. For example, one *cahier* demanded "that no citizen lose his liberty except according to law." However, some *cahiers* also reflected continued reverence for the king, while denouncing the rapacity and bad faith of his advisers and ministers. Most *cahiers* never reached the king.

On May 5, 1789, the nearly 1,200 members of the Estates-General (about 600 of whom represented the third estate) assembled at Versailles. The king greeted the first two estates, but kept the commoners waiting for two hours. When he finished his speech, members of the third estate violated protocol by boldly putting their hats back on, a right reserved for the two privileged orders. On June 17, the third estate overwhelmingly approved a motion by Sieyès that declared the third estate to be the "National Assembly" and the true representative of national sovereignty. The third estate now claimed legitimate sovereignty and an authority parallel, if not superior, to that of the king of France.

But, on June 20, as rumors circulated that the king might take action against them, representatives of the third estate found that their meeting hall had been locked for "repairs." Led by their president, Jean-Sylvain Bailly (1736–1793), an astronomer, the members of the third estate took the bold step of assembling in a nearby tennis court. There they took an oath "not to separate, and to reassemble wherever circumstances require, until the constitution of the kingdom is established and consolidated upon solid foundations." With principled defiance, the third estate demanded that defined limits be placed on the king's authority.

The king declared the third estate's deliberations invalid. Yet on June 23 he announced some substantial reforms, agreeing to convoke periodically the Estates-General, to abolish the *taille* (the tax on land) and the *corvée* (labor tax), to eliminate internal tariffs and tolls that interfered with trade, and to eliminate the *lettres de cachet*. He also agreed that the Estates-General would vote by head, but only on matters that did not concern "the ancient and constitutional rights of the three orders." To the radicalized members of the third estate, the king's concessions were not enough.

The Tennis Court Oath, June 20, 1789.

Louis XVI had dismissed Necker on June 22, but reversed himself after learning that thousands of people in Paris had invaded the courtyard of the Tuileries Palace in Paris to demand that Necker stay on. Necker's contention in 1781 that the kingdom's finances could be put on an even keel without raising taxes had increased his popularity, as had the fact that nobles were pushing for his recall. During these days, most of the clergy and a number of nobles had joined the third estate. Now, after threatening to dissolve the Estates-General by force, on June 27 the king ordered the remaining clergy and nobles of the first two estates to join the third. The new gathering began to constitute itself as the National Constituent Assembly.

Storming of the Bastille

Amid a shortage of food and high prices, many ordinary people now believed that a conspiracy by nobles and hoarders was to blame. Furthermore, the number of royal troops around Paris and Versailles seemed to be increasing. Rumors spread that the National Assembly would be quashed. On July 11, the king once again ordered Necker, who remained unpopular with the court, into exile. He and other ministers were dismissed because the king was convinced they were unable to control the demands for change coming from the Estates-General. Bands of rioters attacked the customs barriers at the gates of Paris, tearing down toll booths where taxes on goods entering the city were collected, thus making foodstuffs more expensive.

On the morning of July 14, 1789, thousands of people—mostly trades-men, artisans, and wage earners—seized weapons stored in the Invalides, a large veterans' hospital. Early that afternoon, the attention of the Paris crowd turned toward the Bastille, a fortress on the eastern edge of the city, where the crowd believed powder and ammunition were stored. For most of the eighteenth century, the Bastille had been a prison, renowned as a symbol of despotism because some prisoners had been sent there by virtue of one of the king's *lettres de cachet*, summarily and without a trial. On that hot summer day, the Bastille's prisoners numbered but seven, a motley crew that included a nobleman imprisoned upon request of his family, a renegade priest, and a demented Irishman, who alternately thought he was Joan of Arc, Saint Louis, and God.

The crowd stormed and captured the Bastille, which was defended by a small garrison. More than 200 of the attackers were killed or wounded. A butcher decapitated the commander of the fortress, and the throng carried his head on a pike in triumph through the streets. The Bastille's fall would be much more significant than it first appeared. The king entered "nothing new" in his diary for that day, July 14. But the crowd's uprising probably saved the National Assembly from being dissolved by the troops the king had ordered to Versailles and Paris. Now unsure of the loyalty of his soldiers, Louis sent away some of the troops he had summoned to Paris, recognized both the newly elected municipal government, with Bailly serving as mayor,

The taking of the Bastille, July 14, 1789.

and a municipal defense force or National Guard (commanded by the Marquis de Lafayette), and capitulated to the popular demand that he recall Necker to office.

On July 17, 1789, the king came to Paris to be received by the municipal council at the town hall, accepting and wearing an emblem of three colors, red and blue for the city of Paris, and white for the Bourbons. By doing so, Louis XVI seemed to be recognizing what became the tricolor symbol of the French Revolution.

The Great Fear and the Night of August 4

News of the convocation of the Estates-General had brought hope to many rural people that the king would relieve their crushing fiscal burdens. They had expressed such hopes in the grievances they sent with their third estate delegates to Versailles. Now, upon news of the fall of the Bastille, between July 19 and August 3 peasants attacked châteaux. In some places they burned title deeds specifying obligations owed to lords. These peasant rebellions helped cause a subsequent panic known as the "Great Fear." Fueled by the rumor of an aristocratic "famine plot" to starve or burn out the population, peasants and townspeople mobilized in many regions of France. To repel the rumored approach of brigands sent to destroy crops, townspeople and peasants formed armed units to defend themselves and save the harvest. New local governments and National Guard units were established to institute reforms and to restore order as the effective authority of the state disintegrated. These events brought to local influence lawyers, merchants, and other "new men" who had formerly been excluded from political life.

News of peasant violence galvanized members of the National Assembly. On August 4, 1789, in an effort to appease the peasants and to forestall further rural disorders, the National Assembly formally abolished the "feudal regime," including seigneurial rights. This sweeping proclamation was modified in the following week: owners of seigneurial dues, or payments owed by peasants who worked land owned by nobles, would receive compensation from the peasants (although, in general, such compensation was not forthcoming and was subsequently eliminated). The Assembly abolished personal labor servitude owed to nobles, without compensation. The members of the National Assembly thus renounced privilege, the fundamental organizing principle of French society. Other reforms enacted the following week included the guarantee of freedom of worship and the abolition of the sale of offices, seigneurial justice, and even of the exclusive right of nobles to hunt. The provinces and cities, too, were required to give up most of their archaic privileges. In these ways, the National Assembly enacted a sweeping agenda that proclaimed the end of what soon became known as the Old Regime.

CONSOLIDATING THE REVOLUTION

The Assembly's decrees destroyed absolutism by redefining the relationship between subject and king. No longer would the king rule by divine right, or buy allegiance by dispensing privileges to favorites. Instead, he would be constrained by powers spelled out in a constitution. The Assembly promulgated the Declaration of the Rights of Man and Citizen, a remarkable document that proposed universal principles of humanity. It next established a new relationship between church and state, creating a national church, making Catholic Church property "national property," and compelling the clergy to swear allegiance to the nation. The National Assembly then turned to the long process of framing a constitution for the new regime, and is therefore sometimes also known as the Constituent Assembly.

In the meantime, Marie-Antoinette denounced the revolutionaries as "monsters," and some of the king's most influential advisers balked at accepting any weakening in royal authority. Fearing the influence of nobles at the court, crowds early in October marched to Versailles, returning to Paris with the king and the royal family. Henceforth, while many nobles, among others, fled France for exile and sought the assistance of the monarchs of

Europe against the Revolution, the king himself became vulnerable to the tide of Parisian popular radicalism. As nobles and clergy led resistance to the Revolution, the Parisian clubs made more radical demands.

The Declaration of the Rights of Man and Citizen

As it set out to create a constitutional monarchy, the Assembly promulgated the Declaration of the Rights of Man and Citizen on August 26, 1789. This set forth the general principles of the new order and intended to educate citizens about liberty. One of the most significant documents in Western political history, the Declaration reflected some of the ideas that Thomas Jefferson had enshrined in the American Declaration of Independence of 1776. Article One proclaims, "Men are born and remain free and equal in rights." The Enlightenment's influence is apparent in the document's concern for individual freedom, civic equality, and the sense of struggle against corporatism, unjust privilege, and absolute rule, a discourse based upon a belief in the primacy of reason. All people were to be equal before the law. All men were to be "equally eligible to all honors, places, and employments . . . without any other distinction than that created by their virtues and talents." No person could be persecuted for his or her opinions, including those concerning religion.

Proclaiming universal principles, the Declaration of the Rights of Man and Citizen clearly placed sovereignty in the French nation. The notion of rights stemming from membership in the "nation," as opposed to that in any corporate group or social estate, was a fundamental change. Laws were to reflect the notion of the "general will," an Enlightenment concept, which would be expressed by national representatives. The nation itself, not the monarch alone, was to be "the source of all sovereignty." The assertion of equality of opportunity, however, was not intended to eliminate all social distinctions. The preservation of property rights assured that differences due to wealth, education, and talent would remain and be considered natural and legitimate. The Declaration thus helped make wealth, not birth, blood, or legal privilege, the foundation of social and political order in modern France.

The Declaration invoked "universal man," meaning mankind. But at the same time, its authors excluded women from the Declaration and did not espouse or foresee equality of the sexes. Nonetheless, many men and women now began to greet each other as "citizen." Indeed, some calls for women's rights arose from the beginning of the Revolution.

The abolition of feudalism and the proclamation of the Declaration of the Rights of Man and Citizen were such monumental achievements that already in 1790 people were referring to the Old Regime as having been that which existed before the representatives of the Estates-General constituted the National Assembly. It remained, however, for Louis XVI to accept the Assembly's work.

"The Baker, the Baker's Wife, and the Baker's Little Boy"

The political crisis was by no means over. The king's closest advisers, the "court party," rejected any constitutional arrangement that would leave the monarch without the power of absolute veto. Royal authority was at stake. Speaking for the patriot party, Sieyès insisted, "If the king's will is capable of equalling that of twenty-five million people . . . it would be a *lettre de cachet* against the general will." The majority of the Assembly, having defeated a motion that an upper chamber like the British House of Lords be created, offered the king in September the power of a "suspending" veto over legislation. The king would be able to delay a measure passed by the Assembly from becoming law for up to four years.

When the king refused to accept these provisions and the decrees of August 4, a flood of pamphlets and newspapers attacked his intransigence. The radical journalist Jean-Paul Marat (1743–1793) quickly found a popular following for his new newspaper, *The Friend of the People*. A physician beset by financial woes, Marat was like one of the ambitious, frustrated "scribblers" whom Voltaire, forty years earlier, had scathingly denounced as hacks. Marat captured with stirring emotion and the colorful, coarse slang of ordinary Parisians the mood of those for whom he wrote. The rhetoric of popular sovereignty, some of it borrowed from the philosophe Jean-Jacques Rousseau, came alive in the outpouring of political pamphlets that undermined popular respect for Louis XVI and even for the institution of monarchy itself.

By October, some "patriots" were demanding that the king reside in Paris, echoing a number of *cahiers*. Like many of the most important events in the French Revolution, the "march to Versailles" began with a seemingly minor event. The officers of the Flanders Regiment insulted the newly adopted tricolor emblem at a reception in their honor attended by the king and queen. According to rumor, they shouted, "Down with the National Assembly!"

On October 5, women from the neighborhoods around the Bastille, having found little at the market, gathered in front of the town hall. From there, some 10,000 people, mostly women, left on foot for Versailles, hoping to convince the king to provide them with bread. Some of them occupied the hall of the National Assembly, where they claimed power in the name of popular sovereignty. Later in the day, a large force of national guardsmen led by Lafayette also arrived at Versailles, hoping to keep order and to convince the king that he should return with them to Paris. Louis cordially greeted the women in the late afternoon, promising them bread. That night Louis XVI announced his acceptance of the Assembly's momentous decrees of the night of August 4.

Nonetheless, violence followed at dawn. When people tried to force their way into the château, royal guards shot a man dead, and the crowds retaliated by killing two guards and sticking their heads on pikes. The crowd insisted that the royal family join it on the road to Paris. Some of the women

À Versailles à Versailles du 5 Octobre 1789

Women of Paris leaving for Versailles.

sang that they were returning to Paris with "The Baker, the Baker's Wife, and the Baker's Little Boy," reflecting the popular notion that the king was responsible for providing bread for his people. The National Assembly, too, left Versailles for Paris. By putting the king and the Assembly under the pressure of popular political will, the women's march to Versailles changed the course of the French Revolution.

Reforming the Church and Clergy

As the National Assembly set about creating a constitution that would limit the authority of the king, it proclaimed Louis "the king of the French," instead of the king of France, a significant change that suggested that he embodied the sovereignty of his people. Alarmed by such changes, the king's brother, the count of Artois, went into exile after the October Days, and was soon followed by more than 20,000 other émigrés, most of whom were nobles, other people of means, and clergymen.

The Assembly turned its attention to reforming the Church. The decrees of August had ended the unpopular tithe payments to the Church, and now the Assembly looked to the Church's wealth to help resolve the state's mounting financial crisis. On October 10, Charles-Maurice de Talleyrand (1754–1838), who had entered the priesthood at the insistence of his family and had been consecrated bishop early in 1789, proposed that Church property become "national properties" (*biens nationaux*). After the Assembly narrowly passed Talleyrand's measure on November 2, some 400 million francs in Church property—roughly 10 percent of the nation's land—began to be offered for sale at auction. The primary beneficiaries of the sale were urban bourgeois and prosperous peasants who could marshal enough cash to buy the land put up for sale.

To raise funds immediately, the Assembly issued paper money (*assignats*), which was backed by the value of the Church lands. Although the law required everyone to accept *assignats* in payment of debts, their value fell dramatically because of a lack of public confidence, and those who used the *assignats* to purchase Church lands or pay debts received a windfall. Even poor peasants were thus able to reduce their debts with inflated currency. Among the consequences of the sale of Church lands, and later of lands owned by noble émigrés, was that more land was brought under cultivation by peasants. The clearing of trees and brush to make room for crops and small-scale farming also put increased pressure on the environment.

The Assembly then altered dramatically the status of the Church itself. On February 13, 1790, it decreed the abolition of the religious orders, deemed politically suspect by many reformers. On July 12, the National Assembly passed the Civil Constitution of the French Clergy. The Assembly redefined the relationship between the clergy and the state, creating, in effect, a national church. Bishops, who could now only publish pronouncements with the authorization of the government, were to be elected by local assemblies at the local level. Ten days later, the king reluctantly accepted these measures affecting the Church.

The Church became essentially a department of the state, which henceforth would pay clerical salaries, the expenses of worship, and poor relief. In November 1790, the National Assembly proclaimed that all priests had to swear an oath of loyalty to the Revolution, and thus accept the Civil Constitution of the French Clergy. His authority directly challenged, Pope Pius VI denounced the Declaration of the Rights of Man and Citizen in March, and in April 1791 he condemned the Civil Constitution of the French Clergy.

The Civil Constitution of the French Clergy altered the course of the Revolution, largely because it was widely resisted and contributed directly to the growth of a counter-revolutionary movement. Between one-half and two-thirds of parish priests refused the oath, and the Assembly prohibited these disloyal, "non-juring" priests from administering the Church sacraments. Nonetheless, many continued to do so with popular support. The issue of the oath split dioceses, parishes, and some households. In some provinces, violence mounted against "non-juring" priests; in others, refractory priests received popular support and protection. Such issues were no small matter, as many Catholics, Louis XVI among them, believed themselves obliged by faith to refuse to take sacraments from the "juring" clergy, that is, those who had taken the oath.

The Reforms of 1791

The Constitution of 1791 formalized the break with the Old Regime by substituting a constitutional monarchy for absolute rule. Although the king retained only the power of a suspending veto, he would still direct foreign policy and command the army. Acts of war or peace, however, required the Assembly's approval.

But France was far from being a republic. In sweeping away the Old Regime, the Revolution had redefined the relationship between the individual and the state by stripping away hereditary legal privileges. Although all citizens were to be equal before the law, when the Assembly abolished titles of hereditary nobility in June 1790, it carefully distinguished between "active" and "passive" citizens. Only "active citizens," men paying the equivalent of three days' wages in direct taxes, had the right to vote in indirect elections—they would vote for electors, wealthier men, who in turn would select representatives to a new legislature (see Map 12.1). Critics such as Marat and the populist orator Georges-Jacques Danton (1759–1794) denounced the restrictive franchise, claiming that the Assembly had merely replaced the privileged caste of the Old Regime with another by substituting the ownership of property for noble title as the criterion for political rights. Rousseau himself would have been ineligible to vote.

In Europe, religious discrimination still characterized many states. In Britain, English Dissenters and Catholics could not hold public office and were excluded from certain professions; in Hungary and the Catholic Rhineland, Protestants faced discrimination. Jews faced intolerance and persecution in much of Europe, excluded, for example, from certain occupations or forced to live in specially designated places. In some parts of Eastern Europe and Ukraine, they suffered violence as well.

Now the National Assembly granted citizenship and civil rights to Protestants and Jews by laws in 1790 and 1791 (Protestants had already been granted civil rights in 1787). The Assembly abolished guilds, declaring each person "free to do such business and to exercise such profession, art or trade as he may choose." It subsequently passed the Le Chapelier Law on June 14, 1791, prohibiting workmen from joining together to refuse to work for a master. This law was a victory for proponents of free trade. The Assembly also passed laws affecting the family: establishing civil marriage, lowering the age of consent for marriage, permitting divorce, and specifying that inheritances be divided equally among children.

The National Assembly abolished slavery in France, but not in the colonies. This exception led to a rebellion by free blacks on the Caribbean island of Hispaniola in October 1790 against the French sugar plantation owners, many of whom were nobles. It was led by Toussaint L'Ouverture (1743–1803), a former slave who had fought in the French army. The National Convention (which would replace the Assembly in September 1792) abolished slavery in the colonies in 1794, hoping that the freed slaves

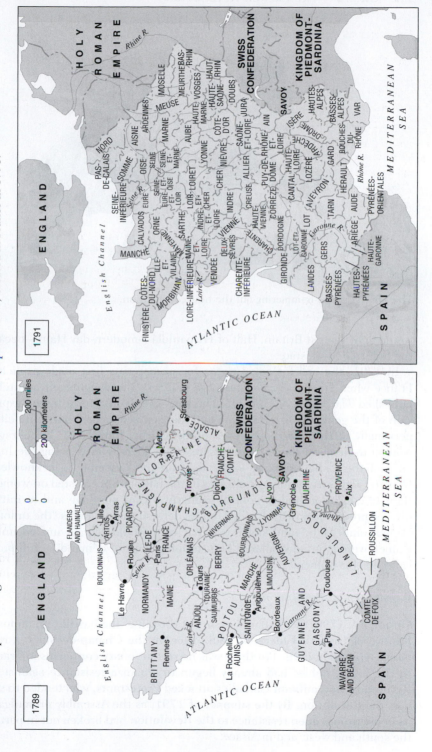

MAP 12.1 FRANCE BEFORE AND AFTER 1789 The map on the left indicates the provinces and provincial capitals in France before the Revolution. The map on the right indicates the administrative districts (départements) created in France in 1790.

The Three Estates hammering out the next constitution.

would fight against Britain. Half of Hispaniola—modern-day Haiti—became the first free black state.

In 1791, the call for equal rights for women was first made explicit in France when Olympe de Gouges (1755–1793), the daughter of a butcher, published *The Rights of Women*. "The law," she wrote, "must be the expression of the general will; all female and male citizens must contribute either personally or through their representatives to its formation." Encouraging women to demand their natural rights—and thereby evidencing the influence of the Enlightenment—she called on the Assembly to acknowledge women's rights as mothers of citizens of the nation. She insisted on women's right to education and to control property within marriage and to initiate divorce proceedings. Olympe de Gouges defined the nation as "the union of Woman and Man," and suggested that men would remain unfree unless women were granted similar rights, stopping short of demanding full political rights for women.

Resistance and Revolution

On July 14, 1790, the first anniversary of the fall of the Bastille, an imposing Festival of General Federation took place on the Champ-de-Mars, a royal parade ground in Paris. But there was no revolutionary consensus in France. In the south, nobles had already begun to organize resistance against the Revolution, and militant Catholics attacked Protestants, who tended to support the Revolution. By the summer of 1791, as the Assembly promulgated its constitution, open resistance to the Revolution had broken out in parts of the south and west, and in Alsace.

Such resistance prompted further calls for even more radical changes. Some of the revolutionaries, who did not accept the distinction between active and passive citizens, called for more democratic participation in political life. From where did this democratic thrust come? The monarchical state had rested on an intertwining network of groups—each with a set of privileges—at virtually every level of society. These included judicial, professional, administrative, and clerical groups, ranging from provincial Estates to artisanal guilds. Participatory and sometimes even democratic procedures within such bodies (or *corps*) may have instilled a tendency toward democracy that affected the course of the Revolution and pushed France toward a republic.

The first clubs were established by political factions among the deputies to the National Assembly. Some of the Assembly's most radical members split off to form the Jacobin Club, so-called because it met in the house of the religious order of the Jacobins. The Cordeliers Club brought together the radicals of Paris, while supporters of the cause of constitutional monarchy, whose members broke with the Jacobins in July 1791, gathered at the Club of the Feuillants. Monarchists formed royalist clubs. Moreover, some women began their own political clubs, such as the Club of Knitters, or joined the Fraternal Society of Patriots of Both Sexes. By 1793, there were at least 5,000 clubs in France. During the first years of the Revolution, however, there was little in France that was not political, and the political clubs were not the only place where political debate occurred. In Paris, there were also meetings of neighborhood "sections," which had first been defined as electoral districts for the convocation of the Estates-General.

Parisian revolutionaries became increasingly known as *sans-culottes*. They defined themselves by what they were without—the fancy knee britches, or *culottes*, which were associated with the aristocracy. The sans-culottes were shopkeepers, artisans, and laborers who were not opposed to private property, but who stood against unearned property, and especially against those people who seemed to have too much property, or who did not work for a living. They demanded that a maximum price be placed on bread, which alone absorbed more than half of the earnings of the average working family. Sans-culottes were for "the people," as they put it. They were defined by their political behavior. Even aristocrats could be sans-culottes if they supported the Revolution. Likewise, laborers or peasants could be called "aristocrats" if they seemed to

A female sans-culotte.

King Louis XVI wearing the Phrygian cap.

oppose the Revolution. In a world in which symbols played a crucial political role, sans-culottes could be identified by the Phrygian cap, a symbol of freedom drawn from the Roman Republic—close-fitting, red in color, with a tricolor emblem—in contrast to the three-cornered hat that had been worn by urban social elites. The language of the sans-culottes also quickly indicated who they were; they called everyone "citizen" and used the familiar (*tu* and never *vous*), egalitarian form of address. The political ideal of the sans-culottes was that popular sovereignty had to be practiced every day in direct democracy, in revolutionary clubs and in the sections.

The Flight to Varennes

Fearing the growing violence of the Revolution and counting on the support of the other monarchs of Europe, Louis XVI and his family tried to flee France in June 1791. The king's goal was to throw his support behind the foreign enemies of the Revolution and return to France to revoke the concessions that he had made. Apprehended by the National Guard in Varennes, the royal family was prevented from continuing their journey into exile and freedom.

The king's attempt to flee turned public sentiment further against him, and strengthened support for a republic. The day after his flight, the Cordeliers Club called for the establishment of a republic, but the majority of the Assembly feared civil war. On July 17, 1791, at the Champ-de-Mars in Paris, people came to sign (or put their "X" on) a petition resting on the "Altar of the Fatherland" that called on the National Assembly to replace the king "by all constitutional means." The National Guard opened fire, killing fifty people. Bailly, the moderate mayor of Paris, and Lafayette, the commander of the National Guard in Paris, declared martial law. However, even Louis XVI's formal acceptance of the constitution on September 14, 1791, could not stem the popular tide against the monarchy.

WAR AND THE SECOND REVOLUTION

The Revolution now entered a new, more radical phase. The king's flight seriously weakened the constitutional monarchists within the Assembly.

(*Left*) Georges–Jacques Danton. (*Right*) Maximilien Robespierre.

The leaders of the Parisian population—Danton, Marat, and Maximilien Robespierre—were Jacobins who had given up on the idea that a constitutional monarchy could adequately guarantee the liberties of the people. Elections brought to Paris a Legislative Assembly, which met on October 1, 1791. It replaced the Constituent Assembly, which had dissolved following the proclamation of the constitution the previous month. Republicans—now identified with the "left" as monarchists were with the "right," due to the location of the seats each group occupied in the Assembly—became a majority in March 1792.

In the meantime, French émigrés at the Austrian and Prussian courts were encouraging foreign intervention to restore Louis XVI to full monarchical authority. The republican followers of Jacques-Pierre Brissot (1754–1793), former radical pamphleteer and police spy as well as a flamboyant orator, called for a war to free Europe from the tyranny of monarchy and nobility. The members of this faction became known as the Girondins because many were from the district of Gironde, in which the major Atlantic port of Bordeaux is located. Under Girondin leadership, the Assembly's proclamations took on a more aggressive tone. The French declaration of war against Austria led to the Second Revolution, the formation of a republic, and, ultimately, a Jacobin-dominated dictatorship, which imposed the "Terror."

Reactions to the French Revolution in Europe

The French Revolution had a considerable impact on the rest of Europe. The early work of the National Assembly, particularly the abolition of feudal rights and the establishment of a constitutional monarchy found considerable favor among educated people in Britain, the Netherlands, and some German and Italian states. Some lawyers and merchants in other lands applauded, for example, measures taken to reduce the independence of the Catholic Church. The promulgation of the principles of national sovereignty and self-determination, however, threatened the monarchies of Europe. The threat posed by the French Revolution brought about a rapprochement between Austria and Prussia, rivals for domination in Central Europe, as well as a wary alliance between Great Britain and Russia.

The Prussian government's first reaction to the Revolution had been to try to subvert the alliance between France and Austria and to undermine Austrian authority in the Southern Netherlands (Belgium). In Vienna, the Habsburg emperor Leopold II was initially preoccupied with demands from the Hungarian nobility for more power. In 1789, a rebellion drove Austrian forces out of the Southern Netherlands and led to the establishment of a republic that survived only until Austrian troops returned in force in 1790.

In London, some radical Whigs greeted with enthusiasm the news of the fall of the Bastille and the first steps toward constitutional monarchy in France. But in 1790, the British writer Edmund Burke attacked the Revolution in *Reflections on the Revolution in France*. He contended that the abstract rationalism of the Enlightenment threatened the historic evolution of nations by undermining monarchy, established churches, and what he considered the "natural" ruling elite.

The Englishman Thomas Paine (1737–1809; see Chapter 11) wrote pamphlets denouncing monarchical rule and unwarranted privilege. *The Rights of Man* (1791–1792) defended the Revolution against Burke's relentless attack. Political societies supporting the Revolution, in which artisans played a major role, sprang up in Britain during the early 1790s. A small group of English women also enthusiastically supported the Revolution. Mary Wollstonecraft (1759–1797), a teacher and writer, greeted the Revolution with optimism, traveling to France to view events firsthand. Angered that the Assembly limited the right to education to men only, she published *Vindication of the Rights of Woman* (1792), the first book in Britain demanding the right for women to vote and hold elected office.

The rulers of the other European states felt threatened by the proclamation of universal principles embodied in the Declaration of the Rights of Man and Citizen. The Revolution also posed the threat of French expansion, now on behalf of carrying the revolutionary principles of "liberty, equality, and fraternity" to other lands. Besieged by exiles from France eager to tell tales of their suffering, the rulers of Prussia, Austria, Naples, and Piedmont

Olympe de Gouges (*left*), whose book *The Rights of Women* was published in France in 1791. It detailed the notion of equal rights that Mary Wollstonecraft (*right*) would take up the next year in Britain with the publication of her *Vindication of the Rights of Woman*.

undertook the suppression of Jacobin sympathizers in their states. In Britain, the seeming threat of foreign invasion helped affirm British national identity (see Chapter 11). Popular respect for the British monarchy and probably also for nobles soared as anti-French and anti-Catholic feelings came to the fore. Pitt the Younger's government lashed out at the development of popular politics in Britain, suspending the freedoms of association, assembly, and the press, as well as the writ of *habeas corpus*. "Coercion Acts" facilitated the arrest of those advocating parliamentary reform.

Thus, Louis XVI's virtual imprisonment in the Tuileries Palace in Paris and the thunderous speeches in the Assembly proclaiming the necessity of "a war of peoples against kings" worried the crowned heads of Europe. On August 27, 1791, Emperor Leopold II of the Holy Roman Empire (brother of Marie-Antoinette, who had not seen him in twenty-five years) and King Frederick William II of Prussia promulgated the Declaration of Pilnitz. It expressed their concern about the plight of the French monarchy and stated the common interest of both sovereigns in seeing order restored in France. Despite Robespierre's speeches warning the deputies that the Revolution must first deal with its enemies within France before waging war abroad, the Assembly, egged on by General Charles François Dumouriez (1739–1823), minister of foreign affairs, in April 1792 declared war on Austria. The stated reason was fear that an Austrian invasion from the Southern Netherlands was imminent. The declaration of war soon seemed a rash move, as the army had been devastated by the desertion of two-thirds of its officers (85 percent of its officers had been nobles before the Revolution). Moreover, Prussia soon joined with Austria in fighting the French. The early stages of the war produced French defeats at the hands of Austrian and Prussian armies.

A Second Revolution

The war sealed the fate of the monarchy and the royal family. As France faced the possibility of foreign invasion by Austria and Prussia, the popular fear that aristocrats and clergymen were betraying the Revolution brought down the monarchy. Early defeats on the northern frontier by Austrian troops and soaring bread prices (in part due to the requisitioning of food for the army) compounded popular anxiety and led to a new revolutionary groundswell, particularly in Paris.

In early April 1792, women marched through the capital demanding the right to bear arms. On June 20, a crowd stormed into the Tuileries Palace and threatened the royal family, shouting, "Tremble, tyrants! Here come the sans-culottes!" Strident calls for the end of the monarchy echoed in clubs and in the sections. On July 11, the Assembly officially proclaimed the *patrie,* or nation, to be "in danger," calling on all citizens to rally against the enemies of liberty within as well as outside of France. The Assembly encouraged the sections to admit the "passive" citizens who had previously been excluded because they had failed to meet tax requirements. Troops from Marseille, among volunteers called up to defend the front, sang a new revolutionary song, "The Marseillaise," penned by Rouget de Lisle. It became the anthem of the Revolution. In the meantime, the Jacobins pressed their attack against the monarchy.

In the Brunswick Manifesto (July 1792), Austria and Prussia warned the French that they would be severely punished if the royal family were harmed. All but one of the forty-eight sections of Paris responded by demanding that the king be immediately deposed. Popular discontent and Jacobin agitation came together in August. A radical committee overthrew the city council and established a revolutionary authority, the Commune of Paris. On August 10, sans-culottes from the Paris sections attacked the Tuileries Palace. The invaders killed 600 of the king's Swiss Guards and servants after they had surrendered. The royal family escaped and found protection in the quarters of the Legislative Assembly. The Assembly immediately proclaimed the monarchy suspended and ordered the royal family's imprisonment.

The popular revolution doomed France's first experiment in constitutional monarchy. On September 2, 1792, a Prussian army entered French territory and captured the eastern fortress town of Verdun. The proximity of the allied armies and the fear of betrayal at home led to the imprisonment in Paris of many people suspected of plotting against the Revolution. When a rumor circulated that the prisoners were planning to break out of prison and attack the army, mobs dragged the prisoners from their cells and killed them. During these September Massacres, more than 1,200 people, includ-

The September Massacre of 1792 in the abbey of Saint-Germain-des-Prés in Paris.

ing 225 priests, perished at the hands of crowds who acted as judges, juries, and executioners.

But just as Paris seemed vulnerable to foreign invasion, a ragtag army of regular soldiers and sans-culottes stopped the Prussian and Austrian advance with effective artillery barrages on September 20, 1792, near the windmill of Valmy, near Châlons-sur-Marne. The German poet Johann Wolfgang von Goethe, amazed by the victory of such ordinary people over a highly trained professional army, wrote, "From this time and place a new epoch is beginning." An officer trained under the Old Regime called the resultant warfare of the revolutionary armies a "hellish tactic," which saw "fifty thousand savage beasts foaming at the mouth like cannibals, hurling themselves at top speed upon soldiers whose courage has been excited by no passion."

The Revolution had been saved by the same people who had first made it. Delegates to a new assembly called the National Convention were selected by universal male suffrage in elections. The Jacobins dominated. The delegates arrived in Paris to draft a republican constitution. Their first act was unanimously to abolish the monarchy and proclaim the republic on September 21, 1792, even before news of Valmy had been learned.

The revolutionary armies of proud, loyal citizen-soldiers, however badly armed, pushed Prussian troops back across the Rhine and entered Mainz in October. On November 6, Dumouriez defeated the Austrians at Jémappes in the Austrian Netherlands, which was soon controlled by the French revolutionary army (see Map 12.2). To supply French troops, arms manufacturers turned out 45,000 guns in one year, and a Parisian factory produced 30,000 pounds of gunpowder every day.

MAP 12.2 EXPANSION OF REVOLUTIONARY FRANCE, 1792–1799   The map indicates French revolutionary army offensives and foreign anti-revolutionary army offensives. It also shows areas annexed by the French, areas occupied by the French, and dependent republics established by revolutionary France.

Emboldened by these unexpected military successes, the National Convention on November 19, 1792, promised "fraternity and assistance to all peoples who want to recover their liberty." French troops captured Frankfurt and occupied much of the Rhineland. The Convention also declared the outright annexation of the Alpine province of Savoy, belonging to the Kingdom of Sardinia, and the Mediterranean town of Nice, captured at the end of September. They declared them within the "natural frontiers" of France—a claim that contradicted the principles of popular sovereignty and self-determination contained in the annexation decrees themselves. On December 15, 1792, the Convention abolished all feudal dues and tithes in those territories occupied by French armies.

The governments of Britain and the Dutch Republic viewed the occupation of the Austrian Netherlands as a great threat. When it appeared that both states were considering joining Austria and Prussia in taking action against France, the Convention on February 1, 1793, declared war on Britain and the Dutch Republic. Spain and the Kingdoms of Sardinia and Naples joined this First Coalition against France.

When correspondence between Louis XVI and the Austrian government was discovered, his trial became inevitable. Accused of treason, the king defended himself with grace and dignity. He called on the Convention to look after his family as he had tried to watch over those of France. But with the words "one cannot reign innocently" ringing in the hall, the Convention condemned the king to death. On the morning of January 21, Louis XVI was guillotined. The huge throng roared its approval as the executioner held up the severed royal head, symbol of the Old Regime, for all to see.

As the Convention and the more radical Paris Commune vied for authority, the French Republic, still at war, began to split apart. The Girondins and the Jacobins quarreled bitterly. The Girondins were popularly identified with the economic liberalism that characterized the port cities and with the desire to carry the Revolution aggressively beyond the frontiers of France. Opposed to centralizing power in Paris, they wanted a significant

The execution of Louis XVI.

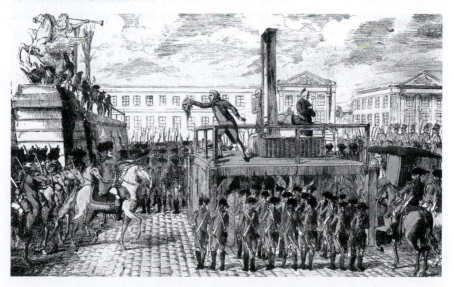

degree of local political control. The deputies of the far left, principally the Jacobins and their followers, sat on the raised side of the Tuileries Hall where the Convention met. The far left became known as "the Mountain" (their followers the *Montagnards*). The political center became known as "the Plain." Backed by the Parisian sans-culottes, the Jacobins insisted on the necessity of centralizing authority in the capital to save the Revolution from internal subversion and foreign armies. The Girondins, more moderate, believed that the Revolution had gone far enough. The Jacobins accused them of secretly supporting the monarchy and demanded swift punishment for traitors.

From the point of view of the Jacobins, those who were not for them were against the Revolution. The sense of vulnerability and insecurity was heightened by reverses in the field. The armies of the First Coalition defeated the French in the Austrian Netherlands in March 1793. Dumouriez then betrayed the Revolution, preparing to march his soldiers to Paris to put Louis XVI's son on the throne as Louis XVII. When his army refused to follow him, Dumouriez fled across the border to join the Austrians and other émigrés. In the meantime, the allies recaptured the left bank of the Rhine River.

Counter-Revolution

The Counter-Revolution began in regions where religious practice still seemed strong and where the Civil Constitution of the French Clergy had met with considerable resistance (see Map 12.3). A full-scale insurrection against the Revolution began in March 1793. This revolt in the western part of France became known as the Vendée, after the name of one of the most insurrectionary districts (the old provinces having been divided into *départements* in 1790). In August 1793, the revolutionary government decreed mass conscription, the *levée en masse,* which initiated the concept of the nation at arms: "Young people will go to battle; married men will forge arms and transport supplies; women will make tents, uniforms, and serve in the hospitals; children will pick rags; old men will have themselves carried to public squares, to inspire the courage of the warriors, and to preach hatred of kings and the unity of the Republic." The unpopularity of military conscription in defense of the republic also generated resistance.

South of the Loire River, the counter-revolutionary forces principally emerged from the relatively isolated bocage, or hedgerow country, where the old noble and clerical elites had been relatively unaffected by the economic changes of the past few decades, specifically the expansion of the market economy. In Brittany, which had enjoyed a relatively light tax burden during the Old Regime, the revolutionary government was hated for having ended that privilege, thereby increasing taxes. Both sides fought with a brutality, including mass executions and systematic pillage, that recalled the Thirty

MAP 12.3 THE COUNTER–REVOLUTION   The map indicates areas of federalism and counter-revolutionary activity, including major uprisings.

Years' War (1618–1648) in Central Europe. In insurrectionary areas during 1793–1794, perhaps a quarter of the population perished, as many as 250,000 people, in part because the revolutionary troops, facing guerilla warfare, saw local civilians as potential threats.

The Terror

Faced with foreign invasion and civil insurgency, the Jacobins further centralized government authority and implemented the "Terror" against those considered enemies of the Revolution. The Convention set aside a planned Constitution of 1793 (which was to have replaced the Constitution of 1791).

The rights of the accused were limited, and new special courts prosecuted anyone considered disloyal to the republic. On March 19, 1793, the Convention passed a law permitting the immediate trial of armed insurgents without a jury. The Jacobin-dominated Convention established a Committee of Public Safety of nine and then twelve members, which gradually assumed more and more power as it oversaw the Terror. The Convention also decreed a special war tax, including a forced levy on wealthy people, and in May 1793 imposed the "Maximum"—a maximum price on grain. These measures of centralization and government interference in the economy led to an irreversible break between the Jacobins, who believed in state controls, and the Girondins, who believed in economic freedom.

Military requisitions of foodstuffs accentuated hardship. Poor people rioted against the high price of grain. In Paris, the Society of Revolutionary Republican Women took to the streets, demanding laws against hoarding and calling for women to be granted citizenship. A group called the *enragés* (the "enraged") demanded that bakers be penalized if they charged more than the maximum price for bread.

In June, pushed on by crowds from the radical sections of Paris, the Convention expelled twenty-nine Girondin deputies, accusing them of supporting hoarders, and it ordered the arrest of some of them. Insurgents in Toulon turned over half of the French fleet to the British. In July, Charlotte Corday, a royalist noblewoman, stabbed Marat to death in his bathtub. Tax revenue and foreign trade fell by half. *Assignats,* more of which had rolled off the government presses as the financial crisis continued, plunged further in value.

Two young radical Jacobin leaders strode forward to take charge of the Terror. Louis Antoine Saint-Just (1767–1794), a precocious, icy young deputy whose mother had once had him incarcerated for running off with the family silver, waged war on royalists, hoarders, and Girondins. "Those who make revolutions by halves dig their own grave," he warned.

Maximilien Robespierre (1758–1794) emerged as the leading figure on the Committee of Public Safety. He knew that the Mountain drew its support from the sans-culottes, some of whom supported the Terror. But he also believed that the popular

Jacques-Louis David's *The Death of Marat*.

movement remained a threat to the orderly transformation of political life in France. Historians have offered interpretations of Robespierre that range from the view that he was a popular democrat who saved the essence of the Revolution from counter-revolutionaries to the suggestion that he was actually a precursor of twentieth-century totalitarianism.

Robespierre was the son and grandson of lawyers from the northern town of Arras. After his irresponsible father abandoned his family, Robespierre depended on scholarships for his schooling. At age eleven, he was chosen to read an address in Latin to the royal family at his school in Paris. It was raining and the royal family, it was said, without acknowledging the young student, ordered their driver onward. The royal coach splashed Robespierre with mud.

After completing his law degree, Robespierre defended a number of poor clients, including a man unjustly accused of stealing from an abbey. After he was elected to the third estate, Robespierre gradually established a reputation in Paris for his well-organized and thoughtful but colorless speeches. Contemporaries noted the prissiness of the impeccably dressed, slight man with very pale skin and chestnut hair always perfectly powdered. A favorite of the Parisian sans-culottes, the man they nicknamed "the Incorruptible" called in 1793 for "a single will" of the nation to save the Revolution.

Insurrections by supporters of the Girondins against the Jacobins and the authority of the Convention broke out in Lyon, Marseille, Bordeaux, and Caen, where merchants and lawyers played prominent roles in failed "federalist revolts" against centralized revolutionary authority emanating from Paris. Lyon fell to Jacobin troops on October 9, 1793, and bloody reprisals followed.

The "Law of Suspects" promulgated by the Convention in September deprived those accused of crimes against the nation of most of their remaining rights. The Convention banned clubs and popular societies of women. Olympe de Gouges was among the Girondins guillotined. Marie-Antoinette, though hardly a feminist, also went to the scaffold.

The Jacobins were so intent on destroying the Old Regime and building a new political world that they instituted a new calendar in October 1793. The old calendar gave way to a new republican calendar based upon "weeks," or cycles of ten days, and "months" taking their names from more secular notions of the changing of the seasons (such as *Germinal,* meaning "the budding," *Ventôse,* meaning "windy," and so on). September 22, 1792, the first year of the republic, became, retroactively, day one of the "year I."

The Jacobins adopted new revolutionary symbols to take the place of Old Regime symbols and to help maintain revolutionary enthusiasm. Following the execution of Louis XVI, the revolutionaries chose a female image for liberty and the republic, which was ironic in light of their denial of political rights to women. The female image of the republic appears gentle, non-threatening, and virtuous, representing the abstract virtues of liberty, popular sovereignty, community, and nation. Contemporaries contrasted republican virtue with the abuses of power that seemed to have characterized the Old Regime. They did so even as Jacobin representatives of the Revolution imposed their will wherever they were resisted in the provinces.

During the "year II" (which began in September 1793), radical revolutionaries undertook an ambitious campaign of "de-christianization," a war on religious institutions and symbols. They closed down churches and removed crosses standing in public places. The campaign failed, unable to overcome centuries of firmly implanted beliefs and traditions, even among many people who supported the Revolution. It also turned many clergy who had accepted the Civil Constitution away from the Revolution, generating further resistance.

Outside of Paris, "representatives on mission," armed with dictatorial authority in the name of the Convention, tried to maintain order. They worked with local "surveillance committees" and "revolutionary tribunals" of Jacobins. Some of these revolutionary officials sent counter-revolutionaries to the guillotine. "Revolutionary armies" of artisans and day laborers guarded requisitioned provisions for the military and oversaw the melting down of church bells for war use.

Yet the Terror was never uniformly implemented. Between 11,000 and 18,000 people perished at the hands of the Committee of Public Safety (a fraction, by comparison, of the deaths that had resulted from the Thirty

A Revolutionary Tribunal during the Terror.

Years' War or the American Civil War). About 300,000 royalists, Girondins, or other "enemies of the Revolution" were imprisoned for some period during the Terror. About 15 percent of those killed were nobles or clergy. Thus, nobles and clergy suffered disproportionately in terms of their number in the population as a whole (5 to 8 percent). However, artisans and peasants constituted by far the largest number of those dispatched by the revolutionary tribunals. The majority of these were arrested near the northern and eastern frontiers that had been invaded by foreign armies or in the counter-revolutionary west where civil war raged. During the winter of 1793–1794, perhaps as many as several thousand prisoners—including priests and nuns—captured from the counter-revolutionary armies of the Vendée were taken out into the swirling waters of the Loire River in boats that had holes bored in them and drowned at the orders of a cruel revolutionary official. In all, several thousand people perished.

In the meantime, the tide of the war had turned in favor of the aggressive French armies. Significant French victories on the battlefield undercut the argument that the Terror was necessary because of the immediate external threat to the republic. A French army defeated the Austrians in the Austrian Netherlands in June 1794, forcing them out of Belgium. Another French force reached the Rhine River and captured Mainz. A third French army recaptured Savoy from the Kingdom of Sardinia. The Spanish army retreated across the Pyrenees Mountains.

The Terror then struck the *enragés* leaders in March 1794 after they demanded even more economic controls and an intensification of the "dechristianization" campaign. They were brought before the Revolutionary Tribunal of Paris, condemned, and guillotined. The Committee of Public Safety then went after Danton and his followers, who believed that the Terror was no longer necessary, and thus had been labeled the "Indulgents." They too were condemned and guillotined. Real and imagined conspiracies provided the justification for the Terror, which now seemed without end. "Who will be next?" was whispered among even those loyal to the most radical members of the Committee of Public Safety. In May, Robespierre survived an assassination attempt.

Robespierre sought to establish a secularized "Cult of the Supreme Being" that would serve as a "constant reminder of justice" to bind the people to the new values of republicanism. With the elimination of the *enragés* and Danton and many of his followers, Robespierre devoted his energies to creating a "Republic of Virtue." Early in June 1794, the republic celebrated the "Festival of Reason." The cathedral of Notre Dame in Paris became a "temple of reason." A popular female opera singer, dressed as Liberty, wearing a Phrygian cap and holding a pike, bowed before the flame of reason. The painter Jacques-Louis David constructed huge statues of monsters like Anarchy and Atheism made of pasteboard. After Robespierre set fire to them, a statue of Wisdom rose out of the ashes.

The Terror took on a momentum of its own. Saint-Just warned, "We must punish not merely traitors, but also the indifferent." The Jacobins arrested the Marquis de Condorcet (1743–1794) for alleged counter-revolutionary activity. Condorcet, an influential philosophe of the late Enlightenment, had been elected to the Assembly in 1791. He believed that all people should have a voice in approving acts of government, albeit indirectly, and that all citizens should be equal before the law. He had campaigned against the death penalty and slavery, and he defended political equality and the rights of women. Condorcet died of apoplexy—or committed suicide—in his cell in the spring of 1794, shortly before he was to be executed. The Revolution seemed to have turned on and destroyed the enlightened reason that had arguably helped bring it about.

THE FINAL STAGES OF THE REVOLUTION

Moderate Jacobins and other members of the Convention, fearing that they might be next in line to be purged, overthrew the Jacobin dictatorship. They established a new government called the Directory, which ended the Terror. Caught between staunch Jacobins on the left and monarchists on the right, the period of the Directory was marked by great political instability, ongoing wars abroad, and economic hardship at home. Although the Directory consolidated some of the gains of the Revolution, it too would be overthrown by conspirators led by the Abbé Sieyès and one of the rising stars of the revolutionary army, Napoleon Bonaparte.

Thermidor

The Revolutionary Tribunal of Paris used new powers granted by the Committee of Public Safety in June 1794 to send 1,376 people to their deaths over a period of six weeks. Afraid that they would be next on Robespierre's list, moderates in the Convention began to plot against Robespierre and his allies. They were led by Paul Barras (1755–1829), a follower of Danton, and Joseph Fouché (1758–1820). On July 27, 1794 (the 9th of Thermidor), Robespierre haltingly addressed the Convention, calling for one more purge. But, anticipating his own downfall, Robespierre also murmured, "I ask for death." That night, Robespierre and Saint-Just were arrested at the virtually unguarded town hall of Paris. Robespierre attempted suicide, shattering his jaw with a shot.

Robespierre and the others were executed without trial, their fate as swift and pitiless as that of the Terror's victims. They were followed to the scaffold by more than a hundred of their allies. In the provinces, particularly in the south, the revenge against the Jacobins by their enemies was swift and brutal. Lazare Carnot (1753–1823), a talented military engineer, brilliant administrator ("the organizer of victory"), and one of the twelve members of the Committee of Public Safety, survived because he had opposed Robespierre. Moreover, the continuing war effort desperately required his administrative talent.

After dismantling the Paris Commune, the victors of Thermidor—the name taken from the period in the revolutionary calendar in which Robespierre fell—set about establishing a new national government. Order was only slowly and incompletely restored in the countryside. The Thermidorians greatly reduced the powers of the Committee of Public Safety on July 31, 1794, and then abolished it completely. In November 1794, Jacobin Clubs were banned.

The Directory: Politics and Society

In 1795 the Thermidorians produced a constitution that created a bicameral (two-house) legislative assembly and a collective executive of five directors. The latter provided the name "the Directory" for this period of the Revolution. The two assemblies included the Council of the Ancients (250 members), which discussed and voted on legislation proposed by the second assembly, the Council of Five Hundred. Two-thirds of the members of the new councils were elected from among the members of the existing Convention. The two councils elected the five directors who formed the collective executive authority, or Directorate. Beginning in 1797, one-third of the members of each council and one of the five directors were to be replaced each year.

People with property benefited from the Thermidorian reaction. By the Constitution of 1795, all male taxpayers could vote, but they selected electoral assemblies for which only about 30,000 men were eligible, a smaller group than in the indirect elections of 1789–1791. But although about 2 million men could vote (out of some 7 million men of voting age), the system of indirect election favored the selection of the wealthiest citizens to serve in the assemblies.

The period of the Directory was marked by a decided turn against the asceticism associated with Robespierre's Republic of Virtue. The *jeunesse dorée,* or gilded youth, drawn from the bourgeoisie and old nobility, set the social and cultural tone of the day. Wearing square collars and fancy clothes, wealthy young men smashed busts of Marat. The red-colored symbols of the sans-culottes—such as the Phrygian cap—quickly disappeared. Women who could afford to do so wore long flowing white robes of opulence and sensuality, with plunging necklines that would have horrified Robespierre. The familiar (*tu*) form of address, identified with section and club meetings, gave way to the formal *vous* more characteristic of the Old Regime. Crowds in which women played a prominent part demanded that churches be reopened. Boisterous social events amused the middle class; among them the macabre "Dance of the Victims," a ball to which only those with a relative who had perished in the Terror could be admitted. Some revelers turned up with their

The return of high society during the Directory.

hair cut away from the back of their neck, mimicking the final haircut of those about to be sent to the guillotine.

Under the Directory, the comforts of the wealthy, some of whom had made their fortunes during the Revolution (by buying Church lands or supplying the military), contrasted sharply with the deprivations of the poor. The economy lay in shambles. The winter of 1795 was cruelly harsh. The abolition of the Maximum spelled the end of cheap bread, which rose in price by thirteen times that spring in Paris. The price of basic commodities soared. Near Paris, people scrambled to eat the carcasses of dead army horses, and in mountainous areas people searched for berries and edible roots while trying to stay warm. Peasants suffered the military requisition of food supplies.

Instability

The Directory may have ended the Terror, but it brought neither stability nor peace to France, despite peace agreements concluded with Prussia in April 1795. Prussia accepted the French annexation of the left bank of the Rhine River, the Austrian Netherlands, and the Dutch United Provinces (which became the "Batavian Republic"). In the meantime, French armies continued to press forward against the Austrian armies in Central Europe and Italy. Mass desertion and heavy casualties drastically reduced the size of the French army, which, after reaching a million men in the summer of 1794, fell to less than 500,000 a year later.

War compounded social and political instability in 1795. That spring, the Directory repressed two small popular demonstrations by crowds demanding a return to controls on the price of bread. Encouraged by the Convention's move to the right, royalists also tried to seize power. The king's son had died in a Paris prison in June 1795, and so the count of Provence, Louis XVI's brother, was now heir to the throne. An army of nobles supported by the British landed at Quiberon Bay in Brittany on June 27, but French forces turned back the invaders with ease. On October 5, 1795, royalists attempted an insurrection in Paris, where they found support in the more prosperous districts. The government called in Napoleon Bonaparte (1769–1821), a young Corsican general, who turned away the insurgents with a "whiff of grapeshot."

Instability continued. François-Noël Babeuf (1760–1797), who was called Gracchus, plotted to overthrow the Directory. Influenced by Rousseau and espousing social egalitarianism and the common ownership of land, Babeuf concluded that a small group of committed revolutionaries could seize power if they were tightly organized and had the support of the poor. Babeuf organized the "Conspiracy of the Equals," finding support among a handful of Parisian artisans and shopkeepers. In May 1796, Babeuf and his friends were arrested; they were guillotined a year later after a trial. The Directory took advantage of the discovery of this plot to purge Jacobins once again.

Caught between the intransigent, dogmatic followers of Robespierre and the Jacobins on the left and the royalists on the right, and lacking effective and charismatic civilian leaders, the Directory's difficult tightrope act grew more precarious in an atmosphere of uncertainty, intrigue, and rumors of coups d'état.

In 1797, elections returned many royalists to the Council of Five Hundred. Fearful that they might press for peace with France's enemies in the hope of obtaining a restoration of the monarchy, the Directory government annulled the election results. The coup d'état of the 18th Fructidor (September 4, 1797) eliminated two of the directors, including Carnot. In May of the next year, the directors refused to allow recently elected deputies to take their seats on the Council of Five Hundred.

For all of its failures, the Directory did provide France with its second apprenticeship in representative government. The Constitution of 1795 was an important transition between the political system of the Old Regime, based primarily upon monarchical absolutism and noble privilege, and modern representative government grounded in the sanctity of property.

The Directory had rejected cautious British suggestions that a workable peace might be forged without France having to give up its conquests of the Rhineland and the Austrian Netherlands. Perhaps fearful that a more bellicose ministry in Britain might replace that of William Pitt the Younger if such a peace were signed, the French fought on.

Napoleon Bonaparte, who had swept aside the royalist insurrection, now commanded the Army of Italy, checking in with Paris only when it suited him. His armies overwhelmed the Austrian troops in northern Italy. The Treaty of Campo Formio (October 17, 1797) left France the dominant foreign power in Italy. This victory, and Napoleon's boldly independent diplomatic negotiations in the Italian campaigns, made him the toast of Paris. The Austrians joined the Prussians in recognizing French absorption of the left bank of the Rhine River and annexation of the Austrian Netherlands. Reorganized in July 1797 as the Cisalpine Republic, much of the north of Italy became a feeble pawn of France.

Despite these victories, years of war had exhausted the French nation and damaged the economy. France's financial situation deteriorated even further. Inflation was rampant, and the collection of taxes was sporadic at best. *Assignats* were now virtually worthless. Many bourgeois were dissatisfied, having lost money when the Directory cancelled more than half of the national debt in 1797.

In May 1798, Napoleon sailed with an army to Egypt, over which Turkey was sovereign; he hoped to strike at British interests in India. Fearing that France sought to break apart the Ottoman Empire and extend its interests in an area Russia had always wanted to dominate, Russia allied with Britain. Austria also joined the alliance, which became the Second Coalition (1799–1802). Austria hoped to undo the Treaty of Campo Formio and to prevent further French expansion in Italy, where French forces had sent the pope into exile and established a Roman Republic.

The combined strength of the Coalition powers for the moment proved too much for the overextended French armies in Italy. In Switzerland, a combined Russian and Austrian army defeated a French force. When Irish rebels rose up against British rule in 1798, France sent an invasion force to aid the insurgents, in the hope of launching an invasion of England. After the defeat of the Irish insurgents and French troops who landed ashore, a French fleet attempting to land more soldiers was defeated off the coast. British troops crushed a series of Irish rebellions in a bloody struggle in which 30,000 people were killed, and the British navy captured one of the French ships and turned back the rest.

In the meantime, coalition members quarreled over strategy and eventual goals. Russian Tsar Paul (ruled 1796–1801) withdrew from the Second Coalition in October 1799, as he was irritated with the British for insisting that the Royal Navy had the right to stop and search any vessel on the seas.

The Eighteenth Brumaire

The wily Abbé Sieyès (who once replied "I survived" when asked what he had done during the Revolution) became a director in the spring of 1799. He believed France needed a government with stronger executive authority.

Because the role of the army had grown enormously, he concluded that it would emerge as the arbiter of France's political future. In the face of endemic instability, Sieyès decided in 1799 to overthrow the Directory. The go-between was Talleyrand, the foreign minister. The career of Talleyrand provides another remarkable example of revolutionary survival; a detractor once claimed that Brie cheese was "the only king to whom he has been loyal." Sieyès contacted General Napoleon Bonaparte. On November 9, 1799 (the 18th Brumaire), General Bonaparte announced to the hastily convened councils that another Jacobin conspiracy had been uncovered and that a new constitution had to be framed to provide France with a stronger executive authority. The deputies were justly dubious. Some demanded his immediate arrest. Napoleon's response was incoherent and ineffective, but the quick thinking of his brother, Lucien, president of the lower assembly, saved Bonaparte from one of his few moments of indecision. Lucien rejected the call for a vote to outlaw Napoleon, and he ordered troops to evict members who opposed him. Those who remained delegated complete power to Sieyès and General Bonaparte. Would Napoleon, whose rise to power would have been almost unthinkable without the French Revolution, be the heir of the French Revolution, or its destroyer?

A contemporary British caricature of the 18th Brumaire: "The Corsican Crocodile dissolving the Council of Frogs!!!"

The Corsican Crocodile dissolving the Council of Frogs!!!

PERSPECTIVES ON THE FRENCH REVOLUTION

The French Revolution, which began in Paris, swept across Europe. In France, it marked a significant break with the past, although, to be sure, important continuities from the Old Regime helped shape the modern world. In other countries, too, the Revolution effected major changes. These included in some places the abolition of feudalism, curtailment of clerical privileges, and establishment of a more centralized governmental structure. But while some people welcomed the export of the French Revolution, others did not, viewing "liberation" by the French as indistinguishable from conquest. The French presence engendered a patriotic response in Russia, Spain, and some of the German and Italian states, contributing to the emergence of nationalist feeling there.

Like the contemporaries who witnessed the Revolution, modern historians also have had a variety of interpretations of it. Many of them still disagree as to the causes, effects, and significance of the Revolution, debating the dramatic events with some of the same passion as those who experienced it firsthand.

European Responses to the Revolution

In countries over which revolutionary armies swept, enthusiastic shouts for "liberty, fraternity, and equality!" echoed in German, Dutch, and Piedmontese, then disappeared in a sea of French muskets, military requisitions, and even executions. The revolutionary wave did bring about sweeping changes in some of the "liberated" territories, and these changes continued even as Napoleon consolidated his authority in France (see Chapter 13). Thus, in Piedmont, French control reduced the influence of the nobility and left a heritage of relative administrative efficiency. The abolition of feudalism in some of the conquered German states, northern Italy, and the Kingdom of Naples increased the number of property owners. The French conquerors proclaimed the rule of law and curtailed some of the influence of the clergy.

But the French faced the realities of almost constant warfare and, increasingly, local resistance. As the wars dragged on and the economic situations of the "republics" grew worse, the benefits brought by the French seemed increasingly less important. Ruined merchants and former officials joined nobles and clerics in opposing rule by France or its puppets. As the Civil Constitution of the French Clergy led to a violent reaction against the Revolution in France, anticlerical measures in the occupied territories had the same effect. The peoples of the Rhineland, the Netherlands, and Flanders bitterly resented the revolutionaries' de-christianization campaign. Increasingly, the French presence bred contempt and hatred. Bavarian, Dutch, Piedmontese, Austrian, and Swiss patriots found willing listeners. The French occupation gave rise to general opposition and a new wave of national feeling among the conquered. In Great Britain, the French Revolution also contributed to the accentuation of British nationalism in the face of a perceived threat by its old Catholic enemy in a new guise.

The French conquests in Europe were themselves an exercise in statemaking, largely unanticipated and unwanted by the local populations. Between 1795 and 1799, the Directory established satellite "sister republics" directly administered by France. The Helvetic Republic (Switzerland), the Batavian Republic (the Netherlands), the Cisalpine Republic (Milan), and the Parthenopean Republic (the Kingdom of Naples) were founded with the goal of shoring up alliances against the other great powers. But in the Italian states, only the Cisalpine Republic generated any local enthusiasm for the French invaders, and then only briefly. People "liberated" from the rule of kings and princes found themselves governed by a revolutionary bureaucracy administered from Paris.

The French found support and hired officials principally from the middle class, which had already provided officials in the old state structure. But the French invasions gradually generated a hatred for the revolutionary invaders and in some places a concomitant nationalist response. This was especially true within the German states, where many writers and other people in the upper classes hoped one day that "Germany"—300 states, 50 free cities, and almost 1,000 territories of imperial knights of the Holy Roman Empire— would one day be politically unified.

Historians' Views of the Revolution

Marxist historians long dominated the historiography of the French Revolution. They have described the Revolution as the inevitable result of a bourgeois challenge to the Old Regime, dominated by nobles. Thus, Marxists have interpreted the Revolution in terms of the rise of the bourgeoisie and its struggle for social and political influence commensurate with its rising economic power during the eighteenth century. Marxists have insisted that the nobility compromised the authority of the absolute monarchy by refusing to be taxed; then, according to this interpretation, the emboldened bourgeoisie allied with urban artisans and workers to bring down the absolute monarchy. They have described the emergence of the bourgeoisie as the dominant social class in France, insisting on its growing role in the country's increasingly capitalist economy.

This traditional Marxist economic interpretation of the French Revolution has been largely discredited. Some historians have noted that differences between aristocrats and bourgeois, and within both social groups, had become considerably blurred during the eighteenth century; that most of the "bourgeois" members of the Estates-General were not drawn from commerce and manufacturing but rather from law; and that, in any case, the upper middle class and nobles by the time of the Revolution shared a common obsession with money, not privilege. Thus, one cannot accurately depict the Revolution as having been simply a victory for the bourgeoisie.

Moreover, the Revolution did not expedite capitalism but may even have retarded it, by launching France and Europe into a long series of costly wars.

Views critical of the "bourgeois revolution" thesis have also emphasized that within France the complex nature of local political power, divided among provincial Estates and parlements, and among various groups enjoying formal privileges or monopolies and municipalities, limited the actual prerogatives of absolute monarchy. Many historians now see the Revolution as affirming the victory of men of property—a rubric that included both nobles and bourgeois—over titled nobles born into status and power.

A related interpretation has seen the Revolution as part of an essentially democratic "Atlantic Revolution" stretching across the Atlantic Ocean. By this view, the American War of Independence was the first manifestation of an essentially political quest for popular sovereignty. It influenced, in turn, the French Revolution and subsequent attempts in other European countries to gain political rights, as well as movements for independence in Spain's Latin American colonies early in the nineteenth century.

More recently, another revisionist school has argued that a new political culture was already in place in the last decades of the Old Regime. An extreme version of this interpretation sees the French monarchy as a state well on the way to reforming itself through the collaboration of liberal nobles before the Revolution interrupted this process. One view sees in the 1750s and 1760s the origins of this new, revolutionary political culture, seen in the political and ideological opposition to Louis XV and particularly in the rhetorical violence of the Revolution's first year.

None of these varying interpretations, however, diminishes the significance of the French Revolution in transforming the Western world by providing its first modern European democratic experience. This is why its origins and nature continue to generate excitement and debate today, well more than 200 years after the fall of the Bastille.

CHAPTER **13**

NAPOLEON AND EUROPE

The royalist, religious writer François-René de Chateaubriand once called his enemy Napoleon "the mightiest breath of life which has ever animated human clay." In a rare moment of introspection, Napoleon once remarked, "It is said that I am an ambitious man but that is not so; or at least my ambition is so closely bound to my being that they are both one and the same."

Yet, far more than his imposing will, Napoleon's career was shaped by and reflected the breathtaking changes brought by the French Revolution. Statemaking and the emergence of nationalism, accompanied by the increased secularization of political institutions, slowly but surely transformed the European continent.

An admirer of the Enlightenment, Napoleon claimed that he was the true son of the French Revolution. He personally supervised the writing of the new constitution, which made wealth, specifically propertied wealth, the determinant of status. Napoleon's reign was also a watershed in statemaking: he further centralized the French state and extended its reach, making it more efficient by codifying laws and creating new bureaucratic structures and a new social hierarchy based upon state service.

Napoleon saw himself as a savior who carried "liberty, equality, and fraternity" abroad, freeing the European peoples from sovereigns who oppressed them. From his final exile on the distant Atlantic island of Saint Helena, Napoleon claimed to have created European unity. But in the process of "liberating" other nations from the stranglehold of old regimes, he also conquered them.

NAPOLEON'S RISE TO POWER

Napoleon's rise to power should be seen in the context of the French Revolution. With the emigration of most of the officer corps during the early

479

stages of the Revolution, a generation of talented generals had risen rapidly through the ranks by virtue of their remarkable battlefield accomplishments during the revolutionary wars that had raged across much of Western and Central Europe since 1792. During the Directory, generals became increasingly powerful arbiters in political life. Napoleon manipulated the consuls and ultimately overthrew the Directory.

The Young Bonaparte

Of the strategically important Mediterranean island of Corsica, Jean-Jacques Rousseau in *The Social Contract* (1762) wrote, "I have a presentiment that one day this small island will astonish Europe." The year before, the Corsican patriot Pascale di Paoli (1725–1807) had managed to evict the Genoese from Corsica. But in 1768 the French took Corsica. Carlo Buonaparte, one of Paoli's followers, remained on the island rather than join Paoli in exile in England.

On August 15, 1769, Buonaparte's wife, whose family could trace its noble origins back to fourteenth-century Lombardy, gave birth to a son, Napoleon, named after a cousin who had been killed by the French. It is one of the strange ironies of history that Napoleon would have been British had his father followed Paoli into exile. In 1770, the French government accepted the Buonaparte family as nobles. The island's governor arranged for the young Buonaparte to receive an appointment to the royal military school at Brienne, in Champagne, which Napoleon entered as a boy in 1779. There he was exposed not only to a rigorous program of study but also to the humiliating condescension of the other students. He was an outsider, and the other students mocked his strong Corsican accent—Napoleon's first language was the patois of his island, a mix of Genovese and Tuscan—and his relatively humble economic situation. During the summer of 1789, he penned a history of his island in which the French were portrayed as murderous exploiters and tormenters, and Corsicans their victims. Unusually bright but also brooding, melancholy, and at least once even suicidal, he earned appointment to the artillery section of the national military academy in Paris, passing the examinations in a single year.

Antoine-Jean Gros's painting of the young Napoleon in *Bonaparte at Arcole* (1796).

Napoleon and the Revolution

With the outbreak of the Revolution, Napoleon returned to Corsica in September 1789. There he helped organize the National Guard and drew up a petition to the National Assembly in Paris asking that Corsica formally become part of France, with its people enjoying the rights of citizenship. In this way, Napoleon distanced himself from those Corsicans who wanted independence, thus parting ways with his hero Paoli, who had returned from England and joined the island's royalists. Napoleon favored the Revolution for three reasons: he wanted to see a curtailment of the abuses of the Old Regime; he hoped that the Revolution might end his island's status within France as little more than a conquered territory; and he thought the Revolution might provide him with an opportunity for promotion.

Napoleon became a Jacobin. He commanded a volunteer force that on Easter Sunday, 1792, fired on rioters supporting the cause of the Catholic Church. When Paoli's victorious forces turned the island over to the English, the Buonapartes were forced to flee. Sent by the Committee of Public Safety to fight federalist and royalist rebels and their British allies in the south, in December 1793 Napoleon planned the successful artillery siege of the port of Toulon, which was held by British forces.

Useful political connections and the lack of direct involvement in the bitter factional struggles in Paris may have saved Napoleon from execution in the Terror or during Thermidor. The result was that Napoleon's star continued to rise (with the help of his own determined campaign to construct a heroic public image of his exploits), while some of his Jacobin friends went to the guillotine. In the Paris of Thermidor, Napoleon helped put down a royalist uprising on October 6, 1795. He attracted the attention of—and soon married—Josephine de Beauharnais, the lover of the corrupt Paul Barras, one of the directors, and the widow of a member of the National Assembly who had been guillotined during the Terror. In 1796, the directors made Napoleon commander of the Army of Italy. It now seemed appropriate to eliminate the Italian spelling of his name; Buonaparte became Napoleon Bonaparte. Spectacular successes against the Austrians and their allies in Italy, including at the Battle of Arcole (November 1796), made him the toast of Paris. He later recalled that, after victory over Austrian forces at the Battle of Lodi (May 1796), which opened the way to Milan, "I realized I was a superior being and conceived the ambition of performing great things, which hitherto had filled my thoughts only as a fantastic dream. I saw the world flee beneath me, as if I were transported in air."

Napoleon was now conducting military and foreign policy virtually on his own, pillaging and looting Italy of art treasures as he pleased in the name of "liberty." His forceful and virtually independent pursuit of the war, and the subsequent peace he arranged with Austria at Campo Formio on October 18, 1797, gave France control of the Austrian Netherlands, Venetia, and the satellite Cisalpine Republic in northern and central Italy. For the moment, only Great Britain remained as an enemy.

Dreaming of an eastern empire, Napoleon then turned his attention to the Middle East. In 1798, he set off on a spectacular voyage to Egypt, part of the Ottoman Empire, thus undertaking the first try by a Western power to occupy a country in the Middle East. He was accompanied by 35,000 soldiers and a shipload of scientists, including mathematicians, physicians, zoologists, and engineers, a few of the latter already dreaming of carving a canal through the Isthmus of Suez that would give the French an overwhelming advantage in trade with the Far East. In Cairo he founded the Institute of Egypt, which greatly influenced the origins of Egyptology. Thus, Napoleon cloaked his invasion as a "civilizing mission."

After pausing en route long enough to capture the island of Malta, Napoleon defeated Egyptian forces at the Battle of the Pyramids in July 1798. But the tiny British admiral Horatio Nelson (1758–1805), who could see out of only one eye, had lost an arm, and had few teeth left, trapped and destroyed the French fleet on August 1, 1798, in the Battle of the Nile. Russia and Austria, their respective interests threatened by French campaigns in the east, now formed a Second Coalition against France, which Turkey also joined. Temporarily stranded in Egypt because of the naval defeat, and with his officers having to use the Greek historian Herodotus's *Histories* as their guide to Egypt, the undaunted Napoleon set off to conquer Syria. In Palestine his army stopped at Jaffa, where it massacred the population. Forced to retreat to Egypt by dwindling supplies and disease, Napoleon achieved a final victory there over the Turks with the annihilation of several more villages and their inhabitants. Napoleon then returned to France.

In Paris, Abbé Emmanuel Sieyès was plotting to overthrow the Directory. Such a venture now required the participation of one of the powerful, popular young generals whom the incessant warfare had catapulted to prominence. Napoleon, who could be portrayed as the potential savior of France, now helped piece together a political constituency from among the quarreling factions of the Directory. With the coup d'état of the 18th Brumaire (November 9, 1799), Sieyès and Napoleon overthrew the Directory.

CONSOLIDATION OF POWER

After the overthrow of the Directory, the conspirators established a new government, the Consulate. It brought political stability to France. It did so by concentrating strong executive authority in the eager hands of Napoleon, who oversaw the drafting of a constitution and made peace with the Catholic Church. Designated "consul for life" in 1802, Napoleon crowned himself emperor two years later. In the meantime, he continued to wage wars against Britain, Austria, Russia, and Prussia, four rivals driven into coalitions by French expansion. By 1809, although he had failed in his goal of

bringing Britain to its knees, a series of remarkable victories enabled
Napoleon to forge a great empire, the largest in Europe since that of Rome.

Establishment of the Consulate

With the fall of the Directory in 1799, Napoleon Bonaparte, at the age of
thirty, became first consul, the most powerful man in France in a new,
stronger executive authority of three consuls, replacing the five directors.
The Constitution of 1799, promulgated in December, gave lip service to universal suffrage, but reflected the authoritarian character Sieyès intended.
Indirect election for each political institution reduced the political body
of the nation to a small number of notables. A Senate, appointed by the
consuls, chose men from a list of 6,000 "notabilities" to serve in a Tribunate. A Council of State, whose members were appointed by the first consul, would propose legislation. The Tribunate would discuss the proposed
legislation, and a Legislative Body would vote on the laws but could not
debate them. There was more than a little truth to the oft-repeated story
that one man who asked what was in the new constitution received the reply,
"Napoleon Bonaparte." The constitution was submitted to voters in a
plebiscite (voters could vote either yes or no). More than 99 percent of the
all-male electorate approved the document. The plebiscite became a fundamental Napoleonic political institution, embodying his principle of "authority from above, confidence from below."

The Consulate provided political stability by institutionalizing strong executive authority. France's districts (*départements*) each received an appointed
prefect, whose powers, delegated by the central government in Paris, sur-
passed those of the intendants of the Bourbon monarchs. Napoleon's
brother Lucien, as minister of interior, extended effective executive authority
to the most distant corners of the nation, curtailing royalist and Jacobin
opposition. Napoleon ruthlessly suppressed the press, reducing the number
of newspapers in Paris from seventy-three to thirteen, cowing survivors with
threats, or winning their allegiance with bribes.

The Concordat

Napoleon made peace with the Catholic Church, bringing it under state
supervision. Deep hostility remained between priests who had sworn allegiance to the nation during the Revolution—the "juring" clergy—and those
who had refused. Influenced by the Enlightenment, Napoleon believed the
Church should not have an institutional role in the affairs of state. But he
was also a cynical pragmatist. "There is only one way to encourage morality,"
he once said, "and that is to reestablish religion. Society cannot exist without
some being richer than others, and this inequality cannot exist without religion. When one man is dying of hunger next door to another who is stuffing
himself with food, the poor man simply cannot accept the disparity unless

some authority tells him, 'God wishes it so . . . in heaven things will be different.'" An agreement with the Church also was intended to undercut popular support for the monarchist cause by restoring some of the Church's prerogatives, but not any that would threaten the government's authority. Napoleon thus shrewdly sought to detach the Church from the quest for a restoration of the monarchy.

With the death in 1799 of Pope Pius VI (pope 1775–1799), who had refused any accommodation with the Revolution, his successor, Pius VII (pope 1800–1823), was eager to end a decade of religious turmoil. In 1801, Napoleon signed a Concordat with the papacy that helped solidify some of the changes brought by the Revolution, declaring Catholicism "the religion of the majority of citizens" in France. A majority of bishops refused to accept the Concordat. The pope would henceforth appoint new bishops, but on the recommendation of the first consul, that is, Napoleon. The Church also abandoned all claims to those ecclesiastical lands that had been sold as "national property" during the first years of the Revolution. The Concordat helped restore ecclesiastical influence in France, reflected by an increase in religious observance and in the number of people entering the clergy. Napoleon also pleased the Church by abandoning the confusing official calendar put in place in 1793, reestablishing Sundays and religious holidays.

The Organic Articles, which Napoleon promulgated without consulting the pope, regulated the Gallican (French) Church's status in France and reduced the pope's authority. The Church would now be subject to virtually the same administrative organization and policing as any other organization;

Napoleon and Pope Pius VII signing the Concordat in 1801, reconciling the Catholic Church with France after the Revolution.

a "minister of religion" would sit with the other ministers in Paris. The state would pay clerical salaries. No papal bull could be read in France's churches without permission of the government, and the clergy would have to read official government decrees from the pulpit. Under Napoleon, the Church gained the freedom of religious practice, but at the expense of some of its independence. Primary-school students were required to memorize a new catechism:

> *Question:* What are the duties of Christians with respect to the princes who govern them, and what are, in particular, our duties toward Napoleon . . . ?
> *Answer:* . . . Love, respect, obedience, fidelity, military service. . . . We also owe him fervent prayers for his safety and for the spiritual and temporal prosperity of the State.

Napoleon granted Protestants and Jews state protection to practice their religion. An article of the Concordat guaranteed freedom of worship for people in both religions (who together made up less than 5 percent of the population, the vast majority of whom were Protestants). One set of Organic Articles supervised Calvinists, another Lutherans. An imperial decree in 1808 organized Judaism into territorial consistories, although rabbis, unlike priests and Protestant ministers, were not to be paid by the state.

Napoleon's settlement with the Church alienated some of his cautious supporters on the left, notably the group known as the Ideologues. After a solemn ceremony at Notre Dame Cathedral in Paris celebrating the Concordat, one general put it bluntly to Napoleon—"A fine monkish show. It lacked only the presence of the hundred thousand men who gave their lives to end all that."

Napoleon's Leadership

One of his staff would later describe Napoleon as an "ever-restless spirit." He ate rapidly and could work days on end with very little sleep. He dictated more than 80,000 letters in his extraordinary career. Napoleon seemed to absorb every bit of information that arrived in his office or field headquarters and rapidly mastered subjects related to military or administrative concerns. But he often ignored matters that did not particularly interest him, such as economics and naval warfare, in which France lagged behind Britain.

Napoleon was more than just an optimist. He believed that his wildest dreams of conquest and empire would inevitably become reality. Everyone feared his rages, although he could be surprisingly understanding and generous toward subordinates when he believed they erred. He delegated very little meaningful authority, mistrusting even his closest advisers, but he tolerated opposing viewpoints. Napoleon's style of leadership became ever more tyrannical. He made up his own mind, and that mind invariably chose war.

Wars of Conquest and Empire

Napoleon had brought stability to France, but France was still at war with the Second Coalition: Great Britain, Austria, and Russia. In February 1800, when Austria turned down his overtures for peace on the basis of the Treaty of Campo Formio (1797), Napoleon returned to the battlefield, retaking Milan and defeating an Austrian army in June 1800. With the Treaty of Lunéville (February 1801), Austria reaffirmed the conditions of the Treaty of Campo Formio, accepting French gains in Italy, as well as French control over the Southern Netherlands (Belgium).

With Austria defeated and Russia tied up by a war against the Ottoman Empire, the British government signed the Peace of Amiens in March 1802. France kept all of its significant gains on the continent, and Britain returned all of the French colonies it had captured. Great Britain gained only the end of hostilities.

In Central Europe, Napoleon was now free to dismember the Holy Roman Empire and to dictate the territorial reorganization of the small German states. France had absorbed the left bank of the Rhine River, fulfilling the nationalistic dreams of a France extending to its "natural frontiers." Since this expansion came at the expense of Prussia and Austria, these two powers had to be compensated. By the oddly named Imperial Recess of 1803, the two most powerful German states absorbed a number of small, independent German states, ecclesiastical territories, and most of the free cities. The rulers of Baden, Bavaria, Hesse-Kassel, and Württemberg, the other largest German states, also added to their domains. France's position in Italy also was solidified. Piedmont remained a French possession, with Napoleon naming himself president of the Italian Cisalpine Republic. After imposing a Federal Constitution on the cantons of Switzerland that transformed them into the Helvetic Republic, Napoleon forced a defensive alliance on that strategically important country. By 1802, France was at peace for the first time in a decade. Napoleon had brought his nation to a position of dominance in Europe not seen since the time of Charlemagne a thousand years earlier.

No longer satisfied with the title "first consul," in 1802 Napoleon became "consul for life," a change approved by another plebiscite. Napoleon then prepared the establishment of a hereditary empire in France. Although thousands of émigrés took advantage of a declared amnesty to return to France, an alleged conspiracy against Napoleon's life by a group of royalists in 1804 led him to act against the Bourbons and to expedite his plan to become emperor. Napoleon accused Louis de Bourbon-Condé, the duke of Enghien (1772–1804)—a member of the Bourbon family who had emigrated to Baden—of involvement in the conspiracy. French troops moved into Baden to arrest him. The duke was hurriedly tried and executed near Paris, despite the lack of any evidence of his involvement in plans to assassinate Napoleon. Public opinion throughout much of Europe was outraged. The German composer Ludwig van Beethoven crossed out the dedication to Napoleon of his Third Symphony ("Eroica," meaning "heroic") shouting, "So he is also nothing more than an ordinary man? Now he will trample on the rights of mankind and indulge only his own ambition; from now on he will make himself superior to all others and become a tyrant!" One of the royalist conspirators, before his own execution, lamented, "We have done more than we hoped to do; we meant to give France a king, and we have given her an Emperor."

The Tribunate, Senate, and another plebiscite quickly approved the change from the Consulate to an empire. On December 2, 1804, Napoleon was anointed emperor by Pius VII. Instead of waiting for the pope to crown him, Napoleon snatched the crown from the pontiff and placed it on his own head. A new constitution presented a telling contradiction: "The government of the republic is entrusted to an emperor." Once an unknown officer who had scraped by with little money amid the spendthrift glitter of Thermidor, Bonaparte began to wear a coat of red velvet that would have been fit for Louis XIV.

Napoleon was no more temperamentally suited to live with peace than with defeat. Jealous of Britain's naval and commercial supremacy in the

Jean-Louis David's *Emperor Napoleon Crowning the Empress Joséphine in the Cathedral of Notre Dame* (1805–1808).

Mediterranean and the Western Hemisphere, he began to goad Britain into a new war. Haiti, the western side of the island of Hispaniola, had proclaimed its independence from France in 1801 under the leadership of Toussaint L'Ouverture (see Chapter 12). In 1802, in response to pressure from sugar planters, Napoleon restored French control of Haiti and reinstituted slavery in the French colonies. French troops captured L'Ouverture and took him to France, where he soon died. However, tropical disease killed most of the French troops occupying Haiti, and the British prevented the arrival of reinforcements. The French army surrendered, and in 1804 Haiti, which had been France's richest colony, again became independent. With his plans to extend France's empire to the Caribbean having come to naught, Napoleon shouted "Damn sugar, damn coffee, damn colonies!"

Seeking to recoup the financial losses France had incurred from war, Napoleon sold the huge Louisiana Territory to the United States in 1803 for 60 million francs (then about 11 million dollars). In retrospect, this was a paltry sum for a territory that virtually doubled the size of what was then the United States. Napoleon's hope that its former colony would emerge as a rival to Britain also lay behind the sale.

In July 1805, Russia and Austria joined Britain to form the Third Coalition against Napoleon. Undaunted, Napoleon readied an army and ships at the port of Boulogne on the English Channel for an invasion of Britain. A French decoy fleet lured Horatio Nelson's fleet into pursuit, hoping to inflict a crushing defeat on the Royal Navy. But the hunter soon became the hunted. When the French fleet sailed from the Spanish Mediterranean port of Cádiz on October 21, 1805, it sighted the Royal Navy. Turning to sail back to port, the French vessels were left vulnerable to attack by two columns of ships that succeeded in breaking the French line. As Nelson lay dying of a wound (which might have been avoided, had he covered up his shiny medals and epaulets that attracted a French marksman's eye), his fleet earned one of naval history's most decisive victories at Cape Trafalgar, not far from Gibraltar. Any chance for a French invasion of England evaporated. Great Britain controlled the seas.

The French armies were more successful on the continent. They defeated the Austrians at Ulm in October 1805, capturing 50,000 troops. Napoleon finally coaxed the Russians and Austrians into open battle. At Austerlitz on December 2, 1805, Napoleon tricked his opponents into an attack on his intentionally weakened right flank. He then divided the two armies with a crushing attack at their vulnerable center. When the dust cleared after the battle, the Russians and their Austrian allies had suffered 30,000 casualties, the French fewer than 9,000. Austria asked for peace, giving up the remnants of imperial territories in Italy and Dalmatia. Napoleon's allies, Bavaria, Baden, and Württemberg, once again gained Habsburg territories.

In the wake of Austerlitz, the hesitant King Frederick William III (ruled 1797–1840) of Prussia abandoned his tentative agreement to join the Third Coalition, instead signing an alliance with France. In July 1806,

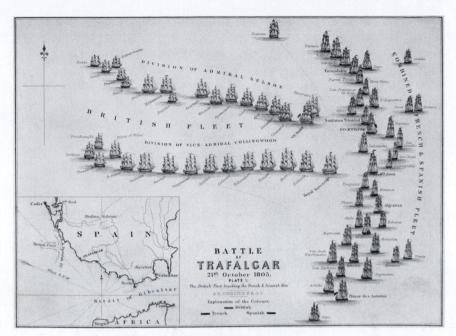

The Battle of Trafalgar.

Napoleon organized the Confederation of the Rhine, composed of sixteen German states, excluding Prussia and Austria (see Map 13.1). Napoleon named himself "Protector" of the Confederation, whose members agreed to accept French garrisons in southern Germany and to support Napoleon if war broke out again. This made the Holy Roman Empire even more irrelevant than it had been for a very long time. In 1806, Francis II (Francis I of Austria) simply dissolved the clumsy entity by abdicating as Holy Roman emperor.

As French power in Central Europe grew, the British government convinced Frederick William to join the alliance against Napoleon. But Napoleon's forces humiliated the Prussian army at Jena near Nuremberg on October 14, 1806, and then occupied Berlin. In February 1807, the French and Russian armies fought to a bloody draw in a Polish snowstorm. Had Austrian and British troops been sent to support the Russians, Napoleon might well have been soundly defeated. But Austria was still reeling from the defeat at Austerlitz, and the British were preoccupied with defending their commercial interests in the Western Hemisphere. Napoleon sent for fresh troops from France and added 30,000 Polish soldiers, some attracted by speculation that the emperor might create an independent Polish state.

After defeating the Russian army at the Battle of Friedland (June 1807), Napoleon met with Tsar Alexander I (ruled 1801–1825) on a raft in the middle of a river. Frederick William, the king of Prussia, paced anxiously on

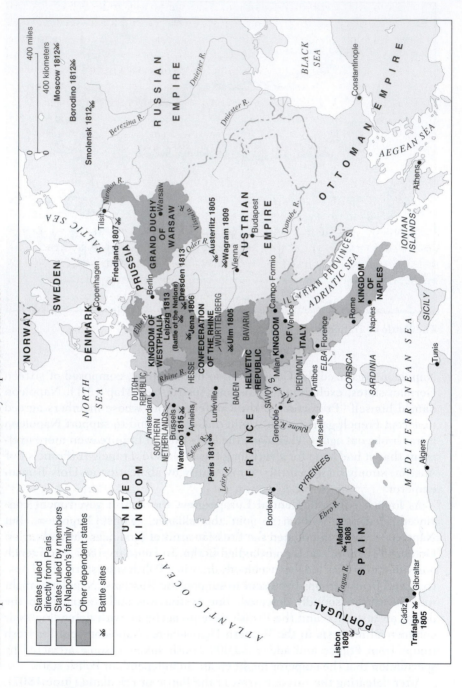

MAP 13.1 THE EMPIRE OF NAPOLEON   This map shows the areas conquered by Napoleon, including dependent states and states incorporated directly into France or ruled by Napoleon's relatives.

Legend:
- States ruled directly from Paris
- States ruled by members of Napoleon's family
- Other dependent states
- ⚔ Battle sites

400 miles
400 kilometers

NORWAY

SWEDEN

DENMARK

Copenhagen

NORTH SEA

BALTIC SEA

UNITED KINGDOM

ATLANTIC OCEAN

Tilsit
Friedland 1807 ⚔
Niemen R.

PRUSSIA
Berlin

GRAND DUCHY OF WARSAW
Warsaw
Vistula R.

RUSSIAN EMPIRE

Smolensk 1812 ⚔
Borodino 1812 ⚔
Moscow 1812 ⚔
Berezina R.
Dnieper R.

KINGDOM OF WESTPHALIA
Leipzig 1813 (Battle of the Nations) ⚔
Dresden 1813 ⚔
Elbe R.
Oder R.

HESSE
Jena 1806 ⚔

CONFEDERATION OF THE RHINE
WÜRTTEMBERG

Austerlitz 1805 ⚔
Wagram 1809 ⚔
Vienna
Budapest
Danube R.

AUSTRIAN EMPIRE

Dniester R.

OTTOMAN EMPIRE

Constantinople

BLACK SEA

AEGEAN SEA
Athens

DUTCH REPUBLIC
Amsterdam

SOUTHERN NETHERLANDS
Brussels
Waterloo 1815 ⚔
Amiens
Lunéville
Seine R.
Paris 1814 ⚔
Loire R.

BADEN
Rhine R.

HELVETIC REPUBLIC

BAVARIA
Ulm 1805 ⚔

KINGDOM OF ITALY
Milan
Venice
Campo Formio

ILLYRIAN PROVINCES
ADRIATIC SEA

FRANCE
Grenoble
Rhône R.
SAVOY
PIEDMONT
Antibes
Marseille

Florence
Rome
ELBA

KINGDOM OF NAPLES
Naples

SARDINIA
CORSICA

SICILY

IONIAN ISLANDS

MEDITERRANEAN SEA
Algiers
Tunis

Bordeaux
PYRENEES
Ebro R.

SPAIN
Madrid 1808 ⚔
Tagus R.

PORTUGAL
Lisbon 1809 ⚔
Cádiz
Trafalgar 1805 ⚔
Gibraltar

the shore as he awaited the outcome. The news was indeed bad. By the Treaty of Tilsit (July 1807), Prussia lost territory in western Germany and in Poland, which became, respectively, the Kingdom of Westphalia and the Grand Duchy of Warsaw, the latter annexed by Napoleon's ally, Saxony. The king of Saxony became the grand duke of Warsaw by virtue of a personal union. Russia was forced to accept the territorial settlements in Western Europe as definitive. In return, the tsar received a promise of French support in Russia's current quarrel with the Ottoman Empire. France thus tacitly agreed to back Russia's long-standing ambitions in southeastern Europe. Finally, the tsar agreed to close Russian ports to British ships.

When Austria challenged Napoleon by invading Bavaria in 1809, Napoleon moved rapidly against Vienna, capturing the Habsburg capital. He then crossed to the left bank of the Danube River and defeated the Habsburg army in July at Wagram, a battle in which 300,000 men participated and 80,000 were killed or wounded. Defeat forced Austria to surrender Illyria to France and other territory to Bavaria and Russia, which was still technically but uneasily allied to France. With Austria defeated and weakened, Prussia discouraged and dismembered, Russia neutralized, and Britain once again left alone to challenge France, Napoleon's position in Europe seemed invincible. Through conquest, the establishment of satellite states, and alliances with smaller powers, Napoleon had constructed a vast empire.

The Corsican Warrior

Napoleon has been considered one of the most brilliant military leaders in modern history. Yet his talents lay not in originality but in his stunningly innovative adaptations of military strategies and tactics developed in the eighteenth century and during the Revolution. Before mass military conscription, warfare had usually involved relatively limited numbers of soldiers. Armies had not moved rapidly. Since the beginning of the Thirty Years' War (1618–1648), wars had been fought over dynastic honor, commercial rivalry, and disputed territories (see Chapters 7 and 11). Old Regime armies had consisted largely of mercenaries commanded by nobles. Most battles had been fought in precise, drilled ranks, by two relatively small armies in line formation directly facing each other.

In the eighteenth century, technological and tactical improvements in artillery augmented its importance in warfare. Artillery pieces became lighter and therefore could be moved more easily. Improvements in roads also helped expedite the movement of cannon, as well as troops. Properly positioned artillery, launching powerful shells, could now play a decisive role against infantry. The artillery became a more respected part of the army; talented officers, Napoleon not the least of them, found a chance for promotion that they would not have had elsewhere.

Warfare changed when armies were no longer made up of mercenaries but rather of "citizen-soldiers" with greater commitment to their cause. Thus, during the French Revolution, committed sans-culottes were first mobilized as citizen-soldiers in the *levée en masse* proclaimed in August 1792. They fought to defend the nation, winning the stunning victory over the Austrian army at Valmy (September 1792; see Chapter 12). The Revolution inaugurated a period of warfare in Europe in which more soldiers entered battle than ever before. Between 1800 and 1815, perhaps as many as 2 million men served in or allied with Napoleon's armies. Napoleon harnessed French nationalism to win the commitment of his armies.

The Prussian general and military writer Karl von Clausewitz (1780–1831) described how warfare, which he defined as "an extension of state policy by other means," had changed. Whereas the wars of most of the eighteenth century had been those of kings and of states, not entire peoples, now "war had again suddenly become an affair of the people, and that of a people numbering thirty million, every one of whom regarded himself a citizen of the state."

Napoleon's genius was his ability to organize, oversee, and assure the supplying of and communication between larger armies than had ever before been effectively assembled, and to move them more rapidly than anyone before him. "Everything is in the execution," as he put it. He built on the French innovation in 1792–1793 of using combat divisions that combined

French citizens drawing lots to determine who would be conscripted to fight in Napoleon's wars.

infantry, cavalry, and artillery, and he subdivided his armies into corps, each with its own sense of pride.

Napoleon founded a military school in 1803 that produced 4,000 officers by 1815—there were lots of vacancies as the wars took their toll. As in the administration of the empire, however, Napoleon refused to delegate responsibility for crucial strategic and tactical decisions to his subordinates. In the long run, this would cost him dearly.

The infantry remained the heart of Napoleon's armies and his military planning (there were never more than 4 artillerymen for every 1,000 foot soldiers). Napoleon perfected the "mixed order" formation developed in the eighteenth century, which combined stretching troops across the field in a thin line about three men deep and bunching them in columns not only for marching but also for attack. Napoleon kept some battalions in columns, others in lines, which allowed battlefield flexibility. When he saw the opportunity, he launched an attack by outflanking his opponent and striking against the enemy's lines of communication. When he confronted an army stretched out before him, skilled marksmen threw the opponent's advance forces into disarray. Napoleon then brilliantly assessed the opposing army's weakest point. The concentration of deadly artillery fire—Napoleon once referred to the twelve-pound cannons as his "beautiful daughters"—prepared the way for the assault of the infantry columns. The speed of his army's movements was such that Napoleon could rapidly attack and defeat part of an enemy army before reinforcements could arrive. Instead of stopping to celebrate victory, Napoleon sent his troops, particularly the cavalry, to pursue the enemy. Victory became a rout.

Napoleon's armies, unlike the professional armies of the Old Regime, lived off the land, simply requisitioning what they needed. This did not make the French troops very popular, even in those lands officially incorporated into the empire. But it did allow the imperial army to travel far afield, in great numbers, marching up to twenty miles a day. Such speed seemed incredible for the period, since each infantryman carried with him about sixty pounds of equipment.

Finally, Napoleon enjoyed intense loyalty from his officers and troops, even up to the bitter end. He took to the field with his troops and rewarded good work with promotions and decorations, sometimes given on the field of battle. The emperor's own courage was also a source of inspiration to his troops. During one battle, the Imperial Guard refused to fight until Napoleon had moved to a safer place. He treated his soldiers with demonstrable respect and even affection because they seemed willing to die for him. At least 400,000 did just that.

The Napoleonic adventure offered even the most humble soldier a chance for glory. Yet the risks of injury and death were considerable. Disease sometimes killed more soldiers than battlefield wounds. (Napoleon had the good fortune to be wounded only twice in his long military career.) Soldiering was a tough life. In good times, soldiers ate reasonably well—bread, vegetables,

Napoleon used titles and awards as pillars of the empire. Jacques-Louis David's *Oath of the Army after the Distribution of Standards* shows the eagerness of the army to defend Napoleon and the empire.

even some meat, and drank wine or rum. But after defeat, or when they were far inside inhospitable territory, soldiers were fortunate just to find enough to eat. Medical care remained inadequate, despite improvements that included caring for wounded soldiers while the battle was still raging, rather than afterward when it often was too late. Major surgery—including the countless amputations occurring after each major battle—was often fatal. Napoleon, however, remained far more concerned with able-bodied soldiers than with the wounded or sick.

THE FOUNDATIONS OF THE FRENCH EMPIRE

The Napoleonic empire was a significant episode in the long story of statemaking in Europe. Continuing the tradition of eighteenth-century monarchs, Napoleon sought to make state administration more efficient and uniform. His aggressive conquests brought centrally controlled, bureaucratic government and a centralized legal system to much of the continent. For this reason, it is possible to see him as the embodiment of "enlightened absolutism" awaited by the philosophe Voltaire.

Napoleon created a new social hierarchy based not on blood but on service to the state, particularly in the army and bureaucracy, and on ownership of property. Beyond French borders, the empire was based on an imperial system in which Napoleon made his relatives and marshals heads of state. Thus, he gave the throne of Westphalia to his brother Jérôme, as earlier he had transformed the Cisalpine Republic in northern Italy into a monarchy ruled by his stepson, Eugène de Beauharnais. He named his brother Louis king of Holland. His brother Joseph became king of Naples and later king of Spain. Everywhere that French armies conquered, Napoleon's daunting will imposed change.

Institutional Foundations: Imperial Centralization

Napoleon's Council of State, the most prestigious and important administrative body of the empire, oversaw finance, interior affairs, and war. Members advised the emperor and drew up laws and regulations for approval by the Legislative Body. Napoleon attached to the council a corps of young, bright, apprentice bureaucrats who would assume important administrative posts in the future. The Senate, Legislative Body, and Tribunate lost all but their ceremonial roles, and Napoleon completely eliminated the Tribunate in 1807. Even the members of the Council of State found their influence on the emperor increasingly reduced.

Napoleon established the Bank of France in 1800, which facilitated the state's ability to borrow money. He followed the Directory's policy of abandoning the grossly inflated paper money of the Revolution. This stabilized France's currency. He facilitated the assessment and collection of taxes, ordering a land survey of the entire country upon which direct taxes were to be based. And he expanded the number of indirect taxes collected on salt (which had also been a principal source of revenue for the Old Regime monarchy), tobacco, and liquor, as well as on goods brought into any town of over 5,000 inhabitants.

The empire followed the Revolution, and particularly the Directory, in making higher education the responsibility of the state. With about half the population illiterate, Napoleon believed that schools could create patriotic and obedient citizens through teaching secular values that would ultimately link education to nationalism. In 1802, Napoleon established state secondary schools (*lycées*), thirty-seven of which were operating six years later, for the relatively few boys who went to secondary school. Students read only textbooks approved by the emperor. In 1808, Napoleon created France's first public university system, charging it with "direct[ing] political and moral opinions."

Legal Foundations: The Napoleonic Code

Napoleon wanted to be known to history as the new Justinian, the Roman lawgiver. The Civil Code of 1804, which became known as the Napoleonic Code, may have been the emperor's most lasting legacy. Many of the *cahiers*, or lists of grievances submitted to Louis XVI on the eve of the Revolution, had asked that French laws be uniform. During the constitutional monarchy, the Convention had begun the process of codifying French laws, but it had been interrupted by the vicissitudes of the Revolution. While the fundamental division in French law had been between the written Roman law in the south and customary law based upon regional and local traditions in the north, there were many different legal codes in France. Napoleon ordered the Council of State to seek advice from a battery of lawyers to codify the laws of the land. Napoleon personally participated in many critical discussions and debates. The Napoleonic Code made the rights of property owners sacrosanct: the majority of the articles concerned private property.

The code, over 2,000 articles long, enshrined the equality of all people before the law and granted the freedom of religion. The subsequent Penal Code of 1810 proclaimed the "freedom of work," reaffirming the Le Chapelier Law of 1791 that forbade the formation of workers' or employers' associations (the latter were extremely rare). The "freedom" guaranteed in relations between employers and workers left workers legally subordinate to their employers and unable to strike. Furthermore, workers were required to carry small passports that had to be handed over to municipal officials, police, or employers when requested.

The Napoleonic Code reflected Napoleon's traditional attitudes toward the family. He considered the family the most important intermediary between the state and the individual, a means of guaranteeing social order. Rejecting scattered demands during the Revolution for the equality of women, the code reaffirmed the patriarchal nature of the traditional family. It made women and children legally dependent on their husbands or fathers. The code granted men control of family property. A woman could not buy or sell property or begin a business without her husband's permission, and any income she earned would pass to his descendants, not hers. A woman worker's wages, too, went to her husband, and women had no control over their children's savings. As during the First Republic, the state recognized divorce, but it was now more difficult to obtain. More articles in the Napoleonic Code established conditions for the sale of cattle than addressed the legal status of women. In cases of adultery, women risked penalties that were far more severe than those for men. Only adult males could officially witness a legal document. Napoleon complained: "In France women are considered too highly. They should not be regarded as equal to men. In reality they are nothing more than machines for producing children."

As in the Old Regime, parents could put their offspring in jail and retained authority over their children's marriages. The code required equal inheritance of all children (the parents could dispose of a certain percentage, based on a sliding scale, as he or she wished), ending primogeniture (inheritance by the eldest son) in northern France, where it still existed. Yet siblings often found ways to keep the family property together; one brother could buy out his brothers' shares in an inherited property. The end of primogeniture also may have provided an impetus for French couples to have fewer children in an effort to avoid further division of property.

The Napoleonic Code—despite its obvious inequities, imperfections, and the fact that it was sometimes promulgated by a conquering army—served as the basis for the codification of laws and the reorganization of judicial systems in Switzerland, Piedmont-Sardinia, and the Netherlands. At the end of his life, Napoleon claimed, "My glory is not to have won forty battles . . . but what nothing will destroy, what will live eternally, is my Civil Code."

Social Foundations: The Imperial Hierarchy

Napoleon once wrote, "My motto has always been: a career open to all talents." He considered the end of social distinctions by birth to be one of the most lasting accomplishments of the French Revolution. The empire favored the aspirations of the middle classes. The elimination of legal barriers to social ascension left wealth, largely defined by the ownership of property and service to the state (rewarded by grants of property, titles, and pensions), as the main determinant of status. Yet imposing obstacles to social mobility remained. It took wealth to acquire the background, education, and reputation to take one's place in the imperial hierarchy.

The army and the bureaucracy were the two pillars of the empire. Napoleon created an elite of "notables," as they were called, rewarding those who served him well with prestigious titles and lucrative positions. At the pinnacle of the new hierarchy were eighteen marshals, appointed in 1804 from the ranks of the Senate and including generals who had earned fortunes waging war. Napoleon began to restore titles abolished by the Revolution: prince in 1804, duke two years later, followed by count, baron, and chevalier. But unlike the titles of the Old Regime, these titles, which could be hereditary, did not stem from the ownership of a certain estate or château, but rather were awarded for service to the state.

Between 1808 and 1814, Napoleon created 3,600 titles. Yet Napoleonic notables totaled only one-seventh of the number of the nobles in France on the eve of the Revolution. Some of the new notables had already become rich through purchase of ecclesiastical and émigré lands sold during the Revolution. More than half of all men granted titles by the emperor had rendered service in the military. The emperor often repeated that "in the backpack of each soldier, there is a marshal's baton." The civil service was the second most important avenue to a Napoleonic title. Some Italians, Dutch, Germans, and others from conquered lands found that the French Empire offered them dignified and sometimes even lucrative careers.

In May 1802, Napoleon established the Legion of Honor to reward those who served the nation with distinction. It was, predictably enough, organized along military lines, with commanders, officers, and knights. Indeed 97 percent of those so decorated by Napoleon served in his military forces. Yet a former Jacobin member of the Council of State complained that the award, a decorated cross that could be displayed prominently on one's coat, was nothing more than a "bauble." Napoleon replied, "You may call them baubles, but it is by baubles that mankind is governed." The subjects of territories incorporated into the empire were eligible to receive the Legion of Honor. When Rome became part of Napoleon's immense empire, the following parody on the Legion of Honor appeared on the walls of the Eternal City:

In fierce old times, they balanced loss
By hanging thieves upon a cross.
But our more humane age believes
In hanging crosses on the thieves.

THE TIDE TURNS AGAINST NAPOLEON

French rule generated resistance in countries absorbed into Napoleon's empire through conquest. Napoleon manipulated factional splits in some countries, co-opted local elites where he could, brushed aside rulers as he pleased, and tried to establish compliant new regimes, some handed over to his brothers. But ultimately French rule over such an extended empire collapsed. Napoleon's failure to force British submission by strangling its economy with his "Continental System," which aimed to cut off Britain from its continental markets, kept his major enemy in the field, or more appropriately, on the high seas. In Spain, resistance against French rule became a full-fledged rebellion (the Peninsular War) that, with British assistance, sapped imperial resources. Moreover, French occupation of some of the German states gave rise to German nationalism, solidifying resistance. Prussian and Austrian military reforms led to stronger opponents in the field. And in a final ill-considered expansion of imperial aggression, Napoleon in 1812 decided to invade Russia. The destruction of his "Grand Army" in the snowdrifts and howling winds of Russia was the beginning of the end.

The Continental System

Knowing that the war was costing the British government huge sums (between 60 and 90 percent of the state's annual revenue), in November 1806 Napoleon announced his Continental System. It prohibited trade with Britain, which he hoped would strangle the British economy by closing all continental ports to British ships. French merchants and manufacturers, as well as the state, would earn fortunes supplying the captive markets of the continent. Increased hardship might even cause damaging unrest in Britain.

But the blockade of the continental ports was far easier said than done. The continental coastline is enormous, the British navy was strong (despite the loss of 317 ships between 1803 and 1815), and the merchants and smugglers resourceful. British merchants continued to find American markets for their goods. The banning of British imports did lead to the development of some important innovations in France (for example, the Jacquard loom for silk weaving and the planting of the sugar beet to compensate for the loss of sugar from the West Indies). But France's relative lack of available coal and iron ore, its lack of capital accumulation and investment, and the overwhelming allocation of the nation's material and human resources to war prevented French merchants from taking up the slack left by the absence of British goods in continental markets.

In response to Napoleon's Continental System, the British government's "Orders in Council" of November and December 1807 demanded that trading ships under all flags purchase a license in a British port. This decision placed Britain at loggerheads with the United States, one of France's principal trading partners. Napoleon retaliated with the Milan Decrees, threatening to seize any ship that had traded with Britain or that had even accepted a search by British authorities. Yet, in 1809, British imports could still be readily found on the continent. The French, suffering a sharp decline in customs revenue, began tolerating violations of the Continental System, even selling special licenses and placing hefty taxes on the importation of British goods to bring in more revenue. The blockade came completely apart in the midst of an economic depression that began in 1811.

Napoleon counted on Britain's deepening crisis with the U.S. government, which opposed the boarding and searching of its vessels by British

British Prime Minister William Pitt the Younger and Napoleon carve up the world.

inspectors, to bring Anglo-American relations to a breaking point. But even the War of 1812 between the British and the United States, which ended with the exhausted British capitulating, could not destroy the British economy. Moreover, the fact that French agents had encouraged an Irish insurrection against British rule in 1798 lingered in the memory of the British upper class, adding to their resentment of France. Tory governments, which governed Britain throughout the entire revolutionary and Napoleonic periods, remained committed to defeating Bonaparte (and repressing dissent at home), despite the staggering economic cost of the war.

The Peninsular War

Napoleon's obsession with bringing Britain to its knees led him into the disastrous Peninsular War (1808–1813) in Spain. In 1807, Napoleon had reached an agreement with Charles IV (ruled 1788–1808), the incompetent king of Spain, that permitted French troops to pass through his kingdom to conquer Portugal, Britain's ally (an arrangement that had functioned to guarantee Portugal's independence from Spain and had also provided Portuguese wine with a ready market for thirsty British people of means). A French army marched on Lisbon, and the Portuguese royal family fled to Brazil. An insurrection in March 1808 led to the abdication of Charles IV and the succession of his son Ferdinand VII (ruled 1808, 1814–1833) to the throne. Believing that the kingdom of Spain was on the verge of falling like an apple into his hands, Napoleon forced Ferdinand to abdicate that same year, and summoned his older brother, Joseph Bonaparte (1768–1844), from his wobbly throne in Naples to become king of Spain.

But Napoleon did not count on the resistance of the Spanish people. Ecclesiastical reforms imposed by Joseph and Napoleon, including the reduction in the number of monastic convents by two-thirds and the abolition of the Inquisition, angered the Church, which remained a powerful force in Spanish life. Napoleon found some allies among the urban middle class, but the Spanish nobility joined their old allies, the clergy, in opposition to the invaders. French forces were easy targets for the small, mobile groups of Spanish guerrillas, who attacked and then quickly disappeared into the Spanish landscape. British troops led by Arthur Wellesley, later duke of Wellington (1769–1852), arrived to help the Spanish and Portuguese fight the French. By 1810, about 350,000 French troops were tied up in the Iberian Peninsula. Fighting for "Church and king," Spaniards sustained what arguably was the first successful guerrilla war in modern Europe. Napoleon's "Spanish ulcer" bled France.

Stirrings of Nationalism in Napoleonic Europe

One of the lasting effects of the Napoleonic period was the quickening of German and, to a lesser extent, Italian national identity. The French revolutionaries had called for a war against the tyrants of Europe. But Napoleon

Francisco Goya's *The Third of May, 1808* depicts the execution of citizens of Madrid by French soldiers after the fall of the city during the Peninsular War.

seemed blind to the fact that the exportation of the principles of the French Revolution might encourage resentment and even nationalist feeling against the French in those countries conquered by his armies. Gradually the French discovered that nationalism was a double-edged sword. Some people in states conquered by French armies not only resented the occupation of their lands but they also began to long for the existence of a territorial state organized around their own nationality.

In any case, Napoleon sought to curry favor in each conquered state in exchange for support against his enemies. Napoleon may indeed have intended that Westphalia, created by the Treaty of Tilsit (1807) out of former Prussian territories and other smaller states that had fought against him, would become a model state. He ended serfdom and gave peasants the right to own land, to move through the kingdom as they pleased, and to send their children to school. But his principal goal was to bolster the Confederation of the Rhine's north flank against possible attacks against his interests.

Napoleon considered conquered territories sources for military conscripts and raw materials, or as potential markets for French goods. In Italy, French authorities forbade the importation of textile machinery and imposed disadvantageous tariffs, fearful of competition with their own industries. With the exception of Jacobin anti-clericals, intellectuals, and merchants who stood to profit from the French occupation, most people expressed little enthusiasm for the Napoleonic regime. In the Netherlands, the French occupation virtually brought the prosperous Dutch trading economy to a standstill. Poles soon began to doubt Napoleon's promise to reestablish Polish independence; some Polish nobles began to look to the Russian tsar for help, others to the king of Prussia. Among those territories conquered by Napoleon, open insurrections were relatively rare, although in the Austrian Tyrol, peasants sang nationalist songs as they fought against the French in 1813. The French armies waged war brutally against those who dared oppose them, burning villages and executing civilians, particularly in Spain, Tyrol, and southern Italy.

The impact of the French invasions on nationalism was perhaps clearest in the numerous German states. At first, some German intellectuals had praised Napoleon, but that soon changed. Attacks by German writers against French occupation mounted in 1807. That year, the French executed a Nuremburg bookseller accused of selling anti-French literature. Two years later, Napoleon escaped an assassination attempt by a young German student, the son of a Lutheran minister, who shouted "Long live Germany!" as he was executed. Gradually German writers espoused the view that people of the German states shared a common culture based upon language, tradition, and history. Only in the middle of the eighteenth century had German writers begun to write in their own language; before then, they considered French the language of culture. Like some composers, they began to discover elements of a common culture, drawing on language, literary texts, folk traditions, and other German cultural traditions to express themselves. This emotional quest for cultural and political institutions that would define "Germany" reflected some rejection of the rational tradition of Enlightenment thought identified with France.

Some German nationalists believed that the multiplicity of states in Central Europe stood in the way of eventual German unification. The Holy Roman Empire had been swept away in 1806. Napoleon destroyed the religious settlement imposed by the Treaty of Westphalia, which in 1648 had ended the Thirty Years' War. Napoleon may have helped the cause of German nationalism by eliminating some tiny states, increasing the territory of the middle-sized states at the expense of the former. About 60 percent of the population of the German states passed from one ruler to another during the revolutionary and Napoleonic eras. Yet in states such as Hanover and Württemburg, German particularism—local identity—was considered part of being German. Forty separate German states survived. Baden, Bavaria, and Württemberg, although much smaller and less powerful than Austria and Germany, emerged from the period with their independence and separate traditions for the most part intact.

Even though any possible political unification of Germany seemed distant, if not impossible, German nationalism nonetheless contributed to the determination with which the people of the German states resisted Napoleon. Johann Gottlieb Fichte (1762–1814) called on "the German nation," which he defined as including anyone who spoke German, to discover its spiritual unity.

In Spain, as we have seen, people of all classes came to view the French as invaders, not liberators. A constitution proposed by the Spanish Cortes in 1812 at Cádiz, which was not under French control, nonetheless reflected the influence of the French Revolution. It proclaimed freedom of the press, established an assembly to be elected by a relatively wide electorate, and abolished the Inquisition. But the constitution, although never implemented because of the eclipse of Spanish liberals in the wake of conservative reaction, was also a self-consciously nationalist document. Some Spaniards, too, were becoming more aware of their own shared linguistic, cultural, and historical traditions.

Military Reforms in Prussia and Austria

The successes of Napoleon's armies led Prussia (particularly in view of the devastating Prussian defeat at Jena in 1806), and, to a lesser extent, Austria, to enact military reforms. In 1807, a royal decree abolished serfdom in Prussia, with military efficiency in mind. Peasants were now free to leave the land to which they had been attached and to marry without the lord's permission. A decree three years later allowed peasants to convert some of the land they worked into their own property. Other reforms removed class barriers that had restricted the sale of land between nobles and non-nobles and that had served to keep middle-class men from assuming the military rank of officer (and had also prevented nobles from taking positions considered beneath their status). The Prussian military commander Baron Heinrich Karl vom und zum Stein (1757–1831) appointed some commoners to be officers and cashiered some of the more inept noble commanders. Stein established a ministry of war, taking away some important decisions from the whims of the king and his inner circle. In 1807, the Stein ministry abolished serfs' ties to the land, but the labor obligations and seigneurial dues of serfs remained in effect. This reform improved the loyalty of peasant-soldiers to the state. Stein called for greater patriotic participation in the national affairs of Prussia. Thus he and many other statesmen who resisted Napoleon continued to think in Prussian, not "German" terms. The elimination of most forms of corporal punishment enhanced troop morale, as did the rewarding of individual soldiers who served well. Stein also organized a civilian militia, which provided a proud, patriotic reserve of 120,000 part-time soldiers.

The Empire's Decline and the Russian Invasion

Napoleon now confronted the fact that he still had no legitimate children to inherit his throne. Although he loved his wife Josephine, he was as unfaithful to her during his lengthy absences as she was to him. Napoleon arranged for a bishop in Paris to annul his marriage—the pope having refused to do so—allowing him to remarry with the Church's blessing. Napoleon then considered diplomatically useful spouses. When the Russian tsar would not provide his younger sister, Napoleon arranged a marriage in 1810 with Marie-Louise (1791–1847), the daughter of Austrian Emperor Francis I. She had never even met Napoleon, but that in itself was not as unusual as the fact that the French emperor had an old enemy, the Archduke Charles (brother of Francis I and Napoleon's opponent during the 1809 war with Austria), stand in for him at the wedding ceremony, while he remained in Paris. Napoleon thus entered into a *de facto* alliance with the Habsburgs, Europe's oldest dynasty. Within a year, Marie-Louise presented Napoleon with a son and heir.

For the first time since Napoleon's remarkable rise to power, dissent also began to be heard openly inside France. Deserters and recalcitrant conscripts dodged authorities in increasing numbers beginning in about 1810. Royalist and Jacobin pamphlets and brochures circulated, despite censorship. Royalists objected to Napoleon's disdainful treatment of the pope, who excommunicated the emperor after France annexed the Papal States in 1809. Napoleon responded by simply placing Pius VII under house arrest, first near Genoa, and then near Paris in Fontainebleau.

Napoleon had become increasingly unable to separate options that were feasible or possible from those that were unlikely or indeed impossible to achieve. One of the emperor's ministers remarked: "It is strange that Napoleon, whose good sense amounted to genius, never discovered the point at which the impossible begins. . . . 'The impossible,' he told me with a smile, 'is the specter of the timid and the refuge of the coward . . . the word is only a confession of impotence' . . . he thought only of satisfying his own desires and adding incessantly to his own glory and greatness . . . death alone could set a limit to his plans and curb his ambition."

Napoleon's advisers now expressed their doubts about the emperor's endless plans for new conquests. Talleyrand had resigned as foreign minister in 1807, after the execution of the duke of Enghien. Talleyrand now symbolized the "party of peace," which opposed extending the empire past limits that could be effectively administered. In 1809, he began to negotiate secretly with Austria about the possibility of a monarchical restoration in France should Napoleon fall.

Napoleon's interest in expanding French influence in the eastern Mediterranean and his marriage to a Habsburg princess virtually assured war with Russia, which had reopened its ports to British and neutral vessels carrying English goods. Believing that he could enforce the continental blockade by defeating Russia, Napoleon prepared for war, forcing vanquished Austria and Prussia to agree to assist him. In the meantime, the tsar signed a peace treaty with the Ottoman Empire, freeing Russia to oppose Napoleon. Alexander I lined up the support of Sweden. There Jean-Baptiste Bernadotte

(1763–1844), once one of Napoleon's marshals, had been elected crown prince in 1810 and thus heir to the Swedish throne by the Swedish Estates (he would succeed the childless Charles XIII in 1818 as King Charles XIV). In return, the tsar offered Sweden a free hand in annexing Norway.

In June 1812, Napoleon's "Grand Army," over 600,000 strong, crossed the Niemen River from the Grand Duchy of Warsaw into Russia. Napoleon hoped to lure the Russian armies into battle. The Russians, however, simply retreated, drawing Napoleon ever farther into western Russia in late summer.

The Grand Army may have been the largest army ever raised up to that time, but the quality of Napoleon's army had declined since 1806 through casualties and desertions. Some of his finest troops were tied up in Spain. Half of the Grand Army consisted of Prussian, Italian, Austrian, Swiss, or Dutch conscripts. Officers now were by necessity more hurriedly trained. As the Grand Army was almost constantly at war, there was no chance to rebuild it to Napoleon's satisfaction.

In Russia, disease, heat, and hunger took a far greater toll on Napoleon's army than did the rearguard action of enemy troops. The Grand Army finally reached the city of Smolensk, 200 miles west of Moscow, in the middle of August; there the emperor planned to force the tsar to sign another humiliating peace. However, the Russian troops continued to retreat deeper into Russia. Napoleon's marshals begged him to stop in Smolensk and wait there. Tempted by the possibility of capturing Moscow, Napoleon pushed on until his army reached Borodino, sixty miles from Moscow. There the two armies fought to a costly draw in the bloodiest battle of the Napoleonic era, with 68,000 killed or wounded before the Russian army continued its retreat. Napoleon entered Moscow on September 14, 1812. He found it virtually deserted. Fires, probably set by Russian troops, spread quickly through the wooden buildings. Almost three-quarters of the city burned to the ground. The tsar and his armies had fled eastward.

Over 1,500 miles from Paris, without sufficient provisions, and with the early signs of the approaching Russian winter already apparent, Napoleon decided to march the Grand Army back to France. The retreat, which began on October 19, was a disaster. Russian troops picked off many among the retreating forces, forcing them to take an even longer route to Smolensk, 200 miles away. The Russians were waiting for Napoleon's beleaguered armies at the Berezina River, where they killed thousands of French soldiers. The emperor himself barely escaped capture by the Cossacks. The freezing winter then finished off most of what was left of Napoleon's Grand Army.

The retreat from Moscow was one of the greatest military debacles of any age. A contemporary described some of the French troops as "a mob of tattered ghosts draped in women's cloaks, odd pieces of carpet, or greatcoats burned full of holes, their feet wrapped in all sorts of rags . . . skeletons of soldiers went by, . . . with lowered heads, eyes on the ground, in absolute silence. . . ." Of the more than 600,000 men who had set out in June from

The retreat of the Grand Army in Russia, November 1812.

the Grand Duchy of Warsaw (Napoleon's defeat ended the hopes of Polish nationalists for independence), only about 40,000 returned to France in December. (Indeed, a mass grave of frozen soldiers of the Grand Army was discovered in Lithuania in 2003.) After racing ahead of the groans of the dying and the frozen corpses, Napoleon issued a famous bulletin that was sent back to Paris: "The health of the emperor has never been better."

Napoleon arrived at the Tuileries Palace in December 1812. In the wake of a military disaster of such dimensions that press censorship and duplicitous official bulletins (the expression "to lie like a military bulletin" became current) could not gloss over it, the mood of the French people soured.

Undaunted, Napoleon demanded a new levy of 350,000 more troops. This call, coming at a time of great economic hardship, was greeted with massive resentment and resistance. Instead of negotiating a peace that could have left France with the left bank of the Rhine River, Napoleon planned new campaigns and further expansion.

The Defeat of Napoleon

Napoleon now faced allies encouraged by his devastating defeat. In February 1813, Russia and Prussia signed an alliance, agreeing to fight Napoleon until the independence of the states of Europe was restored. Napoleon earned two costly victories over Russian and Prussian troops in the spring of 1813, but his casualties were high. Great Britain, still fighting the French in Spain, formally joined the coalition in June. Napoleon rejected Austrian conditions for peace, which included the dissolution of the Confederation of the Rhine, and Austria joined the coalition in August 1813. Napoleon's strategy of winning the temporary allegiance, or at least neutrality, of one of the other four European powers had failed.

In August 1813, Napoleon defeated the allies at Dresden, but then learned that Bavaria had seceded from the Confederation of the Rhine and joined the coalition against France. In October, his troops outnumbered two to one, Napoleon suffered a major defeat at Leipzig (in the Battle of the Nations) and retreated across the Rhine River into France. His armies, ever more filled with reluctant, raw recruits, lacked adequate supplies. An insurrection in the Netherlands followed by an allied invasion restored the prince of Orange to authority there. Austrian troops defeated a French army in northern Italy. The duke of Wellington's English forces drove the French armies from Spain and back across the Pyrenees. Forced to fight on French soil for the first time, Napoleon's discouraged armies were greeted with hostility when they tried to live off the land as they had abroad. Opponents of Napoleon, including some for whom a Bourbon restoration seemed a possibility, now spoke more openly in France.

Early in 1814, the allies proposed peace (perhaps insincerely, assuming the French emperor would refuse) if Napoleon would accept France's natural frontiers of the Rhine River, the Alps, and the Pyrenees. Napoleon stalled. An allied army of 200,000 moved into eastern France. In Paris, the Legislative Body approved a document that amounted to a denunciation of the emperor, though it never reached the public. Even Napoleon's normally dutiful older brother Joseph encouraged the members of the Council of State to sign a petition calling for peace.

The allies were determined not to stop until they had captured Paris. After overcoming stiff French resistance, the main allied force swept into the

(*Left*) Arthur Wellesley, the duke of Wellington. (*Right*) Charles Maurice de Talleyrand.

French capital in March 1814. Tsar Alexander I of Russia and King Frederick William III of Prussia rode triumphantly into the city. At Fontainebleau, Napoleon's marshals refused to join in his frantic plans for an attack on the allies in Paris and pressured him to abdicate. Talleyrand called the Senate into session. It voted to depose Napoleon. The allies refused to consider Napoleon's abdication in favor of his three-year-old son. Without an army and, perhaps for the first time, without hope, Napoleon abdicated on April 6, 1814, and then took poison, which failed to kill him. The long adventure finally seemed at an end.

MONARCHICAL RESTORATION AND NAPOLEON'S RETURN

The allies sought the restoration of the Bourbon monarchy. The French Senate, too, expressed its wish that Louis XVI's brother, the count of Provence, return to France as Louis XVIII. By the Treaty of Fontainebleau (April 11, 1814), the allies exiled Napoleon to a Mediterranean island off the coast of Italy. Bonaparte would be emperor of Elba. Marie-Louise refused to accompany him, preferring to be duchess of Parma, receiving the title by virtue of being a member of the Austrian royal family.

The Bourbon Restoration

The count of Provence entered Paris on May 3, 1814, as King Louis XVIII (ruled 1814–1815; 1815–1824). With more than a little wishful thinking, he

announced that this was the nineteenth year of his reign (counting from the death of the son of Louis XVI, who had died in 1795 in a Paris prison without ever reigning). The allies worked out a surprisingly gracious peace treaty with France, largely thanks to Talleyrand's skilled diplomacy. The Treaty of Paris, signed on May 30, 1814, left France with Savoy and small chunks of land in Germany and the Austrian Netherlands—in other words, the France of November 1, 1792. France could now rejoin the monarchies of Europe.

Louis XVIII signed a constitutional "Charter" that granted his people "public liberties," promising that a legislature would be elected,

Louis XVIII, king of the French. Note the perhaps unconscious Napoleonic pose.

based on a very restricted franchise. Although the document affirmed monarchical rule by divine right, it confirmed some of the important victories of the Revolution, including equality before the law and freedom of expression and religion, although Catholicism would be the religion of the state (see Chapter 15). A coterie of fanatical nobles and their followers (the Ultra-royalists) convinced the king to enact some measures, however, that were highly unpopular. Many in France disapproved of the substitution of the white flag of the Bourbon family for the tricolor, the description of the Charter as a "gift" from the king to the French people, the retiring of 14,000 officers at half pay, the restoration of returned émigrés to high positions in the army, and the return to their original owners of national lands that had not been sold. But most of the French were simply exhausted from years of wars and sacrifice.

The 100 Days

In March 1815, just months after his exile, Napoleon boldly escaped from Elba and landed near Antibes on the French Mediterranean coast. He knew that he retained considerable popularity in France. Furthermore, so much time had passed and so many dramatic events had occurred since the execution of Louis XVI that one of the monarchy's staunchest supporters claimed, with some exaggeration, "The Bourbons were as unknown in France as the Ptolemies."

The word that Napoleon had landed in France stunned everyone. Marshal Ney, who had offered his services to the Bourbons, promised to bring Napoleon back to Paris in a cage. But upon seeing Napoleon, Ney fell into his arms. Regiment after regiment went over to Napoleon as he marched north. With Bonaparte nearing Paris, Louis XVIII and his family and advisers fled to Belgium, which had become part of the Kingdom of Holland. Soon Napoleon again paced frenetically through the Tuileries Palace, making plans to raise new armies.

It was not to be. The allies quickly raised an enormous army of more than 700,000 troops. Napoleon led an army of 200,000 men into the Austrian Netherlands, engaging Prussian and British forces south of Brussels on June 16, 1815. He forced the Prussians to retreat and ordered one of his generals to pursue them with his army. Napoleon then moved against the British forces commanded by Wellington, his old nemesis. The armies met near the village of Waterloo on June 18, 1815. Wellington had skillfully hidden the extent of his superior infantry behind a ridge. Napoleon watched in horror as a Prussian army arrived to reinforce Wellington. The general sent in pursuit of the Prussians, like all Napoleon's commanders, had been taught to follow Napoleon's directives to the letter and not to improvise. He held back until it was too late. When the imperial guard broke ranks and retreated, much of the rest of the French army did the same. The defeat was devastating and total.

The Battle of Waterloo, June 18, 1815.

Napoleon abdicated a second time. He surrendered to British forces near the western coast of France, while hoping to find a way to sail to America. This time the exile would be final. The allies packed Napoleon off to the small island of Saint Helena, in the South Atlantic, 1,000 miles away from any mainland. The closest island of any size was Ascension, a British naval base, some 600 miles distant. Louis XVIII returned to take up the throne of France a second time, 100 days after fleeing Paris.

On Saint Helena, Napoleon's health gradually declined. He died on May 5, 1821, his last words being "France, army, head of the army, Josephine." He died of an ulcer, probably a cancerous one, despite stories to this day that he was poisoned by arsenic.

NAPOLEON'S LEGACY

Napoleon's testament, a masterpiece of political propaganda, tried to create a myth that he saved the Revolution in France. "Every Frenchman could say during my reign,—'I shall be minister, grand officer, duke, count, baron, if I earn it—even king!'" And in some ways, Napoleon was indeed the heir to the French Revolution. He guaranteed the survival of some of its most significant triumphs. Napoleon considered his greatest achievement "that of establishing and consecrating the rule of reason." His Napoleonic Code proclaimed the equality of all people before the law (favoring, however, men over women), personal freedom, and the inviolability of property. Napoleon furthered the myth, and to some extent the reality, of the "career open to talent," which aided, above all, the middle class, but even peasants in some cases. He consolidated the role of wealth, principally property ownership, as the foundation of the political life of the nation. This increased the number of citizens eligible to participate in political life, however limited by imperial strictures. Furthermore, Napoleon helped turn nationalism into an aggressive secular religion, manipulating this patriotic energy and transforming it into an ideology inculcated by French schools.

Napoleon's reforms, built upon those of the French Revolution, extended into states conquered by his imperial armies. The French imposed constitutions and state control over the appointment of clergy, standardized judicial systems, and abolished ecclesiastical courts. Napoleon created new tax structures, standardized weights and measures, ended internal customs barriers, abolished guilds, and established state bureaucracies that were extensions of French rule in the "sister republics" founded by the Directory. In addition to abolishing serfdom and proclaiming equality before the law in Poland, the French occupation also ended residual peasant seigneurial obligations (such as the requirement to provide labor services to the lord) virtually everywhere, and abolished noble and ecclesiastical courts in northern Italy and the Netherlands. The Napoleonic Code proclaimed freedom of worship, and the French conquest of other European states, including Baden, Bavaria, and the Netherlands, helped remove onerous restrictions on Jews. But under pressure from French planters, Napoleon also reestablished slavery in Haiti in 1802.

Yet Napoleon's success in implementing reforms varied from place to place, depending on existing political structures, the degree of compliance by local elites, and the international situation. In southern Italy, for example, which Napoleon's armies conquered relatively late and where the structures of state authority had always been particularly weak, the French presence had little lasting effect. As the Napoleonic wave subsided, nobles and clergy regained domination over the overwhelmingly rural, impoverished local population.

Napoleon claimed from Saint Helena that he was trying to liberate Europe, but he had actually replaced the old sovereigns with new ones—himself or his brothers. "If I conquered other kingdoms," he admitted, "I did so in order that France would be the beneficiary." Wagons returned from Italy full of art and other treasures, which became the property of Napoleon and his family, his marshals, or the state. French conquests helped awaken nationalism in the German states and Spain.

To the writer Germaine de Staël (1766–1817), the daughter of the Swiss banker Jacques Necker, Louis XVI's minister, Napoleon "regarded a human being as an action or a thing . . . nothing existed but himself. He was an able chess player, and the human race was the opponent to whom he proposed to give checkmate." In the end, his monumental ambition got the best of him.

About 2 million men served in Napoleon's armies between 1805 and 1814; about 90,000 died in battle and more than three times that number subsequently perished from wounds or disease; over 600,000 were later recorded as prisoners or "disappeared." Reflecting in 1813, Napoleon put it this way: "I grew up on the battlefield. A man like me does not give a damn about the lives of a million men." Indeed, Napoleon's armies may have suffered as many as 1.5 million casualties. The Napoleonic Wars killed about one in five of all Frenchmen born between 1790 and 1795.

Napoleon's final legacy was his myth. From Saint Helena, he claimed, "If I had succeeded, I would have been the greatest man known to history." The rise of romanticism helped make the story of Napoleon, the romantic hero, part of the collective memory of Western Europe after his death. Long after Waterloo, peddlers of songs, pamphlets, lithographs, and other images glorified Napoleon's life as earlier they had the lives of saints. "I live only for posterity," Napoleon once said. "Death is nothing, but to live defeated and without glory is to die every day." Rumors of his miraculous return to France were persistent long after his death. So powerful was his legend that even the most improbable seemed possible.

Of the changes in the post-Napoleonic period that profoundly transformed the way Europeans lived, none arguably had more important social, political, and cultural consequences than the Industrial Revolution. Having begun in England in the middle decades of the eighteenth century, it accelerated in that country during the first decades of the nineteenth century. It spread to Western Europe in particular, but affected regions in other places as well. The Industrial Revolution and its critics would help shape the modern world.

FURTHER READINGS

GENERAL

Michael Anderson, *Approaches to the History of the Western Family, 1500–1914* (1980).

Philippe Ariès, *Centuries of Childhood: A Social History of Family Life* (1962).

Philippe Ariès and Georges Duby, eds., *A History of Private Life* (5 vols., 1987–1993).

Geoffrey Barraclough, *The Origins of Modern Germany* (1979).

Richard Bonney, *The European Dynastic States, 1494–1660* (1991).

John Bossy, *Christianity in the West, 1400–1700* (1985).

Fernand Braudel, *Capitalism and Material Life, 1400–1800* (1975).

———, *The Mediterranean World in the Age of Philip II* (1992).

Peter Burke, *Popular Culture in Early Modern Europe* (1978).

Carlo Cipolla, *Before the Industrial Revolution: European Society and Economy, 1000–1700* (1980).

Carlo Cipolla, ed., *The Fontana Economic History of Europe* (6 vols., 1976–1977).

Eric Cochrane, *Italy, 1530–1630* (1988).

John Darwin, *After Tamerlane: The Global History of Empire since 1405* (2008).

Georges Duby and Michelle Perrot, eds., *A History of Women in the West* (5 vols., 1992–1994).

Elizabeth Eisenstein, *The Printing Revolution in Early Modern Europe* (1993).

Norbert Elias, *The Civilizing Process* (1994).

J. H. Elliott, *Empire of the Atlantic World* (2007).

R. F. Foster, *Modern Ireland, 1600–1972* (1988).

Jack Goldstone, *Revolution and Rebellion in the Early Modern World* (1991).

Avner Greif, *Institutions and the Path to the Modern Economy: Lessons from Medieval Trade* (2006).

Paul Hohenberg and Lynn Lees, *The Making of Urban Europe, 1000–1950* (1985).

Hahil Inalcik, *The Ottoman Empire: The Classical Age, 1300–1600* (1973).

Charles Ingrao, *The Habsburg Monarchy, 1618–1815* (1994).

Henry Kamen, *European Society, 1500–1700* (1984).

John Keegan, *The Face of Battle* (1976).

———, *A History of Warfare* (1993).

Paul Kennedy, *The Rise and Fall of the Great Powers* (1987).

H. G. Koenigsberger, *Early Modern Europe, 1500–1789* (1987).
———, *The Habsburgs and Europe, 1516–1660* (1971).
Joel Mokyr, *Twenty-Five Centuries of Technological Change: An Historical Survey* (1990).
Geoffrey Parker, *The Military Revolution: Military Innovation and the Rise of the West, 1500–1800* (1988).
Donald Quataert, *The Ottoman Empire, 1700–1922* (2007).
Colin Russell, *Science and Social Change in Britain and Europe, 1700–1900* (1983).
Raffaella Sarti, *Europe at Home: Family and Material Culture 1500–1800* (2002).
James Sheehan, *German History, 1770–1866* (1990).
Bonnie G. Smith, *Changing Lives: Women in European History since 1700* (1989).
Charles Tilly, *Coercion, Capital, and European States, AD 990–1990* (1990).
———, *The Contentious French: Four Centuries of Popular Struggle* (1986).
Charles Tilly, ed., *The Formation of Nation States in Western Europe* (1975).
Mack Walker, *German Home Towns: Community, State, and General Estate, 1648–1871* (1971).
Immanuel Wallerstein, *The Modern World System* (1974).
Piotr Wandycz, *The Price of Freedom: A History of East Central Europe from the Middle Ages to the Present* (1992).
Eric R. Wolf, *Europe and the People without History* (1983).
E. A. Wrigley, *Population and History* (1969).

CHAPTER 1. MEDIEVAL LEGACIES AND TRANSFORMING DISCOVERIES

Kenneth R. Andrews, *Trade, Plunder and Settlement: Maritime Enterprise and the Genesis of the British Empire, 1480–1630* (1984).
Robert Bartlett, *The Making of Europe: Conquest, Colonization and Cultural Change, 950–1350* (1993).
M. W. Beresford, *New Towns of the Middle Ages* (1988).
Marc Bloch, *Feudal Society* (2 vols., 1961).
Brenda Bolton, *The Medieval Reformation* (1983).
John Boswell, *Christianity, Social Tolerance, and Homosexuality: Gay People in Western Europe from the Beginning of the Christian Era to the Fourteenth Century* (1980).
———, *The Kindness of Strangers: The Abandonment of Children in Western Europe from Late Antiquity to the Renaissance* (1988).
Rosalind B. Brooke and Christopher Brooke, *Popular Religion in the Middle Ages* (1984).
Alfred W. Crosby, *Ecological Imperialism: The Biological Expansion of Europe, 900–1900* (1986).
R. O. Crummey, *The Formation of Muscovy, 1404–1613* (1987).
Natalie Zemon Davis, *Trichster Travels: A Sixteenth-Century Muslim Between Worlds* (2006).
Georges Duby, *Rural Economy and Country Life in the Medieval West* (1968).
Edith Ennen, *The Medieval Woman* (1989).
Robert Fossier, *Peasant Life in the Medieval West* (1988).
Paul Freedman, *Out of the East: Spices and the Medieval Imagination* (2008).

Bernard Hamilton, *Religion in the Medieval West* (1986).
Denys Hay, *Europe in the Fourteenth and Fifteenth Centuries* (1989).
———, *Europe, the Emergence of an Idea* (1968).
Norman Housley, *The Later Crusades, 1274–1580* (1992).
William C. Jordan, *Europe in the High Middle Ages* (2001).
Emmanuel Leroy Ladurie, *Montaillou: The Promised Land of Error* (1979).
Angus MacKay, *Society, Economy and Religion in Late Medieval Castile* (1987).
Richard Mackenney, *Sixteenth-Century Europe: Expansion and Conflict* (1993).
H. E. Mayer, *The Crusades* (1988).
Michel Mollat, *The Poor in the Middle Ages* (1986).
R. I. Moore, *The First European Revolution, c. 970–1215* (2000).
John H. Mundy, *Europe in the High Middle Ages, 1150–1309* (1991).
J. H. Parry, *The Age of Reconnaissance: Discovery, Exploration and Settlement, 1450–1650* (1981).
Daniel Waley and Peter Denley, *Later Medieval Europe, 1250–1520* (2001).

Chapter 2. The Renaissance

William J. Bouwsma, *The Waning of the Renaissance, 1550–1640* (2002).
Judith Brown, *In the Shadow of Florence* (1982).
Eugene Brucker, *Renaissance Florence* (1983).
Peter Burke, *The Italian Renaissance: Culture and Society in Italy* (1987).
———, *Popular Culture in Renaissance Europe, 1450–1620* (1986).
Christopher S. Celenza, *The Lost Italian Renaissance: Humanists, Historians, and Latin's Legacy* (2004).
Carlo Ginzburg, *The Cheese and the Worms: The Cosmos of a Sixteenth-Century Miller* (1982).
———, *Night Battles* (1985).
Richard Goldthwaite, *The Building of Renaissance Florence* (1981).
Anthony Grafton and Lisa Jardine, *From Humanism to the Humanities: Education and the Liberal Arts in Fifteenth- and Sixteenth-Century Europe* (1986).
J. R. Hale, *Renaissance Europe* (1977).
———, *War and Society in Renaissance Europe, 1450–1620* (1986).
Denys Hay and John Law, *Italy in the Age of the Renaissance, 1380–1530* (1989).
Dale Kent, *The Rise of the Medici* (1979).
Margaret King, *Women in the Renaissance* (1991).
Lauro Martines, *April Blood: Florence and the Plot against the Medici* (2003).
———, *Power and Imagination: City-States in Renaissance Italy* (1988).
Garrett Mattingly, *Renaissance Diplomacy* (1988).
Margaret Meserve, *Empires of Islam in Renaissance Historical Thought* (2008).
John M. Najemy, *A History of Florence, 1200–1575* (2006).
J. G. A. Pocock, *The Machiavellian Moment: Florentine Political Thought and the Atlantic Republican Tradition* (1975).
John Stephens, *The Italian Renaissance: The Origins of Intellectual and Artistic Change before the Reformation* (1990).
Hugh Thomas, *The Conquest of Mexico* (1993).

CHAPTER 3. THE TWO REFORMATIONS

Cornelis Augustijn, *Erasmus: His Life, Works, and Influence* (1991).

Philip Benedict, *Christ's Churches Purely Reformed: A Social History of Calvinism* (2002).

William J. Bouwsma, *John Calvin: A Sixteenth-Century Portrait* (1987).

Euan Cameron, *The European Reformation* (1991).

Anwar Chejne, *Islam and the West: The Moriscos: A Cultural and Social History* (1983).

William A. Christian, Jr., *Local Religion in Sixteenth-Century Spain* (1981).

A. G. Dickens, *The English Reformation* (1989).

Carlos Eire, *From Madrid to Purgatory: The Art and Craft of Dying in Sixteenth-Century Spain* (1995).

———, *War against the Idol: The Reformation of Worship from Erasmus to Calvin* (1986).

Ronnie Po-Chia Hsia, *Social Discipline in the Reformation: Central Europe, 1550–1750* (1989).

———, *Society and Religion in Münster, 1535–1618* (1984).

Lisa Jardine, *Erasmus, Man of Letters: The Construction of Charisma in Print* (1993).

David Kirby, *Northern Europe in the Early Modern Period: The Baltic World, 1492–1772* (1990).

Sherrin Marshall, ed., *Women in Reformation and Counter-Reformation Europe: Public and Private Worlds* (1989).

Bernd Moeller, *Imperial Cities and the Reformation* (1982).

John W. O'Malley, *Trent and All That: Renaming Catholicism in the Early Modern Period* (2000).

Steven E. Ozment, *Flesh and Spirit: Private Life in Early Modern Germany* (1999).

———, *The Reformation in the Cities: The Appeal of Protestantism to Sixteenth-Century Germany and Switzerland* (1975).

———, *When Fathers Ruled: Family Life in Reformation Europe* (1983).

Eugene R. Rice, Jr., and Anthony Grafton, *The Foundations of Early Modern Europe, 1460–1559* (1994).

Thomas Robisheaux, *Rural Society and the Search for Order in Early Modern Germany* (1989).

John D. Roth and James M. Stayer, eds., *Companion to Anabaptism and Spiritualism, 1521–1700* (2007).

Robert W. Scribner, *For the Sake of Simple Folk: Popular Propaganda for the German Reformation* (1984).

Lewis Spitz, *The Protestant Reformation* (1987).

Keith Thomas, *Religion and the Decline of Magic* (1971).

Tessa Watt, *Cheap Print and Popular Piety, 1550–1640* (1991).

Merry E. Weisner, *Women and Gender in Early Modern Europe* (1993).

CHAPTER 4. THE WARS OF RELIGION

Susan Dwyer Amussen, *An Ordered Society: Gender and Class in Early Modern England* (1988).

Stuart Clarke, *Thinking with Demons: The Idea of Witchcraft in Early Modern Europe* (1997).
Natalie Zemon Davis, *The Gift in Sixteenth-Century France* (2000).
———, *The Return of Martin Guerre* (1983).
Eamon Duffy, *The Voices of Morebath: Reformation and Rebellion in an English Village* (2001).
Bruce Gordon, *The Swiss Reformation* (2002).
Mark Greengrass, *France in the Age of Henry IV: The Struggle for Stability* (1995).
Brad S. Gregory, *Christian Martyrdom in Early Modern Europe* (1999).
R. J. Knecht, *Francis I* (1992).
———, *The French Civil Wars* (2000).
Geoffrey Parker, *Europe in Crisis, 1598–1648* (1979).
Geoffrey Parker, ed., *The Thirty Years' War* (1988).
N. M. Sutherland, *The Massacre of St. Bartholomew and the European Conflict, 1559–1572* (1973).

CHAPTER 5. THE RISE OF THE ATLANTIC ECONOMY: SPAIN AND ENGLAND

Ralph Davis, *The Rise of the Atlantic Economies* (1973).
Jan de Vries, *The Economy of Europe in an Age of Crisis, 1600–1750* (1978).
J. H. Elliott, *The Count-Duke of Olivares: The Statesman in an Age of Decline* (1987).
———, *Imperial Spain, 1469–1714* (1964).
G. R. Elton, *England under the Tudors* (1991).
Felipe Fernandez-Armesto, *The Spanish Armada: The Experience of War in 1588* (1989).
John Guy, *Tudor England* (1988).
Henry Kamen, *Empire: How Spain Became a World Power, 1492–1763* (2004).
John Lynch, *Spain, 1516–1598* (1994).
———, *Spain under the Habsburgs, 1516–1700* (2 vols., 1964–1969).
Colin Martin and Geoffrey Parker, *The Spanish Armada* (1988).
Geoffrey Parker, *The Grand Strategy of Philip II* (2000).
———, *Philip II* (1978).
Carla Rahn Philips, *Galleons for the King of Spain* (1986).
Penry Williams, *The Tudor Regime* (1979).
Joyce Youings, *Sixteenth-Century England* (1984).

CHAPTER 6. ENGLAND AND THE DUTCH REPUBLIC IN THE SEVENTEENTH CENTURY

Michael Braddick, *God's Fury, England's Fire: A New History of England's Civil Wars* (2008).
Harold J. Cook, *Masters of Exchange: Commerce, Medicine, and Science in the Dutch Golden Age* (2007).
Bruce R. Galloway, *The Union of England and Scotland, 1603–1608* (1986).
Pieter Geyl, *The Revolt of the Netherlands, 1555–1609* (1966).
Christopher Hill, *God's Englishman: Oliver Cromwell and the English Revolution* (1975).

———, *The World Turned Upside Down* (1972).

Derek Hirst, *Authority and Conflict: England, 1603–1658* (1986).

Ronald Hutton, *The British Republic, 1649–1660* (1990).

Jonathan I. Israel, *The Dutch Republic: Its Rise, Greatness, and Fall, 1477–1806* (1995).

J. R. Jones, *The Revolution of 1688 in England* (1972).

Anna Keay, *The Magnificent Monarch: Charles II and the Ceremonies of Power* (2008).

Mark Kishlansky, *A Monarchy Transformed: Britain, 1603–1714* (1996).

Mark Knights, *Representation and Misrepresentation in Later Stuart Britain: Partisanship and Political Culture* (2005).

Peter Laslett, *The World We Have Lost: England before the Industrial Age* (1983).

Brian P. Levack, *The Formation of the British State: England, Scotland, and the Union, 1603–1707* (1987).

John Morrill, *The Revolt of the Provinces: Conservatism and Revolution in the English Civil War, 1630–1650* (1980).

Geoffrey Parker, *The Army of Flanders and the Spanish Road, 1567–1659* (1972).

Steven C. Pincus, *1688: The First Modern Revolution* (2009).

Maarten Prak, *The Dutch Republic in the Seventeenth Century* (2005).

J. L. Price, *Culture and Society in the Dutch Republic during the Seventeenth Century* (1974).

Simon Schama, *An Embarrassment of Riches: An Interpretation of Dutch Culture in the Golden Age* (1988).

J. A. Sharpe, *Early Modern England: A Social History, 1550–1760* (1990).

Kevin Sharpe, *The Personal Rule of Charles I* (1995).

Lawrence Stone, *The Causes of the English Revolution, 1629–1642* (1990).

David Underdown, *Fire from Heaven: Life in an English Town in the Seventeenth Century* (1992).

———, *Revel, Riot, and Rebellion: Popular Politics and Culture in England, 1603–1660* (1985).

Keith Wrightson, *Earthly Necessities: Economic Lives in Early Modern Britain* (2000).

———, *English Society, 1550–1760* (1982).

CHAPTER 7. THE AGE OF ABSOLUTISM, 1650–1720

Perry Anderson, *Lineages of the Absolutist State* (1974).

William Beik, *Absolutism and Society in Seventeenth-Century France: State Power and Provincial Aristocracy in Languedoc* (1985).

Joseph Bergin, *Cardinal Richelieu: Power and the Pursuit of Wealth* (1985).

Paul Bushkovitch, *Peter the Great* (2001).

James B. Collins, *The State in Early Modern France* (2001).

J. H. Elliott, *Richelieu and Olivares* (1984).

Richard J. Evans, *The Making of the Habsburg Empire, 1550–1770* (1979).

Pierre Goubert, *Louis XIV and Twenty Million Frenchmen* (1972).

Ragnhild Hatton, *Europe in the Age of Louis XIV* (1979).

Lindsey Hughes, *Russia in the Age of Peter the Great, 1682–1725* (1998).

Sharon Kettering, *French Society, 1589–1715* (2001).

Robert Mandrou, *Introduction to Modern France, 1500–1640* (1975).

Roland Mousnier, *Peasant Uprisings in Seventeenth-Century France, Russia, and China* (1970).

David Parker, *The Making of French Absolutism* (1983).

Theodore Rabb, *The Struggle for Stability in Early Modern Europe* (1975).

Orest Ranum, *The Fronde: A French Revolution* (1993).

———, *Paris in the Age of Absolutism* (2003).

John Stoye, *The Siege of Vienna: The Last Great Trial between Cross and Crescent* (2007).

CHAPTER 8. THE NEW PHILOSOPHY OF SCIENCE

Herbert Butterfield, *The Origins of Modern Science, 1300–1800* (1965).

John Fauvel, Raymond Flood, Michael Shortland, and Robin Wilson, eds., *Let Newton Be! A New Perspective on His Life and Works* (1988).

A. R. Hall, *The Revolution in Science, 1500–1750: The Formation of the Modern Scientific Attitude* (1983).

Margaret Jacobs, *The Cultural Meaning of the Scientific Revolution* (1988).

Hugh Kearney, *Science and Change, 1500–1700* (1971).

Alexandre Koyr, *The Formation of the Modern Scientific Attitude* (1983).

T. S. Kuhn, *The Structure of Scientific Revolution* (1989).

Robert K. Merton, *Science, Technology, and Society in Seventeenth-Century England* (1970).

Ingrid D. Rowland, *Giordino Bruno, Philosopher, Heretic* (2008).

Londa Schiebinger, *The Mind Has No Sex? Women and the Origins of Modern Science* (1990).

R. S. Westfall, *Never at Rest: A Biography of Isaac Newton* (1993).

B. H. G. Wormald, *Francis Bacon: History, Politics, and Science, 1561–1626* (1993).

CHAPTER 9. ENLIGHTENED THOUGHT AND THE REPUBLIC OF LETTERS

Keith Baker, *Inventing the French Revolution: Essays in the Political Culture of Eighteenth-Century France* (1990).

Roger Chartier, *The Cultural Origins of the French Revolution* (1991).

Maurice Cranston, *The Noble Savage: Jean-Jacques Rousseau, 1754–1762* (1991).

———, *Philosophers and Pamphleteers: Political Theorists of the Enlightenment* (1986).

Thomas E. Crow, *Painters and Public Life in Eighteenth-Century Paris* (1985).

Robert Darnton, *The Business of Enlightenment* (1979).

———, *The Great Cat Massacre* (1985).

———, *The Literary Underground of the Old Regime* (1985).

Peter Gay, *The Enlightenment: An Interpretation* (2 vols., 1966–1969).

———, *Voltaire's Politics: The Poet as Realist* (1988).

Dena Goodman, *The Republic of Letters: A Cultural History of the French Enlightenment* (1984).

Norman Hampson, *A Cultural History of the Enlightenment* (1969).

Carla Hesse, *The Other Enlightenment: How French Women Became Modern* (2001).

Darrin M. McMahon, *Enemies of the Enlightenment: Anti-Philosophes and the Birth of the French Far Right, 1778–1830* (1998).

J. M. McManners, *Death and Enlightenment: Changing Attitudes to Death among Christians and Unbelievers in Eighteenth-Century France* (1982).

Roy Porter and Mikulás Teich, eds., *The Enlightenment in National Context* (1981).

John Robertson, *The Case for the Enlightenment: Scotland and Naples, 1680–1760* (2005).

Franco Venturi, *Italy and the Enlightenment: Studies in a Cosmopolitan Century* (1972).

CHAPTER 10. EIGHTEENTH-CENTURY ECONOMIC AND SOCIAL CHANGE

M. S. Anderson, *Europe in the Eighteenth Century, 1713–1783* (1982).

C. A. Bayly, *Imperial Meridian: The British Empire and the World, 1780–1830* (1989).

David A. Bell, *The Cult of the Nation in France: Inventing Nationalism, 1680–1800* (2001).

Maxine Berg, *The Age of Manufacturers, 1700–1820: Industry, Innovation, and Work in Britain* (1985).

Peter Borsay, *The English Urban Renaissance: Culture and Society in the Provincial Town, 1660–1770* (1989).

Christopher Leslie Brown, *Moral Capital: The Foundations of British Abolitionism* (2008).

P. J. Corfield, *The Impact of English Towns, 1700–1800* (1982).

Douglas Hay, et al., *Albion's Fatal Tree: Crime and Punishment in Eighteenth-Century England* (1975).

Steven L. Kaplan, *Provisioning Paris: Merchants and Millers in the Grain and Flour Trade during the Eighteenth Century* (1984).

Emmanuel LeRoy Ladurie, *The Peasants of Languedoc* (1974).

Paul Langford, *A Polite and Commercial People: England, 1727–1783* (1989).

P. J. Marshall, *The Making and Unmaking of Empires: Britain, India, and America c. 1750–1783* (2005).

G. E. Mingay, *Land and Society in England, 1750–1980* (1994).

J. H. Parry, *Trade and Dominion: The European Overseas Empires in the Eighteenth Century* (1971).

Roy Porter, *English Society in the Eighteenth Century* (1986).

Isser Woloch, *Eighteenth-Century Europe: Tradition and Progress, 1715–1789* (1982).

CHAPTER 11. EIGHTEENTH-CENTURY DYNASTIC RIVALRIES AND POLITICS

Paul Avrich, *Russian Rebels, 1600–1800* (1972).

Bernard Bailyn, *The Ideological Origins of the American Revolution* (1992).

C. B. A. Behrens, *The Ancien Régime* (1967).

———, *Society, Government, and the Enlightenment: The Experiences of Eighteenth-Century France and Prussia* (1985).

David Bell, *Lawyers and Citizens: The Making of a Political Elite in Old Regime France* (1994).

John Brewer, *Party Ideology and Popular Politics at the Accession of George III* (1976).

———, *The Sinews of Power: War, Money, and the English State, 1688–1783* (1989).

Linda Colley, *Britons: Forging the Nation, 1707–1837* (1992).

———, *In Defiance of Oligarchy: The Tory Party, 1714–1760* (1982).

———, *The Ordeal of Elizabeth Marsh: A Woman in World History* (2008).

Tim Harris, *Revolution: The Great Crisis of the British Monarchy, 1685–1729* (2006).

Olwen Hufton, *The Poor of Eighteenth-Century France, 1750–1789* (1974).

Maya Jasanoff, *Edge of Empire: Lives, Culture, and Conquest in the East, 1750–1850* (2005).

Isabel de Madariaga, *Catherine the Great: A Short History* (1990).

Sara Maza, *Private Lives and Public Affairs: The Causes Celebres of Prerevolutionary France* (1993).

Edward Pearce, *The Great Man—Sir Robert Walpole* (2007).

Edmund Sears Morgan, *Benjamin Franklin* (2003).

———, *The Birth of the Republic, 1763–1789* (1977).

Daniel Roche, *The People of Paris* (1987).

Robert M. Schwartz, *Policing the Poor in Eighteenth-Century France* (1988).

Wayne Te Brake, *Regents and Rebels: The Revolutionary World of an Eighteenth-Century Dutch City* (1989).

Franco Venturi, *The End of the Old Regime in Europe, 1776–1789* (2 vols., 1991).

CHAPTER 12. THE FRENCH REVOLUTION

Nigel Aston, *Religion and Revolution in France, 1780–1804* (2000).

Jean-Paul Bertaud, *The Army of the French Revolution: From Citizen-Soldiers to Instrument of Power* (1988).

T. C. W. Blanning, *The French Revolutionary Wars, 1787–1802* (1996).

Howard G. Brown, *Ending the French Revolution: Violence, Justice, and Repression from the Terror to Napoleon* (2006).

Richard Cobb, *The Police and the People: French Popular Protest, 1789–1820* (1972).

William Doyle, *Origins of the French Revolution* (1988).

Marianne Elliott, *Partners in Revolution: The United Irishmen and France* (1982).

Alan Forrest, *Conscripts and Deserters: The Army and French Society during the Revolution and Empire* (1989).

———, *The French Revolution and the Poor* (1981).

Francois Furet, *Interpreting the French Revolution* (1992).

David Garrioch, *The Making of Revolutionary Paris* (2002).

Dominique Godineau, *The Women of Paris and Their French Revolution* (1998).

Carla Hesse, *Publishing and Cultural Politics in Revolutionary Paris, 1789–1810* (1991).

Patrice Higonnet, *Sister Republics: The Origins of French and American Republicanism* (1988).

Lynn Hunt, *The Family Romance of the French Revolution* (1992).

———, *Politics, Culture, and Class in the French Revolution* (1984).

Peter Jones, *The Peasantry in the French Revolution* (1988).

Georges Lefebvre, *The Coming of the French Revolution* (1989).

Ted W. Margadant, *Urban Rivalries in the French Revolution* (1992).

Peter McPhee, *The French Revolution, 1789–1799* (2002).

Sarah E. Meltzer and Leslie W. Rabine, eds., *Rebel Daughters: Women and the French Revolution* (1989).

Mona Ozouf, *Festivals and the French Revolution* (1988).

R. R. Palmer, *The Age of the Democratic Revolution: A Political History of Europe and America, 1760–1800* (2 vols., 1959–1964).

———, *Twelve Who Ruled: The Year of the Terror in the French Revolution* (1989).

Jeremy D. Popkin, *Revolutionary News: The Press in France, 1789–1799* (1990).

George Rudé, *The Great Fear of 1789* (1973).

William H. Sewell, Jr., *A Rhetoric of Bourgeois Revolution: The Abbé Sieyès and "What is the Third Estate?"* (1994).

Donald Sutherland, *France, 1789–1815: Revolution and Counterrevolution* (1986).

Timothy Tackett, *Religion, Revolution, and Regional Culture in Eighteenth-Century France: The Ecclesiastical Oath of 1791* (1986).

———, *When the King Took Flight* (2003).

Charles Tilly, *The Vendée* (1964).

Isser Woloch, *The New Regime: Transformations of the French Civic Order, 1789–1820s* (1994).

CHAPTER 13. NAPOLEON AND EUROPE

David A. Bell, *The First Total War: Napoleon's Empire and the Birth of Warfare as We Know It* (2007).

Louis Bergeron, *France under Napoleon* (1981).

Michael Broers, *Europe under Napoleon* (1996).

———, *The Politics of Religion in Napoleonic Italy: The War against God, 1801–1814* (2002).

Philip Dwyer, *Napoleon: The Path to Power* (2007).

Steven Englund, *Napoleon: A Political Life* (2004).

Alan Forrest, *Napoleon's Men: The Soldiers of the Revolution and Empire* (2002).

Alan Schom, *One Hundred Days: Napoleon's Road to Waterloo* (1992).

Jakob Walter, *The Diary of a Napoleonic Foot Soldier* (1991).

Stuart Wolfe, *Napoleon's Integration of Europe* (1991).

D. G. Wright, *Napoleon and Europe* (1984).

CREDITS

INDEX

Page numbers in *italics* refer to illustrations.